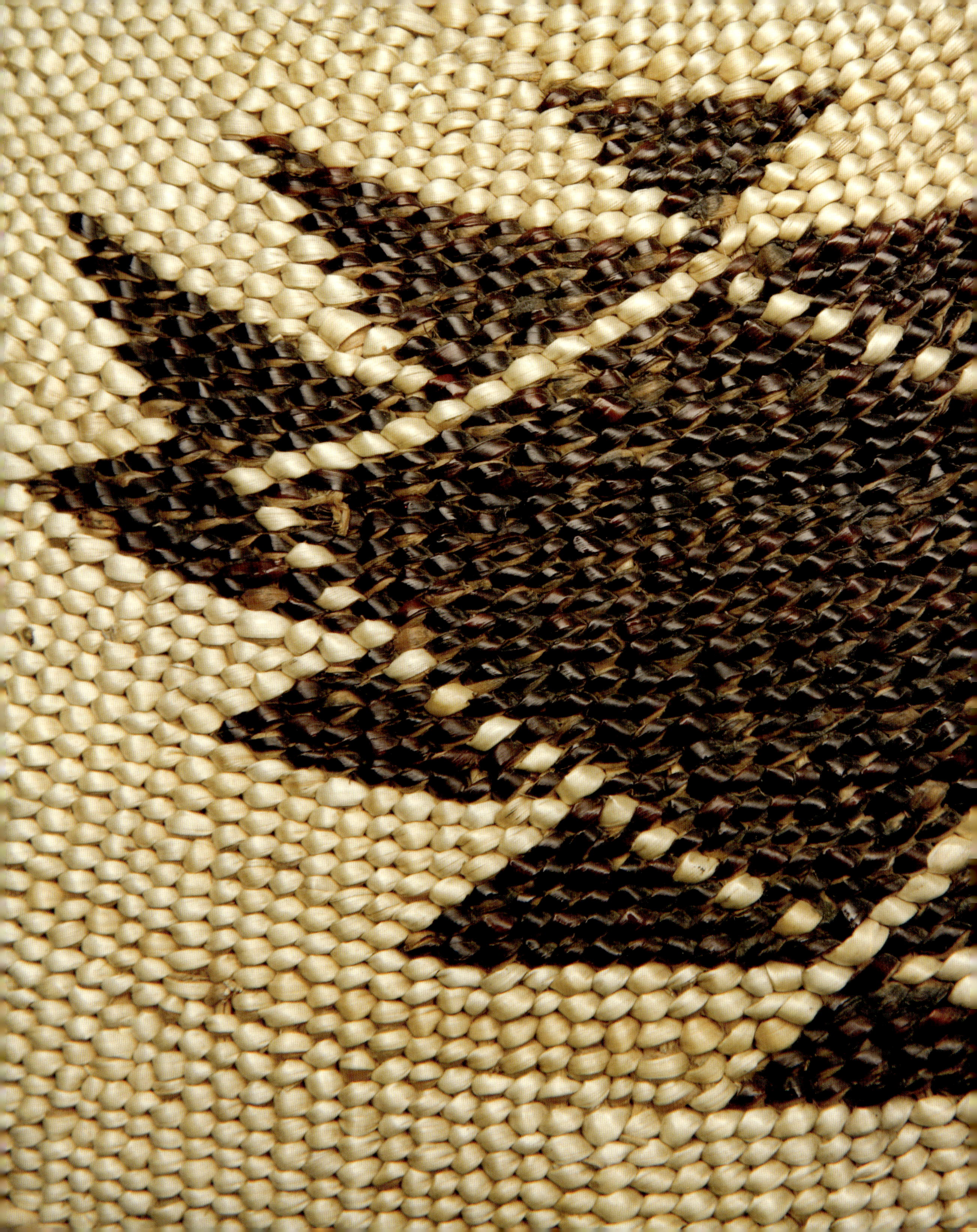

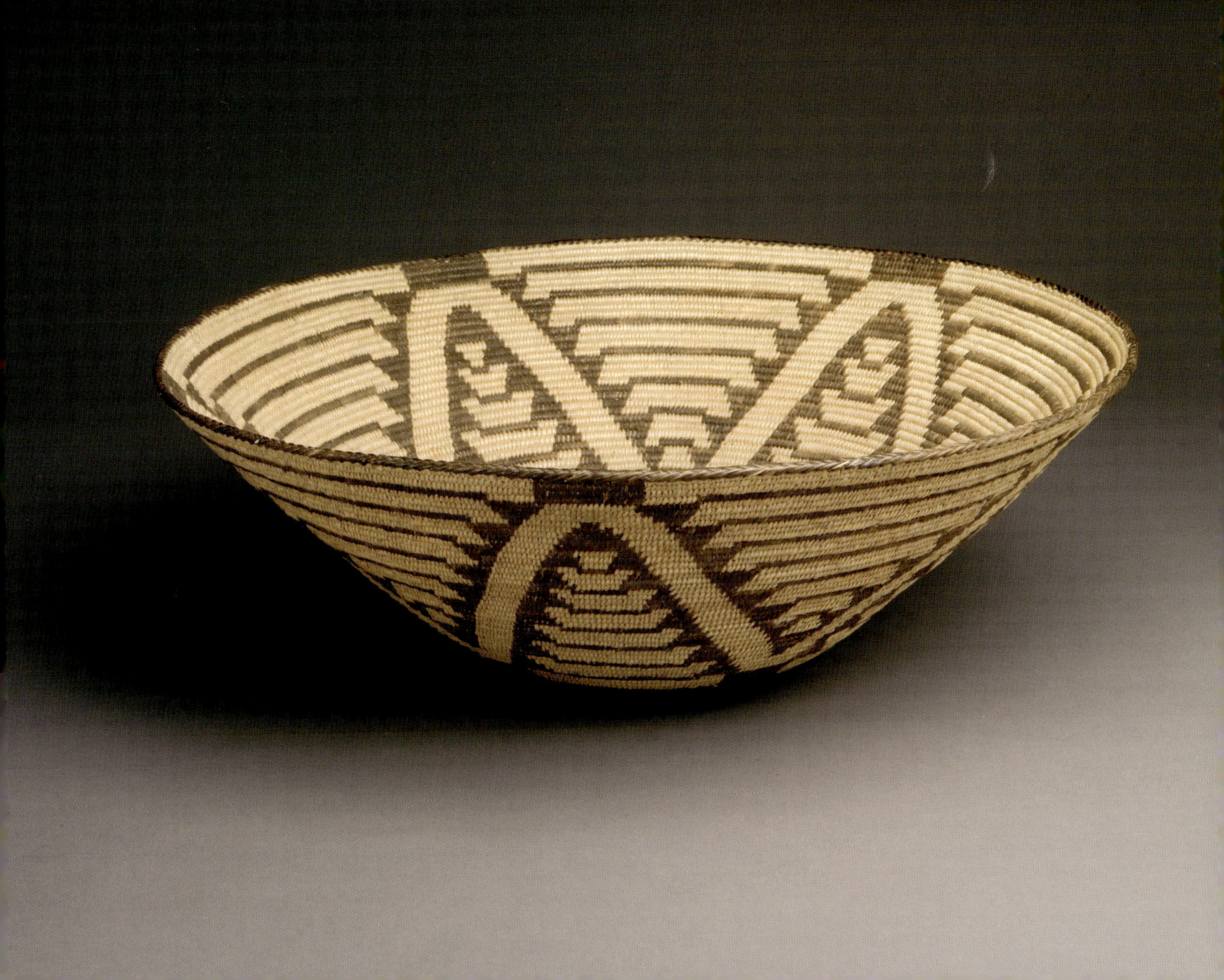

Woven Identities

Basketry Art of Western North America

The Collection of the
Museum of Indian Arts & Culture,
Santa Fe

by Valerie K. Verzuh

Photography by Addison Doty and Blair Clark

Museum of New Mexico Press
Santa Fe

Contents

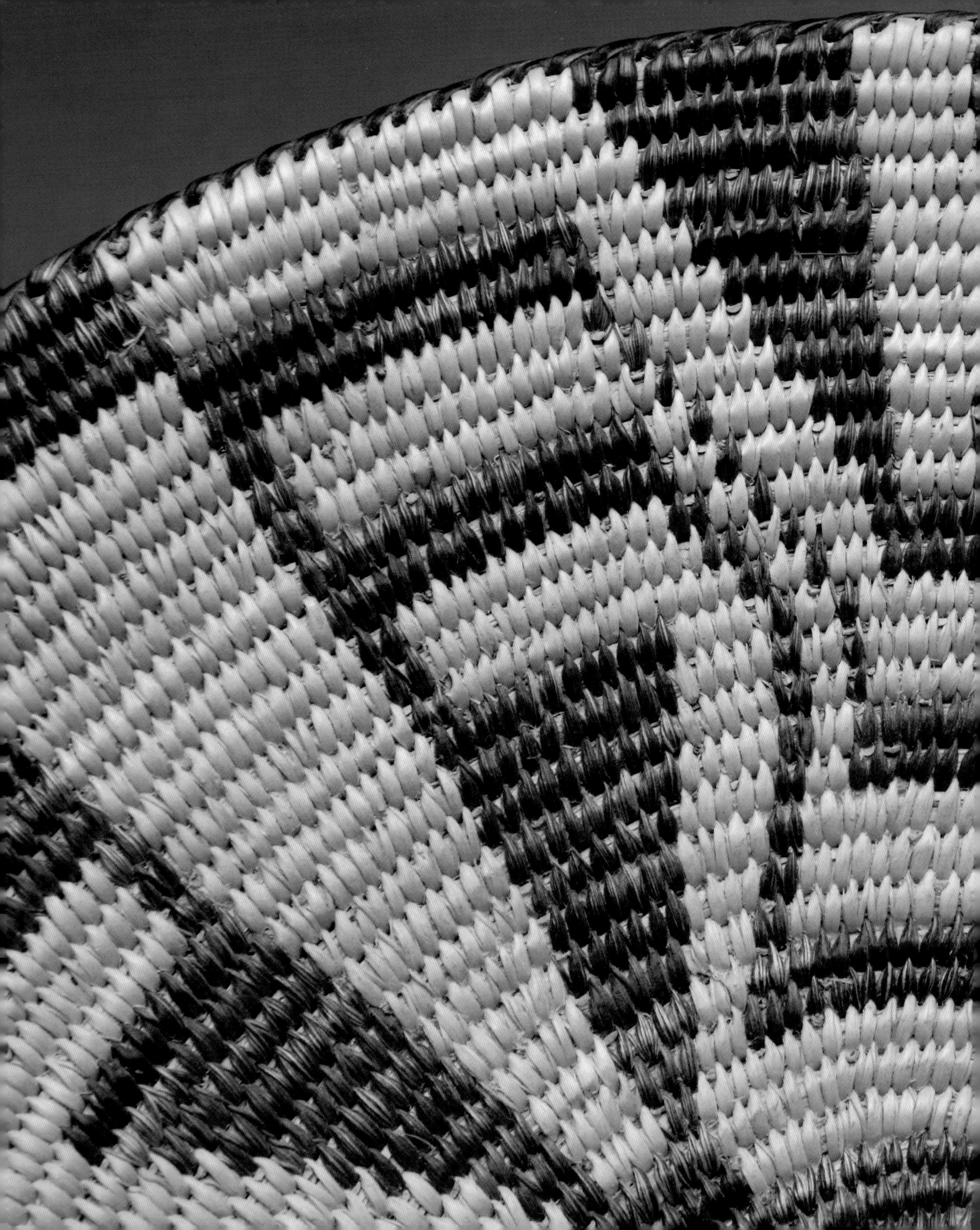

Foreword

Angelo J. Joaquin Jr.
Member, Coyote Clan, Tohono O'odham Nation

Years ago, I asked a Tohono O'odham weaver to make a basket to be presented at a friend's wedding. She asked what design I wanted on the basket. I told her that would be her call. She said that was good because a basket that is not forced is the best. The design, she explained, creates itself as she weaves. I have never doubted the wisdom of this message.

As a member of the Indian Advisory Panel (IAP) for the Museum of Indian Arts & Culture (MIAC) the past decade, I have had the wonderfully rewarding experience of observing how a museum seeks to enhance the education of the Indian and non-Indian public through exhibits, publications, and presentations from the Indian perspective. In my opinion, the exhibits put forth by museums in the past have been interpretations—in the etic or "outsider's" analysis by anthropologists—of Indian cultures. When native peoples are involved, such educational efforts become "presentations" because the base question posed to participants is, "What do you think is valuable for the public to know about you?"

Located in the Southwest and surrounded by two dozen sovereign nations makes it imperative that MIAC takes on this role—as a voice of The People. With the help of the Indian Advisory Panel, which is comprised of members from local tribes, MIAC is, I believe, on the cutting edge in terms of providing genuine information about the residents. It is able to greatly influence the awareness of non-Indians but also to provide a vehicle for transferring traditional knowledge to current members of younger Indian generations.

The collections serve as tangible connectors to our Ancestors. The stories and knowledge imparted by the collections allow young and old to better understand and appreciate the uniqueness of their cultures. Our traditional beliefs must be constantly reinforced to withstand the bombardment of ideas from the dominant culture. A recent auction of Hopi masks in France underlines the complete lack of understanding in the outside world of the vital roles that material culture plays in Native American Culture and the need for continuing education on this subject.

The Indian Advisory Panel advises museum staff on its educational efforts; content is reviewed to ensure that it is respectful of tribal people and that the information is meaningful to the museum visitor. Indeed, the stewardship of the collections is taken seriously and with dedication by both the IAP and museum staff.

It is my hope that the reader of this book will become fully aware that a completed basket, while always a great accomplishment, is only one of several aspects of the basket-weaving process. The acts of thanking the Creator for the plants and thanking the plant for giving of itself through prayer and song are paramount.

Our cultures are based on the spirituality generated through ceremonies, songs, prayers, stories, and other acts of honoring Life. The values and mores leading to a meaningful life are gained by acknowledging and participating in these activities. I truly believe that the passing of each Elder is equivalent to losing a reference library. The museum's collections, however, provide the basis for understanding the Elder's achievements and actions in life.

Acknowledgments

Every exhibition and catalogue is a collaborative effort, and *Woven Identities* is no exception. For their contributions to my knowledge of both the descriptive and interpretive aspects of our basket collection, as well as their generous advice and friendship, I thank consultants Bruce Bernstein, Larry Dalrymple, and John Kania; Judith Finger is responsible for foundation research behind the Material chapter.

I wish to thank the museum's Indian Advisory Panel for reviewing the exhibition and catalogue concept and baskets as well as for their invaluable insights. I am especially indebted to Angelo Joaquin for his contributions to my understanding of the deeper values of Tohono O'odham baskets, to Lee Wayne Lomayestewa for sharing his knowledge of Hopi with me, and to Ulysses Reid of Zia Pueblo who, because he is a weaver himself, was an invaluable resource throughout the project.

Numerous museum staff members contributed their specialized skills to *Woven Identities.* For their assistance I extend my thanks to former Director Shelby Tisdale, Deputy Director Elena Sweeney, Archivist Diane Bird, Curator of Ethnology Tony Chavarria, Director of Education Joyce Begay Foss, Educator Dawn Kaufmann, Librarian Allison Colborne, and Registrar Cathy Notarnicola; and to Monica Vigil. Credit for the fine phraseology and the beauty of this publication goes to the Museum of New Mexico Press, especially Editorial Director Mary Wachs and Art Director David Skolkin. Photographers Addison Doty and Blair Clark are to be commended for their exquisite photographs. And, my eternal gratitude is due to Rebecca Eckman who, while carrying her first child (Mose), spent many hours researching and editing the photos for the Material and Catalogue of the Collections chapters. And, Candy Carlson designed the Exhibition Guide which prompted so many visitors to ask if there was to be a catalogue—indeed there is.

I also extend my appreciation to all of those who read the text in its varying permutations, including (yet again) the incontrovertible basket scholar Bruce Bernstein, Curator of Archaeology Maxine McBrinn, as well as my dedicated volunteers Ross Altshuler, Beth Extract, and Carol Warren.

I am fortunate to have met and spoken with the nearly thirty contemporary basket weavers who participated in Santa Fe's 2011 Indian Market. Those weavers who were able to join us at the museum for a series of educational programs were especially helpful, including Kaitlyn Kayquoptewa and her mother, Patty Wells, Hopi (Second Mesa); Royce Manuel (Akimel O'odham); Terrol Dew Johnson (Tohono O'odham); Jacinthe Two Bulls (Haida); and Loa Balumnaech Ryan (Tsimshian/Gitlan).

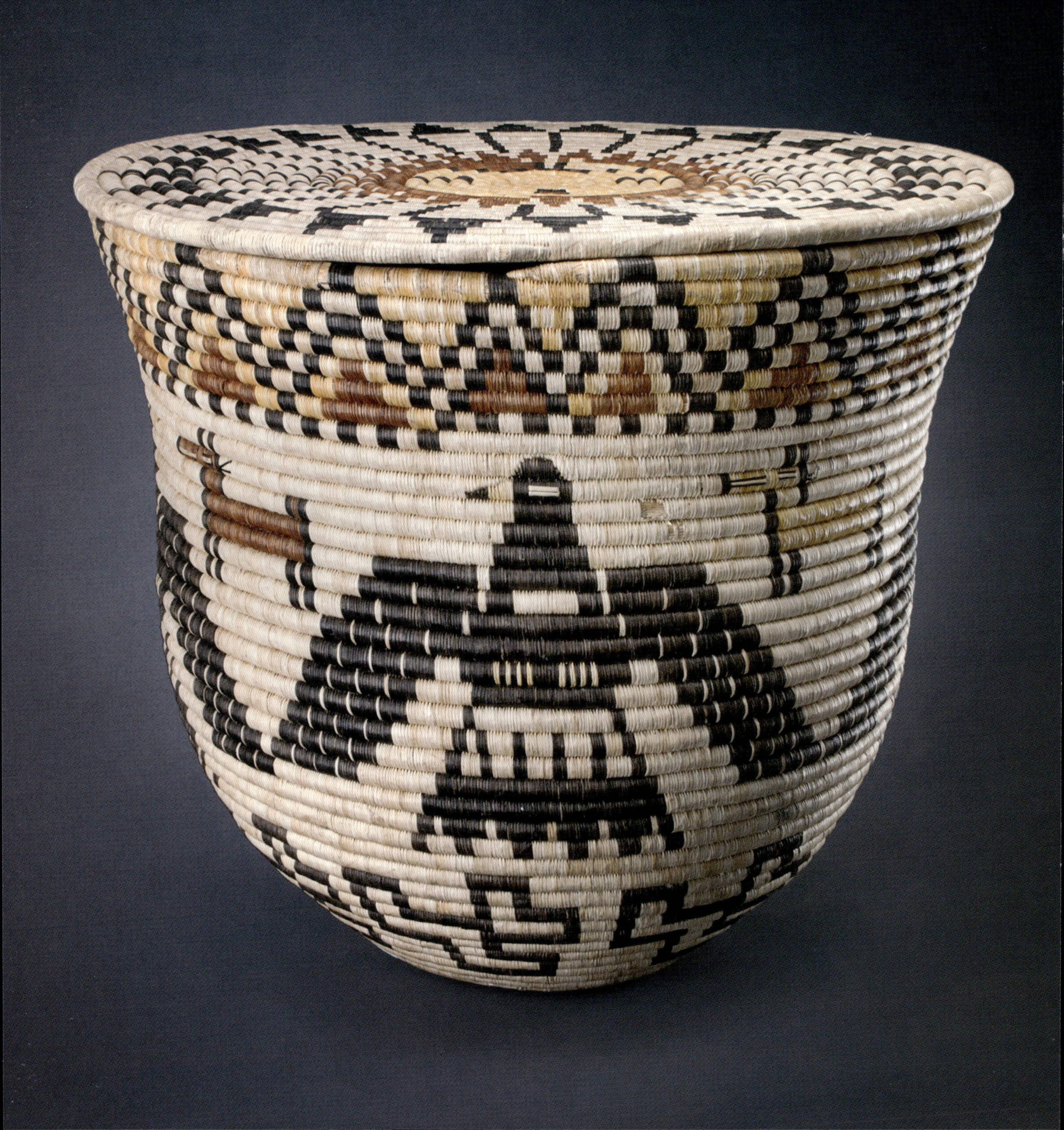

Introduction

Basketry has been practiced for many thousands of years by Indigenous peoples of western North America. Historically, baskets have been made for a variety of purposes, including food gathering, preparation and storage, household furnishings, clothing, and social or ceremonial uses. There are many different types of baskets with countless variations on these types made by different tribes and individual artists. Some basket types are no longer a part of the daily lives of Indigenous peoples; however, other basketry forms continue to play significant roles in Native cultures. Because they are a cultural art form combining both utilitarian and aesthetic qualities, baskets are culture bearers that transmit important traditions and artistic knowledge.

Comprehending the beauty and complexity of a basket by only looking at its outer surface is much like appreciating a book by only looking at its cover. *Woven Identities,* therefore, seeks to go beyond the outer appearance of baskets by examining the five integral elements at the heart of basket weaving—materials, construction techniques, form, function, and design and ornamentaion—and a basket's woven identity: where it was made, when it was made, who made it, and why it was made. An understanding of these elements and how they are united in both utilitarian and "art" baskets is also the key to seeing baskets from the weavers' eye, or point of view. For weavers, the process of collecting and processing materials and constructing a basket is just as important, and in some instances even more so, than the form, function, and design elements of the final product. Therefore, chapters on material and construction begin the basketry discussion in this volume. And, because the significance of the five elements is found to be equally important to weavers regardless of their tribal affiliation, these elements are the overall organizing principle of this publication.

FIG. 1

Storage Basket, c. 1930, Hopi (Second Mesa), Artist unknown, 53.0 x 58.1 cm., 35963

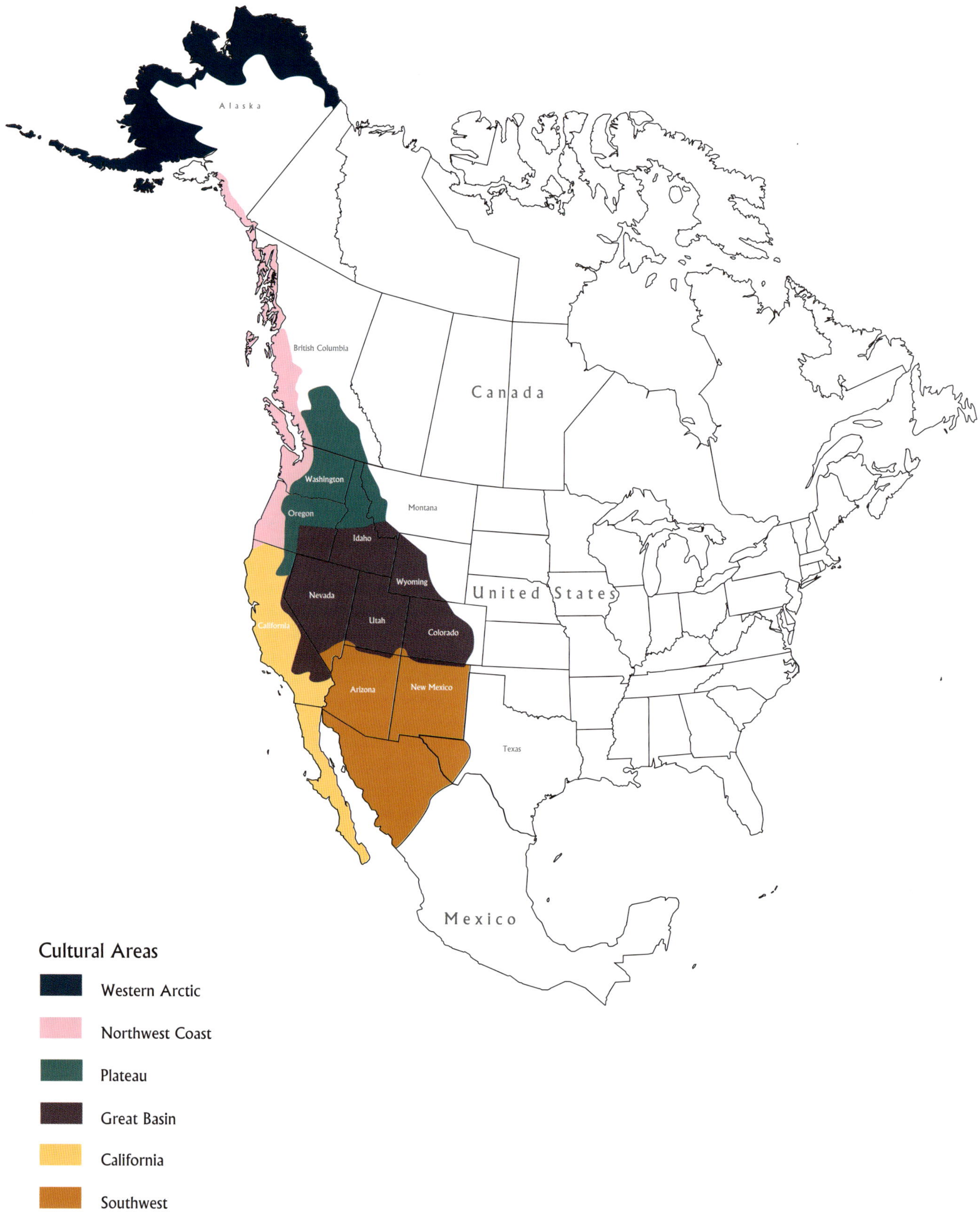
Alaska
British Columbia
Canada
Washington
Oregon
Montana
Idaho
Wyoming
United States
Nevada
Utah
California
Colorado
Arizona
New Mexico
Texas
Mexico
Cultural Areas
Western Arctic
Northwest Coast
Plateau
Great Basin
California
Southwest

The baskets featured in *Woven Identities* are drawn entirely from the Museum of Indian Arts & Culture. This collection consists of approximately 1,500 baskets from (with a few exceptions) six culture areas within western North America: Southwest, Great Basin, Plateau, California, Northwest Coast, and the Arctic. Broad in scope, the collection includes utilitarian baskets, baskets made for sale, and baskets with both traditional and innovative forms. Although the collection's strength resides in the depth and breadth of an assemblage of historic-period baskets, dating between 1870 and 1930, the museum continues to develop the collection by acquiring the work of contemporary weavers whose work exemplifies the vibrant nature of the art today. The following discussions focus on baskets of the above mentioned six culture areas and sixty-one cultural designations (today referred to as bands, tribes, or pueblos) which are well represented in the museum's collection. This selection of baskets does not, however, represent an encyclopedic compilation of all the plant materials, construction techniques, forms, and designs included in the work of the basketmaking cultures of western North America. Also, because women are almost exclusively the basket makers in the post-contact period, throughout this volume basket weavers are referred to primarily by the feminine pronoun. It should be recognized, however, that in some times and places men have woven baskets, and an increasing number do so today.

CULTURE AREAS

The term "culture" is defined here as the beliefs and values that bind a group of people together that are expressed in the people's language, material objects and features, and arts. Simply put, culture is a shared way of life. The term "culture areas" refers to the geographic regions occupied by culturally similar Native Americans before contact with non-Indians. The term is used in *Woven Identities* as an organizational tool but also to express the vastness and ecological diversity of the lands that sustained North American Indians over the thousands of years during which the art of basketmaking arose, as well as to paint a picture of the harsh conditions under which some of the world's finest baskets were created. That their homelands were so vast, and their ways of life so self-sufficient and independent, underscores the great losses felt by Indigenous peoples after contact with foreigners. Not only did Native Americans lose their traditional lands, they also suffered cultural fragmentation, population decline, and acculturation. As native economies broke down, Indigenous peoples were forced to adapt to new ways of life in an often hostile and inhumane society. These cultures have adapted and endured to present times, although they now live on significantly reduced lands and within modern political and social organizations.

Throughout the Indigenous American West, people practiced gathering and hunting as the basis of their livelihood or to supplement the farming of domesticated food crops. Over millennia of interacting with their natural environment, native peoples learned the many uses of indigenous plant materials: they could be woven into baskets and clothing, gathered for food, used to build shelters and construct tools, and used to make medicine. The distinct qualities of baskets—strength, lightness, and ability to serve a multitude of purposes—made them an important part of subsistence lifestyles and particularly suitable for mobile ways of life, when Native peoples circulated throughout their lands (according to the changing seasons) to gather plants, to hunt, and to fish.

Southwest Culture Area

The term "Southwest" refers to the culture area encompassing New Mexico, Arizona, extreme southern and western Texas, southwestern Colorado, western and southern Utah, the southern tip of Nevada, as well as the Mexican states of Sonora, Chihuahua, Coahuila, Durango, Nueva Leon, and Tamaulipas. The first people to come to this culture area over 13,000 years ago were gatherers and hunters and possibly North America's first basket weavers.

This ecologically complex area consists of alpine tundra, coniferous forests, juniper savannas, grasslands, and desert scrub. Although primarily an arid region, the Southwest's topographical diversity includes wide variations in rainfall, climate, and vegetation. The region's rivers supported early sedentary farming communities. Indigenous crops of corn, beans, and squash provided the agricultural base for these villages. After contact with the Spanish in the late 1500s, native farmers added wheat, alfalfa, chili, melons, fruits, and various vegetables to their crops. In the areas where the natural environment could not sustain agriculture, people hunted and gathered wild food.

After AD 200, as sedentary Pueblo communities developed in the Southwest, durable pottery was manufactured and gradually began to supplant basketry for use in many household tasks. Nevertheless, Pueblo women still wove baskets for gathering wild plant foods that continued to supplement

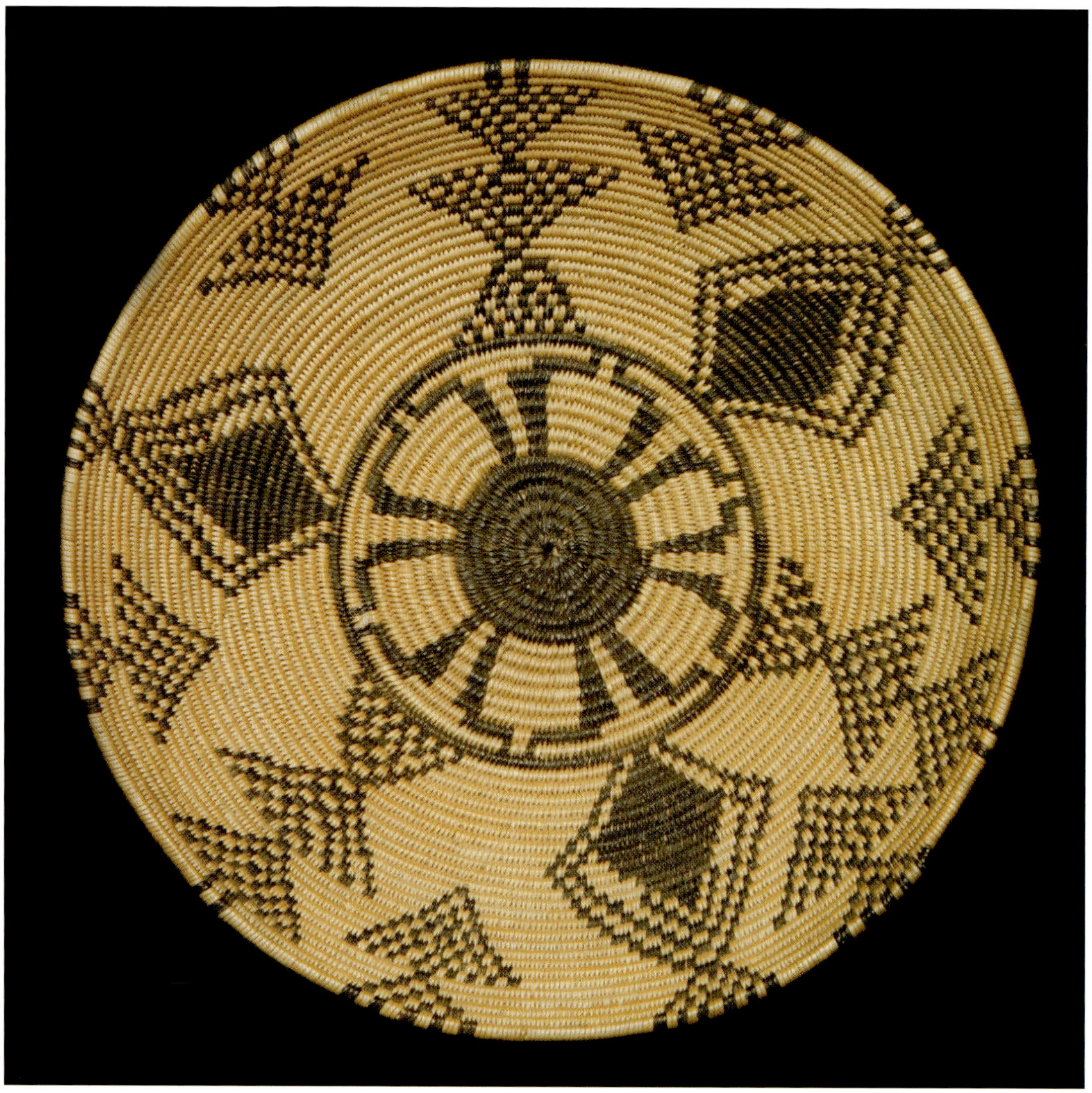

FIG. 2

Tray, c. 1900, Western Apache, Artist Unknown, 6.5 x 30.5 cm., 3119 their diets and adapted others for use with domesticated and introduced crops. Meanwhile, nomadic groups made and used baskets well into the nineteenth century to gather, process, cook, and store the seeds, nuts, berries, roots, and small mammals that were major components in their diet.

Over time, individual histories together with the topographical diversity of the Southwest stimulated the development of differing ways of life, but the Indigenous peoples of the region have remained unified through political, economic, and social interactions.

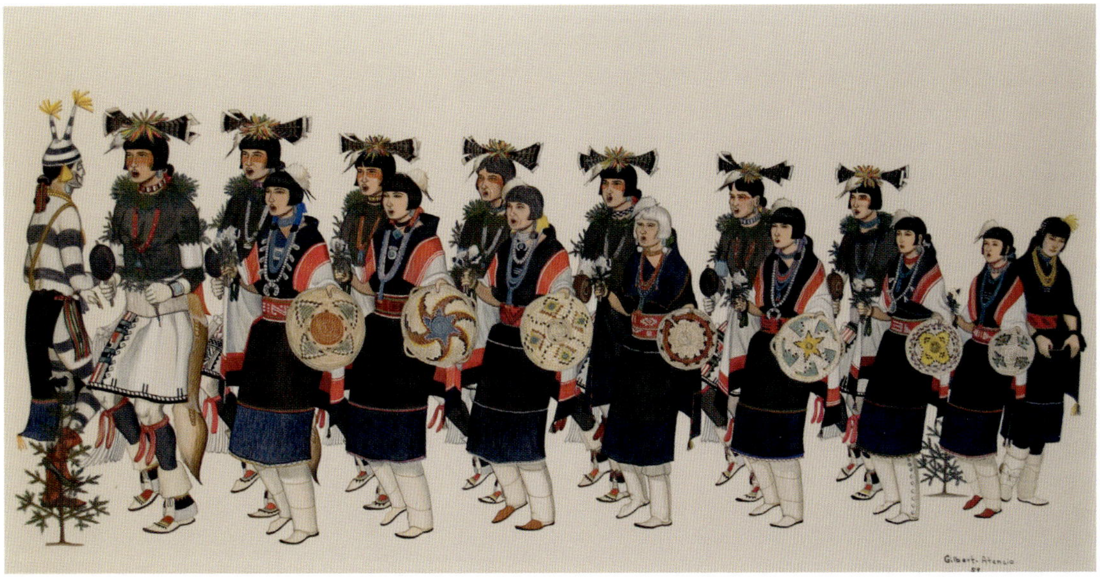

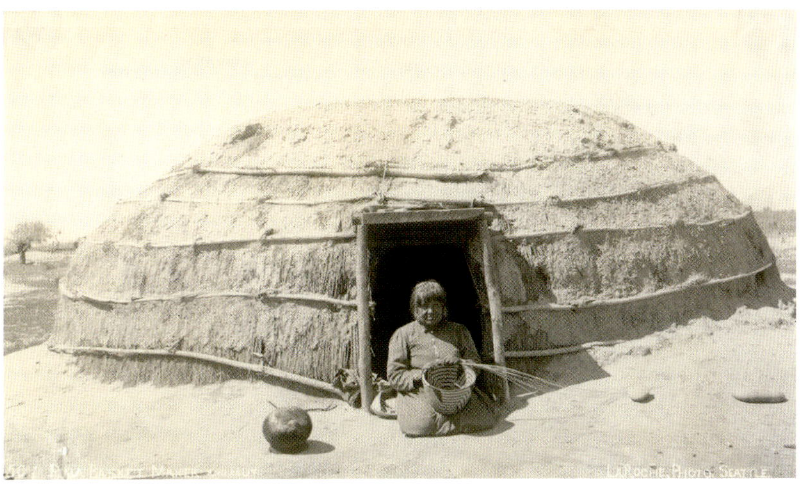

FIG. 3

San Ildefonso Basket Dance, 1959, Gilbert Atencio, San Ildefonso Pueblo, watercolor on paper, 37.0 x 58.5 cm., Museum purchase, 35373

FIG. 4

Akimel O'odham basket weaver, c. 1901. Photo by Frank La Roche. Courtesy of the University of Washington Libraries, Special Collections Division. LAR243.

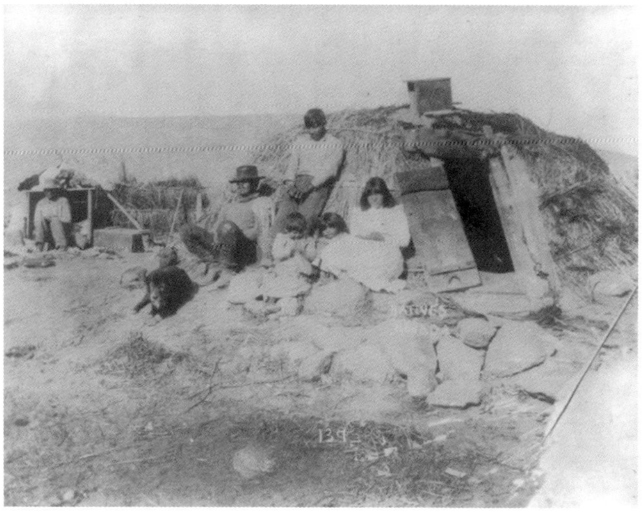

FIG. 5

Paiute family, Goldfield, Nevada, c. 1906. Courtesy of the Library of Congress. LC-USZ62-41448.

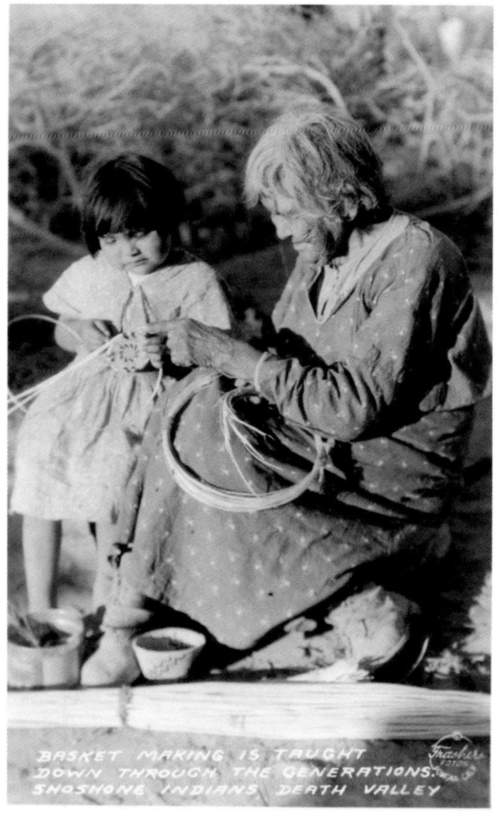

FIG. 6

Panamint Shoshone basket maker teaches young girl to weave, in Death Valley,
California, c. 1900. Courtesy of the Inyo County Museum, Eastern California Museum.

Great Basin Culture Area

The Great Basin Culture Area consists of Utah and Nevada; parts of Colorado, Wyoming, Idaho, Oregon, and California; and the northern edges of Arizona and New Mexico. The region's name refers to the natural basin formed by the Rocky Mountains to the east and the Sierra Nevada mountain range to the west. In this vast dry region, Great Basin people developed a unique style of life: because the natural environment generally could not sustain permanent year-round villages, the populations traveled in family groups or small bands throughout the year, depending on the seasonal availability of food. To accommodate their migrations, Great Basin women wove light, strong basketry containers to carry their personal belongings, food, and babies from camp to camp.

In parts of the southern Great Basin, people lived in small groups along the base of the mountain ranges. They traveled seasonally to a succession of different ecological areas because campsites rarely had a sufficient quantity of food within a short traveling distance. Caves, rock shelters, and woven windbreaks served as temporary shelters. In the northern Great Basin, people stayed longer at several lake, riverine, and marsh areas where resources were more abundant and life more sedentary.

The Great Basin people's first significant contact with foreigners was in the early nineteenth century, when British and American trappers entered their resource-rich northern lands. This was just the beginning of the transformation of their aboriginal ecosystems. By the mid-nineteenth century immigrant trails had been established that crossed the central Great Basin to California and Oregon; with the discovery of gold in 1846, thousands more traveled through the Great Basin on their way to the gold fields. These travelers disrupted and impacted indigenous seasonal migrations, as well as affected the area's delicate ecological balance. Some of these immigrants never made it to their destinations; instead they stayed and settled on the Great Basin landscape.

Permanent foreign settlement began in earnest in the mid-1800s, when over fifty thousand Mormons migrated to the Great Salt Lake region and established a permanent colony. During the following decades, livestock grazing destroyed grasslands along the rivers and springs, and forested areas were clear cut to furnish the needs of mines, towns, and ranches. Because of the continual and increasing demand for land by settlers, during the reservation period (1880–1960) native peoples were removed to government-managed lands that Anglo/Euro-Americans found to be the least desirable.

Plateau Culture Area

The Plateau Culture Area is bordered to the east by the Rocky Mountains and to the west by the Cascade Mountains. It includes parts of Washington, northern Idaho, western Montana, northeastern and central Oregon, the eastern tip of northern California, and southeastern British Columbia, Canada. The region's diverse environment ranges from semi-arid lands to verdant mountain meadows. The geographical term "plateau" refers to a series of high plateaus, or plains, drained by the

FIG. 7

Basket weaver Wash-us-etan-way and a cornhusk bag, 1907. Courtesy of the Maryhill Museum of Art. 1991-06-001.

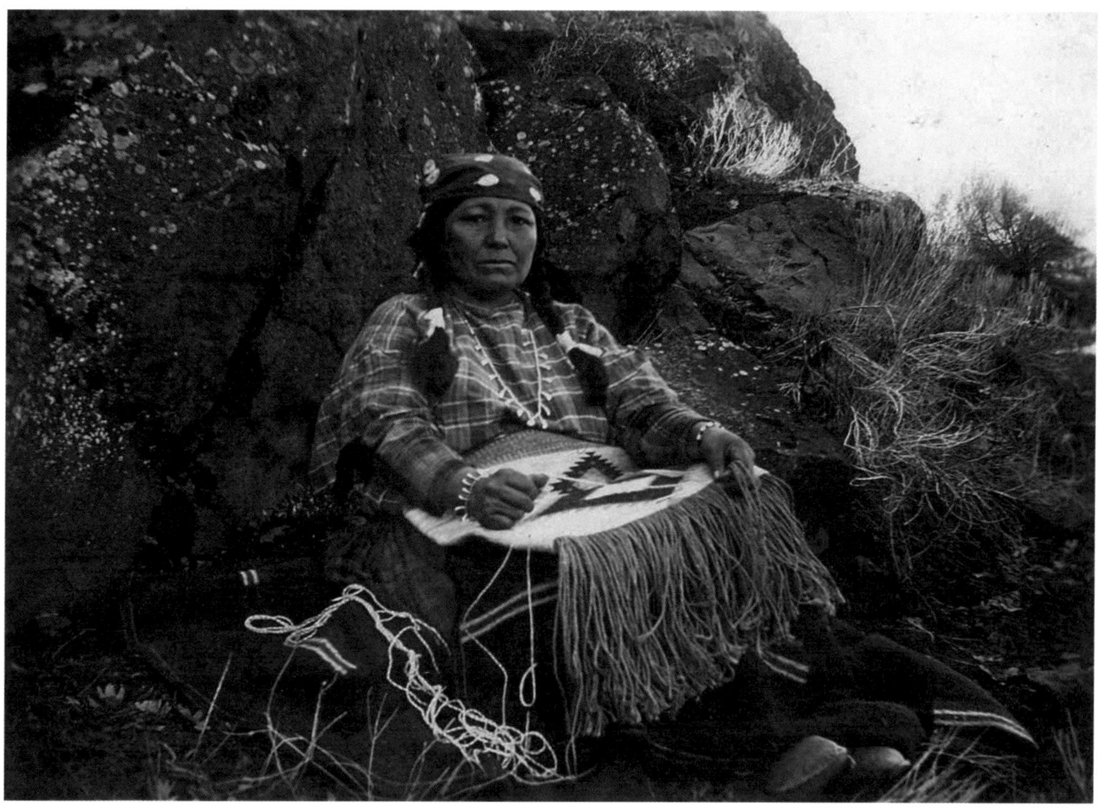

Columbia River and its tributaries in the south and by the Thompson and Fraser rivers in the north.

The Plateau people's most valued food resource was salmon, which they supplemented with various plant foods—primarily roots, tubers, and berries—and small game. Most lived in semi-permanent villages located along fishing streams and rivers; along with groups of related people, they worked and traveled together in the spring, summer, and fall. During the winter, the Plateau people joined together in communal villages. Extensive trade routes circulated resources freely throughout the Plateau, as well as into neighboring regions.

The traditional nomadic way of life began to change dramatically in the early nineteenth century. By the time explorers Lewis and Clark recorded their descriptions of Plateau people in 1805, the acquisition of horses (brought by the Spanish) had initiated culture change. Then, in 1811 fur traders began entering the Plateau; by the 1820s fur-trading posts had been built throughout the area. These explorers and fur trappers and traders introduced diseases to the Plateau people that decimated the Native population. Further cultural and environmental changes occurred when Anglo/Euro-American ranchers and farmers began to settle the narrow valleys of the Plateau region in the early to mid-1800s. In addition, in 1860 gold prospectors overran the Plateau and caused the erosion of stream beds, thus ruining many of the fishing grounds vital to the survival of the Indigenous peoples in the region.

California Culture Area

The California Culture Area corresponds approximately to the present-day state of California and Baja California, Mexico. Before the intrusion of non-Indians, its highly varied ecosystems supported the densest Indigenous population north of Mesoamerica. Pre-contact Californians were food gatherers and hunters, many living in environments rich enough to support year-round villages. An extremely diverse variety of plant species provided the majority of their food, as well as a variety of materials suitable for basket weaving.

The California area includes a wide variety of climates and geographical features—a maritime zone, grasslands and oak woodlands, as well as chaparral, riparian, and forest habitats. All but the most eastern of Indigenous Californians lived where environmental conditions were optimal and food available in amounts that supported established villages. Regions with plentiful resources were home to villages of up to two thousand individuals. The basic social unit was the family; together with groups of related families they formed villages.

California contained some of the most desirable land resources in the American West, and thus contact with non-Indians proved to be intense and devastating to the Indigenous Californians. The first major contact with outsiders was in 1769, when the Spanish established the first of twenty-one missions and presidios along the coast (stretching from San Diego to the San Francisco Bay Area). Due to the introduction of disease by these newcomers, coastal Indigenous populations living near the missions plummeted by approximately 95 percent. Following the secularization of the missions in 1836, Native Americans—who had become separated from their lands and traditional ways of life—sought work in towns, wage labor on private ranches, or a subsistence livelihood on scattered, unoccupied lands.

In 1849 the Gold Rush flooded the state with more foreigners, further destroying Indigenous peoples' delicately balanced relationship with their food supply. As the native economy broke down, people were forced to become part of an inhospitable and alien society. These were the conditions under which California weavers created what arguably are the world's finest baskets.

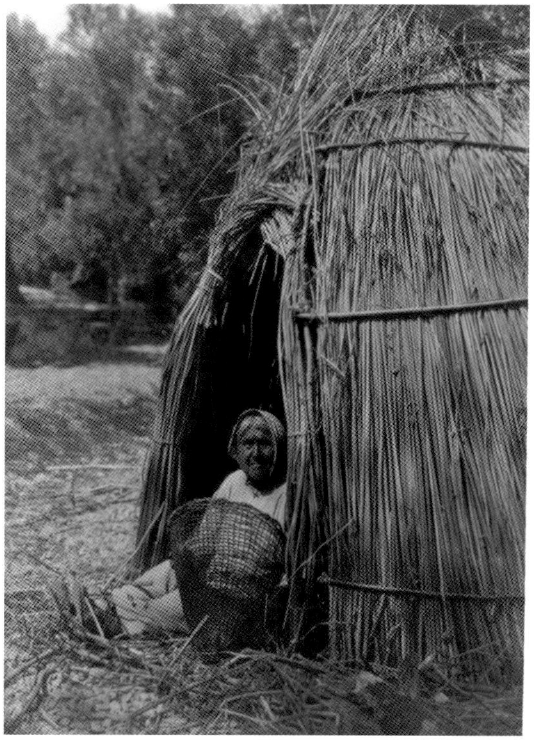

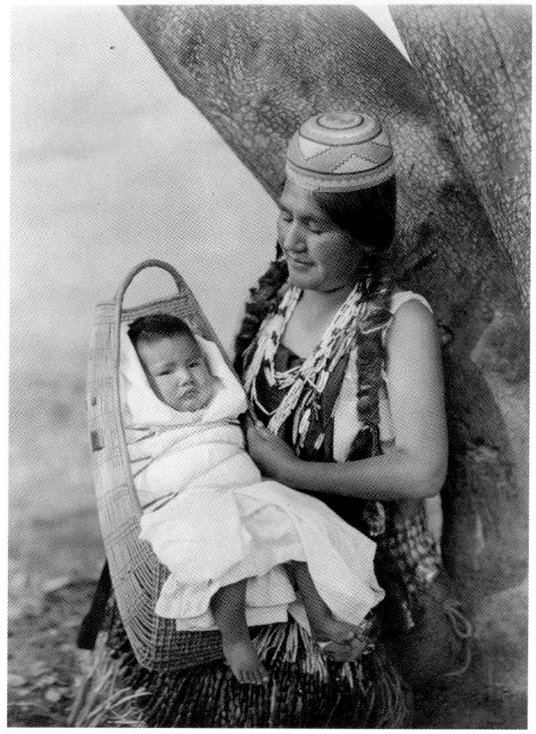

FIG. 8

Pomo woman constructs a tule shelter, 1924. Photo by Edward S. Curtis.
Courtesy of the Library of Congress. LC-USZ62-98673.

FIG. 9

Hupa woman and infant son, 1924. Photo by Edward S. Curtis.
Courtesy of the Library of Congress. LC-USZ62-110505.

Northwest Coast Culture Area

The Northwest Coast is a temperate rainforest extending along the Pacific Coast of North America for more than 2,000 miles. It ranges from the northern tip of California to the panhandle of Alaska and includes western Oregon, Washington, and British Columbia. The eastern boundary is bordered by the Chugach and Saint Elias mountains in Alaska, the Coast Mountains of British Columbia, and the Cascade Range of Washington and Oregon. At its widest point it is only 150 miles across.

Northwest Coast peoples lived in established villages, but it was not uncommon for communities to have separate summer and winter homes. Weather conditions guided seasonal movements and food gathering; during the relatively calm weather of late spring, summer, and early fall, gathering and hunting were the most intense. That was also the time when weavers collected the raw materials necessary for basketmaking. Before contact with non-Indians in the eighteenth century, the Northwest Coast's oceans, rivers, and forests contained plentiful fish (especially salmon) and game to sustain villages, and the lush coniferous forests of the region provided ample basket weaving materials.

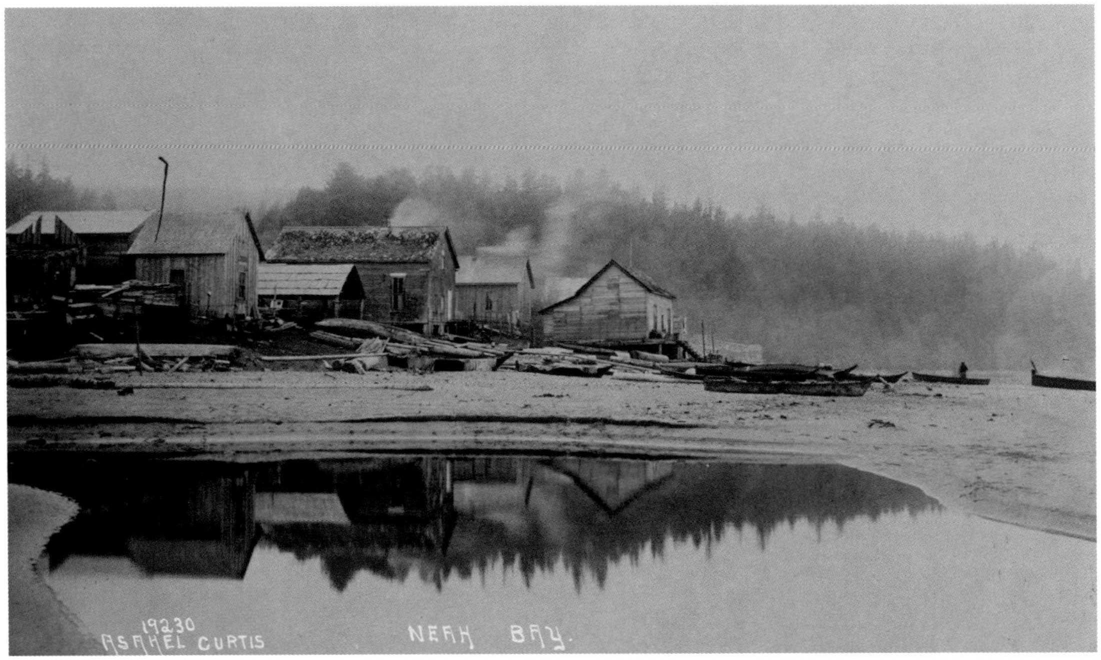

FIG. 10

Neah Bay houses, Makah Indian Reservation, 1910. Photo by Asahel Curtis. Courtesy of the Washington State Historical Society. 1943.42.19230.

FIG. 11

Makah basket weavers, c. 1910. Photo by Asahel Curtis. Courtesy of the Library of Congress. LC-US62-105857.

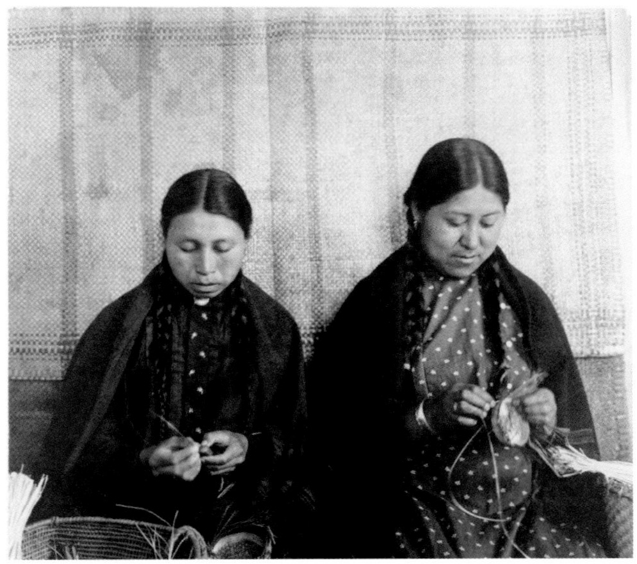

The Northwest Coast peoples' first contact with outsiders was in the late 1700s: Spanish ships docked on the west coast of Vancouver Island, Canada, and by 1800 Russians began establishing settlements in Alaska. By the early nineteenth century foreign fur trappers had reached the lower Columbia River region. They brought new diseases that decimated the Indigenous population. In the 1830s, following the arrival of missionaries, settlers, and commercial logging and fishing enterprises, their indigenous land-based economy was drastically disrupted and their lives changed irrevocably. In less than two generations, Indigenous peoples of the region had lost many of their own traditions and had become part of the cash economy instituted by outsiders. It was during this time period, the 1880s to the 1930s, that women could often be seen selling their baskets directly to tourists on the streets of Northwest Coast cities.

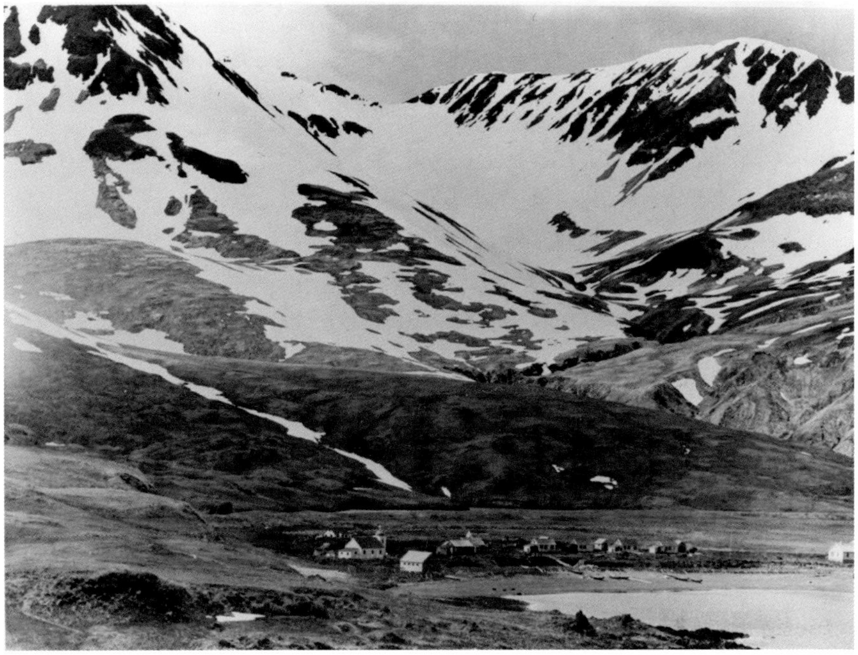

FIG. 12

Attu Island village, 1937. Photo by O. J. Murie. Courtesy of the Library of Congress. LC-USW33-029786-C.

Arctic Culture Area

The Arctic Culture Area extends more than 5,000 miles from eastern Siberia across the northern stretches of Alaska and Canada and all the way to Greenland. The Arctic is largely a tundra landscape with cold, desert-like conditions—the summer temperature reaches highs of 37 to 54 degrees (F). With the exception of the western mountains, Arctic terrain is relatively flat. In summer the treeless tundra is wet and boggy; in winter the extreme cold, snow, and strong winds change the landscape into a hard-packed surface. Despite its harshness, a wide variety of plants and animals thrive there, including the shrubs, sedges, and grasses used for basketry. For subsistence, aboriginal people primarily hunted whales, walrus, seals, and seabirds in coastal areas, and caribou, musk-ox, arctic hare, bears, and smaller animals inland.

The Indigenous peoples of the Western Arctic have a very long history of contact with foreigners, primarily Russians, both because of their proximity to Pacific Coast trading and shipping routes and because of the rich supply of fur resources that drew the foreigners into the interior to trap and trade. As early as the 1760s, Russian expeditions established trade routes along the Pacific Coast (including the Aleutian Islands) and into the Alaskan mainland, bringing them in contact with the Indigenous peoples of the region. However, due to the extremely harsh climate of some areas, where the outsiders rarely ventured, some Indigenous groups did not have significant contact with foreigners until the late nineteenth century.

Of all the people living in the Arctic Culture Area, those from the Aleutian Islands, who identify themselves as the Unangan, had the most intense encounters with outsiders. In the mid-1700s commercial hunters hunted sea otters throughout the island chain; in 1799 the Russian-American

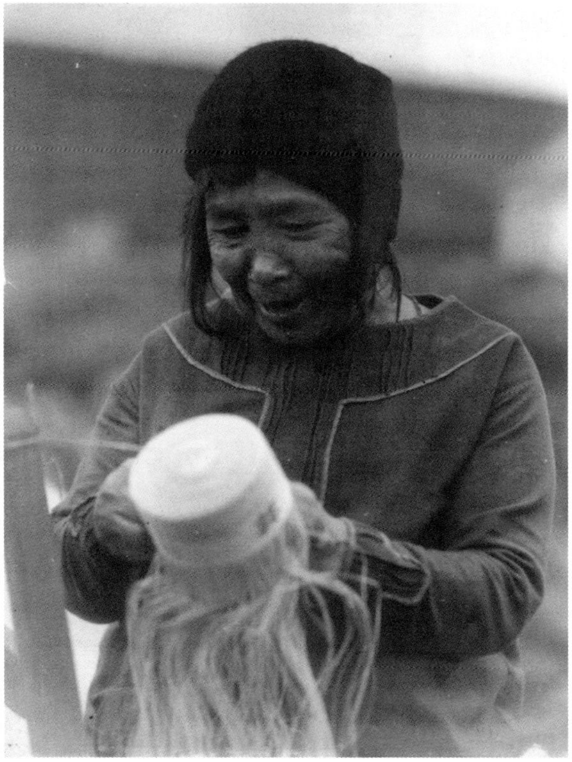

FIG. 13

Unangan basket weaver, Attu Island, c. 1923. Photo by O. J Murie. Courtesy of the University of Alaska Fairbanks, Murie Family Papers. UAF-1990-3-2.

Company was granted an exclusive hunting charter in the area. The intrusion of these non-Indians in their lives, as well as the negative impact that commercial hunting had on the Unangan environment, radically transformed the once independent and self-sufficient lifestyle of these Native peoples. For basket weavers, this meant the adoption of new materials, shapes, and designs while retaining the use of traditional weaving techniques.

THE ART OF BASKET WEAVING

The word "art" is not found in our language. But what do we call a piece of work created by the hands of my family? What will we call that piece which embodies the life of its creator? What will it be if it has a life and soul, while its maker sings and prays for it?

In my home, we call it pottery painted with designs to tell us a story. In my mother's house, we call it a wedding basket, to hold blue corn meal for the groom's family. In my grandma's place, we call it a Kachina doll, a carved image of a life force that holds the Hopi world in place.

We make pieces of life to see, touch, and feel. Shall we call it art? I hope not. It may lose its soul. Its life. Its people.

Michael Lacapa, Apache/Hopi/Tewa

Today when we admire North American Indian baskets as "art" we are responding to them in a way that is quite different from the manner in which they were (and still are) perceived by the people who created and made use of them. It would be unusual to hear a Native American basket maker speak about weaving as creating art for its own sake, for beauty and spirituality and the weaving of baskets are so intertwined in the daily activities of these traditional weavers it is impossible to classify their baskets as only art. Ancestral basket makers would no doubt be amazed to find their baskets in a museum, let alone referred to as art. How would we explain to them that their utilitarian baskets, woven in societies without the notion of art, are now classified as art? It is this blurring of the boundaries between life and art that makes Native American basketry so captivating.

During the 1800s, when Indigenous western North America was being fully colonized by non-Indigenous people, the western "art" world was expanding to include an eclectic range of objects, including those from non-European cultures. Mid-twentieth-century art theorist Andre Malraux saw the purpose behind this new notion of what he called "the first universal world of art" as the creation of a new world, one that would be more balanced, unified, and meaningful (Allan 2009). He recognized the effects of passing time and changing circumstances as the catalysts that transformed objects from non-western cultures, including baskets made by Native American weavers, into works of art in western culture.

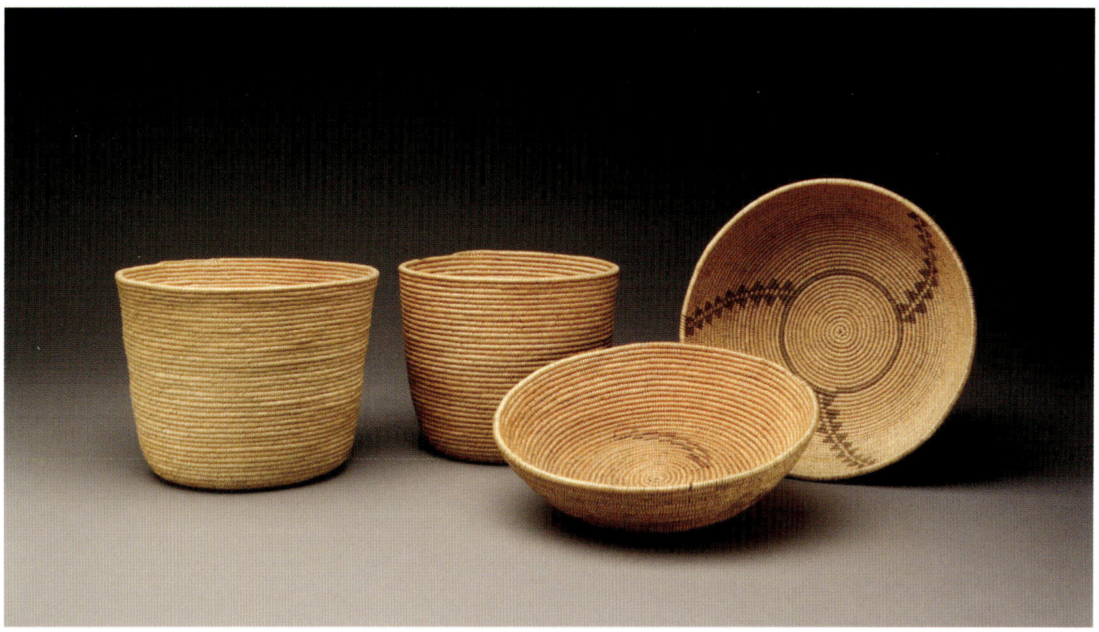

FIG. 14 (Left to right):

Cylinder, c. 1150, Ancestral Pueblo, Artist unknown, 18.5 x 23.8 cm., 53845

Cylinder, c. 1150, Ancestral Pueblo, Artist unknown, 18.5 x 23.8 cm., 53844

Bowl, c. 1150, Ancestral Pueblo, Artist unknown, 8.0 x 27.0 cm., 53846

Bowl, c. 1150, Ancestral Pueblo, Artist unknown, 9.0 x 28.8 cm., 53849

Utilitarian baskets have always been the foundation of basket weaving; as women moved through their daily tasks, they did so with their baskets. For centuries, women have passed their knowledge of basketmaking to the next generation. At one time the art of basketmaking was, of necessity, fully integrated into everyday community and family life. Today, weavers are caught up in the modern world and lead lives in which weaving has become an act of devotion, done when all their other obligations have been met.

For the purposes of creating this exhibition and catalogue, we considered baskets as examples of "cultural art," a concept which is not entirely new (Langer 1966:5–12). Specifically, cultural art expresses the beliefs, values, and ways of doing and knowing things that are common to a group of people. Creating and sharing cultural-art objects gives individuals a sense of belonging to a community. From this perspective, basketry art is an important expression of culture. It helps basket makers and users locate meaning in their lives, understand the world around them, and communicate those understandings to others by means of a visual language unique to them.

Many Native American basket weavers have strong feelings about the concept of art and how it relates to basket weaving. Among them is contemporary Tlingit weaver Teri Rofkar, from Sitka, Alaska:

> We never had a word for art in our culture. The art was part of everything. Art was that berry basket that you used every year that your grandma, your great grandmother or your great-great grandmother did. You know, they last about 200 years. When I say it takes me 200 hours to do one of those baskets, that's ghastly. . . . [B]ut when you think about it and you use it, this beautiful piece which is art most of the year and functional for a small period of time, all of a sudden one hour a year, it's not so bad. Not so bad. We just have a different way of looking at things (Rofkar 2009).

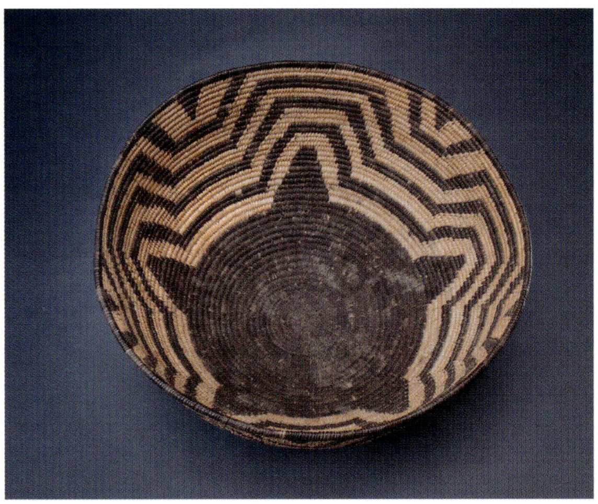

FIG. 15

Saguaro-wine Serving Bowl, c. 1910, Tohono O'odham, Mildred Lewis, 19.5 x 39.5 cm., 57476

In Native American cultures with basket-weaving traditions, baskets have always been objects of great power, meaning, and value. Within this conceptual framework, the state of mind of the basket maker during the gathering and processing of plant materials, as well as the construction of the basket, has consequences for the final product. By following the proper rituals and maintaining the correct attitude the weaver imbues her basket with a life force.

In a parallel vein, Angelo Joaquin, a Tohono O'odham elder and member of the Museum of Indian Art & Culture's Indian Advisory Panel, has distinct views concerning a basket's beauty and value. The world, he explained, was created for the people by four creators: two animals and two humans. The creators included everything the people needed for their physical, mental, and spiritual well-being. Because the creators made plants, animals, and humans equal and invested with power, humans are the stewards, not the lords, of the land. This is why Tohono O'odham weavers are thankful to the plants for giving of themselves, and why they acknowledge their ties as well as their debt to the land when they harvest basketry plants. "Plants have power that transfers to the basket," said Joaquin, "and baskets made of combinations of plants have even more power. If the weaver wove her basket in the culturally correct way, if she said the prayers, if she honored the process, she has made a 'good basket'" (A. Joaquin, pers. comm. 2011). From Joaquin's point of view, it is the spiritual dimension of the basket that determines its worth. It is the process that matters not the result. "Baskets are the by-product," stated Joaquin.

WEAVING TRANSITIONS

Related threads which run through the exhibition and catalogue include how basket weaving has been impacted by the passing of time, as well as the associated cultural, social, and economic changes that have affected Native Americans over the centuries.

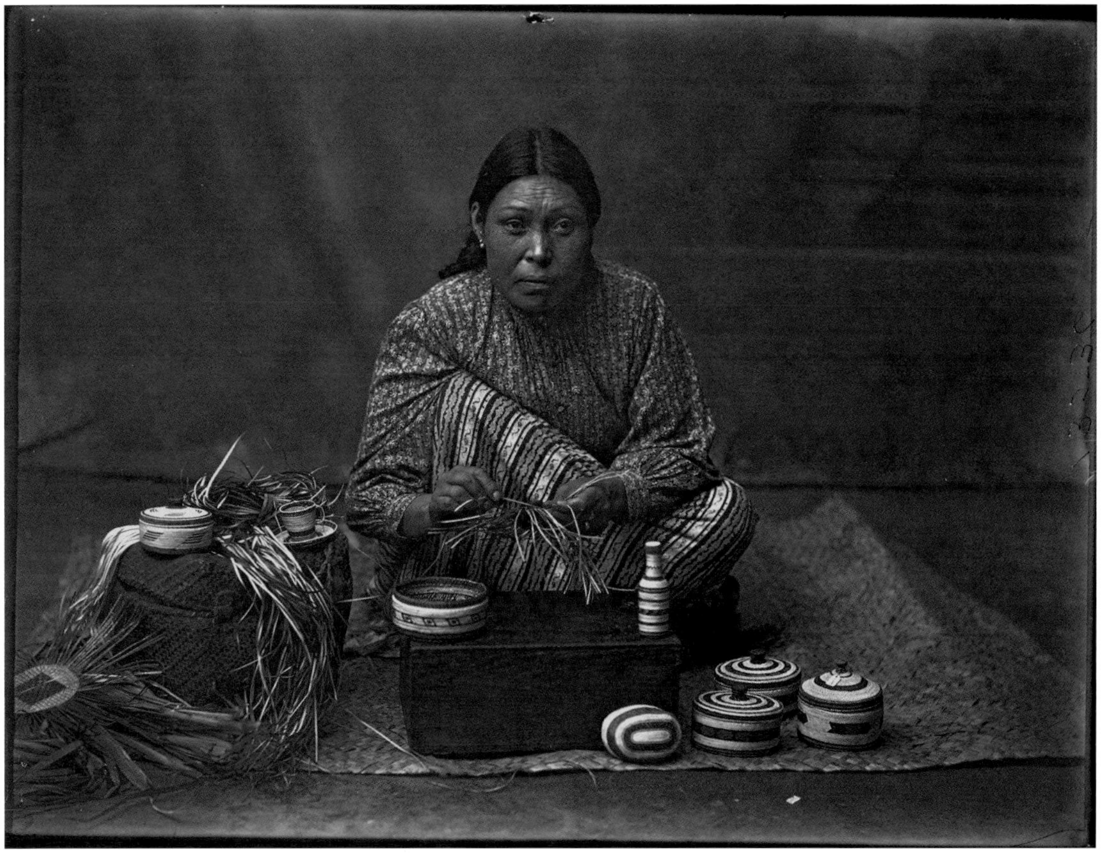

FIG. 16

Nuu-chah-nulth weaver Ellen Curley demonstrates basketmaking at the St. Louis World's Fair, 1904. Courtesy of the Field Museum. CSA 13536-1.

A number of basket weavers from different tribal groups demonstrated their art at the 1904 St. Louis World's Fair. The usual compensation for an event like this would have been travel, food, lodging, and a percentage, if not all, of the profits from the sale of the baskets.

Baskets made during the period 1880 through 1930, a period of transition for Native American communities (and the focus of the museum's collections) are examples of adaptability and endurance; these baskets were made during a time of turmoil and imbalance in the weavers' lives. By 1880 most tribal people in the western United States were relocated on reservations, allotted lands, or had found wage labor within the dominant non-Indian culture. The intrusion of non-Indian people and consequent loss of their homelands, and their self-sufficient and independent way of life made finding new ways to survive in the new wage and market economy essential.

By the late 1880s many basket weavers realized that they were able to help support their families in the new cash economy by selling their baskets. At the same time, the market for their baskets was expanding: baskets of high quality and intricate workmanship were made for or commissioned by dealers, collectors, and museums. In addition, eccentric "trinket" baskets that appealed to tourists and casual collectors became popular.

FIG. 17

Jar with Rattle Lid, c. 1909, Tlingit, Artist unknown, 10.4 x 12.7 cm., 25431

Fancy Gathering Basket, c. 1920, Tlingit, Artist unknown, 19.8 x 14.9 cm., 23445

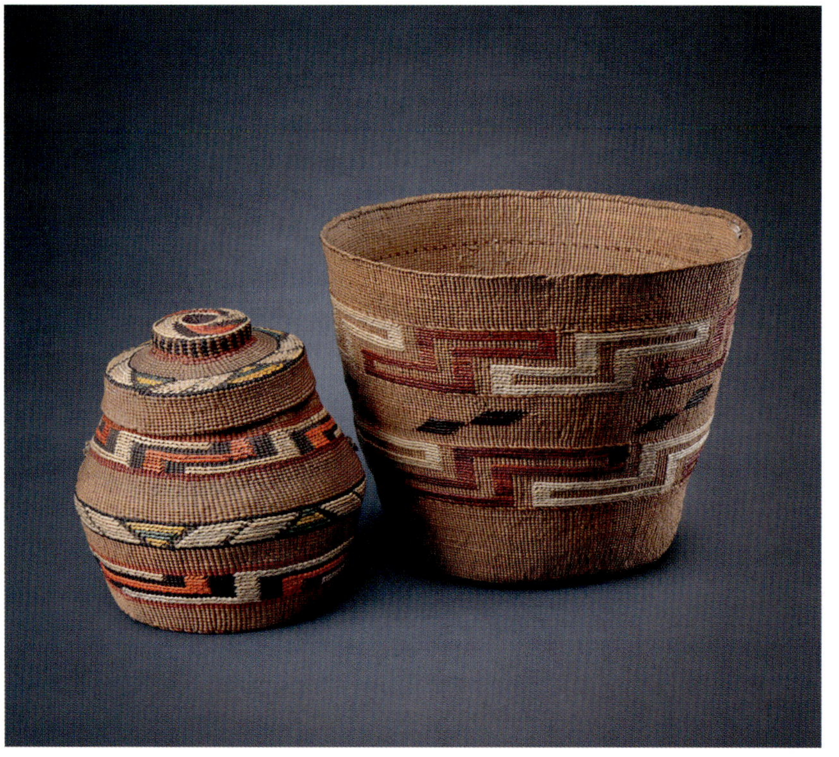

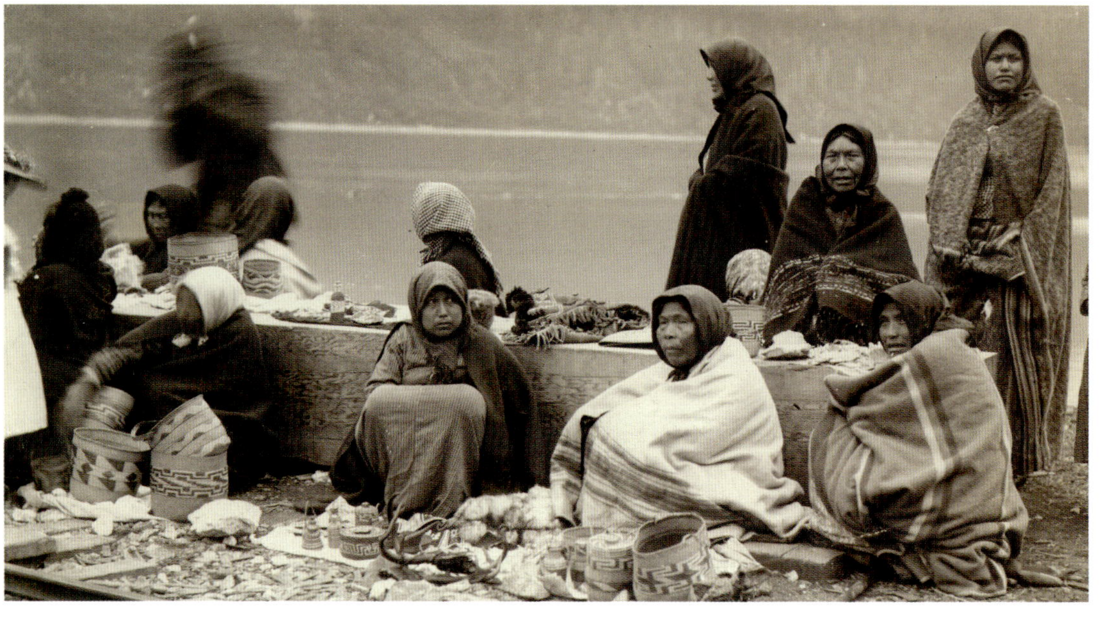

FIG. 18

Tlingit women sell baskets at Treadwell Mines, c. 1894. Photo by Frank LaRoche. Courtesy of the University of Washington Libraries, Special Collections. NA 673.

The area near Juneau, Alaska, was a traditional fish camp for the Indigenous Tlingit Indians. After the discovery of gold, the Treadwell Mines began operations there in 1881. Tlingit women came from nearby villages to sell baskets, beaded clothing, and other wares to gold miners and tourists.

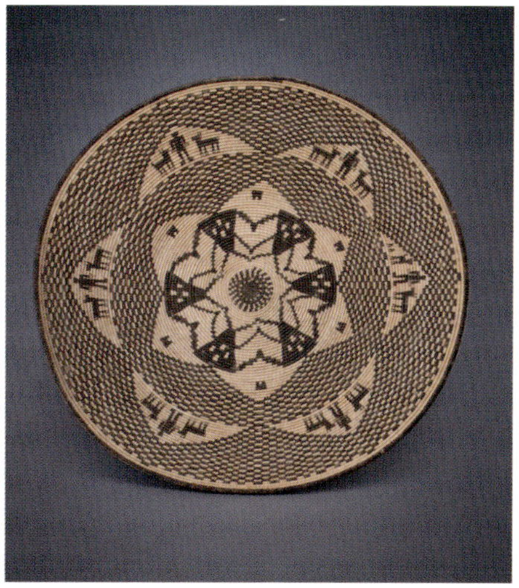

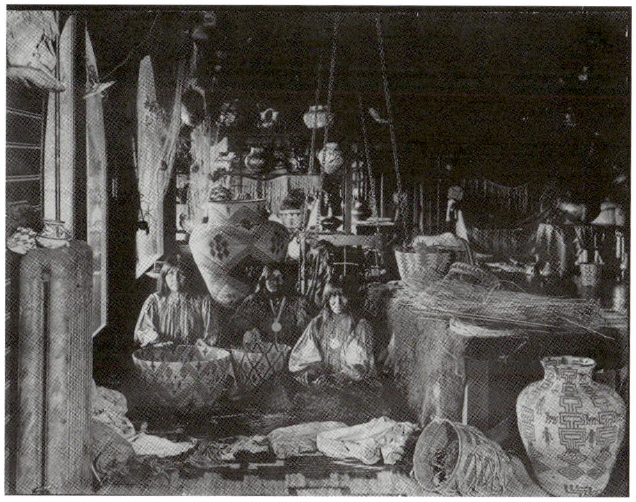

FIG. 19

Tray, c. 1900, Western Apache, Artist unknown, 10.8 x 78.5 cm., 12000

FIG. 20

Yavapai or Western Apache basket-weaving demonstrators at the Alvarado Hotel, Albuquerque, New Mexico, 1903. Courtesy of the Heard Museum, Phoenix, Arizona.

These women probably are demonstrating their art in the Indian Building adjacent to the hotel. The Fred Harvey Company, owners of the Alvarado Hotel, merchandized the arts of the Southwest and attracted tourists in part by hiring Native Americans as salespeople and demonstrators. A few became Harvey Company career employees.

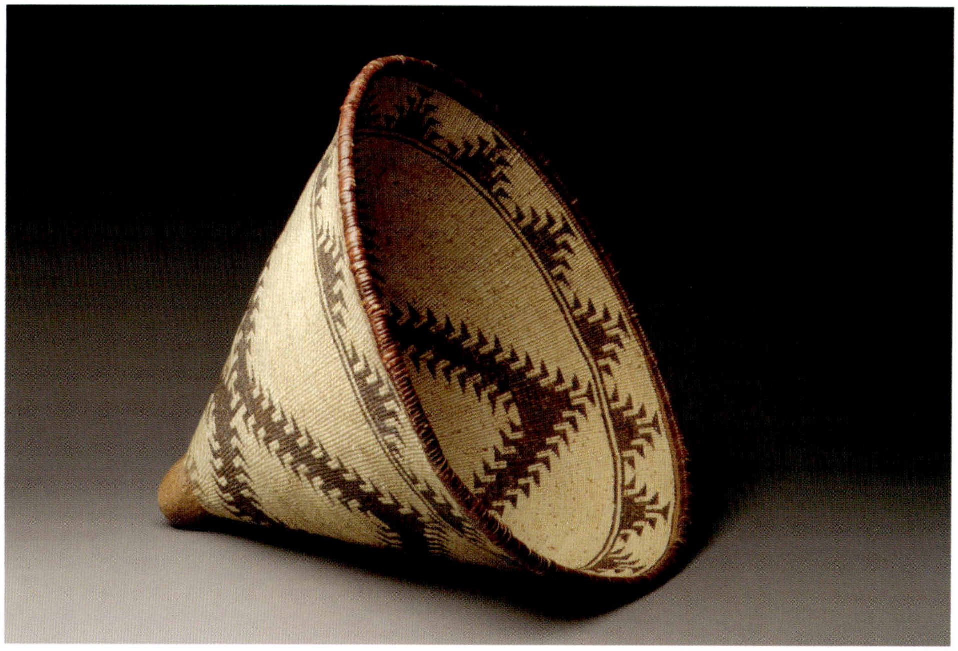

FIG. 21

Carrying Basket, c. 1905, Achumawi, Artist unknown, 48.5 x 53.0 cm., 1852

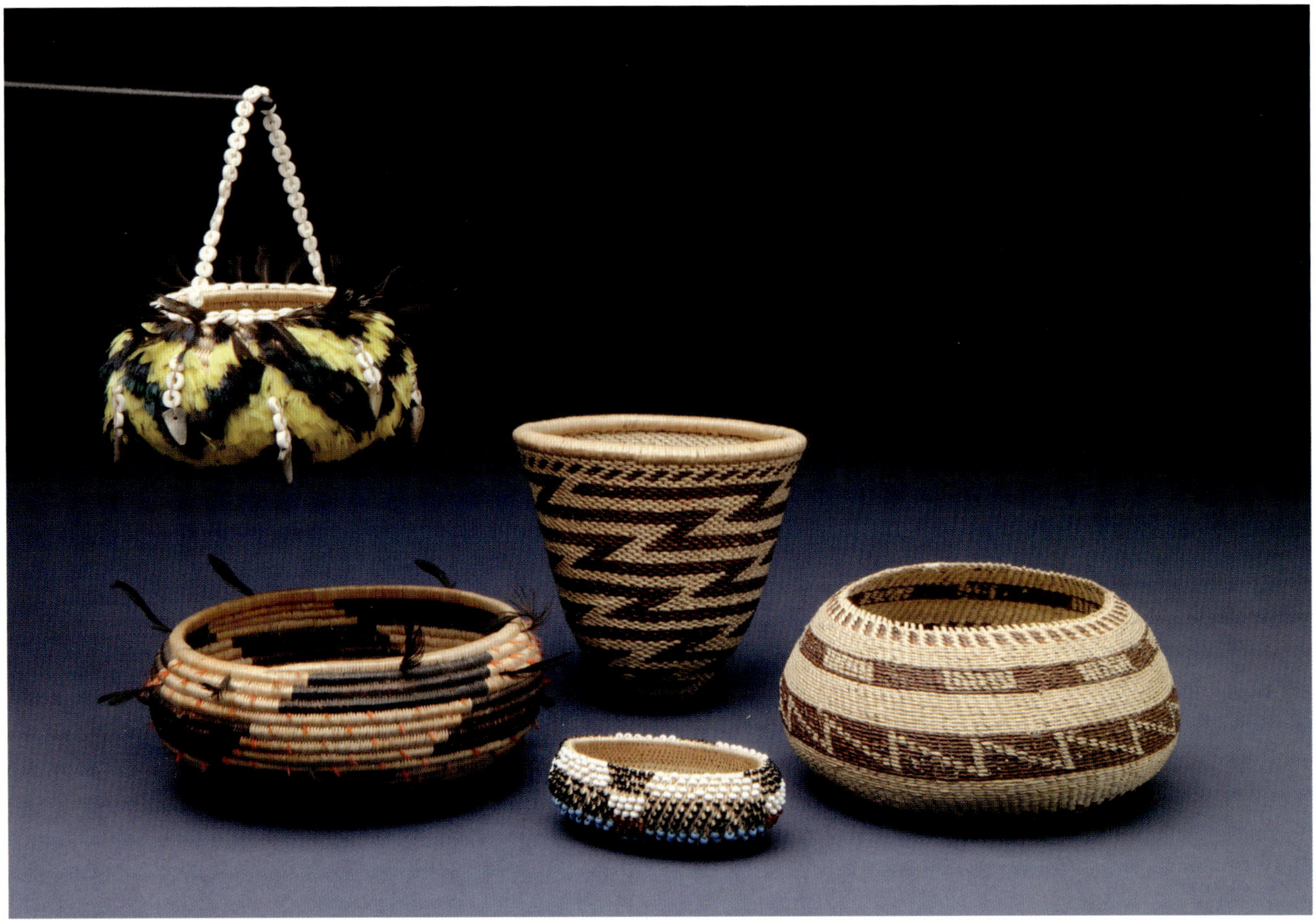

FIG. 22 (Clockwise from lower right):

Trinket Basket, 1906, Pomo, Emily Graves, 6.7 x 10.5 cm., 14325

Gift Basket, c. 1910, Wappo, Artist unknown, 2.4 x 4.6 x 7.0 cm., 14321

Treasure or Gift Basket, c. 1910, Pomo, Artist unknown, 6.0 x 14.1 cm., 14335

Treasure or Gift Basket, c. 1900, Pomo, Artist unknown, 2.5 x 11.6 cm., 14351

Miniature Basket, c. 1901, Pomo, Attributed to Mary Benson, 9.2 x 9.7 cm., 14324

Over the following decades museum curators, fine art dealers, and serious collectors increasingly sought out Indigenous-made baskets that they considered "culturally real and meaningful" and not merely commercial products. The Achumawi carrying basket in figure 21 is a fine example of the meeting of two cultures and two minds: that of the basket's collector, Mary Cabot Wheelwright, founder of the Wheelwright Museum of the American Indian in Santa Fe, New Mexico, and the basket's unknown weaver. Even though we do not know the name of this northern California weaver, we can learn much about her from her basket. For example, after examining the basket's materials, construction, form, and size, we can determine that rather than give in to the demands of the marketplace she stuck to her guns and made an almost wholly traditional basket. The only nod to cultivating the consumer is evident in her use of an elaborated two-dimensional design. For this weaver, making a commercial basket did not mean abandoning her understanding of weaving as a physical expression of her traditional knowledge.

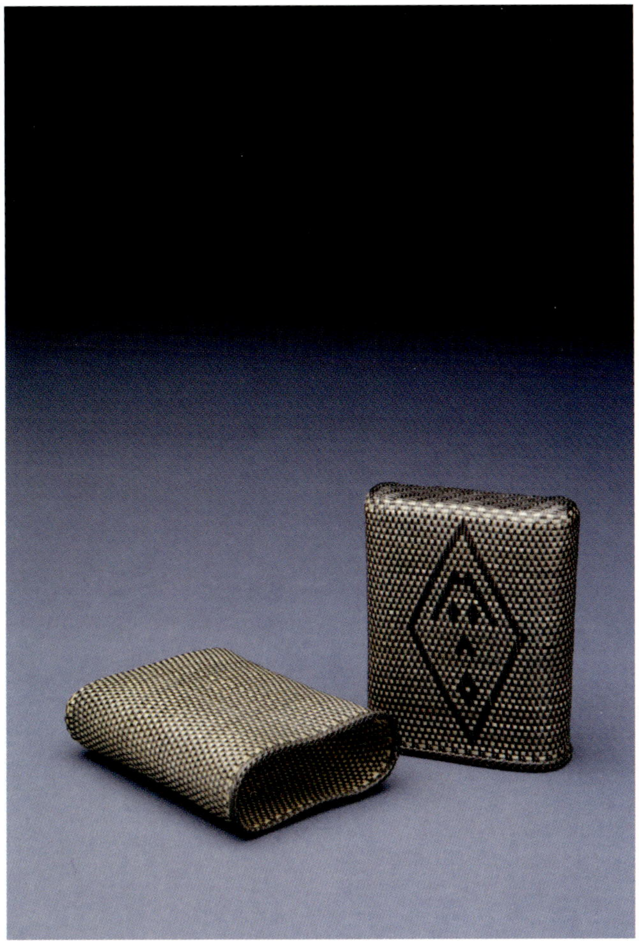

FIG. 23

Cigarette Case, c. 1915, Unangan, Artist unknown, 5.0 x 6.2 x 8.8 cm., 14299

When cultural outsiders look at Native baskets, there are a great many attributes they are unable to see or understand, because the way they observe and learn from things is affected by what they know and believe. Generally, they are looking for connections between objects, even those made by other cultures, and their own known reality (Berger 1972:8–9). Perhaps this is why some basket collectors were particularly attracted to trinket baskets that mimicked objects from their own reality, such as cigarette cases.

On the other hand, the weavers of trinket baskets responded wholeheartedly to the marketplace. They produced baskets for tourists who were not as interested in the cultural or artistic value of baskets as was Mary Cabot Wheelwright when she acquired the carrying basket. Many non-Indian buyers favored small, easily portable baskets that served as souvenirs (and proof to family and friends back home) of their engagement with "strange" and "exotic" cultures. While some basket makers made familiar, utilitarian forms from their own culture, ones they were comfortable weaving, others experimented by weaving baskets based on their astute observations of foreign forms they knew tourists and collectors found appealing or useful, such as the baleen cigarette case in figure 23. For more than a century, these types of "commercial" baskets have helped maintain the cultural practice of basketmaking.

The changes brought on by modern life do not always lead to the degradation or demise of a culture or cultural practice—modernization is not synonymous with cultural loss. Basket weaving is always transforming to fit the changing cultural obligations of the weavers and their communities. Although some contemporary basket weavers acknowledge livelihood as a primary reason for making baskets, they regard their work as more than commodities. Baskets represent Native culture to the world, its spiritual legacy, and each weaver's relation to the natural environment, her community, and her family. The tradition of weaving baskets has never been stagnant as weavers have always kept their art vital by blending new contemporary directions with older traditions. For

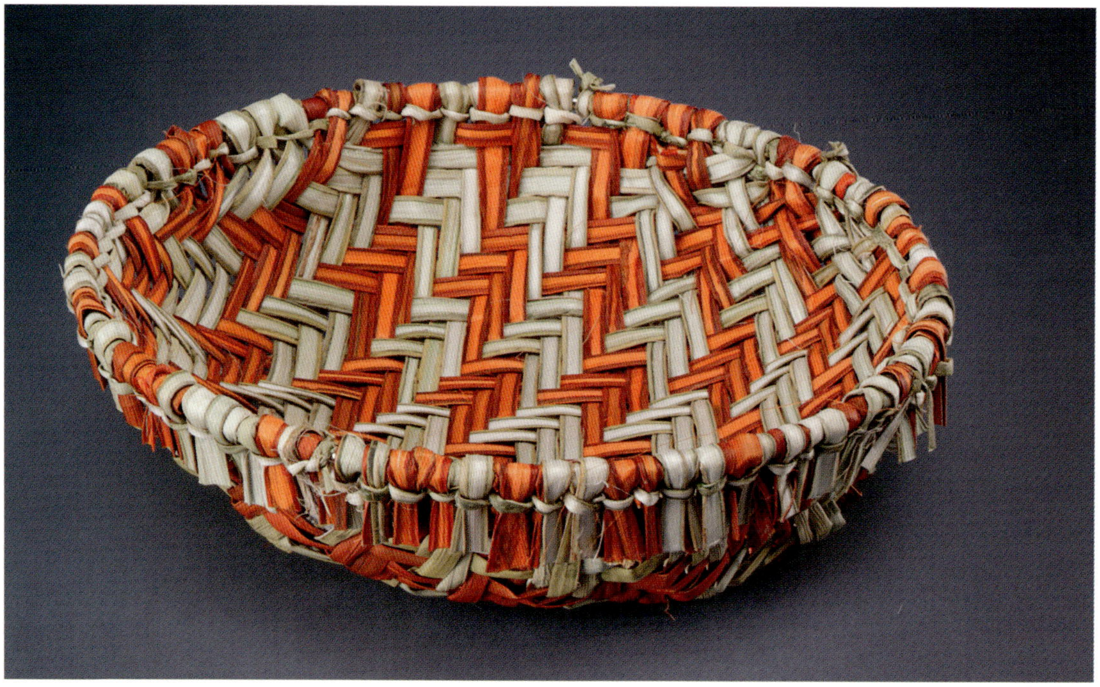

FIG. 24

Bowl, 2012, Hopi (Second Mesa), Kaitlyn Kayquoptewa, 6.5 x 20.5 cm., 58316

Kaitlyn Kayquoptewa made this basket while teaching a class in the plaiting technique at the Museum of Indian Arts & Culture, Santa Fe, in June 2012. She learned to weave from her grandmother and from her mother, Patty Wells. Kayquoptewa was fifteen years old at the time and had been weaving for three years.

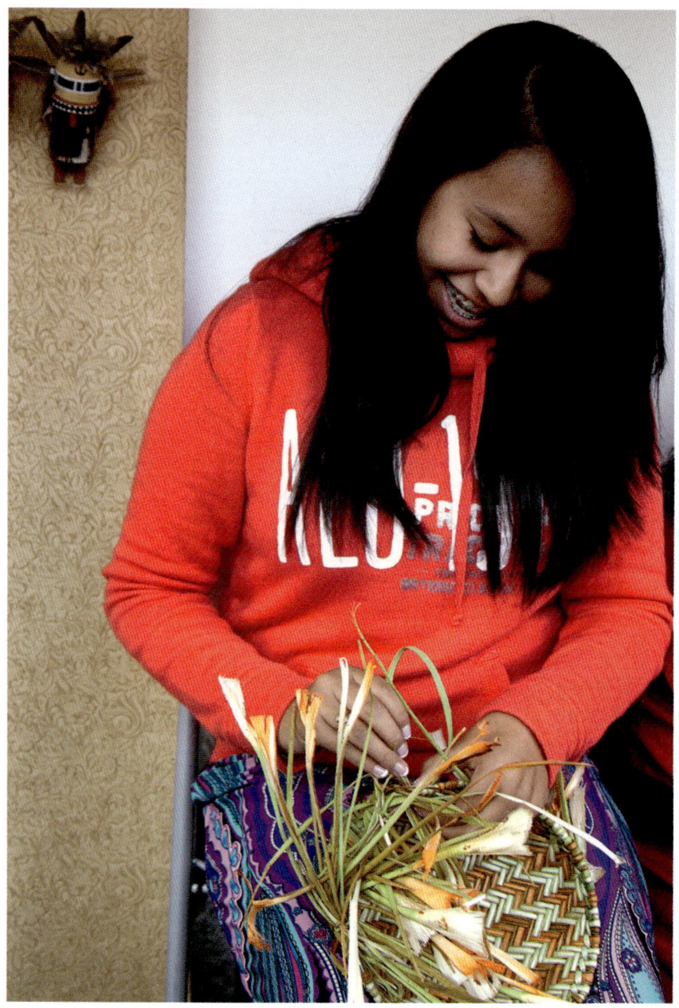

FIG. 25

Kaitlyn Kayquoptewa, Hopi (Second Mesa), Santa Fe Indian Market, 2011. Photo by Clare Lighton.

others, rediscovering old traditions in basketry is personally fulfilling and also a way to teach outsiders about their culture.

FIVE WAYS OF KNOWING BASKETS

North American Indian baskets are cultural histories—documents of the aesthetics, beliefs, lifestyles, natural environment, and technologies of the people who made and used them. These unique baskets are producible and fully comprehensible only within the social context of the weavers. Just as words take on unique meanings within sentences, baskets take on unique meanings within their social contexts. When anthropologist Deborah Neff collaborated with Tohono O'odham basket weaver Frances Manuel on her life history, Neff recognized that in order to understand something from another world we have to try and step outside our taken-for-granted realities and work on understanding difference (Manuel and Neff 2001:206). This means that because baskets are derived from and maintained by social interactions, and are not soley a consequence of utility, their forms and meanings are contingent on social and historical processes (Berger and Luckmann 1966).

Like each basket *Woven Identities* is an exploration of both the concrete and conceptual; it is a study of how weavers have worked with the utilitarian and aesthetic attributes of baskets for centuries to create both functional and cultural art forms. When the baskets included in this catalogue were first collected, little to no information about them was recorded—we know few of the weavers' names, we have few of their words. Nonetheless, each basket has a woven identity and all tell a story if you know the right questions to ask. Museums exist to collect objects as one means of understanding and documenting people, events, places, and times. We study peoples' material culture to learn who they were and how they lived. When exhibiting and representing the lives of peoples with oral cultures—where no written record exists from the point of view of a cultural insider—the histories baskets hold become especially significant. We deduce the identity of each basket—where it was made, when it was made, who made it, who it was made for, and why it was made—by "reading" its individual characteristics.

To understand the language of a basket and to reveal its woven identity, we study five principal traits: materials, construction techniques, form, function, and two-dimensional design and ornamentation. By identifying the materials used in a basket and then determining the geographical availability of those plants, we can establish where the weaver lived and can begin to assign a tribal provenance. For construction, we know that weavers chose techniques based on tribal tradition, personal choice, and the basket's intended use. When determining the form and size of the basket, function drove these attributes, but so did the social milieu in which it was made. Finally, two-dimensional design motifs and the ways they are combined, as well as their subject, are socially determined and thus tend to be unique to each individual tribe.

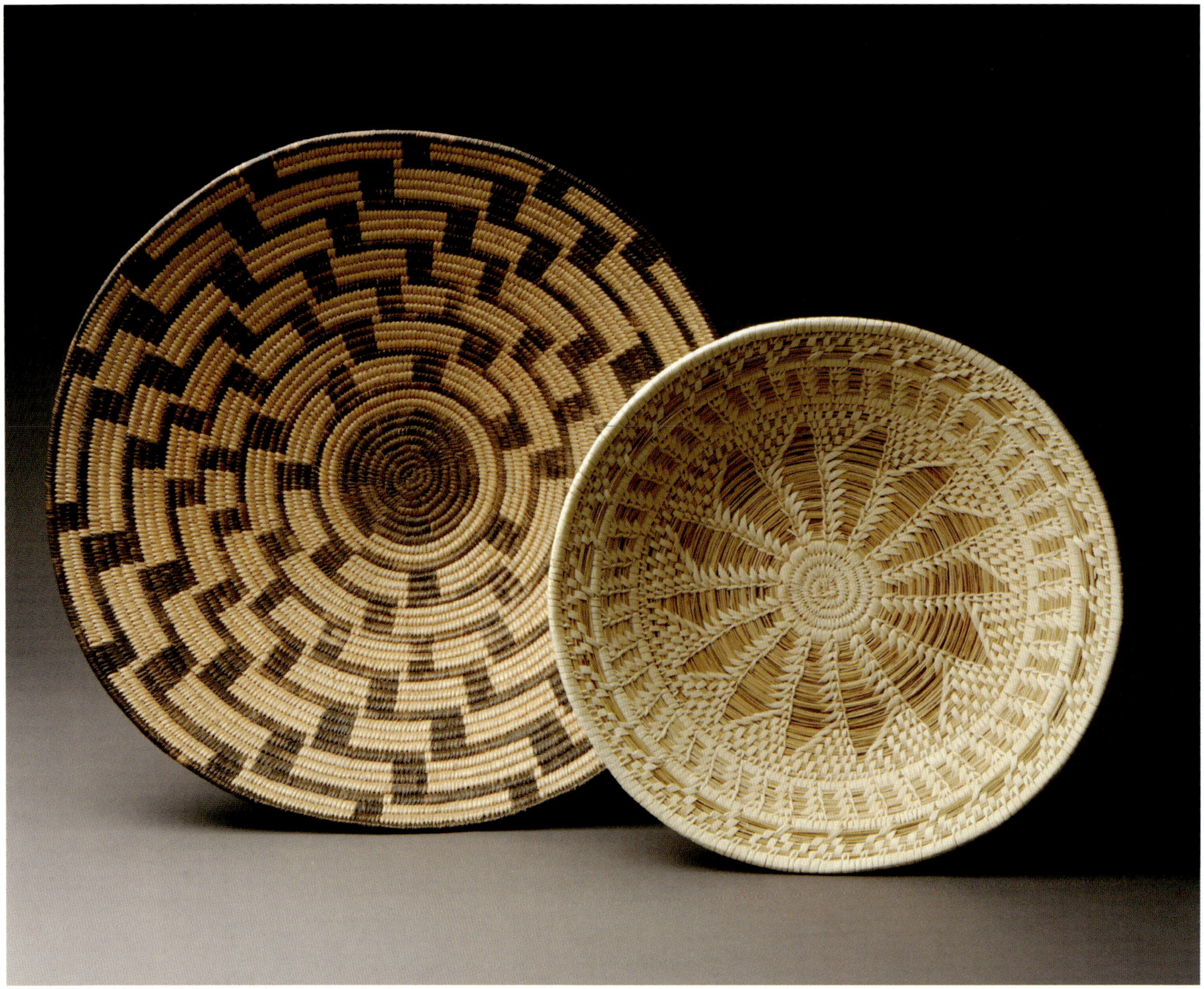

FIG. 26 (left to right):

Bowl, c. 1900, Tohono O'odham, Artist unknown, 14.0 x 48.0 cm., 14411

FOUNDATION: cattail-splint bundle

SEWING ELEMENTS: willow, devil's claw seedpod; with dye

Tray, 1983, Tohono O'odham, Barbara Havier, 7.9 x 35.9 cm., 50014

FOUNDATION: beargrass bundle

SEWING ELEMENT: yucca leaf

In the desert Southwest, certain basketry materials are so valuable that they are saved for weaving baskets intended for internal community use only; baskets made for sale were typically constructed of more easily obtainable plants. Tohono O'odham weavers (as well as the Akimel O'odham) have used willow and cottonwood with devil's claw seedpod as the sewing elements on cattail or beargrass foundations. These materials made sturdy, long-wearing, watertight basket containers for use by the Tohono O'odham peoples. In the late 1800s Tohono O'odham weavers began using the more plentiful yucca sewn on a beargrass foundation for their made-for-sale baskets (Kissell 1916:197).

Chapter 1

MATERIAL

The materials used in a basket are important for helping discover where it was made and by whom. By identifying the geographical availability of plant resources, we can learn where the basket weaver lived and can begin to assign a tribal affiliation. Of the many materials available, a weaver uses only a few—each choice based on tribal tradition and personal choice, as well as on the material's unique utility, color, and surface texture.

> *Basket materials are filled with history, honor, and grace . . .*
> *and weaving with them is medicine for the body, soul, and spirit.*
>
> Terrol Dew Johnson
> Tohono O'odham basket weaver
> (T. Johnson, pers. comm. 2012)

The beauty of basketry begins with wild plants painstakingly tended, selected, processed, and prepared. For thousands of years, weavers coaxed out of their natural environment a vast number of weaving materials, such as roots, rhizomes (underground stems), stems, branches, bark, leaves, and leaves of grass. Wherever they lived, from the desert American Southwest to the Arctic tundra, basket weavers took care to tend and cultivate favored plant species and preserve their habitats. Weavers utilized such horticultural techniques as pruning, weeding, burning, selective harvesting, and coppicing (cutting trees to allow shoots to grow from their stumps) to produce healthy, flawless materials with the desired characteristics of strength, durability, flexibility, uniformity, and beauty (Anderson 2005:210–213).

Over the generations, weavers learned which particular materials were suitable for specific weaving tasks. While some materials are versatile, others can be used for only one or two distinct functions. Some materials have limited geographic availability; others are found in many areas of the western United States. Due to the settling of Indigenous lands by foreigners who disrupted the

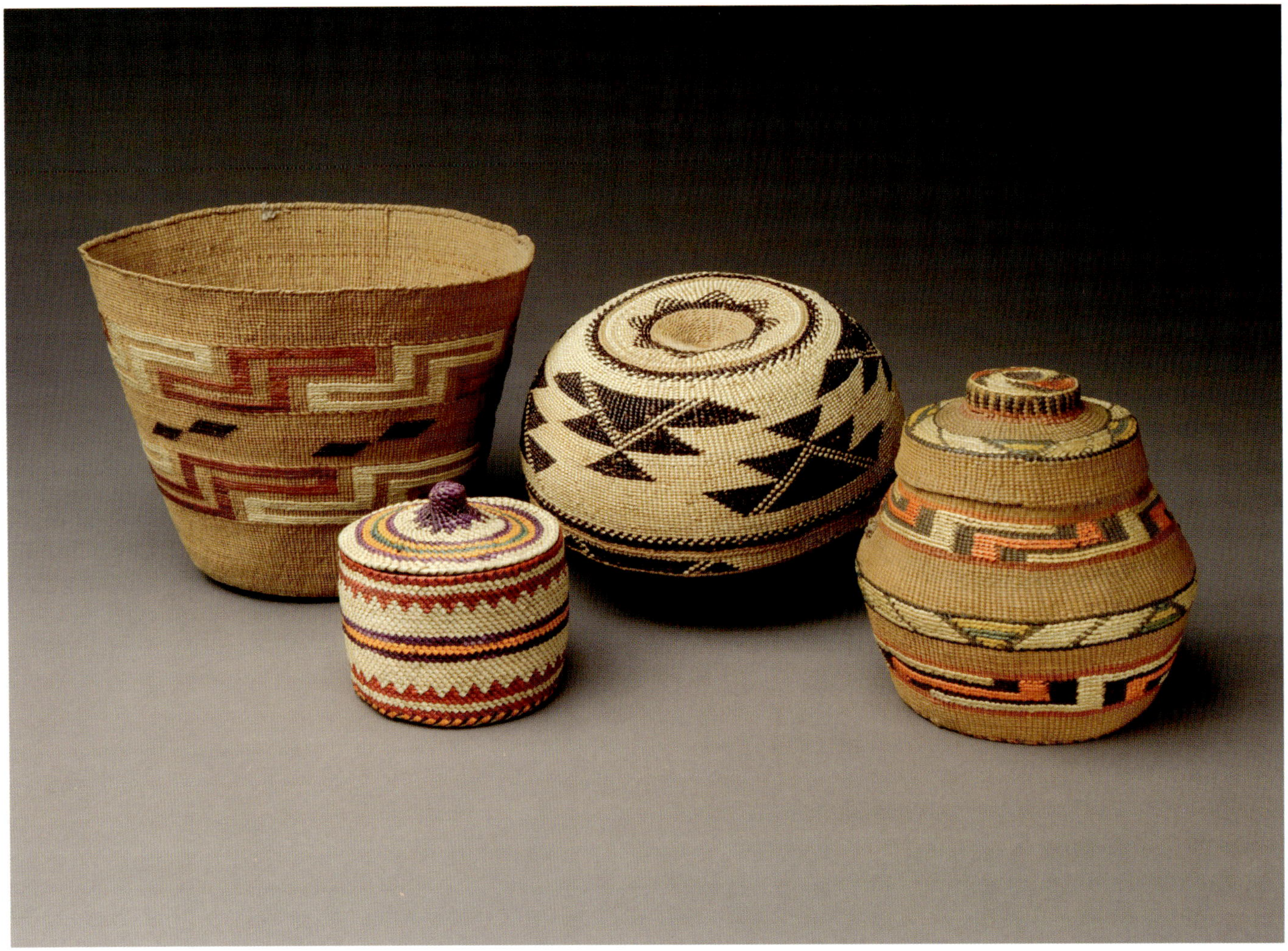

FIG. 27 (Left to right):

Cylinder, c. 1920, Tlingit, Artist unknown, 19.8 x 14.9 cm., 23445

FOUNDATION: spruce root

WEAVING ELEMENTS: spruce root, beach grass; with dye

Lidded Bowl, c. 1970, Makah, Artist unknown, 6.0 x 8.6 cm., 23696

FOUNDATION: cedar bark

WEAVING ELEMENT: beargrass; with dye

Woman's Cap, c. 1930, Lower Klamath River, Artist unknown, 9.0 x 17.0 cm., 23715

FOUNDATION: hazelnut rods

WEAVING ELEMENTS: spruce root, beargrass, maidenhair fern stem

Jar with Rattle Lid, ca. 1909,Tlingit, Artist unknown, 10.4 x 12.7 cm., 25431

FOUNDATION: spruce root

WEAVING ELEMENTS: spruce root, beach grass; with dye

Native American basket weavers consider a number of plant characteristics when choosing materials for their baskets. Most construction techniques require materials that are strong and flexible and in plentiful supply in the weaver's natural environment. Of the many materials available, a weaver uses only a few, each choice based on tribal tradition and personal preference, as well as the material's availability, utility, color, texture, and the ease with which it accepts dyes.

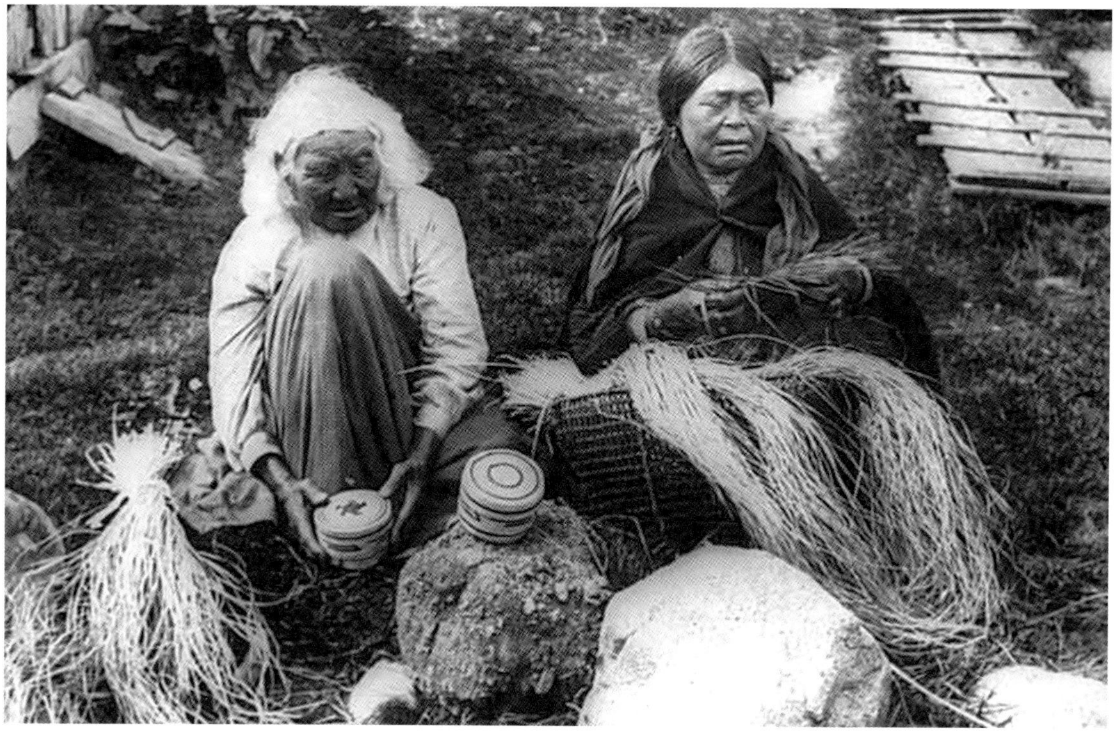

FIG. 28

Makah weavers Ooati and her daughter Susy Ides, c. 1905. Photo by James G. McCurdy. Courtesy of the North Olympic Library Digital Collection. Indn port 035.

These two weavers spent many days collecting and processing materials into the fine foundation and sewing elements they have bundled up for use in their baskets. Contemporary weavers in all parts of western North America have a difficult time finding suitable weaving materials because of the loss of traditional gathering sites to development and private property. In fact, today many culturally significant gathering sites, developed over hundreds of years by generations of weavers, no longer exist. Where traditional gathering sites have actually survived, on private and public lands, access for weavers is often prohibited.

Native peoples' well-tended ecosystems, many of the basketmaking materials included in this chapter are now difficult for weavers to find or access, or in some instances are no longer available at all.

Learning to weave baskets begins with learning where, when, and how to gather and prepare the materials. A weaver who is physically able to collect and prepare her own materials does so in accordance with her beliefs. She follows traditional guidelines of respect and reciprocity by reciting the right prayers and singing the proper songs when gathering and preparing materials. A weaver often knows of special, even secret, locations where she may return year after year to gather just the right materials. In these places, she knows she will find the dye stuffs that give the best color or the plant roots she has sampled and found to be superior to any others (O'Neale 1932:13). By tending her personal collecting areas, the weaver maintains the quality and diversity of plant resources required for weaving.

Material preparation is tedious and time consuming. Weavers can spend days preparing their materials before actually beginning a basket and some tasks, such as dyeing with natural plant dyes or sun bleaching, must be begun weeks or months before the material can be used. The amount of time and specific processes necessary for transforming raw materials into serviceable basket warps (foundations) and wefts (sewing or weaving elements) varies across culture areas, depending upon the type of plants being used.

Across culture areas and plant types, preliminary processing always involves the same steps: cleaning and drying and sizing the materials based on their intended purpose. Materials cleaned of extraneous parts are generally bound together in coils or bundles and then stored to dry and cure in order to prevent uneven shrinking after they are woven into a basket (Bates and Lee 1990:41). Once the materials have cured, the weaver sizes her sewing or weaving elements into an even width and thickness and her foundation materials into an equal and even diameter. Also, at this stage sewing or weaving strands are dyed for decorative effect using either natural or commercial dyes. During the course of weaving, most materials must be lightly moistened or soaked in water to make them pliable. Throughout this process, weavers often recite prayers or sing songs in recognition of weaving as a transformative act in which raw materials are turned into valuable objects.

Plant Materials

BEARGRASS *(Nolina microcarpa)*

This species of beargrass, one of two used in basketmaking (see opposite), is native to New Mexico and Arizona. It is a monocot, or flowering plant, adapted to warm, dry climates. Weavers in the American Southwest, especially the Tohono O'odham in Arizona, use the slender, razor-sharp leaves of beargrass for the bundle foundation in their coiled baskets (see fig. 64). The best beargrass for weaving is gathered from the center of the plant clusters in the summer. The material is dried for four or five days and then trimmed and split prior to use. This species of beargrass is one of the few basket materials that does not need to be moistened before use.

SOUTHWEST
Tohono O'odham

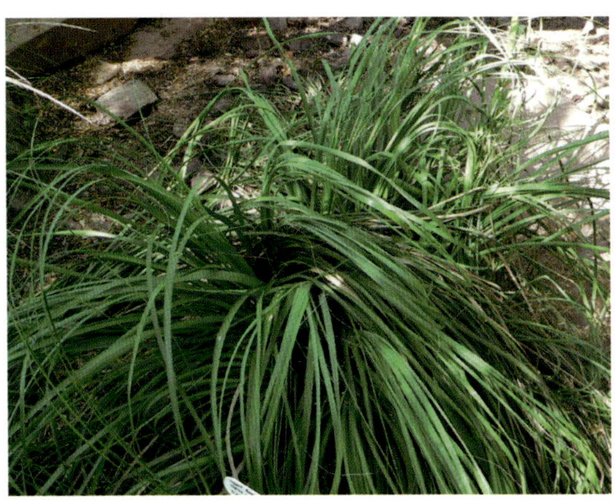

Beargrass *(Nolina microcarpa)*. Photo by Stan Shebs

BEARGRASS *(Xerophyllum tenax)*

This species of beargrass is a member of the lily family and is significantly different from *Nolina microcarpa* (opposite). Weavers harvest the finest beargrass in the summer months. They pull the softest and most pliable leaves from the inside of the plant. They lay these leaves to dry in the sun for two or three days. As they dry, the leaves turn an ivory-white color. Weavers then sort the dried strands by length and width and tie them into coils for storage.

To prepare the dry strands for weaving, basket weavers remove and discard the barbed midrib running down the center of the underside of the beargrass leaf, splitting the remaining strands into the desired thickness and then soaking them in water. When weaving the beargrass strands into a basket, a weaver takes care to keep the smooth glossy side of each strand facing toward the work surface, or outer side, of the basket. Beargrass can be easily dyed for use in the creation of design motifs. Although primarily thought of as a decorative material, beargrass also adds strength and durability to baskets.

CALIFORNIA

Achumawi • Hupa • Karuk • Lower Klamath River • Wintu • Yurok

PLATEAU

Clatsop

NORTHWEST COAST

Cowlitz • Haida • Makah • Modoc • Quinault • Tlingit

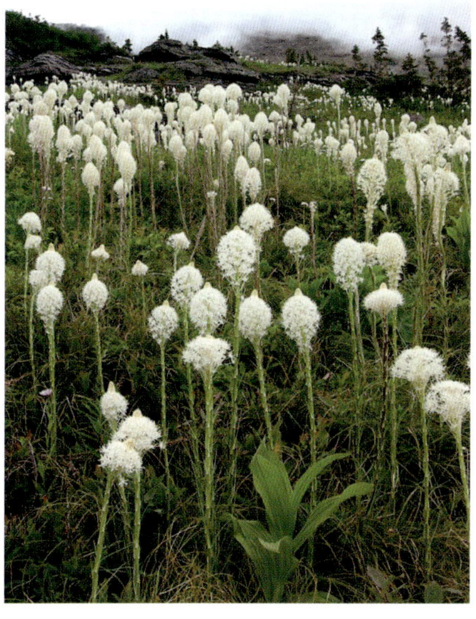

Beargrass *(Xerophyllum tenax)*.
Courtesy of the National Park Service

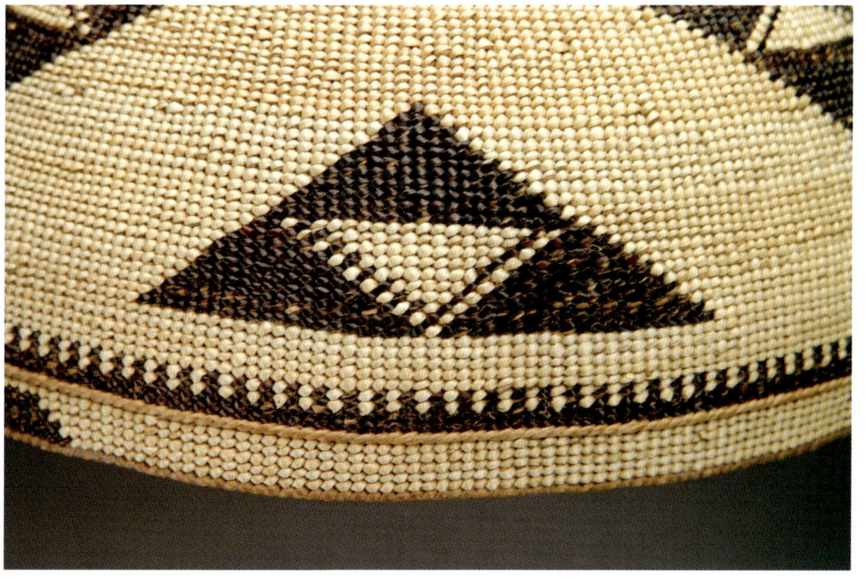

FIG. 29

Woman's Cap, c. 1930, Lower Klamath River, Artist unknown, 9.0 x 19.0 cm., 23716

FOUNDATION: hazelnut rods

WEAVING ELEMENTS: spruce root, beargrass, maidenhair fern stem

BITTER CHERRY *(Prunus emarginata)*

Weavers soften the tough and waterproof bark of bitter cherry trees into sewing elements to create designs on coiled, split-cedar root baskets. Naturally a light reddish brown color, the bark can be darkened by burying it in damp earth or by placing it in a rusty can, methods that turn the bark brown and then black.

NORTHWEST COAST

Ntlakapamuk

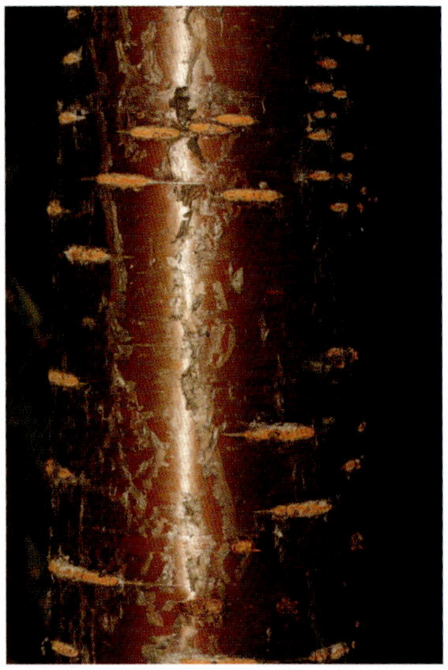

Bitter Cherry. Photo by Walter Siegmund

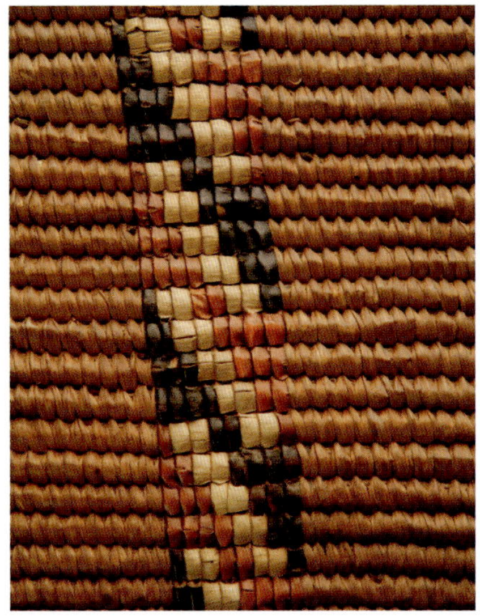

FIG. 30

Storage Basket Model, c. 1890, Ntlakapamuk, Artist unknown, 23.0 x 42.0 x 33.5 cm., 25438

FOUNDATION: cedar root

SEWING ELEMENTS: split cedar-root strand, bitter cherry bark, phragmites; with dye

BRACKEN FERN *(Pteridium aquilinum)*

To make strands for the design elements in coiled baskets, weavers separate out the flat strips of tissue from the bracken fern's rhizomes (underground stems). First, they dig up the rhizomes in the autumn months, after the fronds of the fern have turned yellow, and then split the rhizomes in two and peel off the thick, chunky, outer bark to reveal the yellow-white core. Then the core is split, exposing two dark-brown, ribbon-like strands. The strands must then be scraped smooth and dried before being dyed to the desired black.

GREAT BASIN

Mono Lake Paiute • Washoe

CALIFORNIA

Miwok • Monache • Mountain Maidu • Yokuts

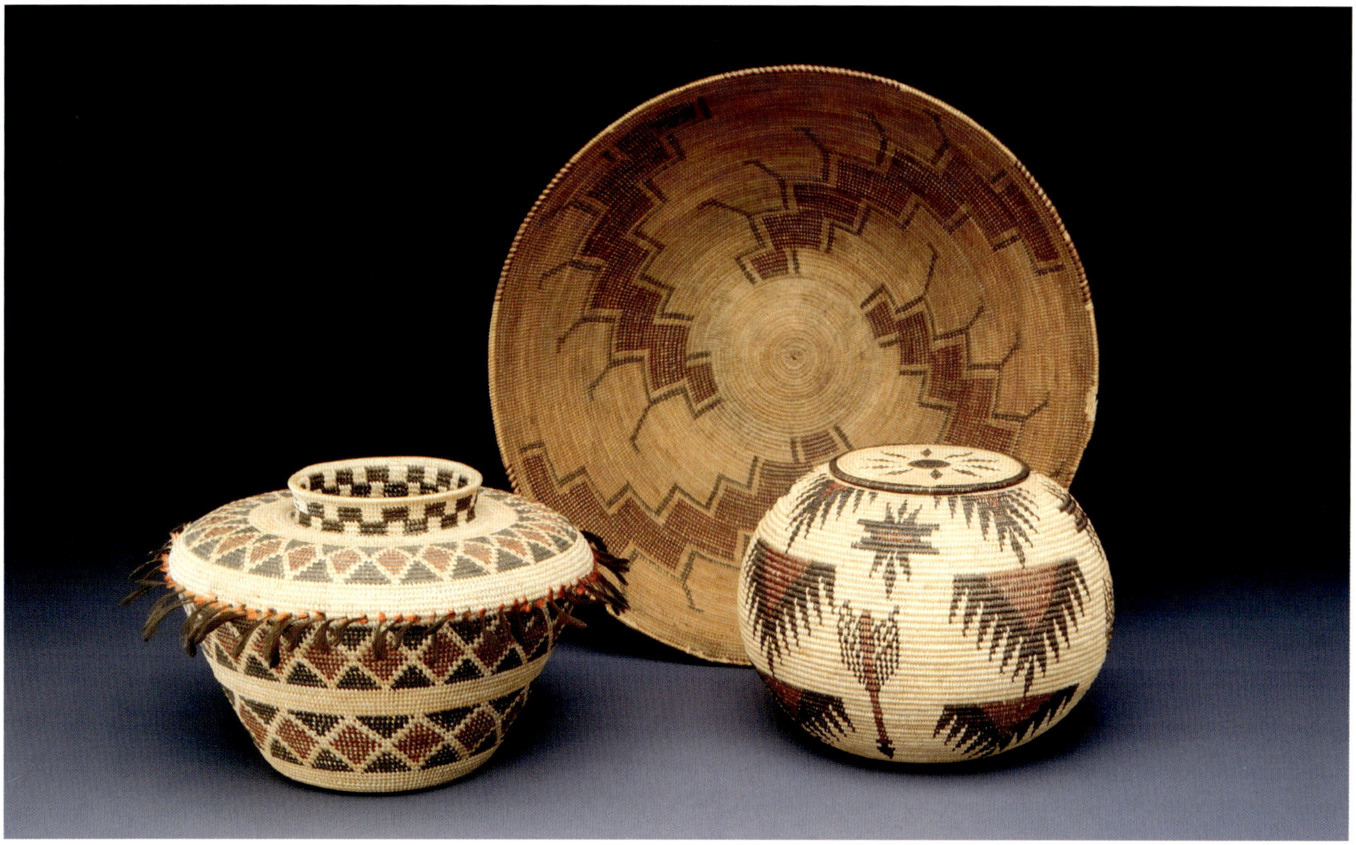

FIG. 31 (Left to right):

Gift Basket, c. 1910, Yokuts, Artist known as "Old Charley's Wife," 16.5 x 28.0 cm., 14304

FOUNDATION: deergrass bundle

SEWING ELEMENTS: sedge rhizome, redbud shoots, bracken fern rhizome; with acorn woodpecker-scalp feathers, quail topknots

Bowl, c. 1910, Yokuts, Artist unknown, 17.0 x 38.0 cm., 14386

FOUNDATION: deergrass bundle

SEWING ELEMENTS: sedge rhizome, bracken fern rhizome, redbud shoots

Bowl, 1912, Mono Lake Paiute and Miwok, Lucy Parker Telles, 17.0 x 21.0 cm., 14308

FOUNDATION: three willow rods

SEWING ELEMENTS: sedge rhizome, redbud shoots, bracken fern rhizome

BULRUSH *(Schoenoplectus spp.)*

A common marsh plant, bulrush is a reddish brown color. Weavers split the small hair roots covering the bulrush rhizomes into two to four strips and then use them as a design material in their coiled baskets. Weavers dye this material to produce colors ranging from dark brown to purple to black (see fig. 82).

Until they lost control of their lands to outsiders, basket weavers had free access to bulrush beds that they carefully tended to ensure a dependable supply of high-quality material. They guarded against overharvesting of the beds; they processed the soil until it was free of gravel, clay, and silt (bulrush plants in beds free of these have the long, straight rhizomes with more high-quality hair roots that weavers prefer); and they dug out overcrowded rhizomes to reduce plant density. Basket weavers also used fire to manage their bulrush beds—fire eliminated old dead stems and restored open water to the bulrush marsh, stimulating the growth of new shoots. And, finally, weavers cleared land to provide soil for bulrush seed germination.

CALIFORNIA
Pomo

PLATEAU
Modoc

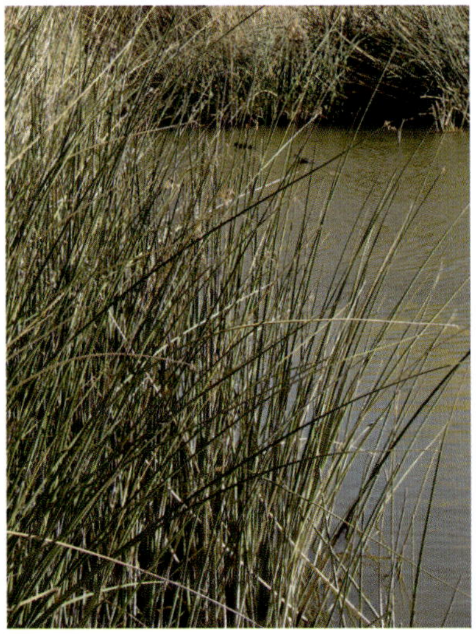

Bulrush. Photo by Forest Starr and Kim Starr

CATTAIL *(Typha angustifolia)*

Cattails are wetland plants with unique flowering stalks and flat blade-like leaves. O'odham weavers of Arizona use the dried and split flower stalks of cattails to form bundle foundations for their coiled baskets.

Klamath and Modoc weavers in northern California use cattail leaves to make the fiber wefts for fine-twined baskets. First they harvest and dry the leaves; then they dampen the leaves and split them into thin strips by starting at the base of the leaf and splitting downward towards the tip. The resulting cattail fibers may be used as plain weaving elements or dyed for use as design weaving elements.

Along the Northwest Coast, cattails grow in shallow fresh water, where weavers gather the plants from early July to early August. They use the soft, pliable, outer edge for the wefts of their baskets.

SOUTHWEST
Acoma • Akimel O'odham • Tohono O'odham

PLATEAU
Klamath • Modoc

NORTHWEST COAST
Makah

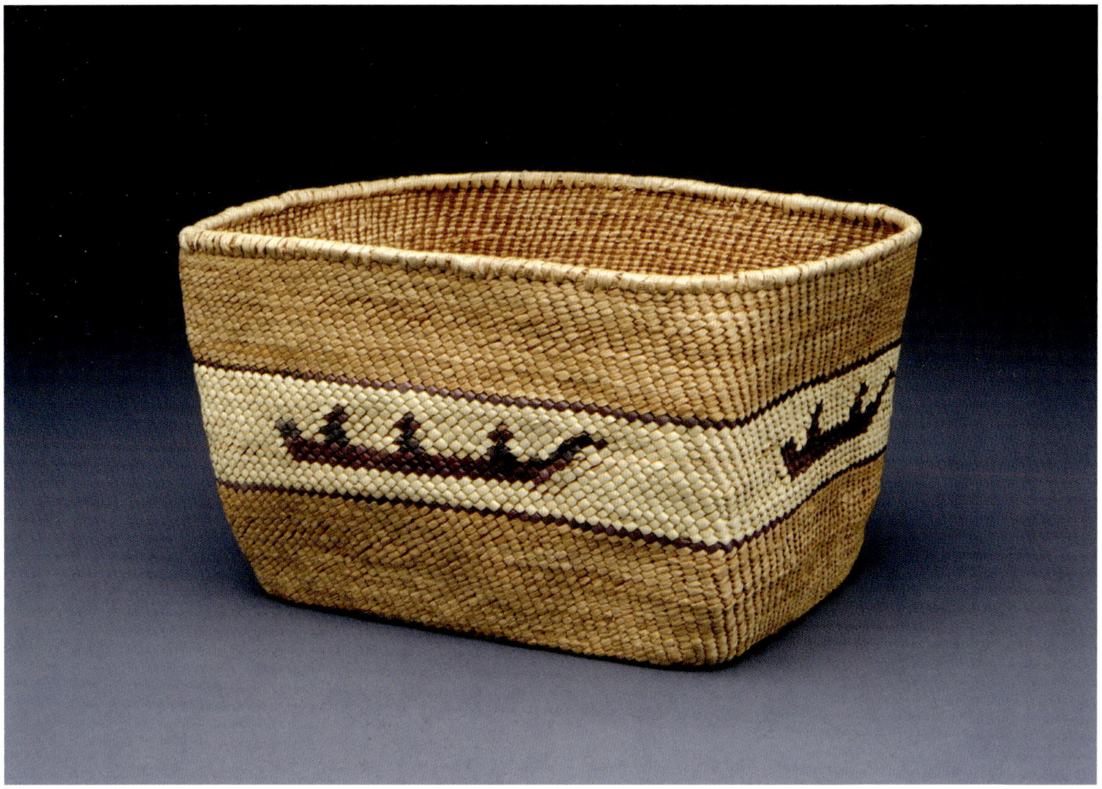

FIG. 32

Rectangular Basket, c. 1910, Makah, Artist unknown, 16.0 x 29.5 x 22.0 cm., 31110

FOUNDATION: shredded cedar-bark bundle

WEAVING ELEMENTS: cattail fiber, beargrass; with dye

WESTERN REDCEDAR *(Thuja plicata)* AND REDCEDAR *(Chamaecyparis nootkatensis)*

Plateau and Northwest Coast basket weavers use both the roots (see fig. 30) and the inner bark of the cedar tree for their baskets. The roots are prepared by boiling them to separate out the inner fibers. One root can yield as many as six weaving strands: Those taken from inside the root are flat and dull and are used for warps (bundle foundations); the ones from next to the skin are convex and shiny and are used for wefts (sewing elements). Weavers gather redcedar bark in May or June, when the sap is beginning to rise and the bark is easy to pull from the tree. They first make a cut in the bark at the bottom of the trunk and then peel off a long strip by pulling upwards and outwards until it comes loose. Only the pliable inner bark is used in baskets, so weavers cut the strip of bark into smaller strips and then strip or cut off the outer bark to reveal the inner bark. The inner bark is soaked in water and then the finer strips of desired width are separated into layers. When exposed to light, the redcedar inner bark of the finished basket turns a reddish-gold color; the inner bark may also be dyed for use as a design material.

PLATEAU

Clatsop • Ntlakapamuk

NORTHWEST COAST

Makah • Nuu-chah-nulth • Quinault • Tsimshian

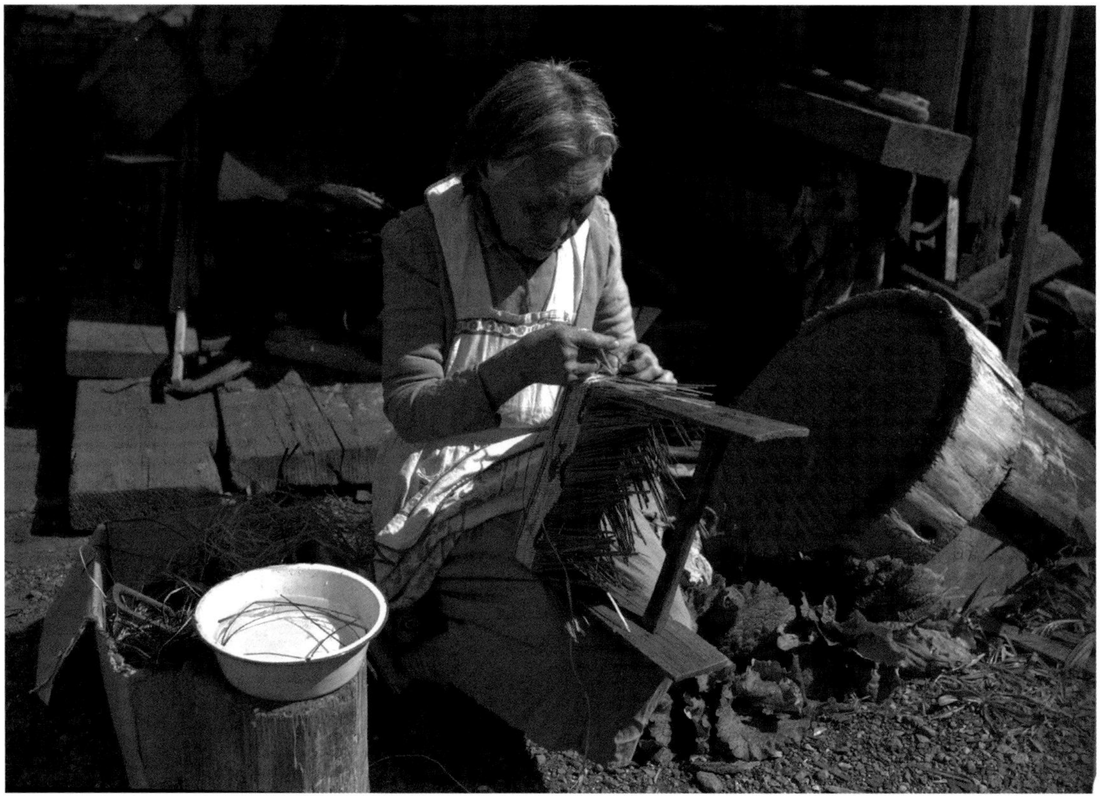

FIG. 33
Emma David, Nuu-chah-nulth, weaves a basket of cedar bark and Swamp grass on a wooden form, May 1951. Photo by R. Kenkham. Courtesy of the Royal British Columbia Museum. pn 4681.

The box to Emma David's right contains plain and dyed swamp grass and an oval, wood, grass splitter with a pair of cutting blades to trim the grass to an even width.

CLIFFROSE *(Purshia stansburiana)*

Traditionally the Paiute made cordage, sandals, blankets, sleeping mats, and clothing from soft cliffrose inner bark. The bark, which shreds easily, is removed from the bush by making a cut at the base of the plant and pulling upward. To prevent damaging the plant, only a thin strip is removed from one side of the trunk. The dull gray color of the rough outer bark conceals the beautiful rust-reds of the inner bark (see fig. 170).

GREAT BASIN

Moapa Paiute • Southern Paiute

CONIFER ROOTS *(Pinus, Sequoia, and Picea)*

The roots of cone-bearing trees such as pine (*Pinus*), redwood (*Sequoia*), and spruce (*Picea*) are the primary twining material used by basket makers in northern California, western Oregon, and Washington (see fig. 27). Gathering conifer roots requires an understanding of the trees' annual growing cycle, as well as the ecological zones in which they grow. For example, in northern California weavers dig roots in the fall; on the Northwest Coast they dig them in the spring. A weaver might sample the roots of a number of trees before harvesting and processing enough roots for the year. If roots from a stand of trees meet the weaver's exacting standards, she will tend and harvest these trees year after year, removing stones and other obstacles so the roots will grow long and straight.

Before being used, all conifer roots must be "cooked" to soften them and remove most of the sap. Historically, weavers steamed the roots on a bed of leafy branches laid over hot embers or over hot river sand heated by a fire. Today many weavers cook their roots in a warm oven until most of the sap has bubbled out. Afterward, the bark and inner pith of each root is easy to remove. Weavers then split the remaining root material into strands and scrape them smooth. Some weavers go a step further and dip a single length into water and then divide it into even thinner strands. The strands from the outer brownish layer of conifer roots, just under the bark, are considered to be the finest weaving material.

PLATEAU
Ntlakapamuk

CALIFORNIA
Achumawi • Hupa • Karuk • Lower Klamath River • Wintu • Yurok

NORTHWEST COAST
Cowlitz • Haida • Makah • Nuu-chah-nulth • Quinault • Tlingit

CORNHUSK *(Zea mays)*

In the early nineteenth century, foreign settlers began occupying Plateau lands for farming, ruining many basketry-plant growing areas and refusing weavers access to others. Plateau basket weavers who had become day laborers in the settlers' corn fields found that they could split the cornhusks and use this new material, along with traditional Indian hemp, for twining their carrying and storage bags. Later, these became known as cornhusk bags.

Cornhusk strands are often dyed bright colors and used in the false embroidery technique to create the design motifs on Plateau carrying bags.

PLATEAU
Umatilla

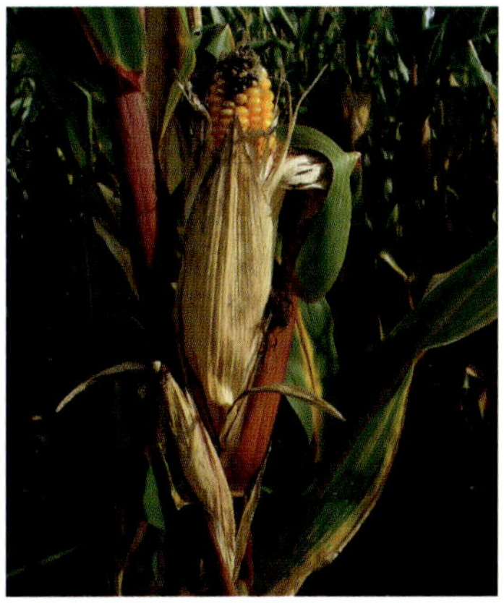

Cornhusk. Photo by H. Zell

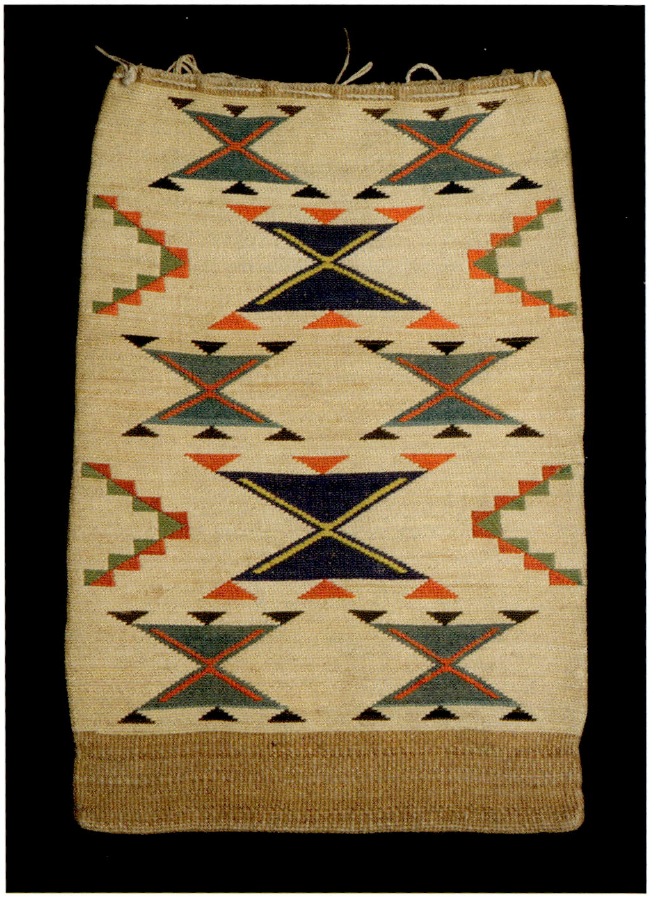

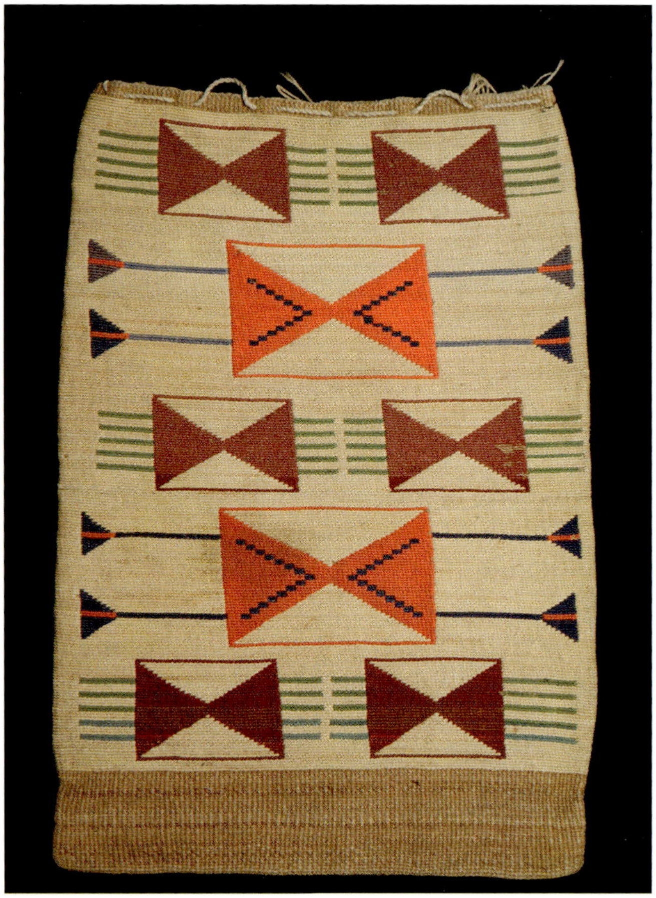

FIGS. 34, 35:

Bag (front and back), c. 1885. Plateau, Artist unknown, 39.7 x 59.2 cm., 53234

FOUNDATION: Indian hemp fiber cordage

WEAVING ELEMENTS: Indian hemp fiber, cornhusk fiber, iris fiber, wool

Cornhusks were not available for Plateau basket weavers until after the 1820s, when farmers began growing corn in the region. Ethnographic accounts indicate that beargrass (*Xerophyllum tenax*) was the material used for false embroidery on flat bags; however, very few examples of early bags exist to confirm this practice.

COTTONWOOD *(Populus fremontii)*

Some basket weavers use long, slender cottonwood tree shoots for both the wefts (sewing elements) and rod foundations of coiled baskets. They peel and then split new shoots into sewing strands, or they peel, scrape, and size them for foundation rods.

SOUTHWEST

Acoma • Havasupai • San Carlos Apache • Western Apache •
White Mountain Apache • Yavapai

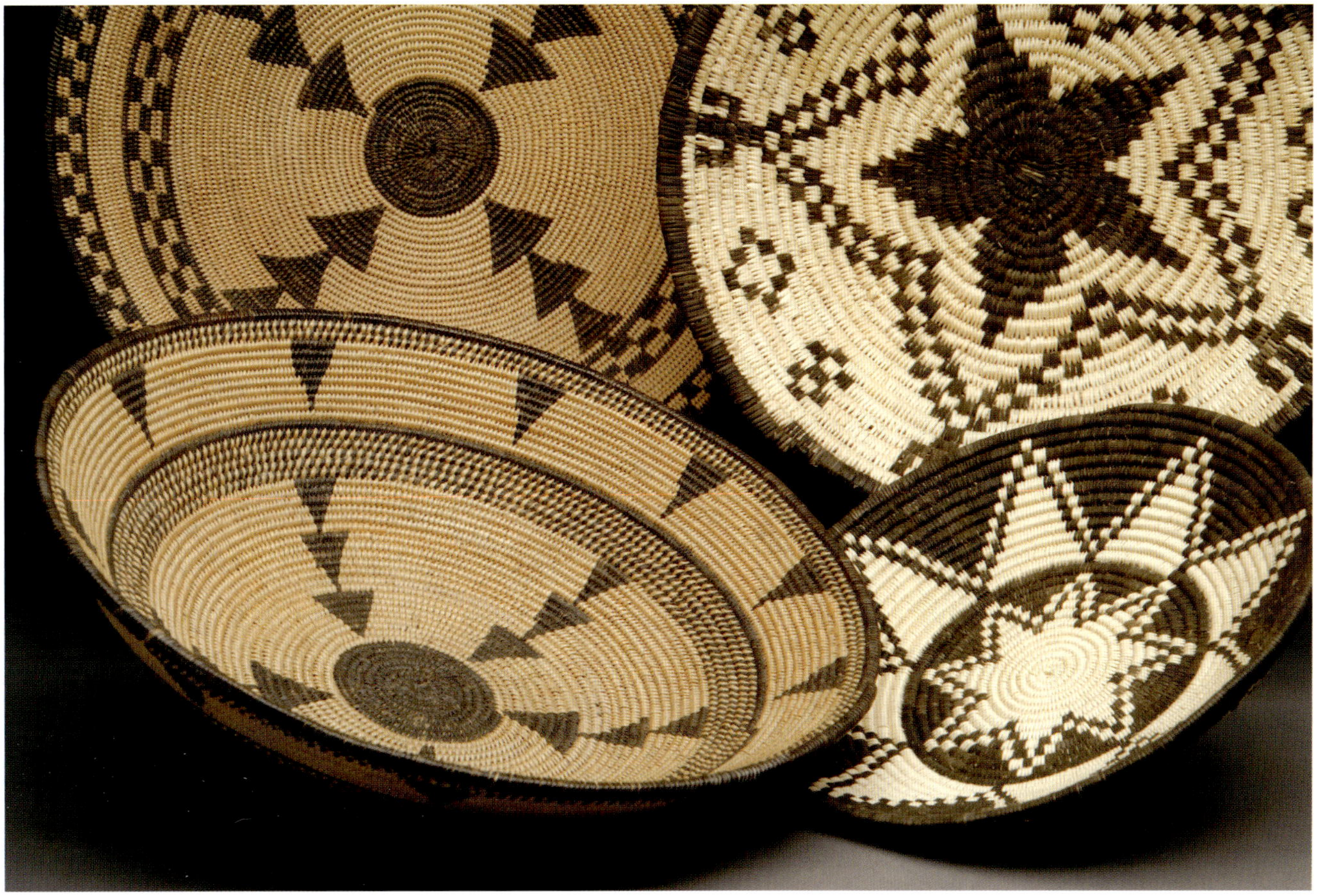

FIG. 36 (Clockwise from upper right):

Tray, 1983, San Carlos Apache, Mary Porter, 7.62 x 36.2 cm., 50065

FOUNDATION: three cottonwood rods

SEWING ELEMENTS: cottonwood shoots, devil's claw seedpod

Tray, 1983, Yavapai, Lillian Shenah, 5.1 x 26.4 cm., 50011

FOUNDATION: three cottonwood rods

WEAVING ELEMENTS: cottonwood shoots, devil's claw seedpod

Tray, c. 1910, White Mountain Apache, Artist unknown, 10.0 x 36.0 cm., 1047

FOUNDATION: three cottonwood rods

SEWING ELEMENTS: cottonwood shoots, devil's claw seedpod

Tray, c. 1900, White Mountain Apache, Artist unknown, 10.0 x 39.0 cm., 31078

FOUNDATION: three cottonwood rods

SEWING ELEMENTS: cottonwood shoots, devil's claw seedpod

Because both willow shoots and cottonwood shoots age to a yellow-tan color, it is difficult to distinguish between the two in finished baskets. The primary differences are that cottonwood shoots are whiter with a rough-matte finish when new and are less durable than willow.

DEERGRASS *(Muhlenbergia rigens,* formerly *Epicampes rigens)*
A native perennial bunchgrass, deergrass provides weavers with a material for the bundle foundations of coiled baskets. In particular, weavers value the flower stalk, or culm, for being flexible and strong. When the stalks get wet they swell, making baskets with deergrass-culm foundations watertight (see fig, 38).

Weavers have learned that deergrass harvested in mid-summer makes the finest baskets. The culms are ready to pick when they let go easily from their sheaths. Deergrass can still be harvested in late summer or fall, but during those times the culms must be cut from the plant. Prior to losing control of their lands to outsiders, weavers burned stands of deergrass to clear other vegetation out of the beds and to induce the growth of the highly desired long, fine, new deergrass culms.

CALIFORNIA
Cahuilla • Kumeyaay • Monache • Tubatulabal • Yokuts

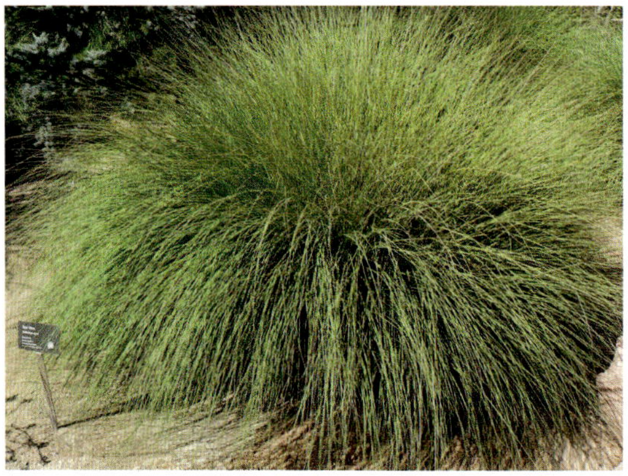

Deergrass. Photo by Stan Shebs

DEVIL'S CLAW *(Proboscidea parviflora)*
Devil's claw is a desert wildflower. One plant may produce fifty or more fruit pods that ripen in late summer or early fall. When ripe the green, fuzzy, outer rind of the fruit dries up to reveal two harvestable seedpods that will mature from a deep gray to a jet black. These two claw-shaped pods contain fibers that become black-colored design elements in coiled basketry.

Weavers gather the pods in the fall before the first frost (that fades the color) and store them for later use. To prepare them for weaving they soak the pods in water and remove the two fibers (front and back) from the pod appendages. Devil's claw varieties that have been domesticated by basket weavers and grown in their own gardens and fields have four usable fibers.

SOUTHWEST
Acoma • Akimel O'odham • Havasupai • Hualapai • San Carlos Apache • Tohono O'odham • Western Apache • White Mountain Apache • Yavapai

GREAT BASIN
Cedar Paiute • Moapa Paiute • Panamint Shoshone • Southern Paiute • Ute

CALIFORNIA
Tubatulabal

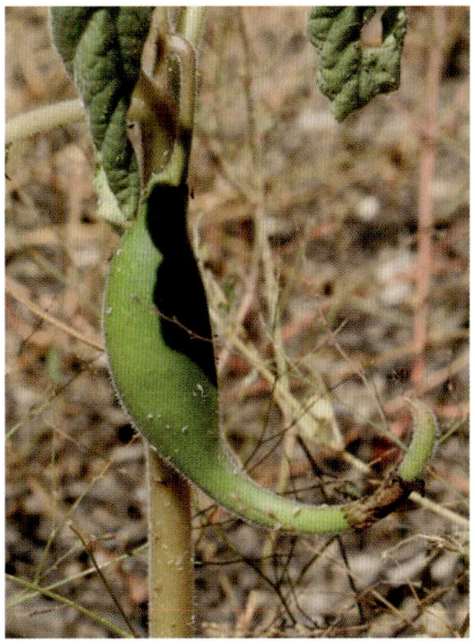

Devil's Claw.
Photo by T. Beth Kinsey.

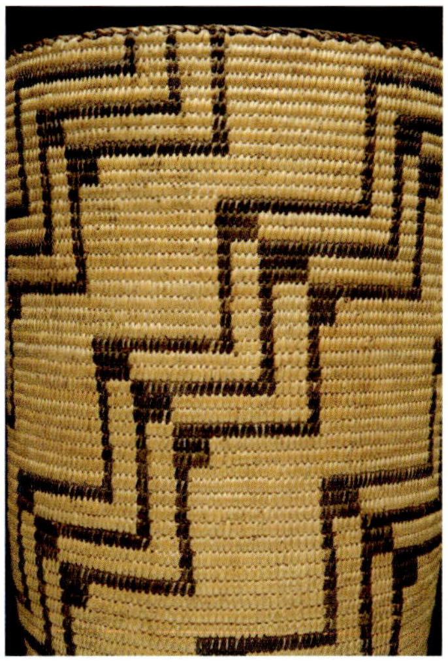

FIG. 37

Cylinder, c. 1890, Akimel O'odham, Artist unknown, 27.5 x 20.5 cm., 14412

FOUNDATION: cattail-splint bundle

SEWING ELEMENTS: willow shoots, devil's claw seedpod

The domestication of devil's claw stemmed from changes in the plant's availability in the natural environment, as well as an increase in the marketability of baskets incorporating the fiber. Mary Lois Kissell reports that in 1910 to 1911, when she was living in O'odham communities in Arizona, most basket makers planted devil's claw in their fields and gardens (Kissell 1916:202). Over time, O'odham weavers chose seeds from plants that produced pods with longer and more (four instead of two) weaving fibers.

DUNEBROOM *(Parryella filifolia)*

Weavers from Hopi Third Mesa use dunebroom stems as warps (foundations) and wefts (weaving elements) in their wicker baskets. They gather them between August and October, after the stems have turned from reddish brown to silver gray, from shrubs that grow in the sandy soils below their mesa. They spend much of their time searching for straight stems of the correct length and a uniform thickness. Because the stems dry out quickly, they must be soaked in water or buried in damp sand to make them flexible for weaving (see fig. 39).

SOUTHWEST

Hopi

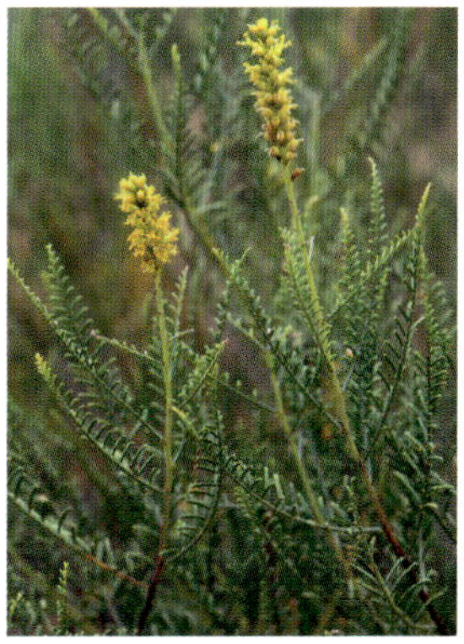

Dunebroom.
Photo by Robert Sivinski

GALLETA GRASS *(Hilaria jamesii)*

Weavers of Hopi Second Mesa use a bundle of galleta-grass leaves (or blades) as the warps (foundation) material for their coiled baskets. They collect the grass from the end of July through August. Hopi basket weavers prefer galleta grass harvested during that time because the grass blades are moist from the rains and the lower part of each blade is still fresh and green (see fig. 1).

SOUTHWEST

Hopi

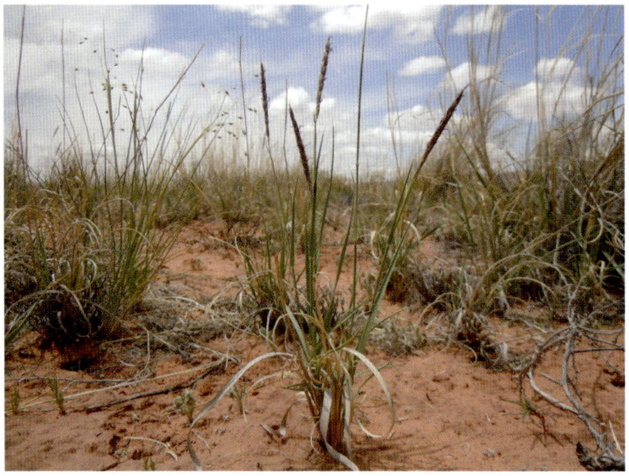

Galleta Grass. Photo by Matt Lavin

HAZELNUT SHRUB *(Corylus spp.)*

California basket weavers use the thin, strong, whole shoots of the hazelnut shrub as warps (foundation) and split the shoots to create the wefts (weaving elements) for twined baskets. They gather the shoots in the spring—April or May—peel them, dry them in the sun, separate them into bunches by length and thickness, and store them for drying and curing. The best shoots are those gathered from second-year growth in tended areas that have been intentionally burned; these new-growth shoots are straight and of the correct thickness for twining; older growth becomes too thick and loses its suppleness (see fig. 29).

CALIFORNIA

Hupa • Karuk • Lower Klamath River • Pomo • Wintu • Yurok

HORSETAIL *(Equisetum palustre)*

Horsetail is a common understory plant in the spruce forests of the Pacific Northwest. It has a deep root system with rhizomes that produce many terrestrial stems, giving it the appearance of a colony. The rhizomatous tissue is covered by a sheath of leaf tissue. Weavers from the Northwest Coast split fibers from this tissue and use them to create a black overlay design in their twined baskets (see fig. 68).

NORTHWEST COAST

Cowlitz

INDIAN HEMP, DOGBANE *(Apocynum cannabinum)*

Indian hemp is a perennial herb found in wetland areas. Weavers gather the long straight stems (without lateral branching) in late fall or winter after the main stalks have died. The phloem (outer bark) of the stems contains bast (strong woody fibers) that is both strong and flexible enough for weaving. Plateau weavers use these fibers as both the foundations (warps) and weaving elements (wefts) for their flexible "cornhusk" or root carrying and storage bags (see figs. 34,35). They spin the Indian hemp bast into two-ply cordage that is suitable for structural warps or for the undecorated top and bottom wefts. Weavers from the Great Basin and Plateau culture areas typically use the cordage for basket handles and loops.

Traditionally, fires set in hemp wetlands during the fall generated long straight stems for next year's harvest. After these lands were converted to farming and ranching by foreign settlers, indigenous Indian hemp became harder to find; weavers were forced to resort to readily available commercial cotton cord for both the warps and wefts of their cornhusk bags, as well as for basket handles.

GREAT BASIN

Paiute

PLATEAU

Umatilla • Wasco-Wishram

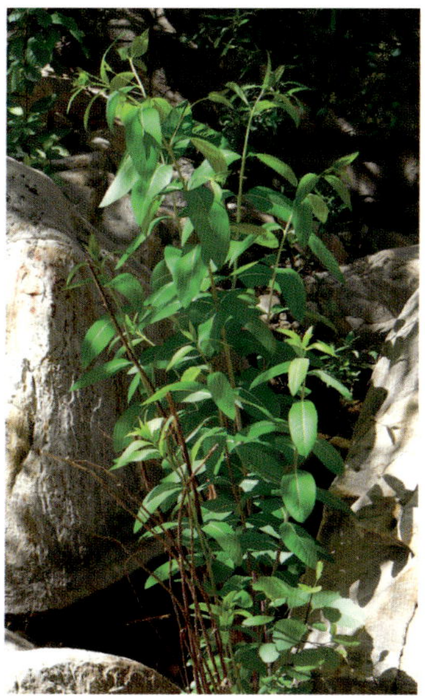

Indian Hemp, Dogbane.
Photo by Stan Shebs

IRIS FIBER *(Iris macrosiphon)*

Iris leaves contain strong fibers that basket weavers have long used to make cordage. Each iris leaf contains only two useable thin fibers on both outside edges that are from one to two feet in length. Weavers harvest the plant from late summer through the fall and into early winter, when the fiber in the leaves has matured and hardened off and the leaf tips are brown. Iris-fiber cordage is used by weavers as the selvage of cornhusk bags or cylindrical carrying bags (see figs. 34, 35).

PLATEAU

Clatsop • Umatilla

JOSHUA TREE ROOT, YUCCA ROOT *(Yucca brevifolia,* formerly *Yucca arborescens)*

California and Nevada desert-dwelling basket weavers use the Joshua tree rootstock core as a design material for coiled baskets. After it is split into two pieces and soaked, the rootstock core turns an orange-red-brown color (see fig. 50).

GREAT BASIN

Havasupai • Panamint Shoshone

CALIFORNIA

Tubatulabal

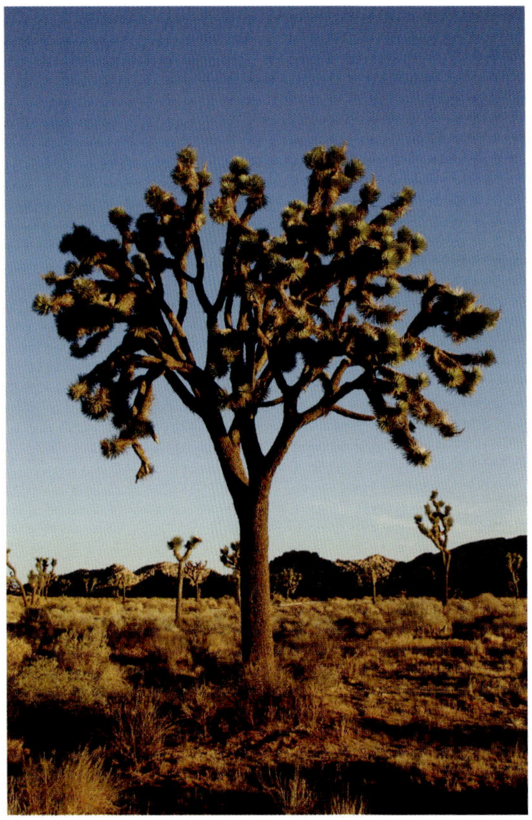

Joshua Tree.
Photo by Jarek Tuszynski

JUNCUS, RUSH *(Juncus spp.)*

Juncus stalks provide weavers with a variety of natural colors—it is red at the base of the stalk and then gradually turns green at the top. Juncus can also be dyed. Weavers, especially those in southern California, use it for both background and design sewing elements in coiled baskets and as both foundations and weaving elements in twined baskets. Today much of the vast California wetland habitats of the *Juncus* species have been claimed for other uses and no longer provide basket weavers with an abundant supply of materials.

CALIFORNIA

Cahuilla • Kumeyaay

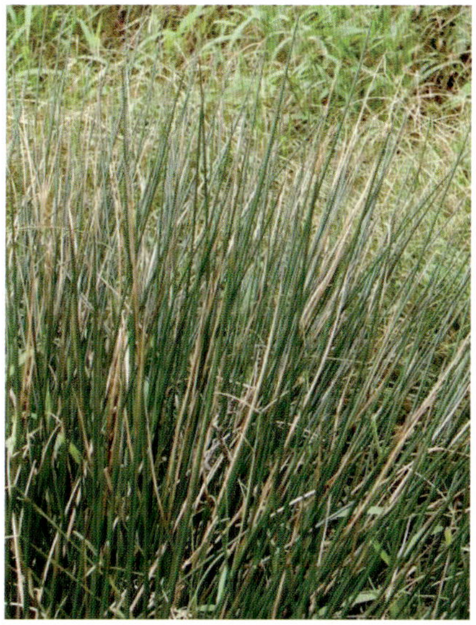

Juncus, Rush.
Photo by Forest Starr and Kim Starr

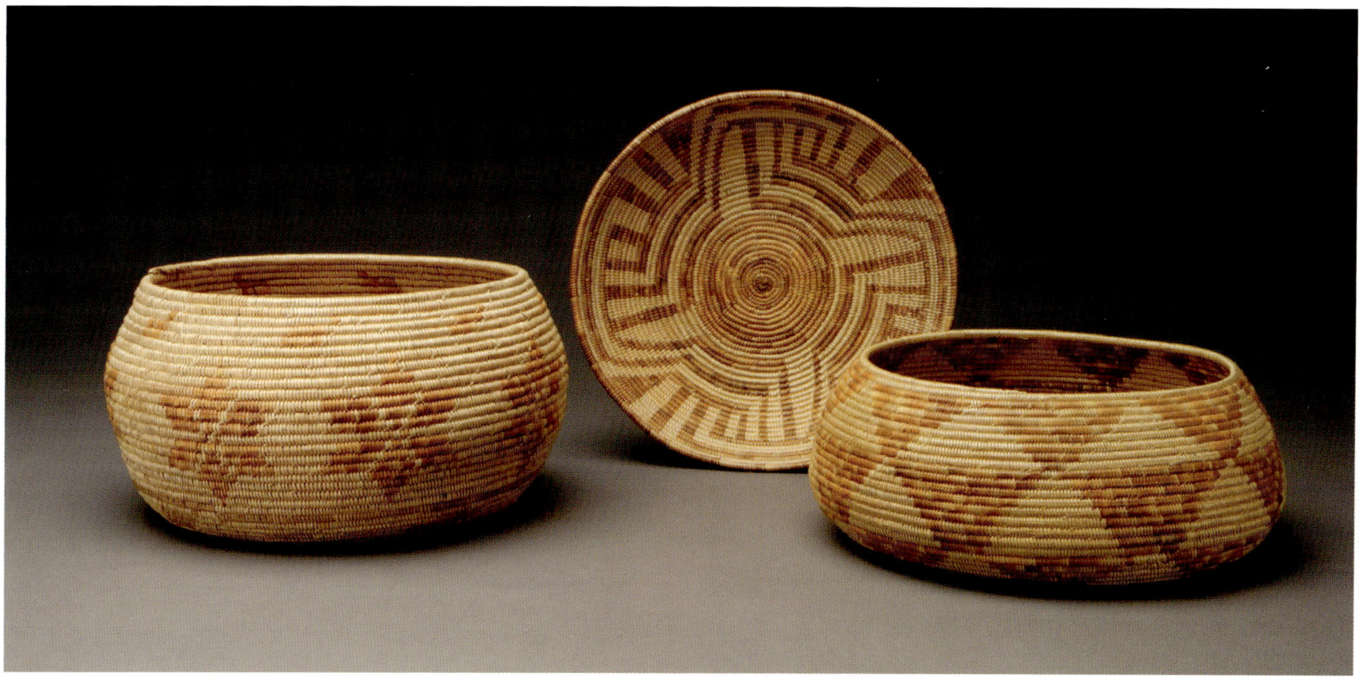

FIG. 38 (Left to right):

Bowl, c. 1895, Cahuilla, Artist unknown, 16.0 x 27.0 cm., 23468

FOUNDATION: deergrass bundle

SEWING ELEMENTS: sumac shoots, juncus stalk

Tray, c. 1900, Kumeyaay, Artist unknown, 6.0 x 26.0 cm., 25024

FOUNDATION: deergrass bundle

SEWING ELEMENTS: sumac shoots, juncus stalk

Bowl, c. 1900, Kumeyaay, Artist unknown, 11.5 x 25.5 cm., 23778

FOUNDATION: deergrass bundle

SEWING ELEMENTS: sumac shoots, juncus stalk

MAIDENHAIR FERN STEM *(Adiantum pedatum)*

Northern California weavers use the strong, shiny, black stems of maidenhair fern as an overlay design material in twined baskets. The best month to harvest quality fern stems is June, when the stalks turn from red on both sides to red on one side and black on the other. Weavers process the stems by splitting apart the two sides and discarding the red side. They scrape the inner green pulp from the black side, dry the strips, and store them for later use (see fig. 29).

CALIFORNIA

Achumawi • Hupa • Karuk • Lower Klamath River • Wintu • Yurok

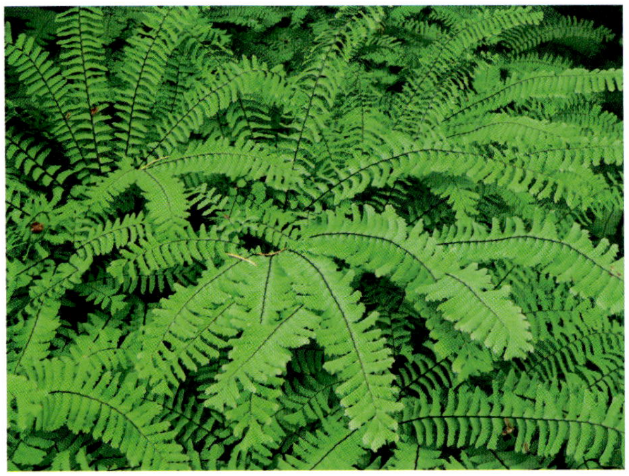

Maidenhair Fern, Photo by Stan Shebs

MAPLE *(Acer macrophyllum)*

In California weavers use young, supple maple shoots for their basketry; prior to the late 1800s, when federal and state laws restricted their activities, these weavers were able to burn, prune, or coppice selected bigleaf maple trees to force the shoots to sprout. The resulting new shoots were harvested and split for use as the wefts (sewing elements) of the weavers' finest coiled baskets (see fig. 121).

CALIFORNIA

Mountain Maidu

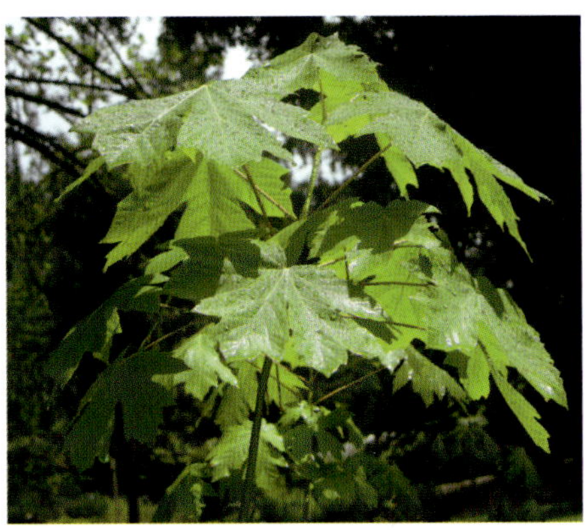

Maple. Courtesy of the The Wild Garden www.nwplants.com

MESQUITE *(Prosopis velutina)*

In the desert Southwest basket weavers principally use mesquite strands as a binding material. Akimel O'odham weaver Alice Manuel says that the bark is shaved from a young tree whose bark is still soft (A. Manuel, pers. Comm., February 2013). In the spring, when the sap just starts running, it is easier to separate the outer bark from the inner bark, which is used as sewing strands.

The dense wood of the mesquite tree is used for tool and basket, especially water jar handles (see fig. 100).

SOUTHWEST

Tohono O'odham • Western Apache

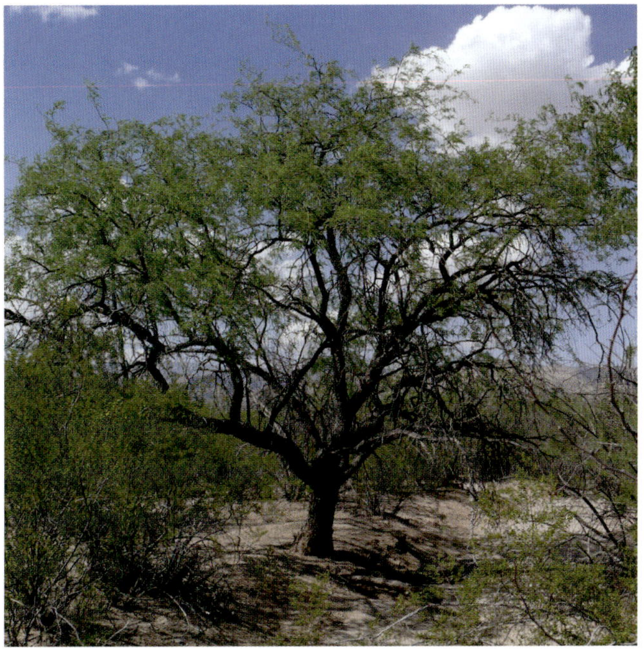

Mesquite Tree.
Photo by Sue Lynn Peterson

PHRAGMITES, GRASS *(Phragmites spp.)*

Northwest Coast and Plateau weavers use phragmites, or grass, as a design material in their baskets. It is often dyed before use. As with other basketry materials, phragmites must be thoroughly dried before use (to avoid an unanticipated amount of shrinkage in the basket), then soaked in water to make it pliable for weaving (see fig. 30).

PLATEAU

Ntlakapamuk

NORTHWEST COAST

Tlingit

RABBITBRUSH *(Chrysothamnus nauseosus spp.)*
Basket weavers of Hopi Third Mesa use the peeled stems of rabbitbrush as the weft weaving elements for wicker plaques and baskets. They harvest it from August to early October when the outer bark is still soft and easy to strip off the stem, the stems are straight and strong, and the plant has turned silver-gray. The stems must be prepared for weaving as soon as they are collected. Weavers loosen the bark at the bottom of each stem with their fingernail or a knife. While holding the peel in their teeth, they use their fingers to strip it off with a downward pull of the stem. The peeled stems are a light green; if the stems are to be dyed, they are bleached in the sun.

SOUTHWEST
Hopi

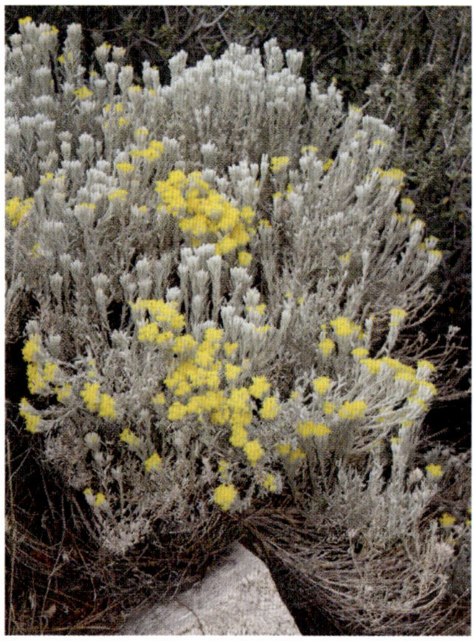

Rabbitbrush.
Photo by Jane Shelby Richardson

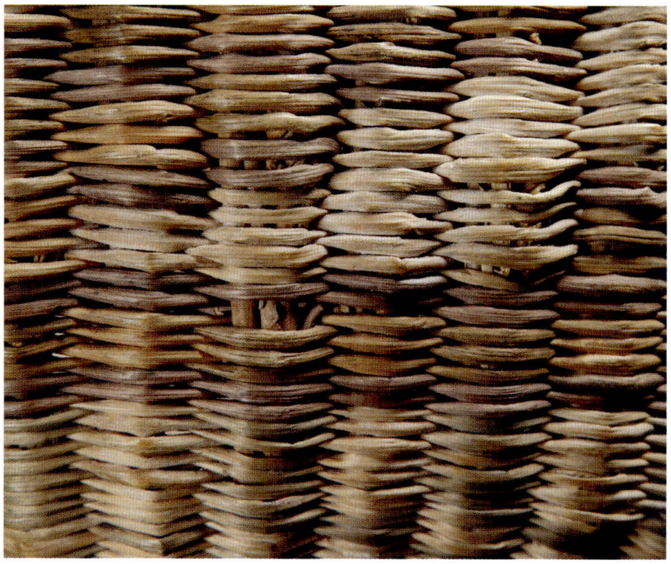

FIG. 39
Cylinder, c. 1900, Hopi (Third Mesa), Artist unknown, 20.5 x 22.5 cm., 48086
FOUNDATION: dunebroom rods
WEAVING ELEMENTS: rabbitbrush stem, yucca leaf; with dye

When making wickerwork baskets, Hopi weavers use almost the entire rabbitbrush plant, with the exception of the roots: the peels and flowers are boiled to make a yellow dye; the prepared stems are boiled in the dye; and the dyed stems are smoked to set the color (Teiwes 1996:37–45).

REDBUD *(Cercis orbiculata,* or *occidentalis)*
California weavers use redbud shrub shoots for both twined and coiled baskets. Weavers gather redbud twice a year: The peeled redbud shoots gathered in the spring or summer are used for the white sewing or weaving elements on coiled and twined baskets; the split unpeeled shoots gathered in the winter are used for the red sewing or weaving elements in basket designs. The whole shoots are used by weavers for the foundation (warps) of twined baskets.

When used for decorative weaving elements (wefts), redbud shoots are split in half along their length beginning at the thick end and working to the thin end. The halves are split again to access and remove the pith (the spongy tissue at the center of the stem). The processed material is coiled and stored to dry and cure for at least a year. To prepare the strands for weaving, basket weavers soak them in water for several hours, reshape them, and then clean them (Anderson 1991:145–157).

GREAT BASIN

Mono Lake Paiute • Washoe

CALIFORNIA

Achumawi • Mountain Maidu • Pomo • Yokuts

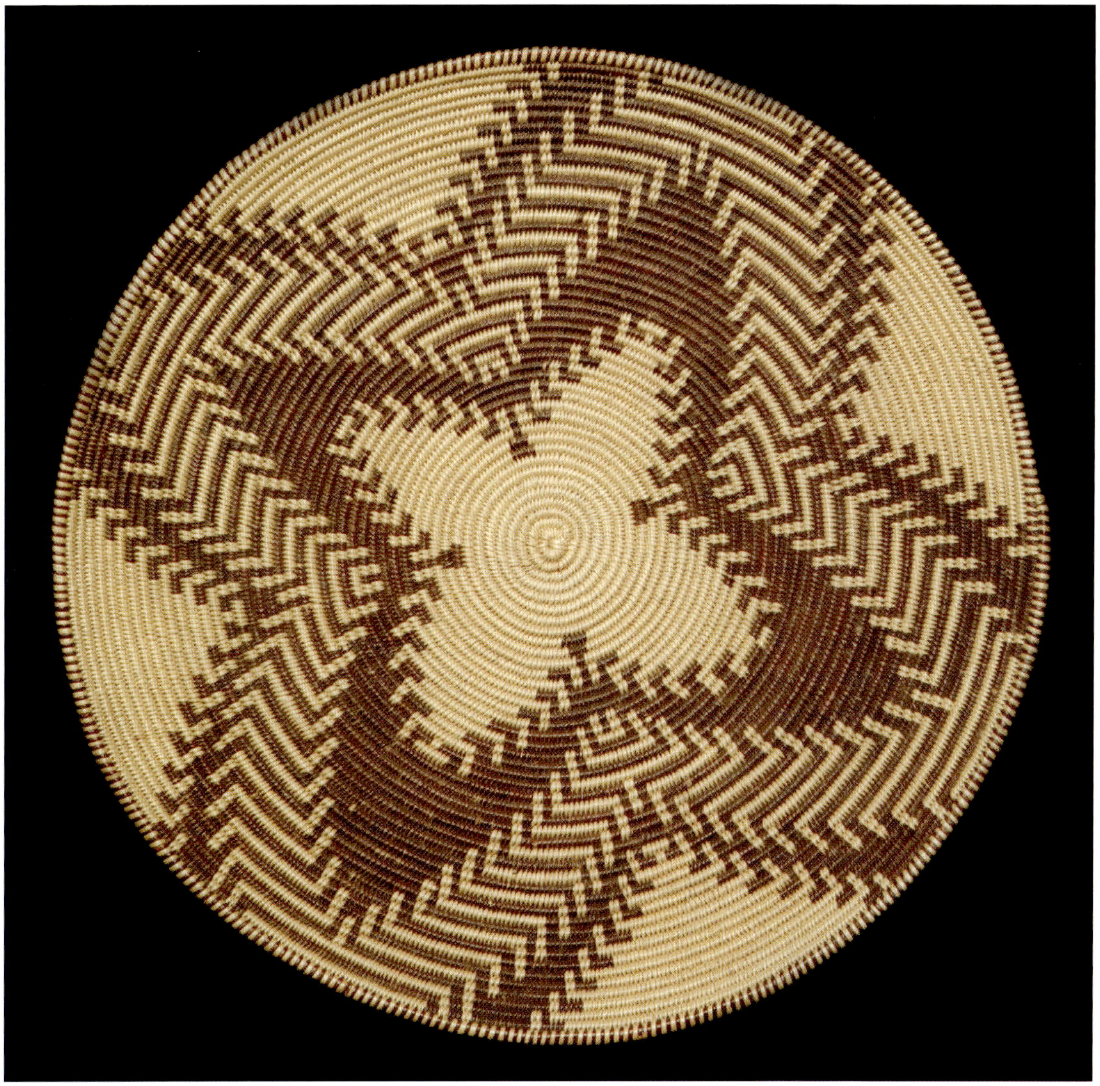

FIG. 40

Tray, c. 1905, Mountain Maidu, artist known as "Big Meadows Susan," 4.0 x 43.5 cm., 14312

FOUNDATION: three willow rods

SEWING ELEMENTS: peeled and unpeeled redbud shoots

SEDGE *(Carex spp.)*

Sedge, which has flat grass-like leaves, grows along rivers and creeks, at the edge of marshes, and in wet meadows. Because it is strong yet very flexible, sedge is a perfect basket-weaving material. Weavers harvest two strands from the tough woody interior of the plant's rhizomes for use as the wefts (sewing elements) in their baskets. Newly processed sedge rhizome is white, and its surface may appear chalky or powdered; as it ages, it turns a darker buff color. By tilling and thinning sedge beds, weavers can harvest rhizomes that are longer, straighter, and more uniform in size; these traditionally-tended sedge plants may produce rhizomes as long as four to six feet in length (see fig. 31).

GREAT BASIN

Mono Lake Paiute

CALIFORNIA

Monache • Pomo • Yokuts • Wappo

NORTHWEST

Makah

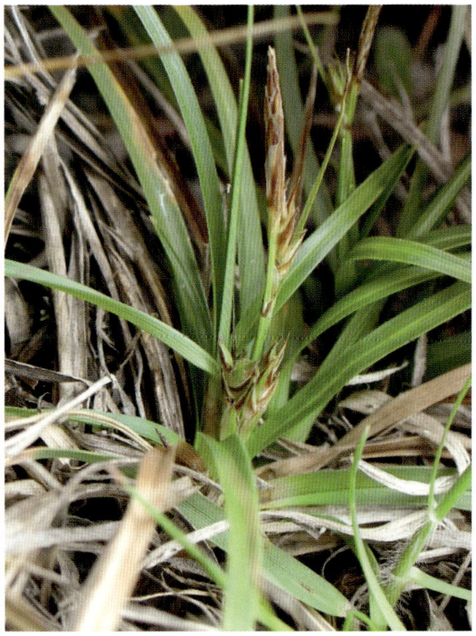

Sedge.
Photo by Robert Steers. Courtesy of the National Park Service

SUMAC, SOUR BERRY, OR BASKET WEED *(Rhus trilobata)*

Weavers harvest the slender new-growth shoots of sumac shrubs for their baskets: For twining, they peel off the bark, processing the whole shoot for use as warps (foundations) and splitting the shoots for use as wefts (weaving elements); for coiling, weavers use sumac strands for the wefts (sewing elements). The material rejected during the processing of the shoots for foundation rods and wefts is used in bundle foundations. Because sumac accepts dye well, the strands are frequently dyed by weavers to use as weft design material. Sumac should be split by hand immediately after gathering—the longer the material sits, the harder it is to split; this process is particularly hard on a basket weaver's body, especially her hands.

SOUTHWEST

Ancestral Pueblo • Diné • Hopi • Hualapai • Jicarilla Apache • Mescalero Apache • Pueblo

GREAT BASIN

Kaibab Paiute • Moapa Paiute • San Juan Paiute • Shivwits Paiute • Southern Paiute • Ute

CALIFORNIA

Cahuilla • Kumeyaay • Tubatulabal

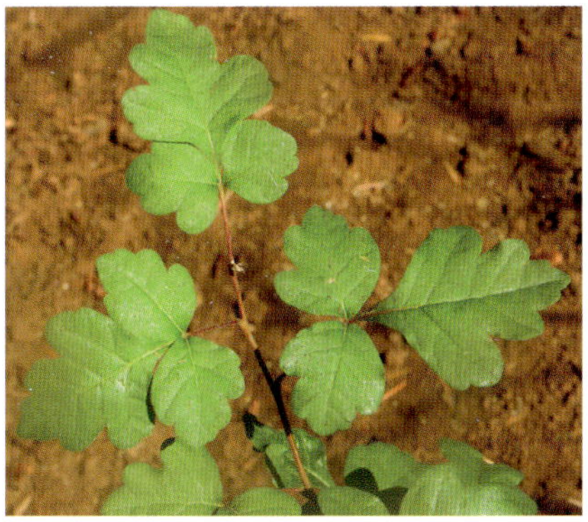

Sumac, Sour Berry, Basket Weed.
Courtesy of The Wild Garden www.nwplants.com

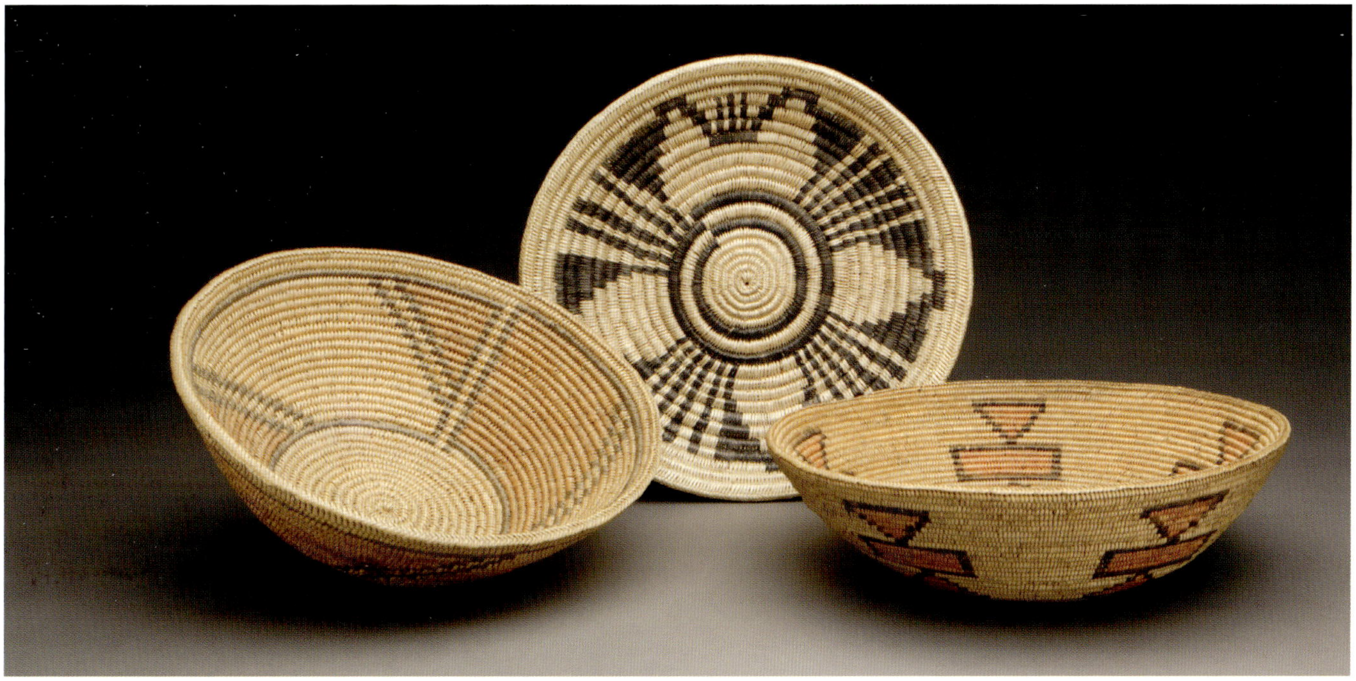

FIG. 41 (Left to right):

Bowl, c. 1880, Pueblo, Artist unknown, 12.5 x 31.5 cm., 14423
FOUNDATION: two sumac rods and sumac bundle
SEWING ELEMENT: sumac shoots; with dye

Tray, c. 1925, San Juan Paiute, Artist unknown, 5.0 x 34.5 cm., 1076
FOUNDATION: three sumac rods
SEWING ELEMENT: sumac shoots; with dye

Tray, c. 1870, Diné, Artist unknown, 10.5 x 34.5 cm., 1100
FOUNDATION: two sumac rods and sumac bundle
SEWING ELEMENT: sumac shoots; with dye

SWAMP GRASS

A number of different types of swamp grass are used in Northwest Coast basketry, including phragmites and wild rye beach grass (see individual listings). The plant grows in swampy marshes along the length of the Northwest Coast. It is difficult to identify one swamp grass species from another once the grass has been processed and woven in a basket. Swamp grass can be easily dyed for use as a design material (see fig. 33).

NORTHWEST COAST

Nuu-chah-nulth

TULE, BULRUSH *(Scirpus spp.)*

Weavers harvest the stems of tule (also known as bulrush) for use in finely woven baskets and coarsely woven work baskets. For fine-twined baskets, the narrow strips of the stems' surface are twisted to separate out the long strands for the wefts (weaving elements); the strips are twisted together into cordage for the warps (foundation). For coarsely woven work baskets, whole or split stems are used for the wefts. The tule threads are naturally green and brown in color; basket weavers sometimes dye them black for use as a design material (see fig. 82).

PLATEAU

Klamath • Modoc • Wasco-Wishram

NORTHWEST COAST

Quinault

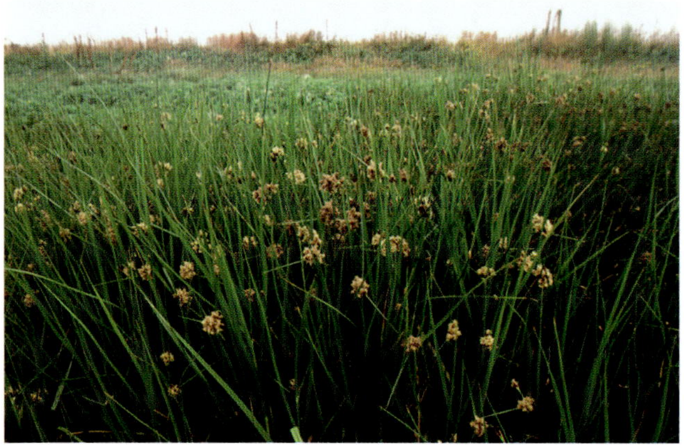

Tule, Bulrush.
Photo by Gordon Leppig and Andrea J. Pickart

WHEAT STRAW *(Triticum vulgare)*

After the Spanish colonists introduced wheat crops to southwest North America in the early eighteenth century, basket weavers began using the easily collected stalks of wheat straw from the fields to form the thick bundle foundations (warps) of large storage baskets (see fig. 118).

SOUTHWEST

Tohono O'odham

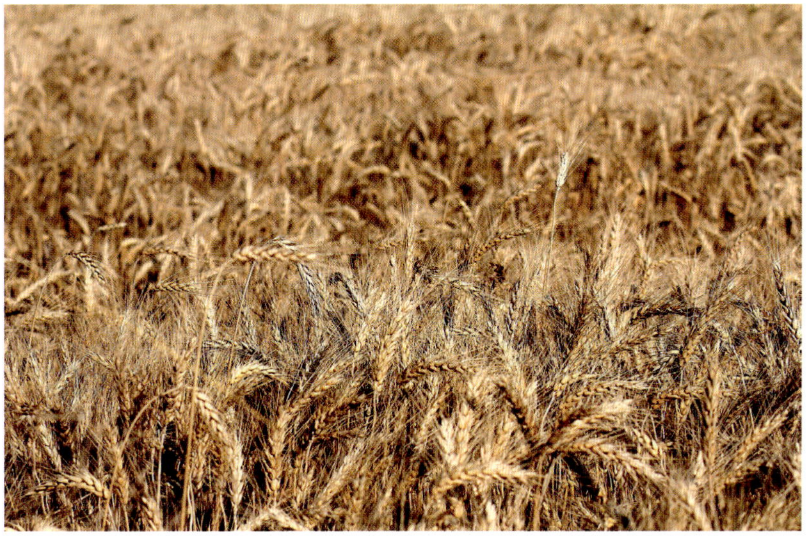

Wheat Straw.
Photo by Peter Valic

WILD RYE BEACH GRASS *(Elymus mollis)*

Basket weavers of the Arctic and Northwest Coast pick or cut wild rye beach grass growing in coastal meadows at its peak growth period in mid-summer. The blades are separated by size and color and then hung in the sun to dry. When drying is complete, the weaver removes the spine from each leaf, discards it, and splits the remaining tissue into thin strands. The resulting material is as fine as the commercial silk threads that some weavers use to decorate their baskets. Wild rye beach grass is used for both warp (foundation) and weft (sewing elements) in almost all Unangan baskets of the Arctic Culture Area. Northwest Coast weavers split the grass blades and use the strands for decorative sewing elements on spruce root baskets. Wild rye beach grass is often dyed for use as a weft design material in both culture areas.

NORTHWEST COAST

Nuu-chah-nulth • Tlingit

ARCTIC

Unangan • Yupik

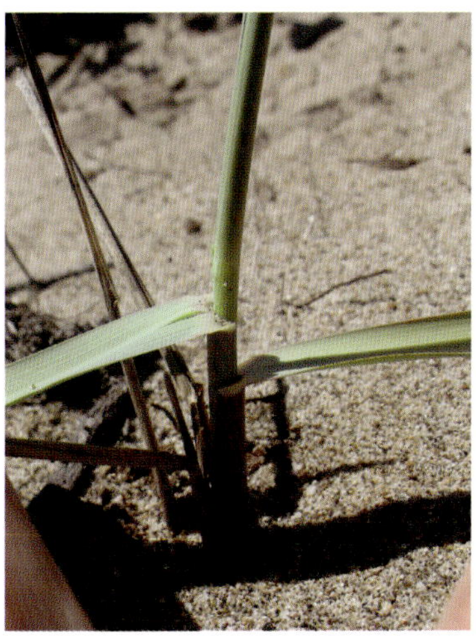

Wild Rye Beach Grass.
Photo by Robert Steers.
Courtesy of the National Park Service

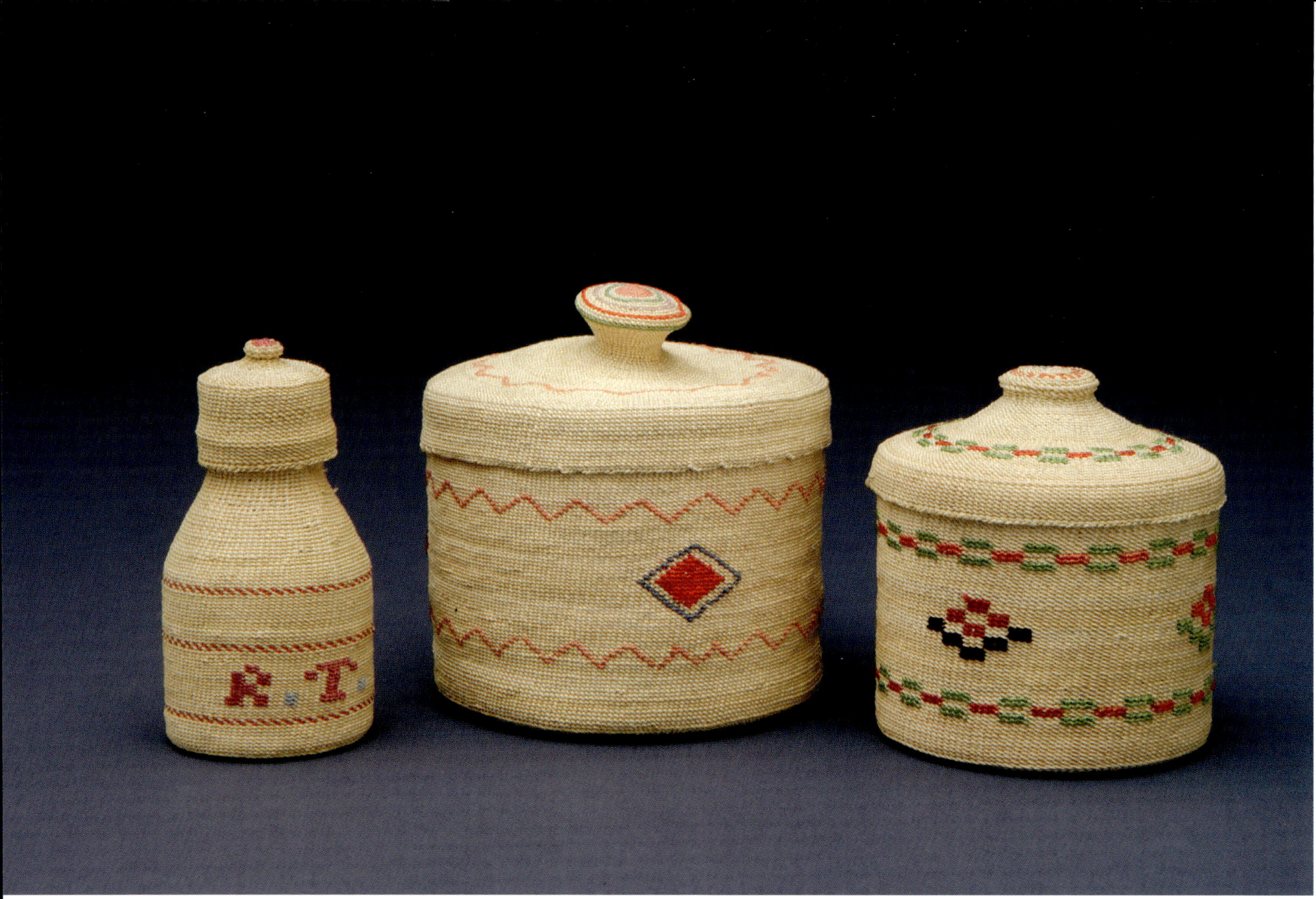

FIG. 42 (Left to right):

Bottle, c. 1920, Unangan, Artist unknown, 7.0 x 3.5 cm., 36011
FOUNDATION: wild rye beach grass bundle
WEAVING ELEMENT: wild rye beach grass; with silk thread

Trinket Basket, c. 1920, Unangan, Artist unknown, 8.0 x 8.0 cm., 36010
FOUNDATION: wild rye beach grass bundle
WEAVING ELEMENT: wild rye beach grass; with silk thread

Trinket Basket, c. 1920, Unangan, Artist unknown, 4.3 x 5.7 cm., 36014
FOUNDATION: wild rye beach grass bundle
WEAVING ELEMENT: wild rye beach grass; with silk thread

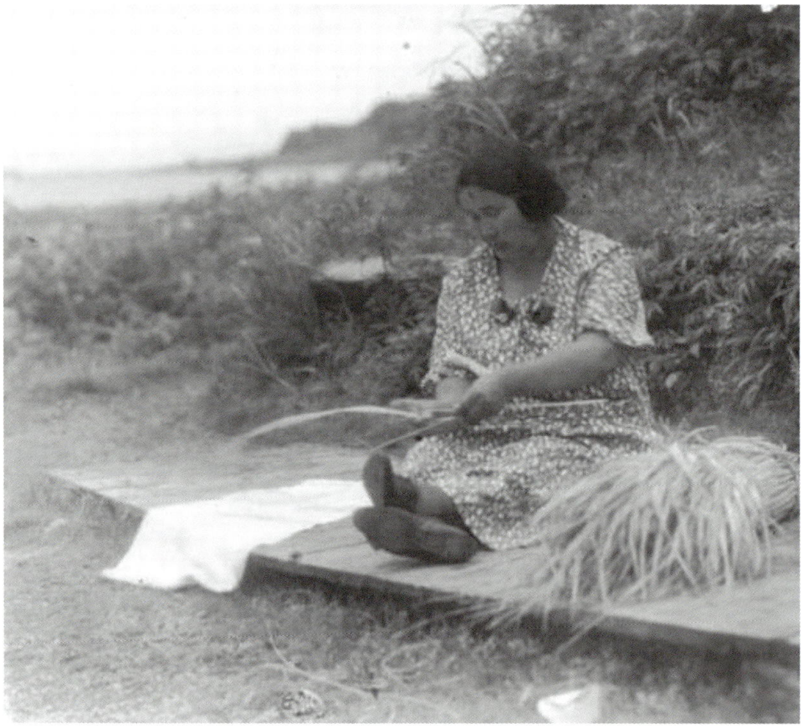

FIG. 43

Unangan basket weaver splits wild rye beach grass, c. 1926. Courtesy of the Archives, Rasmuson Library, University of Alaska Fairbanks. 1990-0003-004.

WILLOW *(Salix spp.)*

Willow shoots are gathered by basket weavers in the winter, spring, and in late summer. When winter shoots are used, weavers must scrape off the bark; on spring or late summer shoots, the bark slips easily off. After the bark is removed, the shoots are bound together in groups of similar length and diameter and then stored for drying and curing. Willow is sometimes dyed, but as it does not accept or retain the color well, basket weavers usually pair it with design materials of different texture or color. When beginning to weave, a basket maker carefully chooses willow shoots of uniform diameter and length. If necessary, she will plane the shoots to create surface smoothness and then turn them into uniform size by pushing the shoots through holes punched in metal, commonly tin can lids; or the weaver may scrape the shoots with a knife. Whole willow shoots are used for the foundation (warps) in coiled and twined baskets, and split willow shoots are used as sewing and weaving elements (wefts) in coiled and twined baskets.

SOUTHWEST

Akimel O'odham • Ancestral Pueblo • Havasupai • Hualapai • Jicarilla Apache • Ohkay Owingeh Pueblo • Pueblo • San Carlos Apache • Santo Domingo Pueblo • Tohono O'odham • Western Apache • White Mountain Apache • Yavapai

GREAT BASIN

Cedar Paiute • Moapa Paiute • Mono Lake Paiute • Paiute • Panamint Shoshone • Southern Paiute • Tubatulabal • Ute • Washoe

CALIFORNIA

Mountain Maidu • Pomo • Wappo

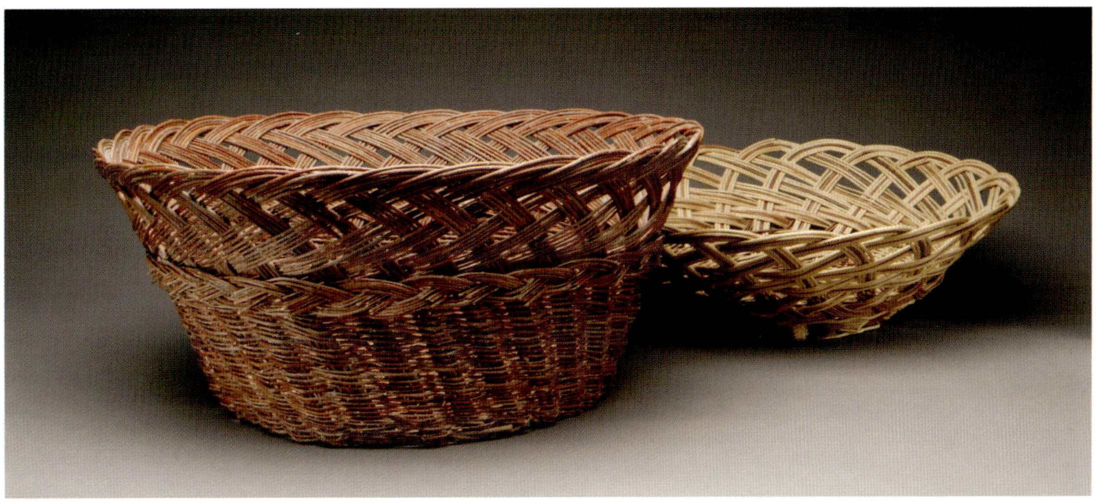

FIG. 44 (Left to right):

Bowl, 1949, Santo Domingo Pueblo, Santiago Tenorio, 28.0 x 62.0 cm., 23499
FOUNDATION: willow rods
WEAVING ELEMENT: willow rods

Bowl, c. 1930, Pueblo, Artist unknown, 21.0 x 57.0 cm., 47702
FOUNDATION: willow rods
WEAVING ELEMENT: willow rods

In the Southwest pueblos men typically weave these sturdy work baskets.

WOODWARDIA FERN, GIANT CHAIN FERN *(Woodwardia spinulosa)*

Basket weavers may gather woodwardia fern stems at any time of year, except the spring months. After the stems are stripped of leaves, they are pounded with a stone to loosen the two long, strong, central fibers. These fibers are hung straight until dry and then wound into coils for storage. Before weaving, the naturally white woodwardia-fern fibers are dyed an orange-red color using alder bark. Northern California weavers use this plant fiber most frequently as a weft overlay design material.

CALIFORNIA

Karuk • Wintu • Yurok

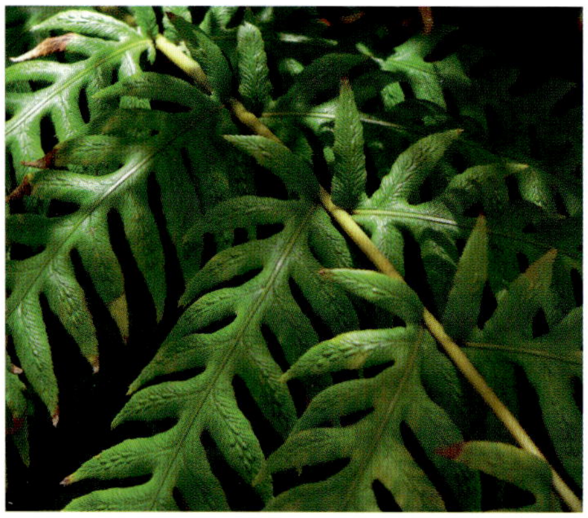

Woodwardia Fern, Giant Chain Fern.
Photo by Stan Shebs

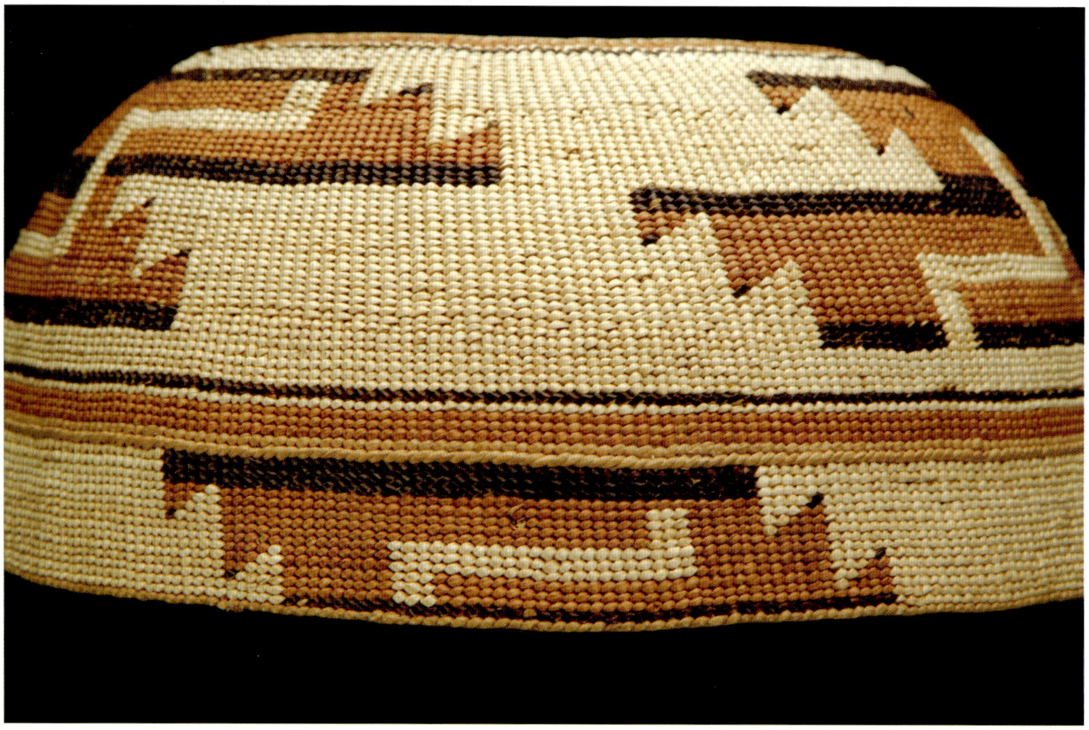

FIG. 45

Woman's Cap, c. 1920, Karuk, Artist unknown, 7.5 x 17.5 cm., 19

FOUNDATION: hazelnut rods

WEAVING ELEMENTS: spruce root, beargrass, alder-dyed woodwardia fern stem, maidenhair fern stem

YUCCA *(Yucca spp.)*, NARROWLEAF YUCCA *(Yucca angustissima)*

There are about four yucca species native to the western United States that become very difficult to tell apart when used as basket-weaving material. San Carlos Apache, Western Apache, and O'odham weavers probably use the deep, thick tap root of banana yucca (*Yucca Baccata*) (naturally red when the outer bark is removed) as a sewing element to create designs in their coiled baskets. In addition, Mescalero Apache weavers may split the banana yucca leaves into separate strands to use them for the sewing elements on their coiled baskets, as well as for foundation bundles.

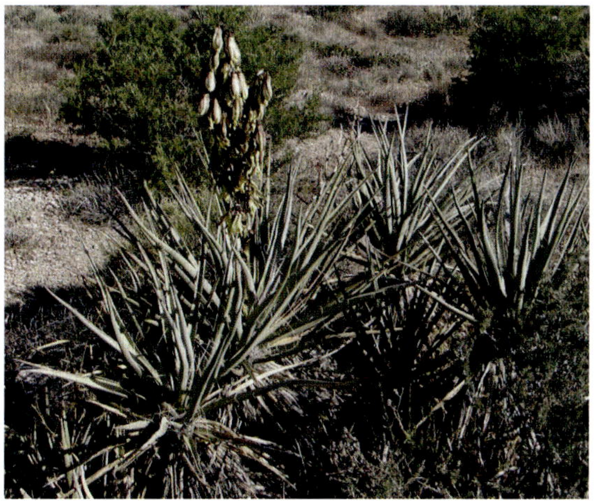

Banana Yucca.
Photo by Stan Shebs

Basket weavers on Hopi Second Mesa use narrowleaf yucca (*Yucca angustissima*) leaves sized into strips for coiled baskets. When creating designs, many of these weavers use the natural colors: After harvesting dried yucca leaves gathered in spring turn yellow; yucca leaves gathered in summer turn white; and those gathered after October keep their green color. Yucca can be colored with subtle vegetal dyes or bright aniline dyes. When creating plaited baskets, the Hopi weavers use whole yucca leaves, without splitting them into strips. Basket weavers on Hopi Third Mesa, who specialize in wicker plaques, use yucca leaves to wrap the rims of their plaques.

Tohono O'odham weavers began using yucca leaves as a weft weaving element in their commercial baskets during the early 1900s. (They saved the more difficult to obtain traditional weaving materials, willow and cottonwood, for baskets made for their own use.) O'odham weavers harvest only the young, tender, inside leaves at the center of the yucca plant. They strip off the stringy edges, split them through the middle, and spread them out on the ground for two to three days to dry. To create individual sewing strands, the midrib is shaved off and discarded (see fig. 26).

SOUTHWEST

Akimel O'odham • Ancestral Pueblo • Hopi • Hualapai • Jemez Pueblo • Mescalero Apache • San Carlos Apache • Tohono O'odham • Western Apache

GREAT BASIN

Moapa Paiute

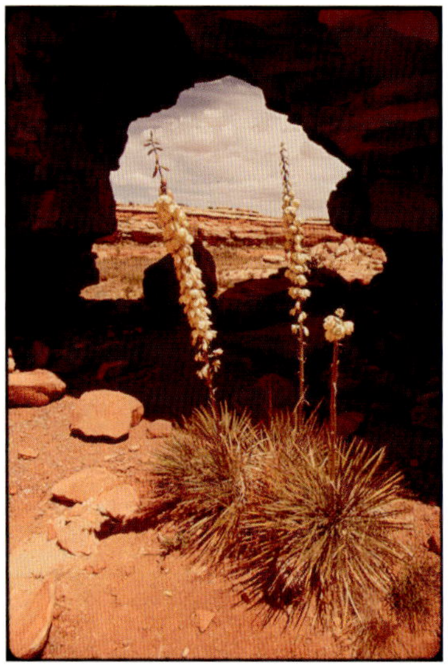

Yucca, Narrowleaf Yucca.
Photo by David Hiser. Courtesy of The United States National Archives and Records Administration

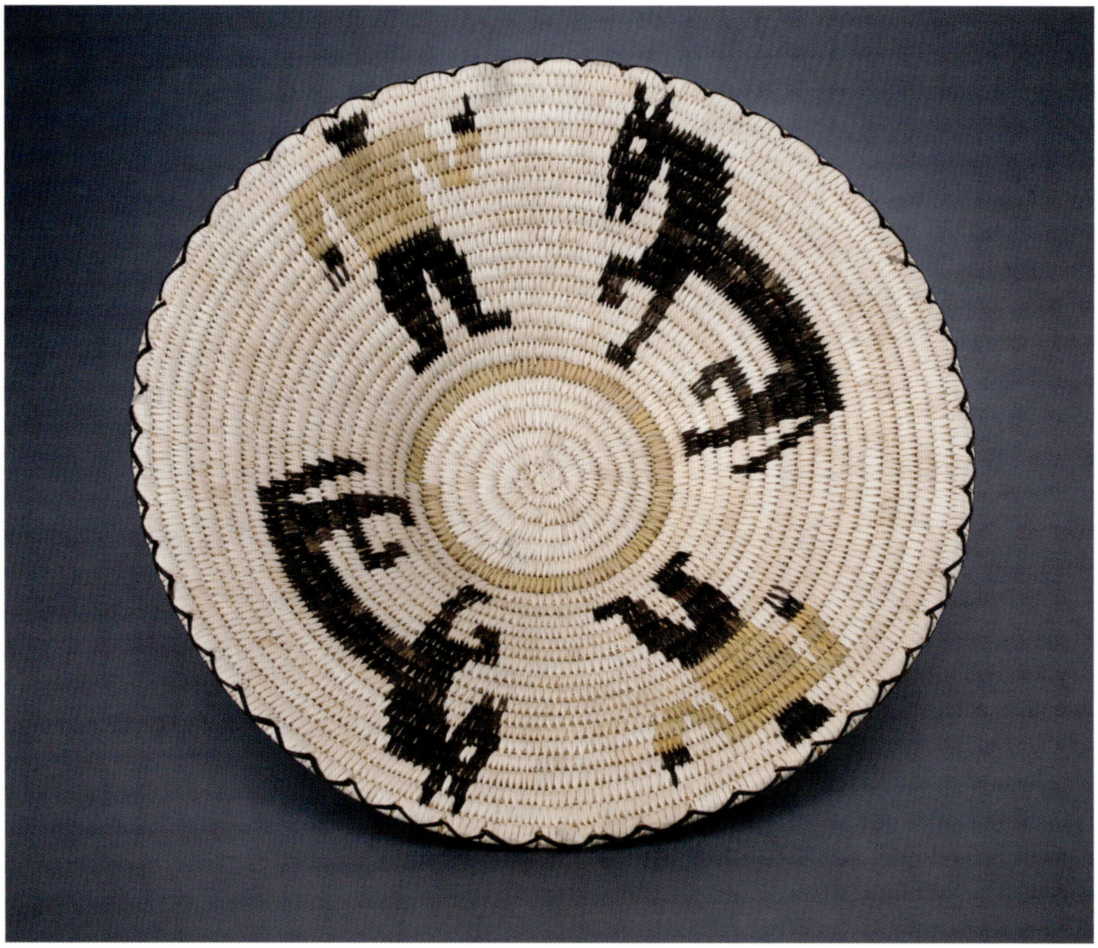

FIG. 46

Bowl, c. 1970, Tohono O'odham, Artist unknown, 9.6 x 46.0 cm., 54644

FOUNDATION: beargrass bundle

SEWING ELEMENTS: yucca leaf, devil's claw seedpod

Animal Materials

BALEEN

Unangan and Inupiat men weave baskets using baleen—the white and black keratinous fibers that serve as a plankton-filtering system in the mouth of the bowhead whale. Traditionally, Inupiat men split and shaved whale baleen to make cordage for nets and lashings. By 1920 the Inupiat had expanded their use of baleen to weaving baskets for the tourist trade. Weaving baleen baskets is still primarily men's work.

ARTIC

Inupiat • Unangan

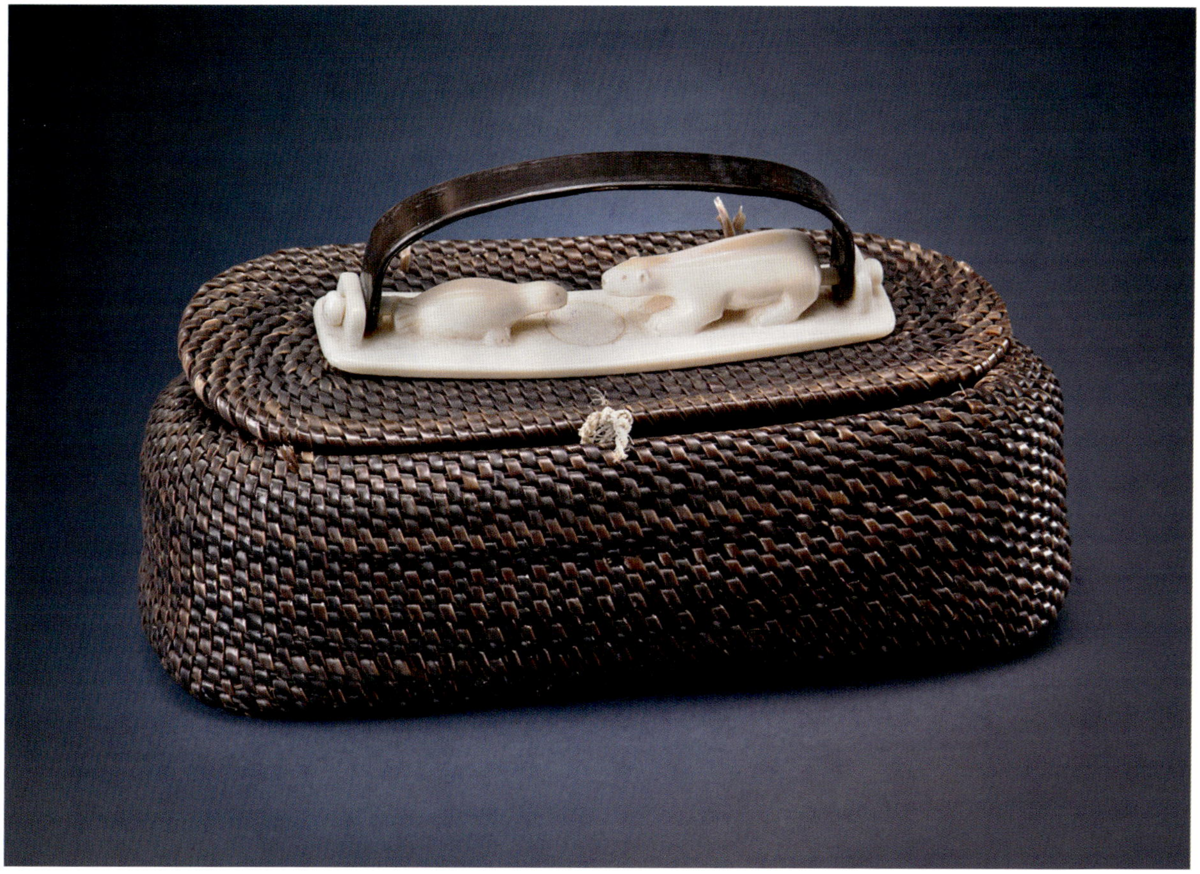

FIG. 47

Box, 1949, Inupiat, George Omnik, 10.0 x 8.0 x 17.5 cm., 50006

FOUNDATION: baleen

SEWING ELEMENT: baleen; with carved ivory

HORSEHAIR

Horsehair is commonly used throughout the Southwest to make handles and straps, including those needed for baskets. The Tohono O'odham acquired horses as early as the seventeenth century, shortly after horses were introduced to the Southwest by the Spanish; however, Tohono O'odham basket makers have only been using horsehair for weaving miniature baskets since the early to mid-twentieth century (Shreve 1943:15). Basket weavers use the long coarse hair of a horse's tail, or the finer hair of its mane, for both the bundle foundation and sewing elements (wefts) of coiled baskets.

SOUTHWEST

Diné • Jicarilla Apache • Tohono O'odham • Ute

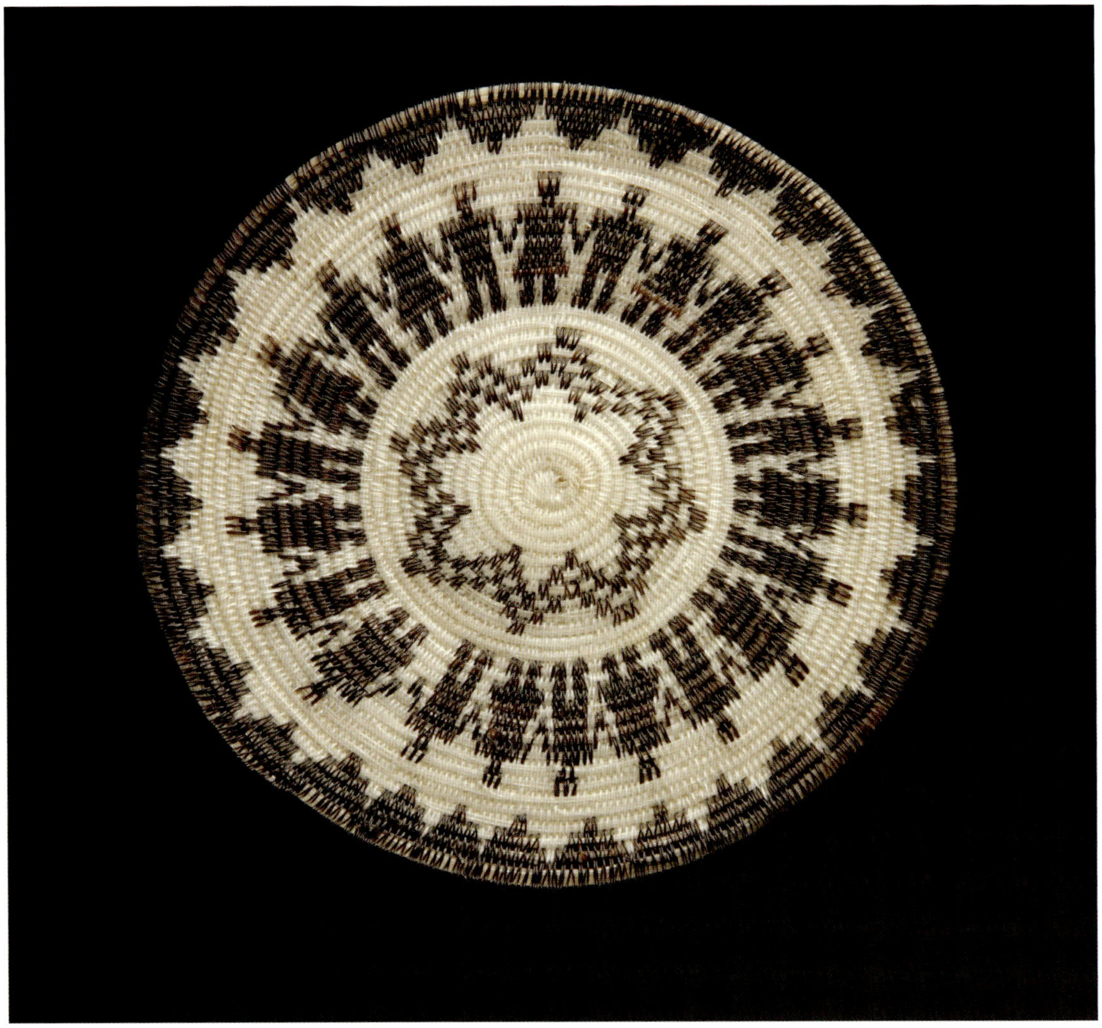

FIG. 48

Miniature Basket, 1983, Tohono O'odham, Norma Antone, 0.3 x 7.3 cm. 50125
FOUNDATION: horsehair
SEWING ELEMENT: horsehair

BIRD FEATHERS AND QUILLS

Pomo weavers of California were renowned for their skilled use of feathers in their coiled gift baskets (also called fancy or treasure baskets). Famous basket weaver Elsie Allen described their importance: "Pomo Feather Baskets of the old days were made almost exclusively to be given as gifts to important or very much revered people. So much work went into these baskets that their value today is almost priceless" (Allen 1972:37). For centuries, Pomo weavers trapped wild birds for food and to acquire feathers for their gift baskets. Because so many of the birds they once used have become protected species, Pomo basket weavers began using the feathers from game birds, including pheasants and ducks.

Before using the feathers, the weavers must dry them; this is done while the feathers are still attached to the bird's skin. As the weaver pulls each feather from the skin, she scrapes the quill clean. When coiling a basket, she lays the quill under a weft (sewing element), which she pulls tight around the feather quill to hold it in place.

CALIFORNIA

Pomo • Tubatulabal • Yokuts • Yurok

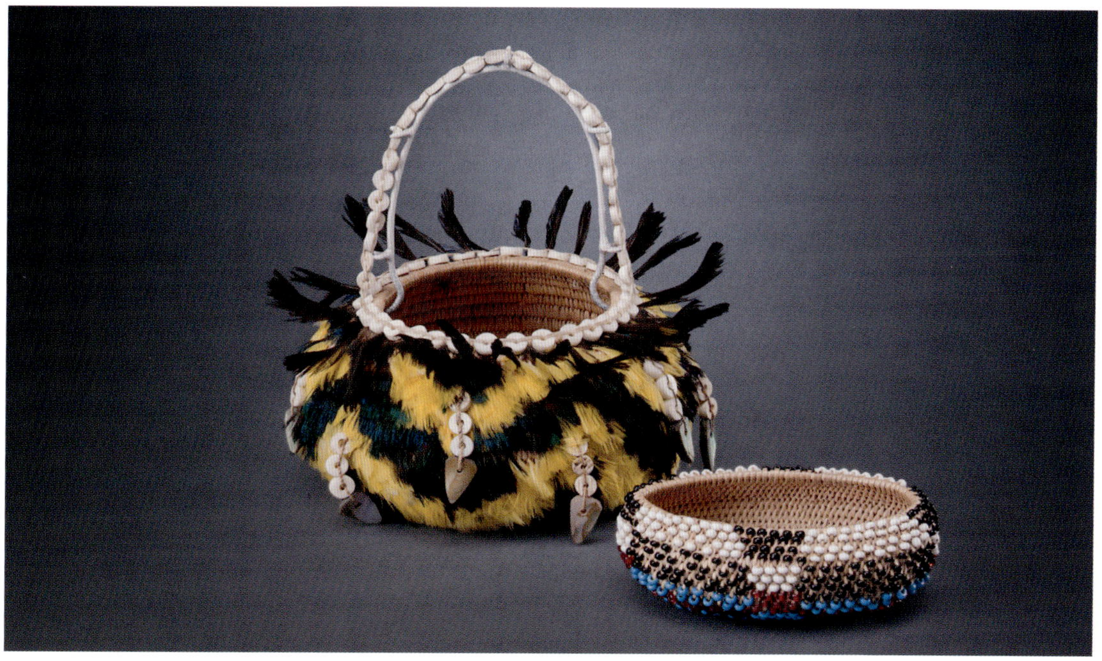

FIG. 49 (Left to right):

Treasure or Gift Basket, c. 1900, Pomo, Artist unknown, 2.5 x 11.6 cm., 14351

FOUNDATION: three willow rods

SEWING ELEMENT: sedge rhizome; with meadowlark feathers, mallard feathers, quail topknots, clamshell disk beads, abalone pendants

Gift Basket, c. 1910, Wappo, Artist unknown, 2.4 x 4.6 x 7.0 cm., 14321

FOUNDATION: single willow rod

SEWING ELEMENT: sedge rhizome; with glass beads

Pomo and Wappo weavers of California made feathered baskets centuries before they came into contact with foreigners. By the early twentieth century, when both of these gift baskets were made, weavers found it almost impossible to get enough wild bird feathers to continue making this type of basket. As a result, many basket weavers in the region began using beads to cover their baskets and create design elements.

PORCUPINE QUILLS

The literal translation of the porcupine's scientific name, *Erethizon dorsatum*, is "irritable back," an excellent description of this rodent's distinctive feature—about 30,000 quills covering the porcupine's back that are used as a defense against predators. Most quills are located close to the porcupine's body, hidden in its long yellow-tipped hair. The quills are gathered from a trapped animal or living animal by causing it to expel quills in defense. Weavers clean the quills to remove hair and skin, and then snip off the pointed ends. Prior to use they are flattened and sized. Basket makers weave them into baskets by passing the weft (weaving element) through the center of each quill (see fig. 82).

PLATEAU

Modoc

Surface Coatings

PIÑON PITCH

Native basket makers of the Southwest coat the surfaces of both coiled and twined baskets with piñon pitch to make them watertight. The pitch, which is gathered from piñon trees in springtime, is heated and spread over the exterior and/or then poured into the basket; the weaver then rotates the basket until the interior is completely coated. Sometimes a rock is added to the pitch and rolled around the inside of the basket to push the pitch further into the basket's crevices (see fig. 109).

SOUTHWEST

Diné • Havasupai • Hualapai • Jicarilla Apache • Pueblo • Western Apache

Chapter 2

CONSTRUCTION TECHNIQUES

Basket construction techniques are just one example of how Native American women manipulate materials from their environment to literally transform the natural into the cultural. Basket weavers choose construction methods based on cultural preference, personal choice, and the basket's intended use. Baskets can, therefore, be identified as being from a particular community or by a particular individual because these objects reflect communal and individual ideas and preferences.

Over the past two centuries, basket weavers have modified and adapted their basketmaking materials, forms, and designs due to the influence of changing lifeways. However, throughout this period construction techniques have remained the same. As historian and author Bruce Bernstein explains, "Weavers may make baskets for sale or in the style of another group, or in non-traditional materials, with the design system of another group, or as a unique contract, but their technique most often does not vary" (Bernstein 1990:223). Contemporary basket makers, for instance, still use construction techniques associated with older utilitarian baskets and with community and family traditions.

Individual basket weavers are the keepers of their personal weaving knowledge; tribal tradition, however, guides who may teach, learn, or apply the art form. It is customary for basket weavers to teach other family members: usually a grandmother or mother teaches a daughter or granddaughter. Weavers from oral cultures learn through listening and imitating; there are no written instructions to follow. Learning to weave in a traditional manner, then, requires sustained observation, patience, repetition, and lifelong practice. These Native basket makers see the use of elements from the natural environment to weave their world as an important responsibility: from a weaver's perspective not using knowledge in the proper or correct way may have spiritual and physical consequences within her culture's cosmology (Schwarz 1997:38–40).

Traditionally, basket weavers have learned construction techniques by memorizing and internalizing the teachings of their elders, as well as by studying existing baskets. Expert weavers

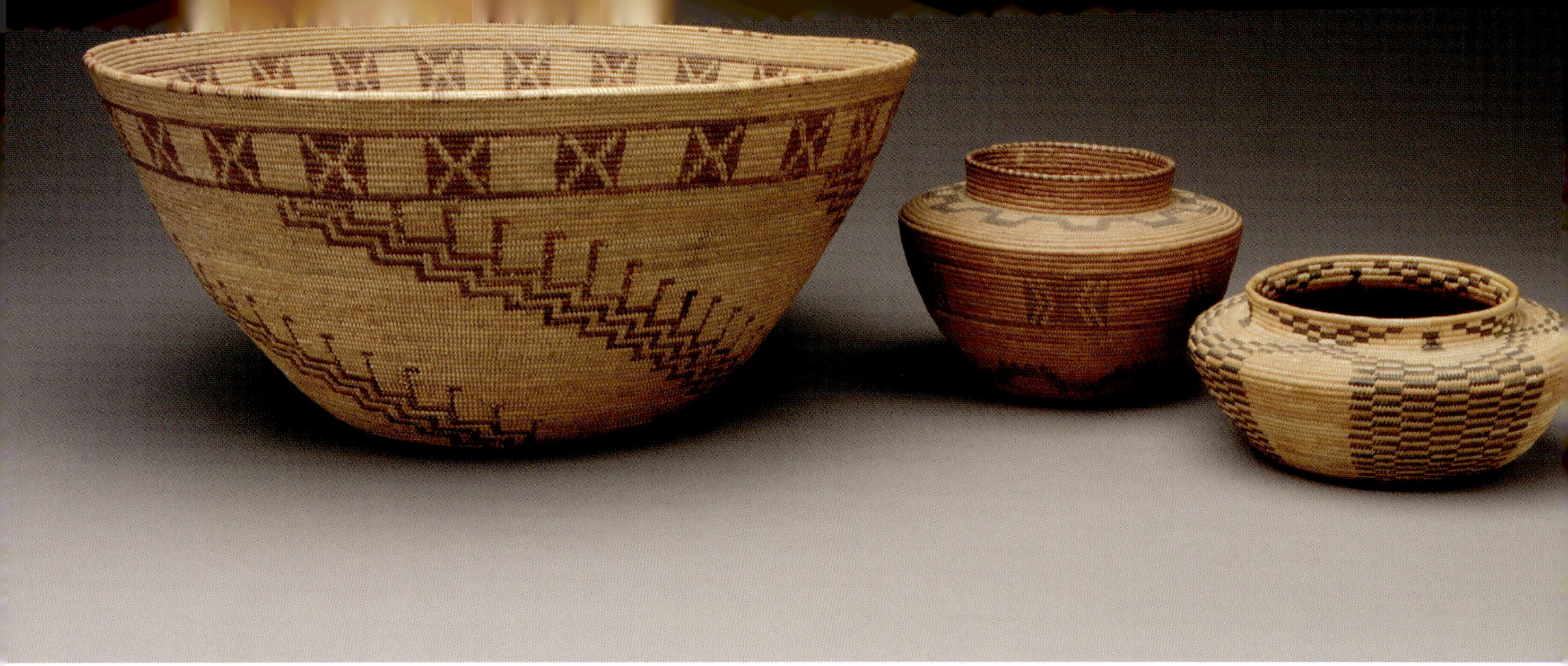

FIG. 50 (Left to right):

Cooking Bowl, c. 1890, Tubatulabal, Artist unknown, 18.5 x 40.0 cm., 23682

CONSTRUCTION: coiling

FOUNDATION: bundle

Gift Basket, c. 1900, Panamint Shoshone, Artist unknown, 12.0 x 17.0 cm., 56963

CONSTRUCTION: coiling

FOUNDATION: rods

Gift Basket, c. 1950, Monache, Artist unknown, 9.0 x 18.0 cm., 47664

CONSTRUCTION: coiling

FOUNDATION: bundle

At first glance it may appear that basket weavers conceive and make use of construction techniques for purely practical reasons. However, upon further examination it becomes clear that they also find pleasure in the beauty inherent in each technique as well as their ability to attain a high degree of accuracy and fineness of stitch. This striving for excellence is a standard in basketmaking for at least two reasons: As weavers perfect their skills, they receive respect from their families and communities; and fine weaving skills result in sturdy utility baskets. Because of the high stitch count in the three baskets illustrated here—each has between thirteen and nineteen stitches to the inch—they are durable and strong.

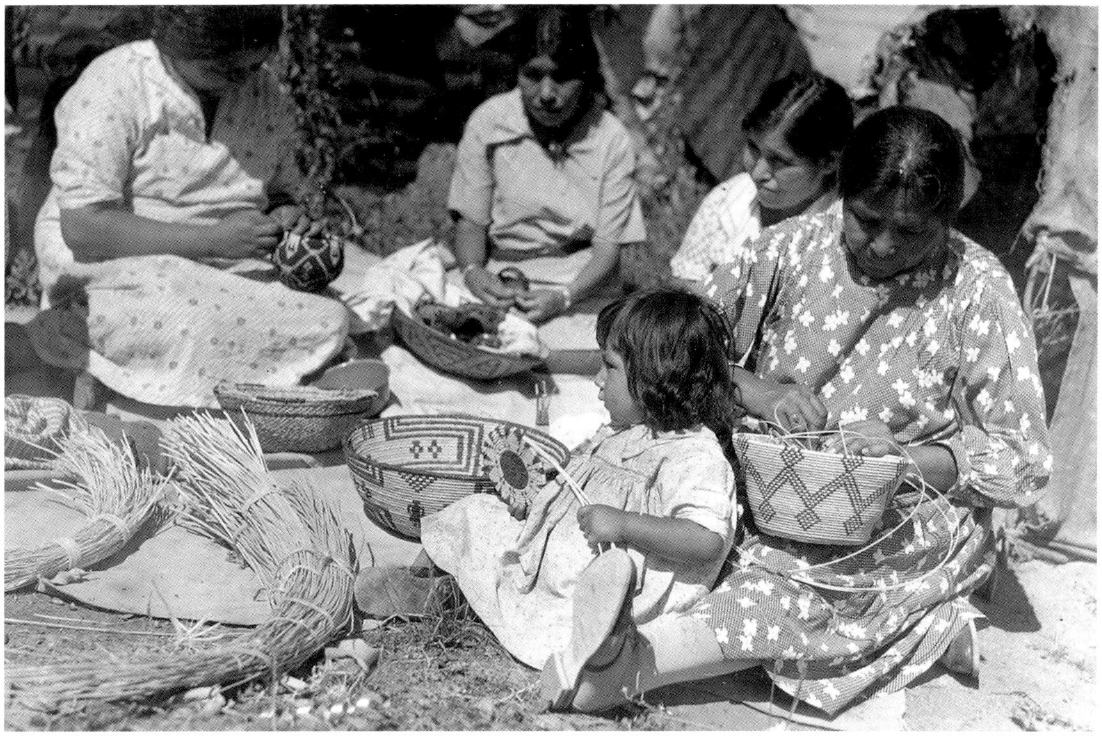

FIG. 51

Viola Jimulla, Yavapai, teaches basketmaking to a group of women. Clockwise from upper left: Grace Jimulla Mitchell, Julia Moore, Edna Moore, Viola Jimulla, and Ruth Mitchell Welch. Courtesy of the Sharlot Hall Museum. INY-2110PE.

then use their skills to explore new applications for their technique. As ethnographer Lila O'Neale learned during her work with Yurok and Karuk basket weavers of northern California, in 1929: "The weaver who can control her technique to effect an unusual shape is admired. It takes ability and effort and is characterized as hard. Only a good weaver would attempt to do this and it is looked upon as high technical proficiency. Weavers must overcome unknown difficulties to develop a tangible something out of a concept" (O'Neale 1995:160).

As with most basket makers throughout the world, Indigenous weavers of western North America construct all their baskets using only four basic techniques: coiling, twining, wicker, and plaiting. Even so, every basket is a unique object of remarkable structural and textural complexity, as each of the four weaves has numerous variations. In basket construction, the units of processed plant fibers are called "elements." An element may be a strand of plant material, such as a leaf or a strip of bark. In addition, elements are either active or passive based on whether they are "moving" (sewing or weaving elements) or "stationary" (foundation elements) and are worked around, under, or over during construction.

All four basket weaving techniques have two essential elements: a warp and a weft. The warp is the stationary foundation around which the weft is sewn (in coiling) or woven (in twining and wicker). The weft consists of those moving elements sewn or woven around the stationary warp.

Coiled baskets have a spiral foundation (warp) sewn together with a moving sewing element (weft). Twined baskets have two or more weaving elements (wefts) that are twisted as they pass between vertical, stationary foundation elements (warps). Wicker baskets have single weaving elements (wefts) that pass over and under vertical, stationary foundation elements (warps). Plaited baskets have two active weaving elements, a variation of warp and weft, which cross at right angles.

Almost all western North American baskets are decorated with two-dimensional designs. (Decoration refers to designs incorporated into the weave; ornamentation refers to three-dimensional design elements, such as feathers or beads.) The most straightforward way of adding design motifs to coiled and twined baskets is by simply substituting one texture or color of weft (sewing or weaving element) for another. Or a weaver may float a design weft element on top of a base weft element, concealing the design weft element behind the base weft element to terminate the design. In wickerwork and plaiting, surface designs are created by alternating weaving techniques or using multi-colored materials. Weavers have also devised more complex design techniques: imbrication and beading (with the coiling method); and overlay and false embroidery (with the twining method).

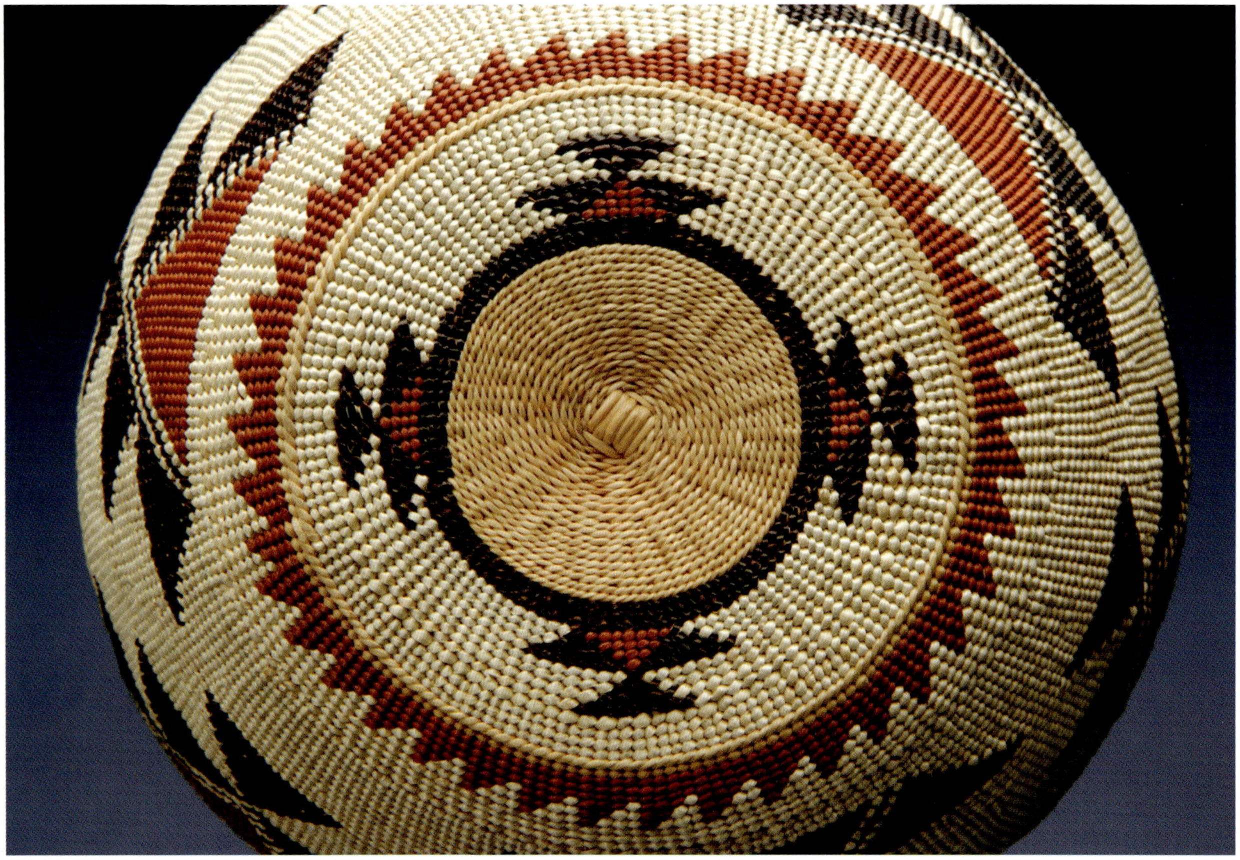

FIG. 52

Woman's Cap (Start detail), c. 1945, Yurok, Artist unknown, 8.0 x 17.1 cm., 54586

CONSTRUCTION: plain twining, overlay

FOUNDATION: rods

A basket "start" sets the tone for the finished work: this is the place where the weaver chooses and knots together her materials. Because basket starts are often culturally determined, as well as personal, much can be determined about the maker of a basket by studying the start. This cap, for instance, has the twined-basket start typical of the basket weaving of the Lower Klamath River region of California.

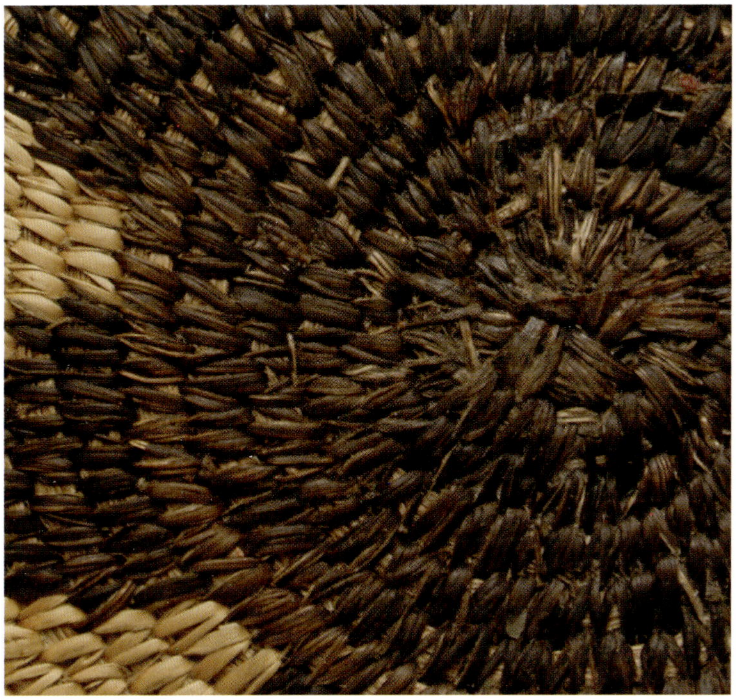

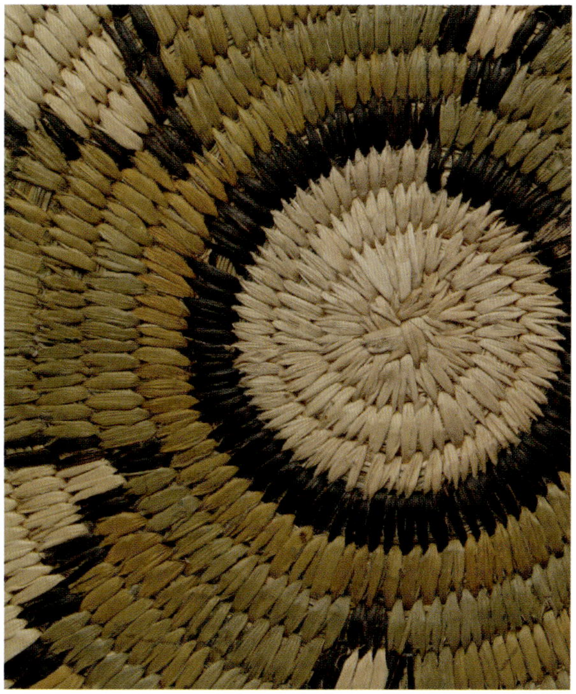

FIGS. 53

Plaque (Start detail), c. 1920, Akimel O'odham, Artist unknown, 2.0 x 18.5 cm., 23325

CONSTRUCTION: coiling

FOUNDATION: bundle

FIGS. 54

Unfinished Tray (Start detail), c. 1930, Tohono O'odham, Artist unknown, 3.0 x 37.0 cm., 907

CONSTRUCTION: coiling

FOUNDATION: bundle

The Akimel O'odham and Tohono O'odham are two closely related tribes of the Sonoran Desert in Arizona and northern Mexico. Evidence of this relationship can be found in how weavers from both tribes start their baskets. Typically, they start their coiled baskets around the four-square knot (illustrated above); the O'odham weavers are the only basket weavers in the Southwest Culture Area to use this distinctive start (Whiteford 1988:121–122).

Every basket has a beginning and an end—or a start and a finish. The start is usually at the bottom center, or in the case of hats at the top center. Because the start has features that can be linked to a specific tribal group or individual, it may reveal information about where a basket was made and by whom. Starts vary according to the basket's form and function and preferences of the basket weaver: she may choose a concave or convex shape, use three-strand twining for strength, or plait a bottom for a twined made-for-sale basket (to save time and materials).

The finish, or rim, is often reinforced on utilitarian baskets by attaching a wooden rod or using a reinforcing stitch. On the other hand, baskets made for sale and not for daily use may have delicate decorative rim finishes (unsuitable for utilitarian baskets). Some rim finishes can be linked to specific cultures and time periods; for instance, the sturdy herringbone finish was typically used on Ancestral Pueblo utilitarian baskets, as seen in figure 55.

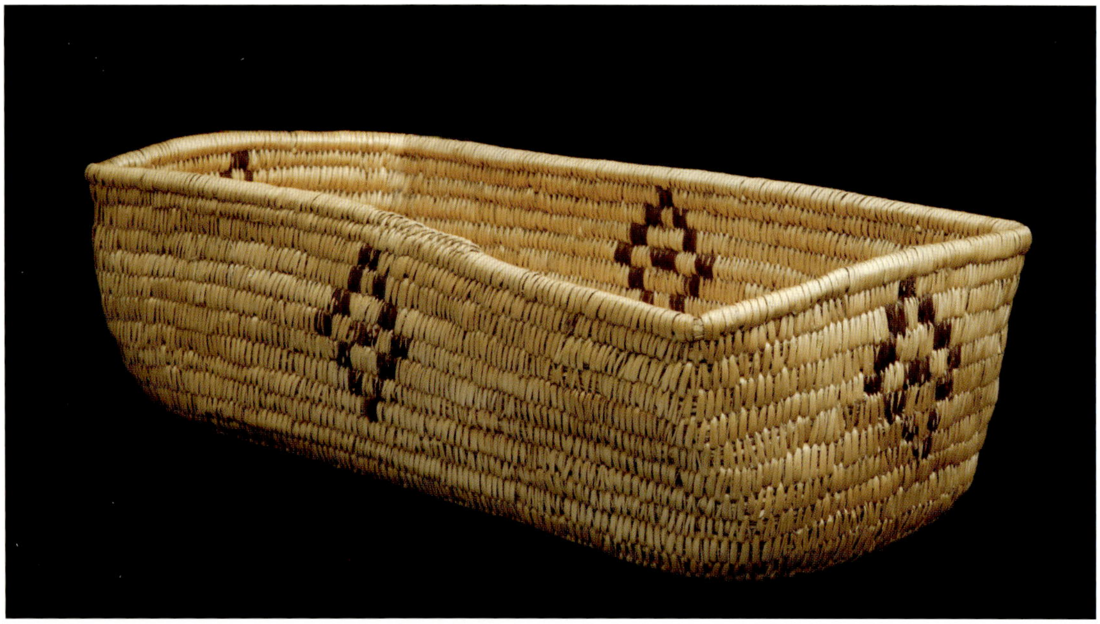

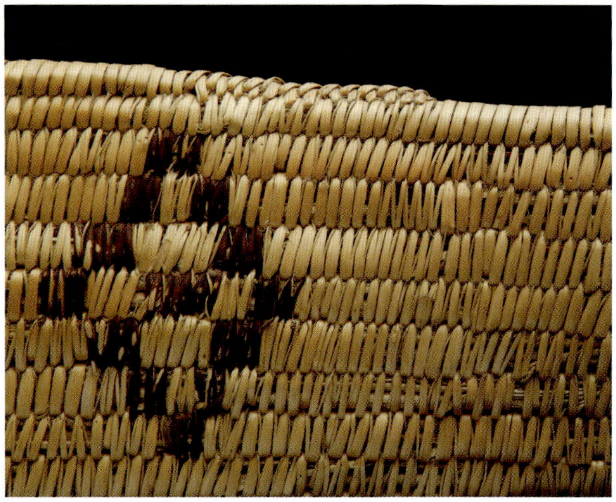

FIG. 55

Box (Rim detail), c. 1150, Ancestral Pueblo, Artist unknown, 9.8 x 16.0 x 35.0 cm., 53847

CONSTRUCTION: coiling

FOUNDATION: two rods and bundle

Throughout the weaving process, basket makers must add and subtract both warp and weft elements for a number of reasons: They size and shape baskets by adding or subtracting foundation elements; when incorporating a design, weavers terminate one sewing element and then start another; or they add materials when a foundation (warp) or sewing element (weft) is used up. The end of the spent material is called the "moving end"; the beginning of the new material is called the "fag end," or "stationary end." Also referred to as splices, the ends may be tucked into the foundation or trimmed. Some weavers may stabilize these ends by wrapping them around each other or by catching them under succeeding stitches.

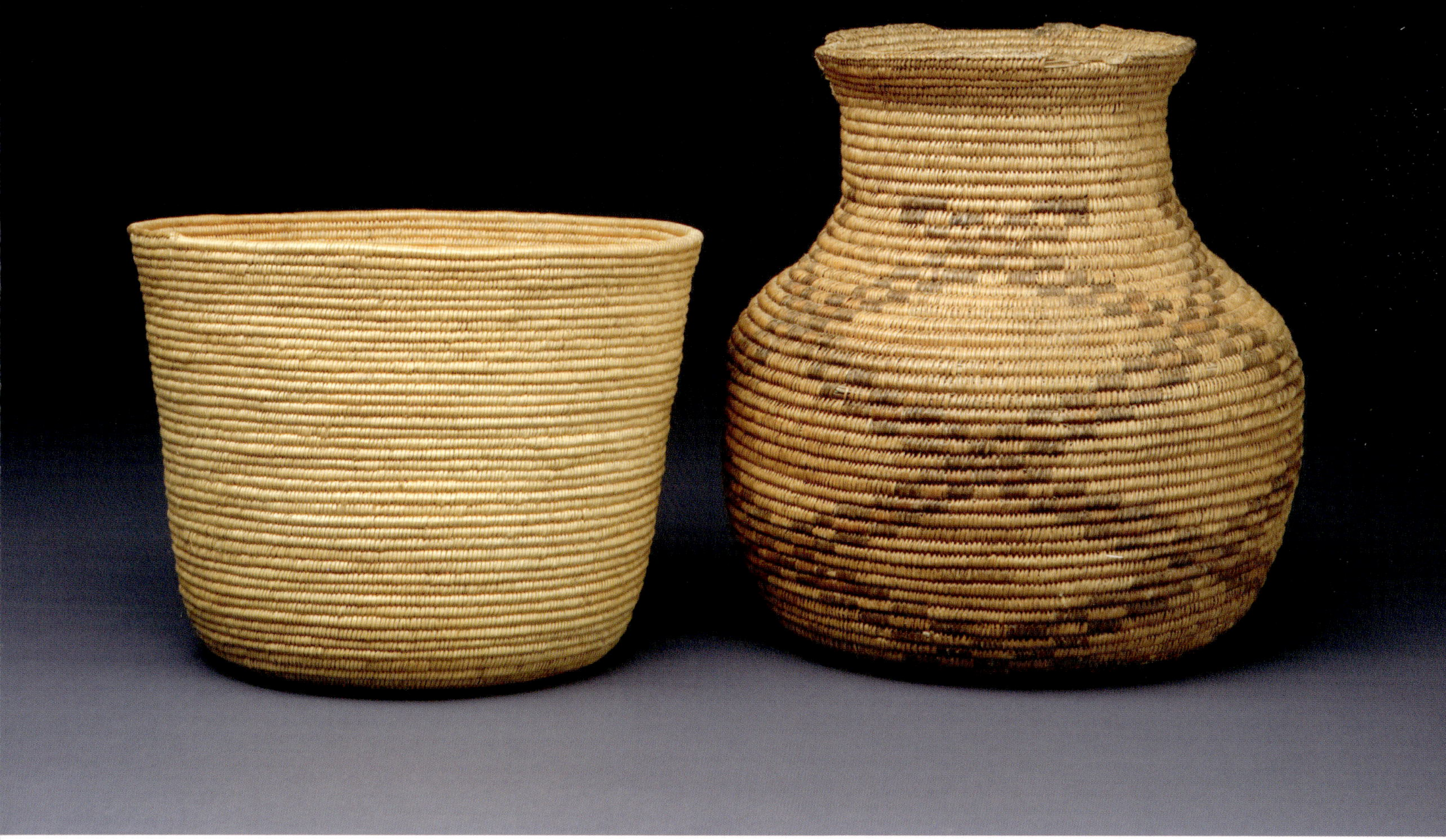

FIG. 56 (Left to right):

Cylinder, c. 1150, Ancestral Pueblo, Artist unknown, 18.5 x 23.8 cm., 53845

CONSTRUCTION: coiling

FOUNDATION: two rods and bundle

Jar, c. 1800, Zuni Pueblo, Artist unknown, 28.0 x 35.0 cm., 1118

CONSTRUCTION: coiling

FOUNDATION: two rods and bundle

The Ancestral Pueblo cylinder basket and the Zuni Pueblo basketry jar were both constructed using two-rod and bundle foundations and finished with herringbone rims. (The herringbone technique was used to construct only one inch of the circa 1150 basket rim; this technique was used to construct the entire rim of the circa 1800 basket.) Ancestral Pueblo weavers appear to have made baskets with two-rod and bundle foundations beginning in the period archaeologists call Basketmaker II (400 BC to AD 400) and through the early twentieth century (Whiteford 1988:159–161). These two baskets demonstrate a continuity of the coiled-basketry technique, made by Pueblo peoples of the Southwest over a period of at least 650 years.

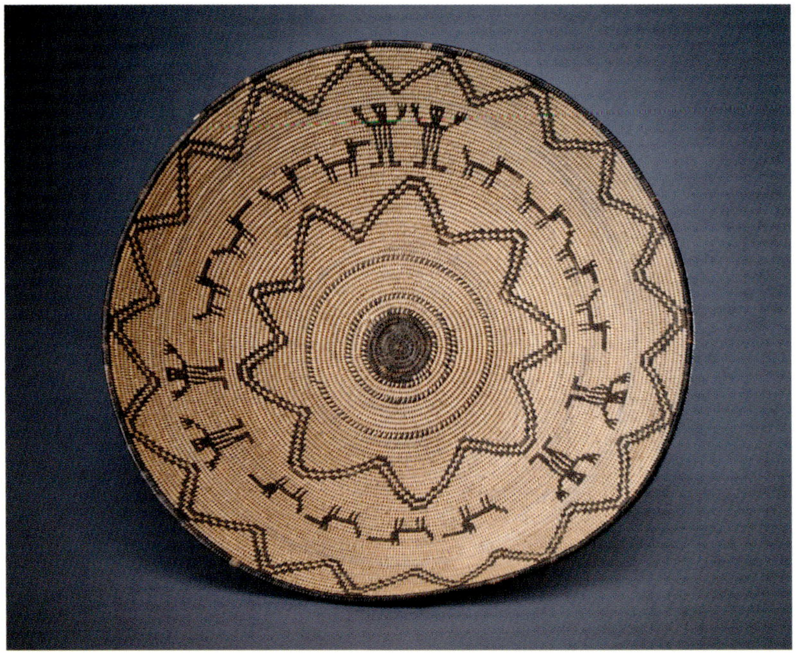

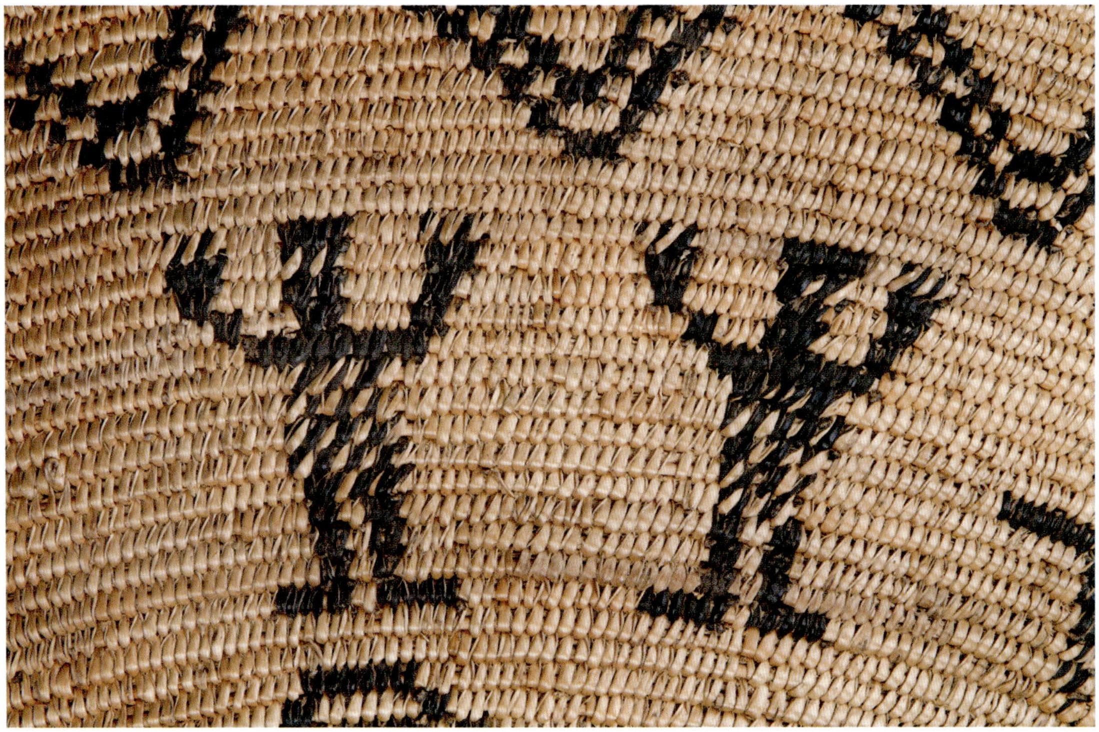

FIG. 57

Tray, c. 1900, Western Apache, Artist unknown, 10.8 x 78.5 cm., 14215

CONSTRUCTION: coiling

FOUNDATION: three rods

One of the irregularities visible on the non-work surface of coiled baskets is the result of the weaver coming to the finish of her sewing splint and leaving the end protruding from the basket. After the weaver finished this tray, she cut off the "moving" ends close to the coils, leaving behind protruding stubs on the surface.

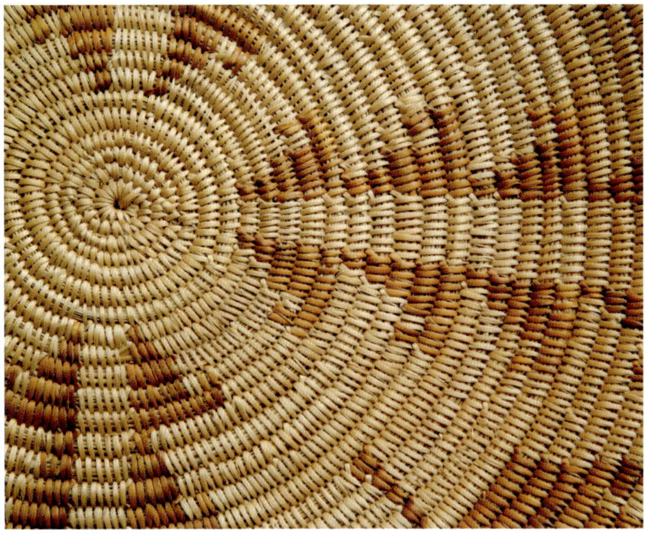

FIG. 58

Tray, c. 1890, Cahuilla, Artist unknown, 8.0 x 33.5 cm., 25026

CONSTRUCTION: coiling

FOUNDATION: bundle

When changing materials for the two-dimensional design in her tray this weaver left the stationary ends of the new sewing materials (or splices) visible. By incorporating them into the design the weaver made the basket surface more interesting.

When working on a basket, a weaver distinguishes between two surfaces: the work surface and the non-work surface. The work surface is the side of the basket facing the weaver as she works—usually the outside of an inward curving or closed-form basket, or the face (front side) of a tray or plaque. It is the surface the weaver sees as she weaves and, therefore, it is the surface where the fineness of her technique is most evident. The non-work surface, on the other hand, is not as well finished as the work surface; this may be evident by the presence of split stitches or unconcealed moving and stationary ends. Some weavers ensure that both surfaces are equally finely woven, making it difficult to identify the work surface.

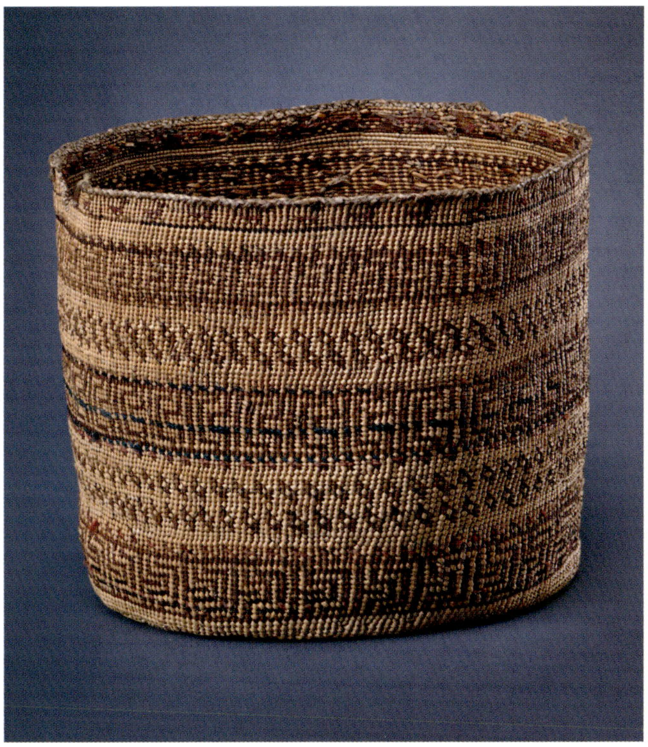

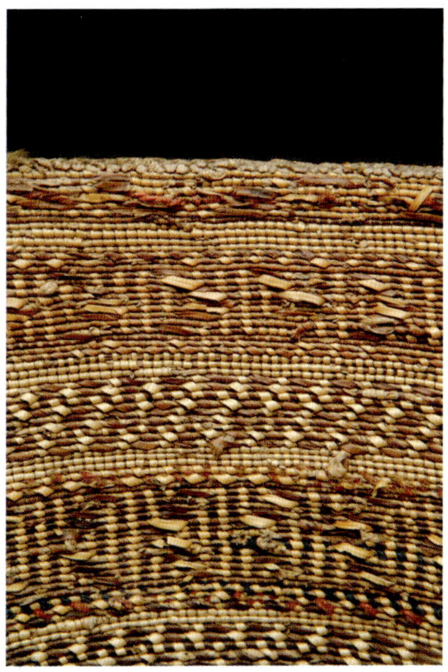

FIG. 59

Fancy Gathering Basket, c. 1840, Clatsop, Artist unknown, 15.0 x 20.0 cm., 45106

CONSTRUCTION: plain and wrapped twining

FOUNDATION: bundle

Once the work surface is established, the weaving direction of coiled and twined baskets can be determined. The direction is either rightward or leftward and is primarily determined by cultural preference. (Whether the weaver is right handed or left handed should not affect the work direction.) Because weaving direction is a social construction and not a personal choice, it is one way to determine the provenance (tribal origin) of a basket.

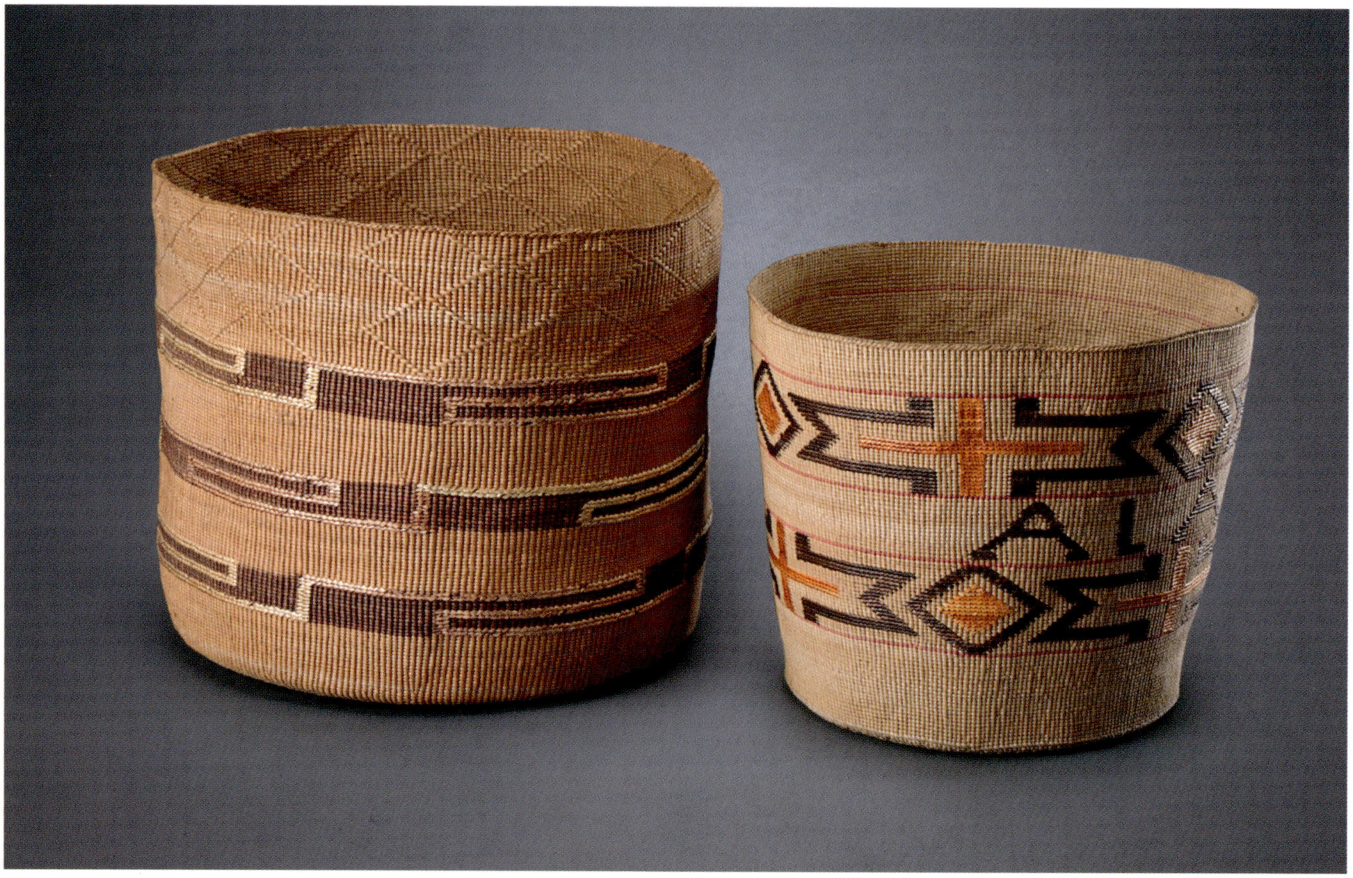

FIG. 60 (Left to right; details opposite):

Cylinder, c. 1890, Haida, Artist unknown, 18.0 x 20.0 cm., 46245

CONSTRUCTION: plain and diagonal twining, false embroidery

FOUNDATION: root

Cylinder, c. 1950, Tlingit, Artist unknown, 15.3 x 18.0 cm., 48638

CONSTRUCTION: plain twining, plaiting, false embroidery

FOUNDATION: root

An example of reading the work direction to determine cultural affiliation is by examining the two Haida and Tlingit baskets in fig. 61. One way of differentiating a Tlingit basket from a Haida is the point of weft material termination on a basket, which can be seen as a jog along vertical rows at a point on the basket wall. (In twined and coiled baskets, a jog is the transition from one row of stitches to the next row.) At the point where a weaver has changed her weft material a visible step in the alignment of the two materials occurs. The angle of this step, or jog, is reflective of orientation of the basket during the weaving process. Simply stated Haida basketry jogs up to the right; Tlingit baskets jog down to the right.

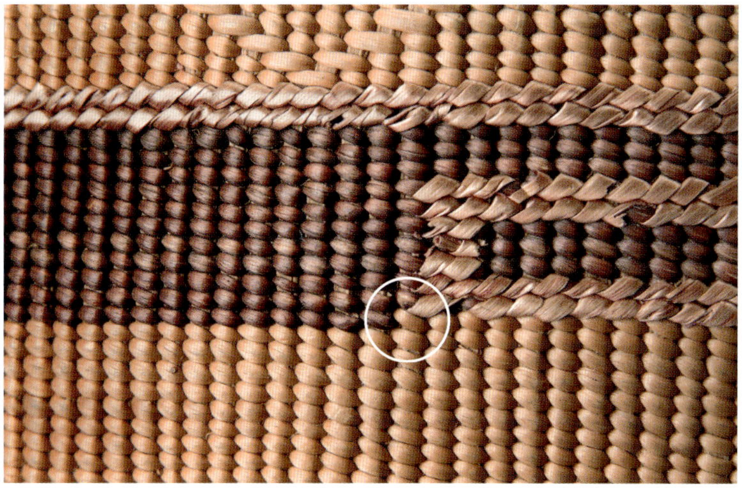

In this Haida basket, the material change highlights the "jog" up to the right, where each row is slightly below the previous one. This jog direction is the by-product of the Haida cultural convention of weaving baskets "upside down" and supported by a mold.

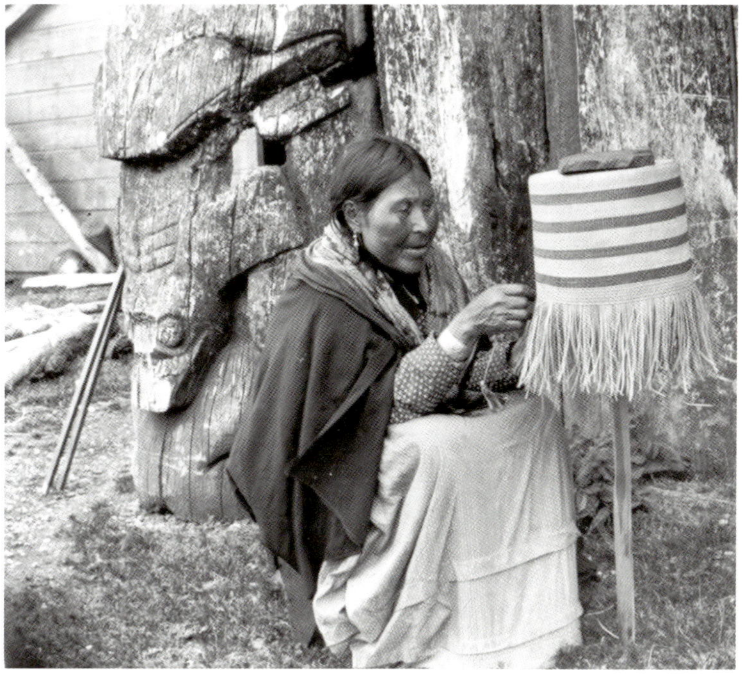

FIG. 61

A Haida woman in the village of Masset weaves a basket supported by a form in the "upside down" position, 1897. Photo by Edward P. Allen. Courtesy of the Field Museum. CSA854.

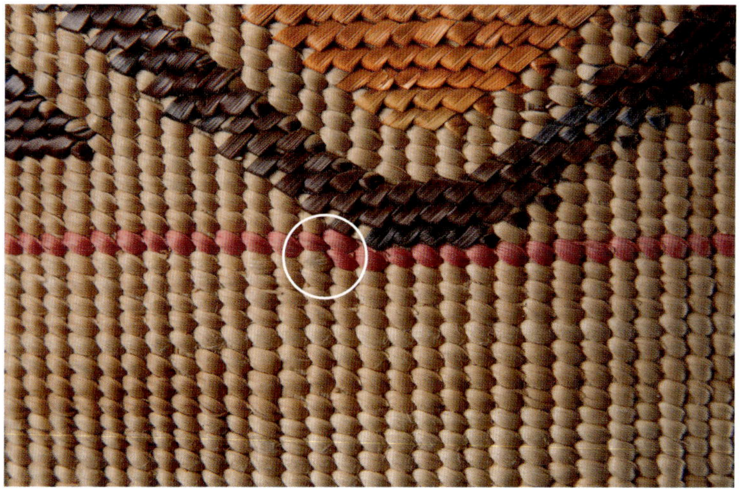

In this Tlingit basket, the material change highlights the "jog" down to the right, as each row is slightly above the previous one. This jog direction is the by-product of the Tlingit cultural convention of weaving baskets in the "right side up" position.

Coiling

Coiled baskets consist of a continuous coil that spirals from the start to the rim. Technically, coiling is a sewing technique. As they work, weavers sew the foundation (warp) with the sewing element (weft), passing it around the foundation and over or through the preceding coil to bind them together. The warp element is passive and the weft element is active in this process. The only tool basket weavers typically use for this construction technique is a sharp awl to punch a hole in the preceding coil's foundation, so they can insert the rigid sewing splint and bind the coils together.

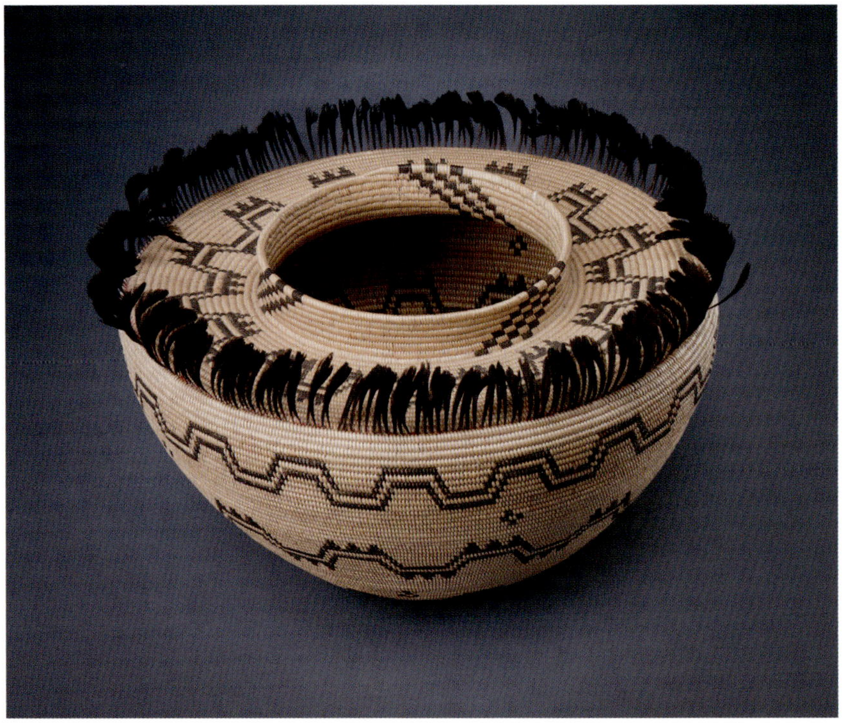

FIG. 62

Jar, 1905, Tubatulabal, Artist known as "Lucy," 16.0 x 25.0 cm., 14315

CONSTRUCTION: coiling

FOUNDATION: bundle

The subtle (or in the case of Lucy's basket, not so subtle) changes in the shape of a coiled basket reside in the weaver's skillful stacking of the coils. When the coils are perfectly aligned, the sides of the basket rise at a straight angle; when the coils are stacked gradually toward the outside, the basket circumference expands; and when the coils are stacked gradually toward the inside it contracts. Another feature of coiled gift or "treasure" baskets is the addition of feathers, a manner of decoration followed for centuries by some basketmaking traditions in the California Culture Area. The weaver of this basket, Lucy, carefully matched the size and quality of the quail topknots, attaching them by catching the base of each feather under a stitch.

STITCHES

Basket weavers can create structural designs and textures by varying the stitches in their coiled baskets. They may split stitches on the work face of a basket; use long stitches that encompass two or more coils, called overstitching; or place stitches close together or wide apart to create closed or open patterns. The Tohono O'odham use a two-stitch technique called the wheat stitch: the first stitch is a spaced stitch that splits a stitch on the coil below it; the second stitch is added to its right (see Fig. 64).

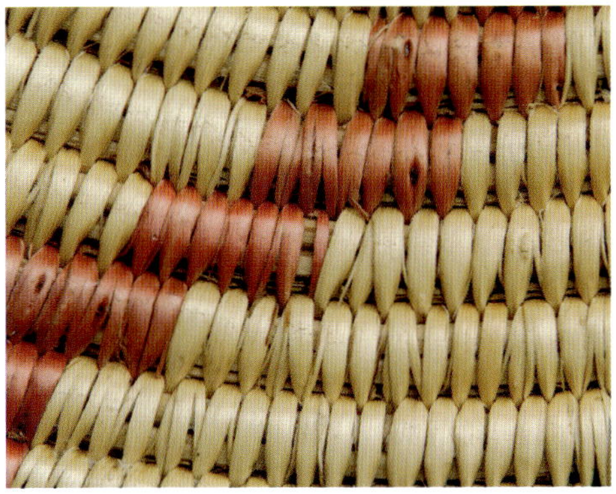

FIG. 63

Tray, c. 1930, Jicarilla Apache, Artist unknown, 10.0 x 41.0 cm., 23528

CONSTRUCTION: coiling

FOUNDATION: three rods

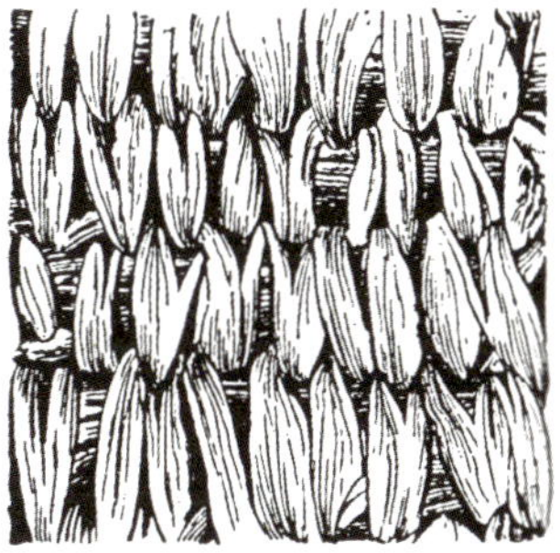

Split and unsplit stitches

FIG. 64

Fruit Bowl, c. 1940, Jicarilla Apache, Artist unknown, 9.4 x 33.0 cm., 23476

CONSTRUCTION: coiling

FOUNDATION: three rod

Tray, 2000, Tohono O'odham, Sadie Marks, 7.5 x 31.5 cm., 55728

CONSTRUCTION: open coiling, split stitches, and wheat stitches

FOUNDATION: bundle

Since the late 1800s, Jicarilla Apache and Tohono O'odham weavers have been creating baskets intended solely for the tourist market. The weavers of these two baskets are from different basketmaking traditions and different time periods, but they created works based on the same concept. The Jicarilla Apache basket weaver used plain coiling for her "fruit bowl" form, which she styled from a foreign prototype. Tohono O'odham weaver Sadie Marks used three stitch types to create the design on her extremely similar form: open coiling or space stitching (which exposes the foundation materials), intentional split stitches, and wheat stitches.

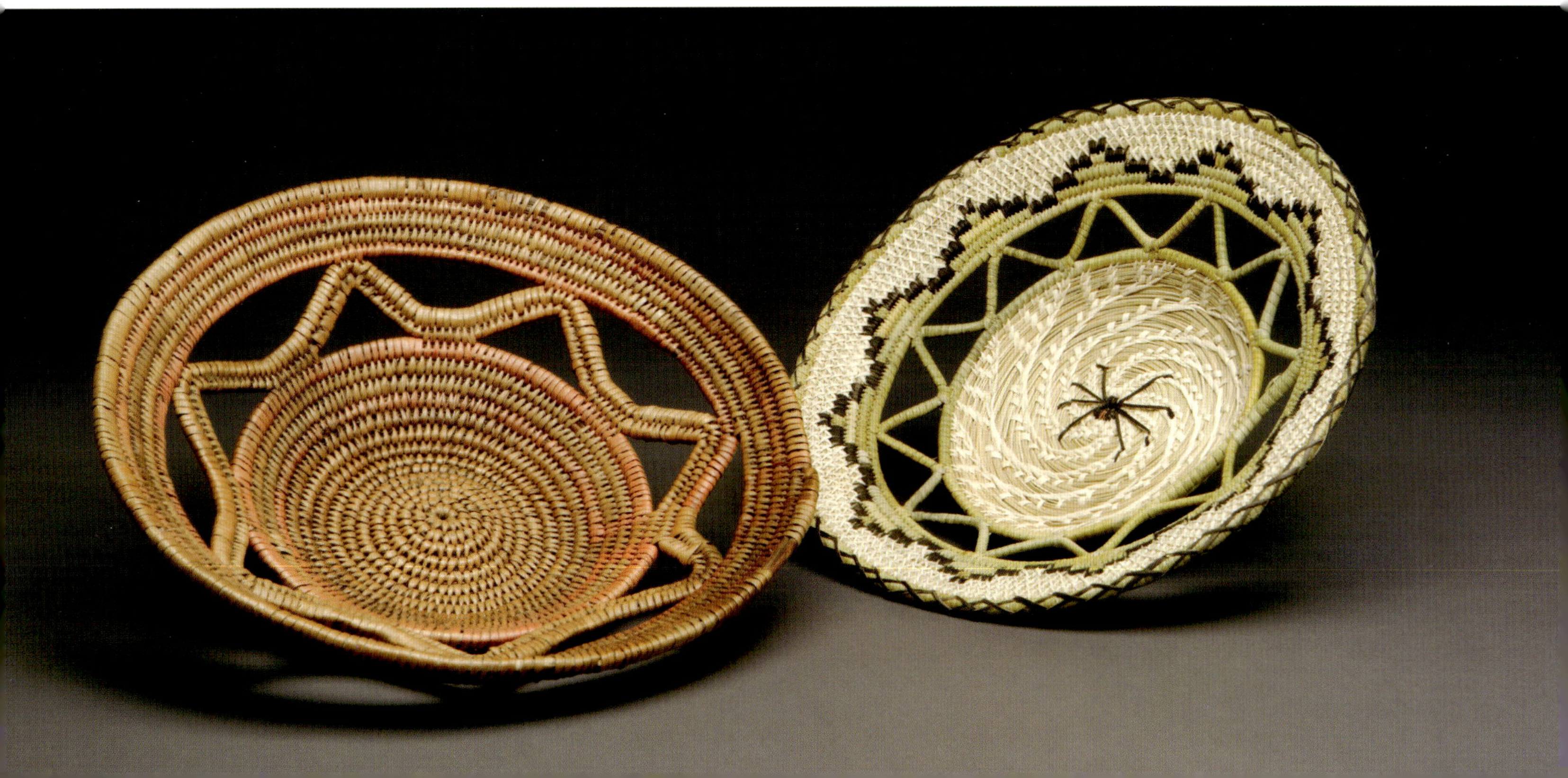

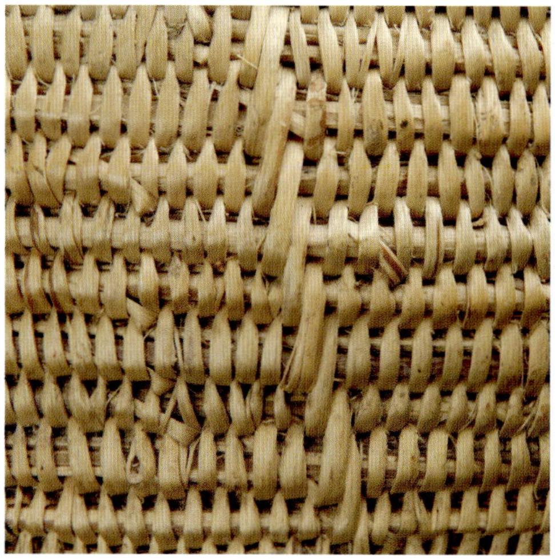

FIG. 65

Water Jar, 1935, Ute, Artist unknown, 32.0 x 25.0 cm., 7498

CONSTRUCTION: coiling, vertical overstitching

FOUNDATION: three-stacked rods

TWO-DIMENSIONAL DESIGNS

To create two-dimensional designs, weavers may add colored or textured stitches to their coiled baskets in two general ways. The first technique involves using a design sewing material to replace a regular sewing element (weft). The Hopi weavers in figure 66 are splicing in material of a different color to make their design (see also fig. 67).

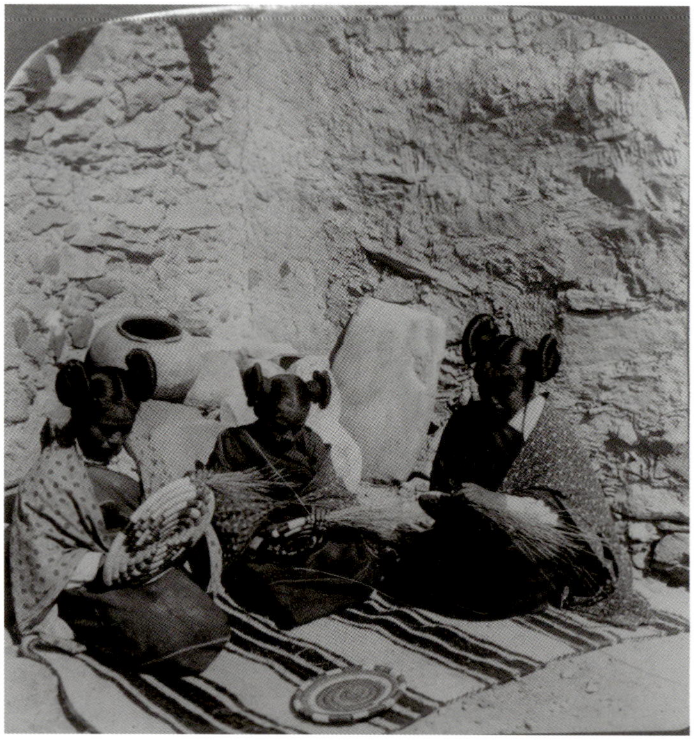

FIG. 66

Three young Hopi weavers coil plaques at Shipaulovi (Second Mesa), c. 1900.
Courtesy of the Palace of the Governors Photo Archives. 85318.

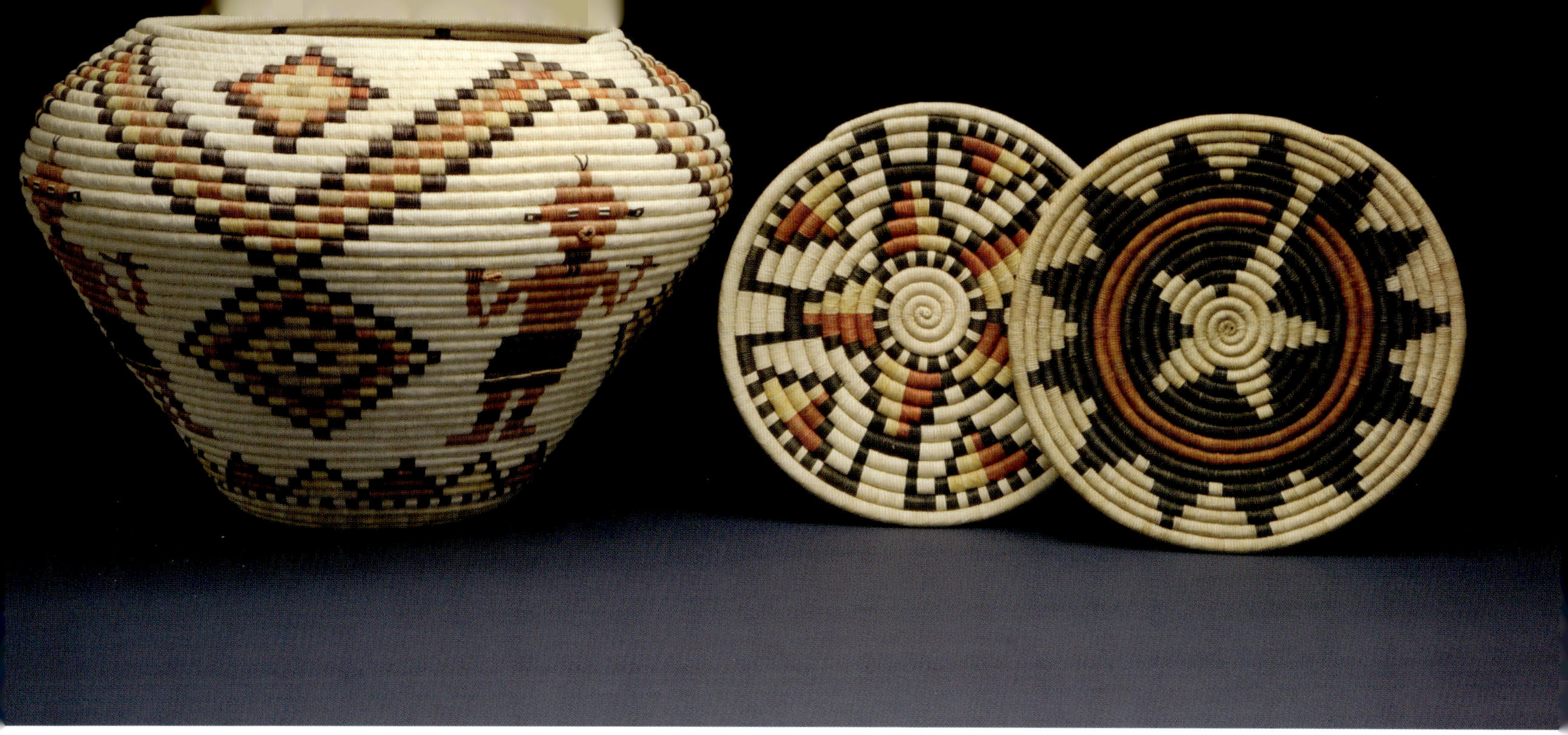

FIG. 67 (Left to right):

Jar, 1990, Hopi (Second Mesa), Elizabeth Nuvayouma, 37.6 x 51.0 cm., 57056
CONSTRUCTION: coiling
FOUNDATION: bundle

Plaque, c. 1930, Hopi (Second Mesa), Artist unknown, 3.3 x 31.4 cm., 1125
CONSTRUCTION: coiling
FOUNDATION: bundle

Plaque, c. 1960, Hopi (Second Mesa), Artist unknown, 3.3 x 32.0 cm., 46261
CONSTRUCTION: coiling
FOUNDATION: bundle

The second method of creating two-dimensional designs in coiled baskets involves the addition of non-functional elements. In other words, the base sewing element is overlaid with a design material. This may be done by beading or imbrication. In the latter, the design material is folded back on itself and stitched in place with the base sewing element and then folded forward to conceal the stitch. In beading, the base sewing element binds the design material to the foundation; widely spaced stitching is used so that the design material is visible as a decorative element.

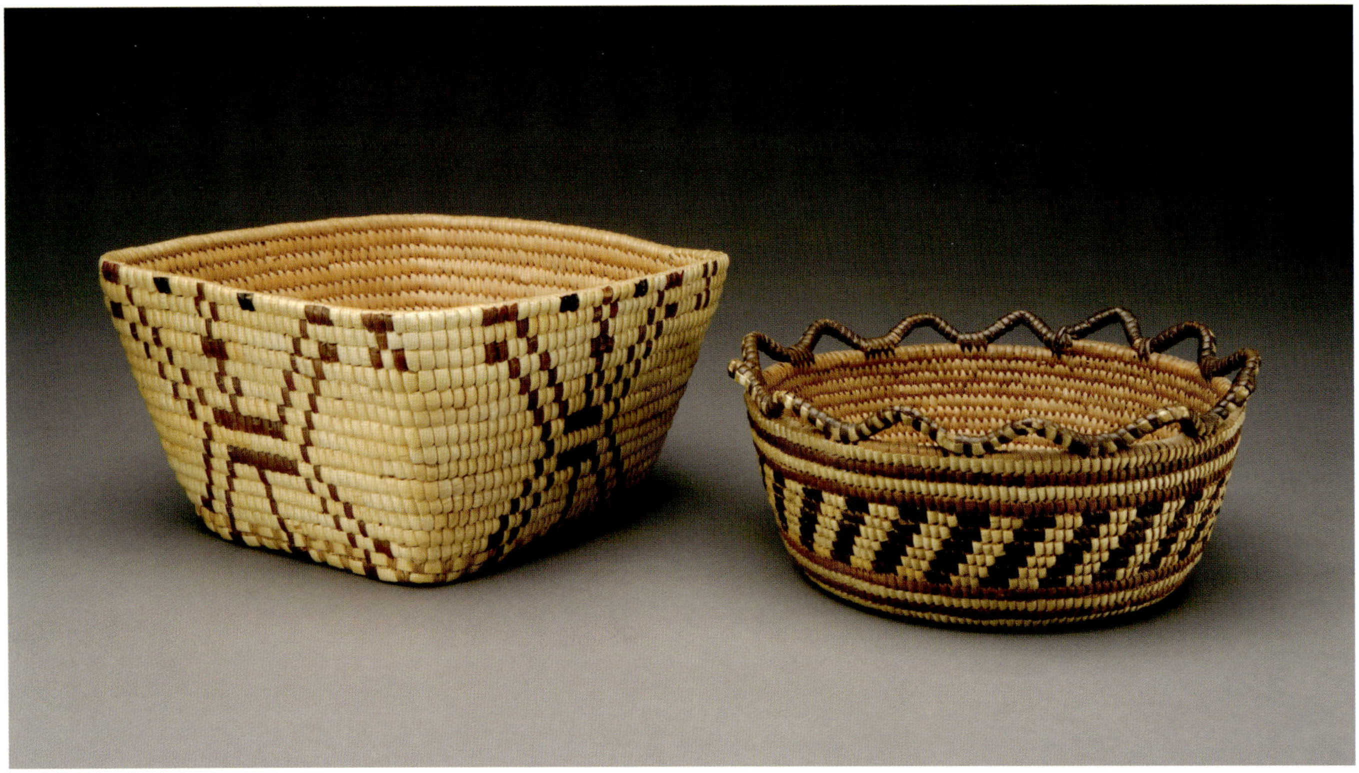

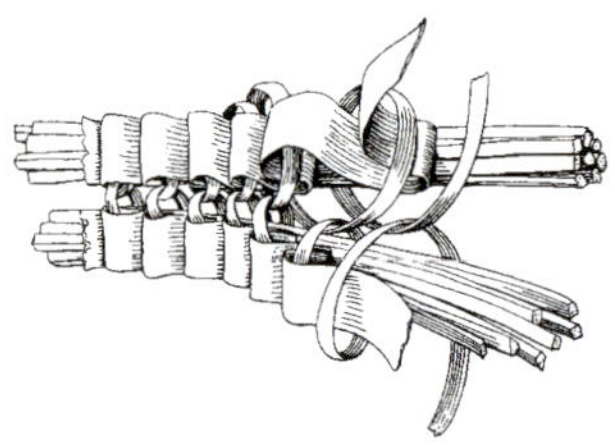

Imbrication

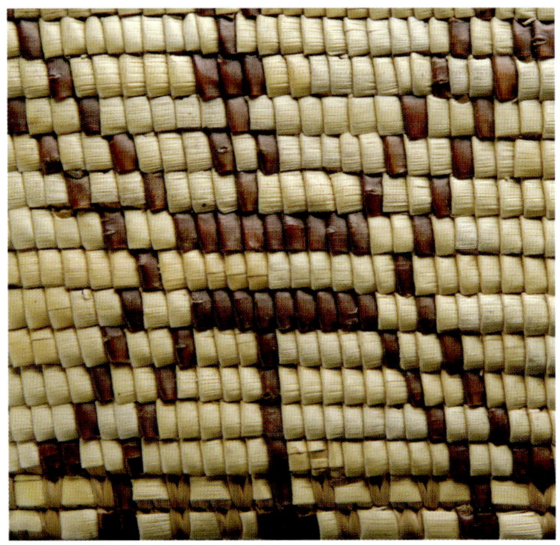

FIG. 68 (Left to right):

Bowl, c. 1890, Ntlakapamuk, Artist unknown, 11.0 x 19.5 x 19.5 cm., 14401

CONSTRUCTION: coiling, imbrication, slat bottom

FOUNDATION: bundle

Bowl, c. 1900, Cowlitz, Artist unknown, 8.5 x 18.5 cm., 31111

CONSTRUCTION: coiling, imbrication, beading

FOUNDATION: bundle

The basket on the left is imbricated with beading on the bottom two rows (visible in the close-up at right). The basket on the right is imbricated with a decorative beading rim element.

FIG. 69

Bowl (detail), c. 1890, Ntlakapamuk, Artist unknown, 11.0 x 19.5 cm., 14401

CONSTRUCTION: coiling, imbrication, slat bottom

FOUNDATION: bundle

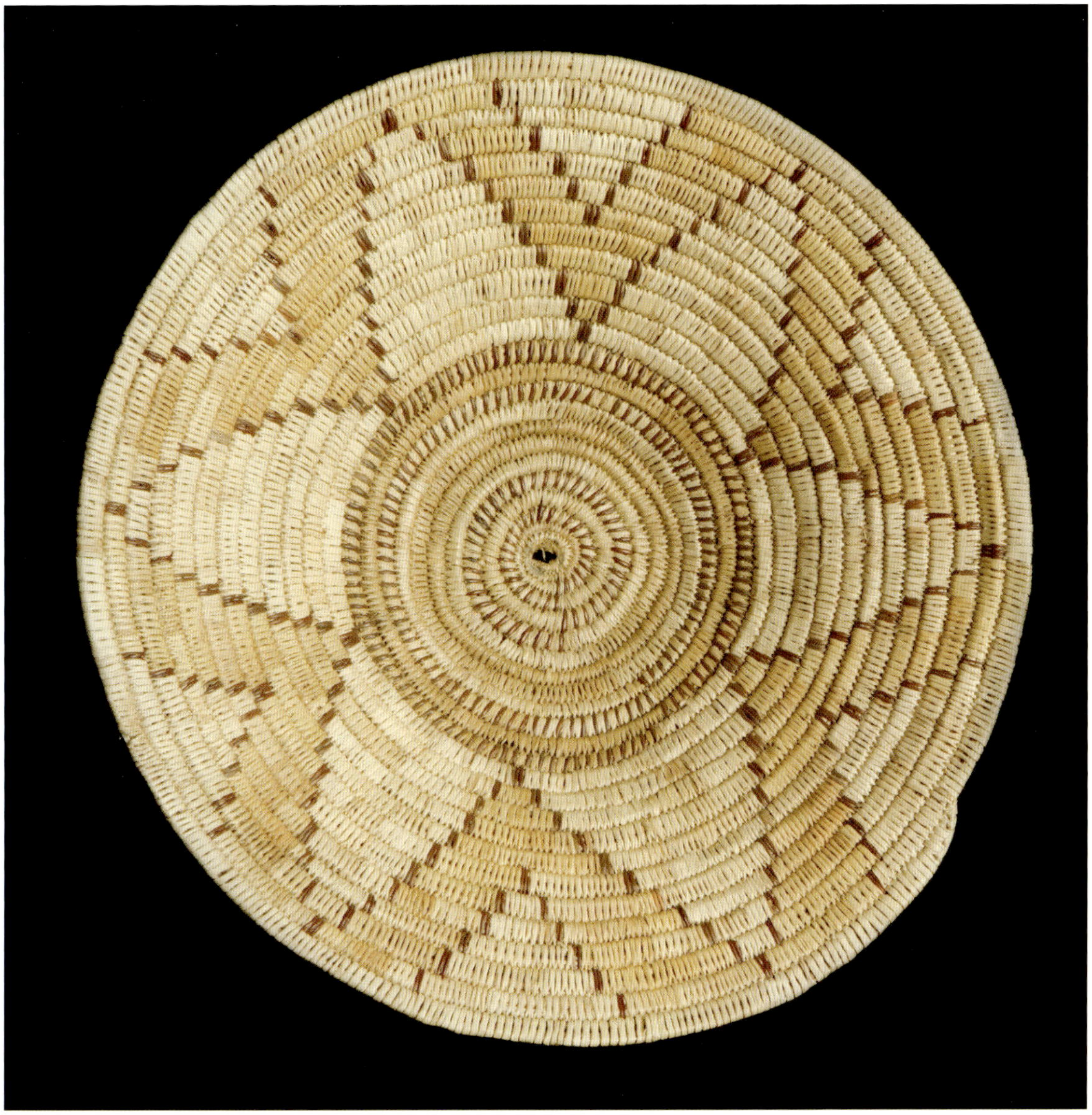

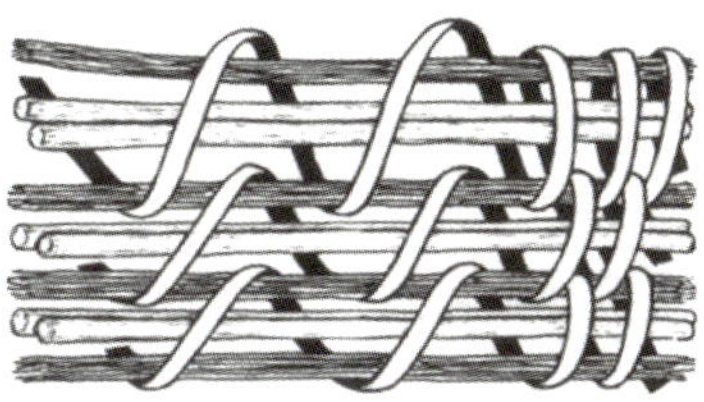

Rod and bundle foundation

FIG. 70

Tray, c. 1930, Mescalero Apache, Artist unknown, 9.0 x 35.5 cm., 11

CONSTRUCTION: coiling

FOUNDATION: two rods and bundle

COILING FOUNDATIONS

In coiled baskets, foundations used include varying numbers of rods; rod and fiber bundle combinations; or the use of fiber bundles alone. Each of these techniques creates baskets that are relatively rigid to flexible. Also, each foundation type produces a unique visual quality: from steeply ridged (three rods) to flat (bundle).

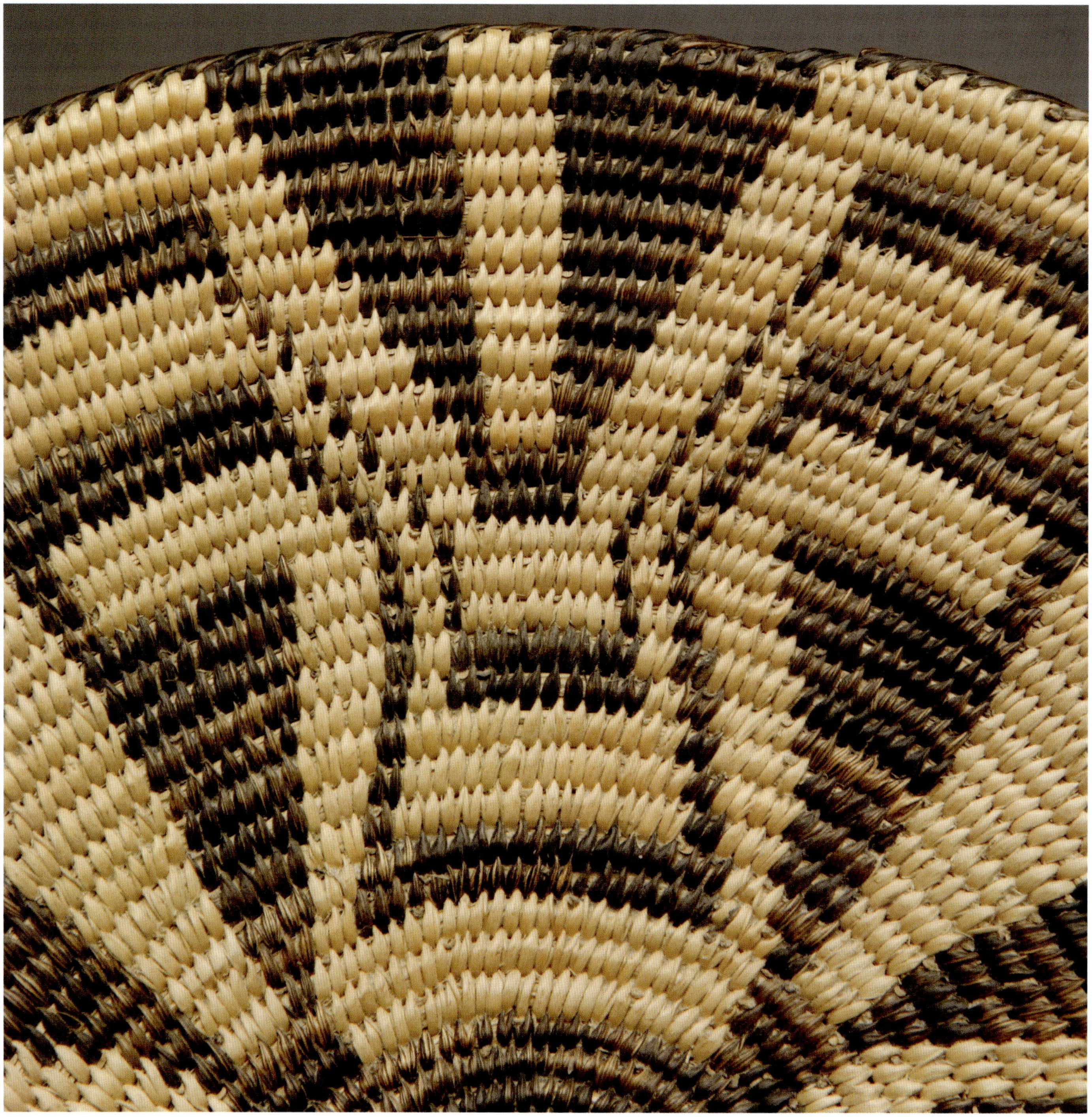

FIG. 71:

Bowl, c. 1919, Akimel O'odham, Artist Unknown
6.5 x 31 cm., 36720
CONSTRUCTION: coiling
FOUNDATION: cattail-splint bundle

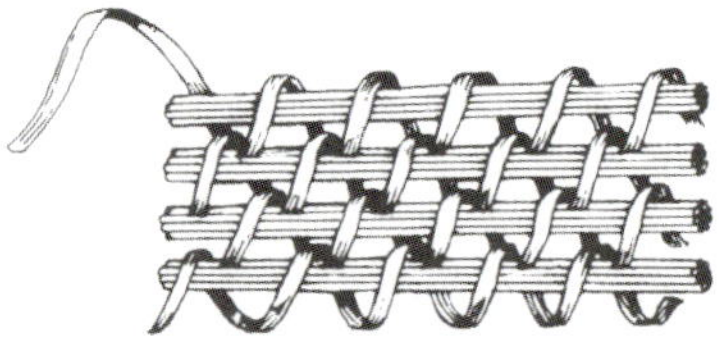

Bundle foundation

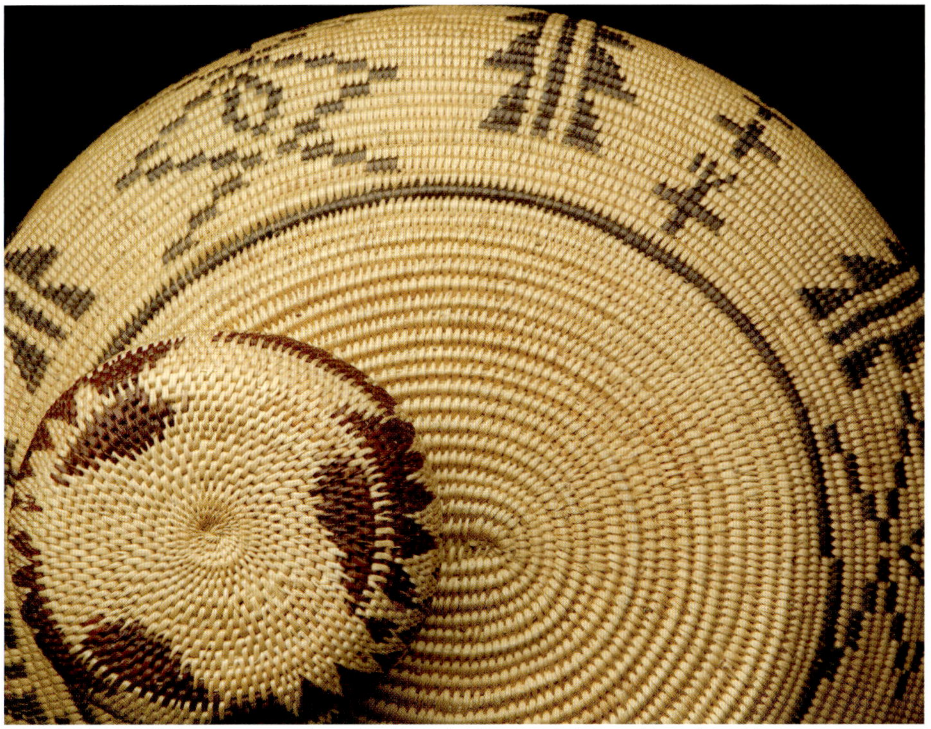

FIG. 72 (Front to back):

Gift Basket, c. 1920, Pomo, Artist unknown, 4.2 x 8.50 cm., 924

CONSTRUCTION: coiling

FOUNDATION: single rod

Bowl, c. 1905, Mono Lake Paiute, Artist unknown, 11.0 x 26.5 cm., 14407

CONSTRUCTION: coiling

FOUNDATION: three rods

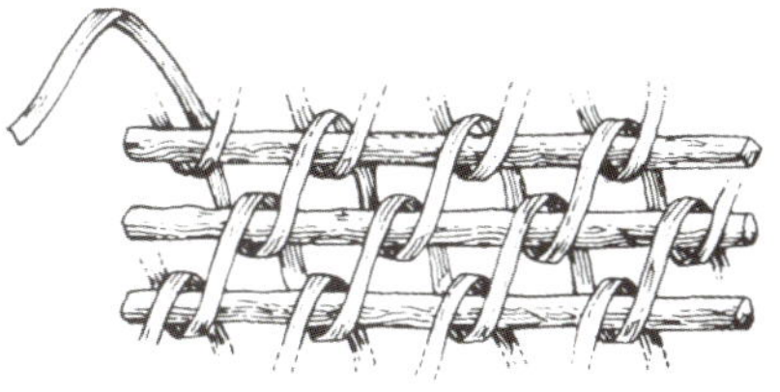

Single rod

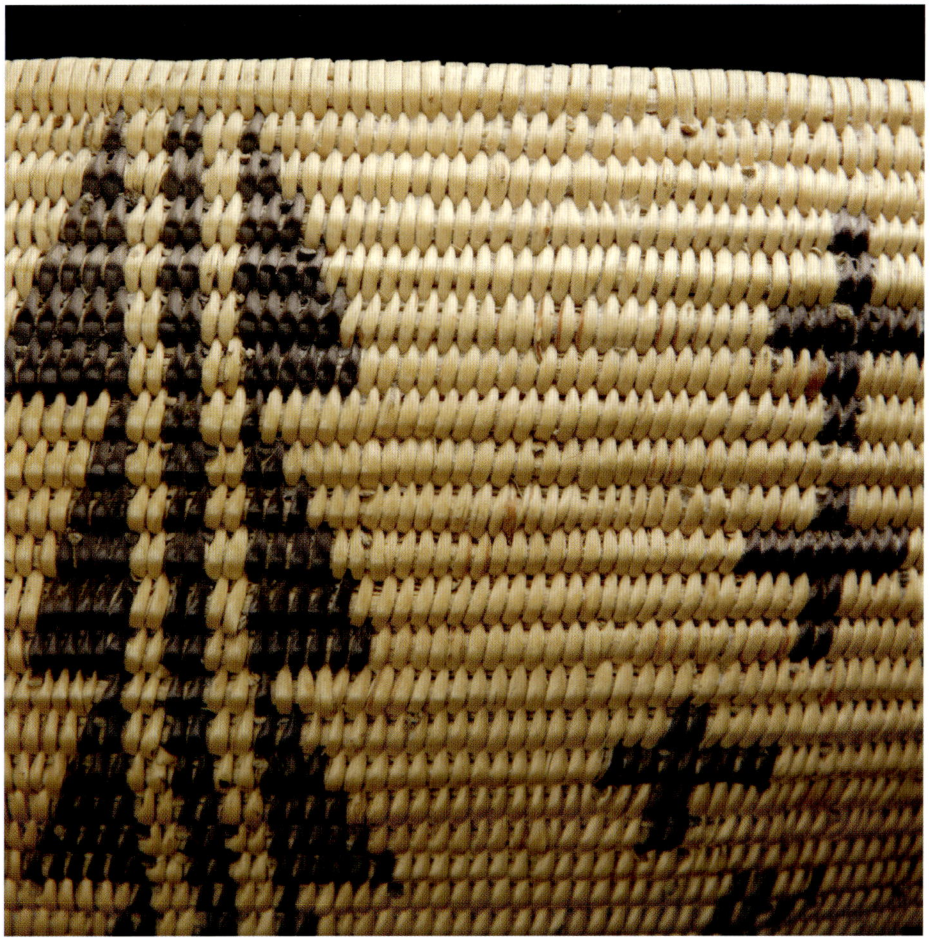

FIG. 73

Bowl, c. 1905, Mono Lake Paiute, Artist unknown, 11.0 x 26.5 cm., 14407

CONSTRUCTION: coiling

FOUNDATION: three rods

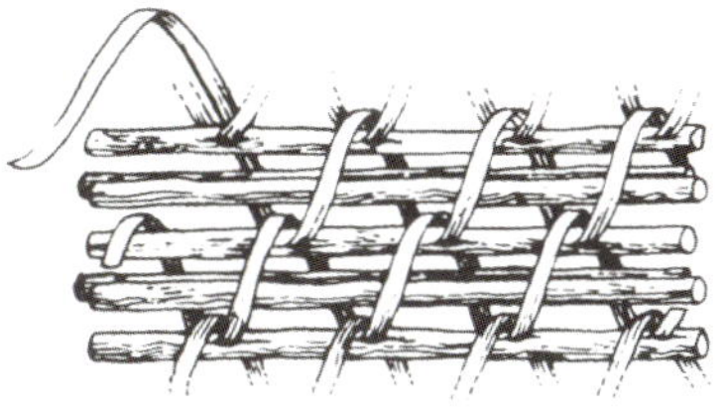

Three-rod foundation

Twining

Twining is a weaving technique in which two to four weaving elements (wefts) cross over or twist around each other between stationary foundation (warp) elements—the wefts are active and the warps are passive. There are numerous variations of twining: A different number of weaving elements may be used; a different number of warps may be crossed by the weaving elements; and the angle of the warps may vary. Each of these variations on twining alters the surface appearance and utility of the basket. For example, some twining methods have a functional application and are used for creating utilitarian baskets, while other twining methods are more decorative and are used for special-occasion baskets and baskets made for sale.

The underlying warp structure of a twined basket serves as the basket's skeletal framework. The weaver forms the basket's shape with the warps—ranging from straight and rigid rods to flexible cordage—by either splicing additional foundation elements in to increase the size or by phasing out warps to decrease the size.

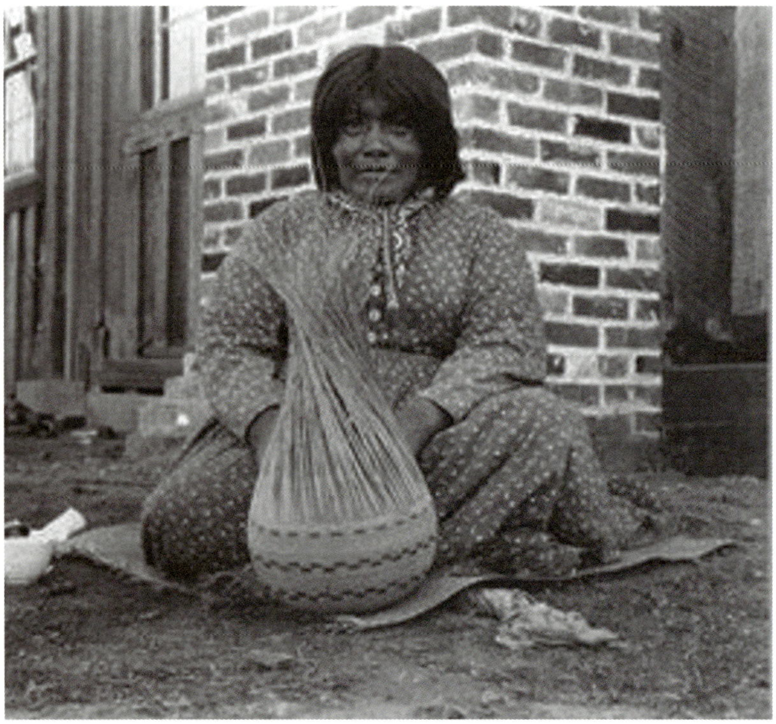

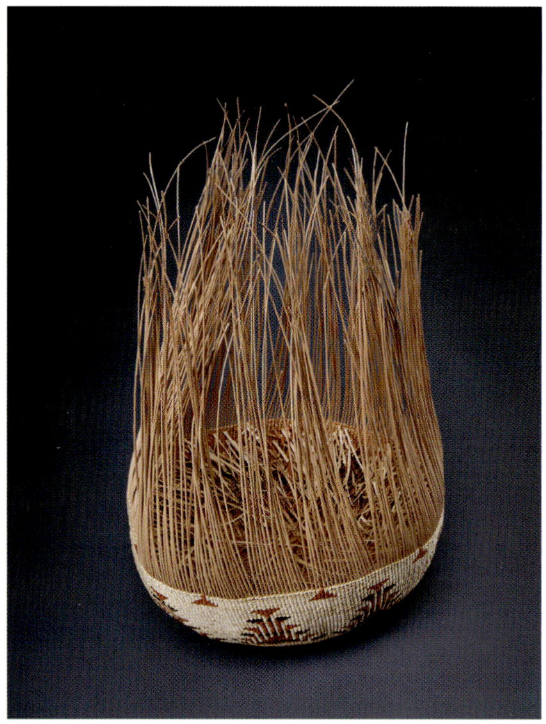

FIG. 73

Pomo basket weaver Eliza Coon, at Yokaya Rancheria, near Ukiah, California, 1906. Photo by Henry W. Henshaw. Courtesy of the Brooklyn Museum Archives. Culin Archival Collection. S01 02 01 005.

FIG. 74

Unfinished Bowl, 1913, Karuk, Artist unknown, 32.0 x 7.0 cm., 14294

CONSTRUCTION: plain twining, overlay

FOUNDATION: rods

CLOSED AND OPEN TWINING

Twining techniques are built on the spacing of weft rows: Closed twining leaves no space between the weft rows, completely concealing the warp; and open twining leaves spaces between the weft rows, exposing the warps. The two methods may be combined in one basket, in which closed and open twining is alternated, with multiple rows of wefts concealing the warps and multiple rows exposing the warps.

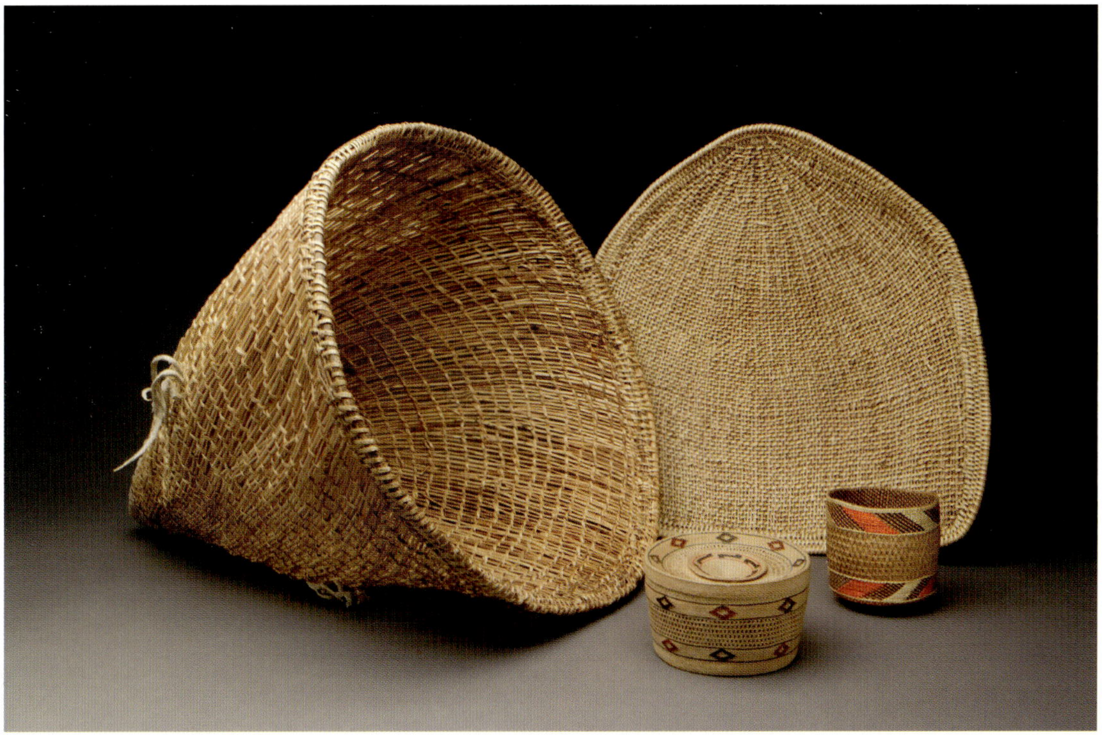

FIG. 75 (Clockwise from left):

Carrying Basket, 1932, Cedar Paiute, Minnie Tom, 62.0 x 52.0 cm., 9971
CONSTRUCTION: open diagonal twining
FOUNDATION: rods

Winnowing Tray, 1932, Cedar Paiute, Minnie Tom, 7.0 x 48.0 x 50.0 cm., 9989
CONSTRUCTION: open diagonal twining, with coiled selvedge
FOUNDATION: rods

Cylinder, c. 1900, Tlingit, Artist unknown, 11.5 x 11.0 cm., 23629
CONSTRUCTION: plain and open cross-warp twining, false embroidery
FOUNDATION: root

Gift Basket, c. 1900, Tlingit, Artist unknown, 8.0 x 14.6 cm., 14317
CONSTRUCTION: plain and open cross-warp twining, false embroidery
FOUNDATION: root

These four baskets demonstrate how open twining can be both utilitarian and decorative. Cedar Paiute Minnie Tom wove the two open-twined baskets as replicas of traditional utility baskets. The two Tlingit baskets, woven for the commercial market, were made using the open-twining method because of its patterned characteristics.

PLAIN TWINING

In the plain twining method, which may be seen at the top and bottom of the basket in figure 76, each turn of the weaving elements (wefts) encompasses the same warp or warps (foundation elements) enclosed by the corresponding turn in the preceding row. The visible turns of the wefts are stacked vertically on the basket, producing a textured surface of vertical columns.

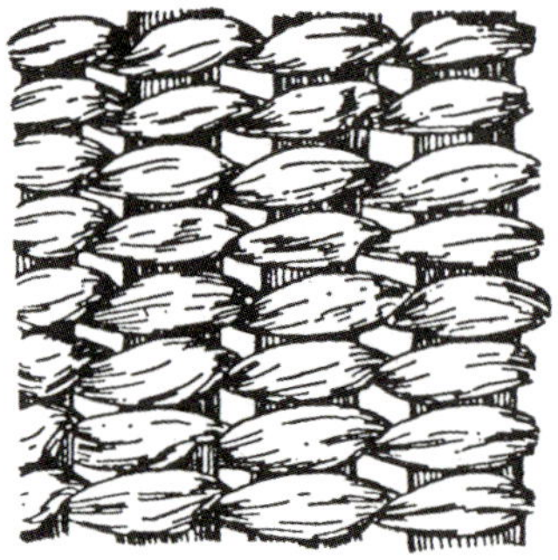

Plain twining

CROSS-WARP TWINING

The cross-warp twining method is a type of open twining in which two sets of warps cross each other producing an "X" pattern.

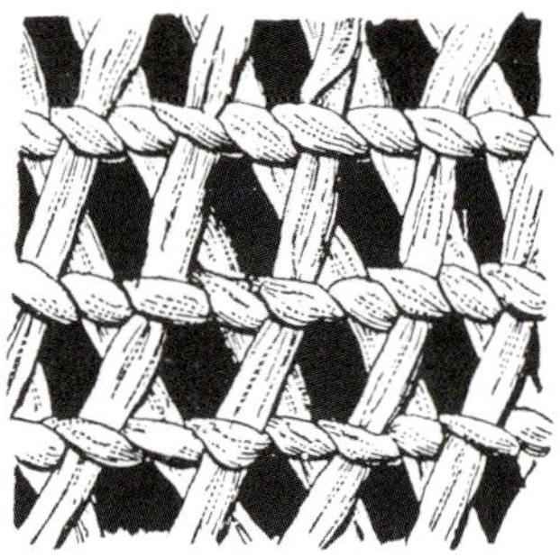

Cross-warp twining with open spacing

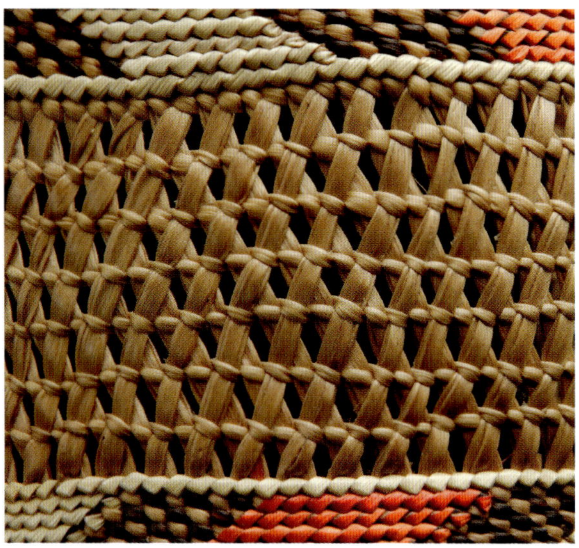

FIG. 76

Cylinder, c. 1900, Tlingit, Artist unknown, 11.5 x 11.0 cm., 23629

CONSTRUCTION: plain and cross-warp twining, false embroidery

FOUNDATION: root

DIAGONAL TWINING

In the diagonal twining method, the sewing elements (wefts) span two or more foundation elements (warps), with each turn shifting horizontally by one or more warps. The shift moves at an angle producing a surface of diagonal rows.

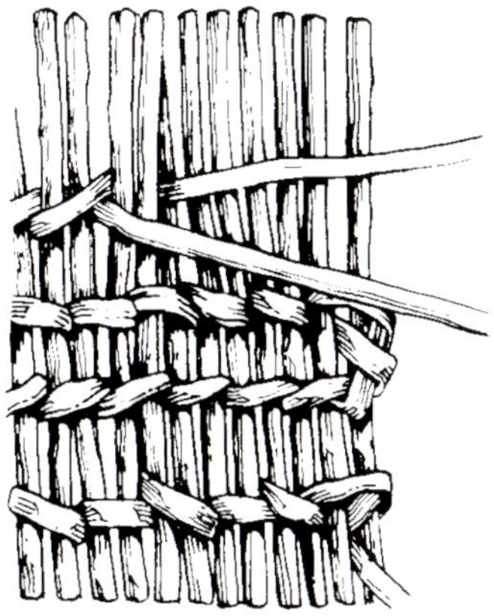

Diagonal twining

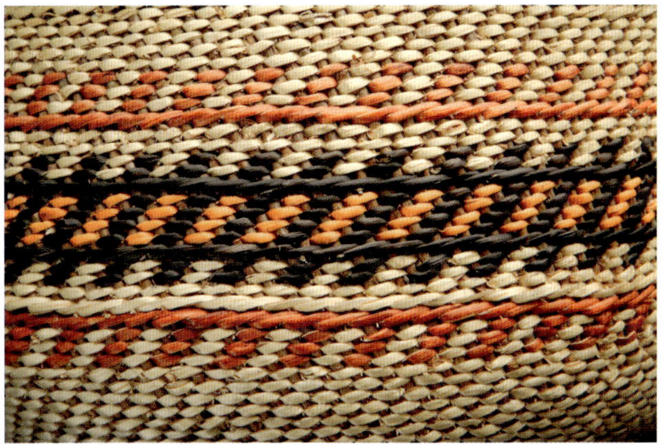

FIG. 77

Bowl, c. 1930, Hualapai, Artist unknown, 13.3 x 23.6 cm., 23722

CONSTRUCTION: diagonal twining

FOUNDATION: rods

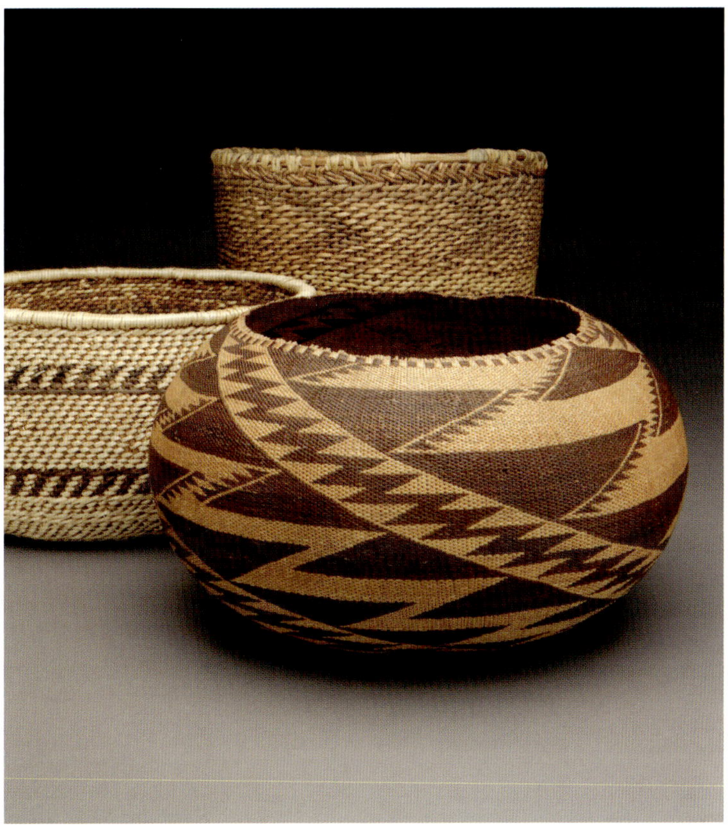

FIG. 78 (Clockwise from front):

Storage Bowl, c. 1906, Pomo, Artist known as "Captain Jack's Wife," 20.0 x 31.0 cm., 28

CONSTRUCTION: diagonal twining

FOUNDATION: rods

Bowl, c. 1930, Hualapai, Artist unknown, 17.7 x 29.5 cm., 10969

CONSTRUCTION: diagonal twining

FOUNDATION: rods

Carrying Basket, c. 1850, Pueblo, Artist unknown, 30.0 x 26.0 cm., 49424

CONSTRUCTION: diagonal twining

FOUNDATION: rods

Although they look quite different, all three of these baskets were constructed using the same diagonal twining as the primary construction technique. The varying surface characteristics are the result of the quality and processing of the materials, as well as the tightness of the weave.

THREE-STRAND TWINING

In three-strand twining, three weft elements are manipulated so that in every turn of the elements around the foundation rods each individual strand passes behind one and in front of two rods. Three-strand twining produces a raised ridge and is used as a decorative element or to strengthen a basket at its stress points (such as the bottom or start). For an example of this method, see the diagram below: the top five rows illustrate three-strand twining, and the bottom five rows illustrate plain twining.

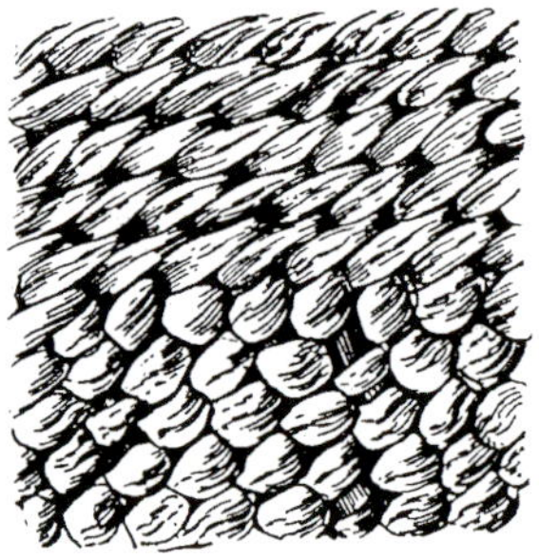

Three-strand twining

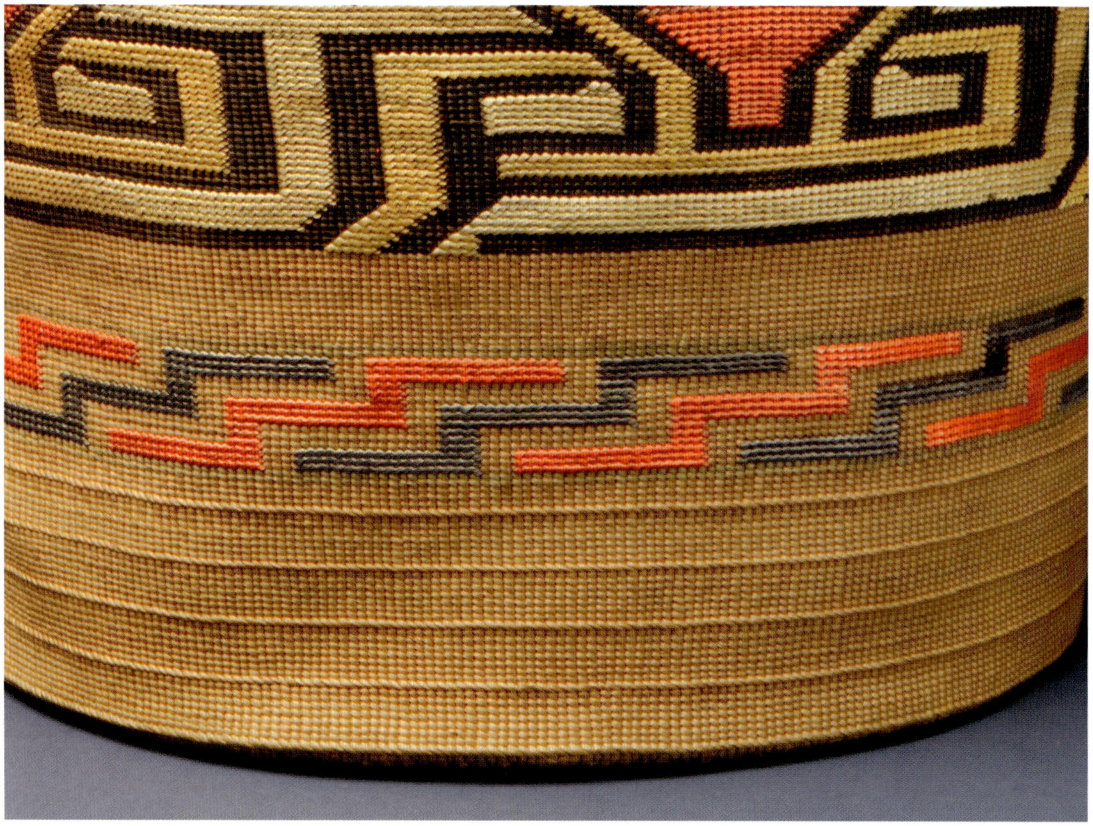

FIG. 79

Fancy Carrying Basket, c. 1900, Tlingit, Artist known as "Mary," 26.2 x 31.0 cm., 1901

CONSTRUCTION: plain and three-strand twining, false embroidery

FOUNDATION: root

LATTICE TWINING

Lattice twining adds strength to the stress points of utilitarian baskets by adding a rigid horizontal element, or supplementary weft, to the basket's exterior surface. This stationary horizontal element is attached to the foundation rods using a two-strand twining technique. (The horizontal, ridged rows on the surface of the Pomo basket in figure 80 are supplementary wefts.)

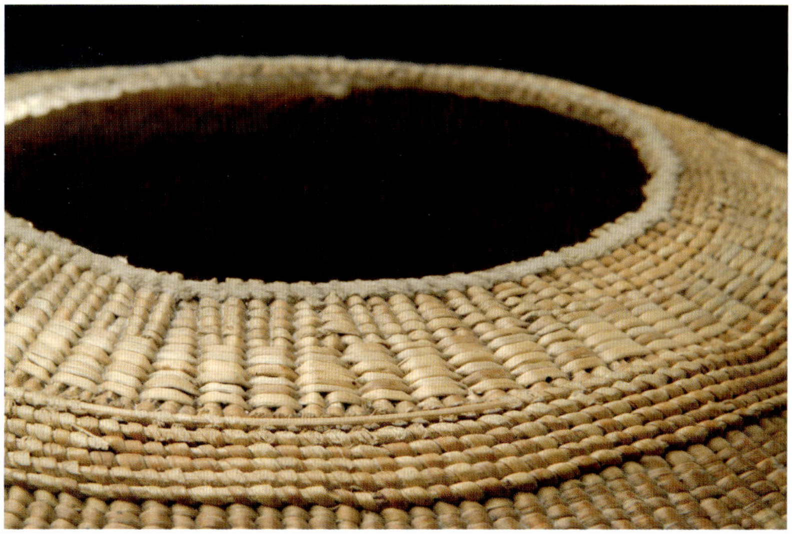

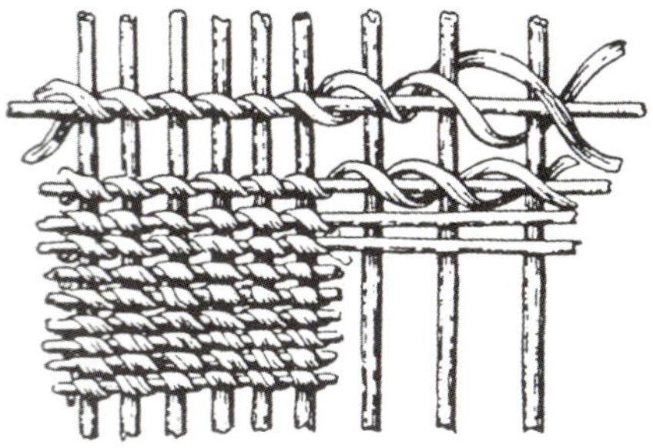

Lattice twining

FIG. 80

Mortar Hopper, c. 1920, Pomo, Artist unknown, 16.0 x 48.5 cm., 23500

CONSTRUCTION: plain, diagonal, and lattice twining

FOUNDATION: rods

WRAPPED TWINING

Wrapped twining incorporates three structural elements: a rigid foundation (warp); a rigid weaving element (weft); and a flexible weaving element (weft). The rigid weaving element remains on the inside surface, moving horizontally without twisting, and the flexible weaving element passes in front of each foundation rod, wrapping around the stationary, rigid weaving element.

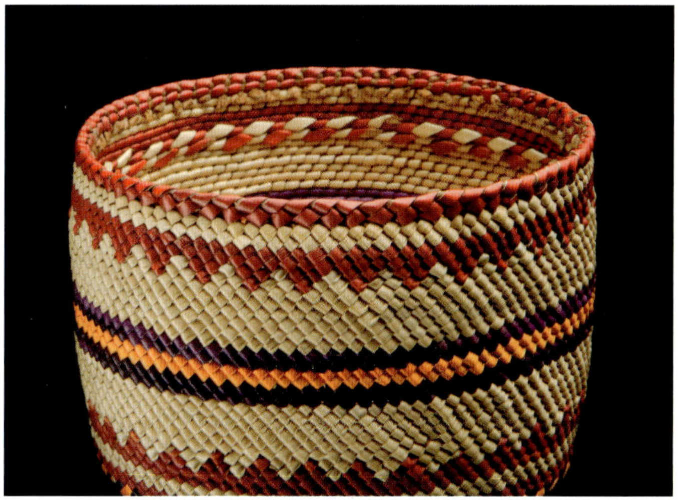

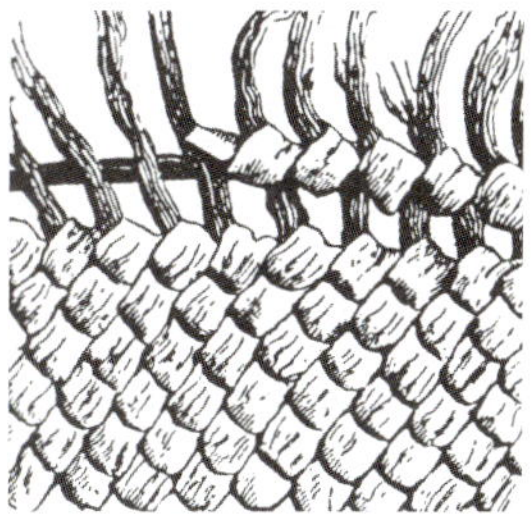

Wrapped twining

FIG. 81

Lidded Bowl, c. 1970, Makah, Artist unknown, 6.0 x 8.6 cm., 23696

CONSTRUCTION: wrapped twining

FOUNDATION: rods

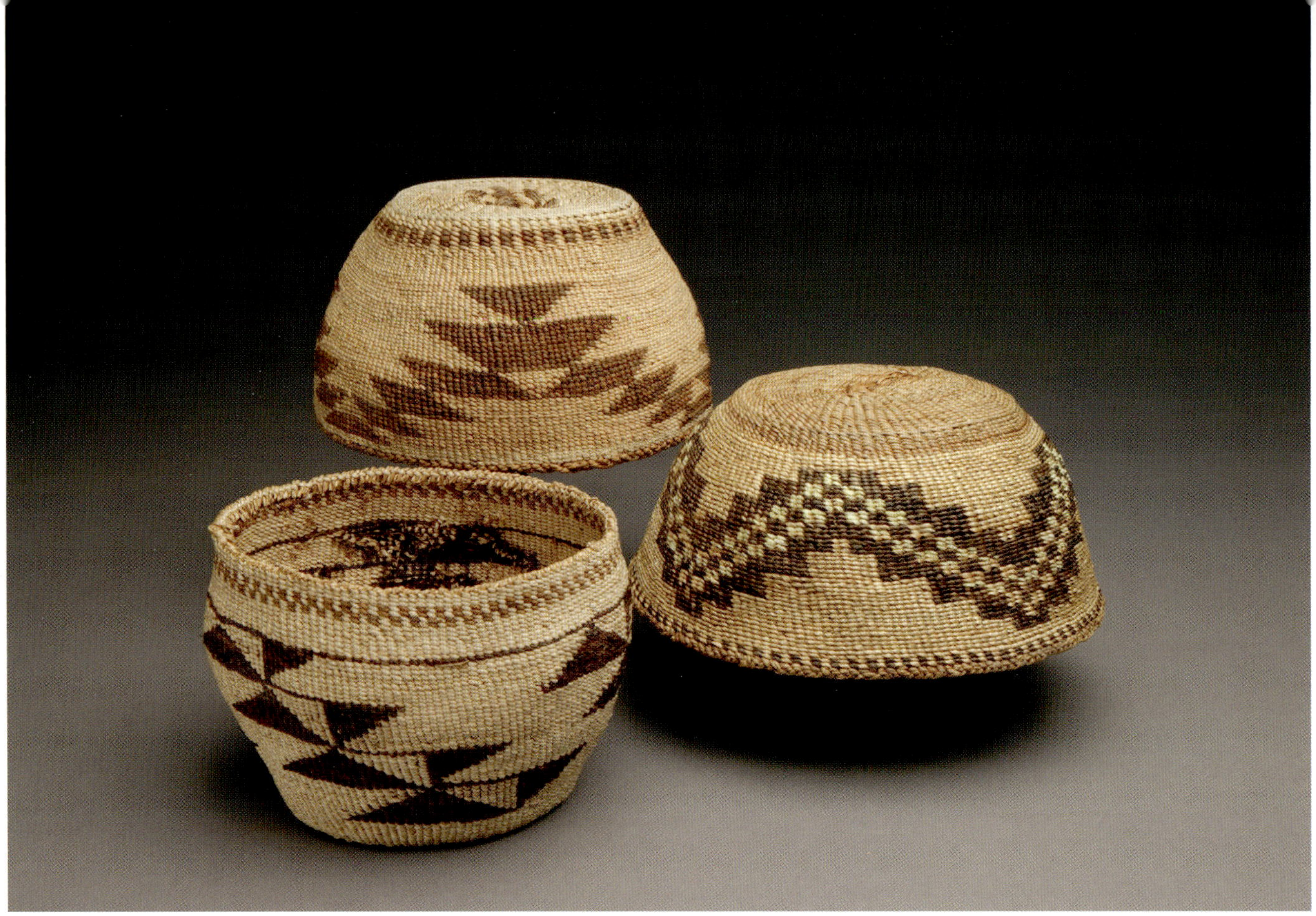

FIG. 82 (Clockwise from right):

Woman's Hat, c. 1900, Modoc, Artist unknown, 10.0 x 20.0 cm., 14260

CONSTRUCTION: plain and wrapped twining

FOUNDATION: twisted cordage

Bowl, c. 1920, Klamath or Modoc, Artist unknown, 10.2 x 15.5 cm., 1786

CONSTRUCTION: plain and wrapped twining

FOUNDATION: twisted cordage

Bowl, c. 1920, Modoc, Artist unknown, 10.0 x 18.0 cm., 35703

CONSTRUCTION: plain and wrapped twining

FOUNDATION: twisted cordage

The Plateau weavers of these three twined baskets used the weft float technique to add design motifs. Instead of splicing and cutting their weft base material to begin or end a design, they carried it behind the added design material, and vice versa.

TWO-DIMENSIONAL DESIGNS

Two-dimensional surface designs in plain- or diagonal-twined baskets may be created by using the overlay method. In this technique, weft elements of design material are paired with one or both of the weft base elements. When two strands of material, a base weft and its overlay, are paired as one element, the design material appears on the work surface on alternating stitches, with the alternate stitch a bare base element. When both wefts are paired with an overlay material, solid lines and motifs of color appear as each stitch brings one of the two overlays to the work surface. If the weaver does not twist the strands passing behind the warps, the overlay material of the back weft strand faces toward the front so that the overlay material does not show on the inside of the basket.

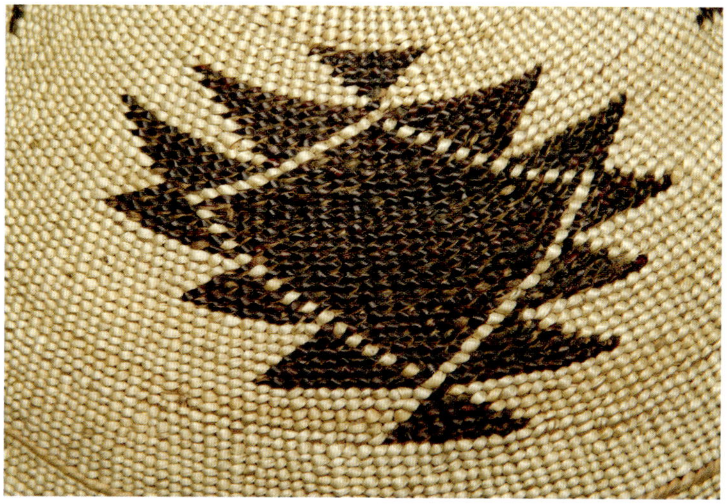

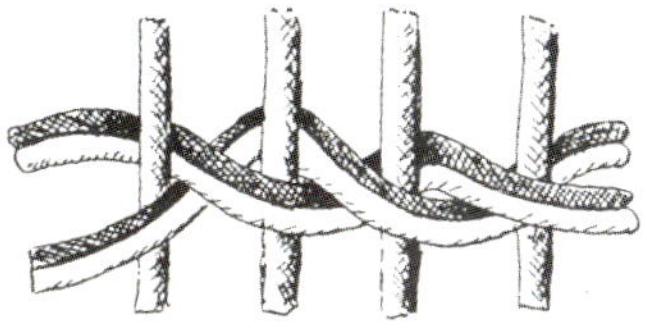

overlay

FIG. 83

Storage Basket Model, c. 1904, Yurok, Artist known as "Mrs. Johnny Jack," 38.0 x 32.0 cm., 14296

CONSTRUCTION: plain twining, overlay

FOUNDATION: rods

In the false embroidery method, a single design material is wrapped around the base weft element as it passes over the warp. False embroidery can only be seen on the work surface, or front, of the basket. A stitch covered by false embroidery appears to slant in the opposite direction of a stitch made in base weft material alone.

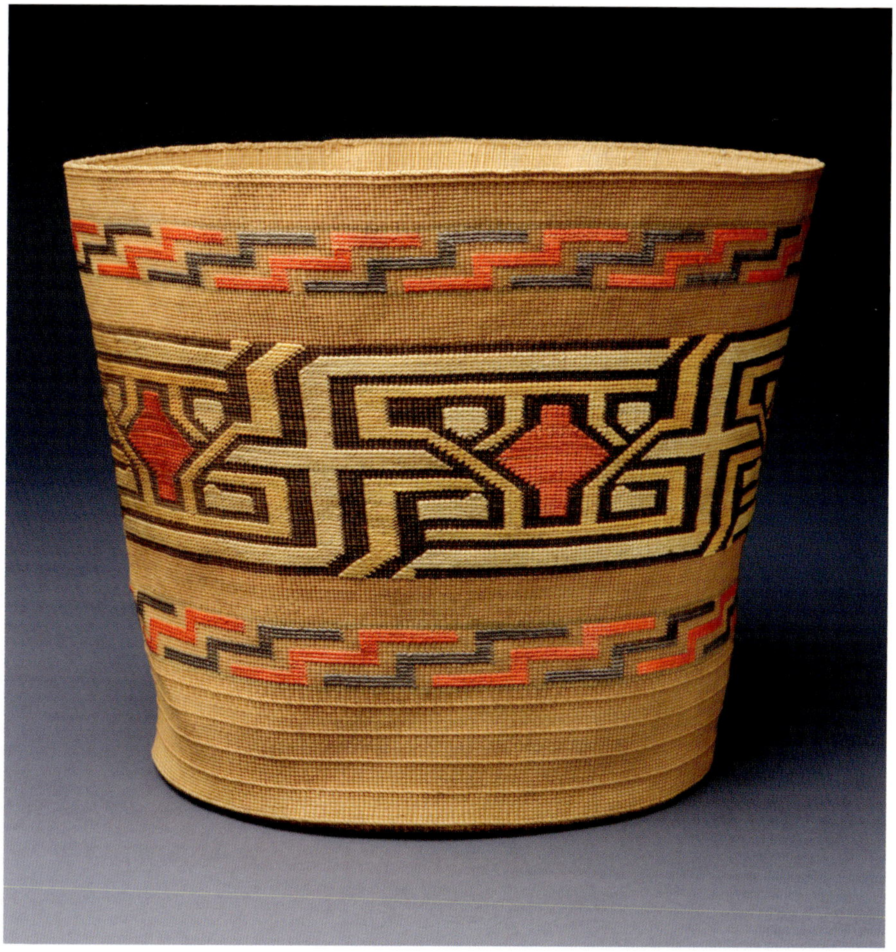

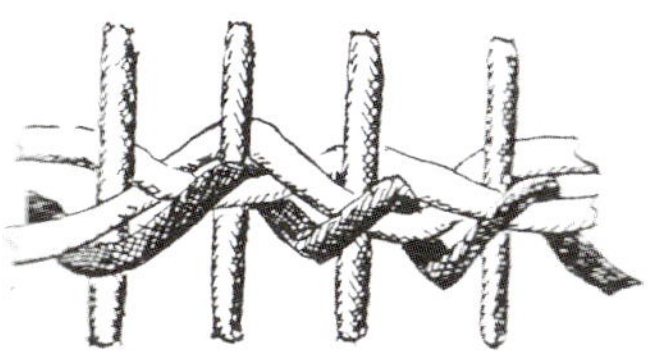

False embroidery

FIG. 84

Fancy Carrying Basket, c. 1900, Tlingit, Artist known as "Mary," 26.2 x 31.0 cm., 1901

CONSTRUCTION: plain and three-strand twining, with false embroidery

FOUNDATION: root

Wicker, or Wickerwork

Wickerwork is built on a stationary foundation of rods radiating spoke-like from a common center, or on a framework of parallel rods. In wickerwork, the basket maker weaves the weft material over and under the stiff foundation (warp) of rods, incorporating design elements by varying the technique or changing the materials.

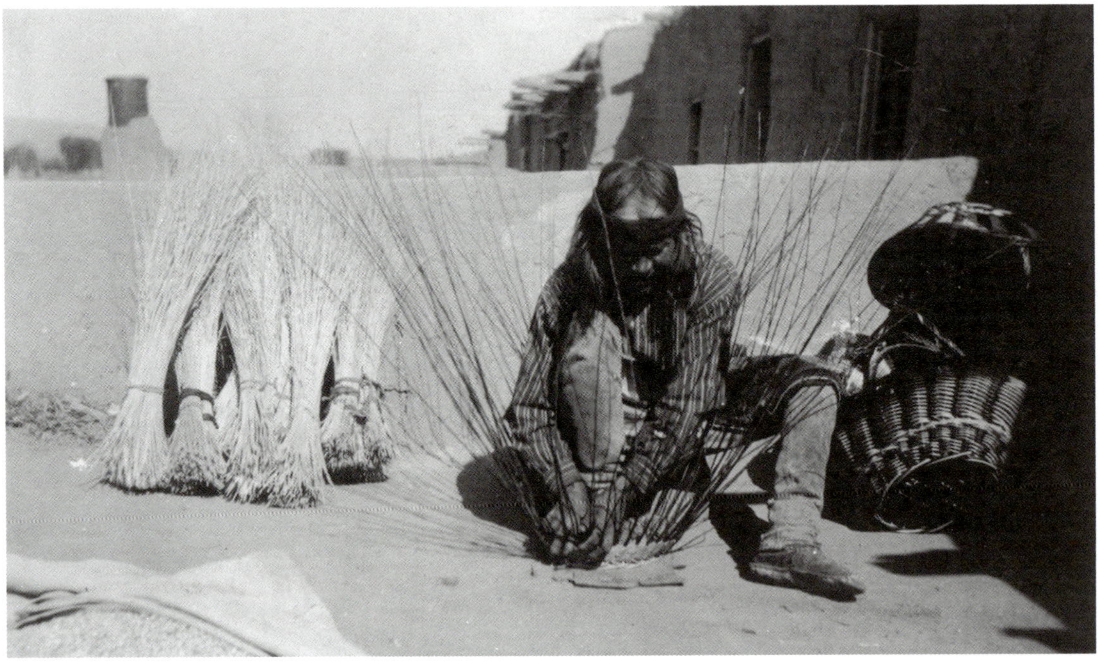

FIG. 85

Male weaver making a wicker basket, San Ildefonso Pueblo, c. 1900. Photo by Mary E. Dissette. Courtesy of the Palace of the Governors Photo Archives. 42328.

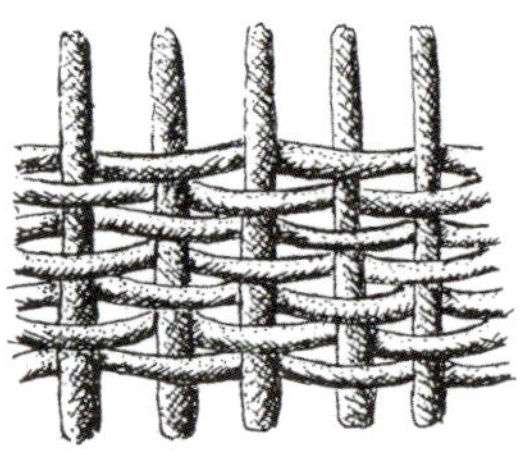

Wicker, or wickerwork

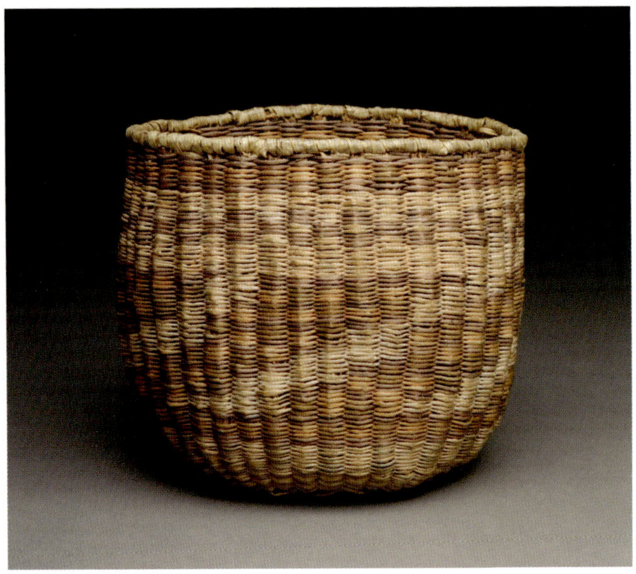

FIG. 86

Cylinder, c. 1900, Hopi (Third Mesa), Artist unknown, 20.5 x 22.5 cm., 48086

CONSTRUCTION: wicker, plaiting

FOUNDATION: rods

Plaiting

Unlike all other types of basket-weaving techniques, plaiting has no distinct stationary foundation (warp) or active weaving (weft) elements. Although there are two sets of elements, both are active and perform the same function. The elements used in plaiting are thin, flat, and flexible with a ribbon-like quality; generally, they are also all the same material and same size. The result is basketry with a flat, tight weave.

PLAIN (OR CHECKER) PLAITING

In the plain-plaiting technique, two sets of elements are crossed in a simple over-one/under-one pattern.

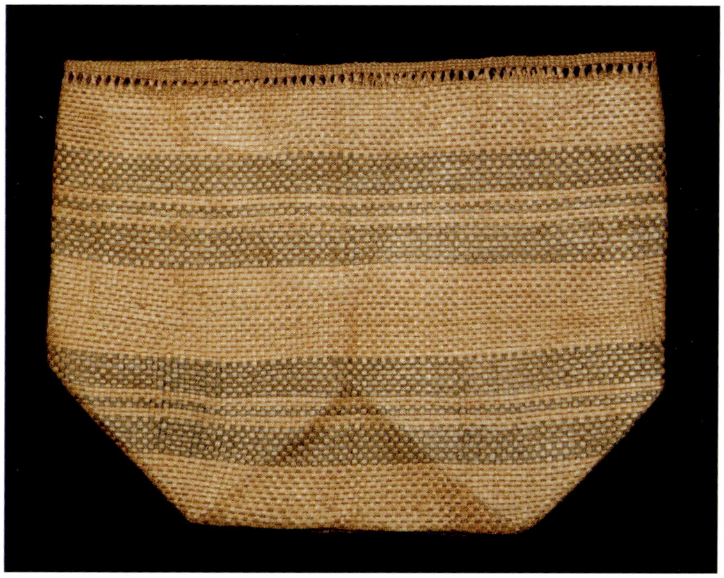

FIG.87

Carrying/Storage Bag, c. 1900, Tsimshian, Artist unknown, 33.0 x 43.0 cm., 14293

CONSTRUCTION: checker plaiting

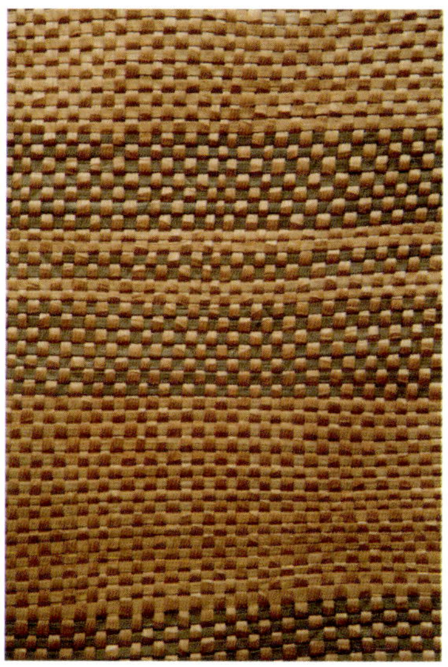

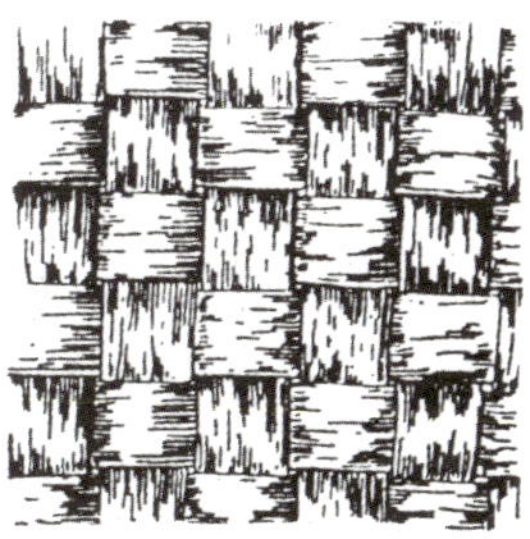

Checker plaiting

DIAGONAL (OR TWILL) PLAITING

In basketry made with the diagonal-plaiting method, two sets of weaving elements are crossed at varying intervals to form diagonal, chevron, herringbone, and diamond patterns. These designs are a variation of the over-one/under-one pattern of plain plaiting. Also known as twill, this type of plaiting is easily recognizable by the diagonal patterning on the basket surface.

Diagonal plaiting

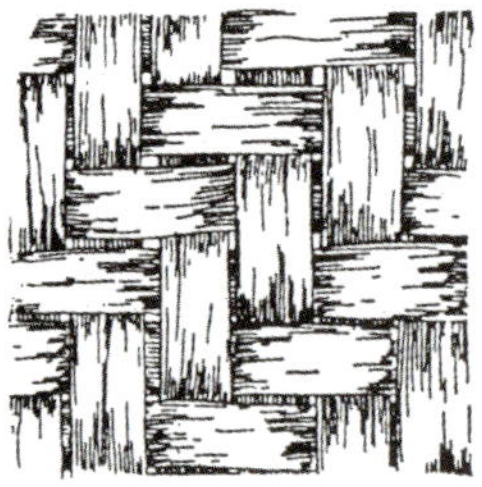

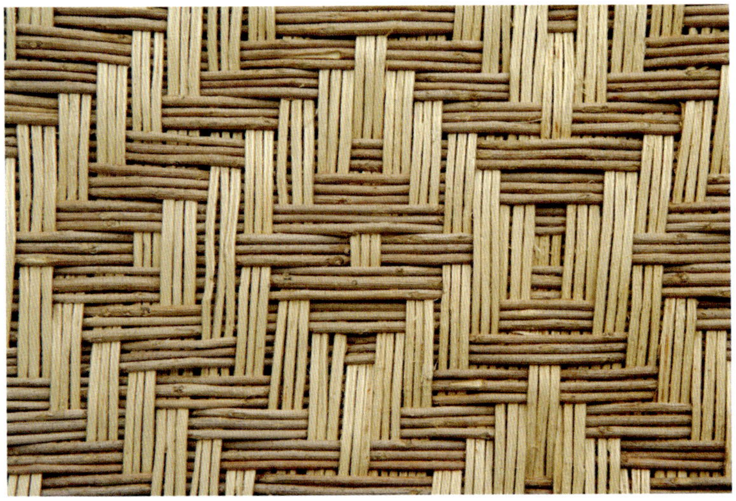

FIG. 88

Piki Tray, 1983, Hopi (Third Mesa), Fermina Banyacya, 48.3 x 33.0 cm., 50126

CONSTRUCTION: diagonal plaiting, wicker

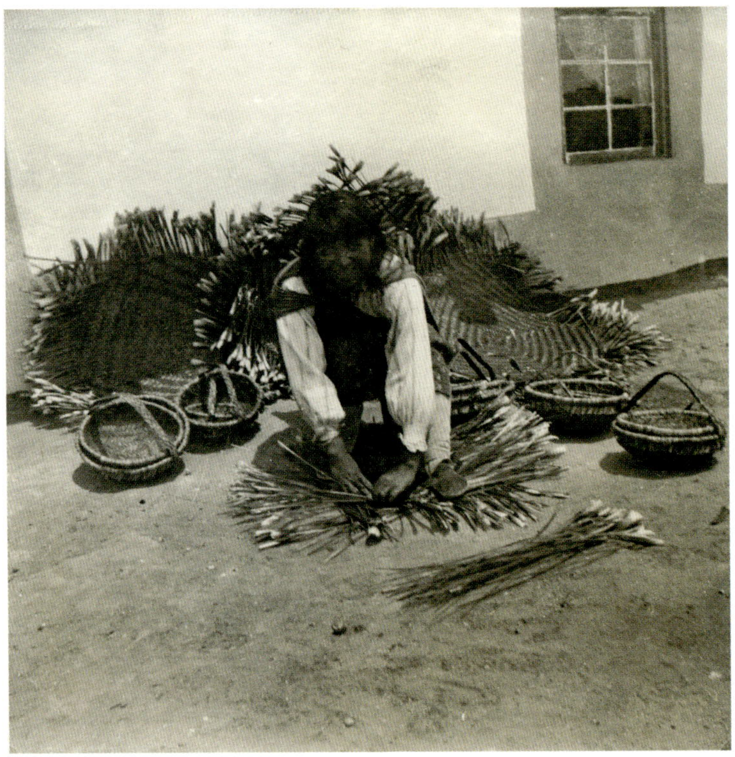

FIG. 89

Jemez Pueblo weaver plaiting basket, c. 1900. Photo by Mary E. Dissette. Courtesy of the Palace of the Governors Photo Archives. 677.

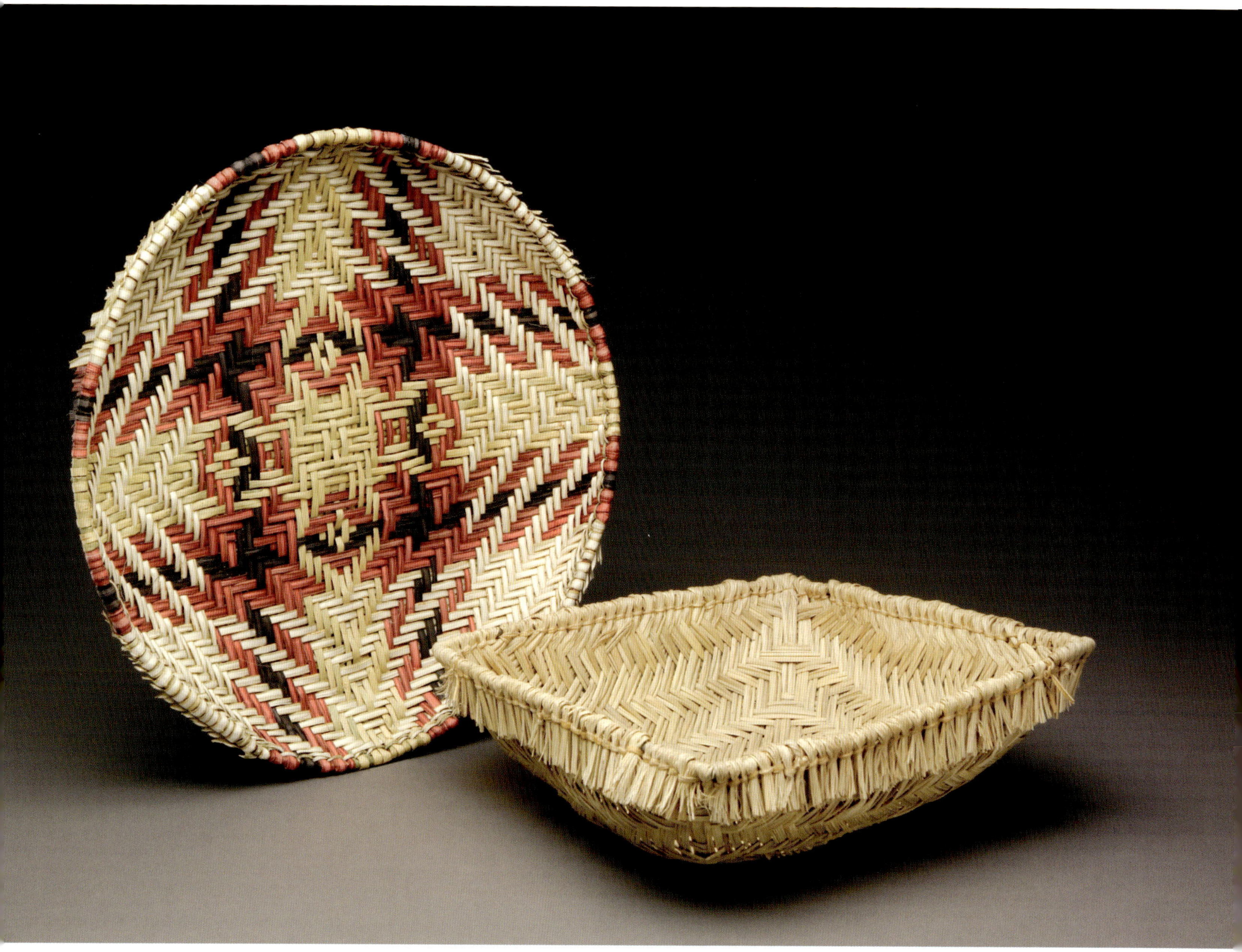

FIG. 90 (Left to right):

Sifter Tray, 1999, Hopi (First Mesa), Kevin Navasie, 75.0 x 42.1 cm., 55666

CONSTRUCTION: diagonal plaiting

Sifter Tray, 1961, Jemez Pueblo, Anita Toya, 12.0 x 31.5 x 32.0 cm., 25838

CONSTRUCTION: diagonal plaiting

TWO-DIMENSIONAL DESIGNS

The design features of plaited baskets are achieved by: using different colored elements; intentional alterations of cross-over intervals to form patterns; or variation in the width of the weaving elements. In addition, basket weavers may construct beautiful monochromatic structural designs, or emphasize designs, by varying the color of the weaving elements.

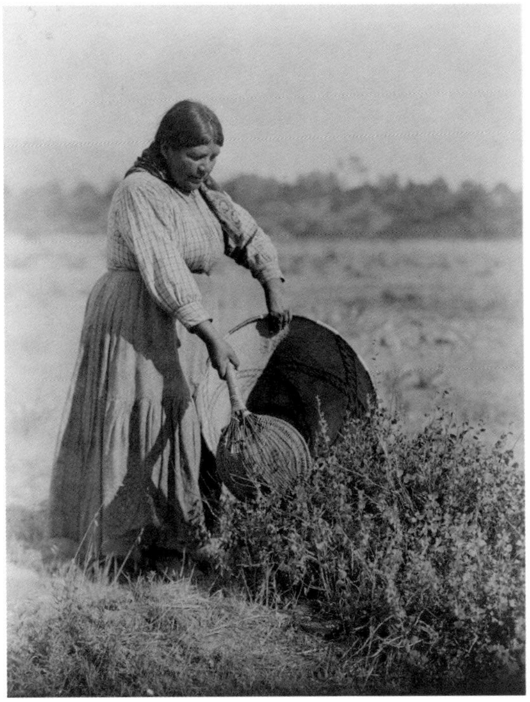

FIG. 91

Gathering Seeds, c. 1924. Photo by Edward S. Curtis. Courtesy of the Library of Congress Prints and Photographs Division. LC-USZ62-116525.

In this historical photo, Cecilia Joaquin, Pomo, uses a seed beater to knock seeds into a burden basket.

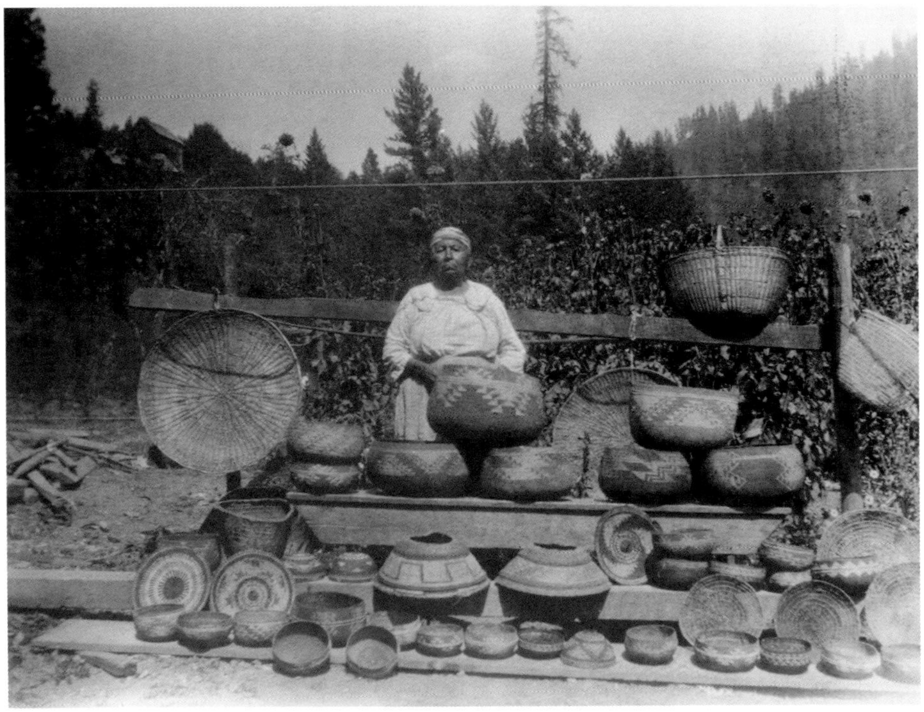

FIG. 92

Mary Jacobs, Karuk, and baskets, 1929. Photo by Lila M. O'Neale. Courtesy of the Phoebe A. Hearst Museum of Anthropology and the Regents of the University of California. 15-9018.

Basket weaver Mary Jacobs (who is wearing a basket cap) stands with the food-processing, cooking, and serving baskets she used at the Karuk New Year's "making." If a Karuk woman was a skilled weaver and had a full complement of fine baskets in good repair, such as Jacobs, she earned the respect and admiration of her community and family.

Chapter 3

FORM AND FUNCTION

One of the hallmarks of western North American basketry is the incredible variety of forms. Basket weavers from various tribal traditions have designed and constructed baskets for the same functions but in shapes and sizes that are often quite different. This is largely because the weavers are influenced by the context in which they make their baskets. The contextual forces that have shaped baskets include function, historical precedence, community and family values, and aesthetics. Working from shared standards as their foundation, community members evaluate the suitability and aesthetics of a basket's form based on both its utility and adherence to tradition. Because baskets are both utilitarian and social constructions, they are expressive of the culturally rich lives of the weavers who create them.

For millennia, baskets have been utilized for an extraordinary range of purposes, sometimes in surprising ways. They have been used for harvesting, carrying, and storing food; as kitchen utensils for food processing and preparation; and for the cooking and serving of meals. In addition, because baskets were objects of value and power they have been appropriate containers for objects of religious significance, medicines, and important personal possessions. Even articles of clothing have been constructed using basketry materials and techniques. Every Indigenous woman who was responsible for weaving her family's baskets may have had a basket weaving repertoire of up to twenty essential types.

In studying the following examples, it becomes clear that in the design and construction of baskets, form does not follow function alone and that each form can be multi-functional. Indigenous basketry forms are also shaped by the availability of materials, a repertoire of culturally appropriate construction techniques, and socially determined factors.

UTILITARIAN FORMS

One of the most important utilitarian forms for the Indigenous peoples of western North America was the carrying basket, also known as the "burden basket." It was central to the way of life of people who were the primary burden bearers before horses and other animals took on this role. When nomadic peoples moved from camp to camp throughout the year, to access seasonal food sources, women loaded these burden baskets with food, clothing, tools, and other smaller utility baskets. And when women went out to gather foodstuffs they collected them in these carrying baskets.

Weavers invented and constructed cone-shaped carrying baskets for gathering and transporting loads of various materials, sizes, and weights. Designed to fit the contours of the female body, the basket's distinctive shape distributes the weight along a woman's spine, so that it becomes the primary load carrying structure. In addition, the cone shape gives the basket a high center of gravity, so the bearer does not have to lean far forward to bring the basket and body into balance. The basket was designed to be carried using a tumpline that typically stretched across the top of a woman's head or sometimes around her shoulders. When carried this way, the basket's load is stabilized and does not roll from side to side.

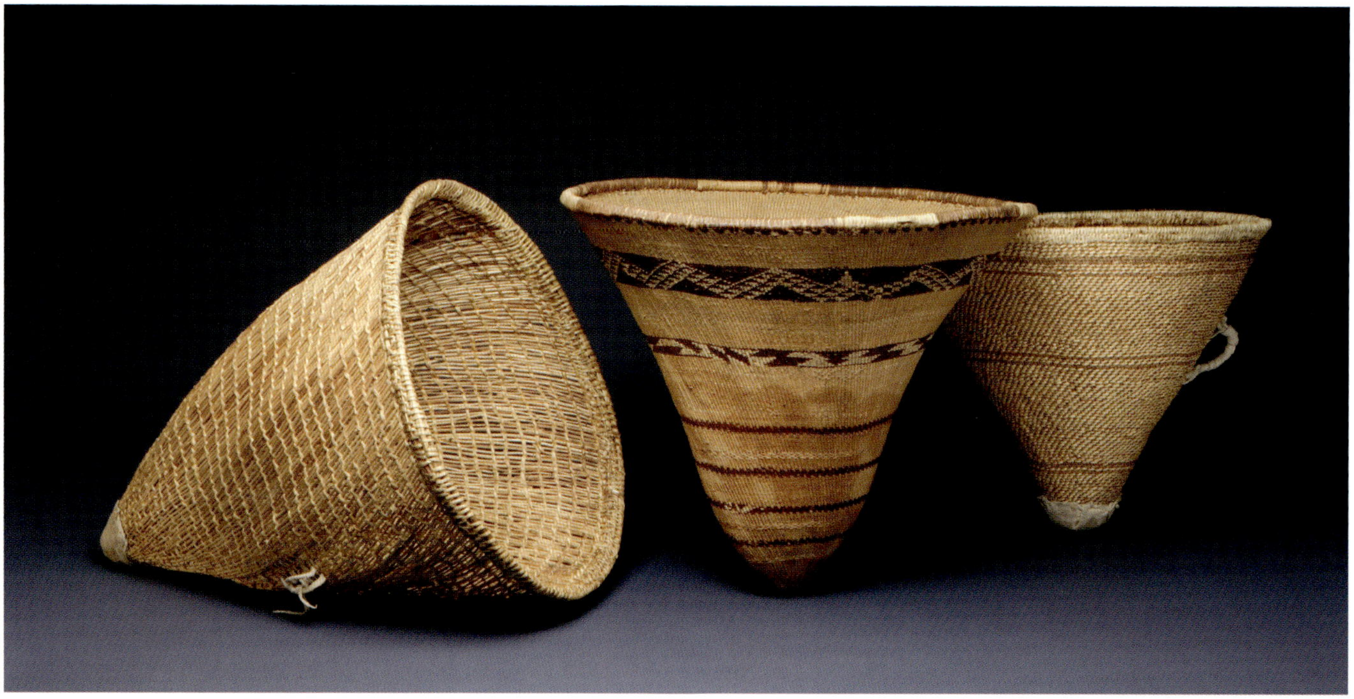

FIG. 93 (Left to right):

Carrying Basket, c. 1900, Hualapai, Artist unknown, 42.9 x 48.0 cm., 10977

Carrying Basket, c. 1895, Pomo, Artist unknown, 48.0 x 58.5 cm., 23265

Carrying Basket, 1932, Cedar Paiute, Minnie Tom, 62.0 x 52.0 cm., 9971

As a group, these three baskets attest to the utility of the cone-shaped carrying basket. Because this type of basket was so functional, its form was shared among weavers from different tribes and culture areas. All three weavers used different construction materials, but they all incorporated the diagonal twining technique to give their baskets additional strength. The two finely-woven closed-twined baskets (on the right) were suitable for collecting and carrying small plant materials such as grass seeds; the more loosely-woven open-weave carrying basket (on the left), which took less time and materials to make, was suitable for carrying larger objects.

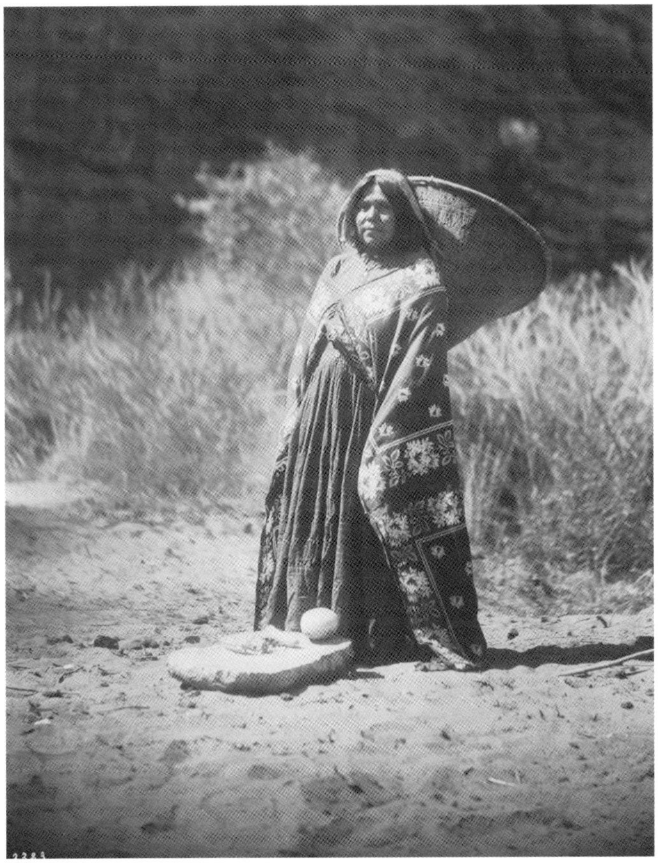

FIG. 94

Ta-ya-ba, Havasupai, demonstrates the use of a carrying basket, c. 1900. Photo by Charles C. Pierce. Courtesy of the California Historical Society Title Insurance and Trust/C. C. Pierce Photography Collection. CHS-3383.

The Pueblo-made burden basket shown in the center of figure 95 may be a prototype for the two Apache baskets on either side of it. However, it is more likely that mutually beneficial exchanges resulted in a basket form that was agreeable to both tribal traditions. The people of the historic-period Southwest pueblos were semi-sedentary farmers whose way of life stretched back for millennia; Athapaskans (including the Apache) were nomads who migrated to the area by circa AD 1300 (John Torres-Nez, pers. comm., November 5, 2012). The Apache, as newcomers to the region, may have been influenced by the cultural traditions of the Pueblo people. The similarities in the weaving techniques of the burden baskets illustrated, then, is likely because the Apache acquired this particular form from Pueblo weavers, adding it to an already rich repertoire.

When ethnologist Grenville Goodwin was conducting fieldwork among the Western Apache, between 1929 and 1939, his informants described two different kinds of burden baskets:

> [One] has crossed sticks on the bottom, and . . . [the other] has no crossed sticks on the bottom and . . . is not ornamented with buckskin as is the first. The first kind we used to pack our belongings in, on our backs, when we moved camp. . . . The second kind we used more for gathering foods in. We used to gather mescal heads in this kind. The juice of roasted mescal we used to smear on the inside of the basket, so that when we gathered small seeds they wouldn't leak out (Ferg 1987:73).

The use of buckskin ornamentation and the lack of crossed sticks in the Apache burden basket shown in figure 95 (see far left side) may be explained as the result of commercialization:

because the basket was not intended for heavy use, the stick reinforcements were unnecessary, and buckskin fringes were added to attract non-Apache buyers. The more conical shape of the basket, as well as the tin tinklers, are also typical features of burden baskets made for sale (Ferg 1987:73).

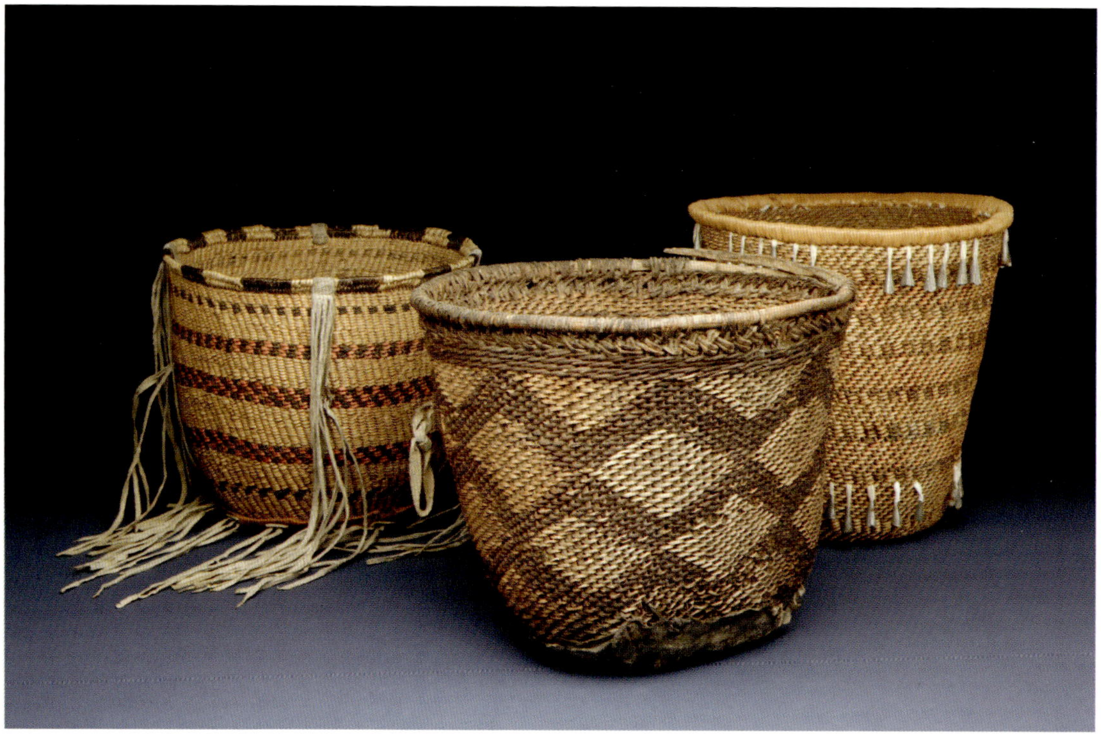

FIG. 95 (Left to right):

Carrying Basket, c. 1920, White Mountain Apache, Artist unknown, 25.0 x 29.0 cm., 12603

Carrying Basket, c. 1850, Pueblo, Artist unknown, 27.0 x 33.0 cm., 45767

Carrying Basket, c. 1910, Mescalero Apache, Artist unknown, 30.5 x 27.9 cm., 56989

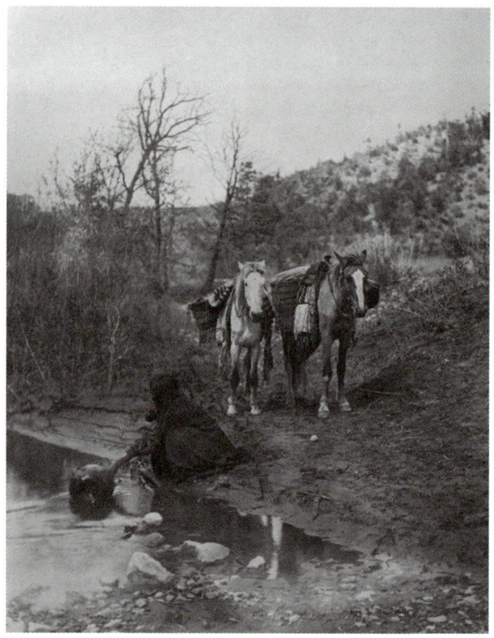

FIG. 96

Western Apache women with pitched water bottle and horses loaded with twined carrying baskets, c. 1910. Photo by Edward S. Curtis. Courtesy of the Palace of the Governors Photo Archives. 76955.

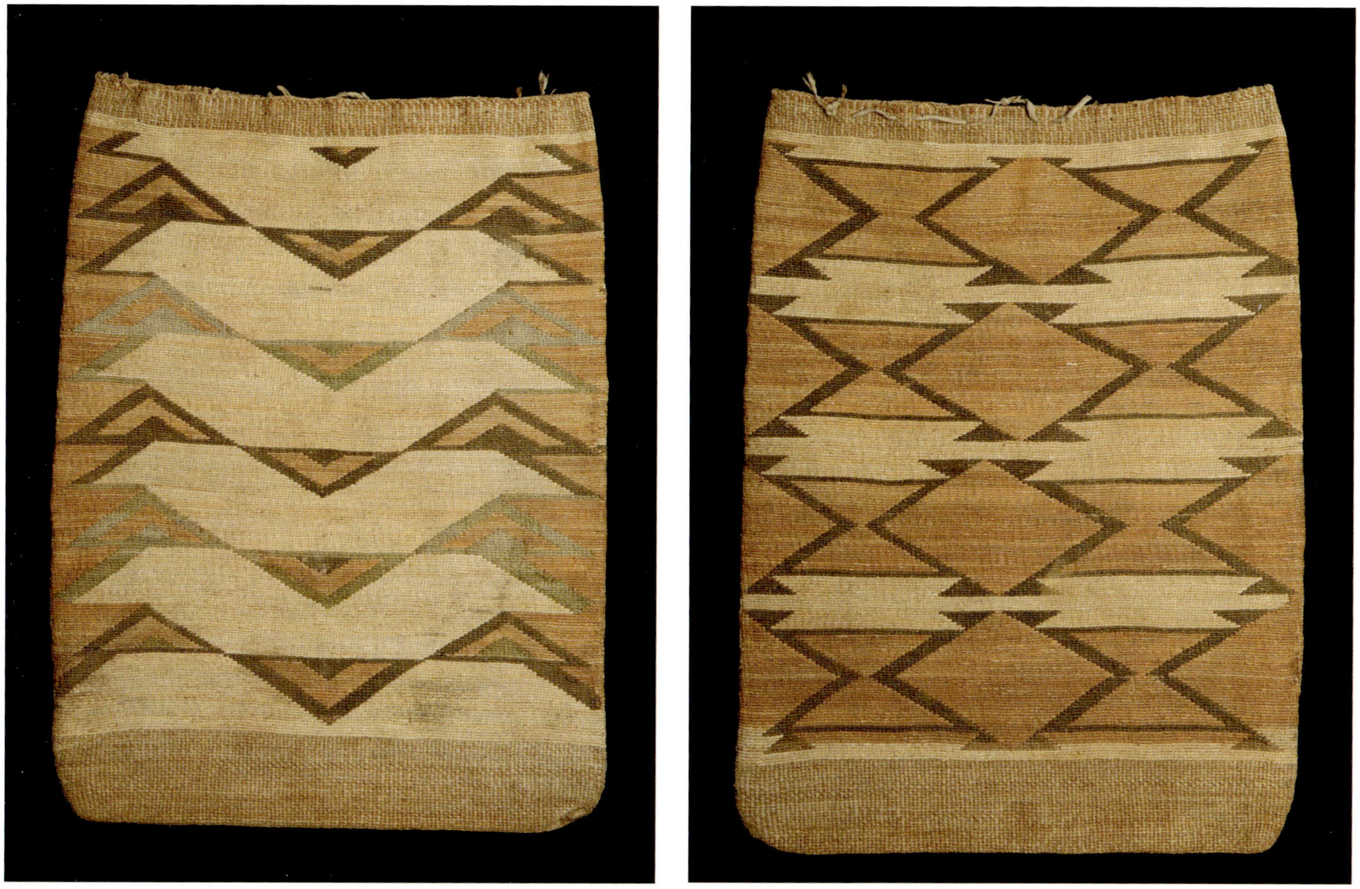

FIG. 97

Carrying Bag (front and back), c. 1900, Plateau, Artist unknown, 63.0 x 47.5 cm., 25030

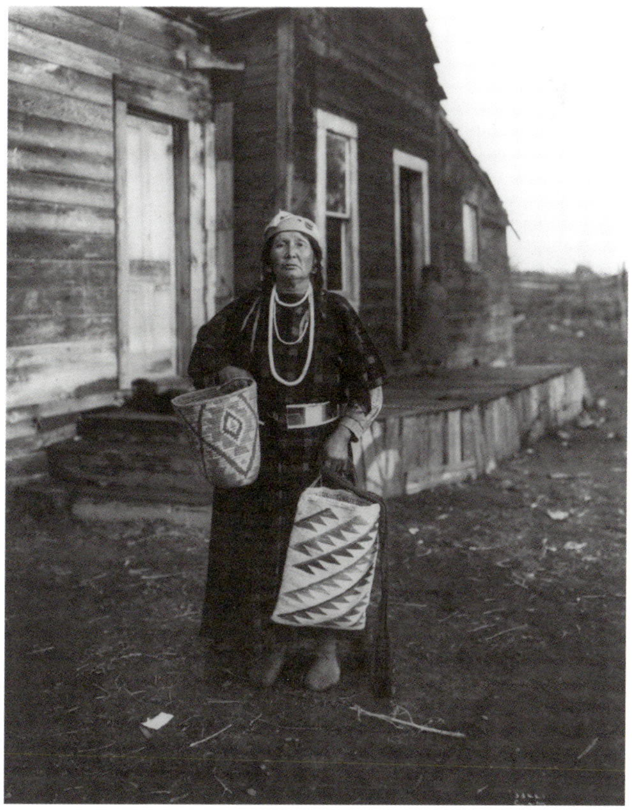

FIG. 98

Mrs. Sluiskin, Yakima, Plateau Culture Area, 1915. Photo by Asahel Curtis. Courtesy of the University of Washington Libraries. Special Collections Division. NA572.

Mrs. Sluiskin holds a gathering basket in her right hand and a carrying bag in her left hand. The photographer did not record whether or not she was the weaver.

Another type of distinctive carrying basket made by Indigenous peoples of western North America is the cornhusk bag. A number of factors determined the shape and size: the construction materials available in the weaver's environment; the materials the weaver chose to use; and the bag's functions/anticipated uses. Made by basket weavers of the Plateau Culture Area, it was constructed out of soft, flexible yet strong plant materials. It functioned as a carrying basket for women gathering edible roots, as a sack in which to store roots in the home, and as a saddlebag after the horse was introduced to the Plateau area in the 1800s. Because it was soft, flat, and flexible, it was easily stored when not in use (see fig. 97).

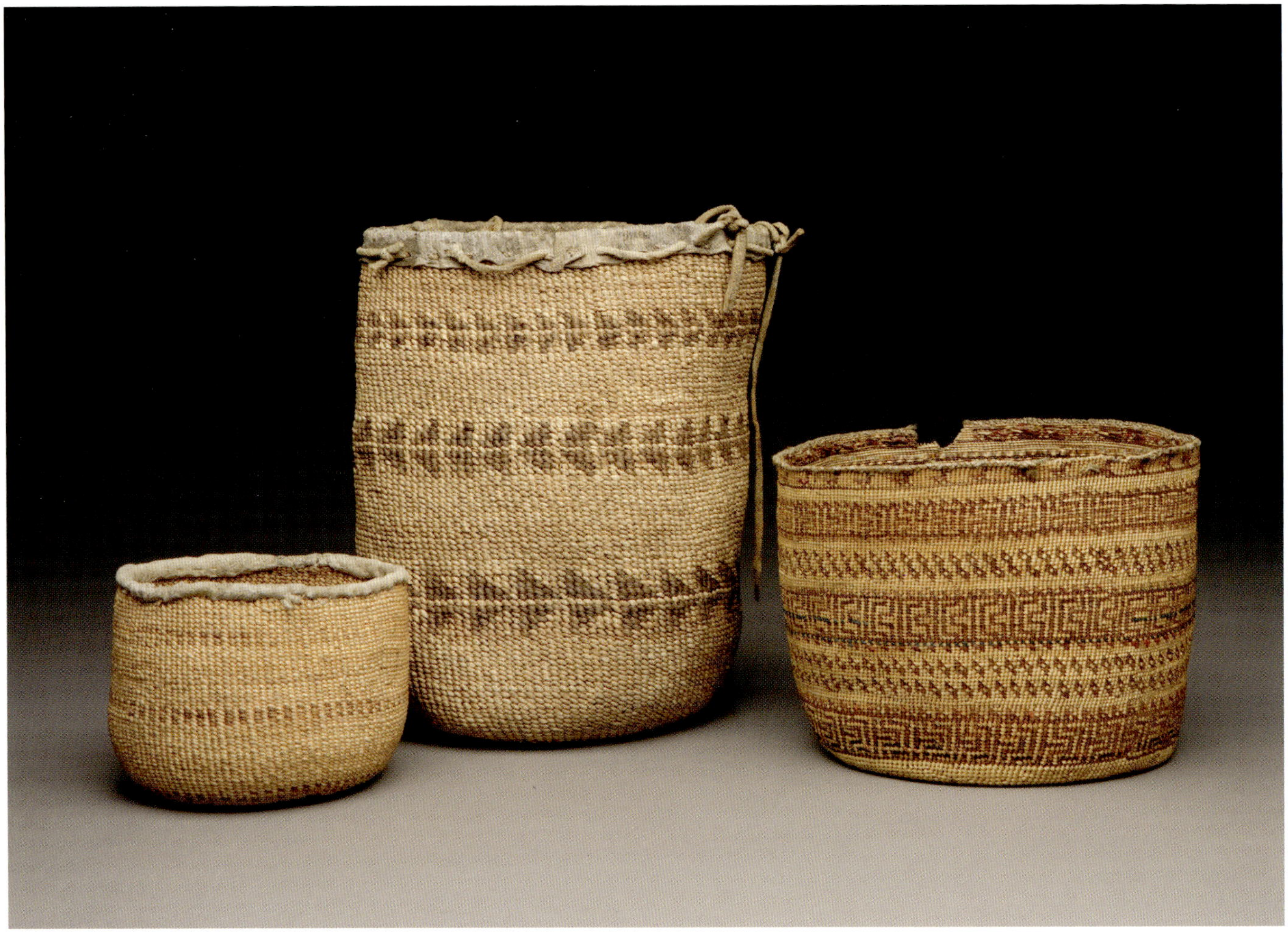

FIG. 99

Miniature Gathering Basket, c. 1880, Wasco-Wishram, Artist unknown, 10.0 x 13.5 cm., 911

Gathering Basket, c. 1880, Wasco-Wishram, Artist unknown, 25.5 x 19.0 cm., 14376

Fancy Gathering Basket, c. 1840, Clatsop, Artist unknown, 15.0 x 20.0 cm., 45106

Both the Wasco-Wishram weavers of the Northwest Coast Culture Area and the Clatsop weavers of the Plateau Culture Area twine their carrying baskets using pliable materials. Women often used these baskets for carrying and storing edible plant roots (which they gathered using a special stick as a shovel).

The O'odham carrying basket, which they call the *kiaha*, is an interesting example of how a basket form largely arose from function but was additionally shaped by (and dependent on) cultural and social contexts. Noteworthy for its bold structural and conceptual frameworks, the *kiaha* was once a common sight in the Indigenous communities of Arizona's Sonoran Desert. Women traditionally used this seemingly unwieldy form to carry large and heavy loads for long distances (see figure 100). The basket features long support sticks that acted as legs on the ground and confined tall loads when the basket was carried. When loading the basket, it was placed on the ground, where it was supported by its "helping stick." The bearer then stooped beneath it, pulled the headband across the top of her head, and let the load rest against her shoulders and back as she stood up. Because it could stand on legs, the *kiaha* also served as a safe interim storage basket during rest stops and as a secure display area for "setting up shop" to sell wares or produce.

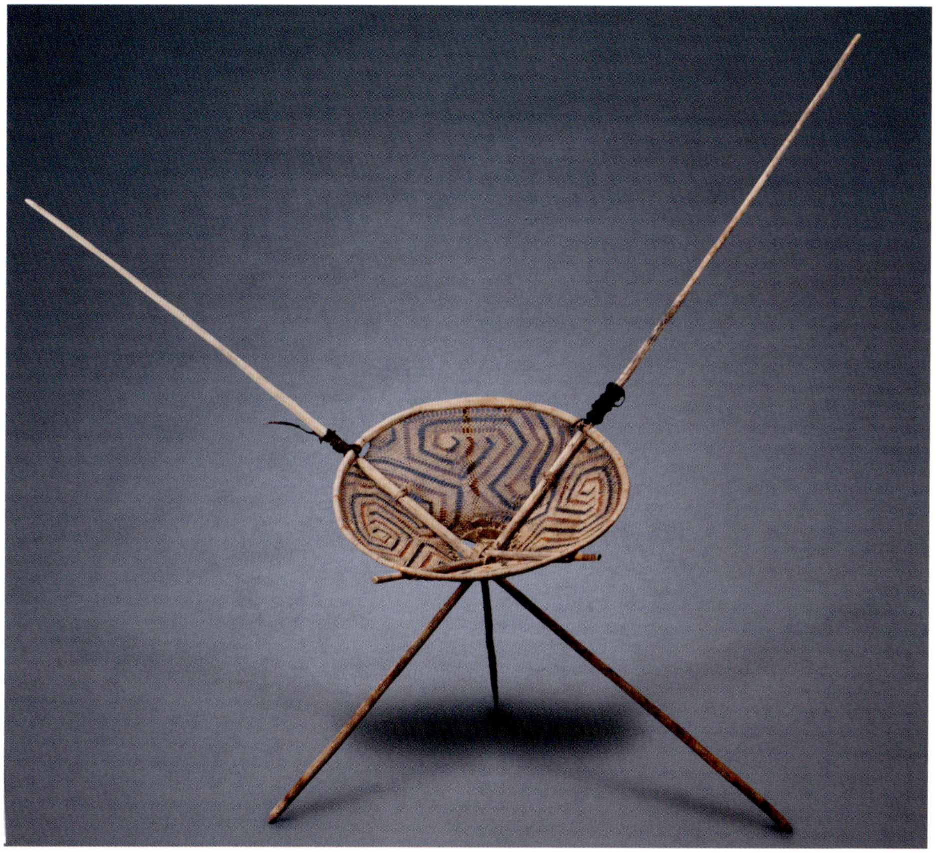

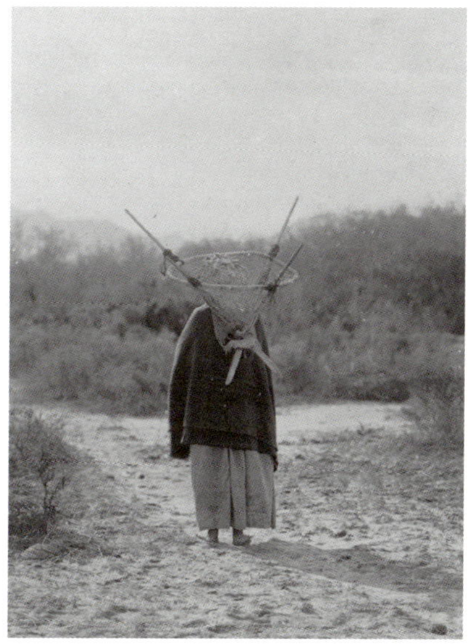

FIG. 100

Kiaha **and Helping Stick**, c. 1900, Akimel O'odham, Artist unknown, 179.0 x 201.0 cm., 36693

The *kiaha* is shown here with its forked helping stick that supports the *kiaha* when it sits on the ground. The stick may also have served as a walking and/or digging stick.

FIG. 101

Akimel O'odham woman with kiaha, c. 1907. Photo by Edward S. Curtis. Courtesy of the Library of Congress. LC-USZ62-111282.

One Native basket weaver is determined to bring back the historic *kiaha* basket form. On August 4, 2012, at the Museum of Indian Arts & Culture in Santa Fe, Royce Manuel—Akimel O'odham basketry artist and knowledge-holder—led a workshop entitled "Binding Our Future to the Past: Agave Workshop." Manuel hopes to bring the *kiaha* back to life for the O'odham by teaching workshops and, more importantly, by holding training sessions for tribal community members. According to Manuel, the knowledge required in making this complex basket form had been lost to his generation because no one had made one for over sixty years. Manuel sought knowledge from ethnographic publications, archives, museums, and the legends connecting the form to his community. He began the trial and error process of constructing a *kiaha* himself by identifying, harvesting, and processing the raw materials he needed. Then he learned how to make cordage and weave it into the *kiaha's* basket, and finally, he reconstructed the weaving techniques needed to construct the *kiaha's* headband and back pad.

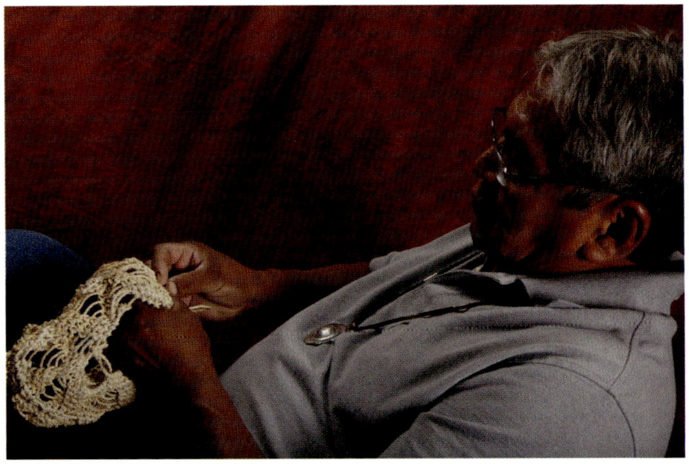

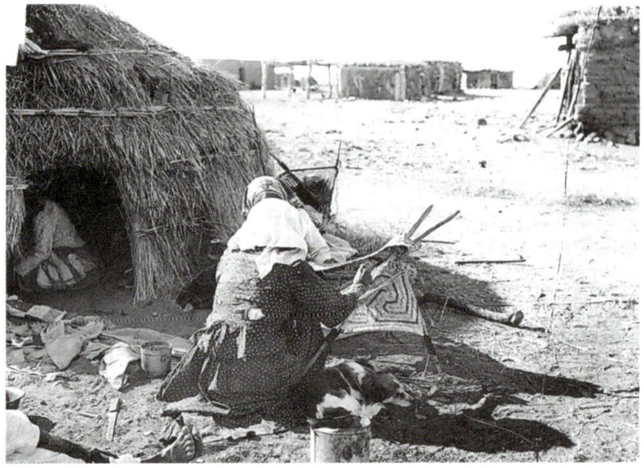

FIG. 102

Royce Manuel, Akimel O'odham, 2010. Photo by Debbie Manuel.

When Royce Manuel visited the Museum of Indian Arts & Culture, he joined the staff in the collection storage area to reconstruct the museum's O'odham *kiaha,* which had been stored flat for decades (see fig. 100). After studying the marks left on the frame from Indigenous use, Manuel saw that it had been put together incorrectly and surmised that it had been purchased, disassembled for transport to the museum, and reassembled by someone unfamiliar with the form. He noted that some parts were missing, including the back pad, the notched sticks to hold the cords at the center of the basket, the stick used to adjust the strap attached to the headband, and the horsehair rope that normally would have been attached to each stick to hold the load in the basket. He also noted that two of the sticks had been cut short, most likely after purchase. He said he had seen this in *kiahas* at a number of museums, as *kiahas* were not designed to fit into exhibit cases.

FIG. 103

Two Tohono O'odham women working on a *kiaha*, 1894. Photo by William Dinwiddie. Courtesy of the National Anthropological Archives. 02749 C.

During the Santa Fe workshop, Manuel shared an O'odham story that was a version of the following legend. As in many other traditional myths and legends of basket-weaving people, it explains the importance of baskets in the spiritual and everyday life of Indigenous peoples, and the connections of baskets and people to traditional lands.

Burden Basket Becomes a Mountain

One day Coyote climbed a hill and sat down to watch the world go by. Suddenly a lovely girl came walking by and he knew this was the girl he wanted to marry.

Strangely, the girl wasn't carrying her burden basket on her back, it was walking along by itself after her. Yet a basket never walks around on its own. It seems that this girl's father was a powerful medicine man and had made this basket especially for his daughter.

The lovely girl was gathering firewood, which she loaded into the basket. She gathered a great deal of wood, and when she was finished she turned to go home, and the basket followed her.

Coyote was thinking of getting that basket and showing people how smart he was so he said, "Hahaha. So the burden basket walks around." The basket just stopped where it was and became a mountain which the people now call Quijo Toa—Burden-Basket Mountain (Saxton and Saxton 1973:211–215).

In addition to carrying baskets, early Indigenous weavers designed and constructed basket forms for the harvesting and processing of nuts and seeds, among the wild foods that were essential dietary staples of the subsistence cultures of western North America. One such form is called the winnowing basket. Before women processed nuts and seeds into flour, they had to remove the hard husks or hulls surrounding the edible meat of nuts and the grains of grass seeds. First, they separated out as much of the husks as they could by hand and then used their winnowing baskets to remove all the remaining loose bits (referred to as chaff). Winnowing the chaff involved tossing the mixture into the air and letting it fall back into the basket, or slowly pouring it into a receptacle on the ground, allowing a breeze to blow the lighter chaff away from the heavier grains.

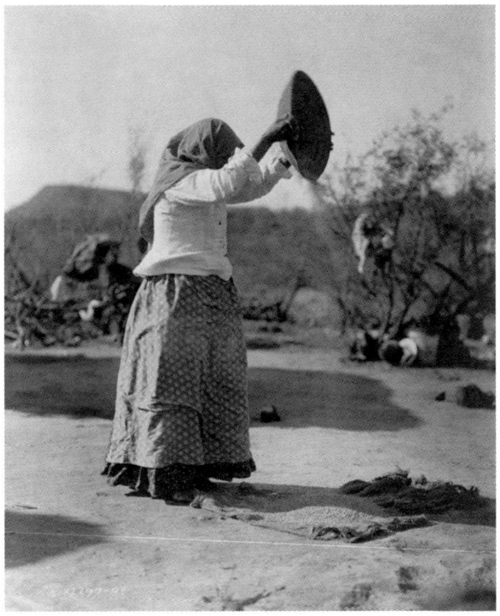

FIG. 104

A Tohono O'odham woman winnowing wheat, c. 1907. Photo by Edward S. Curtis. Courtesy of the Library of Congress. LC-USZ62-123312.

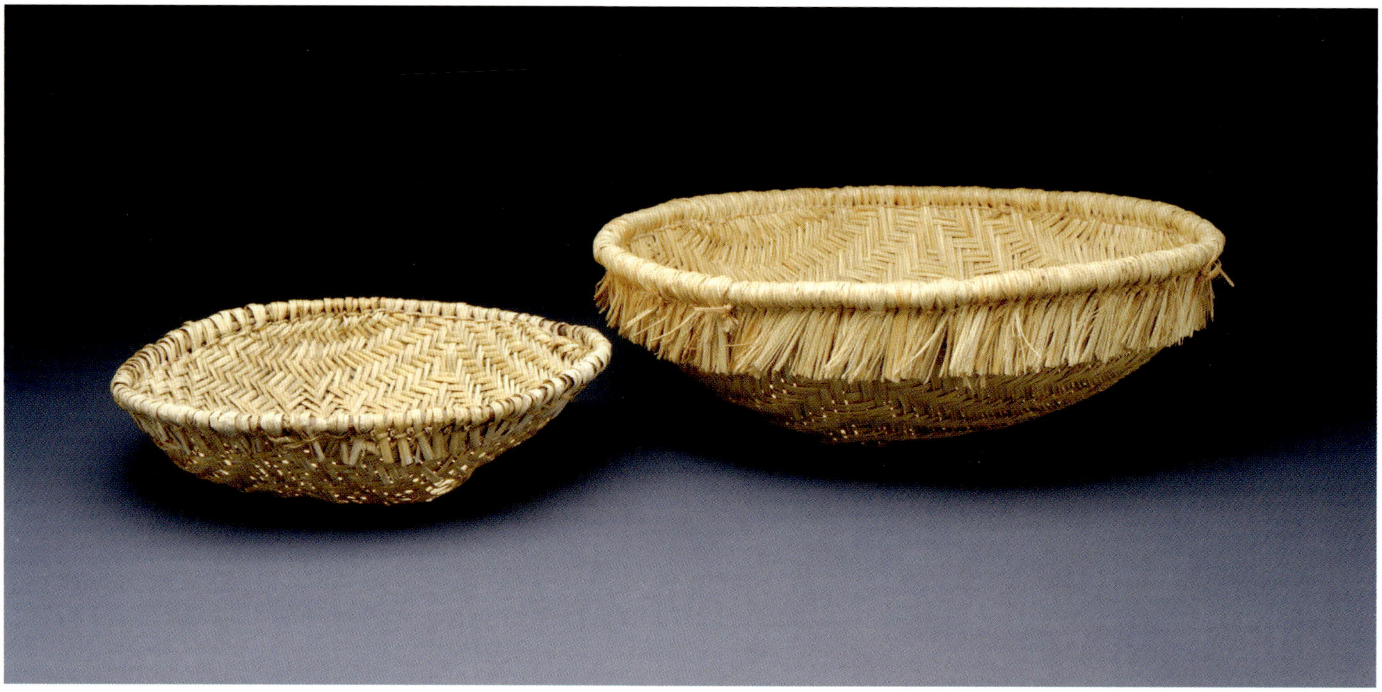

FIG. 105 (Left to right):

Sifter Tray, c. 1940, Hopi, Artist unknown, 10.0 x 37.0 cm., 50187

Ring Sifter, 1955, Jemez Pueblo, Artist unknown, 16.5 x 50.0 cm., 37026

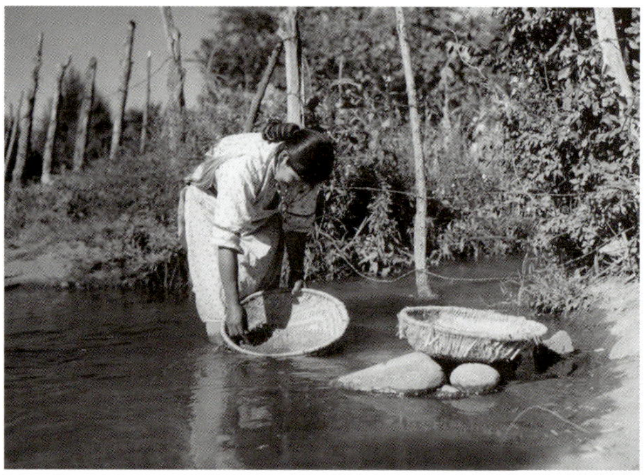

FIG. 106

Perfectitia Baca Toya, Jemez Pueblo, washes wheat in a ring sifter, September 15, 1936. Photo by Ten Broeck Williamson. Courtesy of the Palace of the Governors Photo Archives. 42075.

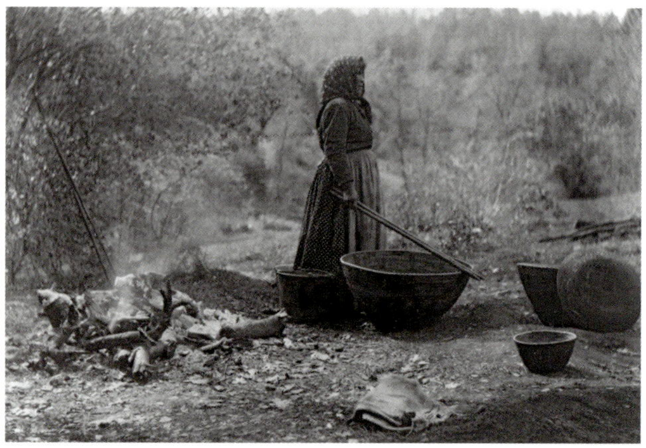

FIG. 107

A woman cooks acorn mush in baskets at a Konkow Maidu feast, Bidwell Bar, California, 1903. The feast was given in honor of visiting Chico Maidu people. Photo by John. W. Hudson. Courtesy of the Field Museum of Natural History, Chicago. 9514.

A more multi-purpose food-processing basket is the plaited sifter, a utensil that crosses cultural boundaries. They were used for washing and winnowing the nuts and seeds used to make different types of flours, as well as for sifting flour. (The flour falls through the interstices in the basket weave. See figure 105.) Sifters also served double duty as food-serving platters.

In Indigenous-made cooking baskets, form unites with material and construction technique in the most purely functional sense. Cooking in baskets made from natural (possibly flammable) materials may seem to be counter-intuitive, but it was a common and commonsense procedure in prehistoric and historic times. The first step in the process was to heat cooking rocks in a fire; next, flour was stirred with water in the cooking basket until well mixed; and finally the red-hot rocks were added to the basket filled with mush. The mixture had to be stirred continuously so the rocks would not scorch the basket; as each rock cooled it was replaced with a hot rock from the fire, until the mush boiled. To keep fire ash from getting into the mush, women usually kept a basket of fresh water at hand to clean the rocks off before they dropped them into the cooking basket.

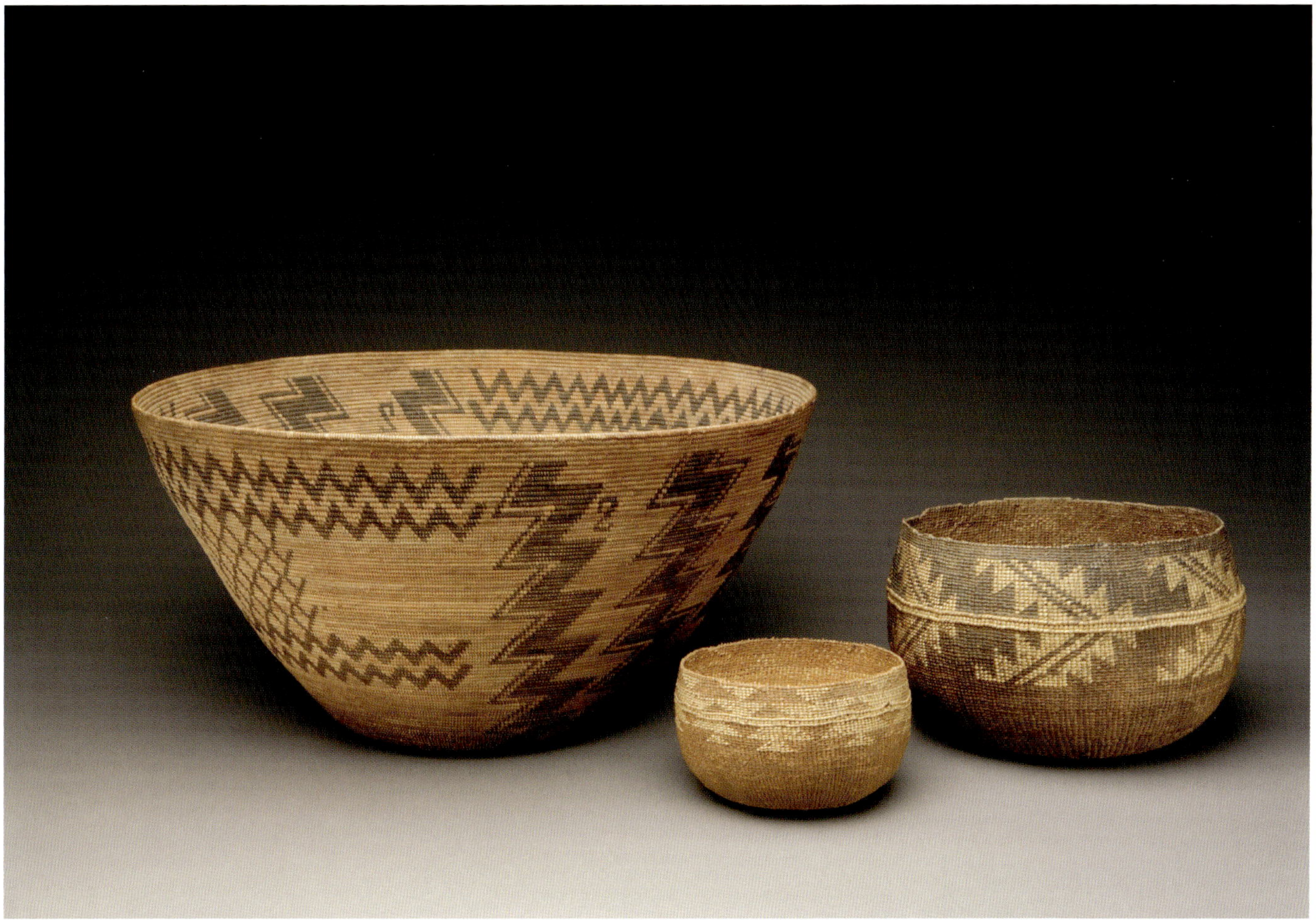

FIG. 108 (Left to right):

Cooking Basket, c. 1885, Monache, 15.4 x 20.8 cm., Artist unknown, 25445

Food Bowl, c. 1920, Yurok, Artist unknown, 9.0 x 16.0 cm., 47663

Cooking Basket, c. 1900, Hupa, Artist unknown, 18.0 x 26.0 cm., 23495

Cooking baskets have flared or straight sides to make it easier to add and remove hot cooking rocks and to stir the mush. The cooking baskets on the left and right were made using different materials and construction techniques, reflecting the different cultural traditions of the weavers. The basket in the center is an individual eating bowl. As all these baskets illustrate, closely coiled or twined baskets can be watertight when they are made from the correct materials.

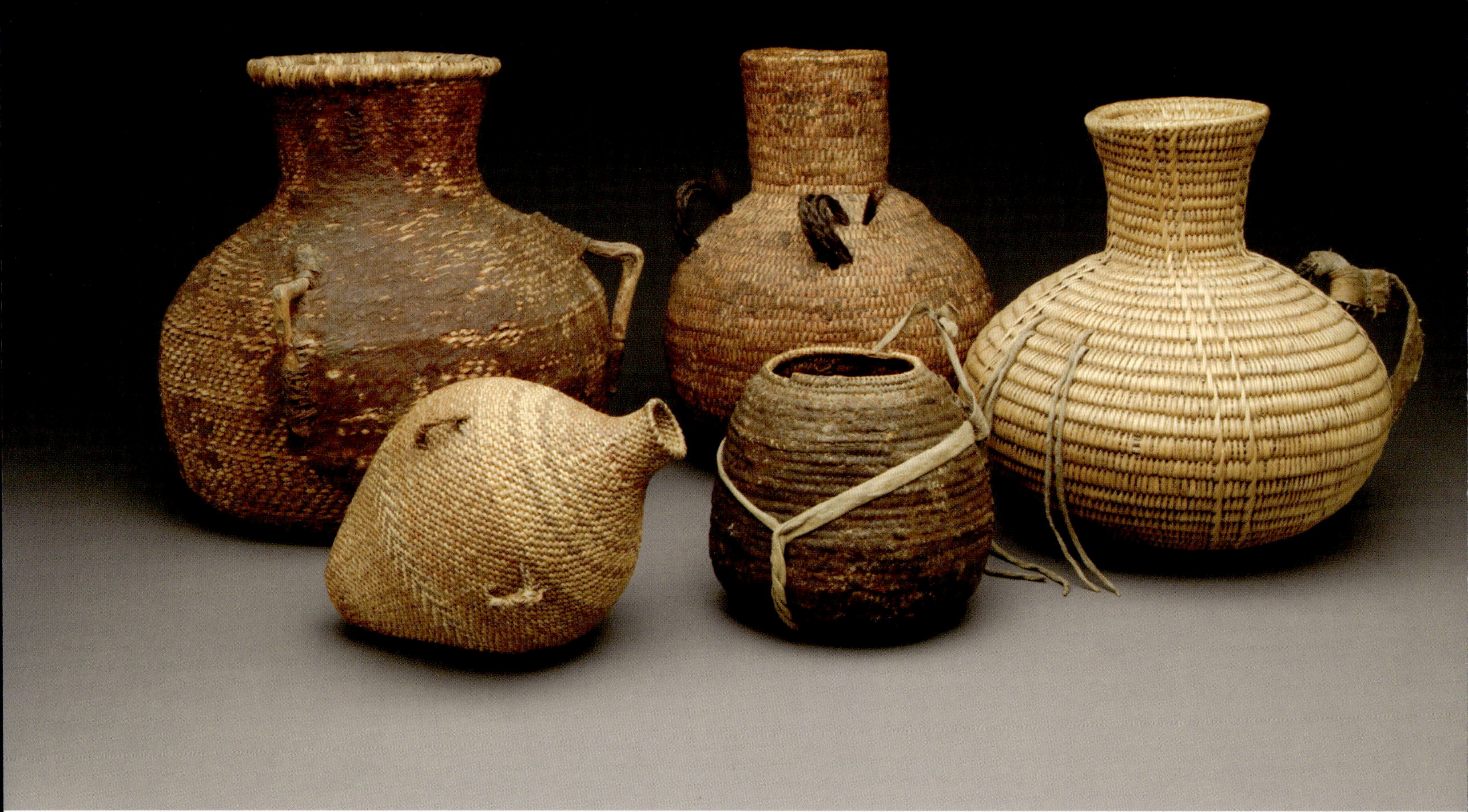

FIG. 109 (Clockwise from far right):

Water Jar, c. 1880, Jicarilla Apache, Artist unknown, 31.0 x 29.0 cm., 16098

Canteen, c. 1800, Pueblo, Artist unknown, 16.5 x 18.0 cm., 11345

Water Jar, c. 1930, Southern Paiute, Artist unknown, 25 x 16.5 cm., 23467

Water Jar, c. 1895, Western Apache, Artist unknown, 33.5 x 34.0 cm., 46562

Water Jar, c. 1910, Diné, Artist unknown, 33.0 x 24.3 cm., 57220

For many thousands of years, weavers of western North America made baskets to meet their household needs. They based their choices of materials, construction techniques, form, and two-dimensional design elements on the function and cultural meaning of the finished basket. After outsiders overwhelmed remote Native lands, baskets such as these water jars, made from locally gathered materials, were gradually replaced with barrels, buckets, pots, jars, and bowls made of wood, metal, ceramic, and glass.

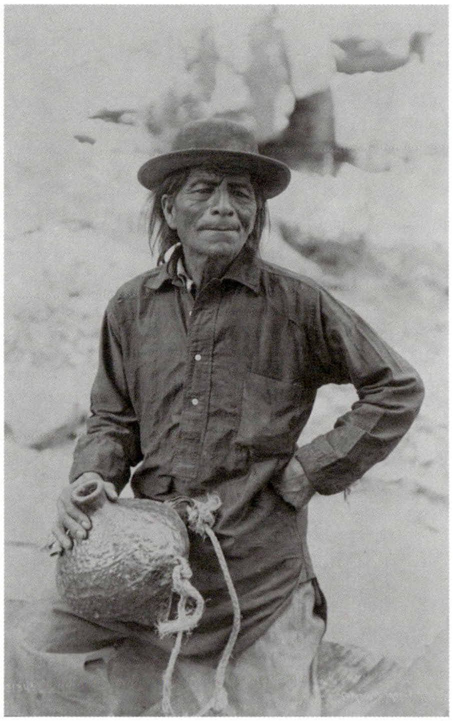

FIG. 110

Captain Burro, Havasupai, holds a basketry water jar coated with pine pitch, 1900. Courtesy of the Palace of the Governors Photo Archives. 82454.

Basketry jars woven to hold water were made in a variety of functional forms. The jars in figure 109 illustrate several types, woven by four different tribes in the Southwest Culture Area. To make them watertight, basket weavers coated these baskets with piñon pitch on the inside (and in some cases on the outside as well). The pitch, as well as the narrow necks of the jars, helped slow the evaporation of water in the hot desert climates in which these baskets were used.

These baskets were made for use, except for the Southern Paiute jar that was woven in circa 1910 and intended for sale. The beautiful form and designs of water jars were popular with collectors in the early twentieth century; presumably, the Paiute weaver left her jar unpitched to better display her virtuoso construction technique and design motifs. The jar is a copy of the type used by individuals, as is the small canteen shown. The three larger jars in the photograph are typical of basketry jars used for collecting and storing water in camps or villages. All would have been fitted with fiber stoppers when in use (Whiteford 1988:84).

Storage baskets were needed by Indigenous people who lived off both wild foods and domesticated crops and stored their surpluses against times of need. For example, people who traveled from camp to camp throughout the year stored dry foods in woven jars, also referred to as ollas. With time and experience, Native basket weavers were able to perfect the shape and size of these light and durable jars. These basketry storage jars were constructed taller than wide, expanding from a constricted base into a globular body, topped by sloping shoulders, with a narrow rimmed opening. This form is well suited for storing foodstuffs, as the constricted base and expanding sides distribute the weight of the contents throughout the basket, preventing materials on the bottom from being crushed, and the narrow neck enables the basket to be secured with a plug.

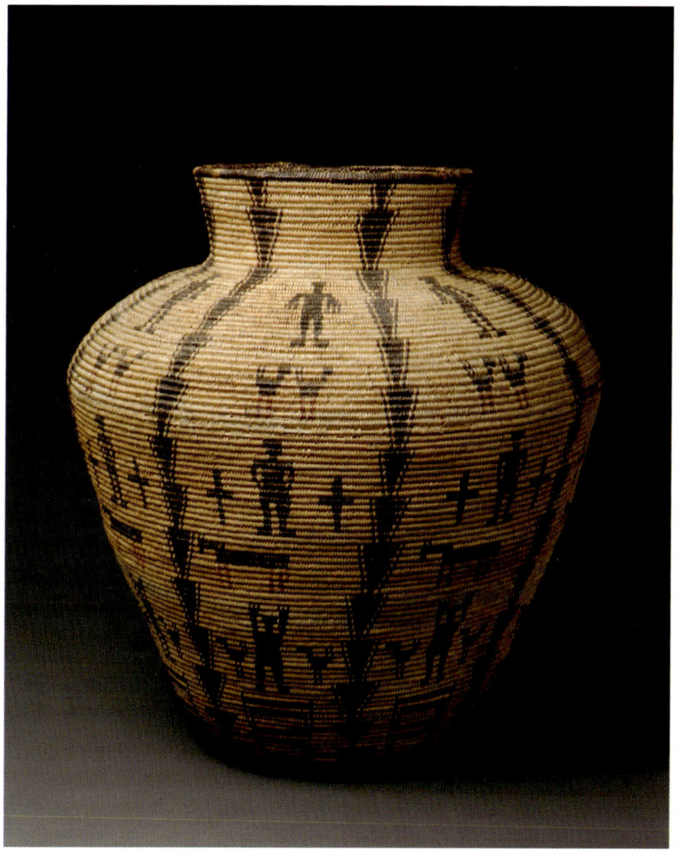

FIG. 111

Jar, c. 1900, Western Apache, Artist unknown, 53.2 x 46.2 cm., 35969

COMMERCIAL BASKET FORMS

Basket forms that remained static, unchanged, may eventually lose their usefulness, relevance, and meaning; thus, Indigenous basket weavers continually adapted their "mental" templates for functional forms. Some basket forms changed when weavers married into another tribal group; these weavers integrated their traditional basketry forms into the forms of the new community. In other instances, basket weavers were influenced by the baskets brought into their community through far-ranging Indigenous trade networks (Marr 1990:272). Beginning in the seventeenth century, changes in Indigenous basketry forms were the result of outsiders intruding in their lives, ushering in Native population decline, loss of Indigenous homelands and self-sufficient ways of life, and the introduction of new foods to the region.

Once the need for traditional utilitarian baskets began to decline, and basket weavers entered the new cash economy introduced by outsiders, many began weaving items solely for the commer-

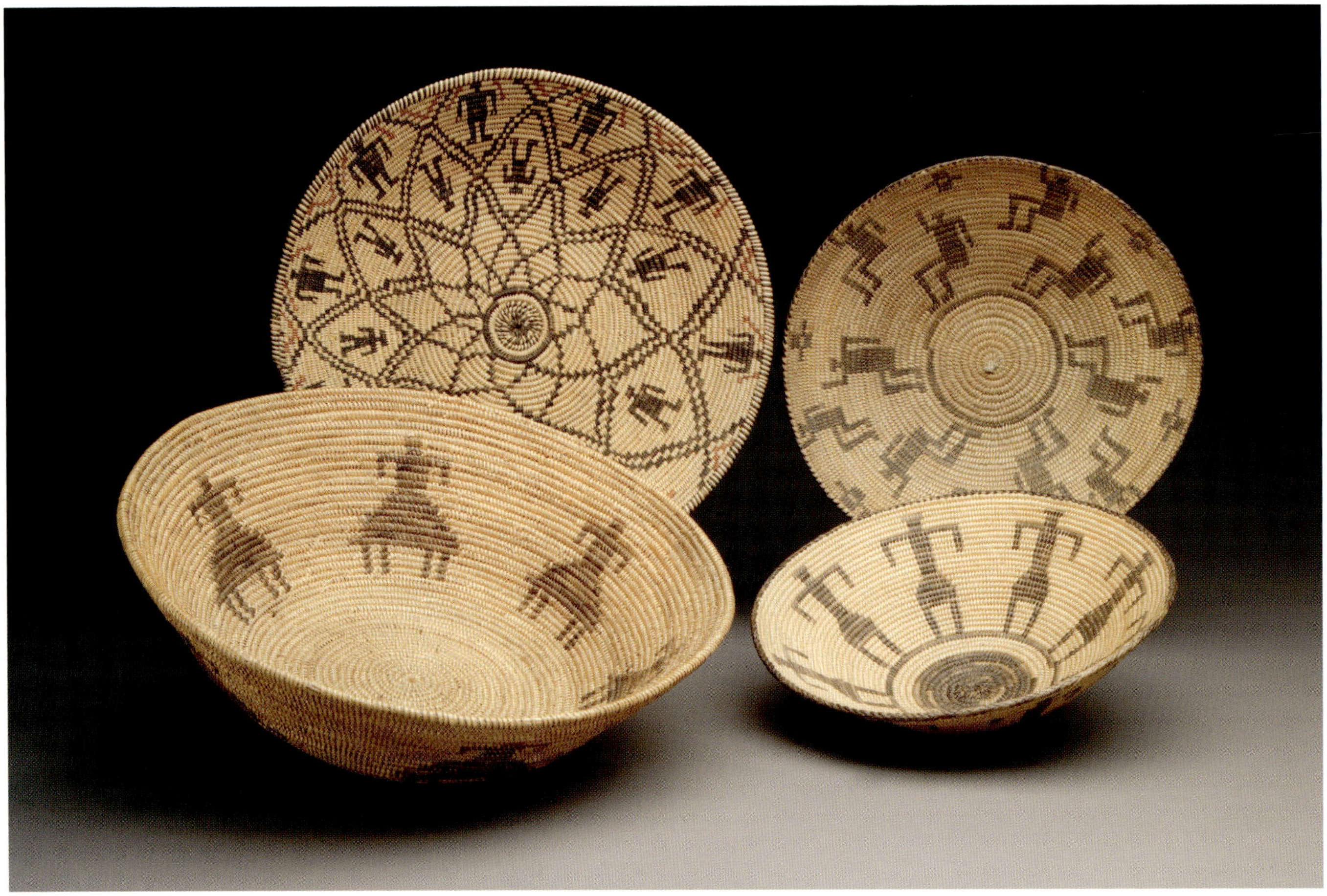

FIG. 112 (Clockwise from upper right):

Tray, c. 1900, Akimel O'odham, Artist unknown, 8.0 x 33.0 cm., 23384
Bowl, c. 1890, Akimel O'odham, Artist unknown, 11.0 x 28.5 cm., 31118
Bowl, c. 1900, Kumeyaay, Artist unknown, 13.0 x 39.0 cm., 14378
Tray, c. 1910, San Carlos Apache, Artist unknown, 9.0 x 39.5 cm., 12604

When weavers recognized the impact of a good design on their basket sales, they developed forms that were essentially canvases for design elements. For example, they began weaving fewer bowls and more tray forms that were made larger and flatter to showcase their design elements.

cial market. In the Southwest Culture Area, with the arrival of Spanish settlers in the early 1600s, Indigenous weavers created serviceable containers to trade across cultural barriers. This type of commerce was already familiar to many basket weavers, whose wares had been part of Indigenous trade networks—networks that had existed for centuries. Nevertheless, trading with the Spanish marked the first step in the transformation of baskets made for personal use into baskets made as commercial products. The new forms of these trade baskets reflected the interactions between the Indigenous peoples of the Southwest and their new non-Native neighbors.

Distinct types of reciprocal influence are evident in a group of five innovatively produced Jicarilla baskets: revival of old forms for sale; adaption of foreign forms for sale; adaption of foreign forms for use in Indigenous households; and adaption of Indigenous forms for use in foreign households (see fig.s 113, 116, 117). The weaver of the water jar seen at left in figure 113 revived a traditional utilitarian form for a basket intended for sale. We know that she wove this basket for sale because if the basket had been woven for personal use the weaver would have coated the inside with piñon pitch to make it watertight. In the pitcher form to its right, a Jicarilla Apache weaver clearly adapted the foreign form of a pitcher to her basketry repertoire; by the 1920s, when she wove this basket, glass or ceramic pitchers were a common sight in local Anglo/Euro-American stores and households. Although the prototype would have held water, this woven copy is not suited to hold liquid of any kind, placing it in the category of tourist or art basket.

In the same way, the clothes hamper and laundry basket in figure 116 were based entirely on Anglo/Euro-American prototypes; they were woven for use either in foreign households, or in acculturated Indigenous households. Sturdy willow baskets (such as those seen in figure 117) were made by Pueblo men for use as storage baskets in their homes. After arrival of the Spanish, and then Anglo/Euro-American settlers, Pueblo weavers sold or traded these baskets (with little or no changes made to the form) for use in foreign households. Although the above-mentioned group of baskets were made for sale and demonstrate reciprocal influences, they were all made with traditional materials, construction techniques, and two-dimensional surface designs.

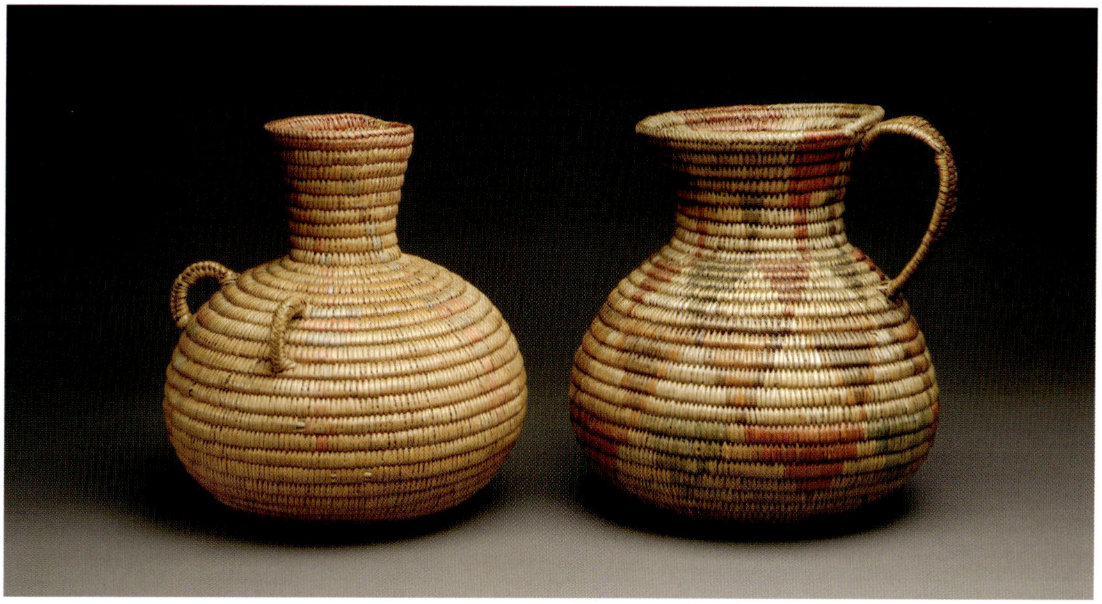

FIG. 113

Water Jar, c. 1935, Jicarilla Apache, Artist unknown, 28.5 x 25.3 cm., 23537

Pitcher, c. 1925, Jicarilla Apache, Artist unknown, 30.0 x 28.7 cm., 23555

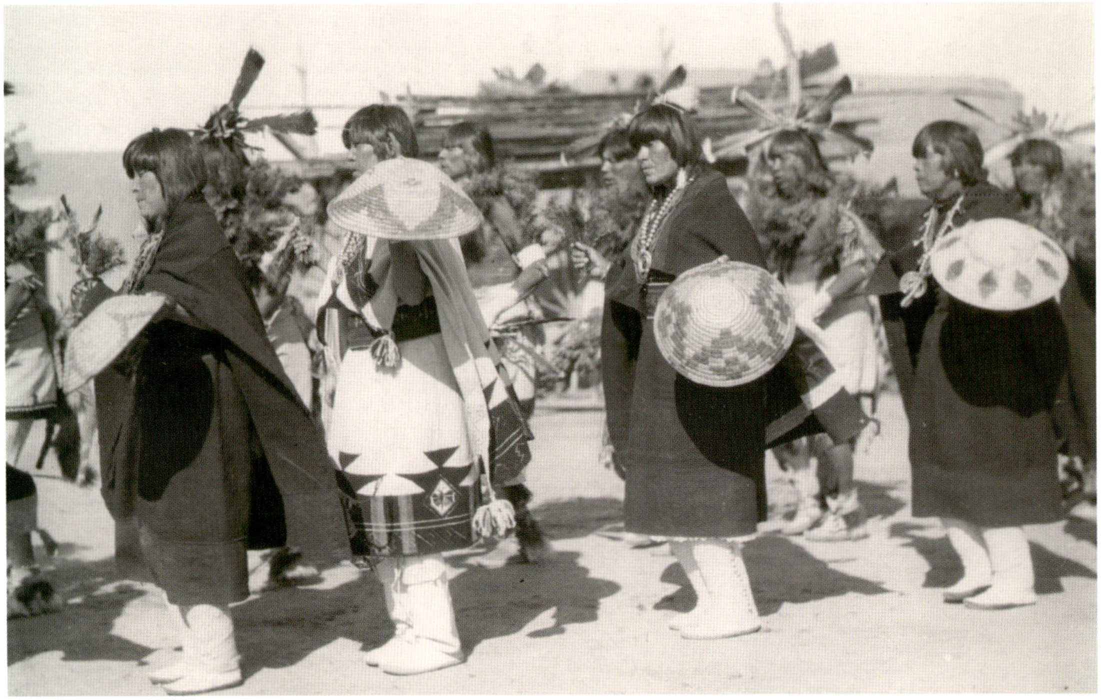

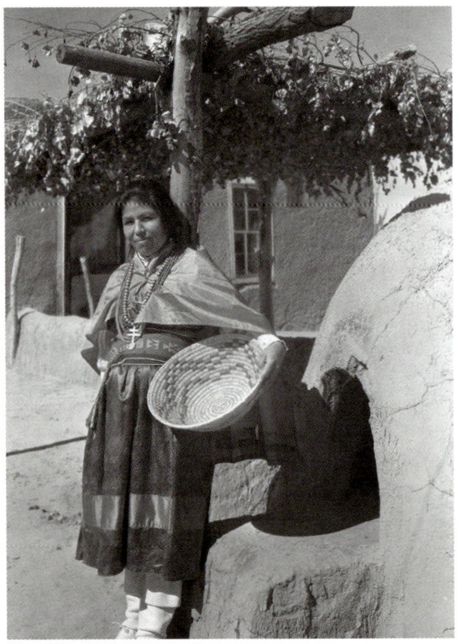

FIG. 114

Basket Dancers at San Ildefonso Pueblo holding Jicarilla Apache baskets, New Mexico,1920. Photo by Sheldon Parsons. Courtesy of the Palace of the Governors Photo Archives. 106876.

FIG. 115

An Ohkay Owingeh Pueblo woman holds a Jicarilla Apache basket, c. 1935. Photo by T. Harmon Parkhurst. Courtesy of the Palace of the Governors Photo Archives. 4488.

Jicarilla Apache weavers traded and sold their baskets both to Native and non-Native people as a source of income. In particular, the Rio Grande pueblos of New Mexico, where women tended to make pottery instead of baskets, provided a ready market for their wares. As the photographs in figures 114 and 115 illustrate, Pueblo women used the baskets for ceremonial and utilitarian purposes.

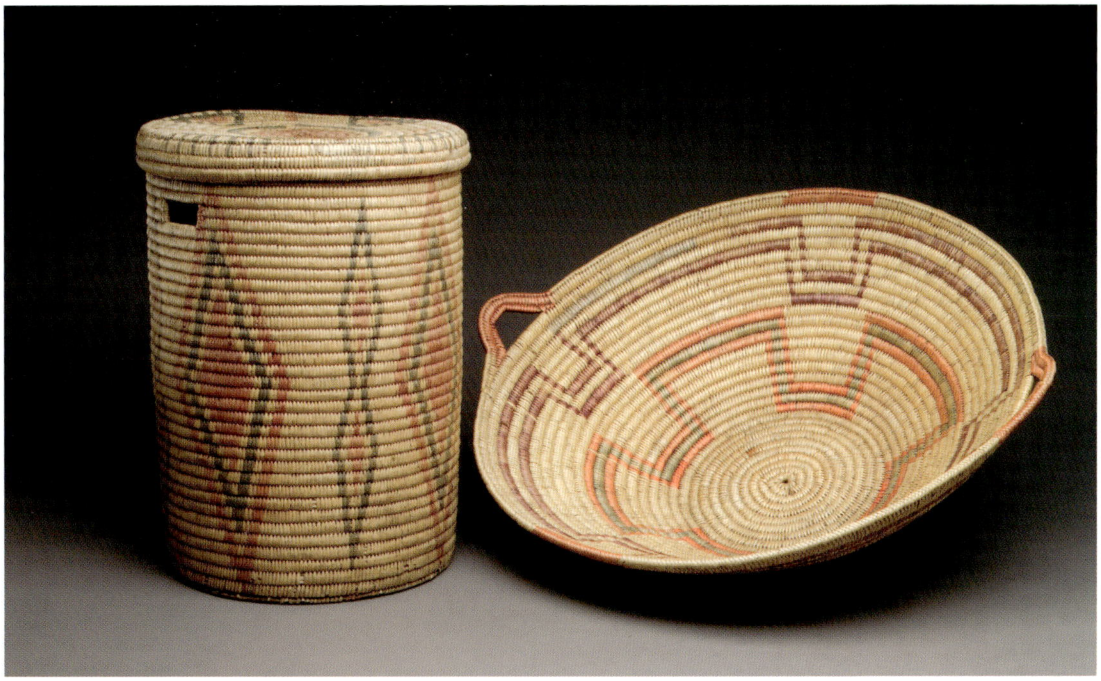

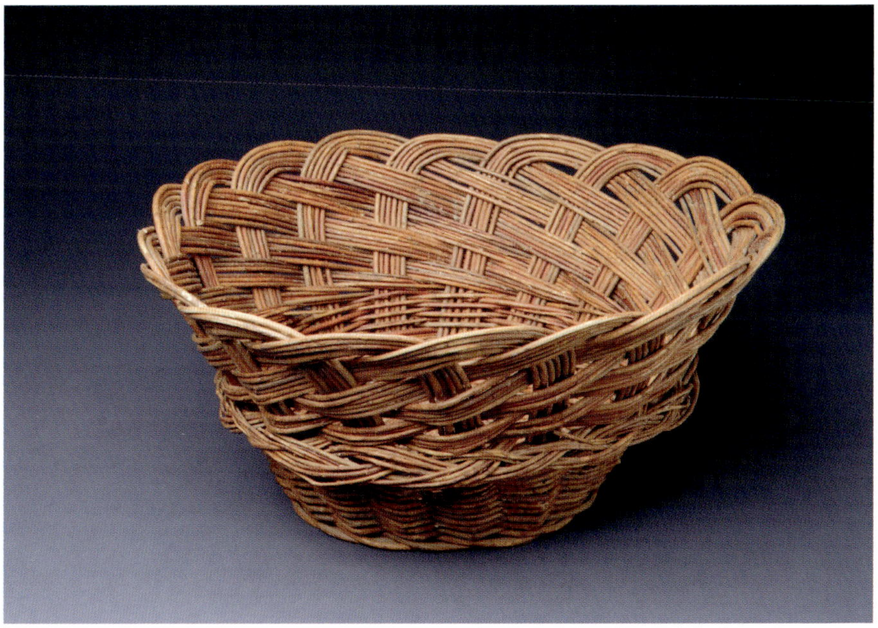

FIG. 116 (Left to right):

Clothes Hamper, c. 1920, Jicarilla Apache, Artist unknown, 48.0 x 32.0 cm., 23538

Laundry Basket, c. 1925, Jicarilla Apache, Artist unknown, 21.0 x 67.0 cm., 23488

FIG. 117

Bowl, 1949, Santo Domingo Pueblo, Santiago Tenorio, 28.0 x 62.0 cm., 23499

By the late 1800s the range of baskets made for the commercial marketplace had expanded to include high-quality examples based on authentic cultural forms for purchase by museums and collectors, as well as trinket baskets and other unusual forms for tourists (see fig. 121). During that time—a period of intense cultural upheaval and foreign influence—modifications to Indigenous basketry forms was far-reaching. When disruptions in the Native social fabric rendered some old utilitarian baskets obsolete, the same forms often appeared in a weavers' commercial repertoire, generally decreased in size and with more elaborate two-dimensional designs (see fig. 120).

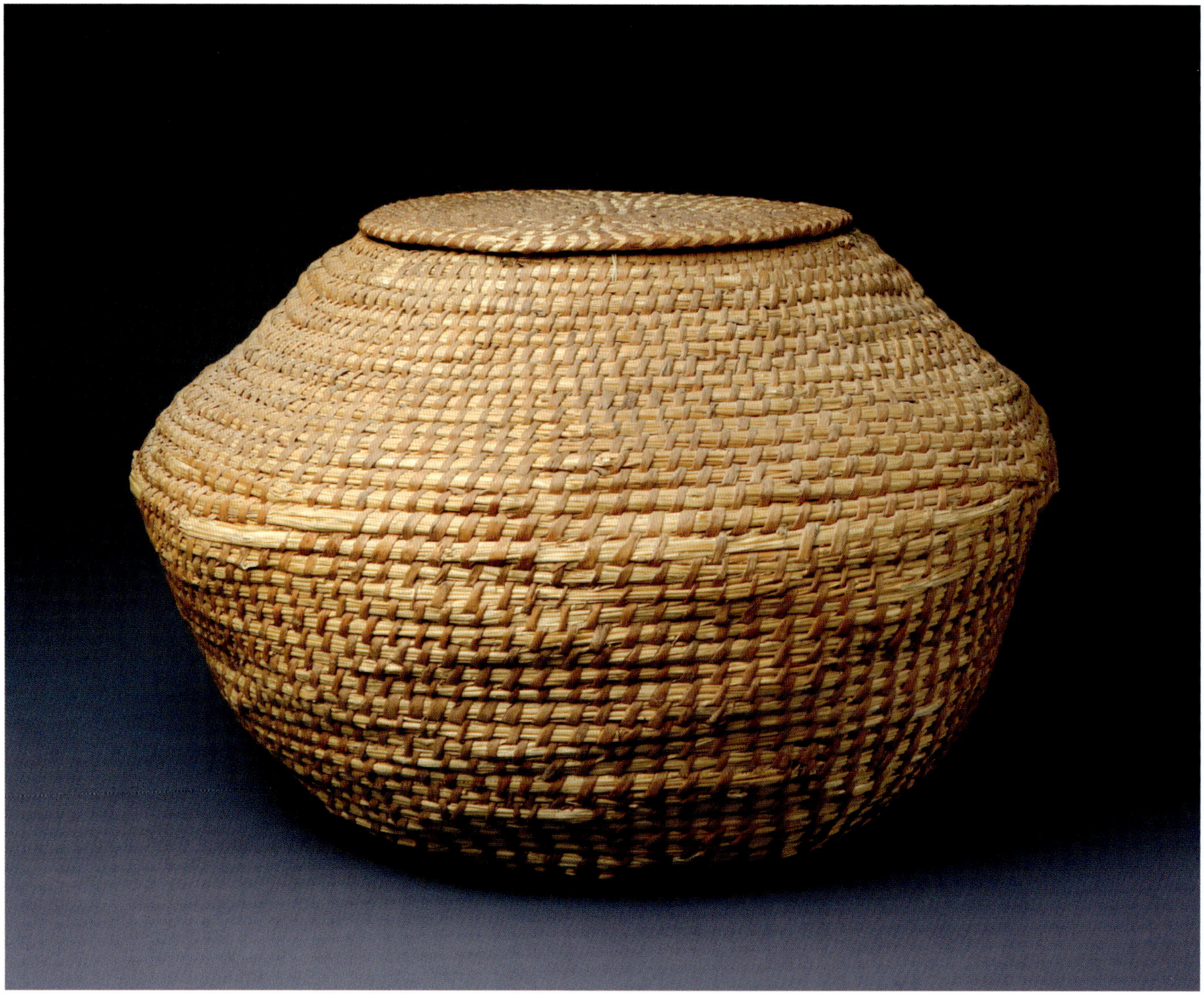

FIG. 118

Storage Basket Model, c. 1900, Tohono O'odham, Artist unknown, 34.0 x 48.0 cm., 35970

Made at the turn of the twentieth century for sale, this basket is a model of a storage basket that earlier would have served as a food cache.

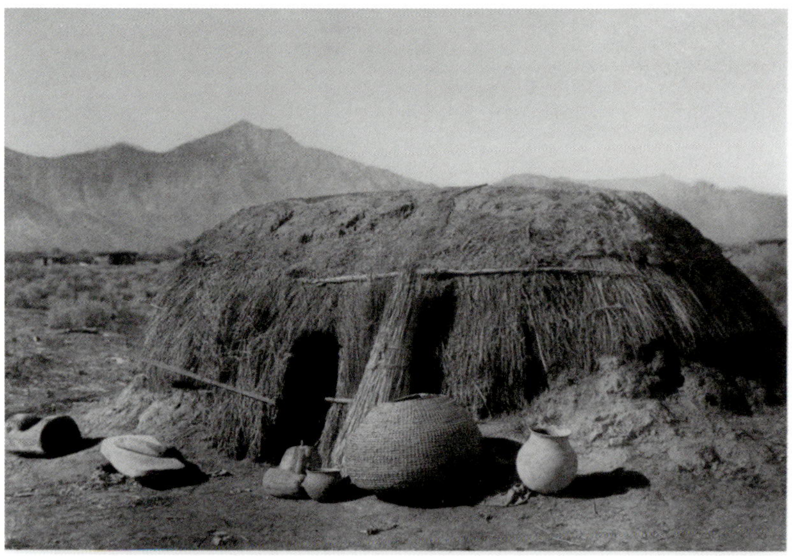

FIG. 119

An O'odham brush house with a full-size storage or granary basket, c. 1907. Library of Congress. LC-US262-101255.

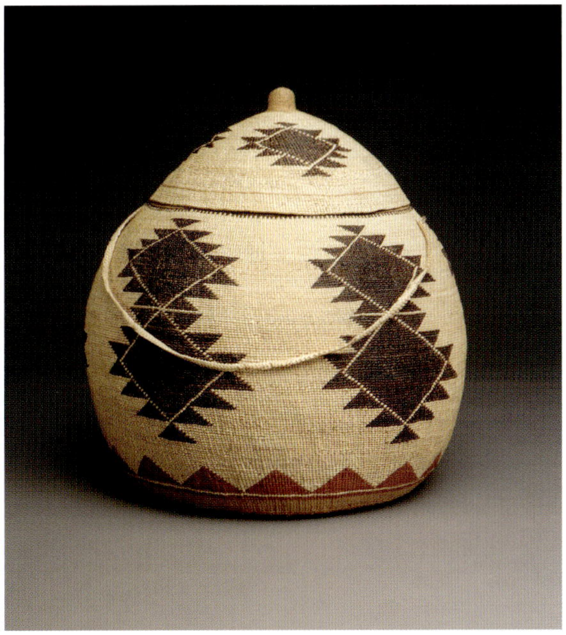

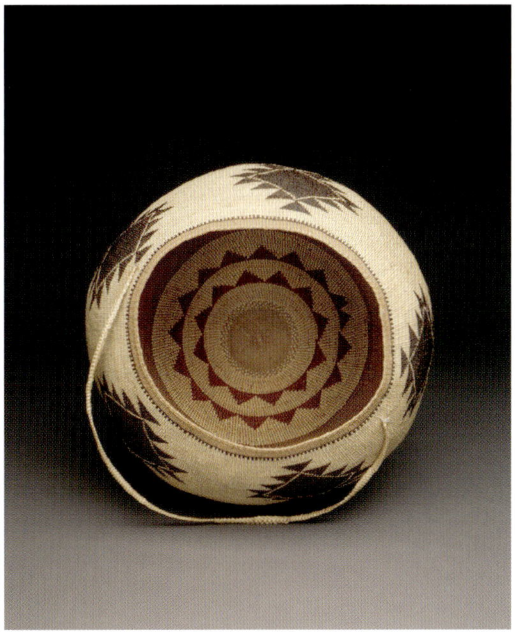

FIG. 120 (Two views):

Storage Basket Model, c. 1904, Yurok, Artist known as "Mrs. Johnny Jack," 38.0 x 32.0 cm., 14296

Mrs. Johnny Jack based this storage basket on a traditional model, which she reduced in size and adorned with added elements (such as the knob on the lid and the handle), references to foreign cultural influences and preferences. With its elaborate surface design, this basket is a show piece exhibiting the skill and artistry of the weaver.

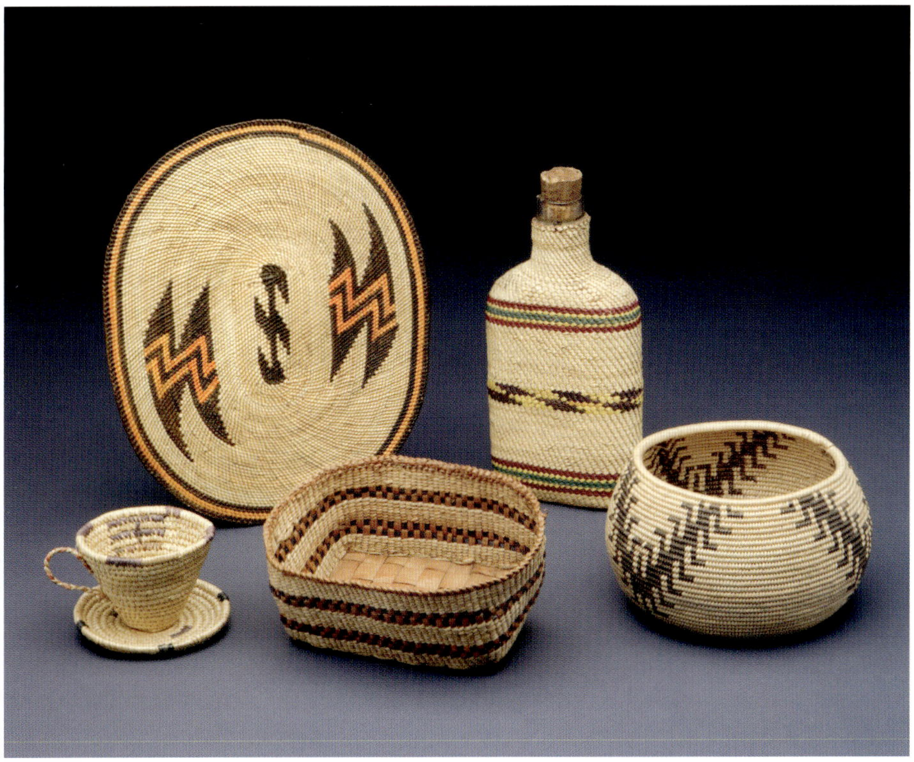

FIG. 121 (Left to right):

Cup and Saucer, c. 1930, Yupik, Artist unknown, 5.5 x 8.5 cm., 48195

Mat, c. 1910, Makah, Artist unknown, 0.1 x 17.4 x 21.7 cm., 23344

Bowl, c. 1920, Nuu-chah-nulth, Artist unknown, 5.5 x 11.1 cm., 23689

Bottle, c. 1920, Makah, Artist unknown, 18.5 x 8.8 cm., 23244

Bowl, c. 1907, Mountain Maidu, Artist known as "Young Bob's Woman," 9.0 x 13.0 cm., 14306

Several fine examples of traditional utilitarian forms that were made for the tourist market in miniature size are illustrated in figure 121. These trinket baskets represent interesting individual choices both by the weavers and the collectors. The teacup and saucer and bottle are miniature adapted Westernized forms. Nevertheless, these baskets are products of creative and inventive minds. For Indigenous weavers, the cultural value of basketmaking resides as much in the knowledge and process of production as it does in the end product. Therefore, even trinket baskets are infused with traditional and artistic qualities by the weaver.

Clothing

There is little more personal or more reflective of our way of living in the world than our clothing. Certainly, one of the first steps in the movement to acculturate Native Americans was to introduce them to western clothing. One common article of clothing worn by Indigenous peoples in the western culture areas is the basketry hat. They have the same social importance whether they were woven in traditional form (such as a ceremonial dance hat) or foreign form (such as a straw boater).

Before the arrival of outsiders, weavers throughout Indigenous western North America based their hat designs on socially constructed models developed within and approved through community consensus. This is evident in the variety of Indigenous headgear and their social contexts, as well as in weavers' fascination with foreign hat forms. The majority of hats were made for everyday use as work caps for both men and women. Some hats—through their culturally rich variety of shapes and designs—transmitted information about the wearer such as status and authority, family and clan, and personal achievements and wealth (the combination of net worth, material goods, and spiritual and behavioral qualities).

Indigenous women often wore practical basketry caps for daily work. For example, Hualapai and Moapa Paiute women wore caps to protect them from the sun of their desert region and to protect their heads from carrying-basket tumplines. Although slightly different in shape, these women's caps shown in figure 122 are rounded in profile; the curved shape made the hat fit a woman's head tightly, to alleviate pressure from the tumpline, and the brim stood out slightly from the wearer's forehead to shade her eyes.

Some of the most well-known caps, esteemed by both community members and collectors, are those produced on the Lower Klamath River of northwest California. One particularly fine example, made by a Yurok weaver, appears in figure 122 at the far left. Women wear these dress caps on ceremonial or important social occasions. Such a cap also is a sign of wealth. Even if a woman were a basket maker, she would not necessarily weave her own fancy hat, unless she were highly skilled: wealthy women obtained their caps from a basket weaver who was known to make the finest ones.

An excellent example of a social construction, the form of these caps was firmly established by each community; weavers diverged very little from the socially established size and shape. The ideal fancy hat is round with a flattened top, and steeply sloping sides which fit the wearer's head tightly around the rim, giving it a high crown. This uniqueness of fit and its consequence for the woven form are simple yet significant steps away from the everyday work hat.

Basketry hats of the Northwest Coast are striking examples of how baskets can be carriers of culture. The type of hat shown on the left in figure 123 is often referred to as an "onion-domed hat" in reference to its idiosyncratic top. This hat form is unique to the Nuu-chah-nulth whale hunt-

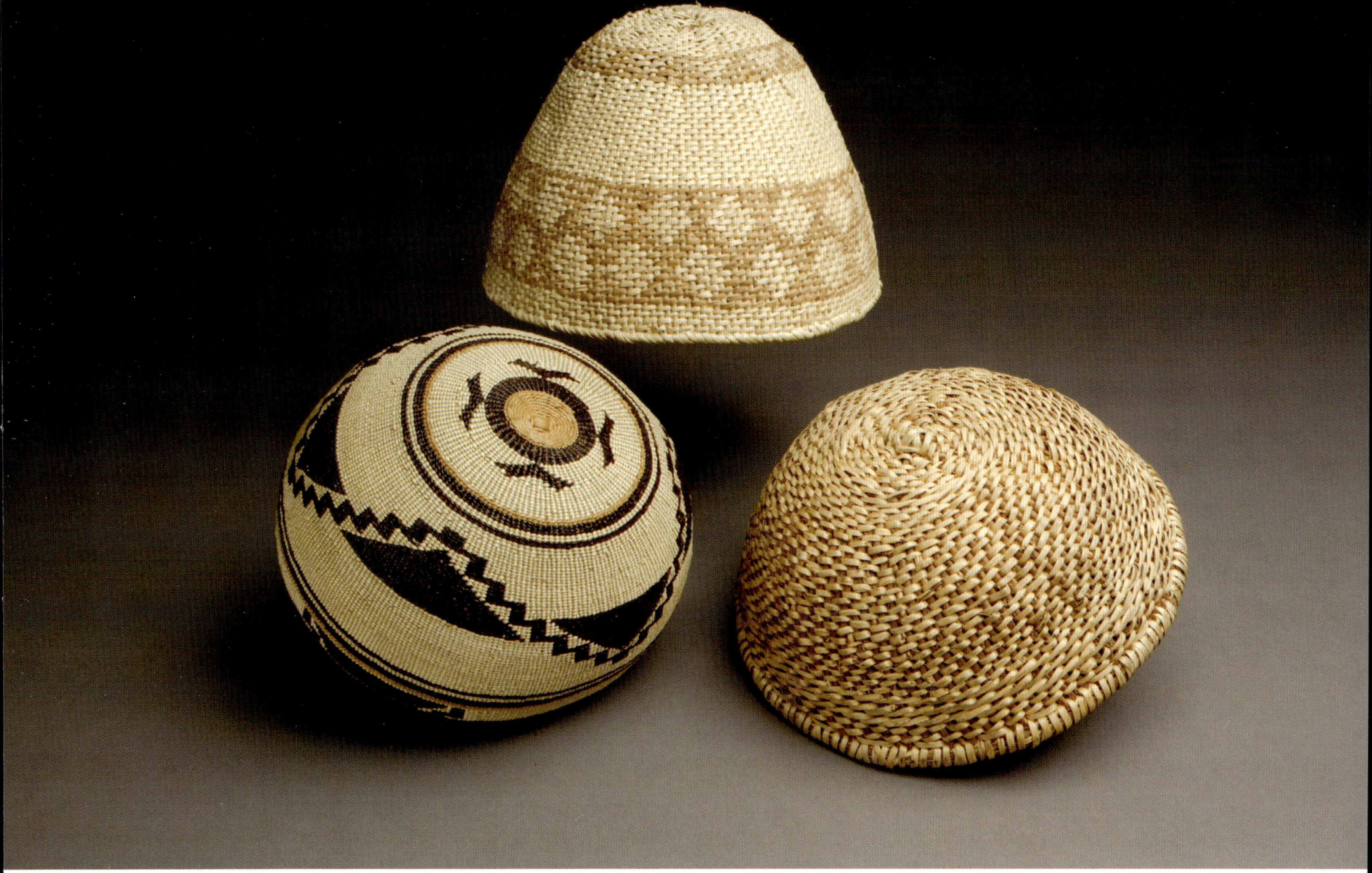

FIG. 122

Woman's Cap, c. 1930, Yurok, Artist unknown, 9.0 x 18.0 cm., 23267

Woman's Cap, 1930, Hualapai, Artist unknown, 10.0 x 20.5 cm., 10979

Woman's Cap, 1932, Moapa Paiute, Artist known as "Tangre," 14.5 x 22.0 cm., 9988

All three of these basketry caps were woven in the 1930s and (because they show no signs of wear) made for the commercial market. Ethnographers commissioned weavers to make the two work caps on the right for the Museum of Indian Arts & Culture: Dr. Alfred L. Kroeber commissioned the Hualapai cap, and Dr. Isabel Kelly commissioned the Paiute cap.

ers of the Nootka Sound region on the coast of British Columbia and to the whale-hunting Makah on the northwest tip of Washington State. The form has a long history on the Northwest Coast: examples have been found in archaeological sites dating back 2,500 years (Croes 1977:154). Later, when British ships under the command of Captain James Cook arrived at Nootka Sound, in 1778, members of this exploratory expedition collected a number of them (Devine 1980:26).

Onion-domed hats were most likely designed and woven only for chiefs and high-ranking whaling men; it is probable that a chief would have commissioned his hat from the best weaver in

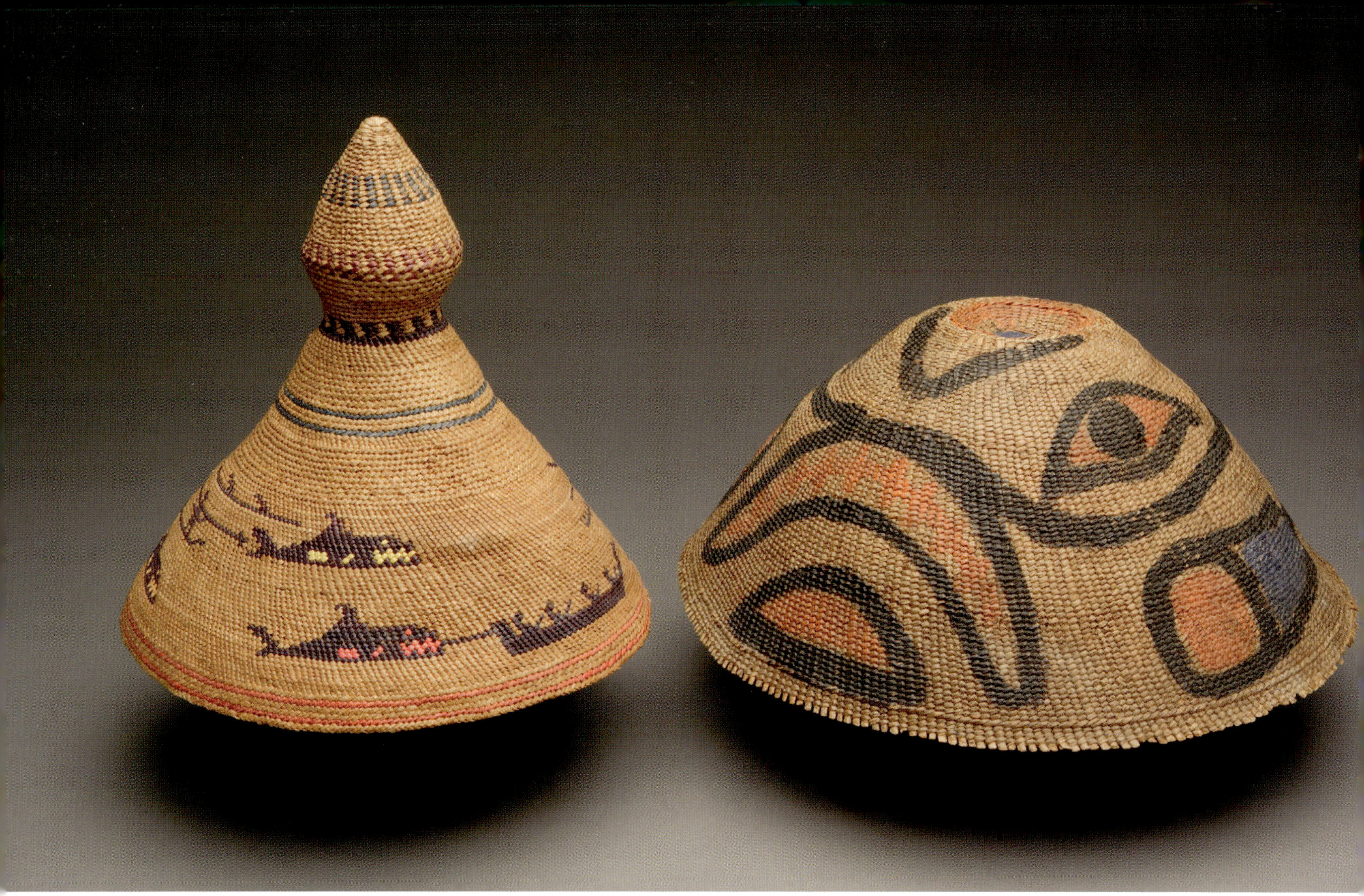

FIG. 123

Whaler's Hat, c. 1900, Nuu-chah-nulth, Artist unknown, 27.0 x 26.5 cm., 48236

Hat, c. 1900, Nuu-chah-nulth, Artist unknown, 17.0 x 35.0 cm., 31092

the village (Winther 2011:49). The onion dome, with its high difficulty of technique, is a deliberate indicator of virtuoso weaving. For Nuu-chah-nulth and Makah basket weavers and their communities, the onion-domed hat is both a status symbol and a testament to the skill of the wearer as a harpooner in the whale hunt (Winther 2011:48).

Another type of headgear made by weavers in the Northwest Culture Area is the rain hat, as seen on the right side of figure 123. This hat form reflects its use as utilitarian rain gear needed in the rainforest climate of the Northwest Coast Culture Area. In addition, this hat has a painted design—a whale portrayed in the form-line style unique to the area—intended to enhance the hat's commercial value. Although made for sale, this rain hat is also representative of the hats made in previous centuries that displayed the wearer's clan symbols and broadcast his identity to all observers.

It was common for Native artisans to make western-style clothing for sale to foreigners in a number of Indigenous materials (such as hide); the only form basket makers created in a western style was hats. Historically, the hat is among the articles of clothing that indicates social distinctions among both Native peoples and Anglo/Euro-Americans. Native basket weavers appear to have understood this, as can be seen in their large repertoires of western-style hats. During the summer months, these weavers probably saw Anglo/Euro-American men and women wearing fiber-made western-style hats, which they reproduced using indigenous plant fibers and their own construction techniques. For example, see the three fine Native-made western-style hats, spanning four decades, illustrated in figure 124.

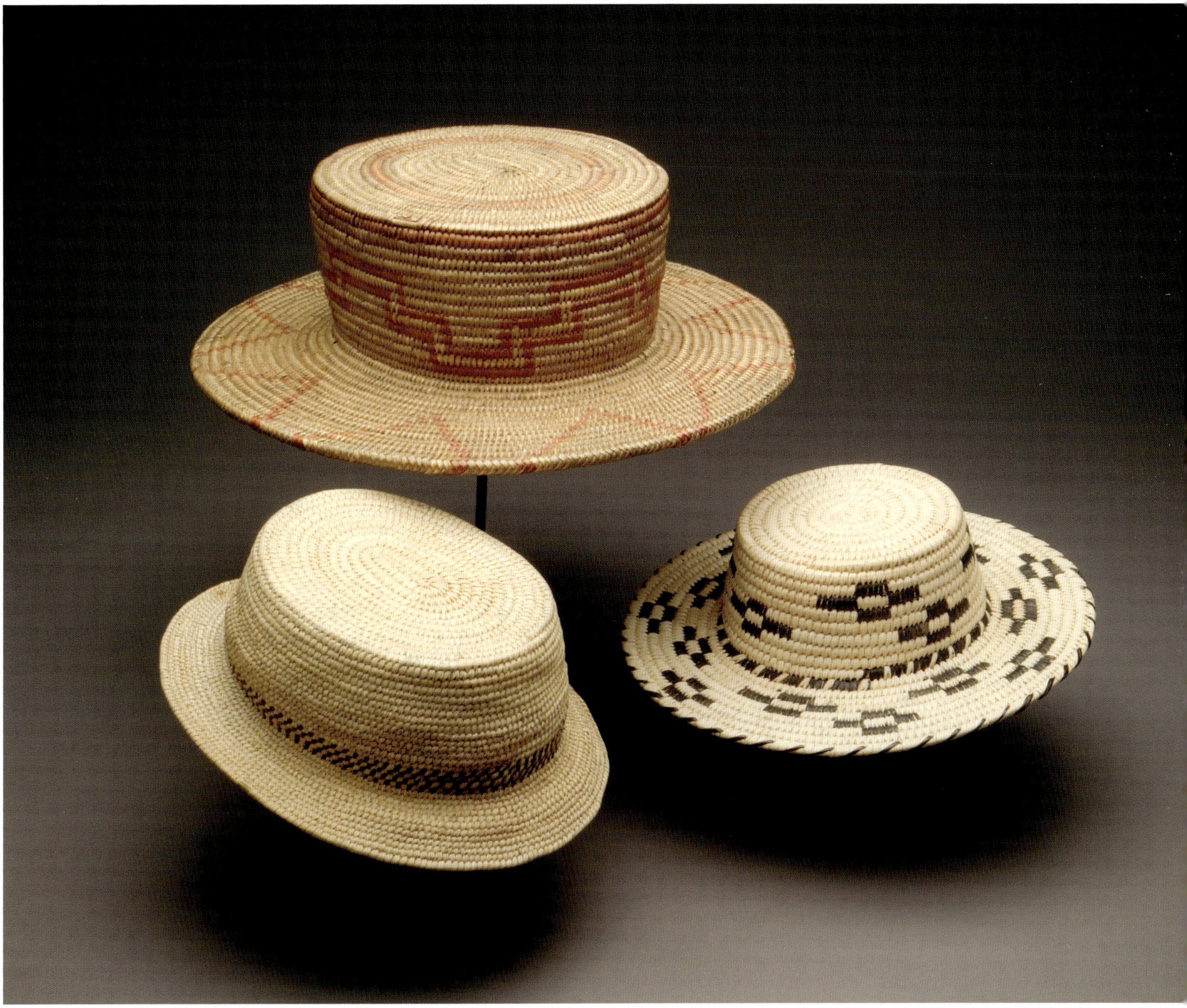

FIG. 124 (Left to right):

Hat, c. 1920, Tohono O'odham, Artist unknown, 8.5 x 25.0 cm., 1730
Hat, c. 1930, Jicarilla Apache, Artist unknown, 10.5 x 35.0 cm., 23526
Hat, c. 1960, Tohono O'odham, Artist unknown, 6.9 x 28.0 cm., 25413

SOCIAL AND CEREMONIAL BASKETS

Despite their struggle to survive over the last two centuries, Indigenous communities of western North America have continued to respect and observe their traditional social, religious, and ceremonial activities. Many of the basket forms that persisted into contemporary community life are those integral to these activities; it is during social and ceremonial occasions that a basket's function as a culture bearer is fully realized. The fact that basket weavers have retained a "mental template" for specific forms and can weave "proper baskets" for these occasions is evidence that the traditional values and beliefs unique to their community are still alive. All of the forms discussed in this section are still woven and celebrated today.

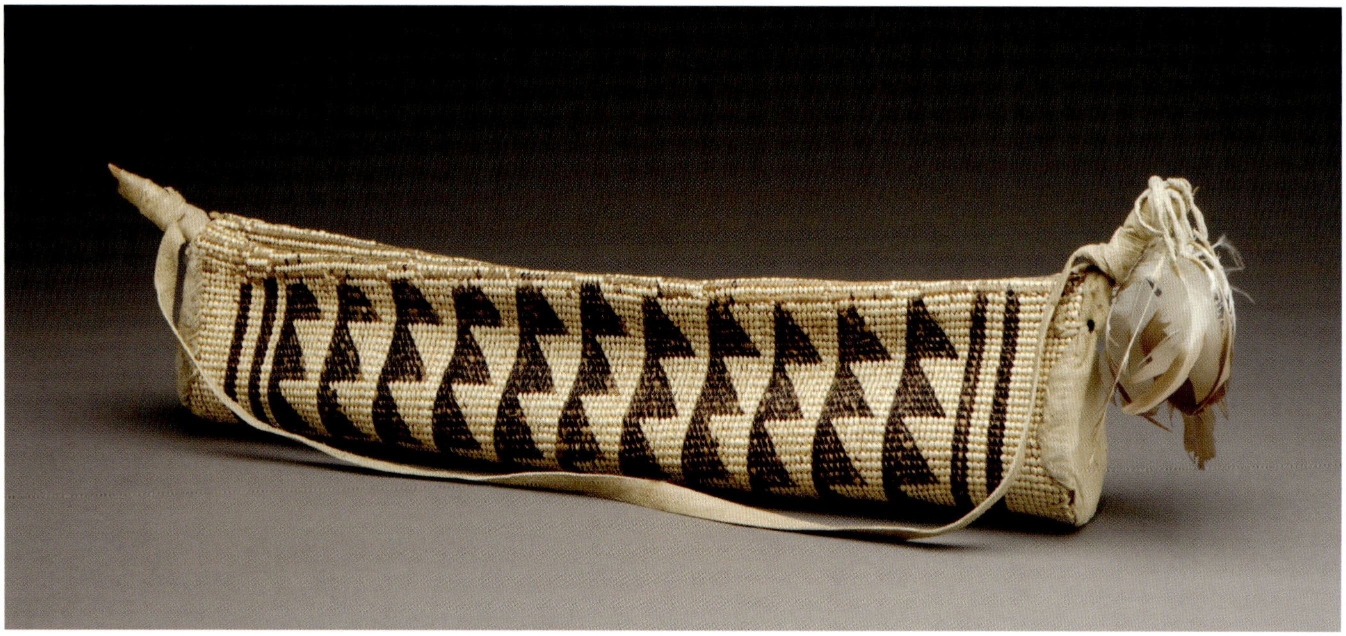

FIG. 125

Jump Dance Basket, c. 1900, Yurok, Artist unknown, 15.0 x 52.0 cm., 14311

Men and women join together to create dance baskets in the Native communities of northern California: women weave a flat mat that men then sew over two rods, closing the ends.

One type of ceremonial basket made by the Yurok of Northern California is carried in the Jump Dance by male dancers. The Yurok have long identified themselves as "Fix the Earth People," and the Jump Dance basket (see figure 125) embodies that belief. The Jump Dance, one of the Yurok's annual World Renewal ceremonies, is essential for reestablishing the balance necessary for maintaining the health of the fragile earth and its people. Anthropologist Alfred Kroeber observed that "not only is the physical world generically reestablished by the ceremony, but sickness, flood, and other calamities are specifically averted by it, and fish and plant foods are made abundant" (Kroeber and Gifford 1949:5).

Reciprocity is another example of how baskets personify the concept of keeping the world in balance. For the Hopi, giving baskets is central to the ritual exchanges that accompany important life stages, including birth, marriage, and death. Marriage exchanges are particularly significant examples, as they symbolize the merging of two families in the eyes of the community and are an occasion when balanced exchanges characterize an ideal union. One such exchange occurs after the groom's family has made the bride's wedding robes; the bride and her family reciprocate, or "pay back," with basketry plaques as soon as possible (Teiwes 1996:53–56).

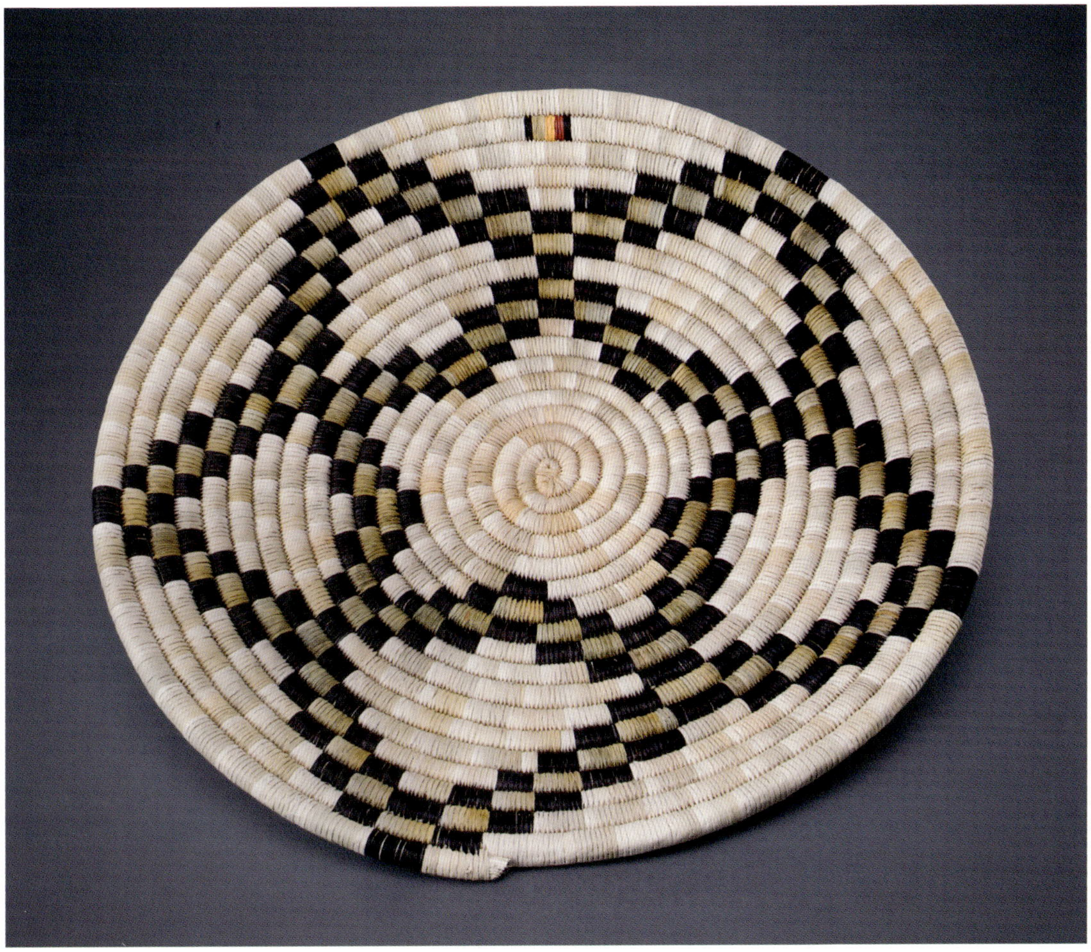

FIG. 126

Groom's Wedding Plaque, 2006, Hopi (Second Mesa), Joyce Ann Saufkie, 4.8 x 42.0 cm., 57190

Mandatory for a wedding payback, this type of Hopi basketry plaque is made for the groom, who will keep it throughout his life. Piled high with cornmeal, the plaque is delivered to the groom's mother on payback day. It is important that the rim coil on the plaque is not finished at the end (Teiwes 1996:57). In one interpretation it symbolizes the unfinished nature or beginning of a groom's life.

Another type of Hopi ceremonial basket is made for the Hopi Basket Dance, which takes its name from the food baskets that female dancers carry during the event. These baskets (or plaques) held during the dance and then given away represent the baskets that Hopi women traditionally weave to harvest, process, store, and prepare food. Other Hopi woven plaques are literally "run after" (Teiwes 1996:53): the winners of footraces associated with ceremonies are given plaques.

When visiting the Museum of Indian Arts & Culture, Hopi (Second Mesa) weaver Patty Wells discovered the coiled plaque shown in figure 127 in the museum's basket storage area. It caught her eye because of the two lines of clay painted across the surface. These, she said, marked the basket as having been given as a prize in a footrace (P. Wells, pers. comm., July 2012). After looking at this same basket, Lee Wayne Lomayestewa, from the Hopi village of Shungopavi (Second Mesa) and a member of the museum's Indian Advisory Panel, explained that footraces still take place during the yearly ceremonial cycle at Second Mesa where this basket was made. The runners, he said, who are Hopi or Hopi family members, begin their race on the flatlands and then ascend on historical trails to the top of the mesa to the finish line.

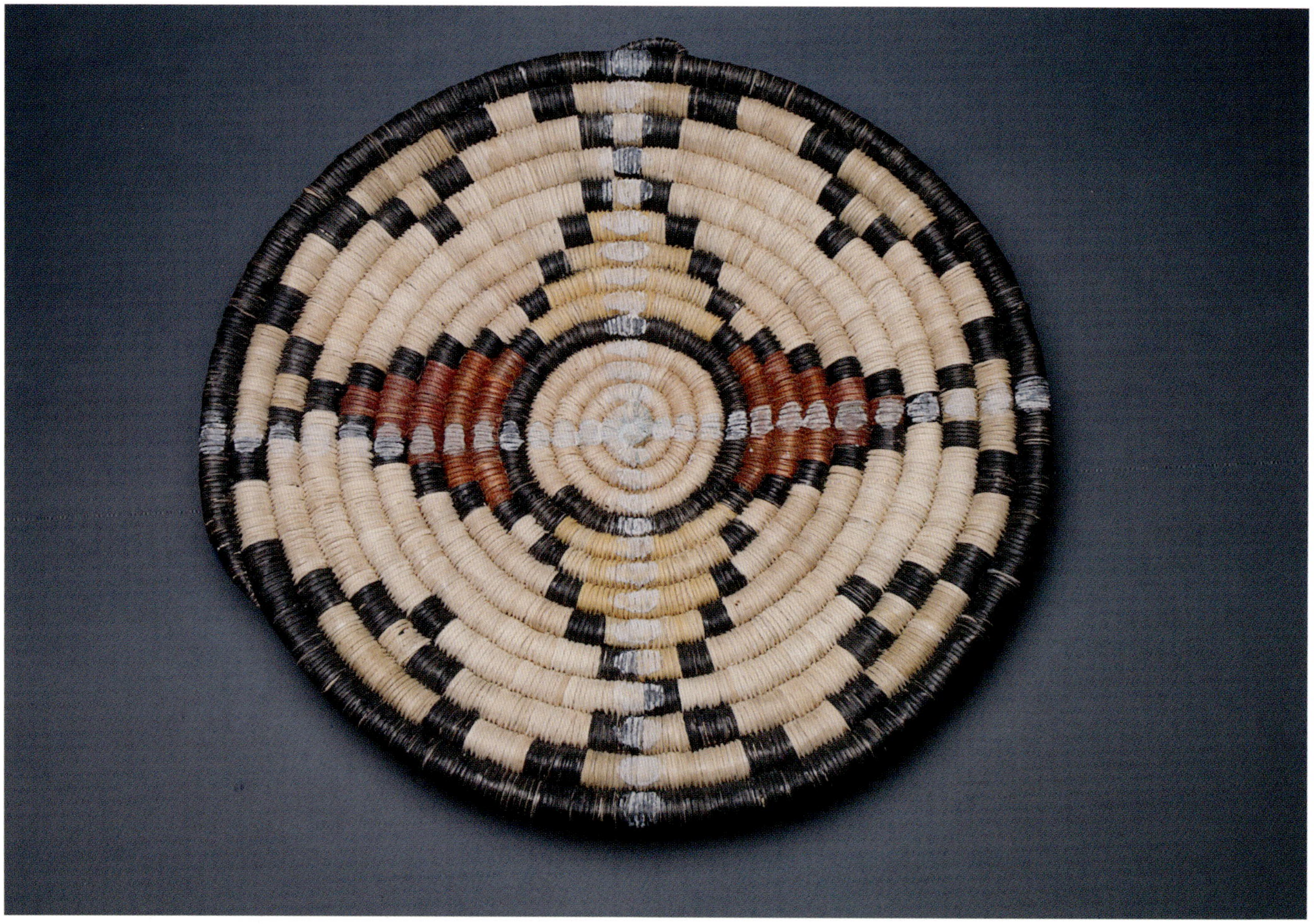

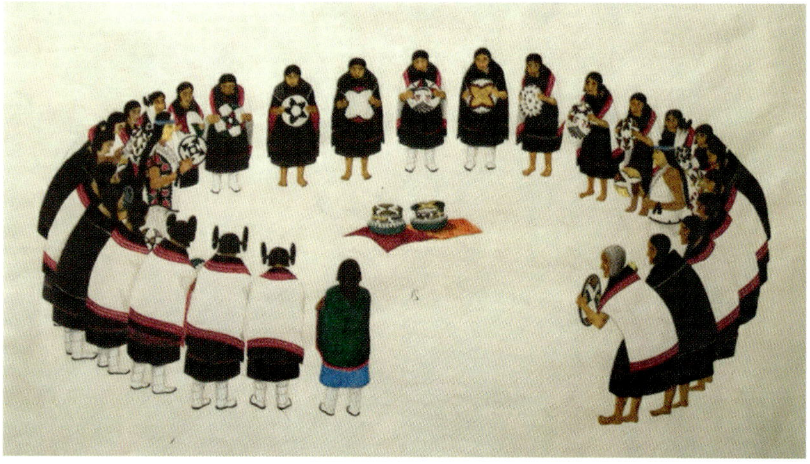

FIG. 127

Plaque, c. 1945, Hopi (Second Mesa), Artist unknown, 1.5 x 27.0 cm., 36609

This Hopi plaque was presented as a prize to the winner of a footrace at Hopi Second Mesa.

FIG. 128

Hopi Basket Ceremony, c. 1921, Fred Nakayoma Kabotie, watercolor on paper, 35.7 x 52.0 cm., Edgar L. Hewett Collection, 35485

A socially and culturally important basket form to the Hopi is the piki tray, on which piki bread is served; the tray is a utilitarian form connected with food preparation and preservation and a cultural form associated with the distribution of food and wealth in both the pre-contact and contemporary Hopi world. Piki bread is a significant food nutritionally, and the piki bread-making tradition is both a community and family event. Mothers teach their daughters the technique of making both the basket and the bread. To make piki bread, women finely grind blue corn and mix it with burnt ash. The resulting meal is blended with water to produce a light batter that is spread thinly over a hot piki stone. The result is wafer-thin bread. Sheets of the bread are folded three times in each direction and then rolled and placed on the specially-made tray. "True" piki trays are those sized to conform to a piki sheet. Trays such as the one shown in figure 129 can hold a pile of three or four dozen piki rolls, or three or four of the unrolled sheets required for specific ceremonies (Teiwes 1996:66).

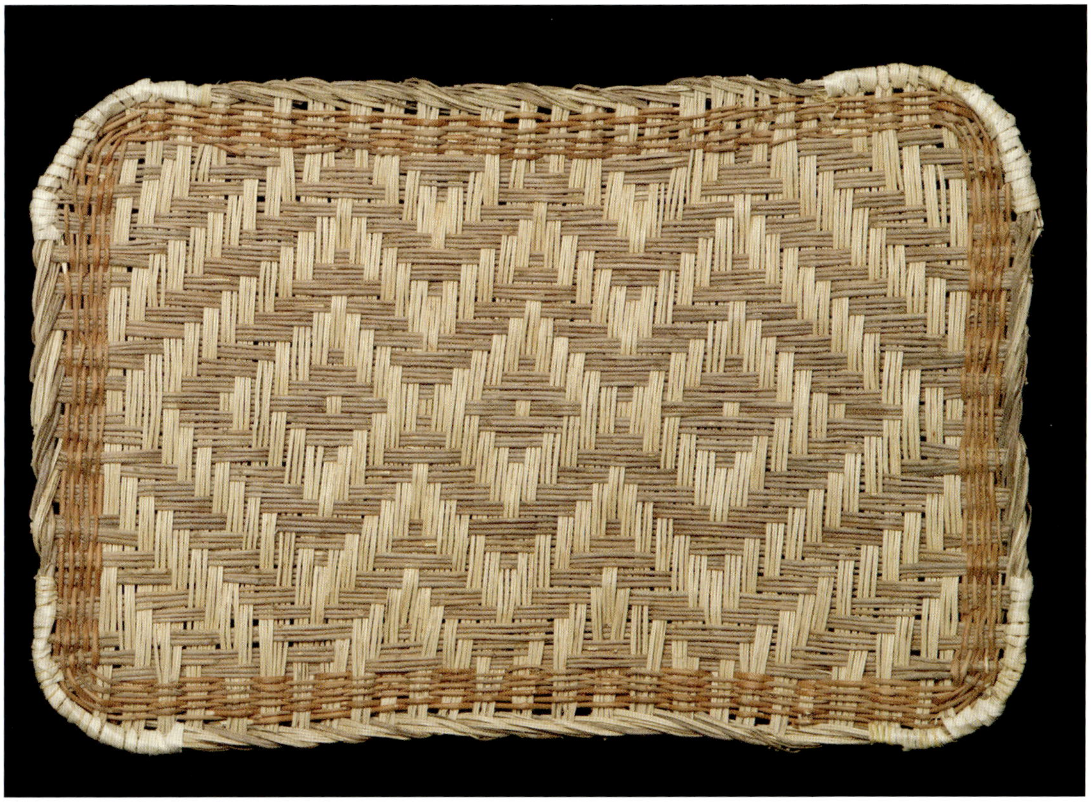

FIG. 129

Piki Tray, 1983, Hopi (Third Mesa), Fermina Banyacya, 48.3 x 33.0 cm., 50126

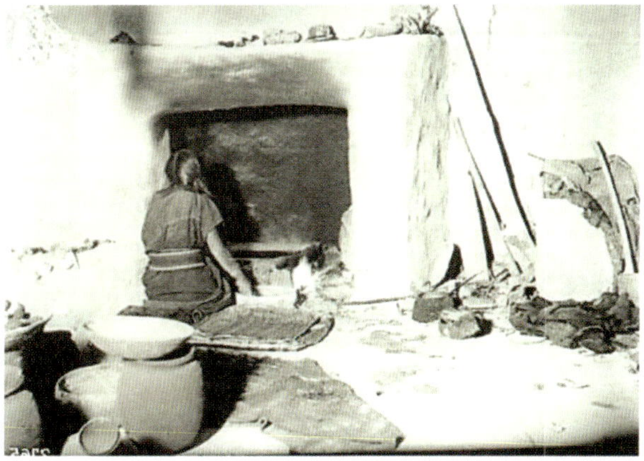

FIG. 130

A woman of Hopi Second Mesa cooks piki bread, c.1906. Photo by Edward S. Curtis. Courtesy of the Library of Congress. LC-USZ62-115802.

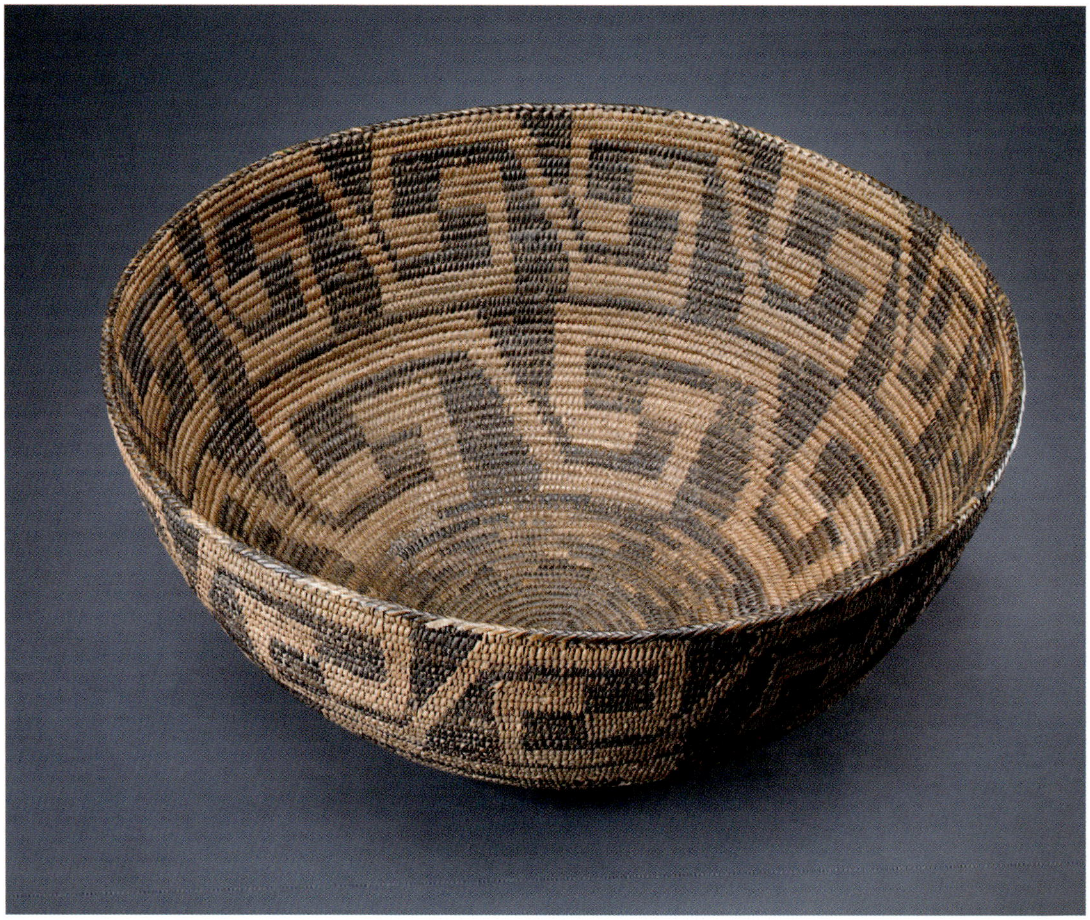

FIG. 131

Saguaro-wine Serving Bowl, c. 1885, Tohono O'odham, Artist unknown, 21.5 x 48.0 cm., 35959

As this catalogue and exhibition reveal, the study of baskets introduces us to amazing places, people, and events—baskets are truly an introduction to another world. One excellent example of this is the basketry bowl woven by the O'odham for holding saguaro-cactus wine. The saguaro cactus, iconic of the landscape of southern Arizona, produces an edible red fruit. When the fruit ripens in June, O'odham women and children knock the fruit from the cacti with long poles made from the woody ribs of dead saguaro. The fresh fruit can be eaten, made into syrup, or the seeds ground into flour. Each family saves some of the fruit's juice to donate to their village saguaro-wine festival. In preparation for this ceremony, the community's medicine men ferment the juice in the village Rainhouse for three days. Then all the men gather to "sing down the rain" and "drink down the clouds" until all the saguaro wine is gone. Afterward, the O'odham plant their crops to take advantage of the rains that will surely saturate their fields.

The late Tohono O'odham basket weaver Frances Manuel relates her experiences harvesting saguaro fruit at her family's camp:

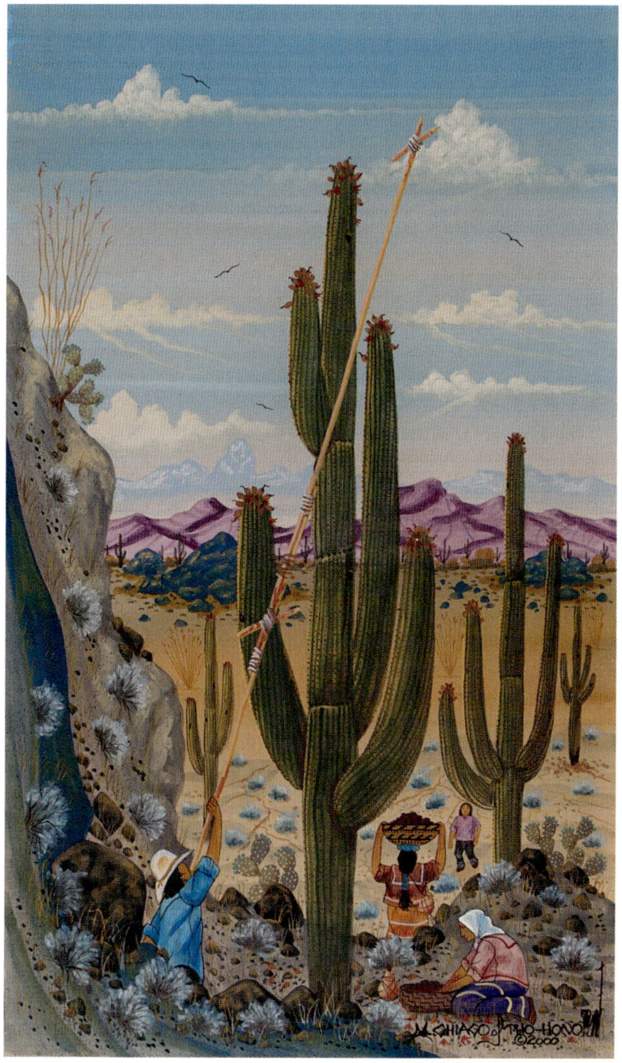

FIG. 132

Picking Saguaro Fruit, 2000, Tohono O'odham, Michael Chiago, watercolor on paper, 52.0 x 35.7 cm., Private collection.

When I got here [to San Pedro], my in-laws used to camp way out on that side of the mountain [pointing to a mountain called Komalk]. That's to harvest saguaro fruit. I would go with them because that's the only time I got out. Well it was hard, hard work, because we had to get up at four o'clock in the morning, and come back and cook breakfast and eat and cook the saguaro, and then start boiling it. Maybe by two o'clock the syrup will be ready and then we'll go after some more. We'd leave it for the night, and the next day we'd go for some more. We'd do it for five days. But boy, everything was good to eat, we'd be so hungry. That's about all we'd do, we'd go to bed early on the earth (Manuel and Neff 2001:25).

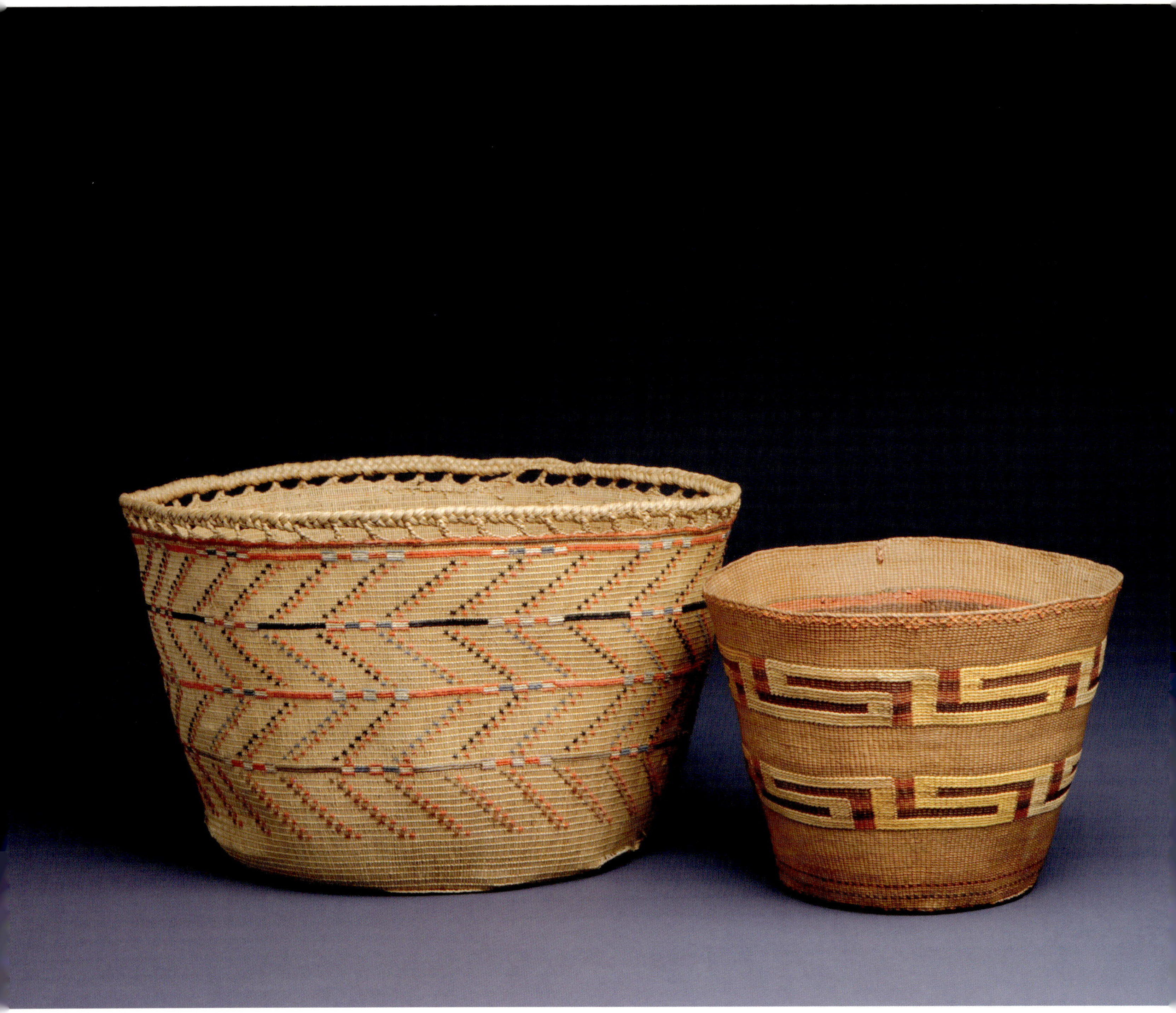

FIG. 133 (Left to right):

Carrying Bag, c. 1900, Unangan, Artist unknown, 20.5 x 31.5 cm., 14320

Fancy Gathering Basket, c. 1885, Tlingit, Artist unknown, 16.0 x 20.4 cm., 25435

In creating their geometric designs, Unangan basket weavers first incorporated split bird quills and then, when they became available as trade items, replaced quills with worsted and silk embroidery thread. Tlingit basket weavers incorporated geometric, principally banded, designs in their work.

Chapter 4

DESIGN AND ORNAMENTATION

The two-dimensional design elements used on Indigenous basketry are distinct, or iconic, in most tribal traditions. The characteristics of a good design vary but usually include the balanced use of culturally appropriate motifs, skilled depiction, and inherent meaning. As a rule, ornamentation is applied primarily to gift, treasure, personal, and ceremonial baskets, as well as to baskets made for sale.

Two-dimensional basket designs are conceptual expressions—they represent thoughts, emotions, and things through a system of symbols that, when commonly understood by a community of people, is akin to a language. The meanings and significance of basket designs are difficult to decipher, therefore, because of the need to understand each basketmaking culture's language and because interpretations of designs vary even within individual communities. This is due in part to the fact that in cultures with oral histories most symbols have no fixed meaning; symbols and designs continuously acquire new meanings, depending on changing contexts (Lévi-Strauss 1966). Additionally, because communicating the nature and meaning of a design is analogous to storytelling, interpretations have the potential to vary with each narrator and narration.

Every symbolic system, whether it is language, math, music, or a visual art like basketry, is a way for people to share ideas. When an Indigenous woman first learns to weave, she learns to read and reproduce a visual language of design principles; she draws from this language every time she creates designs for her baskets. Working within tribal conventions does not necessarily limit a basket weaver's options; instead, it encourages the weaver to focus on experimentation and choice making within the visual language she has learned. A basket weaver will develop a repertoire of designs that are identified with her throughout her life; however, she usually will not construct a design in exactly the same way twice. In the Northwest Coast Culture Area, some weavers create dream designs inspired by the supernatural spirits; however, even within these new designs traditional motifs are incorporated (Schlick 1994:106).

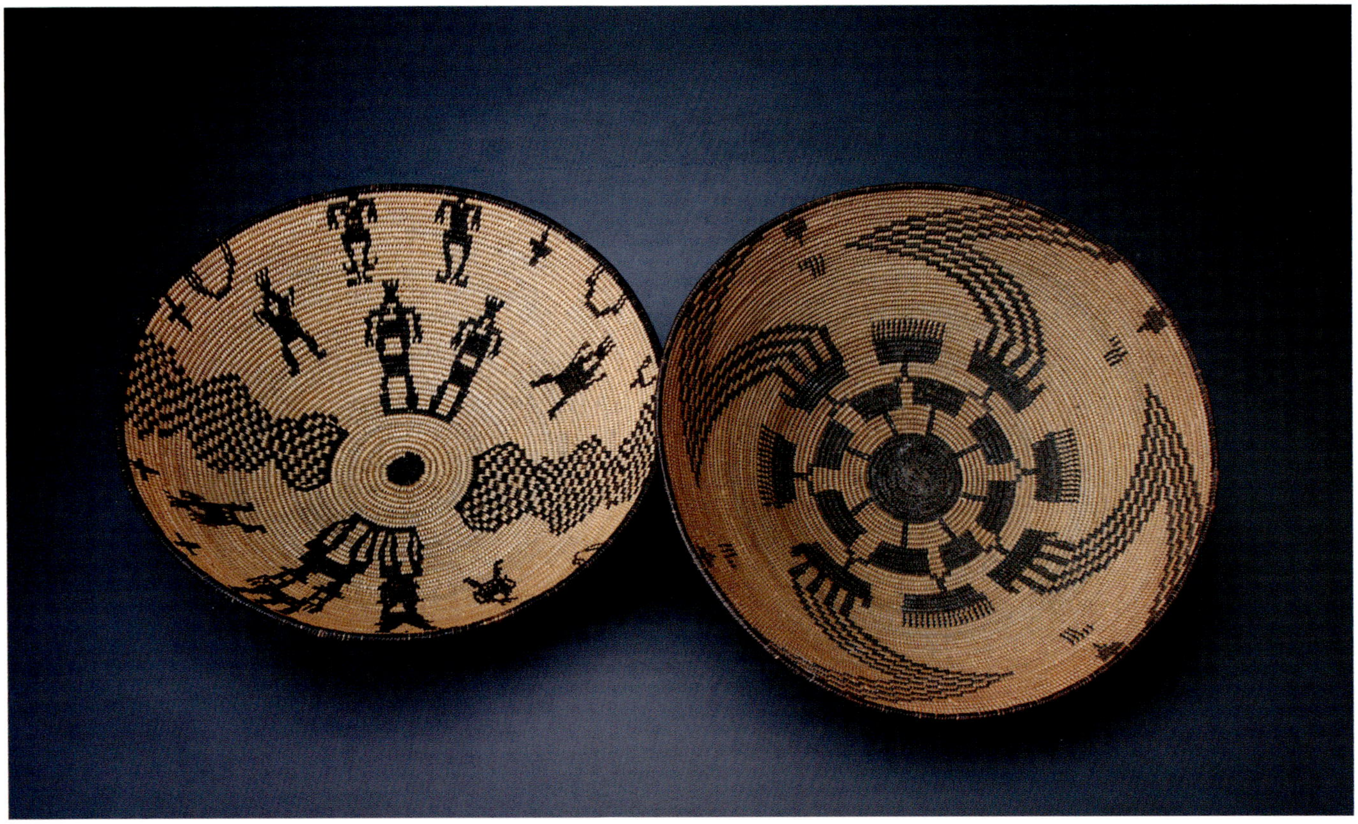

FIG. 134 (Left to right):

Bowl, c. 1905, Western Apache, Artist unknown, 10.0 x 40.5 cm., 23672

Bowl, c. 1900, Western Apache, Artist unknown, 12.5 x 39.5 cm., 31132

Among the designs featured on Western Apache basketry are images relating to the Mountain Spirits, or Mountain Spirit Dancers, also called Gaan Dancers (see basket at left). The Mountain Spirit Dancers personify these sacred beings; by embodying these spirits, the dancers physically manifest the spiritual world. Masked-dance performances of the Apache Gaan Dancers may be used to protect against illness, to cure, and to control the weather (Opler 1941). Natural phenomena are also respected by the Western Apache; in particular, lightning is an important power concept (see the basket at right). In the Apache creation myth, the Creator makes Lightning-Rumbler before creating the Earth, and leaves him in charge of clouds (which are his home) and rain. Lightning is a frequent design motif used in basketry and other art forms throughout the American Southwest.

Metaphors—symbols that express the intangible in terms of the concrete—are a key element of Indigenous art, including basketry. The metaphors may represent natural and cosmological forces, death and renewal, or a mutable and fluid world in which all things are animate and imbued with spirit (Ahtone 2009:380). One way to understand Native American cosmology and religion is in terms of power (Gill and Sullivan 1994:242). To know and convey myths, stories, prayers, and songs; to conceive of and practice ritual; to develop beliefs that identify one locus of power in the natural world; and to be able to call upon creators and communicate with gods are all concepts that signify connections to power and give life meaning.

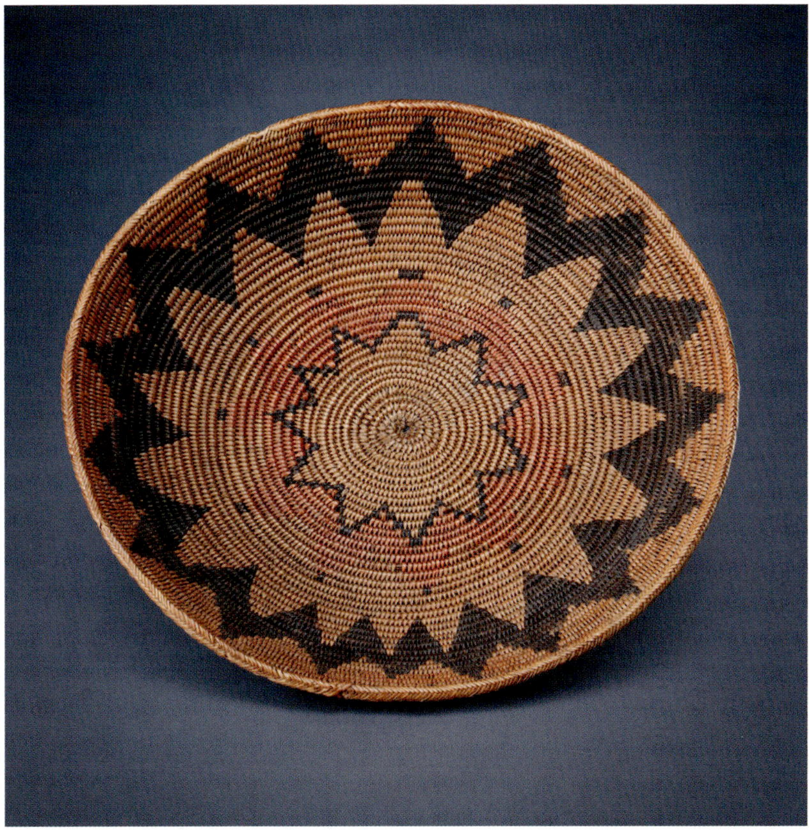

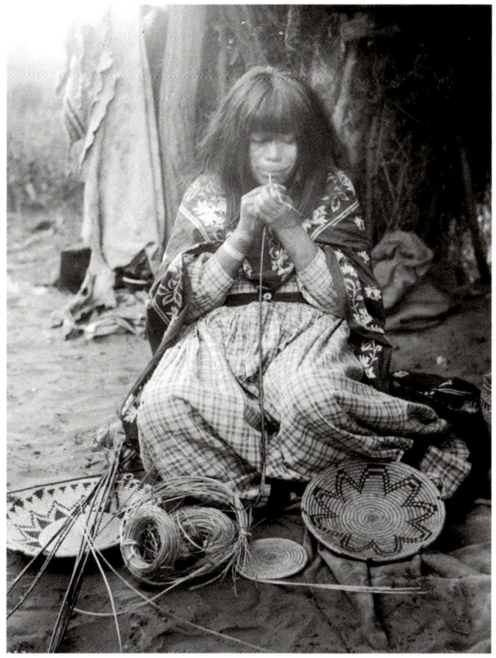

FIG. 135

Tray, c. 1900, Havasupai, Artist unknown, 7.8 x 36.2 cm., 25094

This floral design is executed in bands, a common organizational technique of Havasupai basketry design. The layout begins in the center with a thin black band, followed by a red band, a band of wide-spaced checks, and then a thick black band (repeating the center band).

FIG. 136

Havasupai basket weaver, c. 1900. Photo by Charles C. Pierce. Courtesy of the California Historical Society Title Insurance and Trust/C. C. Pierce Photography Collection. CHS-3371.

Native basket designs are made up of individual elements called motifs. The names of these motifs may be purely descriptive, such as a triangle or square, or may denote a quality or thing in the basket weaver's environment, such as a star or coyote tracks. While many motifs may be named simply as a point of reference, others have names that serve a function. These names may differentiate the concept of a motif in one cultural context from its meaning in another. Or, because a motif's identity is constructed by the weaver, its name may reflect how she wants her audience to perceive it and, by extension, herself, her family, and her community or tribe. Over time, a basket motif's identity may evolve and acquire new attributes, meanings, and names.

Contemporary basket weavers pass down design motifs and their meanings through oral history, and this may also have been true in the past. Cahuilla basket weaver and teacher Donna Largo (1944–2009), who learned to weave from her grandmother and other mentors, passed down a family story that is one account of how the rattlesnake motif came to be:

My grandmother told me a story about the rattlesnake and how it got into the basket. She said the women would all sit around on the ground making baskets and a rattlesnake kept coming toward one lady. And she'd chase him away and chase him away. And he kept coming back. And finally she told the rattlesnake, "If you don't go away, I'm going to put you in my basket." Well, he wouldn't go away, so that's how we got rattlesnakes in our baskets (Bibby 1996:92).

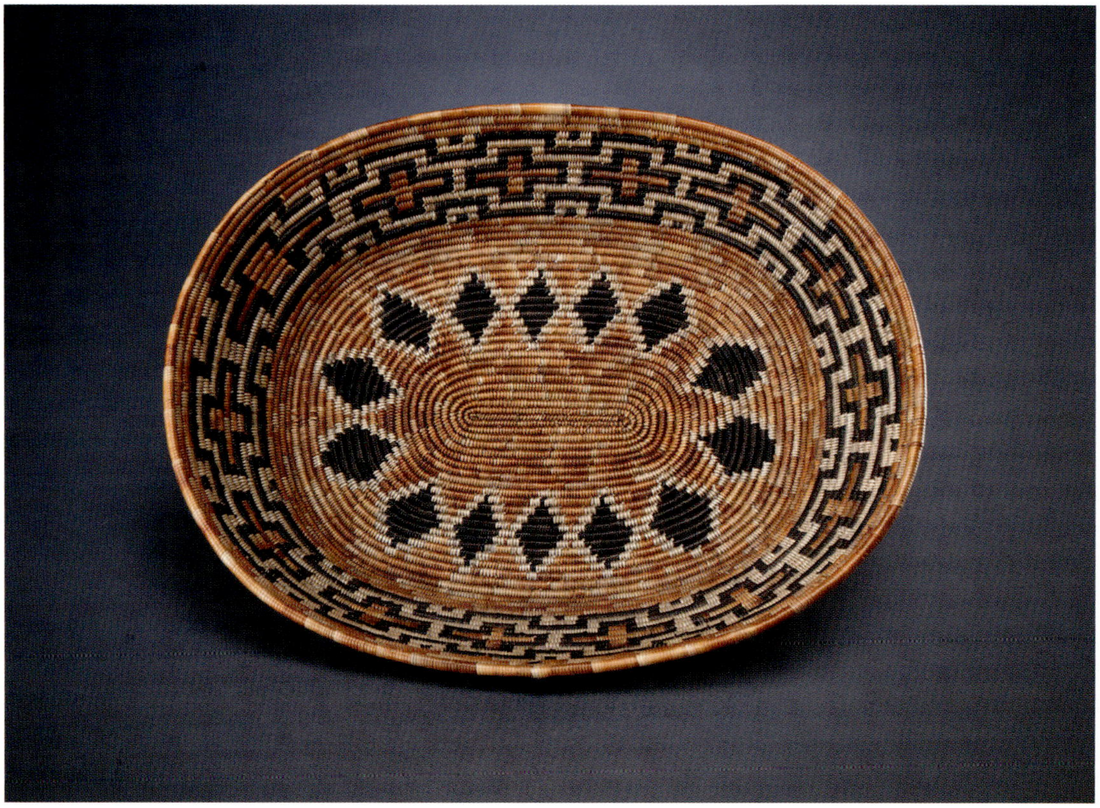

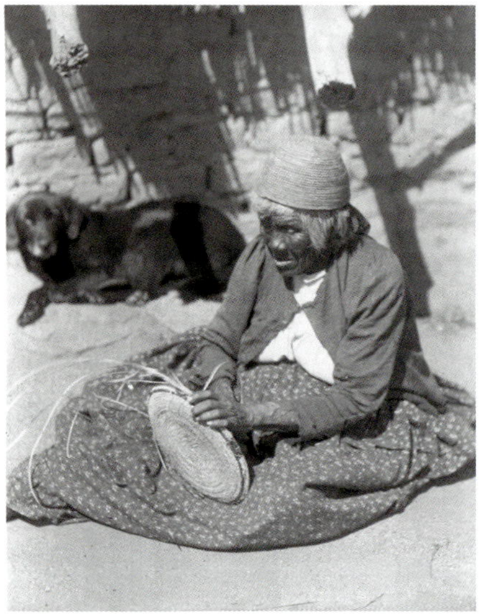

FIG. 137

Tray, c. 1920, Cahuilla, Artist unknown, 7.0 x 36.0 cm., 23774

The center design band of this Cahuilla basket is constructed of diamonds visually associated with the diamond-back rattlesnake (thus named the "rattlesnake design"). Some southern California weavers' snake designs are far more literal and include the snake's head, forked tongue, and rattle.

FIG. 138

Cahuilla basket weaver Maria Casseri, c. 1899. Photo by George Wharton James.
Courtesy of the California Historical Society Title Insurance and Trust/C. C. Pierce Photography Collection. CHS-4747.

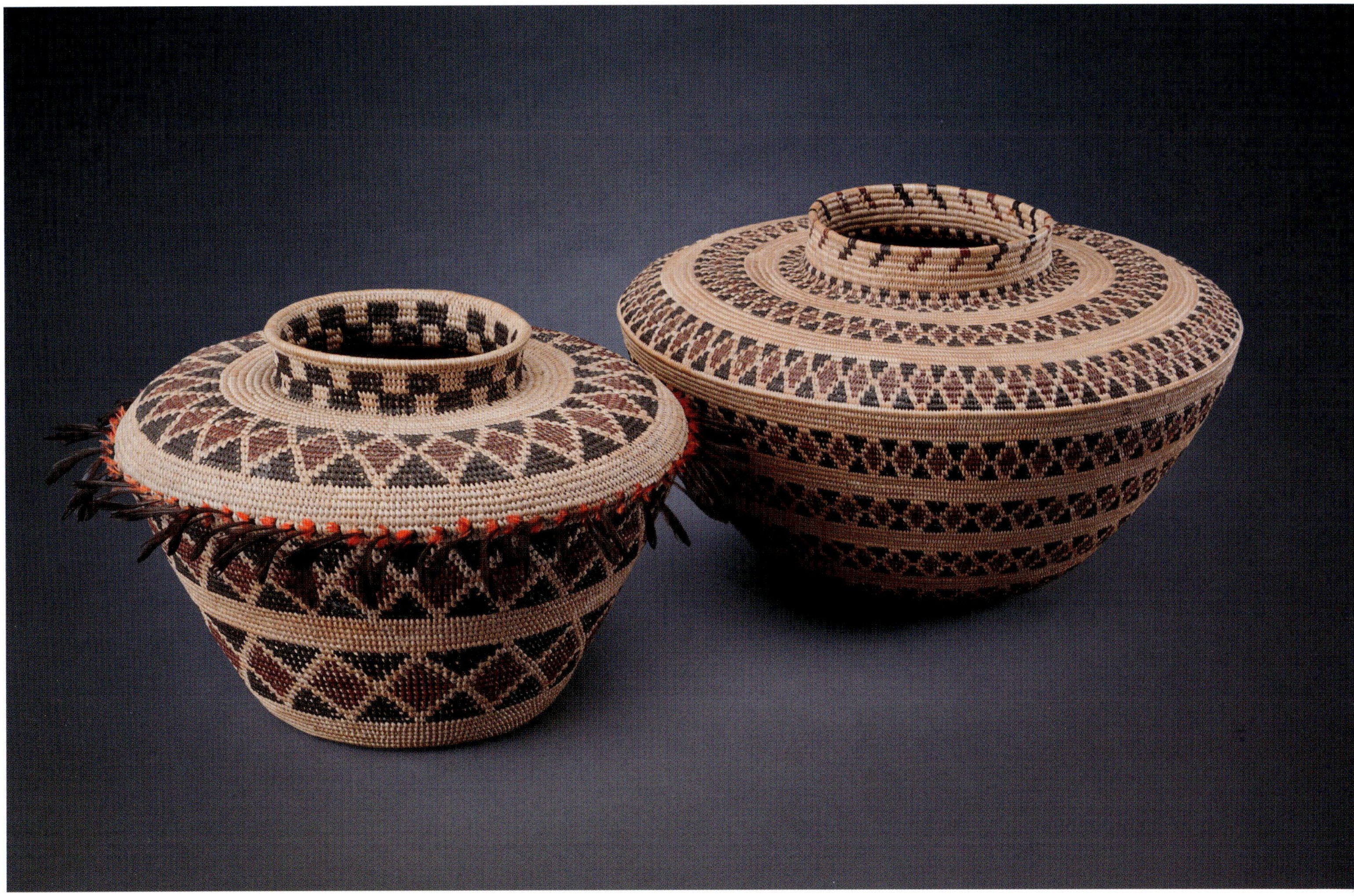

FIG. 139 (Left to right):

Gift Basket, c. 1910, Yokuts, Artist known as "Old Charley's Wife," 16.5 x 28.0 cm., 14304

Jar, c. 1910, Yokuts, Artist known as "Wife of Joe Joloa," 17.5 x 31.0 cm., 14300

Banded-triangle motifs, referred to as "rattlesnake designs," were common on Yokuts baskets of the early twentieth century. Because bottleneck baskets were containers for personal valuables, they are referred to as "treasure," or "gift," baskets.

As the snake story suggests, each tribe's iconic designs are linked to perceptions, experiences, and beliefs that are unique to each culture's worldview. The designs that emerge—geometric, figurative, and narrative designs—are characteristic, then, of each community's visual language. Furthermore, cultural values define the standards by which Indigenous weavers judge design suitability, beauty, and integrity. Contemporary basket weavers often combine new artistic visions (or new designs) with established traditions and motifs. In this way, they keep the traditions alive and vital: when she alters an iconic design or creates a new one with personal or contemporary allusions, a weaver creates baskets that are relevant in the present, enabling her audience to relate to her art in a meaningful way.

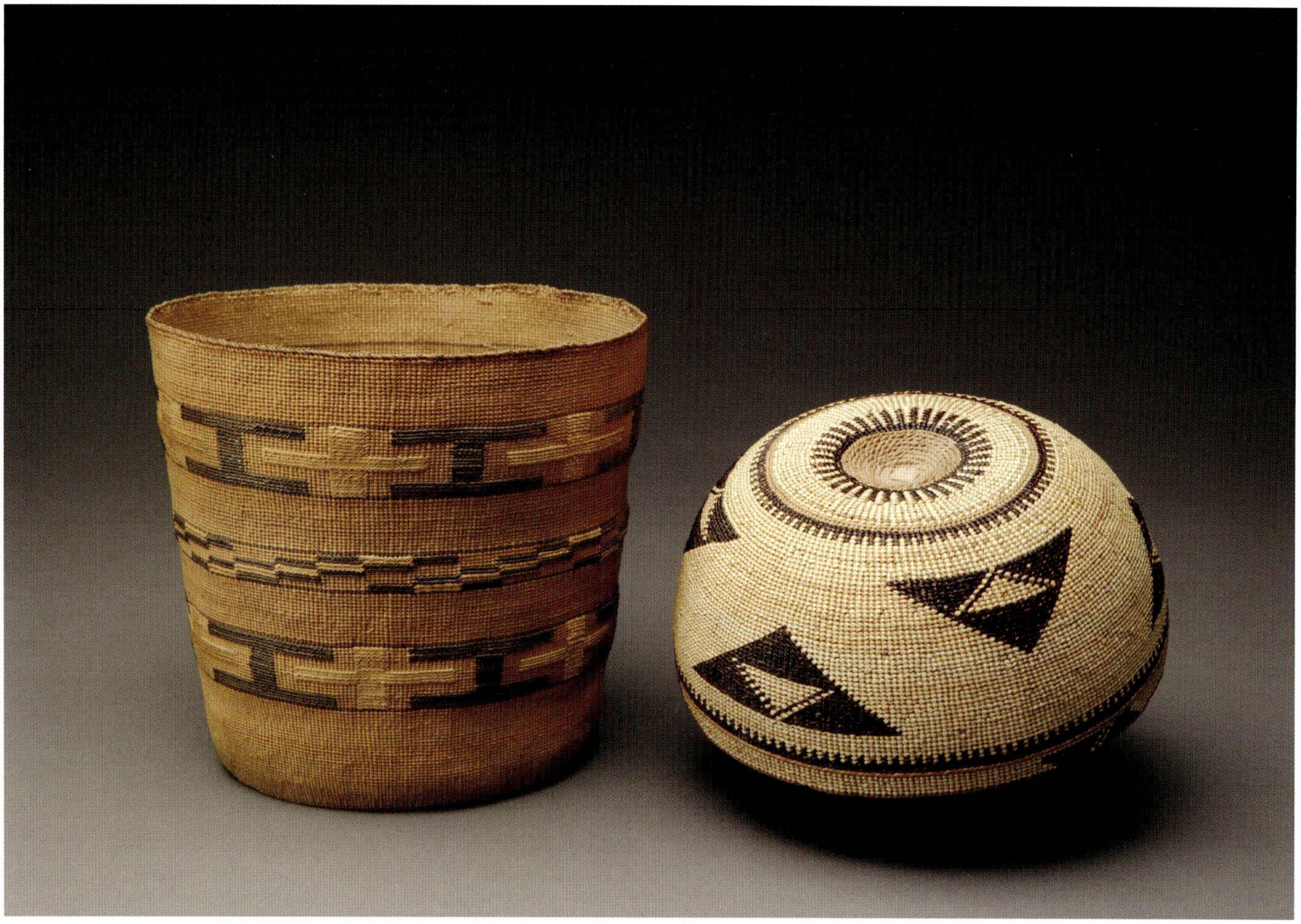

FIG.140 (Left to right):

Cylinder, c. 1950, Tlingit, Artist unknown, 19.0 x 17.5 cm., 48637

Woman's Cap, c. 1930, Lower Klamath River, Artist unknown, 9.0 x 19.0 cm., 23716

Tlingit basket weavers place their designs within bands. For example, in the basket at left the weaver created three distinct design fields using thin, dark, framing lines. (Interestingly, only the framing lines are visible on the inside of the basket.) Similarly, the Lower Klamath River weaver of the basketry cap on the right divided her design into three bands or zones, using a row of wrap twining. Zone one is the crown of the cap, zone two is the wall, and zone three is the narrow band at the rim.

ICONIC DESIGNS

Within every basketmaking culture there are conventions of visual organization that determine how design fields are defined, what motifs are used, and how motifs may be combined to create allover designs. These principles are the basis of Native basketry design: iconic works of art whose common hallmarks traditionally are simplicity, consistency, and geometric abstraction.

Basket weavers generally learn designs through observing and following the example of a skilled weaver who serves as a mentor, and younger basket makers are able to establish bonds with their mentors and perpetuate their tribal traditions by weaving designs which fit within their community's visual conventions. This apprentice relationship, usually contained within families, has led to the standardization of designs that overtime become iconic. The power of a basket weaver's artistry is evident in her use of traditional basket designs that are timely, culturally significant, and emotionally resonant.

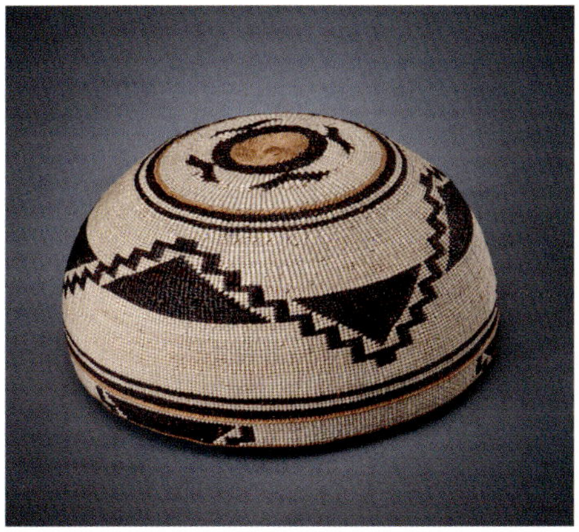

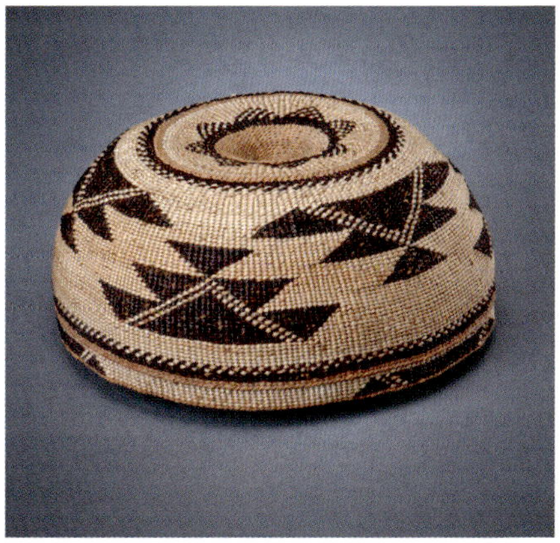

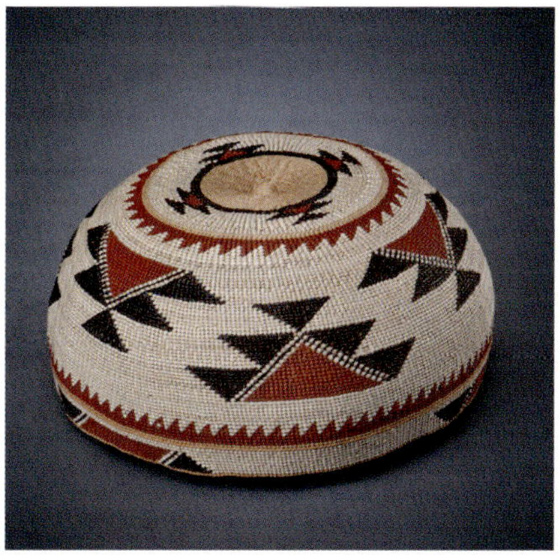

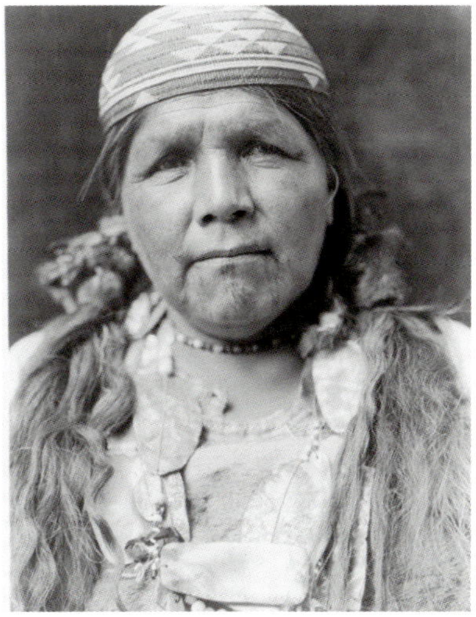

FIG. 141

Woman's Cap, c. 1930, Yurok, Artist unknown, 9.0 x 18.0 cm., 23267

Woman's Cap, c. 1930, Lower Klamath River, Artist unknown, 9.0 x 17.0 cm., 23715

Woman's Cap, c. 1945, Yurok, Artist unknown, 8.0 x 17.1 cm., 54586

These three basketry caps represent a range of designs from the simple to the complex. All of the weavers followed Lower Klamath River tribal design conventions, including the division of the caps into three design fields as well as the proper choice and placement of motifs within each field.

FIG. 142

Hupa shaman, c. 1923. Photo by Edward S. Curtis. Courtesy of the Library of Congress. LC-US62-115024.

GEOMETRIC DESIGNS

Indigenous basket weavers have very specific notions of what constitutes good design. One early example was recorded by ethnologist Lila O'Neale, who interviewed Yurok and Karuk basket weavers living along the Lower Klamath River in California, in 1932. When the weavers evaluated their community's baskets, harmony and moderation were the two design characteristics that won their praise. Harmony was located in the repetition and equal spacing of design motifs, in the division of the basket into primary and secondary design fields, and in the relationship between the designs in each field. Harmony was also the criteria when examining the relationship between basket size and scale of the design; weavers praised those baskets in which the design motifs were scaled to the form. The weavers also praised baskets that exhibited moderation in the elaboration of the design; they felt designs should be reserved and yet not too sparse.

Iconic O'odham basket designs are derived primarily from various lines: straight, curved, concave and convex, parallel and horizontal, and interconnected. Ancestral O'odham basket makers wove together variations of several linear motifs, including the "meander"—a maze-like motif consisting of linear elements filled with twists and turns. A second ancestral design is based on an equilateral cross with four arms bent at 90 degrees, usually with a white center (see figure 145.) A third, often used as an isolated motif, consists of the four-arm cross (its straight arms distinct from the bent-arm cross; fig. 143). A fourth ancestral O'odham iconic motif is the squash blossom flower; the two baskets in figure 144 have four-petal and three-petal squash blossom designs.

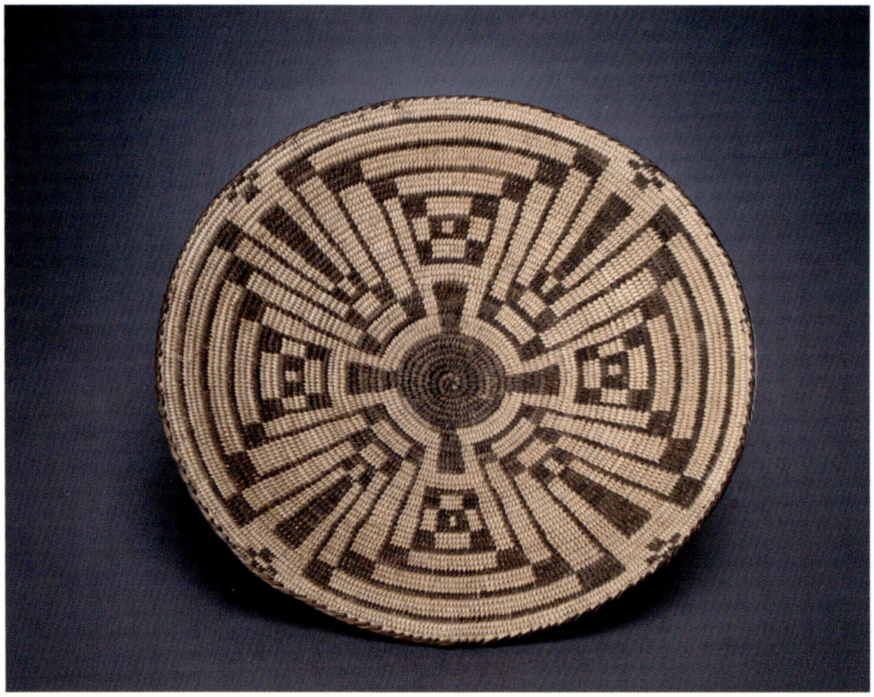

FIG. 143

Tray, c. 1910, Akimel O'odham, Artist unknown, 4.0 x 32.7 cm., 48196

The black-and-white designs created by O'odham basket weavers strike an equilibrium that confounds classification of visual space. In constant visual play, their designs have foregrounds and backgrounds that switch places in endlessly dynamic and visually intriguing ways. Also illustrated here is repetition, the basis of learning and memory in oral cultures and a common feature of O'odham basketry design.

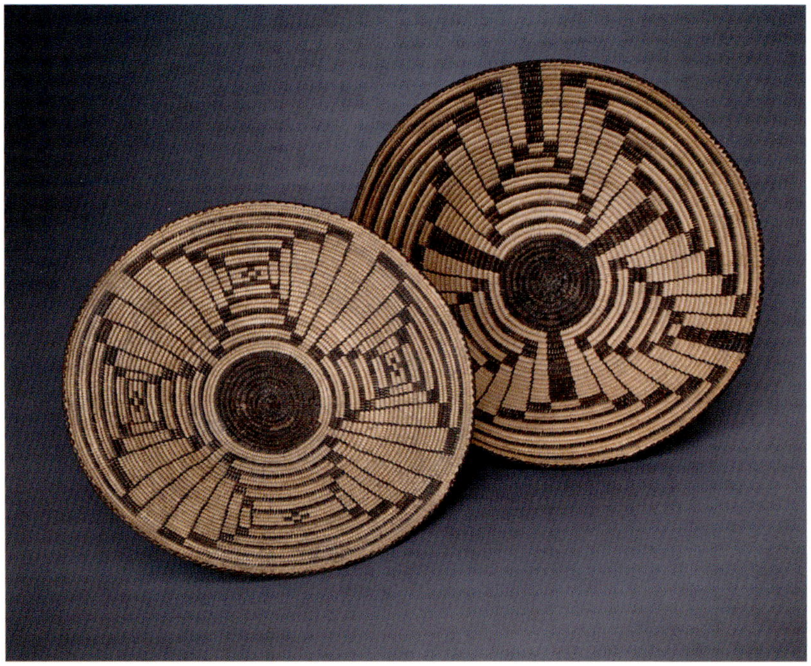

FIG. 144 (Left to right):

Tray, c. 1900, Akimel O'odham, Artist unknown, 7.0 x 41.5 cm., 23381

Bowl, c. 1900, Akimel O'odham, Artist unknown, 14.0 x 45.0 cm., 31083

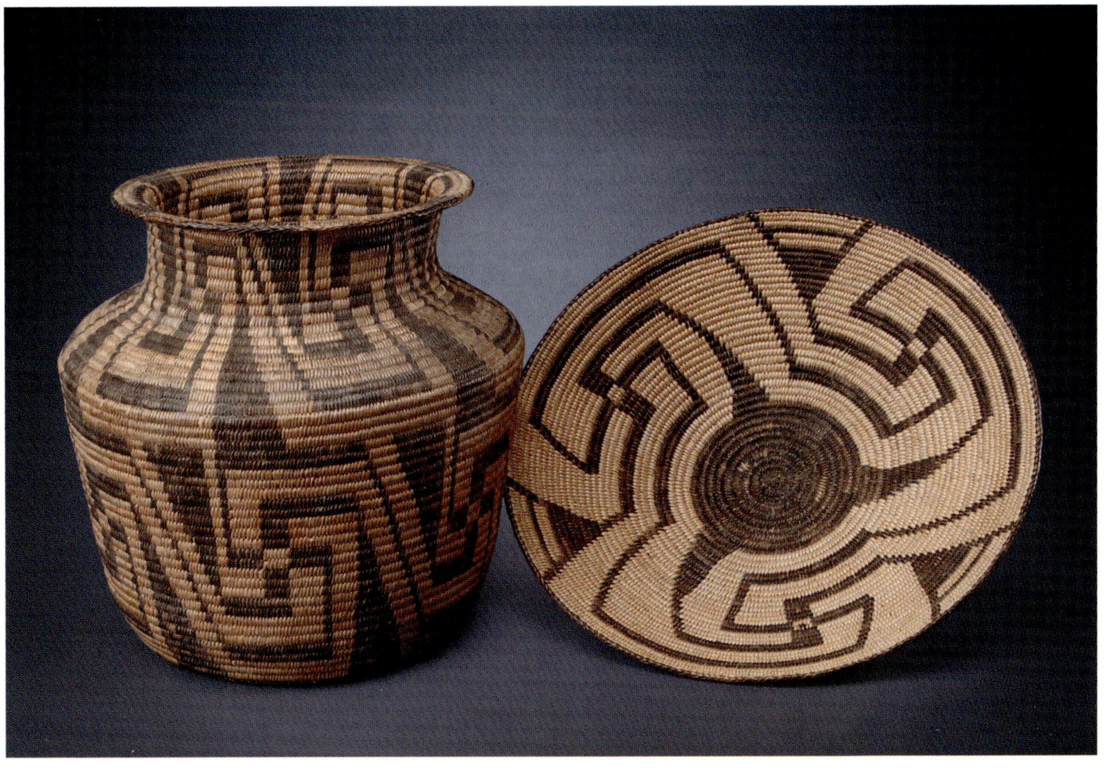

FIG. 145 (Left to right):

Jar, c. 1900, Akimel O'odham, Artist unknown, 36.0 x 29.0 cm., 25425
Tray, c. 1900, Akimel O'odham, Artist unknown, 11.0 x 40.0 cm., 31091

According to O'odham artistic canons, repetition in basket design is a positive trait. In repeating or reproducing a design meticulously, an O'odham weaver displays her control over mind, hand, and material, and achievement and competence (Glassie 1993:162–163). And yet, O'odham basketry artists are able to skillfully create endless subtle variations on these traditional geometric motifs.

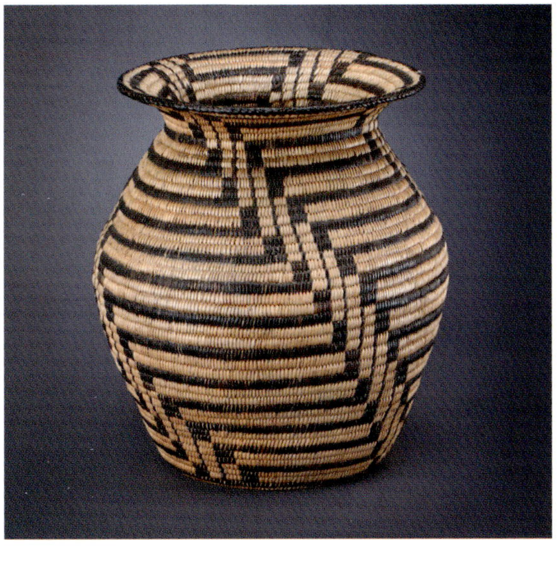

FIG. 146

Jar, c. 1910, Akimel O'odham, Artist unknown, 30.0 x 26.1 cm., 23681

When they began making baskets for the art market, in the late 1880s, Indigenous basket weavers proved their art to be both adaptable and enduring. Design became more important on these baskets made for sale; when skillfully applied, the design motifs complemented the beauty of traditional form by accentuating its shape. For example, in this basket the Akimel O'odham weaver combined two distinct cultural motifs to create a unique design that flows with the form.

The cultural history of many basketmaking tribes have become so intertwined that it is difficult to distinguish one community's basketry style/motifs from the other. One such example is found in the intermixing of basketry traditions of the Yavapai and Western Apache. There is no clear consensus among scholars on how these two basketry traditions became related in pre-contact times (Gifford 1932:249; Robinson 1954:79–84; Tanner 1982:178–181); however, some information on the general historical connections between them are known. According to studies of the Spanish interactions with the two tribes, early Spanish settlers did not recognize the Yavapai as a tribal group distinct from Apachean people (Khera and Mariella 1983:40). Furthermore, during the American reservation period (1880–1960), Western Apache and Yavapai people were interned together at the San Carlos Indian Reservation in Arizona. Social interaction and intermarriage between the two tribes served to blend their two basketry traditions even more. Unfortunately, there are no studies of individual Yavapai or Apache basketry artists from 1880 to 1930, a period when highly skilled basket weavers were experiencing a renaissance of artistic productivity. This may be because anti-Apache sentiments resulting from the Apache Wars (which ended in 1886) precluded Yavapai and Apache basket weavers from promoting themselves to the outside world; or because cultural beliefs may have inhibited sharing the oral histories of the dead. The isolation of Yavapai and Apache tribal lands from railroad lines and tourist attractions may also have curtailed the study of weavers from these two tribes (Dittemore and Notarnicola 1999:59–60).

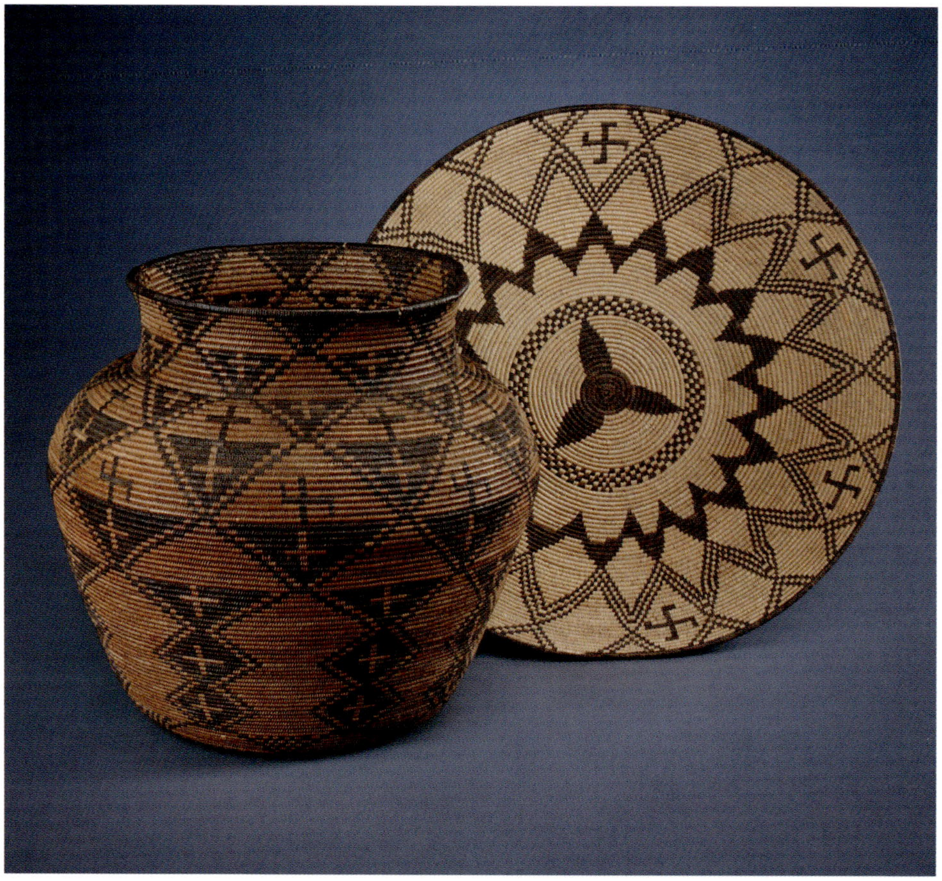

FIG. 147 (Left to right):

Tray, c. 1900, San Carlos Apache, Artist unknown, 7.0 x 51.0 cm., 23633

Jar, c. 1890, Yavapai, Artist unknown, 36.0 x 36.5 cm., 25424

Because the San Carlos Apache and Yavapai have so much in common, both culturally and historically, it is often difficult to tell their basketry apart. The materials and weaving techniques they used are identical, and they used many of the same design motifs. For example, the weavers of these two baskets used similar design motifs—the equilateral cross with four arms bent at 90 degrees and checkerboard linear elements—albeit in slightly different ways. In addition, both weavers used black rim wrapping on their baskets.

FIGURATIVE DESIGNS

The use of figurative designs—such as human figures, animals, plants, insects, and other recognizable things—in Indigenous basketry developed when weavers began making baskets for sale; the new motifs either replaced or were integrated with geometric motifs. One reason figurative motifs were popular with tourists and basket collectors was because these images had meanings easily understood by cultural outsiders, while geometric motifs generally had abstracted meanings known only by cultural insiders.

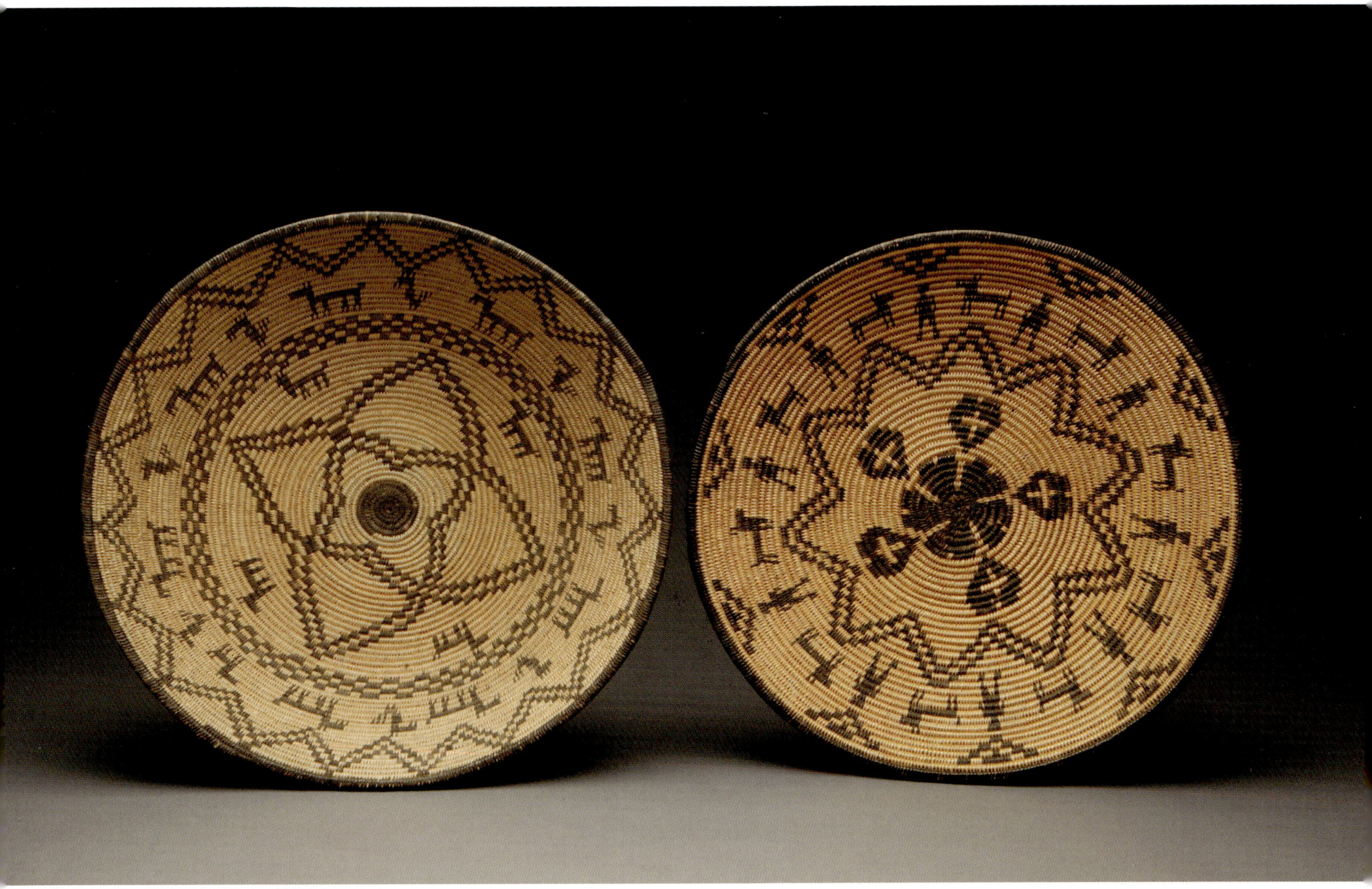

FIG. 148 (Left to right):

Bowl, c. 1905, Western Apache, Artist unknown, 13.5 x 43.5 cm., 49934
Tray, c. 1915, White Mountain Apache, Artist unknown, 8.0 x 42.5 cm., 1050

The earliest designs on Indigenous western North American basketry consist of geometric shapes and abstractions. After colonization, weavers began to increasingly experiment with new motifs inspired by the introduced images, including those on foreign goods and in books, newspapers, and magazines. Weavers continued making baskets with conventional geometric patterns but often combined them with figurative motifs that appealed to the non-Native market.

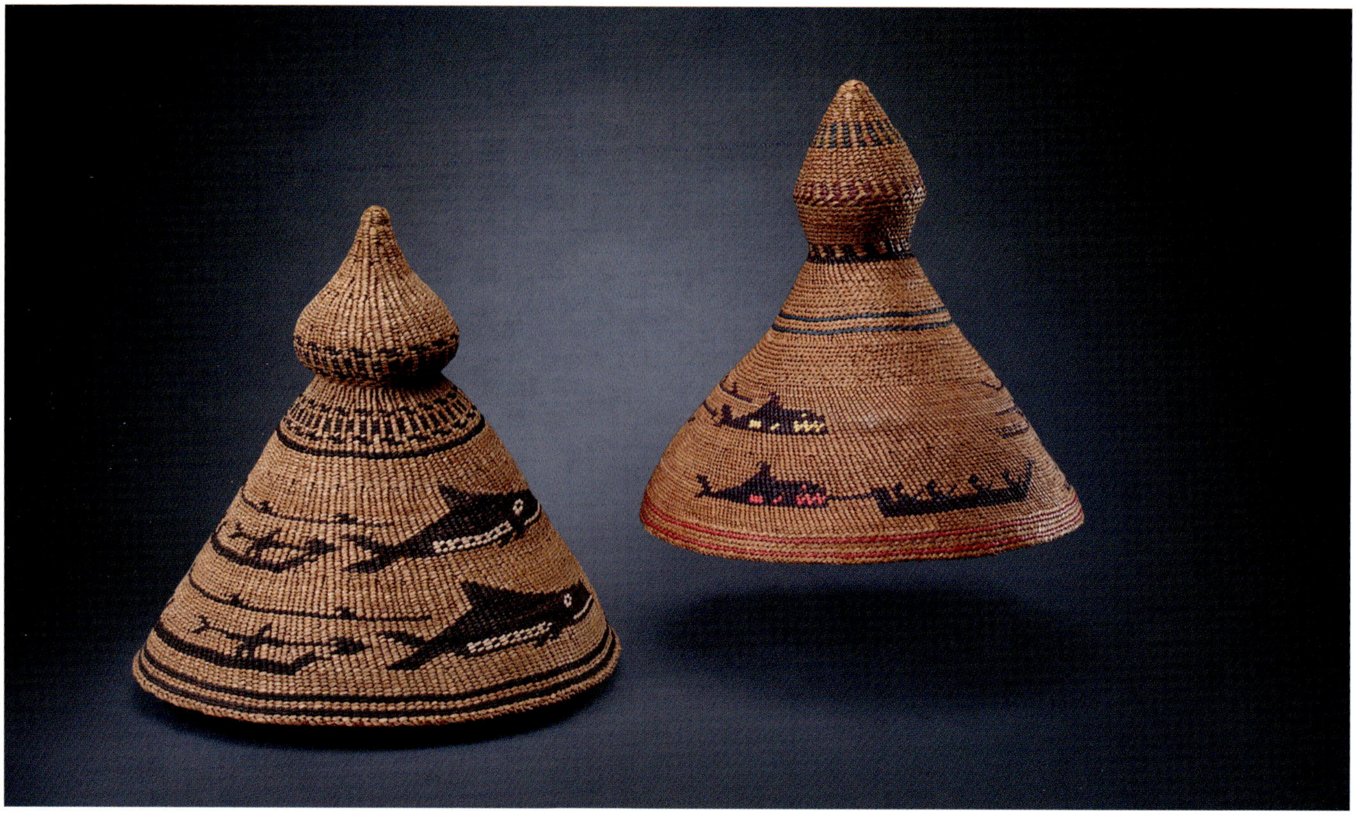

FIG. 149 (Left to right):

Whaler's Hat, c. 1900, Nuu-chah-nulth, Artist unknown, 27.0 x 26.5 cm., 48236

Whaler's Hat, c. 1900, Nuu-chah-nulth, Artist unknown, 20.0 x 27.8 cm., 57849

Whalers' hats were an especially elaborate type of Northwest Coast basketry hat. Usually, they employed both form and design intended to convey information about the wearer's status and achievements.

Some Indigenous basket weavers created figurative designs that reflected important elements of their own worldview. For example, the designs on these two hats in figure 149 by Nuu-chah-nulth weavers portray whale hunts at the dynamic moment when the chiefs are about to throw their harpoons. The whale hunt is oriented on the hats to run counterclockwise, the direction that the chief (who is also the harpooner) moved during a ritual performance he would have enacted prior to his participation in a hunt, as well as the direction the hunters planned to approach and move with the whale, and the way they hoped the whale would move. The hat is not worn during the hunt, but rather it is a visual reminder to the community of the importance of the whale hunt, as well as an expression of the respect that must be shown for the whale (Winther 2011:48). The weavers of these basketry hats took the three-dimensional shape into consideration when creating the designs: their dynamic figurative scenes must be experienced from more than one side.

While some Native basket weavers created figurative designs which reflected elements of their own worldview, others chose to strike out into new territory. For instance, the basket lid made by a Makah weaver (illustrated in figure 150), in about 1900, portrays a double-peacock design—a contemporary motif that was popular in the decorative arts of the aesthetic movement (1860s to early 1900s). The movement was characterized by the cult of the beautiful and an emphasis on the

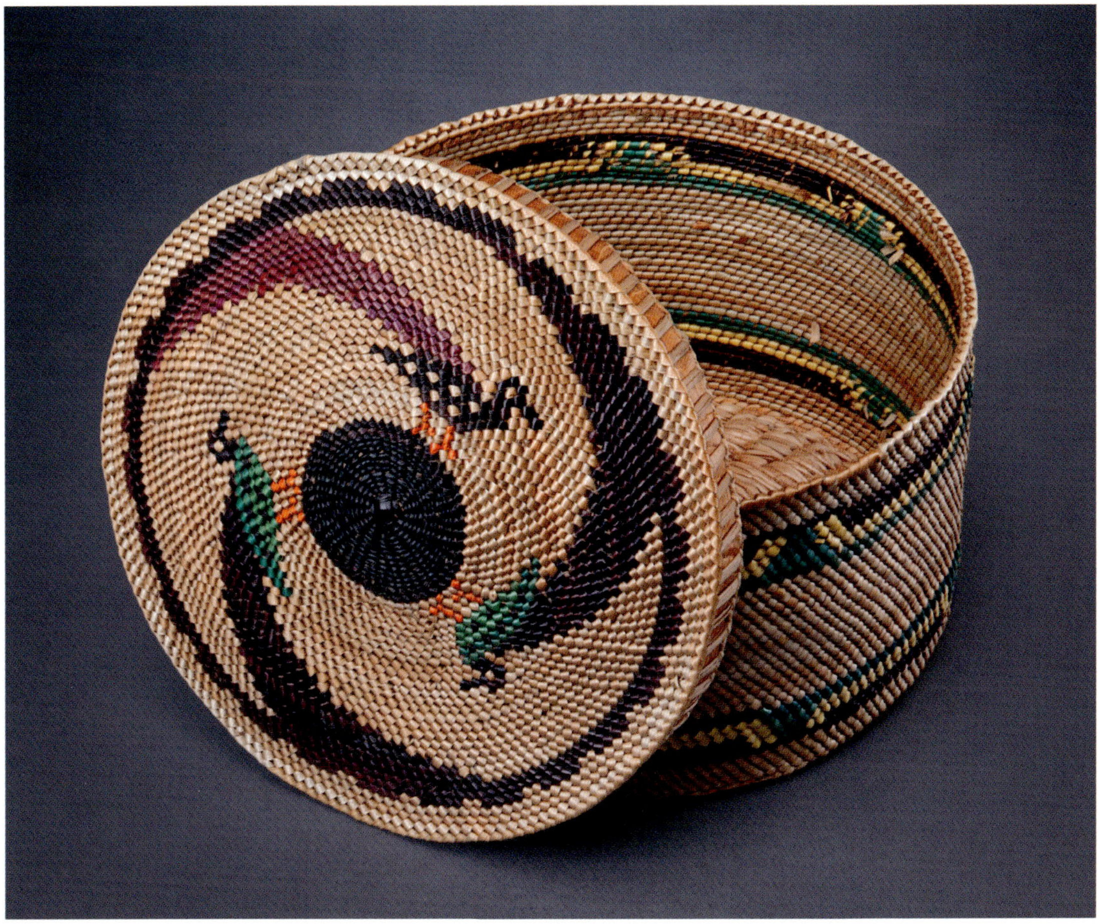

FIG. 150

Lidded Bowl, c. 1900, Makah, Artist unknown, 8.2 x 12.5 cm., 25427

The period of the late 1880s through the early 1900s, when basket weavers began increasingly to create designs for the marketplace, was a time of extraordinary creativity. The selection of designs was no longer based just on community, family, or personal aesthetics but also on the aesthetics and tastes of community outsiders. As basket weavers engaged more and more with people from diverse communities and backgrounds, their basketry designs began to incorporate these new inspirations.

sheer pleasure to be derived from beauty. Aesthete design incorporated motifs from both exotic cultures and historical sources, including stylized forms from nature such as the peacock. The unknown weaver of the Makah basket may have seen an aesthetic movement work of art depicting a peacock, she may have worked for an aesthete, or she may even have been an aesthete herself. Or, the weaver may have copied the motif from a piece of china, as peacock motifs were common on European china patterns at the turn of the twentieth century. Tlingit weaver Teri Rofkar explained that her grandmother told her that when she was weaving she should "go down to the store . . . and find out what the china pattern is for the year. When you're weaving be sure and weave patterns that match the china—all those White ladies are powerless over baskets that match their china" (Rofkar 2008).

NARRATIVE AND CEREMONIAL DESIGNS

Two particularly important narrative designs used in Native basketry are the O'odham "man-in-the-maze" and the Diné "wedding basket." Both can be understood as metaphoric representations of stories that guide an individual or cultural group on their path through life. As she weaves, a basket maker traces her own journey as well as the journey of her people through time and space. Over time, viewers of the basket may read and retell the story by tracing the coils from the start (at the center) to the finish (at the rim).

The man-in-the-maze features a man standing at the entrance of an elaborate labyrinth; the entrance is always portrayed at the top of the maze. The image is closely associated with the beliefs of the Akimel O'odham and Tohono O'odham people. There is no definitive version of its meaning. The man-in-the-maze has been variously interpreted as relating the emergence story of the

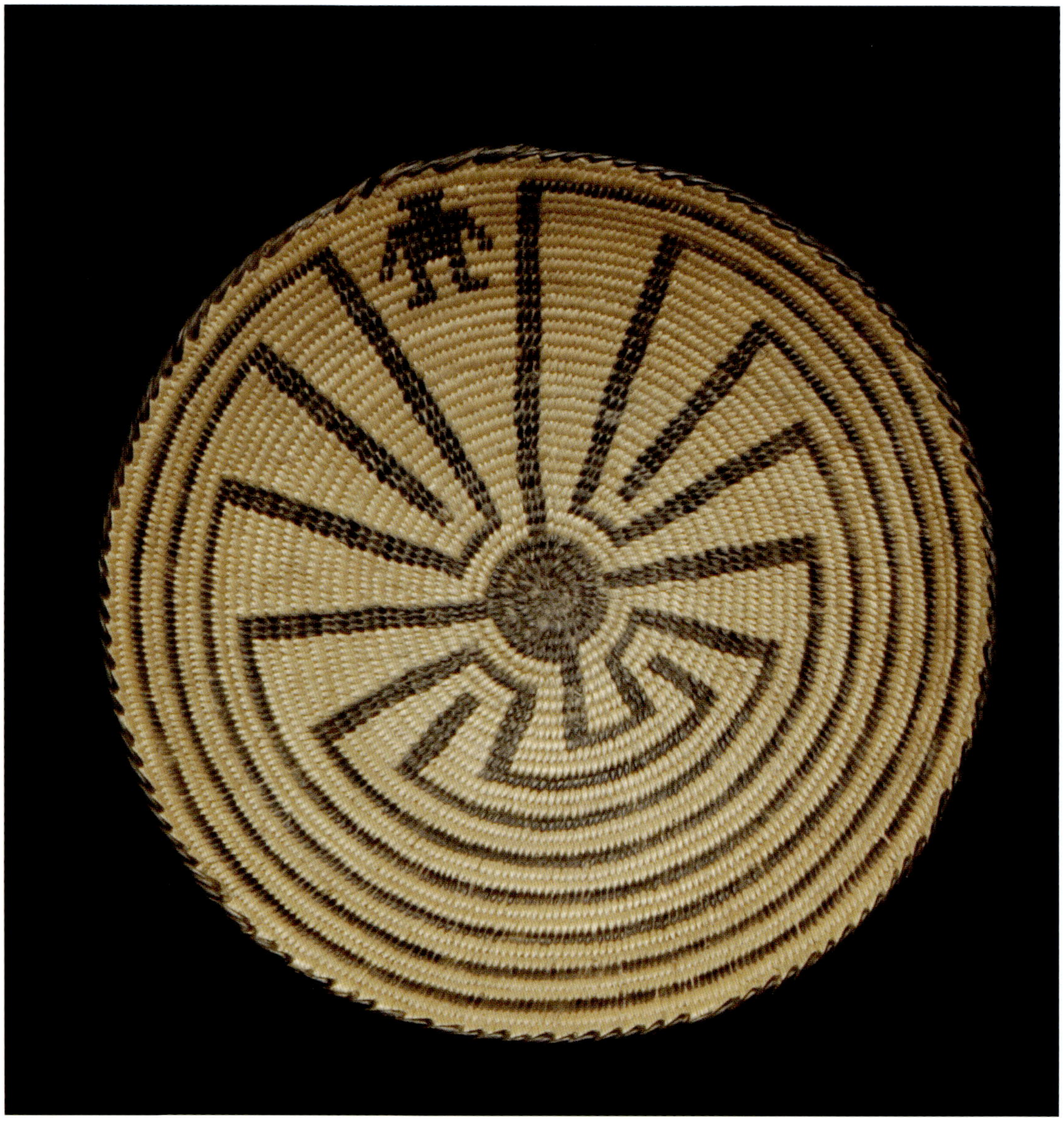

FIG. 151

Tray, c. 1900, Akimel O'odham, Artist unknown, 5.0 x 20.5 cm., 1029

O'odham people, as a depiction of the home of the creator of the Tohono O'odham—I'ito— and as a visual representation of the cycle of life. Akimel O'odham Alfretta Antone (1929–2012) gave the following account of the man-in-the-maze myth:

> Elder Brother lived in the maze . . . and the reason why he lived in the maze was because . . . I think how I'm gonna say this . . . magician or oh, medicine man that can disappear, and that can do things, heal people and things like that . . . that was Elder Brother . . . Se:he . . . they called him . . . he lived in there . . . but he had a lot of enemies so he made that, and to live in there people would go in there but they couldn't find him . . . they would turn around and go back.
>
> But in real life . . . when you look at the maze you start from the top and go into the maze . . . your life, you go down and then you reach a place where you have to turn around . . . maybe in your own life you fall, something happens in your home, you are sad, you pick yourself up and you go on through the maze . . . you go on and on and on . . . so many places in there you might . . . maybe your child died . . . or maybe somebody died, or you stop, you fall and you feel bad . . . you get up, turn around and go again . . . when you reach that middle of the maze . . . that's when you see the Sun God and the Sun God blesses you and say you have made it . . . that's where you die.
>
> The maze is a symbol of life . . . happiness, sadness . . . and you reach your goal . . . there's a dream there, and you reach that dream when you get to the middle of the maze . . . that's how I was told, my grandparents told me that's how the maze is (Myers and Gryder 1988).

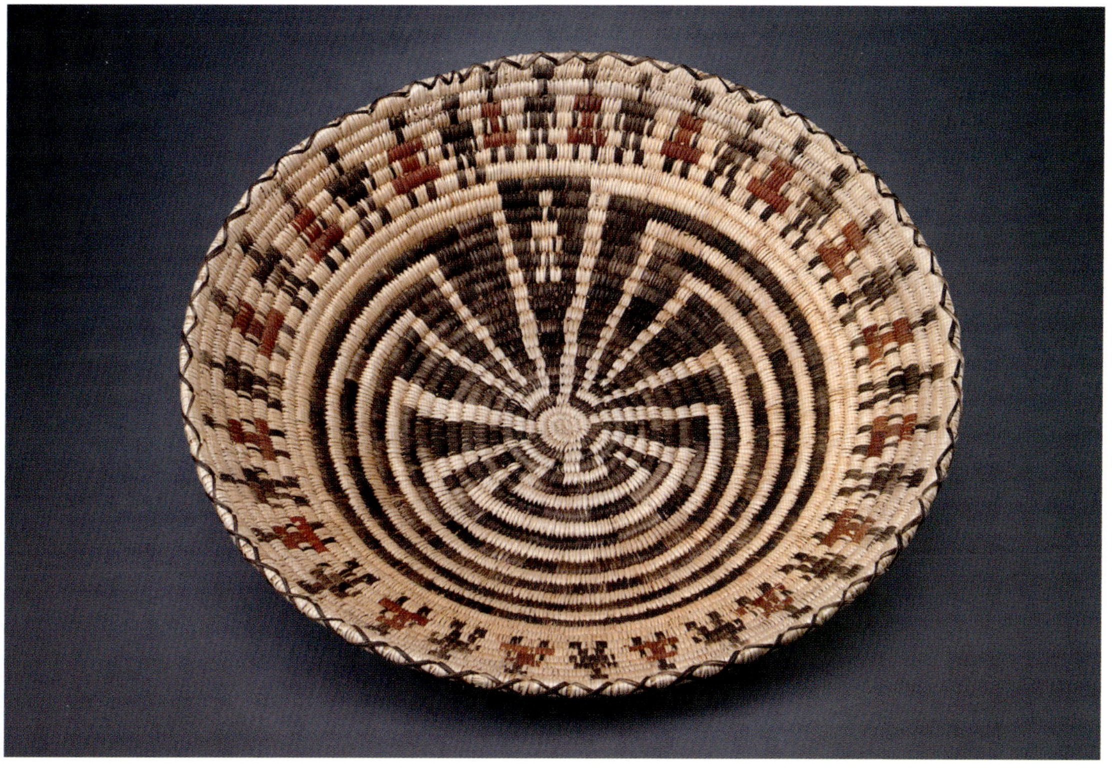

FIG. 152

Tray, 1999, Tohono O'odham, Mildred Lewis, 7.1 x 32.6 cm., 55671

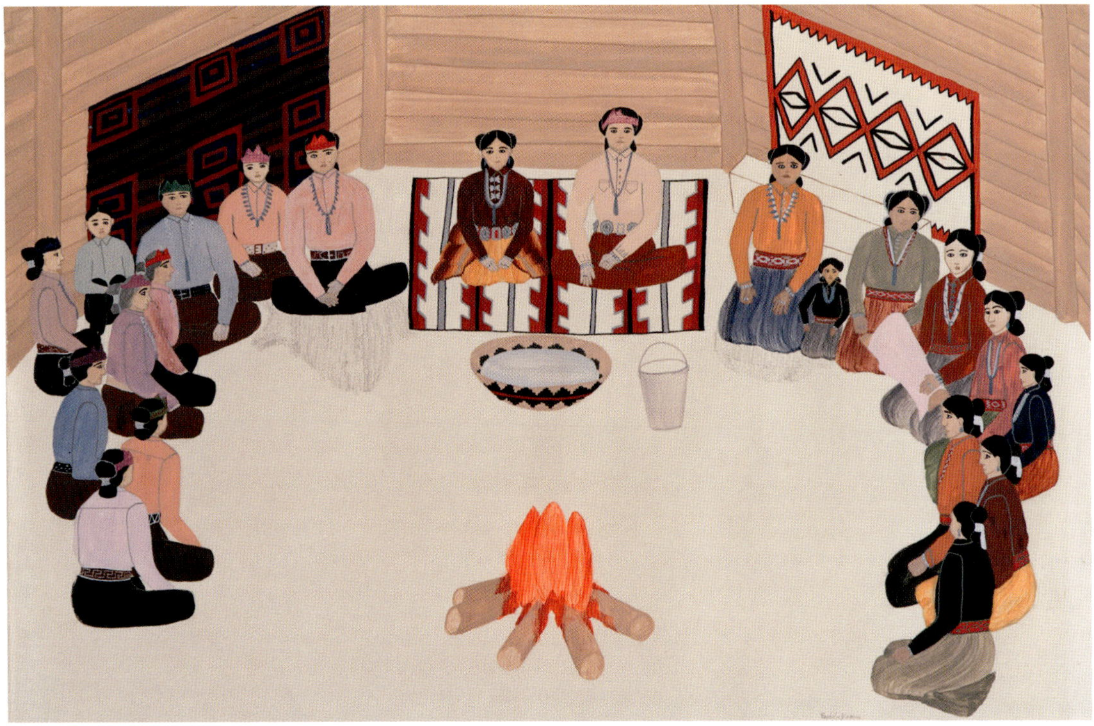

FIG. 153

Navajo Wedding, 1936, Diné, Sybil Yazzie, tempera on board, 35.2 x 48.8 cm., 53983

The man-in-the-maze emblem can be traced back to pre-contact petroglyphs situated throughout the American Southwest. Among the places it can be found is in the rock art of Casa Grande Ruins. Located in the Sonoran Desert of Arizona and occupied from about AD 1350 to 1450, it is one of the largest prehistoric structures in North America.

Today this historically significant design is an honored symbol for the Akimel O'odham, Tohono O'odham, Gila, and Salt River tribes of Arizona and Mexico. The Tohono O'odham have frequently depicted the man-in-the-maze in their art, and basket makers began using the image as early as 1900.

The Diné ceremonial "wedding basket" design—consisting of red bands, black stepped terraces, and white bands—has been woven over and over for more than a century using the exact same specifications. While there are numerous interpretations of its meaning, most in some way relate the design to a map through which the Diné people chart their lives. The white center represents where the People emerged, or the beginning of life; the black stepped terraces may symbolize mountains, or the darkness of struggle and pain; and the red circular bands may either be a rainbow or refer to marriage and the creation of family. The outer band of white is said to represent light or the spirit world. The break in the design may be a pathway to this light or an outlet for the weaver's thoughts, or an entrance through which the Holy People can come and go. Lastly, the herringbone rim finish is said to represent human life; the last coil on the basket rim, finished off at the end of the pathway, allows the medicine man to easily locate this spot in darkness during ritual use (during ceremonies this pathway is always pointed east).

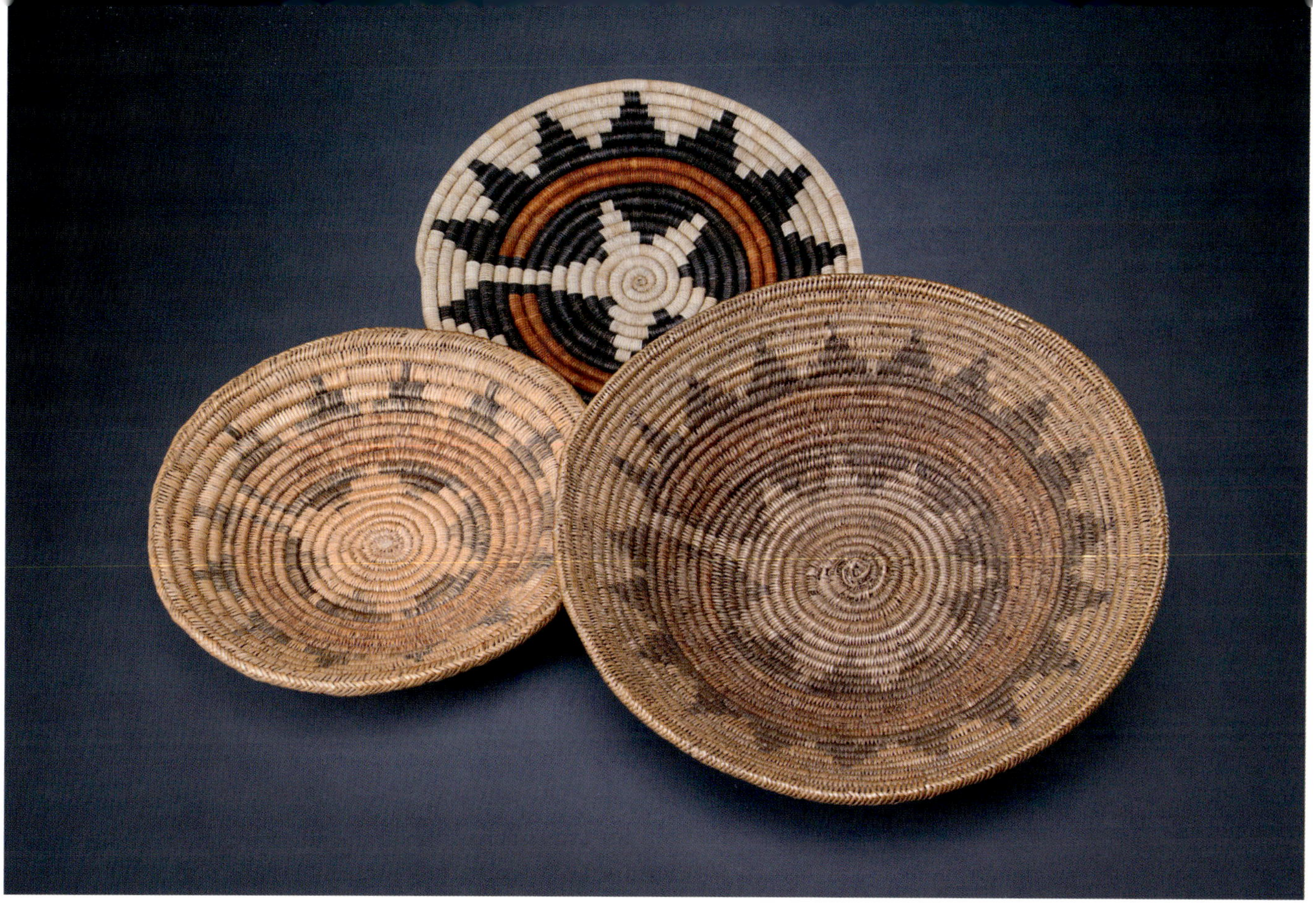

FIG. 154 (Left to right):

Wedding Tray, c. 1930, San Juan Paiute, Artist unknown, 5.0 x 30.5 cm., 57534

Plaque, c. 1960, Hopi (Second Mesa), Artist unknown, 3.3 x 32.0 cm., 46261

Wedding Tray, c. 1900, Diné, Artist unknown, 9.0 x 5.4 cm., 46374

The Diné baskets generally known as "wedding baskets" are actually woven for use in many different ceremonies, including those for weddings and healing. The overall design is always broken at one point, allowing a pathway from the center of the basket to the rim; the rim finish (always finished with a plaited herringbone pattern) ends at the pathway. In Diné ceremonies, the pathway is oriented towards the east.

Although the traditional wedding design originates with the Diné, the design is also woven by the San Juan Paiute and Hopi. As these three baskets illustrate, the use of the same design indicates the close geographic and historical connections of these three tribes. San Juan Paiute basket weavers have traditionally made baskets with this design for sale or trade to the Diné. Hopi weavers originally wove small basketry plaques (about five inches in diameter) with this design for the Havasupai Dance (in which it is attached to the left side of the *K'oonin-katsina's* belt) (Teiwes 1996:149).

The power of a ceremonial basket (such as the Diné wedding basket) is said to reside, in part, in the protective nature of its materials and the care with which it was made. Because it creates and safeguards a space, this "basket power" may be used to protect important personal or ritual objects. Diné baskets serving as containers for ceremonial objects are believed to have enough power to shield their contents from Mother Earth, as well as malevolent thoughts (Simpson 2003:70). Many Diné weavers believe that the act of weaving a ceremonial basket from the center outward parallels life's journey and builds harmony and balance between the weaver and her surroundings.

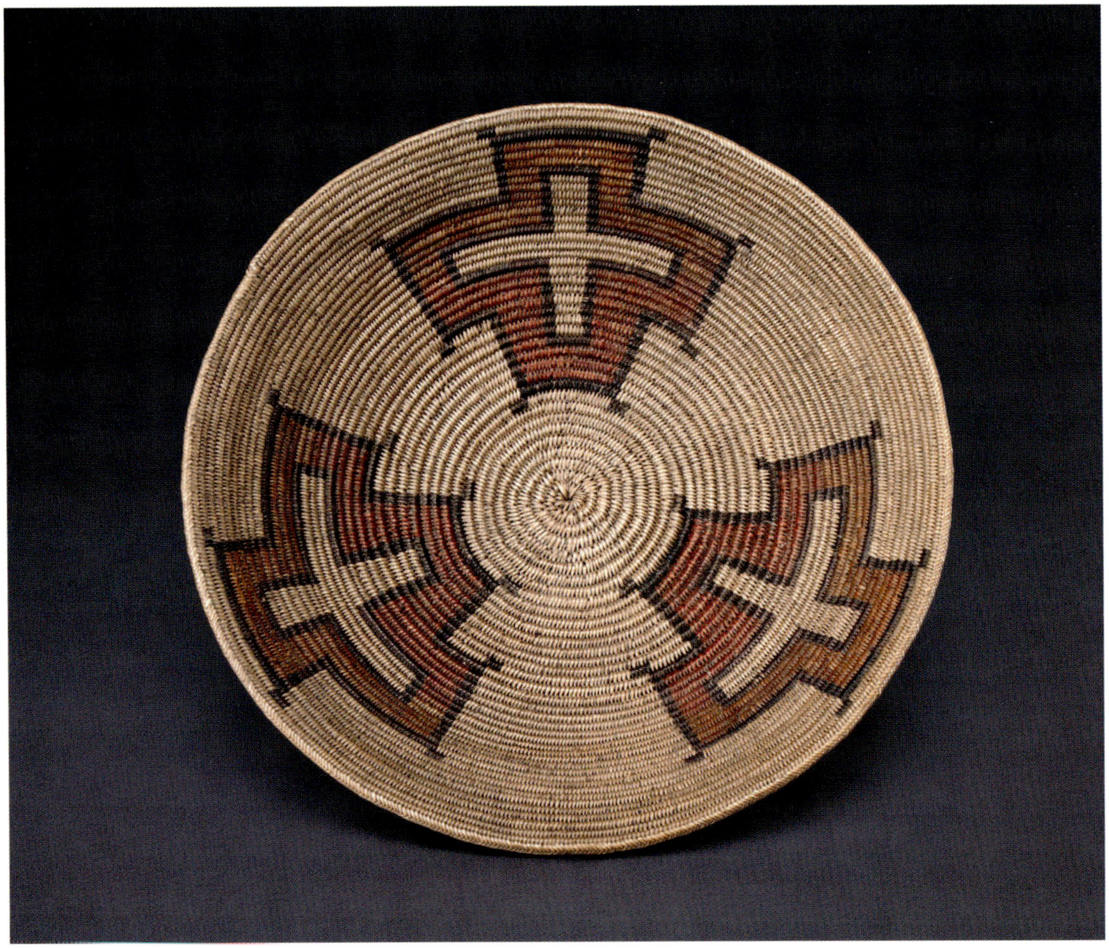

FIG. 155
Bowl, c. 1870, Diné, Artist unknown, 11.8 x 46.6 cm., 23775

Narrative and ceremonial baskets make extensive use of symbolism. For example, the Spider Woman Cross is an important traditional Diné design relating to the female deity who gave the art of weaving to the Diné people (see fig. 155). The cross form is sometimes compared to clouds, and baskets with cross depictions are often used in ceremonies to bring rain. Thus, the alternative name for this symbol is the rain cross. The four arms of the cross are associated with the sacred number four. To the Diné, the four arms also represent the four essential elements (abalone, turquoise, white shell, and jet); the four sacred plants (corn, squash, beans, and tobacco), the four sacred rivers (Colorado, Little Colorado, San Juan, and Rio Grande); and the four sacred mountains that define the four cardinal directions (Mount Blanca in the east, Mount Taylor in the south, San Francisco Peaks in the west, and Mount Herpersus in the north).

Prior to the 1880s baskets filled dual roles in Diné society: they functioned as household wares and as containers and/or drums in sacred ceremonies. Over time, a combination of factors—including the gradual replacement of utilitarian baskets with commercially-manufactured containers and the numerous restrictions dictating when and under what circumstances basket makers could weave ceremonial baskets—led to a sharp decline in the number of Diné women weaving both utilitarian and ceremonial baskets.

During the 1970s, a revival of traditional basket weaving took place in the Diné communities of Utah's Monument Valley. Inspired by the visual art of the prehistoric Mimbres and Ancestral Puebloans, as well as the art of other tribes, sand paintings, and their own culture's designs, Diné weavers of the mid-twentieth century established new basketry conventions concerning the use of human, animal, and other representational motifs, as well as designs depicting traditional beliefs, including those from myths, legends, and tales.

Mary Holiday Black and her family were at the forefront of the Diné basketry renaissance. The Blacks, along with neighboring weavers, expanded design convention; they modified the basic wedding basket design by combining birds, deer, butterflies, or rabbits with traditional motifs. The Black family also incorporated geometric rug designs into their baskets, as well as images of Ye'ii (or Holy People), which are most commonly made visible through Diné ceremonial sand paintings. To date, the pinnacle of this burst of creativity may well be the "story baskets" in which the Black family weavers have depicted themes from prayers, rituals, and traditional narratives.

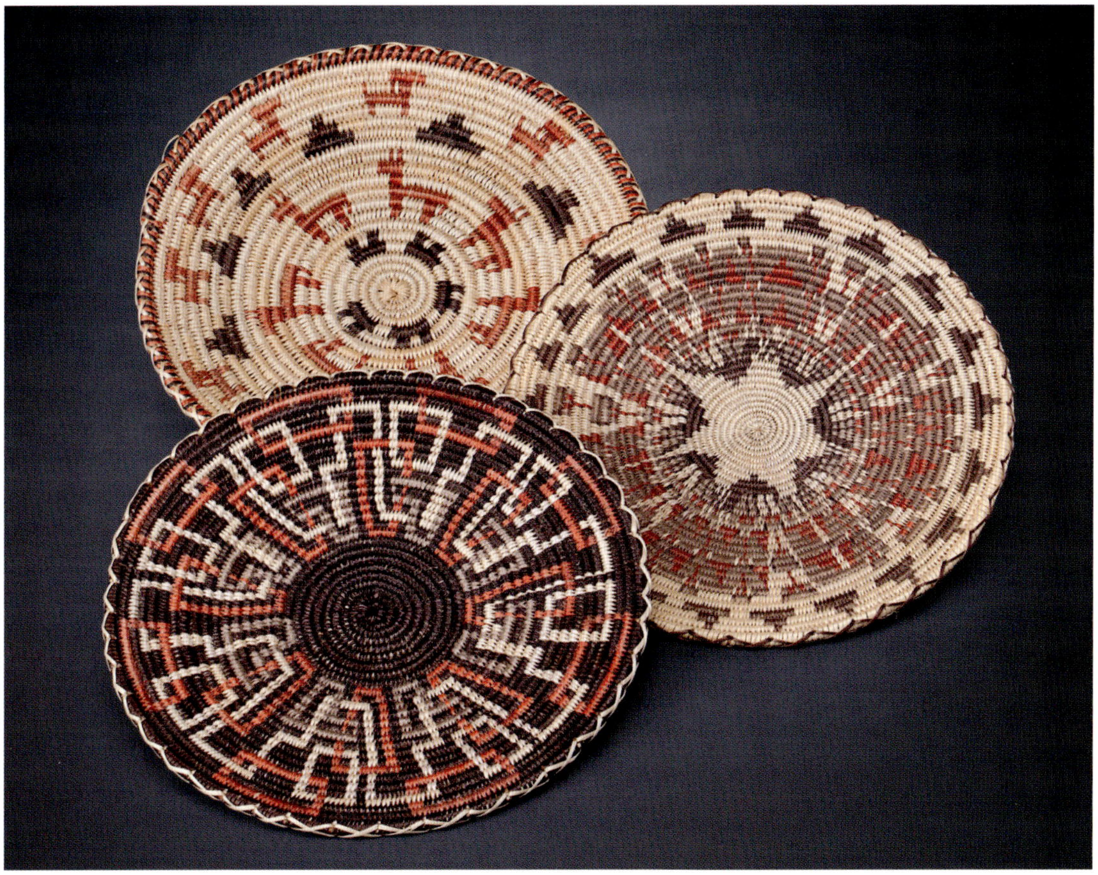

FIG. 156 (Clockwise from upper left):

Plaque, c. 1985, San Juan Paiute, Attributed to Lorraine King, 4.0 x 28.0 cm., 55919

Tray, c. 2005, San Juan Paiute, Louise Owl Tallman, 2.0 x 26 cm., 58044

Tray, c. 2005, San Juan Paiute, Louise Owl Tallman, 2.9 x 26 cm., 58025

As these three baskets illustrate, purely decorative design is displayed to its best advantage on flat trays or plaques. San Juan Paiute weavers call these trays their "design baskets," as these basket forms feature new design inspirations that open up new market opportunities, and stimulate the artistic growth of the weaver (McGreevy 1985: 26).

When most Diné women ceased making baskets in the late nineteenth century, San Juan Paiute women began weaving the hundreds of baskets needed yearly for Diné ceremonies. For more than a century, they have also made baskets to trade and sell to the Hopi. The San Juan Paiutes have lived for the last several hundred years in territory east of the Grand Canyon, bounded by the San Juan and Colorado rivers, with the Diné and Hopi as their neighbors.

For many San Juan Paiute weavers, making baskets for the Diné and Hopi has been the focus of their basketmaking art as well as one of their primary sources of income. However, in the 1970s William Beaver, proprietor of the Sacred Mountain Trading Post in Arizona, who bought and sold their baskets, began giving San Juan Paiute weavers source materials to encourage them to experiment with various design motifs. Among the items he gave them were photographs of baskets in museum collections, images from magazines and auction catalogues, and basketry books (McGreevy 1985:29–30). Today San Juan Paiute weavers make what they call "old-timer baskets"—utilitarian pieces that keep Paiute basket traditions alive—and "wedding baskets" (the mainstay of their economy), as well as "fancy baskets" or "design baskets" to nurture their artistic needs and appeal to the market.

Another important narrative (and ceremonial) image that has appeared in Native basketry is the Katsinam—the supernaturals, or benevolent spirit beings, of the Pueblo people of the American Southwest. Katsinam have been depicted on Hopi basketry for at least one hundred years, as well as on Pueblo pottery for at least seven hundred years. There are hundreds of Katsinam who are associated with rain, clouds, and the dead; also, the word Katsinam refers to the "performers"

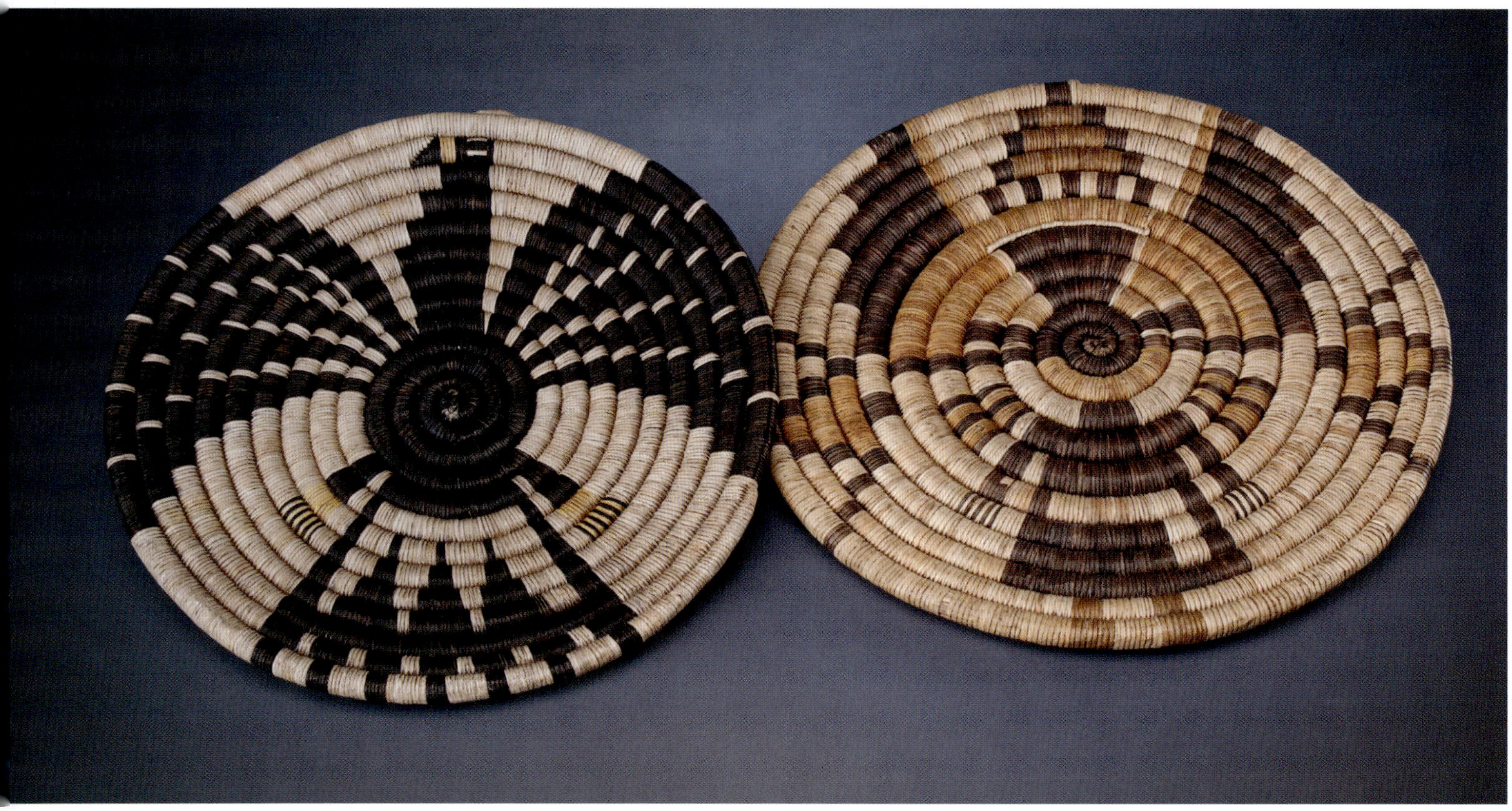

FIG. 157 (Left to right):

Plaque, c. 1880, Hopi (Second Mesa), Artist unknown, 4.5 x 30.0 cm., 43751

Plaque, c. 1925, Hopi (Second Mesa), Artist unknown, 3.4 x 34.2 cm., 36623

(Pueblo Indians who personify the Katsina) in the Katsinam ceremonies. The Katsinam appear at the Hopi villages from December to July of every year; for the Hopi, both the spirit beings and the performers are sacred (Pearlstone 2001:43–45). Today Hopi artists produce Katsina imagery in a variety of media including baskets. In part they do so for economic reasons: Katsina imagery is in great demand by collectors and tourists, and the sale of basketry with this imagery enables the Hopi to earn a livelihood while living in their traditional villages. In addition, Hopi artists weave Katsina imagery to keep their basketry authentic and representative of their worldview.

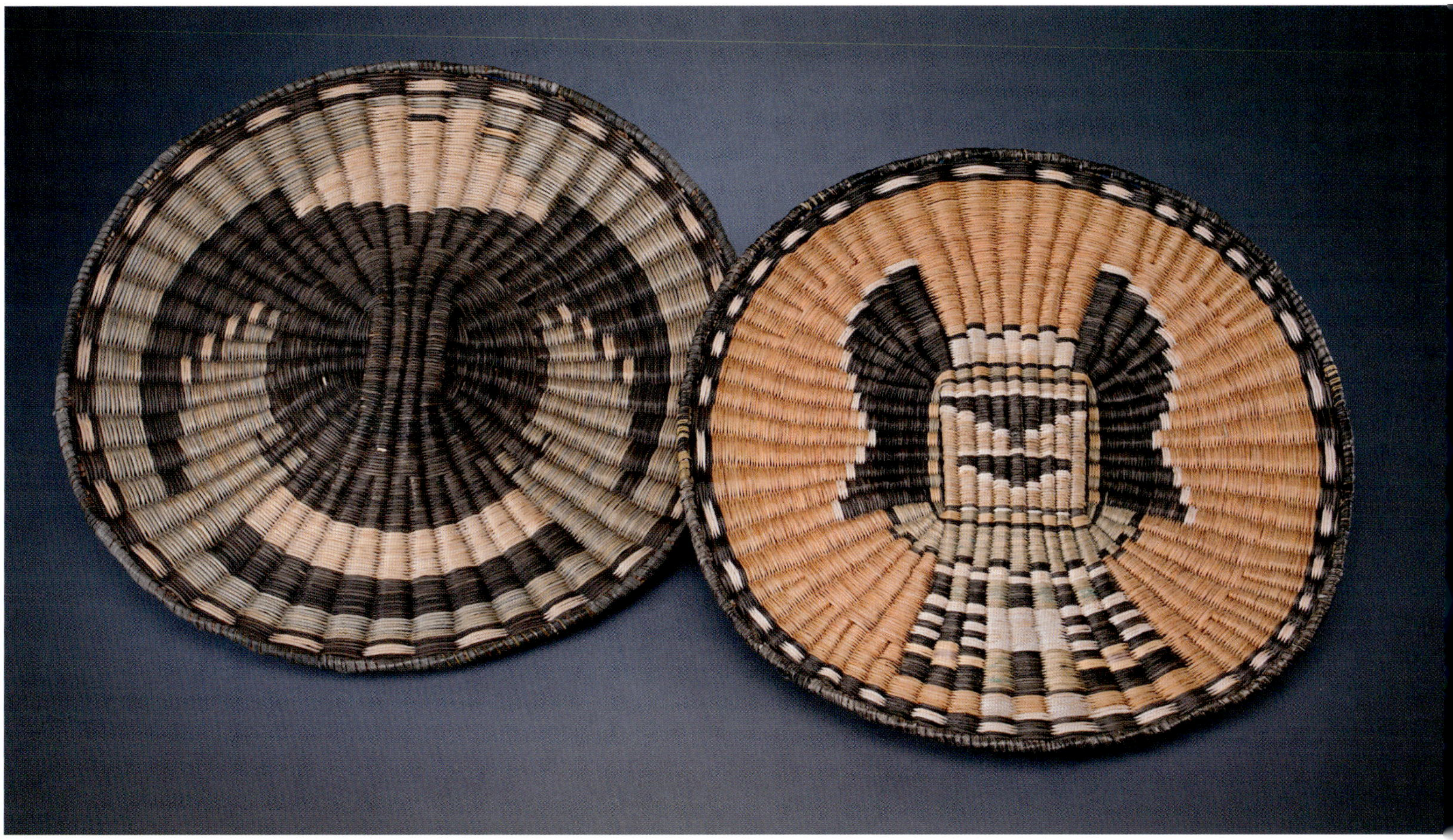

FIG. 158 (Left to right):

Plaque, 1935, Hopi (Third Mesa), Artist unknown, 3.5 x 35.0 cm., 46352

Plaque, c. 1920, Hopi (Third Mesa), Artist unknown, 2.0 x 32.5 cm., 55904

There is a specialization of basket-weaving techniques at the Hopi mesa villages: weavers on Second Mesa use the coil method exclusively and weavers on Third Mesa use the wicker technique exclusively. Although the techniques are different, in figs. 157 and 158 eagles are depicted on the plaques to the left, and Crow Mother is depicted on the plaques to the right.

Crow Mother is believed by some Hopi to be the mother of all Katsinas. She appears in the Bean Dance and supervises the initiation of the children into the Katsina Society. Crow Mother's image can be identified by her distinctive black crow wings that emerge from the sides of her mask.

At the end of the Niman ceremony, which takes places at midsummer in July, the Katsinam who have been at the villages return to their mountain homes to await the cycle of the coming year. At this time, the spirits of the eagles the priests have brought to reside in the village accompany them, bearing prayers and their own observations of the events. After the last dance of the Niman Ceremony, the eagles carry the people's messages to the spirits (Frigout 1979:572).

DESIGN BREAKS

Intentional breaks in the overall design are a component of baskets made by many western North American cultures. These breaks—also referred to as *daus,* pathways, or doorways—are considered expressions of a weaver's cosmology; they are visual notations of how baskets are imbued with life and consequence through the weaver's actions. In 1985 Pomo basket weaver Elsie Allen related her understanding of the purpose of design breaks: "The extra design besides the main design is the weaver's kind of *dau.* Certain weavers had certain kinds of *daus* or certain ways of putting them on a basket—like a signature. All traditional Pomo baskets have the *dau,* so spirits can get in and out of baskets" (Winther 1996:47). The design break is also used by some Native weavers to ensure the imperfection of a basket (see figure 159) or to provide a "way out" so the basket maker's creativity will not be trapped in the basket (see figures 160, 161).

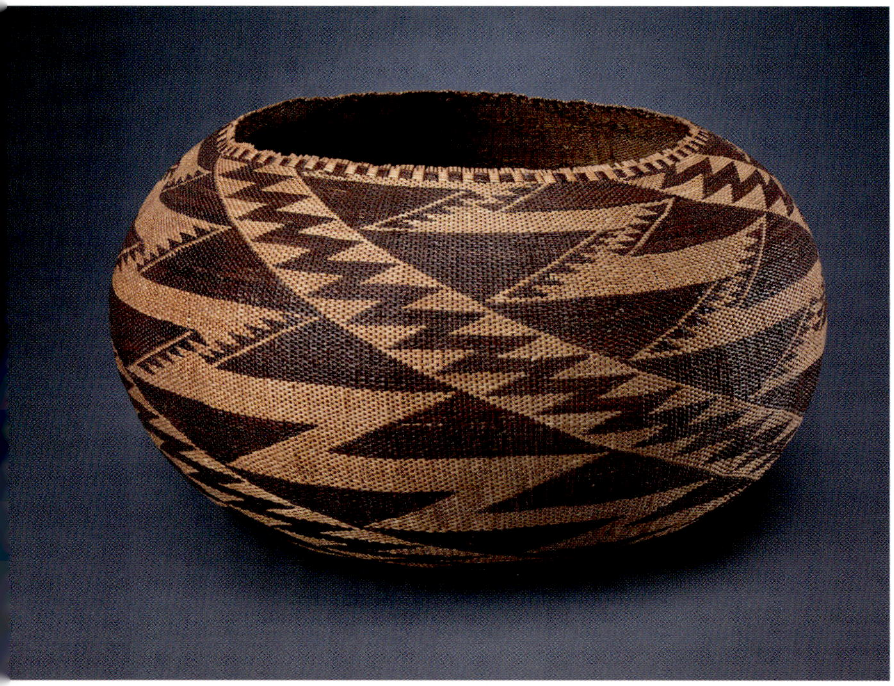

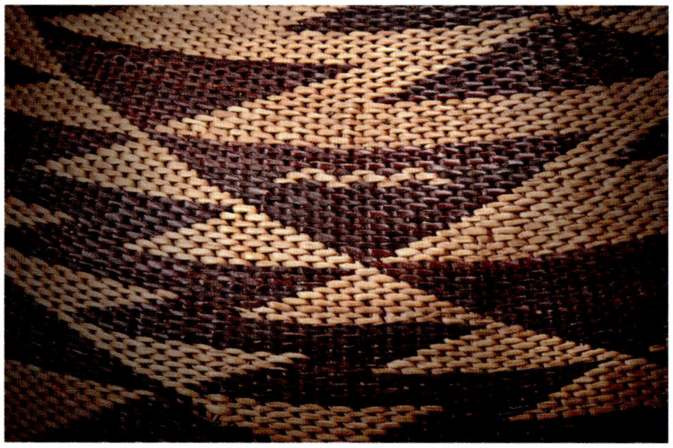

FIG. 159

Storage Bowl, c. 1906, Pomo, Artist known as "Captain Jack's Wife," 20.0 x 31.0 cm., 28

In north-central California, multiple vertical or horizontal design bands are typical of Indigenous twined baskets. In this Pomo storage bowl, there are two distinct, vertical design bands. An interesting feature of Pomo design bands is the elaborate nature of the design break, or *dau* mark. These design breaks are idiosyncratic marks made by the weaver, possibly as a signature mark or possibly intended to ensure the imperfection of a basket. As basketry scholar Bruce Bernstein explains: "This imperfection allows the weaver to make baskets which connote her humanity, and thus, the ability to keep weaving, rather than to achieve a perfection in which all the weaver's talent would be captured. Intentional errors emphasize the process of creation rather than end-product" (Bernstein 1985:7).

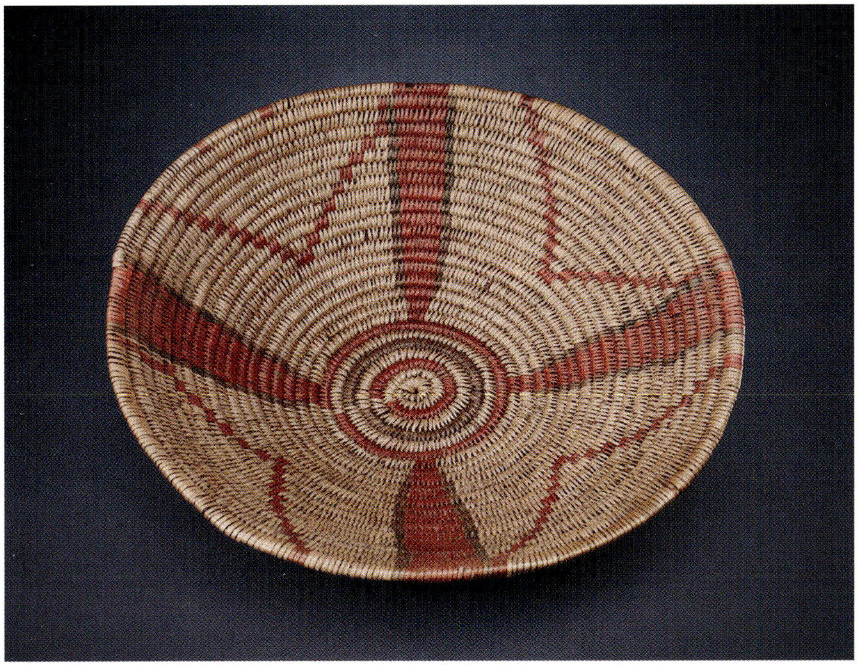

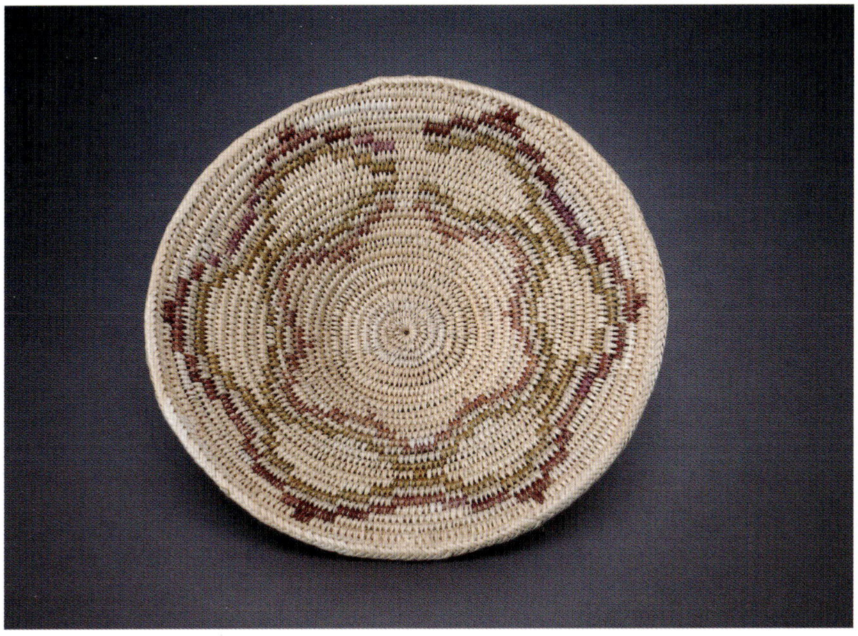

FIG. 160

Tray, c. 1925, Jicarilla Apache, Artist unknown, 12.5 x 50.5 cm., 23486

FIG. 161

Bowl, 1983, Jicarilla Apache, Lydia Pesata, 8.0 x 36.2 cm., 50066

For Jicarilla Apache weavers, the ceremonial break provides a "way out" so that the weavers' creativity will not be trapped in her basket. It also represents the original "sun ladders" that play a major role in the Jicarilla Apache creation myth (Herold 1999:67). Contrary to this, Tsimshian basket weaver Loa Ryan has explained that in her tradition designs always remain closed to prevent evil from entering the basket.

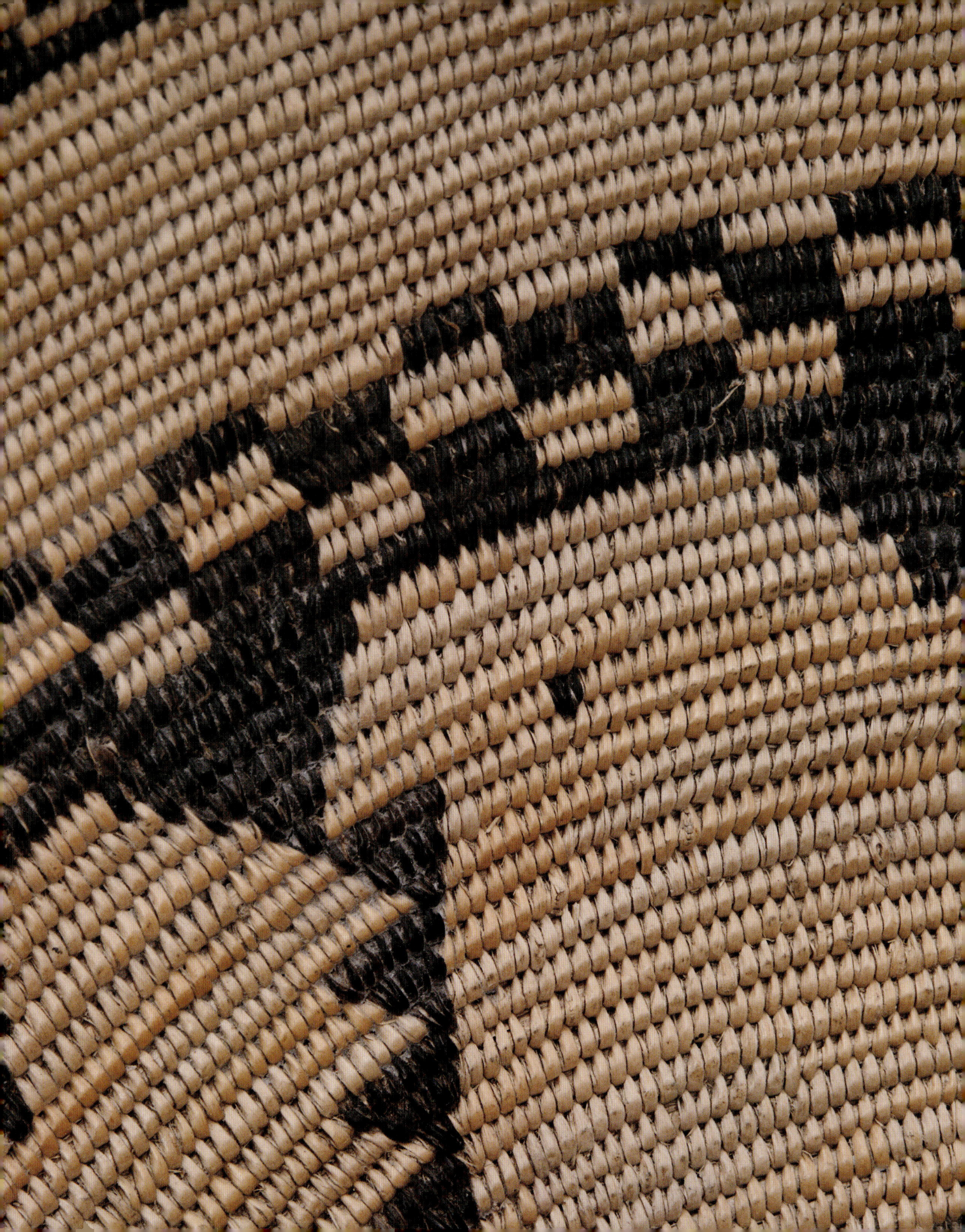

Chapter 5

Creative Visions

I said that my grandmother taught me to make baskets.
Well, I did make baskets and,
later on,
I found myself liking making baskets
and to me
basket weaving is relaxing.
And I don't know how to put it but it's THERE
[softly] you're all together when you are making baskets
there are no other things
like if you're cooking you are thinking about something else,
or if you are washing or walking you're thinking about something.
But basket weaving is the only thing that you are all there.
And sometimes I think about it
and in my imagination
it SHINES
from above
and it tells how to go about it
how to do
what color to use.
And it seems to work that way
it seems that I don't make mistakes
like when you sew you put the sleeve on the wrong side.
But as long as you are all there, there's no mistakes.

—Frances Manuel, Tohono O'odham basket weaver, 1987
(Manuel and Neff 2001:97)

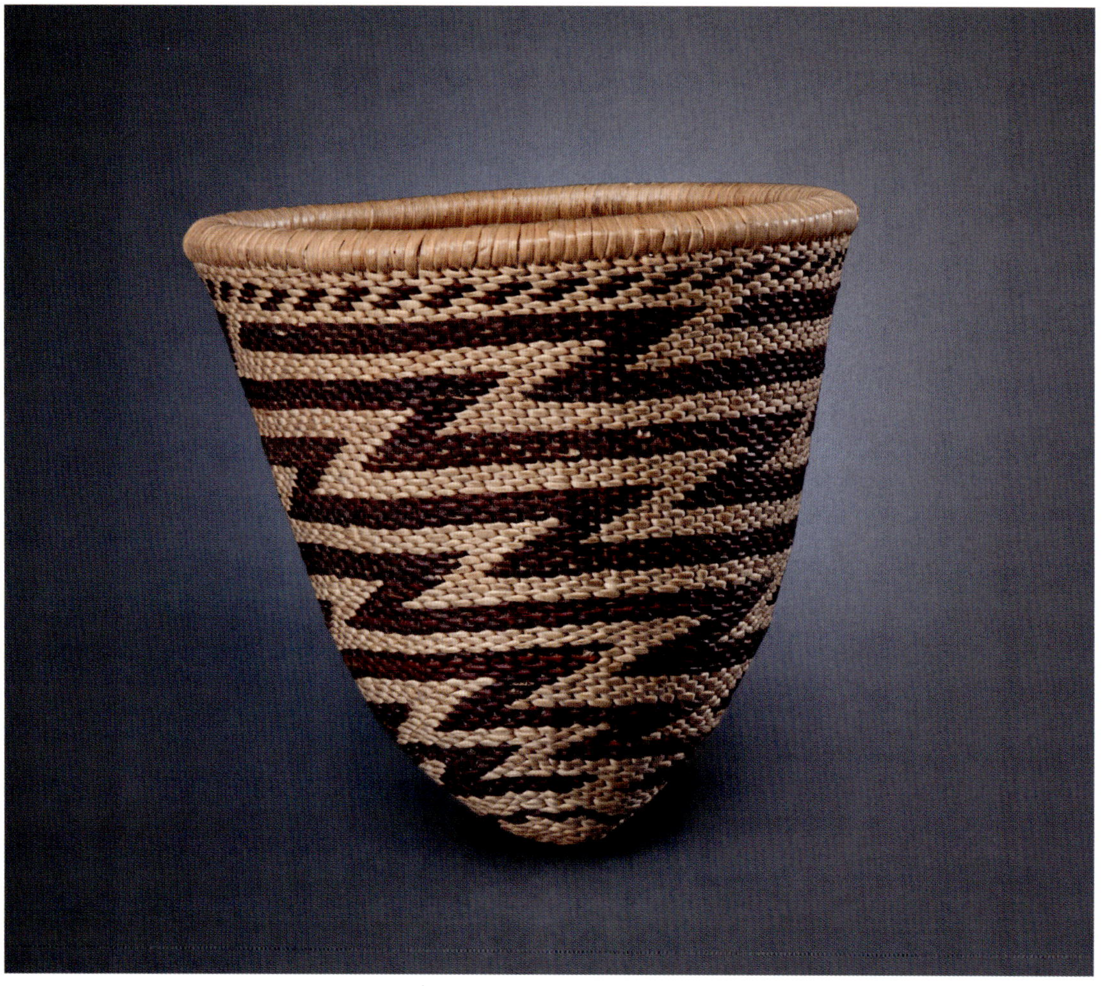

FIG. 162

Miniature Carrying Basket, c. 1901, Pomo, Attributed to Mary Knight Benson, 9.2 x 9.7 cm., 14324

The term "art" suggests a level of creative expertise, whether it is a demonstration of a mastery of materials, technical ability, originality, creative vision, or a combination of these; however, the locus of the value of a Native American basket is not so easily realized. A valued basket may be a type or weave no longer woven and thus comparable to a rare historical document. For basket makers and their communities, a valued basket may be the work of an honored teacher, family member, or ancestor now gone. A truly "good" basket may have a spiritual dimension not visible to the eye.

Culturally, the Western notion of individual artists as superstars has never been recognized by Native American weavers; Native communities do not identify master basket weavers based on their technical or artistic skills alone. The following Native basket weavers, therefore, are not included in this section because they are superstars or "master" weavers but rather because they are grandmothers or mothers who have inspired others; they are women and men who have contributed to the revival of basket weaving; they are teachers who have preserved the art of basketry as part of the life of their community; or because they are women and men for whom weaving baskets is a living art and have invigorated the art form with their skill and originality.

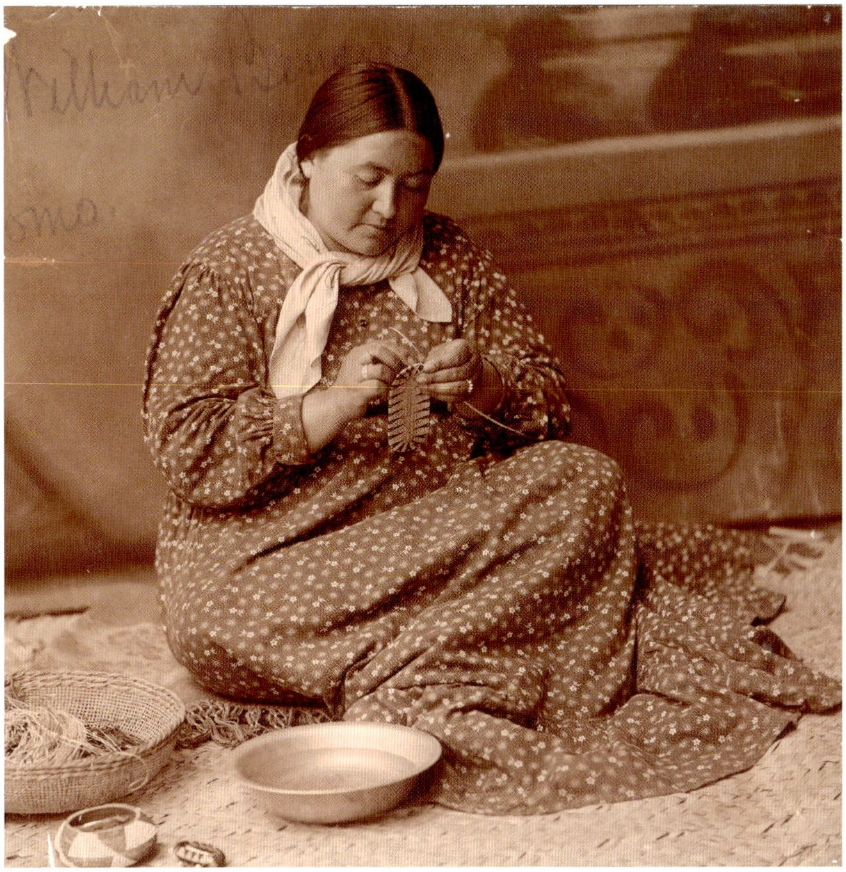

FIG.163

Mary Knight Benson, Pomo, demonstrates weaving at the St. Louis World's Fair, 1904. Photo by Charles H. Carpenter. Courtesy of the National Museum of the American Indian. P17579.

MARY KNIGHT BENSON, Pomo (1878–1937)

Mary Knight was born in 1878 in Knight's Valley, south of Ukiah, California. Her father, John Knight, was a white settler, and her mother, Sarah Joaquin Knight, was a Pomo basket weaver. As with most young Pomo girls, Mary Knight learned to weave from her mother. Because of her mixed heritage, Knight grew up to be a sophisticated woman of two different cultures. Her life at the center of two worlds, Anglo and Indian, proved to be to her benefit as she entered into the commercial art-basket market.

In 1894 Knight married William Benson, also of Anglo American and Pomo descent, and also a skilled weaver. Both Bensons had an early and enduring relationship with basket dealer Grace Nicholson. Because of this, Mary Benson is one of the best-documented weavers of the early twentieth century. Nicholson, based in Pasadena, California, met the Bensons in 1903 on her first buying trip to northern California. From 1903 through 1907, Nicholson, like other collectors of this period, searched for examples of culturally traditional California Indian baskets; she also began commissioning baskets from the Bensons.

In 1916, after she achieved success as an art dealer, Nicholson began providing the Bensons with a monthly stipend in addition to buying their finished work. This arrangement freed the Bensons from wage labor, allowing them sufficient time to gather and process materials and to devote the long hours required for their increasingly fine weaving. The relationship with Nicholson continued for more than two decades (until Mary Benson's death) and produced some of the most exquisite baskets ever made.

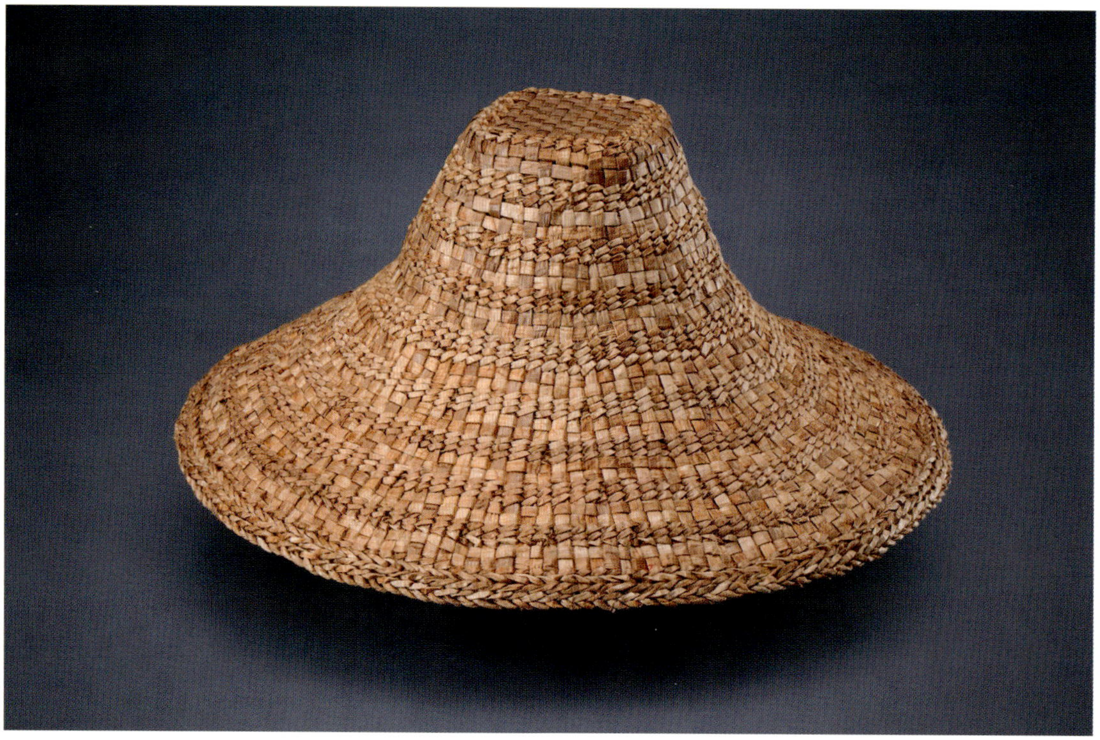

FIG. 164

Hat, 2012, Loa Balumnaech Ryan, Tsimshian, 16.4 x 30.1 cm., 58314

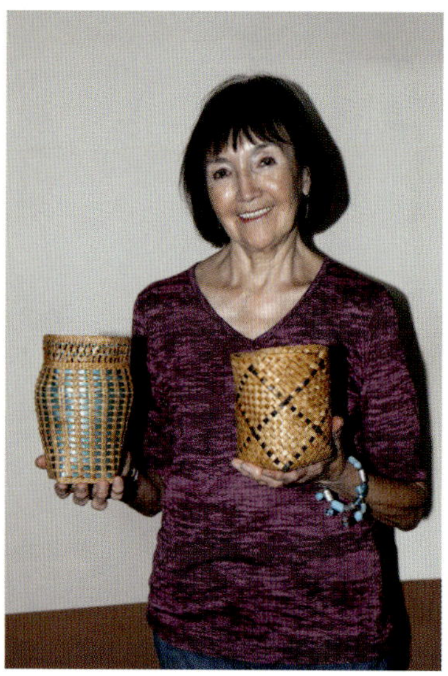

FIG.165

Loa Balumnaech Ryan, Tsimshian, Santa Fe Indian Market, 2011. Photo by Clare Lighton.

LOA BALUMNAECH RYAN, Tsimshian/Gitlan (b. 1939)

Although Ryan was born and raised in the Tsimshian village of Metlakatla, British Columbia, as a child growing up she was never told she was Tsimshian. After learning of her heritage later, she developed a cultural connection that is deep and enduring. Today she proudly identifies herself as an enrolled member of the Metlakatla Band, Tsimshian Nation, and of the house of Xpe Hanax, member of the Raven Clan (Ganhada). Ryan is the great-great-granddaughter of James Lequinisk, chief of the Gitlan tribe. (Balumnaech is her mother's clan.)

Ryan believes she was chosen to be a weaver; in 1990 she began reviving her family's weaving tradition that was last practiced by her great-grandmothers. Because the traditional familial learning chain had been broken, and she was unable to find a Tsimshian weaver willing to teach her, Ryan's basket weaving teachers came from outside both her family and her tribe. One of her most important teachers was Haida weaver Delores Churchill, with whom she apprenticed over four summers, in the early 1990s. Recognizing that there was still a void in her basketry knowledge, Ryan extensively studied Tsimshian baskets in museums, and has since been instrumental in the revival of techniques and forms that were no longer being woven.

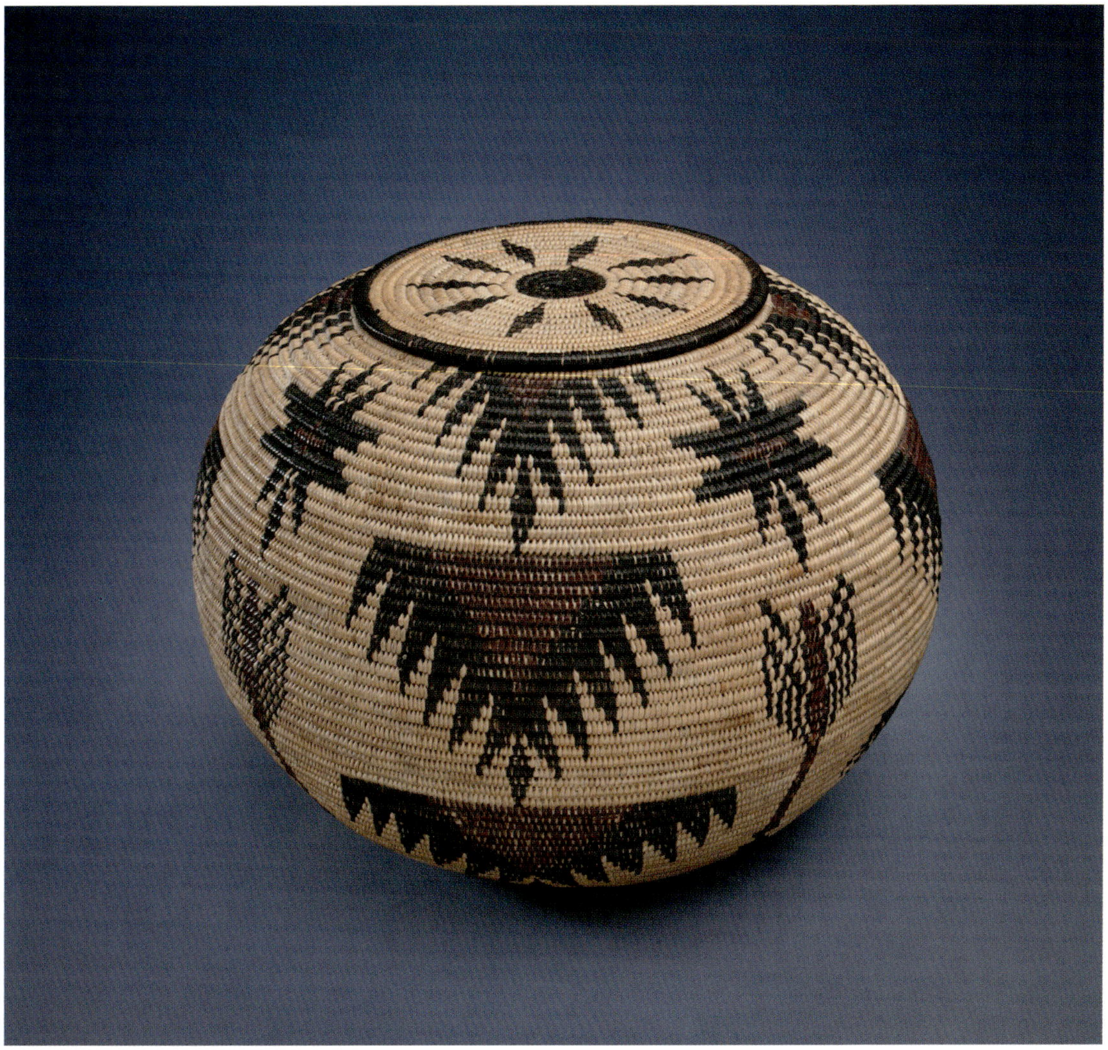

FIG. 166

Bowl, 1912, Mono Lake Paiute/Miwok, Lucy Parker Telles, 17.0 x 21.0 cm., 14308

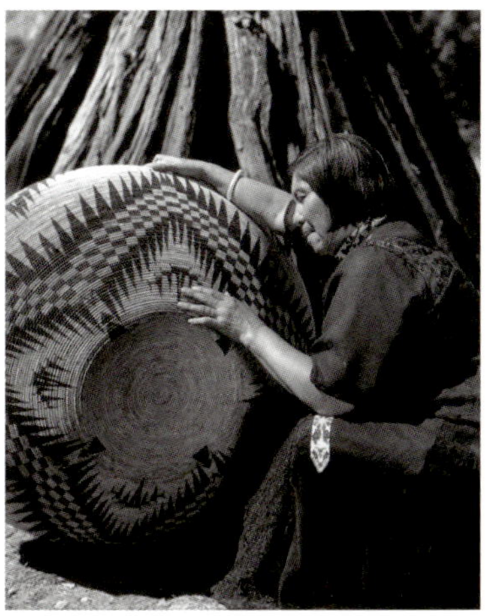

LUCY PARKER TELLES, Mono Paiute Lake/Miwok (1885–1955)

Lucy Parker Telles was born near Mono Lake, the daughter of Louisa Sam Tom (Paiute/Miwok) and Mack Tom (Paiute), a traditional healer. Her family lived both in Yosemite Valley and at Mono Lake, California. Parker Telles married Jack Parker, a Paiute man, about 1900, and they had one son. After Parker's death, Parker Telles married John Telles in 1914, and the

FIG. 167

Lucy Parker Telles, Mono Lake Paiute/Miwok, with one of her baskets, Yosemite National Park, c. 1940. Courtesy of the Yosemite National Park Service Library. RL 2051.

couple lived in Yosemite Valley for most of their lives. Together they raised three children and later two grandchildren. In Yosemite Valley, the Telleses supported their family by working as a laborer (John) and housekeeper (Lucy). As with many basket weavers of this era, Lucy Parker Telles augmented the family income with the sale of her baskets.

Parker Telles learned the art of basketry from her mother and as a young girl wove traditional baskets. By the second decade of the 1900s, she was weaving baskets with new and novel shapes and designs, as well as beaded baskets; all were designed to appeal to the collectors and tourists who frequented Yosemite Valley. By the 1920s Parker Telles was entering her baskets in the Yosemite Indian Field Days basketry competitions, and by 1930 she was recognized as one of the finest basket makers in the region (Bates and Lee 1990:172–177). In the 1930s she was hired to demonstrate basket weaving to Yosemite National Park visitors in the Indian Village at the Yosemite Museum. Parker Telles was one of the few Native American weavers of the first half of the twentieth century who was lucky enough to live in a place where she could make a living from her art.

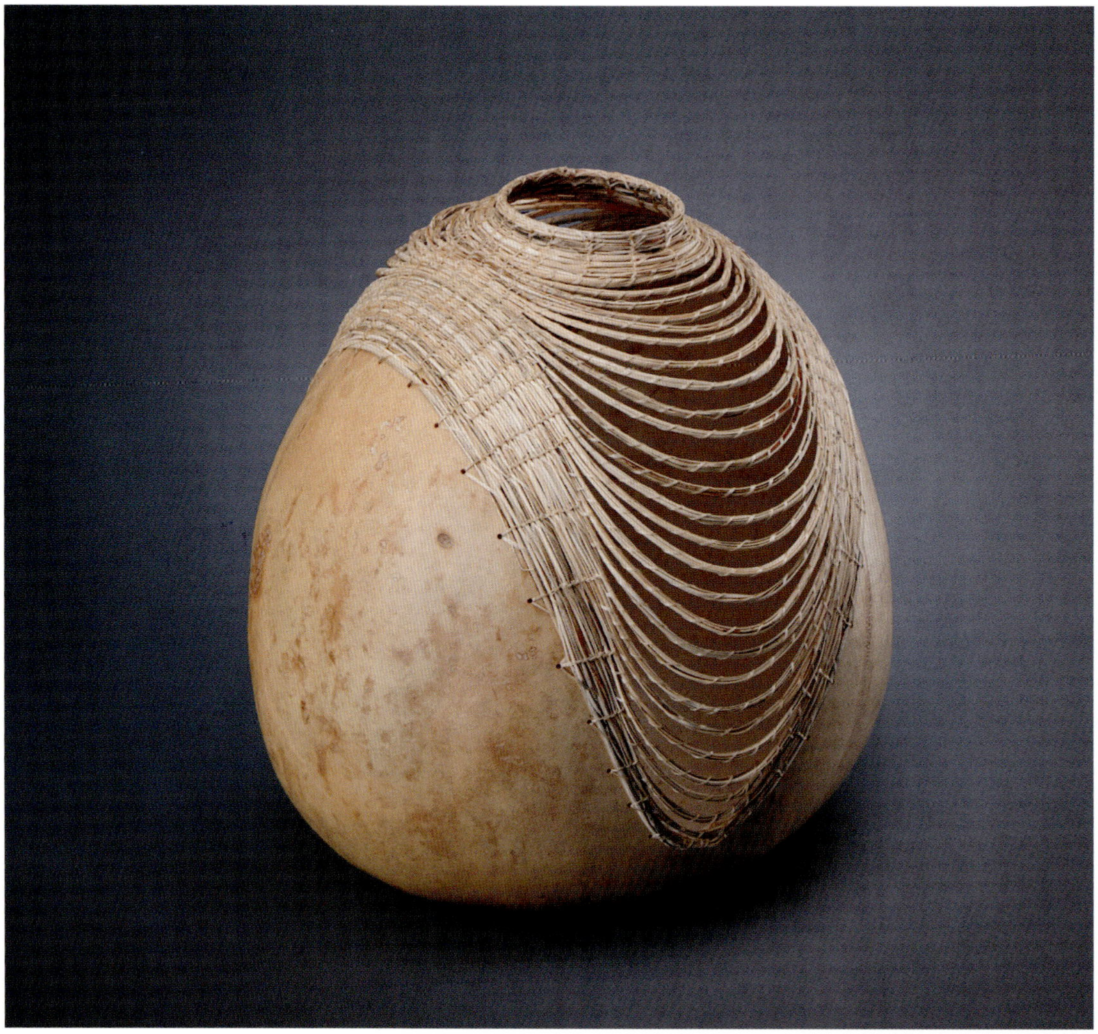

FIG. 168

Gourd Basket, 2012, Tohono O'odham, Terrol Dew Johnson, 6.8 x 23.1 cm., Museum purchase, 58315

TERROL DEW JOHNSON, Tohono O'odham (b. 1973)

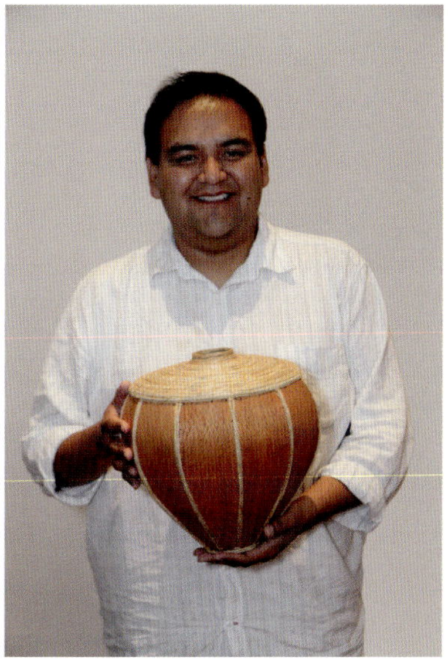

FIG. 169

Terrol Dew Johnson, Tohono O'odham, 2011. Photo by Clare Lighton. Courtesy Tohono O'odham Community Action.

It is not traditional for men to be weavers of fine baskets in Native American cultures; however, Terrol Dew Johnson is one of the exceptions. A contemporary basket weaver and community and health advocate from Sells, Arizona, Johnson lives on the Tohono O'odham Indian Reservation. According to Johnson, he began weaving baskets at age ten because weaving was the only thing he was good at; even as a small child he was "touchy-feely" and good with his hands (T. Johnson, pers. comm. August 17, 2012). Johnson says that both of his parents supported his interest in basketry, particularly his mother, Betty Ann Pancho. Because he felt greatly in debt to his teachers—Margaret Acosta, Lolita Manuel, and Clara Havier—he became a teacher himself. He explained: "Their generosity has helped me learn more than just the techniques of weaving. It helped me understand the heritage of hard work, culture and artistic vision that has driven generations of my ancestors to live artfully in the dry desert" (Folwell 2001:35).

Johnson has said that basket weaving is a "calling" for him and "haunts" him. "Today, my own baskets—both contemporary and traditional—often emerge from the dream process," he explains (Dewhurst, MacDowell, and Hunt 2010:6). "New designs and styles haunt my sleep, calling me to weave them into the waking world, one stitch at a time, until they have taken on a life of their own." The belief that weaving is a calling and baskets are products of inspirations from dream states, or spiritual states, is not uncommon among Native American basket weavers.

In addition to weaving, Johnson is a community activist. In 1996 he co-founded Tohono O'odham Community Action (TOCA). A nonprofit community development organization, TOCA also operates a basketry cooperative, the Tohono O'odham Basketweavers' Association (TOBA). The goal of the cooperative is to break the dependence Tohono O'odham weavers have on outside dealers who buy low and sell high and revitalize basketry both as a viable economic opportunity and respected cultural practice. TOBA has helped market basket weavers' work (with fair trade products as their model) and is working towards reducing artists' reliance on a middleman who takes the profits. TOBA also supports weavers by negotiating what has become a harsh reality for most Indigenous weavers: the permits they now need to acquire before harvesting basketry materials on federal, state, and private lands.

> *In the Tohono O'odham language, we have no word for art. My ancestors never really created formal artwork that was separated from day-to-day life. Instead, Native people have always looked to create artful ways of living, seeking ways to blend beauty and usefulness. We try to live in ways that bring together the material, spiritual and aesthetic worlds. In basketry, beauty and utility are joined together. Some call it art; most basket weavers simply call it life.*
>
> TERROL DEW JOHNSON
>
> (FOLWELL 2001: 34–35)

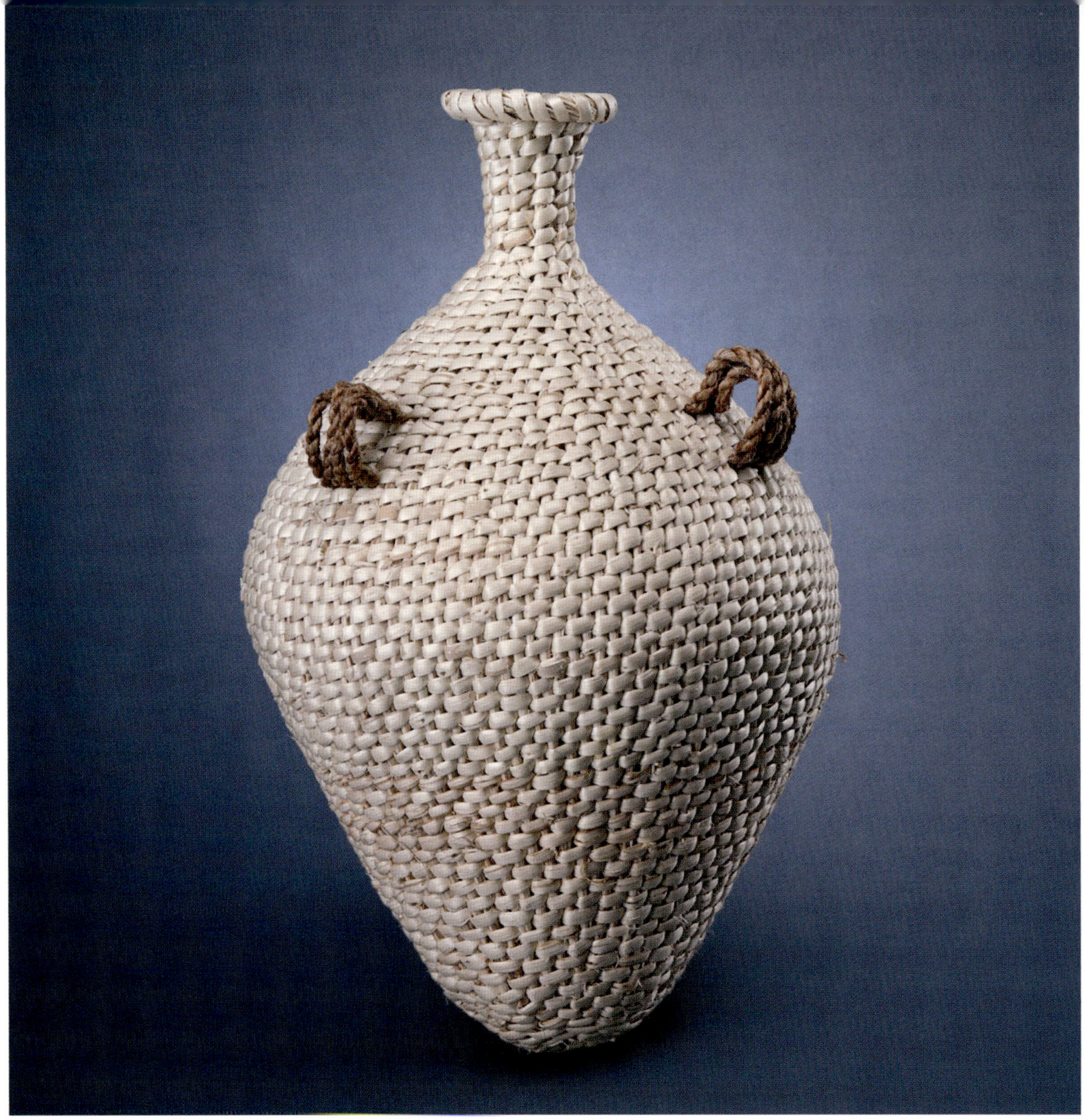

FIG.170

Water Jar, 2012, Moapa Paiute, Everett Pikyavit, 21.4 x 13.2 cm., 58188

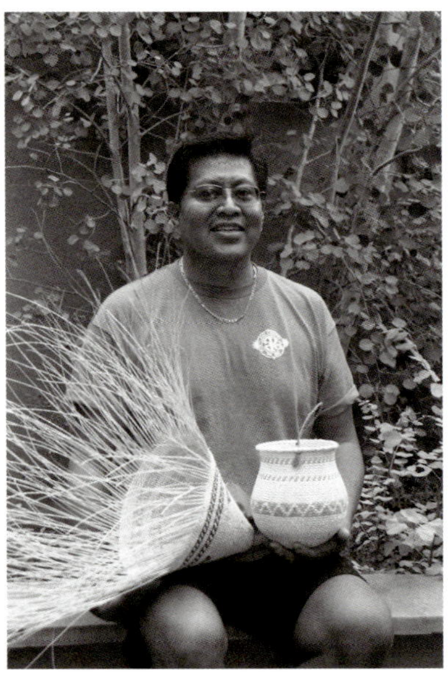

EVERETT PIKYAVIT, Moapa Paiute (b. 1967)

Everett Pikyavit's basket weaving has been influenced by the work of many Southern Paiute basket weavers of the past. However, according to Pikyavit, his greatest source of inspiration was his paternal grandmother, Lila Benson Rogers. He started weaving baskets as an adult, drawing upon what he remembered about his grandmother's techniques, as well as studying historic museum baskets, to decipher how different basket types were made. As with many other basket makers, he found that the process came to him naturally. Pikyavit explained: "As a child I warmly recall sitting

FIG. 171

Everett Pikyavit, Moapa Paiute, 2005. Photo by Katrina Lasko. Courtesy of the School for Advanced Research.

next to my grandmother, Lila, playing with my trucks and other toys, as she worked on her baskets. Sometimes she would gather willows along a creek in Utah or Nevada, collecting different sizes of willow for different baskets, while I would play or wade in the water. It was more just being around her when her hands were always busy. I'd be on the floor playing while she was working and picked things up along the way."

After a visit to the Lost City Museum in Overton, Nevada, in 1999, where he saw traditional Native American baskets, Pikyavit was inspired to gather basketry materials and begin weaving baskets as his grandmother had done before him. Today, as a teacher, he passes on his knowledge to other Southern Paiutes, encouraging them to revive traditional basket materials, techniques, styles, and designs, with the hope that the art and culture of basketry will endure.

MARY HOLIDAY BLACK (B. 1935) AND FAMILY, Diné

> *Every ceremonial basket has a story. There are many basket stories. If we stop making the baskets, we lose the stories.*
>
> MARY HOLIDAY BLACK
>
> (SIMPSON 2003: 131)

A Native American woman may become a basket weaver for cultural, creative, or economic reasons, or to preserve her history by educating the outside world. For the Black family, weaving has meant creating and sustaining a family tradition, while leading their lives within traditional cultural and social patterns. The family's matriarch is Mary Holiday Black (b. 1935), who learned to weave as a

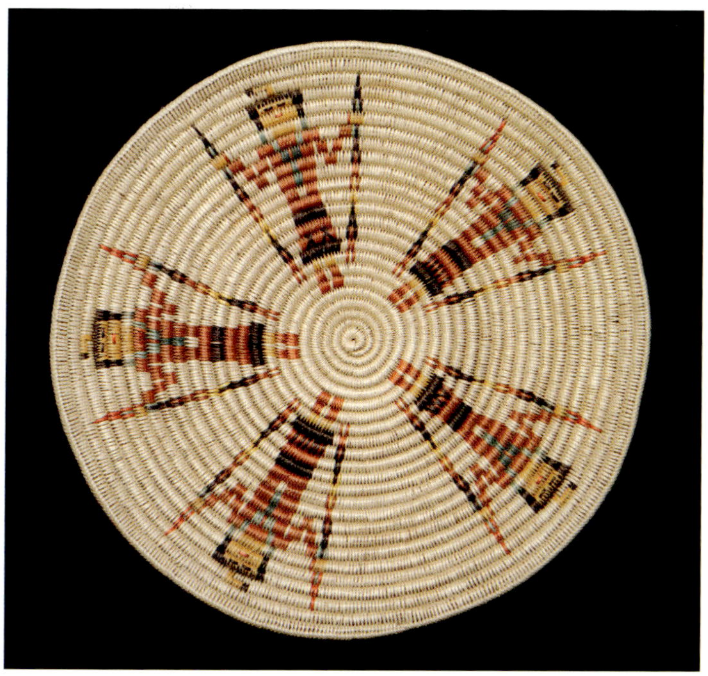

FIG. 172

Tray, 1982, Diné, Sally Black, 10.8 x 56.5 cm., 50016

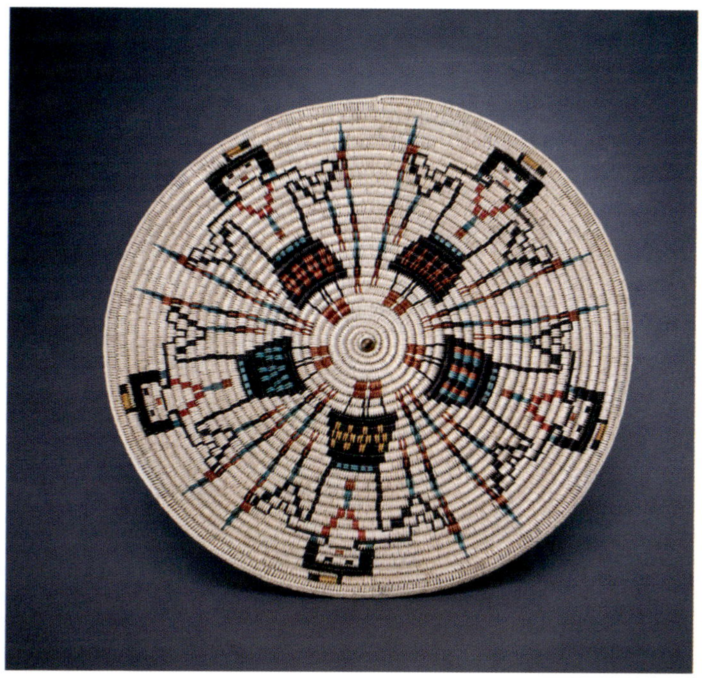

FIG. 173

Tray, 1987, Diné, Sally Black, 2.5 x 68.1 cm., 51300

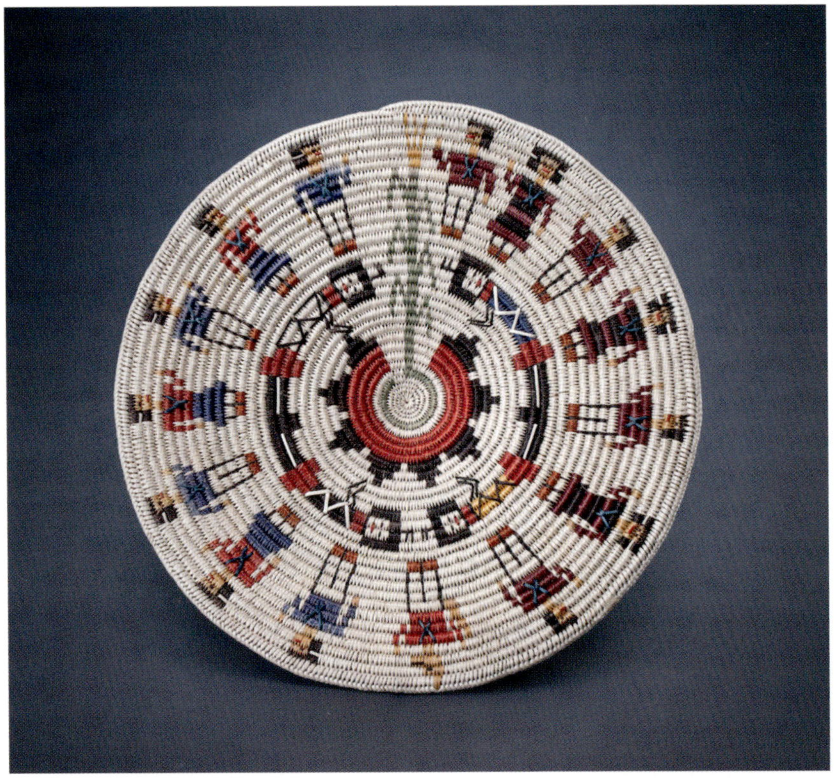

FIG. 174

"Mythology" Tray, 1995, Diné, Agnes Black Gray, 7.2 x 51.0 cm., 54658

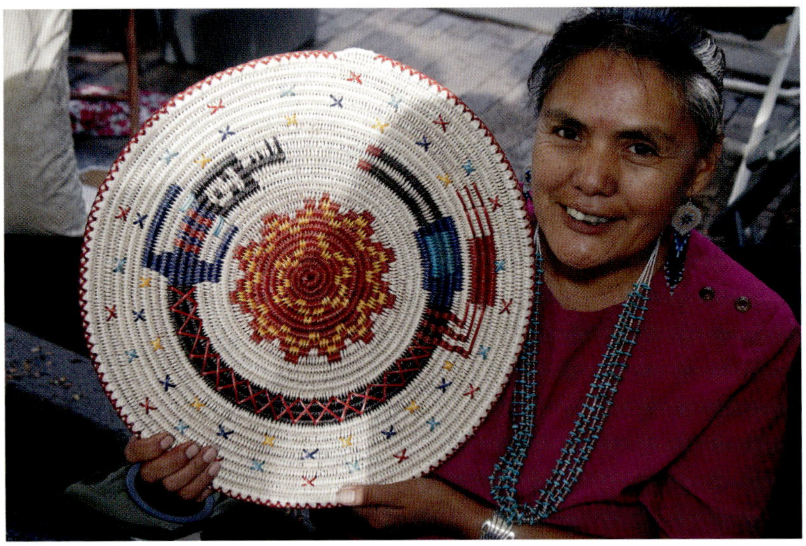

FIG. 175

Sally Black, Santa Fe Indian Market, 2011. Photo by Clare Lighton.

child from her grandmother's relatives. Today, more than a half century later, she heads a family of eleven children—nine of whom are weavers—and a number of grandchildren who also have chosen to weave.

Black and her descendants are part of a group of weavers from Douglas Mesa (located in an isolated corner of the Navajo Reservation in southeastern Utah) who are leading a renaissance in Diné basket weaving. Variations in Diné basket designs were virtually nonexistent through the mid-twentieth century. The wedding basket—a truly ceremonial object and design—dominated the weaving of the few basket makers still practicing the art. Beginning in the 1970s a small number of Diné basket weavers began experimenting with design motifs, establishing a movement to revive Diné basket weaving. The Black family—including Mary's daughters Sally Black, Lorraine Black, and Agnes Black Gray—introduced new motifs into the traditional wedding basket design, such as depictions of plants, insects, animals, and humans. However, their most innovative contribution to Diné basketry are the family's story, or narrative, baskets, which depict Diné legends and myths and transmit important tribal traditions and values.

ARTIST UNKNOWN

Most historic-period Native American baskets in museums and private collections are, at best, documented by tribe, ethnic group, or community; only rarely has the basket weaver's name been recorded. The reasons for this omission are varied and complex. The term "artist unknown," used for instance in this exhibition and catalogue, has come into being because of the collector's and

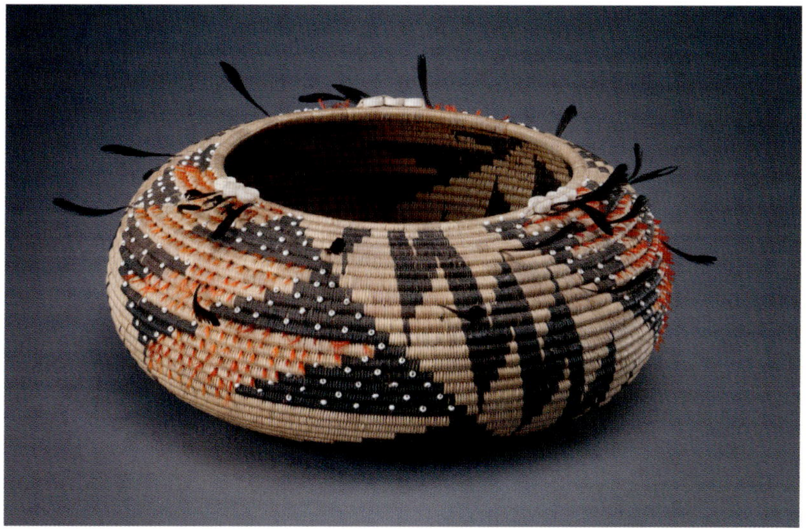

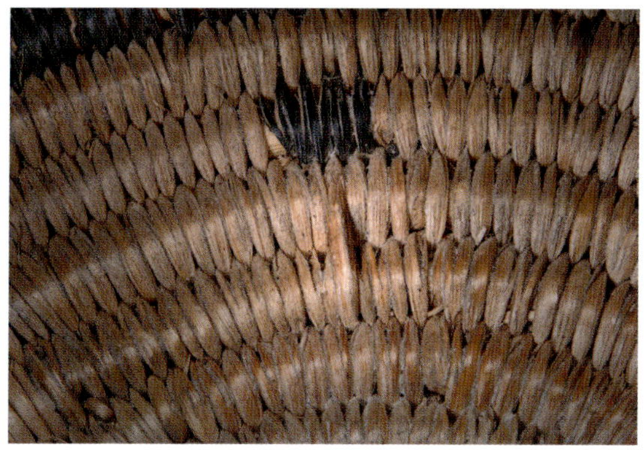

FIG. 176

Treasure, or Gift, Basket, c. 1900, Pomo, Attributed to Laura White Wilbell, 10.0 x 26.0 cm., 14331

Historically, most ethnographers, collectors, traders, and dealers rarely recorded or divulged a basket weaver's name. In the Museum of Indian Arts & Culture's collection, weavers are variously referred to by their husband's name, by their first name alone, and/or by the area where they lived. Because basket weavers cannot sign their works, they have traditionally relied upon their unique weaving style to serve as their signature; however, a few weavers have applied individual marks to their baskets. Throughout the museum's history, curators have been adding artists' names, when known, to catalogue records and exhibition labels: individual weavers have been identified through signature stylistic characteristics, as well as by subtle marks incorporated into the baskets' weave. During the planning of this exhibition, two baskets were attributed to individual weavers. One is the work of Pomo basket weaver Mary Knight Benson, profiled above. The other was made by Laura White Wilbell, Pomo (1855–1942). Wilbell's basket was identified by her great-granddaughter, Susan Billy, who recognized Wilbell's characteristic mark: a weft stitch covering two warps on the interior of the basket.

curator's outdated notions of the role personal identity plays in "primitive" societies, as well as the importance of male versus female work, and the relationship between collectors and basket weavers at the time their baskets were acquired. The term also reflects the difference between basketry as an art form made by an artist and basketry as a craft—a trade or profession. Finally, museums have historically addressed Native American art from an almost exclusively ethnographic point of view, focusing on the cultural characteristics of baskets and ignoring the individual maker.

Over the centuries, many basket weavers have not sought recognition from a dominant culture that has often been hostile and brutal to them. Those who have sought recognition have faced the added challenge of the medium itself, which does not lend itself well to being signed. Through the individualization presented in this exhibition and catalogue, we strive to help weavers from the past through the present in their struggle reclaim their humanity, their power, and their identity.

When critiquing another's work, weavers consider the appropriate use of materials and how well they are prepared; the construction techniques chosen and the skill evident in their execution; and the form and related choice and placement of the two-dimensional design and ornamentation. All of these traits determine the basket's quality and cultural appropriateness. As you experience the works represented in this catalogue—both by known and unknown makers—take note of these qualities, consider the depth of devotion needed by weavers to collect and process materials, and remember the spiritual power that is woven into each basket. These attributes, interwoven with cultural legacy and creative vision, are the hallmarks of the basket weaver's art.

CATALOGUE OF THE COLLECTION

SOUTHWEST

ACOMA

Cooking Bowl, c. 1850
Acoma
Artist unknown
10.0 x 39.0 cm.
Museum collection, 23332
CONSTRUCTION: coiling
FOUNDATION: three cottonwood rods
SEWING ELEMENTS: cottonwood shoots, devil's claw seedpod, cattail fiber; with buckskin

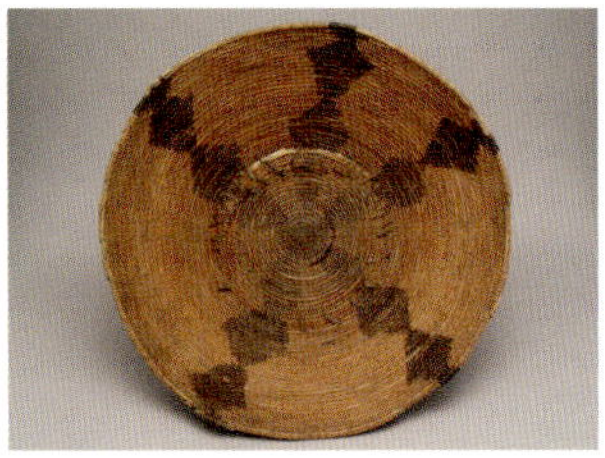

AKIMEL O'ODHAM

Tray, c. 1900
Akimel O'odham
Artist unknown
5.0 x 20.5 cm.
Michael Harrison Collection, 1029
CONSTRUCTION: coiling
FOUNDATION: cattail-splint bundle
SEWING ELEMENTS: willow shoots, devil's claw seedpod

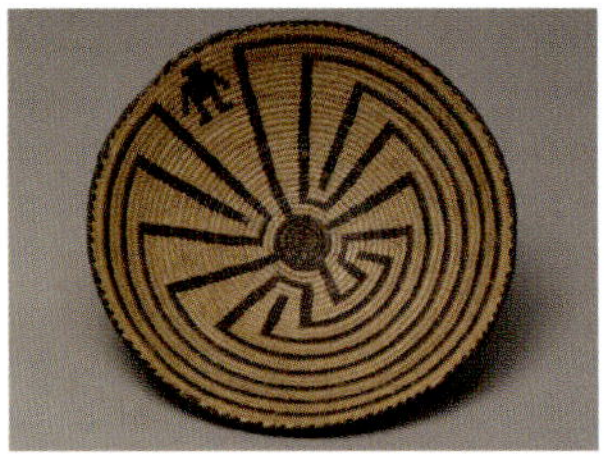

Bowl, c. 1900
Akimel O'odham
Artist unknown
12.5 x 48.1 cm.
Gift of Mrs. J. F. Collins, 1136
CONSTRUCTION: coiling
FOUNDATION: cattail-splint bundle
SEWING ELEMENTS: willow shoots, devil's claw seedpod

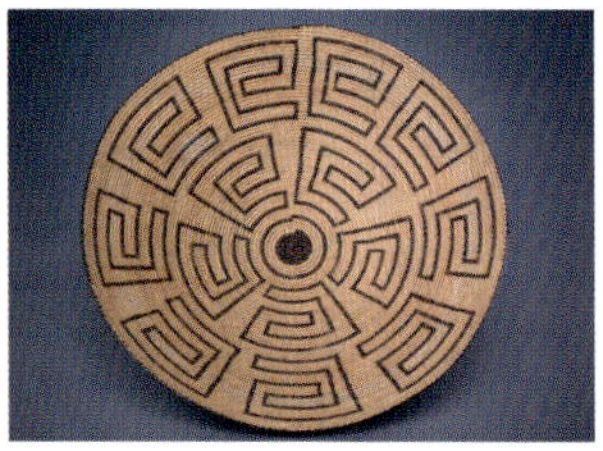

Bowl, c. 1890
Akimel O'odham
Artist unknown
6.5 x 98.0 cm.
Gift of Mrs. J. F. Collins, 1141
CONSTRUCTION: coiling
FOUNDATION: cattail-splint bundle
SEWING ELEMENTS: willow shoots, devil's claw seedpod

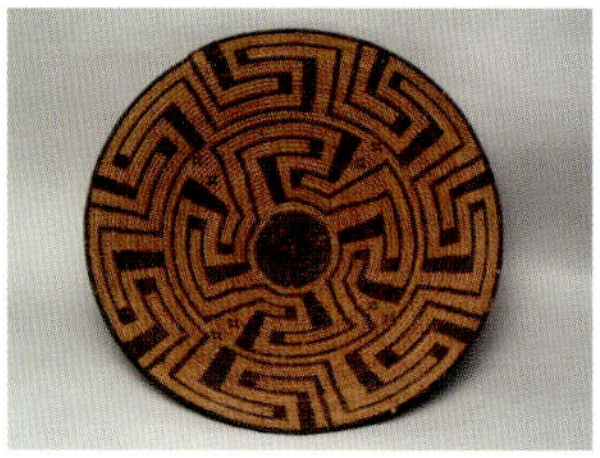

Cylinder, c. 1890
Akimel O'odham
Artist unknown
27.5 x 20.5 cm.
Honorable Daniel H. McMillan Collection, 14412
CONSTRUCTION: coiling
FOUNDATION: cattail-splint bundle
SEWING ELEMENTS: willow shoots, devil's claw seedpod

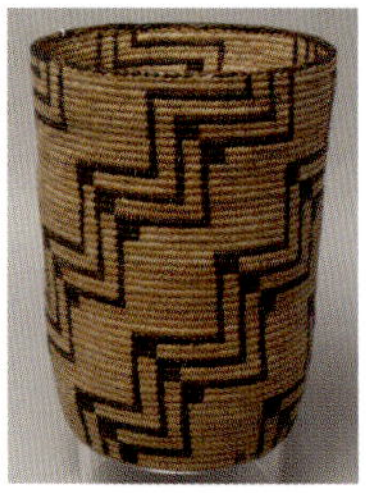

Plaque, c. 1920
Akimel O'odham
Artist unknown
2.0 x 18.5 cm.
Gift of Lydia Trowbridge, 23325
CONSTRUCTION: coiling
FOUNDATION: cattail-splint bundle
SEWING ELEMENTS: willow shoots, devil's claw seedpod

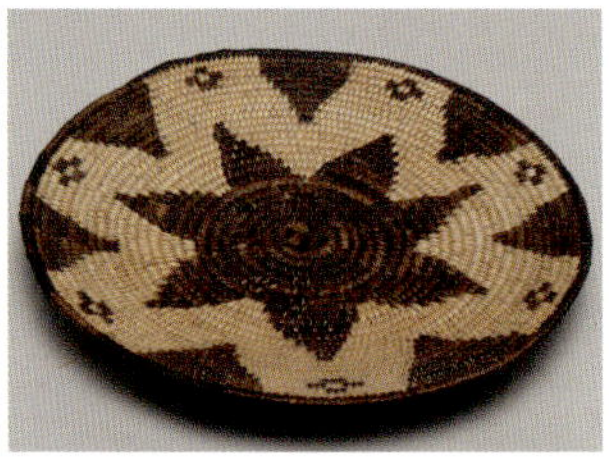

Tray, c. 1900
Akimel O'odham
Artist unknown
7.0 x 41.5 cm.
H. F. Robinson Collection, 23381
CONSTRUCTION: coiling
FOUNDATION: cattail-splint bundle
SEWING ELEMENTS: willow shoots, devil's claw seedpod

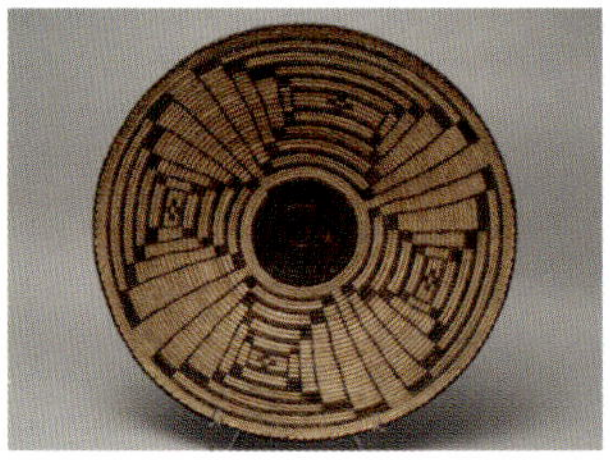

Tray, c. 1900
Akimel O'odham
Artist unknown
8.0 x 33.0 cm.
Gift of S. J. Hess, 23384
CONSTRUCTION: coiling
FOUNDATION: cattail-splint bundle
SEWING ELEMENTS: willow shoots, devil's claw seedpod

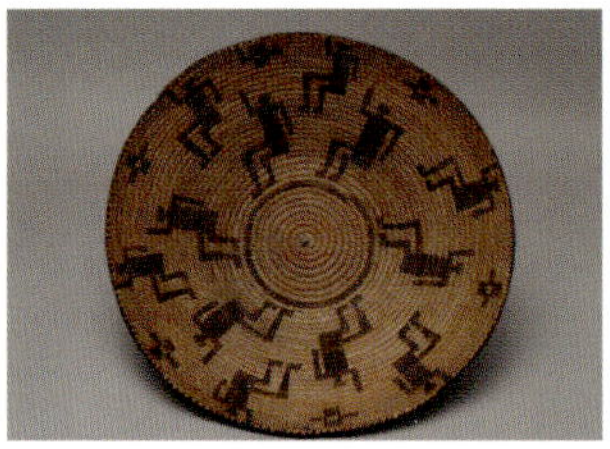

Jar, c. 1910
Akimel O'odham
Artist unknown
30.0 x 26.1 cm.
Museum collection, 23681
CONSTRUCTION: coiling
FOUNDATION: cattail-splint bundle
SEWING ELEMENTS: willow shoots, devil's claw seedpod

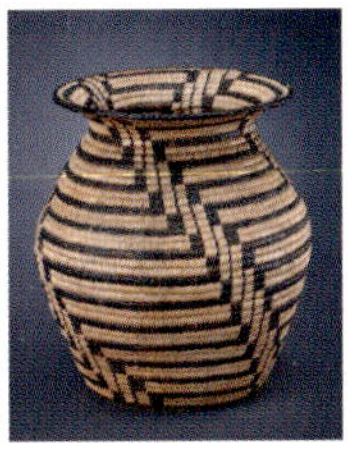

Bowl, c. 1900
Akimel O'odham
Artist unknown
14.0 x 45.0 cm.
Ada Crawford McCormack Collection, 31083
CONSTRUCTION: coiling
FOUNDATION: cattail-splint bundle
SEWING ELEMENTS: willow shoots, devil's claw seedpod

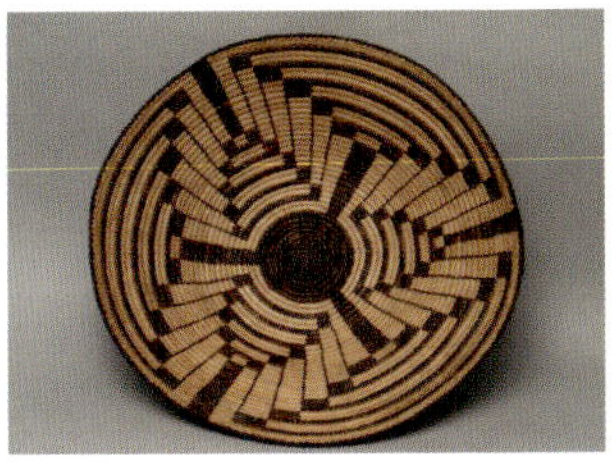

Carrying Basket, c. 1900
Akimel O'odham
Artist unknown
213.0 x 196.0
Historical Society of New Mexico Collection, 36693
CONSTRUCTION: knotless netting, plaiting
WEAVING ELEMENTS: mesquite wood, agave cordage, sotol leaf; with dye, paint, horsehair

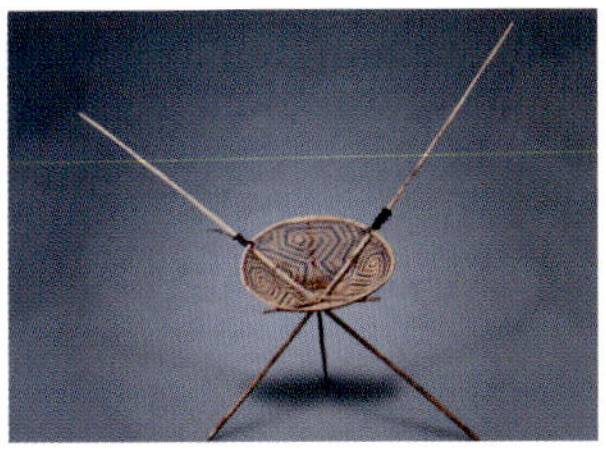

Jar, c. 1900
Akimel O'odham
Artist unknown
36.0 x 29.0 cm.
Gift of Alden Foss, 25425
CONSTRUCTION: coiling
FOUNDATION: cattail-splint bundle
SEWING ELEMENTS: willow shoots, devil's claw seedpod

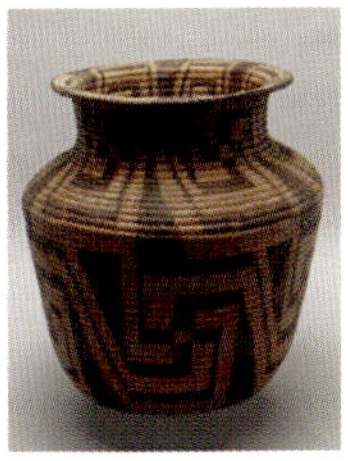

Tray, c. 1900
Akimel O'odham
Artist unknown
11.0 x 40.0 cm.
Ada Crawford McCormack Collection, 31091
CONSTRUCTION: coiling
FOUNDATION: cattail-splint bundle
SEWING ELEMENTS: willow shoots, devil's claw seedpod

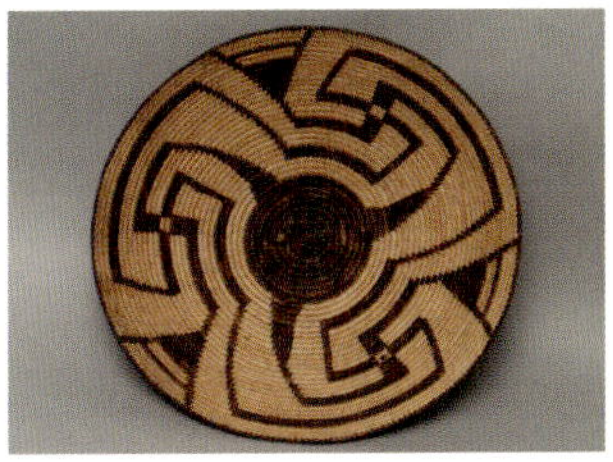

Bowl, c. 1910
Akimel O'odham
Artist unknown
6.5 x 31.0 cm.
Museum collection, 36720
CONSTRUCTION: coiling
FOUNDATION: cattail-splint bundle
SEWING ELEMENTS: willow shoots, devil's claw seedpod

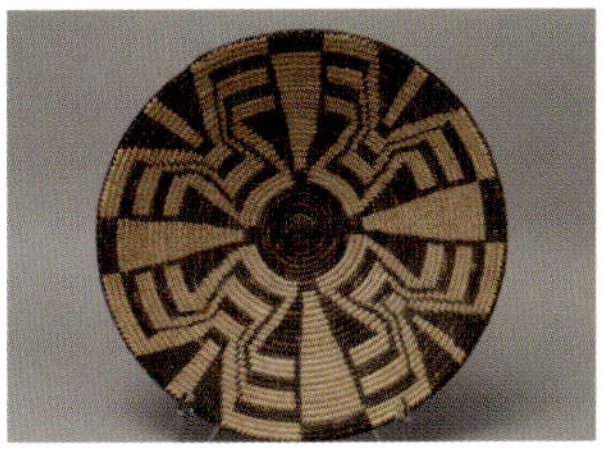

Bowl, c. 1940
Akimel O'odham
Artist unknown
11.0 x 18.0 cm.
Gift of Alden Foss, 25433
CONSTRUCTION: coiling
FOUNDATION: cattail-splint bundle
SEWING ELEMENTS: willow shoots, devil's claw seedpod

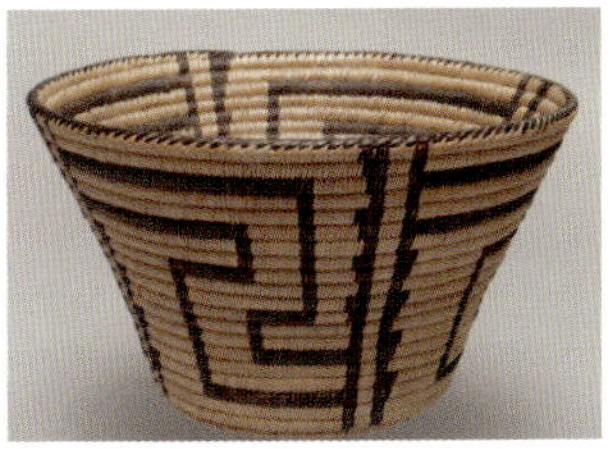

Bowl, c. 1890
Akimel O'odham
Artist unknown
11.0 x 28.5 cm.
Ada Crawford McCormack Collection, 31118
CONSTRUCTION: coiling
FOUNDATION: cattail-splint bundle
SEWING ELEMENTS: willow shoots, devil's claw seedpod

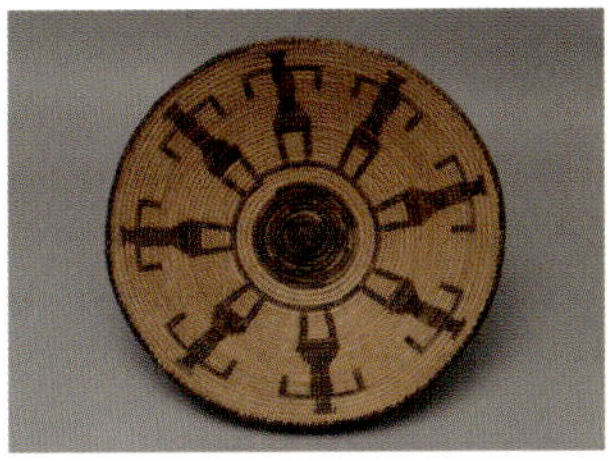

Cylinder, c. 1895
Akimel O'odham
Artist unknown
39.0 x 30.2 cm.
Gift of Mrs. W. H. Langroise, 45705
CONSTRUCTION: coiling
FOUNDATION: cattail-splint bundle
SEWING ELEMENTS: willow shoots, banana yucca root, devil's claw seedpod

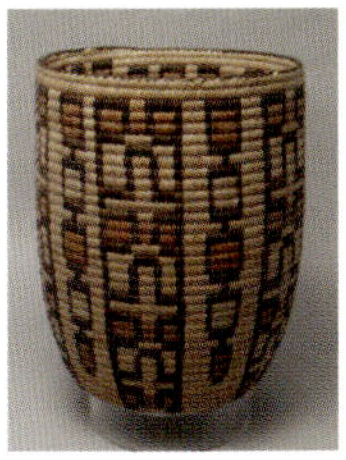

Bowl, c. 1900
Akimel O'odham
Artist unknown
18.5 x 48.0 cm.
Gift of Betty Toulouse, 46369

CONSTRUCTION: coiling

FOUNDATION: cattail-stem bundle

SEWING ELEMENTS: willow shoots, devil's claw seedpod

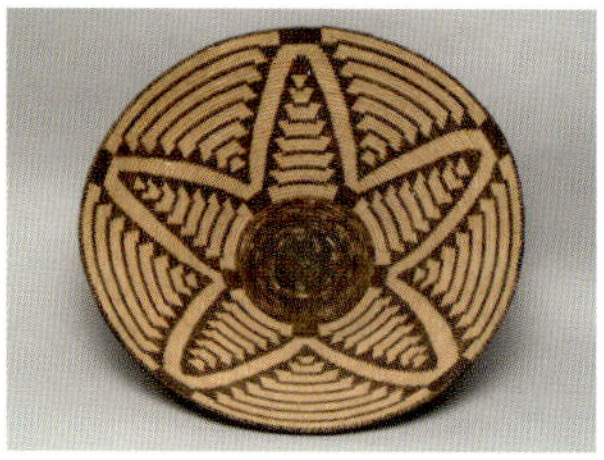

Tray, c. 1910
Akimel O'odham
Artist unknown
4.0 x 32.7 cm.
Bequest of William O. Sweet, 48196

CONSTRUCTION: coiling

FOUNDATION: cattail-stem bundle

SEWING ELEMENTS: willow shoots, devil's claw seedpod

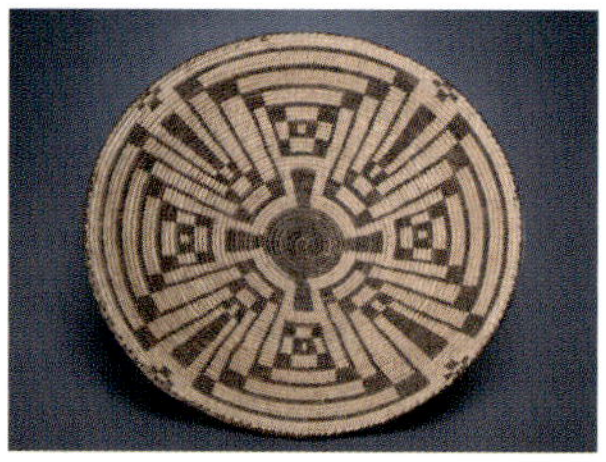

ANCESTRAL PUEBLO

Cylinder, c. 1150
Ancestral Pueblo
Artist unknown
18.5 x 23.8 cm.
Museum collection, 53844

CONSTRUCTION: coiling

FOUNDATION: two sumac rods and sumac bundle

SEWING ELEMENT: sumac shoots

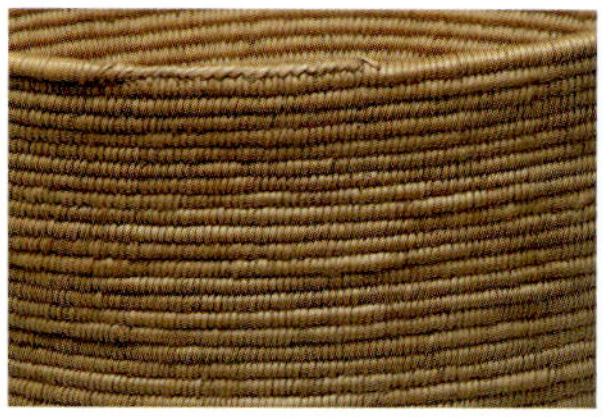

Cylinder, c. 1150
Ancestral Pueblo
Artist unknown
18.5 x 23.8 cm.
Museum collection, 53845

CONSTRUCTION: coiling

FOUNDATION: two sumac rods and sumac bundle

SEWING ELEMENT: sumac shoots

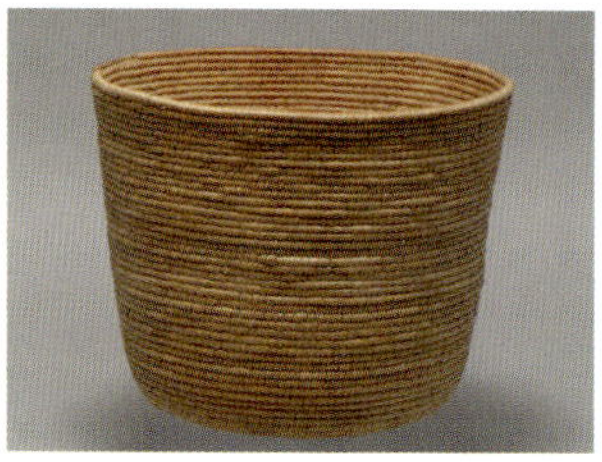

Bowl, c. 1150
Ancestral Pueblo
Artist unknown
8.0 x 27.0 cm.
Museum collection, 53846

CONSTRUCTION: coiling

FOUNDATION: two sumac rods and sumac bundle

SEWING ELEMENTS: sumac shoots, yucca root

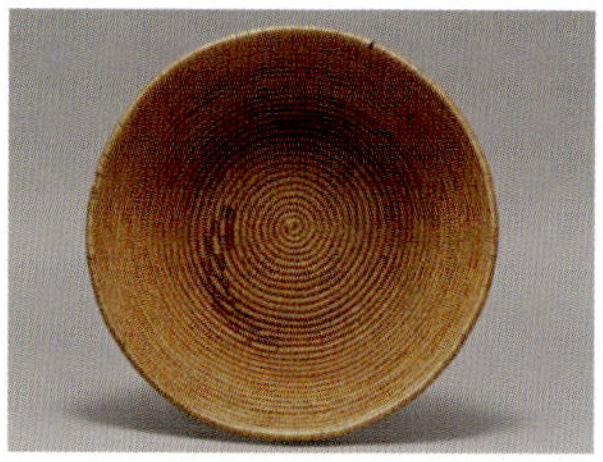

Box, c. 1150
Ancestral Pueblo
Artist unknown
9.8 x 16.0 x 35.0 cm.
Museum collection, 53847

CONSTRUCTION: coiling

FOUNDATION: two sumac rods and sumac bundle

SEWING ELEMENTS: sumac shoots, yucca root

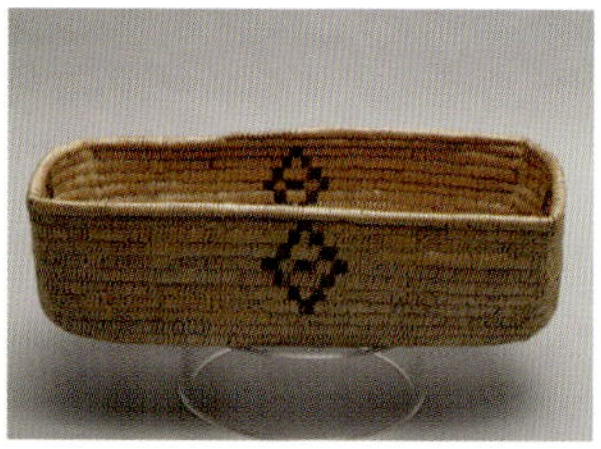

Bowl, c. 1150
Ancestral Pueblo
Artist unknown
9.0 x 28.8 cm.
Museum collection, 53849

CONSTRUCTION: coiling

FOUNDATION: two sumac rods and sumac bundle

SEWING ELEMENTS: sumac shoots, yucca root

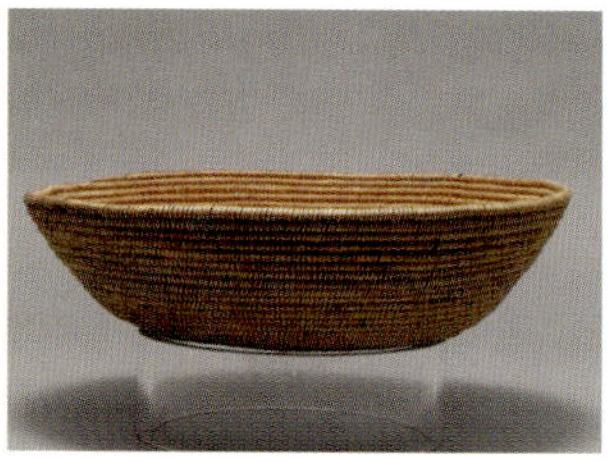

DINÉ

Bowl, c. 1880
Diné
Artist unknown
11.0 x 37.5 cm.
Michael Harrison Collection, 1094

CONSTRUCTION: coiling

FOUNDATION: two sumac rods and sumac bundle

SEWING ELEMENT: sumac shoots; with dye

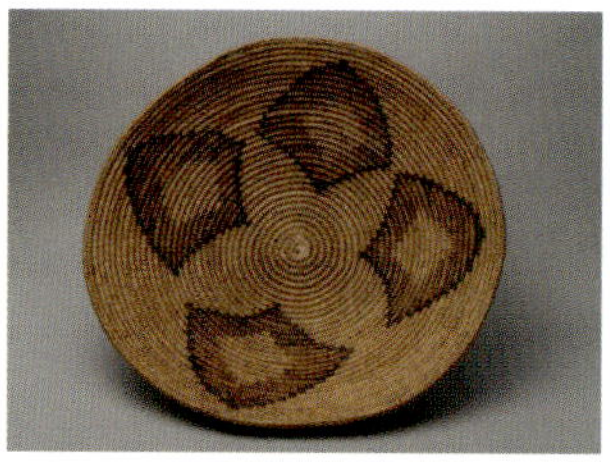

Bowl, c. 1900
Diné
Artist unknown
8.1 x 30.2 cm.
Michael Harrison Collection, 1099

CONSTRUCTION: coiling

FOUNDATION: three sumac rods

SEWING ELEMENT: sumac shoots; with dye

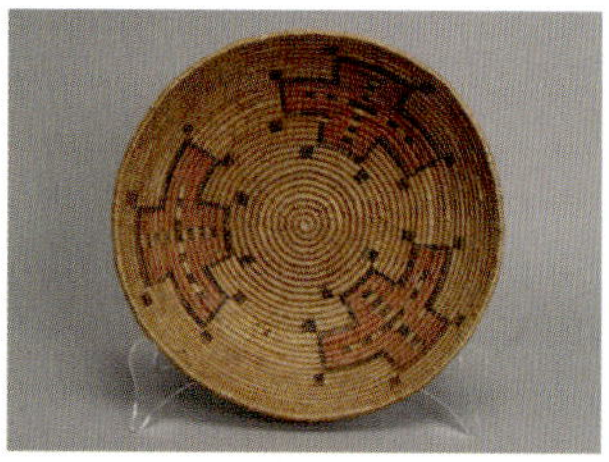

Tray, c. 1870
Diné
Artist unknown
10.5 x 34.5 cm.
Michael Harrison Collection, 1100
CONSTRUCTION: coiling
FOUNDATION: two sumac rods and sumac bundle
SEWING ELEMENT: sumac shoots; with dye

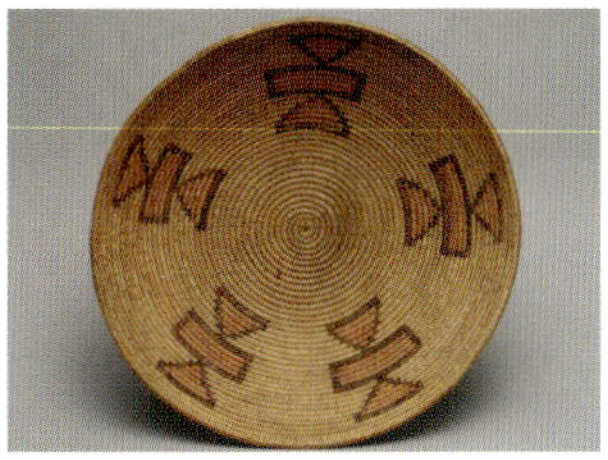

Tray, c. 1850
Diné
Artist unknown
12.5 x 45.0 cm.
Museum collection, 1119
CONSTRUCTION: coiling
FOUNDATION: two sumac rods and sumac bundle
SEWING ELEMENT: sumac shoots; with dye

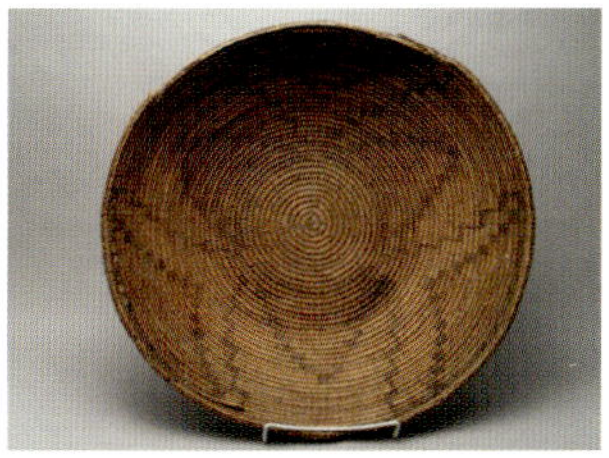

Tray, c. 1890
Diné
Artist unknown
7.5 x 31.5 cm.
Museum collection, 11342
CONSTRUCTION: coiling
FOUNDATION: two sumac rods and sumac bundle
SEWING ELEMENT: sumac shoots; with dye

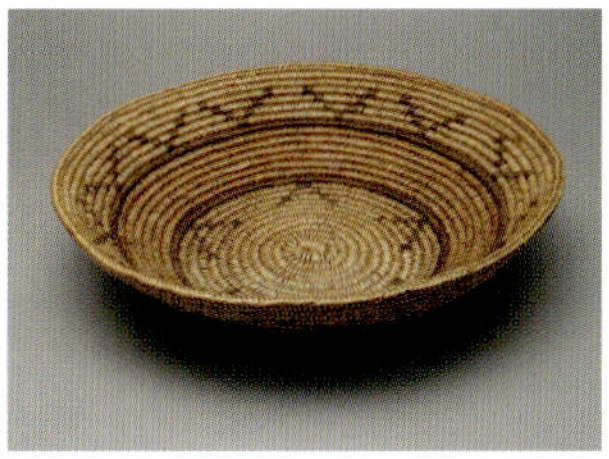

Tray, c. 1890
Diné
Artist unknown
9.5 x 27.5 cm.
Museum collection, 14415
CONSTRUCTION: coiling
FOUNDATION: two sumac rods and sumac bundle
SEWING ELEMENT: sumac shoots; with dye

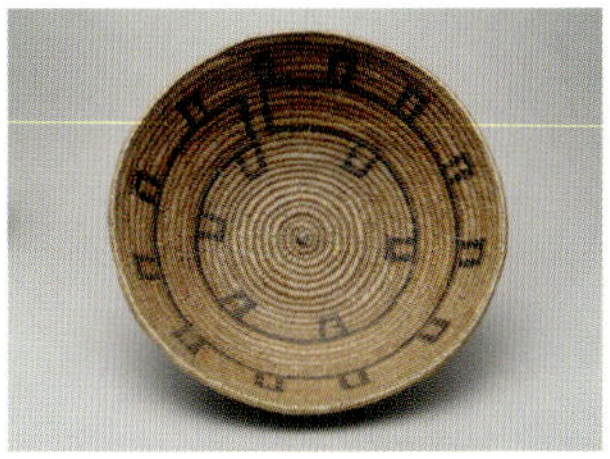

Bowl, c. 1870
Diné
Artist unknown
11.8 x 46.6 cm.
H. F. Robinson Collection, 23775
CONSTRUCTION: coiling
FOUNDATION: two sumac rods and sumac bundle
SEWING ELEMENT: sumac shoots; with dye

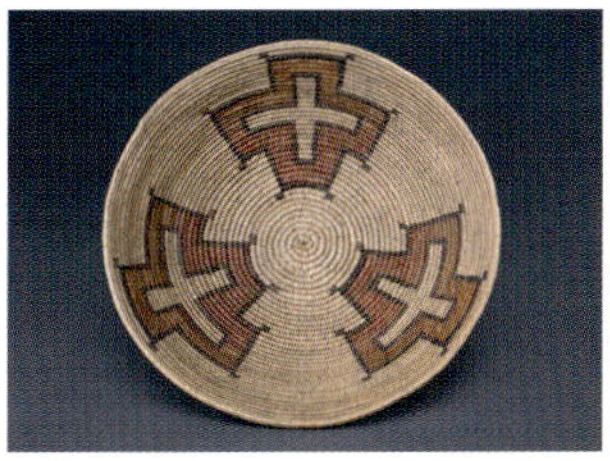

Tray, c. 1875
Diné
Artist unknown
9.0 x 29.5 cm.
Ada Crawford McCormack Collection, 36692
CONSTRUCTION: coiling
FOUNDATION: two sumac rods and sumac bundle
SEWING ELEMENT: sumac shoots; with dye

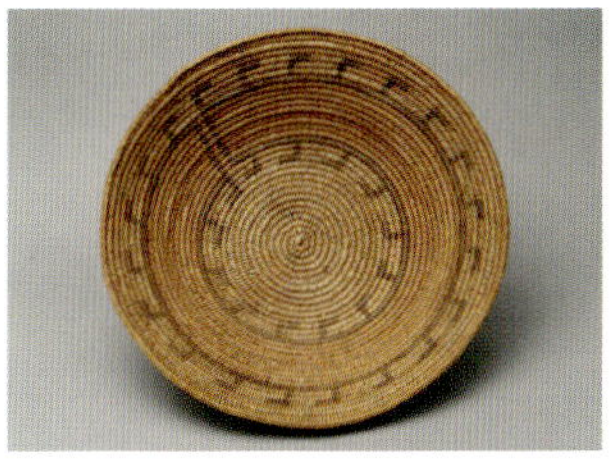

Wedding Tray, c. 1900
Diné
Artist unknown
9.0 x 5.4 cm.
Gift of Betty Toulouse, 46374
CONSTRUCTION: coiling
FOUNDATION: three sumac rods
SEWING ELEMENT: sumac shoots; with dye

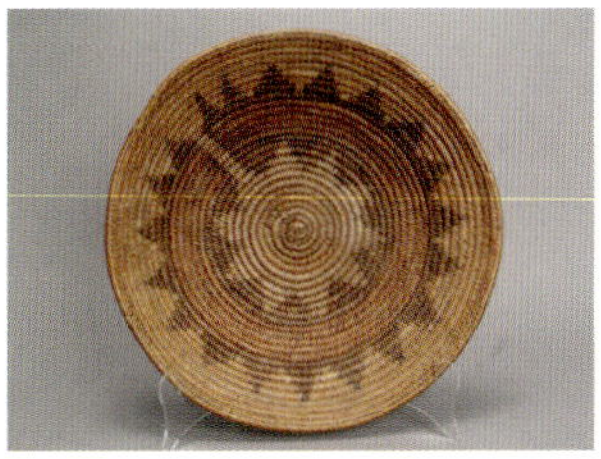

Tray, 1982
Diné
Sally Black
10.8 x 56.5 cm.
Museum collection, 50016
CONSTRUCTION: coiling
FOUNDATION: five sumac rods
SEWING ELEMENT: sumac shoots; with dye

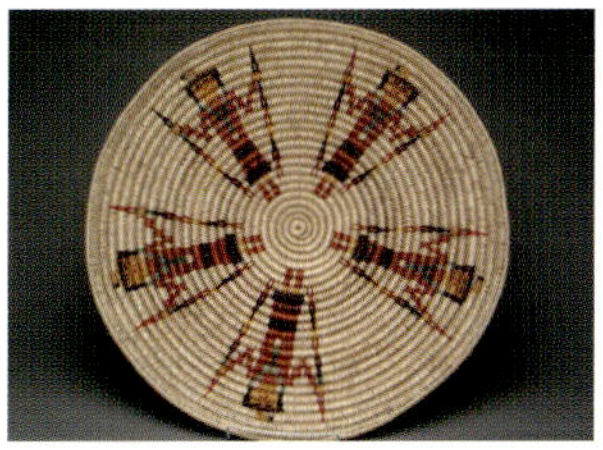

Tray, 1987
Diné
Sally Black
2.5 x 68.1 cm.
Museum purchase, 51300
CONSTRUCTION: coiling
FOUNDATION: five sumac rods
SEWING ELEMENT: sumac shoots; with dye

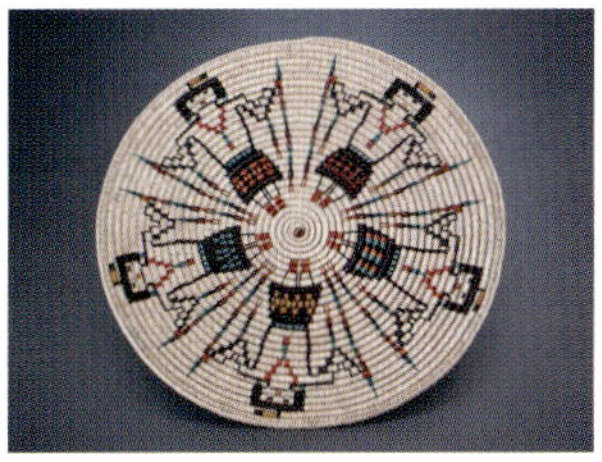

"Mythology" Tray, 1995
Diné
Agnes Black Gray
7.2 x 51.0 cm.
Gift of Steven P. Simpson, 54658

CONSTRUCTION: coiling

FOUNDATION: five sumac rods

SEWING ELEMENT: sumac shoots; with dye

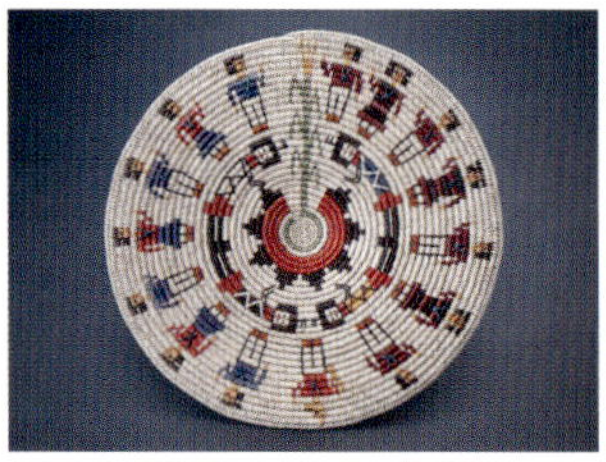

Tray, 1999
Diné
Peggy Rock Black
6.4 x 33.7 cm.
Gift of Friends of Indian Arts, 55667

CONSTRUCTION: coiling

FOUNDATION: two sumac rods

SEWING ELEMENT: sumac shoots; with dye

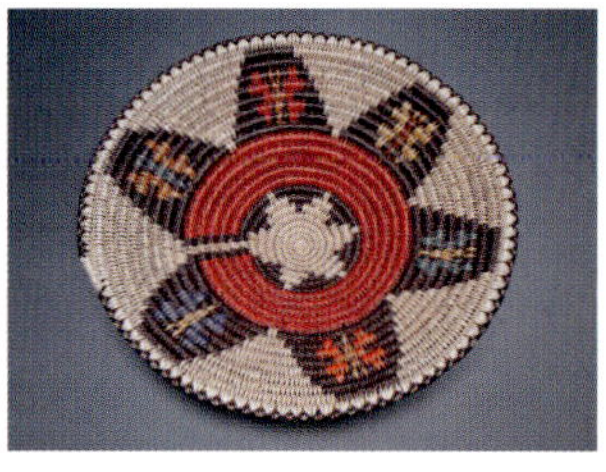

Water Jar, c. 1910
Diné
Artist unknown
33.0 x 24.3 cm.
Gift of John W. Broome, 57220

CONSTRUCTION: coiling

FOUNDATION: two stacked rods

SEWING ELEMENTS: sumac shoots, horsehair; with piñon pitch

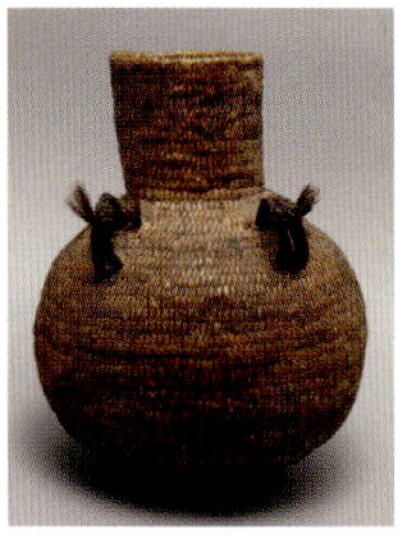

HAVASUPAI

Bowl, c. 1930
Havasupai
Artist unknown
9.2 x 19.2 cm.
Michael Harrison Collection, 941

CONSTRUCTION: coiling

FOUNDATION: three willow rods

SEWING ELEMENTS: willow shoots, devil's claw seedpod

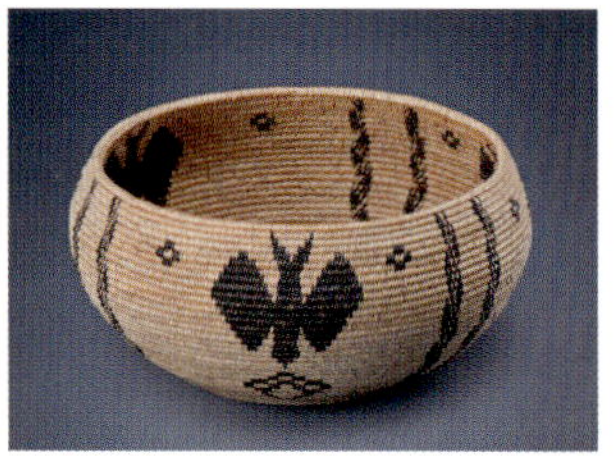

Bowl, c. 1925
Havasupai
Artist unknown
10.5 x 14.0 cm.
Michael Harrison Collection, 942

CONSTRUCTION: coiling

FOUNDATION: three willow rods

SEWING ELEMENTS: willow shoots, devil's claw seedpod

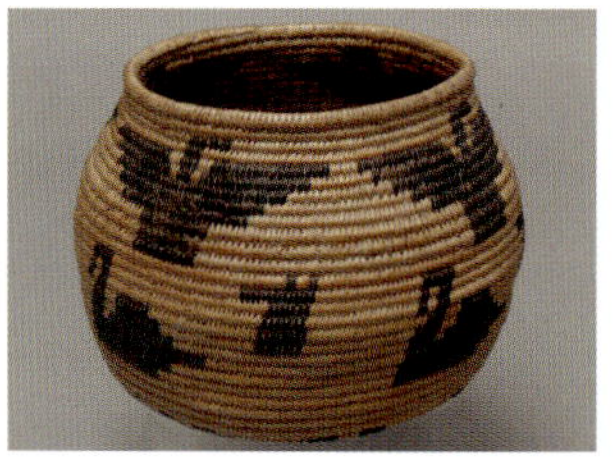

Jar, c. 1920
Havasupai
Artist unknown
16.0 x 15.5 cm.
Michael Harrison Collection, 948

CONSTRUCTION: coiling

FOUNDATION: three willow rods

SEWING ELEMENTS: willow shoots, devil's claw seedpod

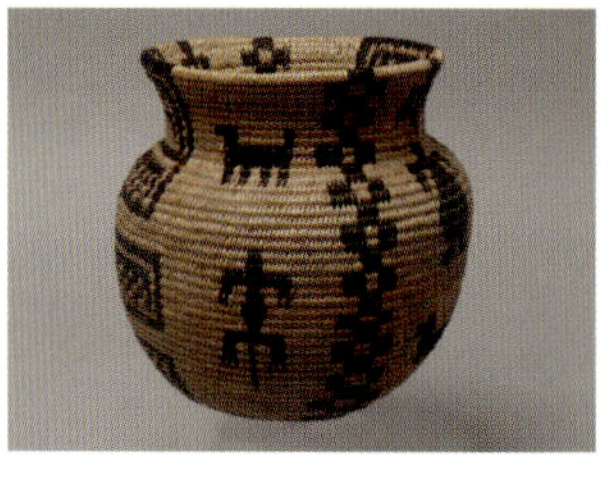

Bowl, c. 1925
Havasupai
Artist unknown
5.0 x 10.5 cm.
Michael Harrison Collection, 949

CONSTRUCTION: coiling

FOUNDATION: three willow rods

SEWING ELEMENTS: willow shoots, Joshua tree root, devil's claw seedpod

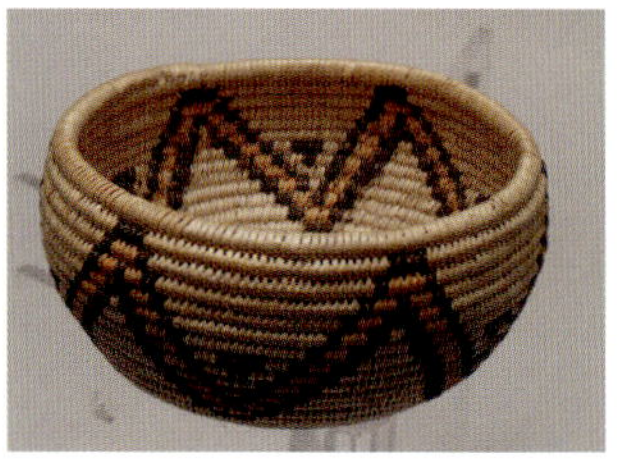

Bowl, c. 1925
Havasupai
Artist unknown
6.5 x 17.5 cm.
Michael Harrison Collection, 955

CONSTRUCTION: coiling

FOUNDATION: three willow rods

SEWING ELEMENTS: willow shoots, devil's claw seedpod

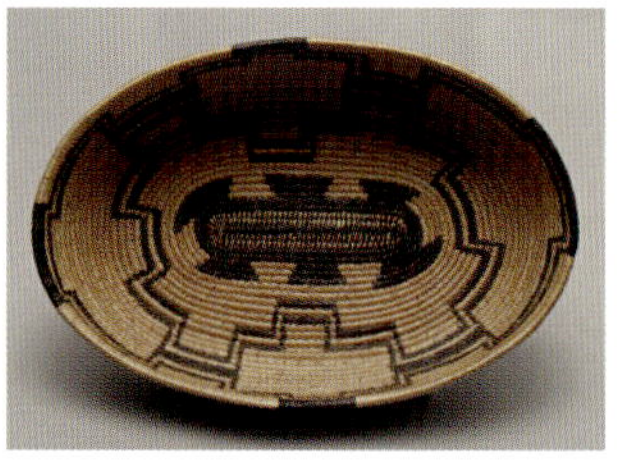

Bowl, c. 1915
Havasupai
Artist unknown
13.0 x 25.5 cm.
Michael Harrison Collection, 959

CONSTRUCTION: coiling

FOUNDATION: three willow rods

SEWING ELEMENTS: willow shoots, devil's claw seedpod

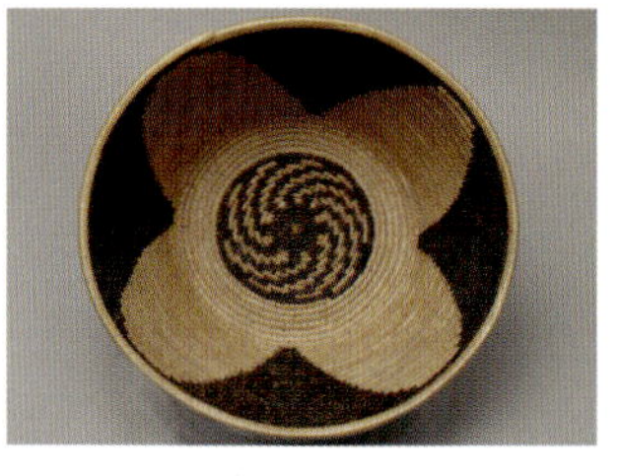

Bowl, c. 1930
Havasupai
Artist unknown
10.5 x 19.0 cm.
Michael Harrison Collection, 962
CONSTRUCTION: coiling
FOUNDATION: three willow rods
SEWING ELEMENTS: willow shoots, devil's claw seedpod

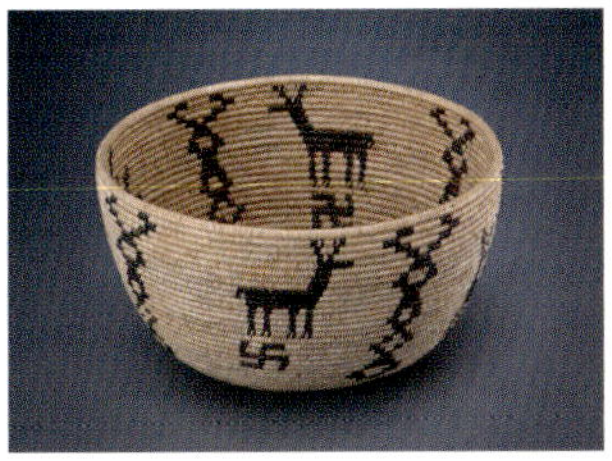

Tray, c. 1935
Havasupai
Artist unknown
3.0 x 28.0 cm.
Michael Harrison Collection, 972
CONSTRUCTION: coiling
FOUNDATION: three willow rods
SEWING ELEMENTS: willow shoots, devil's claw seedpod

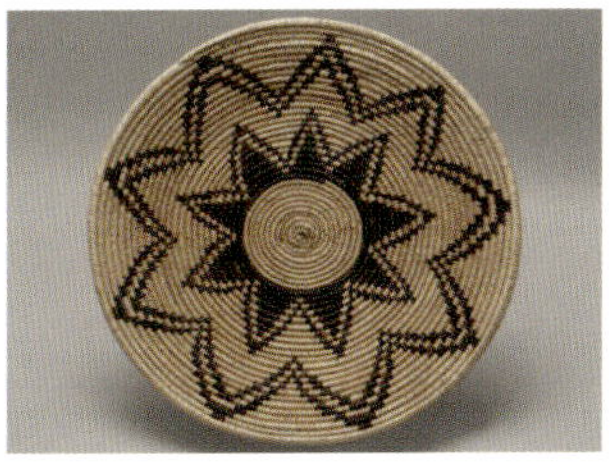

Plaque, c. 1925
Havasupai
Artist unknown
2.0 x 26.0 cm.
Michael Harrison Collection, 1027
CONSTRUCTION: coiling
FOUNDATION: three willow rods
SEWING ELEMENTS: cottonwood shoots, devil's claw seedpod

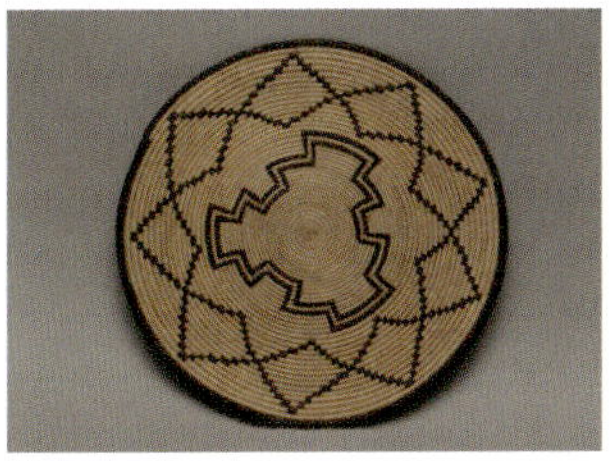

Water Jar, c. 1890
Havasupai or Hualapai
Artist unknown
24.5 x 19.5 cm.
Museum collection, 23417
CONSTRUCTION: coiling
FOUNDATION: two willow rods
SEWING ELEMENTS: willow, wool; with piñon pitch

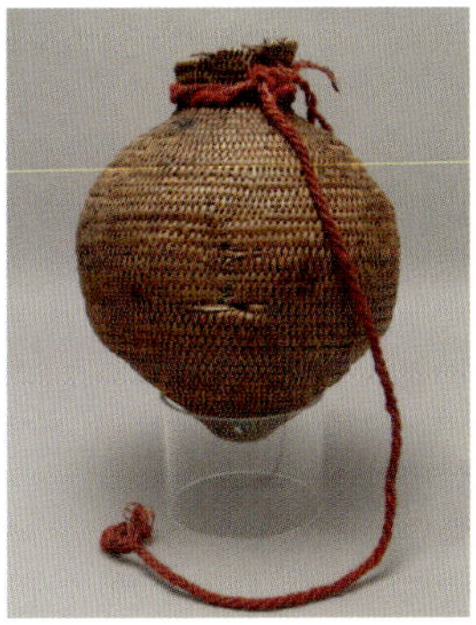

Tray, c. 1900
Havasupai
Artist unknown
7.8 x 36.2 cm.
Gift of Grace Brownell Daniels, 25094
CONSTRUCTION: coiling
FOUNDATION: three willow rods
SEWING ELEMENTS: willow shoots, Joshua tree root, devil's claw seedpod

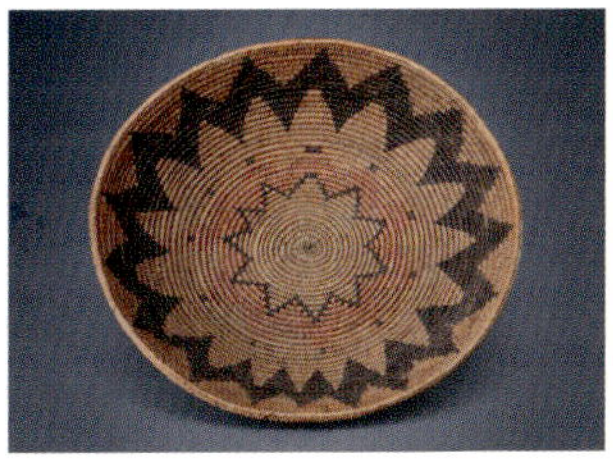

HOPI

Cylinder, c. 1925
Hopi (Second Mesa)
Artist unknown
17.0 x 22.5 cm.
Michael Harrison Collection, 982
CONSTRUCTION: coiling
FOUNDATION: galleta-grass bundle
SEWING ELEMENT: yucca leaf; with dye

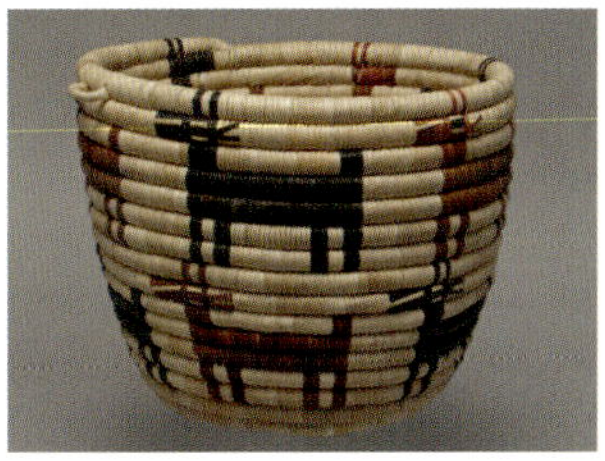

Plaque, c. 1890
Hopi (Second Mesa)
Artist unknown
4.0 x 46.0 cm.
Michael Harrison Collection, 1008
CONSTRUCTION: coiling
FOUNDATION: galleta-grass bundle
SEWING ELEMENT: yucca leaf; with dye

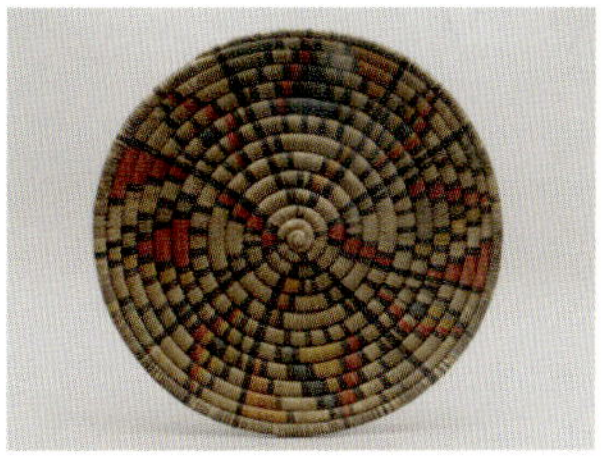

Plaque, c. 1925
Hopi (Third Mesa)
Artist unknown
1.0 x 67.5 cm.
Michael Harrison Collection, 1025
CONSTRUCTION: wicker
FOUNDATION: dunebroom rods
WEAVING ELEMENTS: rabbitbrush stem, yucca leaf; with dye

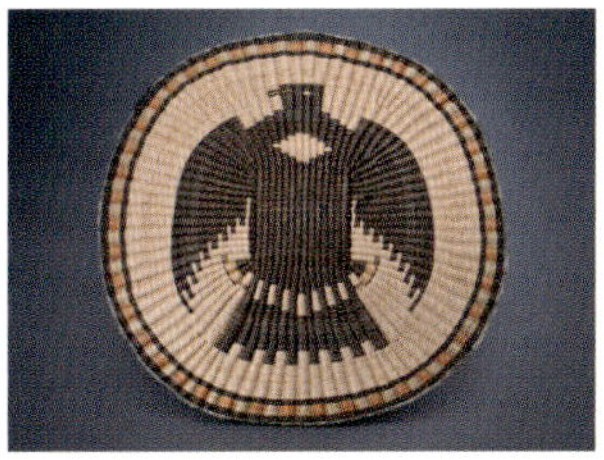

Plaque, c. 1930
Hopi (Second Mesa)
Artist unknown
3.3 x 31.4 cm.
Gift of Dr. Kenneth Chapman, 1125
CONSTRUCTION: coiling
FOUNDATION: galleta-grass bundle
SEWING ELEMENT: yucca leaf; with dye

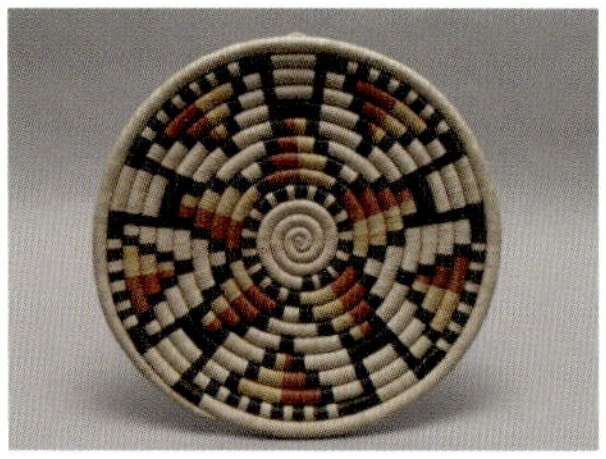

Plaque, c. 1920
Hopi (Third Mesa)
Artist unknown
3.0 x 36.0 cm.
Gift of Dr. Kenneth Chapman, 1130
CONSTRUCTION: wicker
FOUNDATION: dunebroom rods
WEAVING ELEMENTS: rabbitbrush stem, yucca leaf; with dye

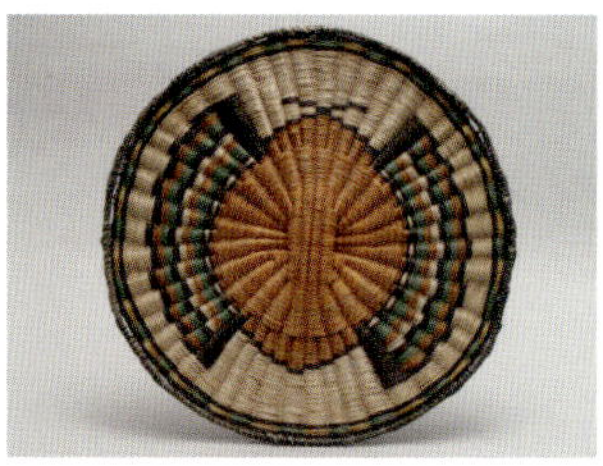

Plaque, c. 1890
Hopi (Third Mesa)
Artist unknown
6.0 x 47.5 cm.
Gift of A. W. Rogers, 23453
CONSTRUCTION: wicker
FOUNDATION: dunebroom rods
WEAVING ELEMENTS: rabbitbrush stem, yucca leaf; with dye

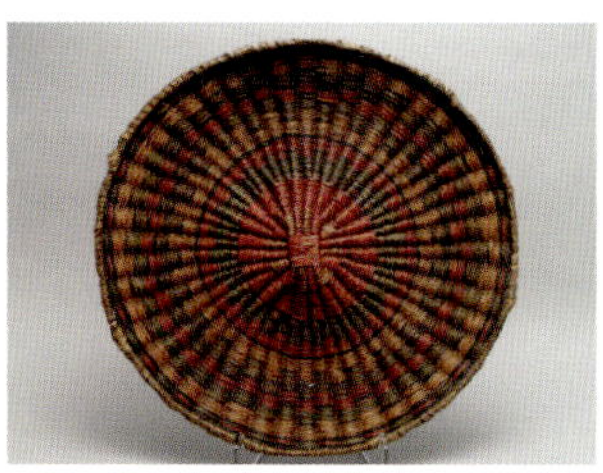

Plaque, c. 1900
Hopi (Third Mesa)
Artist unknown
3.0 x 29.0 cm.
Museum collection, 23636
CONSTRUCTION: wicker
FOUNDATION: dunebroom rods
WEAVING ELEMENTS: rabbitbrush stem, yucca leaf; with dye

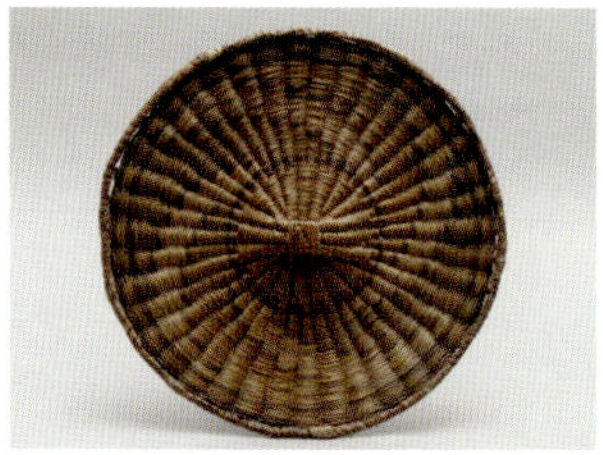

Plaque, c. 1900
Hopi (Third Mesa)
Artist unknown
4.5 x 40.0 cm.
H. F. Robinson Collection, 23643
CONSTRUCTION: wicker
FOUNDATION: dunebroom rods
WEAVING ELEMENTS: rabbitbrush stem, yucca leaf; with dye

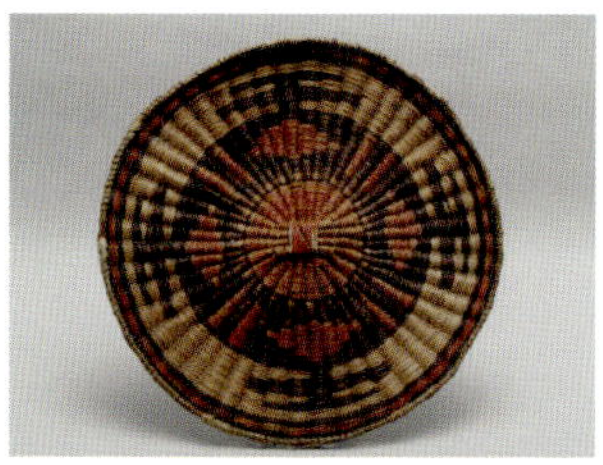

Plaque, c. 1920
Hopi (Third Mesa)
Artist unknown
5.5 x 24.0 cm.
Museum collection, 35708
CONSTRUCTION: wicker
FOUNDATION: dunebroom rods
WEAVING ELEMENTS: rabbitbrush stem, yucca leaf; with dye

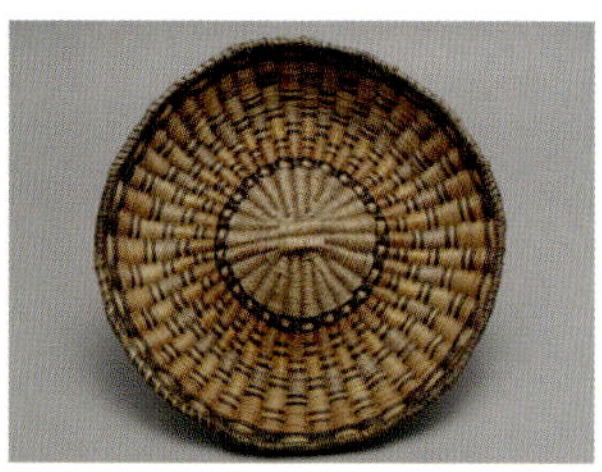

Storage Basket, c. 1930
Hopi (Second Mesa)
Artist unknown
53.0 x 58.1 cm.
Nelson Collection, 35963
CONSTRUCTION: coiling
FOUNDATION: galleta-grass bundle
SEWING ELEMENT: yucca leaf; with dye, blue clay

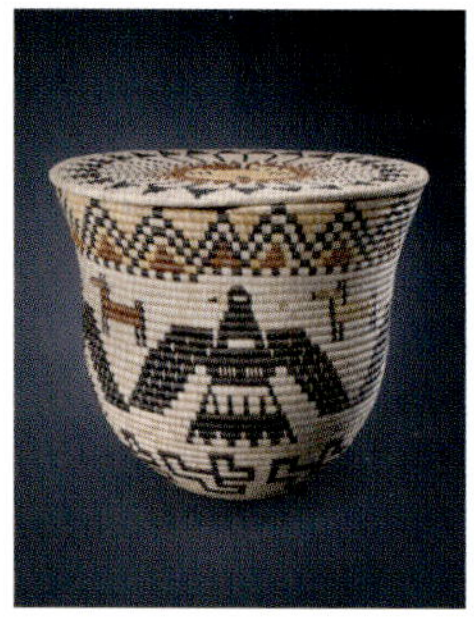

Plaque, c. 1945
Hopi (Second Mesa)
Artist unknown
1.5 x 27 cm.
Gift of Thomas Bahti, 36609
CONSTRUCTION: coiling
FOUNDATION: galleta-grass bundle
SEWING ELEMENT: yucca leaf; with dye, blue clay

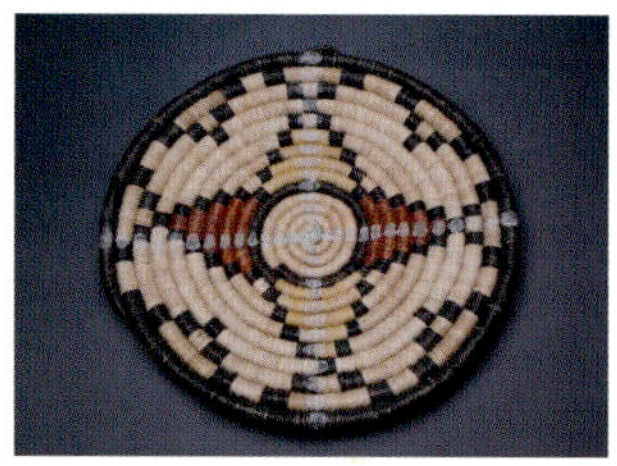

Plaque, c. 1925
Hopi (Second Mesa)
Artist unknown
3.4 x 34.2 cm.
Nelson Collection, 36623
CONSTRUCTION: coiling
FOUNDATION: galleta-grass bundle
SEWING ELEMENT: yucca leaf; with dye

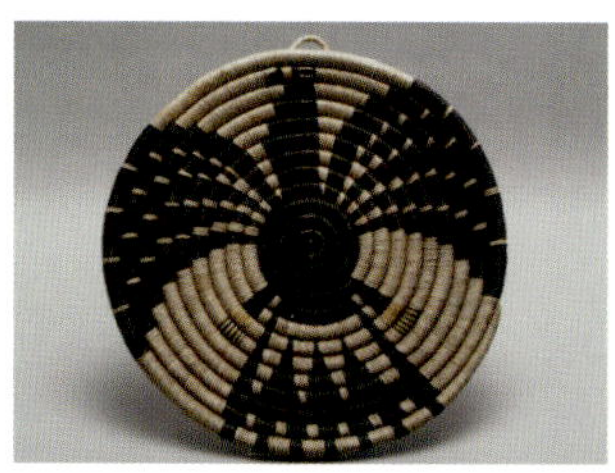

Plaque, c. 1880
Hopi (Second Mesa)
Artist unknown
4.5 x 30.0 cm.
Gift of Mrs. Reed Holaman, 43751
CONSTRUCTION: coiling
FOUNDATION: galleta-grass bundle
SEWING ELEMENT: yucca leaf; with dye

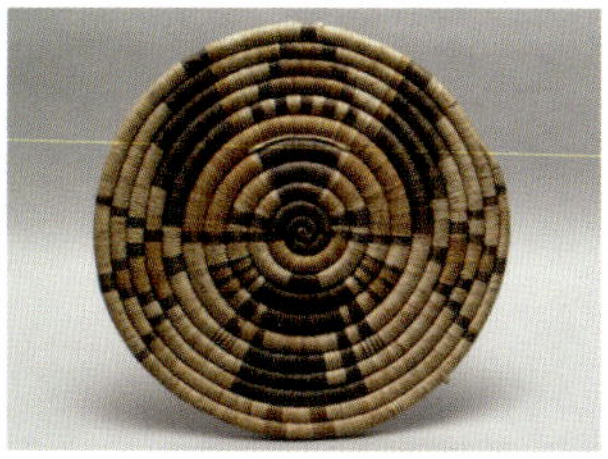

Plaque, c. 1960
Hopi (Second Mesa)
Artist unknown
3.3 x 32.0 cm.
Gift of Pansy Stockton, 46261
CONSTRUCTION: coiling
FOUNDATION: galleta-grass bundle
SEWING ELEMENT: yucca leaf; with dye

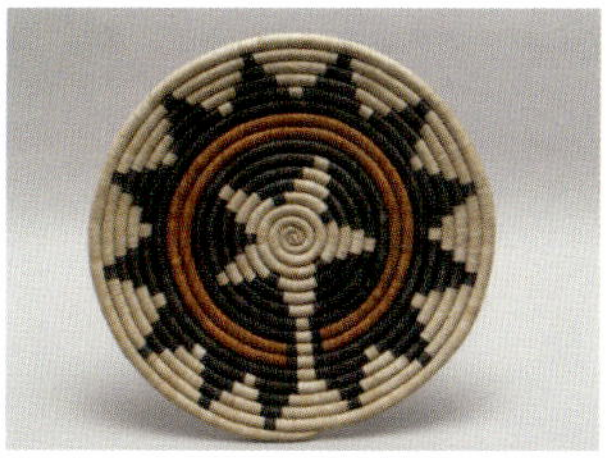

Plaque, 1935
Hopi (Third Mesa)
Artist unknown
3.5 x 35.0 cm.
Gift of Frieda Lauerman, 46352
CONSTRUCTION: wicker
FOUNDATION: dunebroom rods
WEAVING ELEMENTS: rabbitbrush stem, yucca leaf; with dye

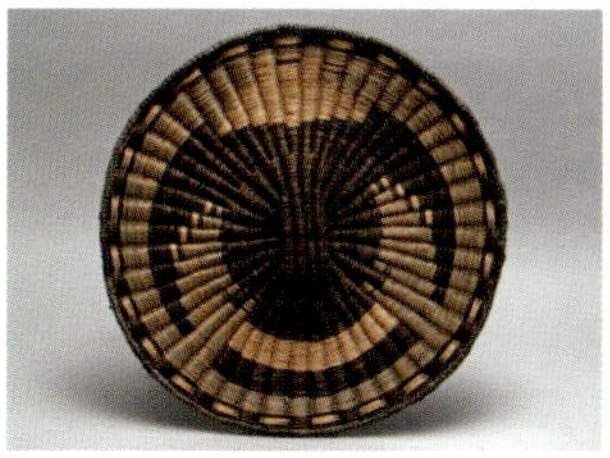

Cylinder, c. 1900
Hopi (Third Mesa)
Artist unknown
20.5 x 22.5 cm.
Madeleine P. and William C. Ilfeld Collection, 48086
CONSTRUCTION: wicker, plaiting
FOUNDATION: dunebroom rods
WEAVING ELEMENTS: rabbitbrush stem, yucca leaf; with dye

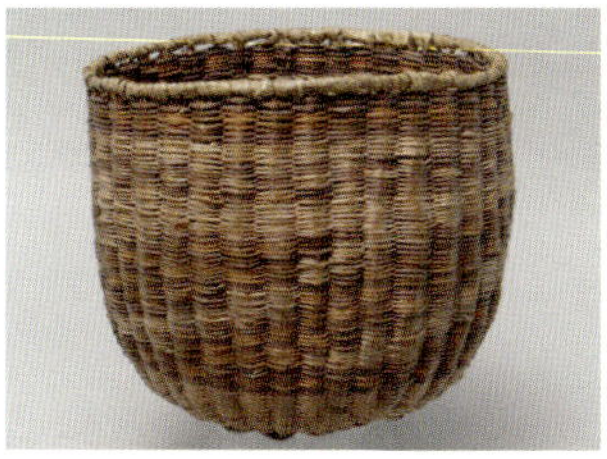

Piki Tray, 1983
Hopi (Third Mesa)
Fermina Banyacya
48.3 x 33.0 cm.
Museum purchase, 50126
CONSTRUCTION: diagonal plaiting, wicker
FOUNDATION: dunebroom rods
WEAVING ELEMENTS: dunebroom shoots, sumac shoots, yucca leaf

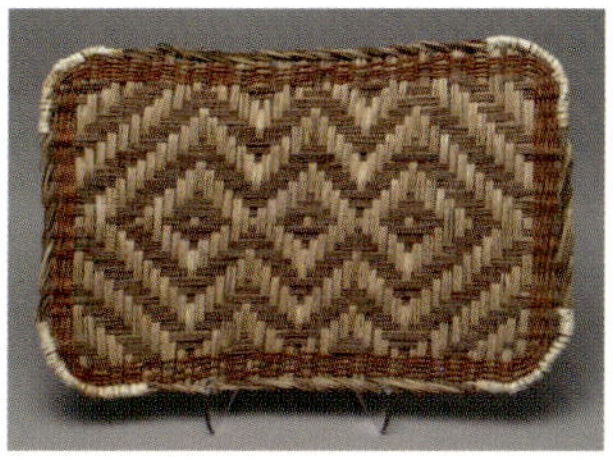

Sifter Tray, c. 1940
Hopi
Artist unknown
10.0 x 37.0 cm.
Gift of Dr. Leo N. Bushman, 50187
CONSTRUCTION: diagonal plaiting
WEAVING ELEMENT: yucca leaf; with sumac stick

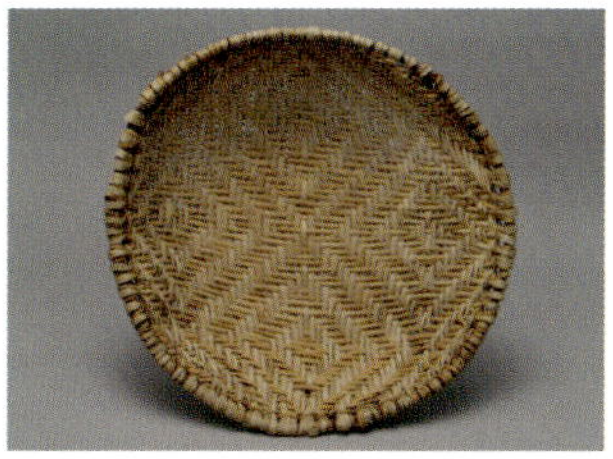

Sifter Tray, 1999
Hopi (First Mesa)
Kevin Navasie
75.0 x 42.1 cm.
Gift of Friends of Indian Art, 55666
CONSTRUCTION: diagonal plaiting
WEAVING ELEMENT: yucca leaf; with tamarisk stick, dye

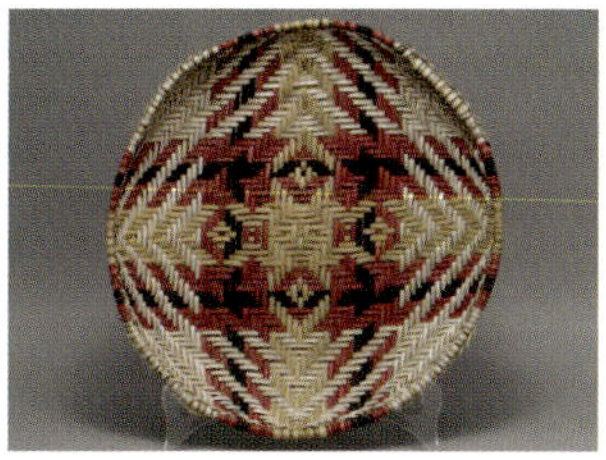

Plaque, c. 1920
Hopi (Third Mesa)
Artist unknown
2.0 x 32.5 cm.
Gift of Melody Damon, 55904
CONSTRUCTION: wicker
FOUNDATION: dunebroom rods
WEAVING ELEMENTS: rabbitbrush stem, yucca leaf; with dye

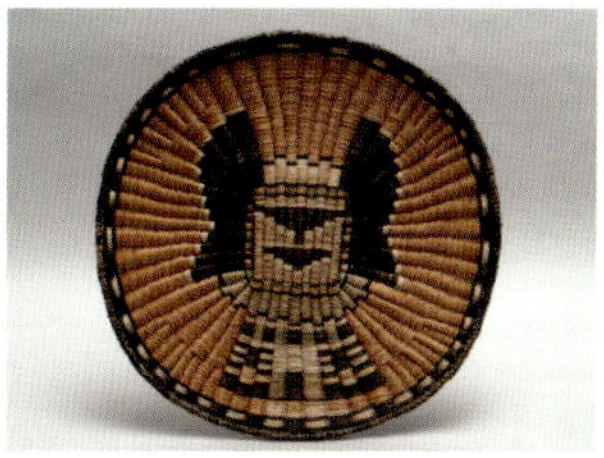

Plaque, c. 1890
Hopi (Third Mesa)
Artist unknown
2.0 x 29.5 cm.
Gift of Maurcena Eby Wells, 57015
CONSTRUCTION: wicker
FOUNDATION: dunebroom rods
WEAVING ELEMENTS: rabbitbrush stem, yucca leaf; with dye

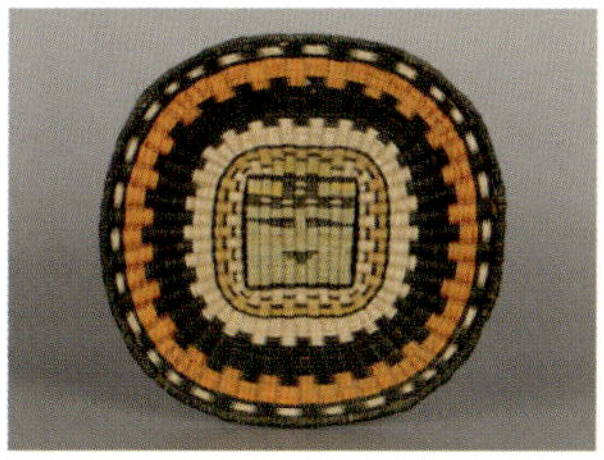

Plaque, c. 1970
Hopi (Third Mesa)
Rometa Vicente
2.0 x 33.0 cm.
Museum collection, 57028

CONSTRUCTION: wicker

FOUNDATION: dunebroom rods

WEAVING ELEMENTS: rabbitbrush stem, yucca leaf; with dye

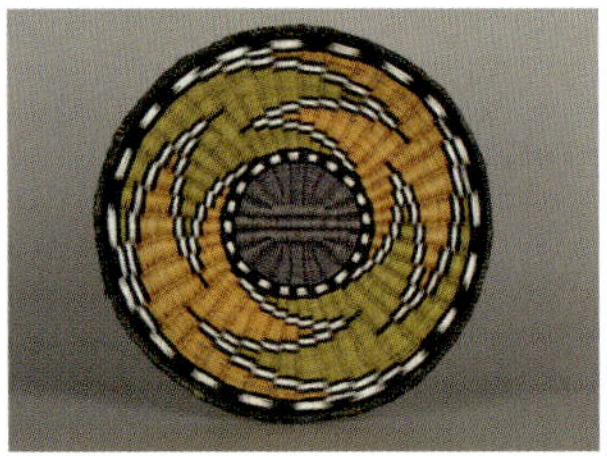

Plaque, c. 1970
Hopi (Third Mesa)
Artist unknown
2.0 x 36.0 cm.
Gift of Maurcena Eby Wells, 57038

CONSTRUCTION: wicker

FOUNDATION: dunebroom rods

WEAVING ELEMENTS: rabbitbrush stem, yucca leaf; with dye

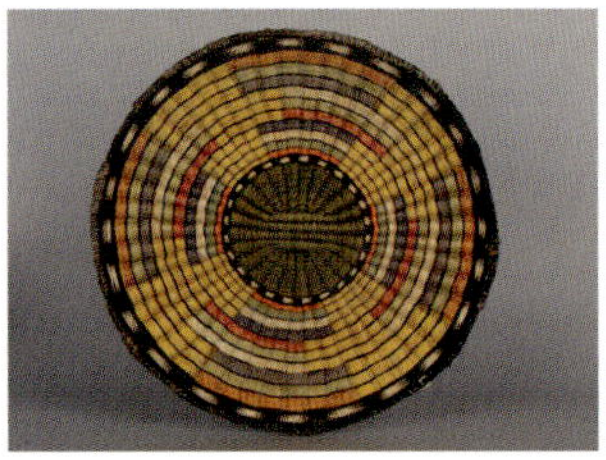

Jar, 1990
Hopi (Second Mesa)
Elizabeth Nuvayouma
37.6 x 51.0 cm.
Gift of Robert J. Dellenback, 57056

CONSTRUCTION: coiling

FOUNDATION: galleta-grass bundle

SEWING ELEMENT: yucca leaf; with dye

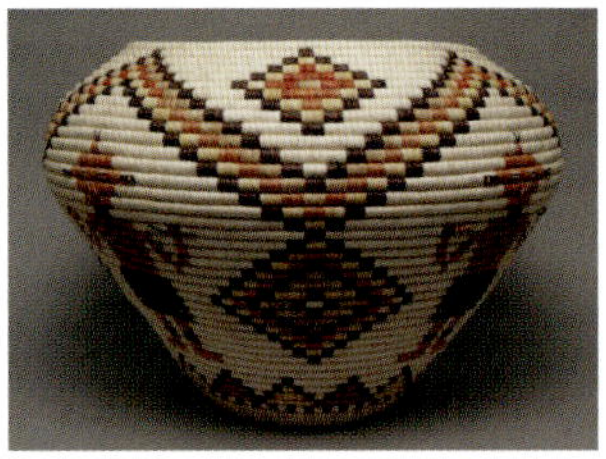

Groom's Wedding Plaque, 2006
Hopi (Second Mesa)
Joyce Ann Saufkie
4.8 x 42.0 cm.
Museum purchase, 57190

CONSTRUCTION: coiling

FOUNDATION: galleta-grass bundle

SEWING ELEMENT: yucca leaf; with dye

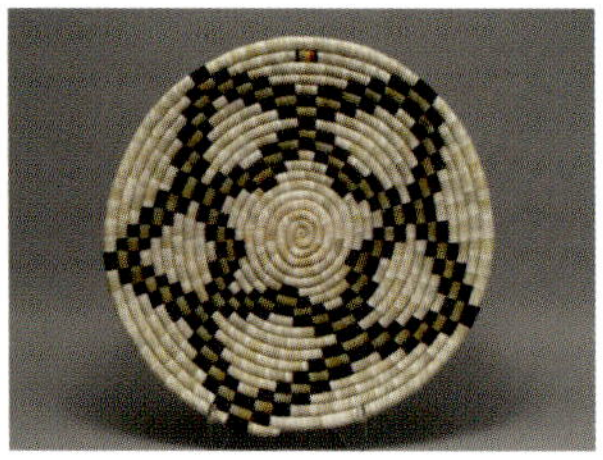

Bowl, 2012
Hopi (Second Mesa)
Kaitlyn Kayquoptewa
6.5 x 20.5 cm.
Museum purchase, 58316

CONSTRUCTION: diagonal plaiting

WEAVING ELEMENT: yucca leaf; with metal ring, dye

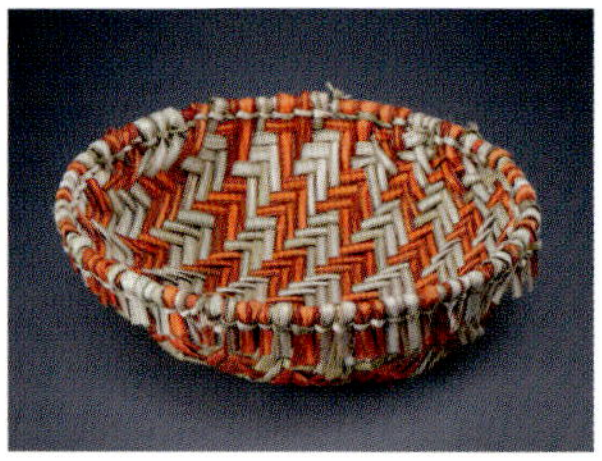

HUALAPAI

Seed Beater, c. 1925
Hualapai
Artist unknown
29.2 x 7.6 cm.
Collected by Dr. Alfred L. Kroeber, 10918

CONSTRUCTION: plaiting

WEAVING ELEMENTS: sumac shoots, yucca leaf

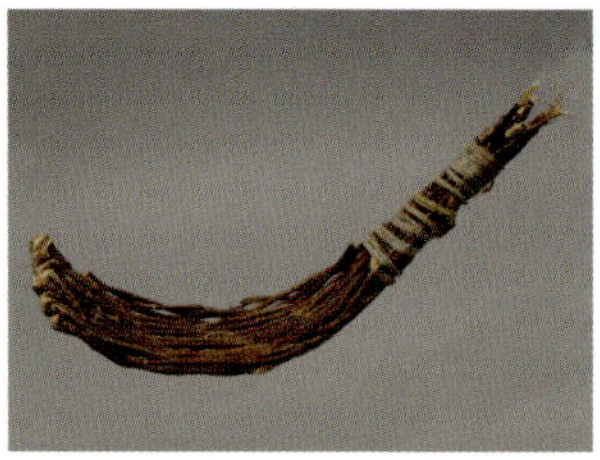

Bowl, c. 1900
Hualapai
Artist unknown
7.6 x 37.0 cm.
Collected by Dr. Alfred L. Kroeber, 10923

CONSTRUCTION: diagonal and three-strand twining

FOUNDATION: sumac rods

WEAVING ELEMENT: sumac shoots; with peach pulp

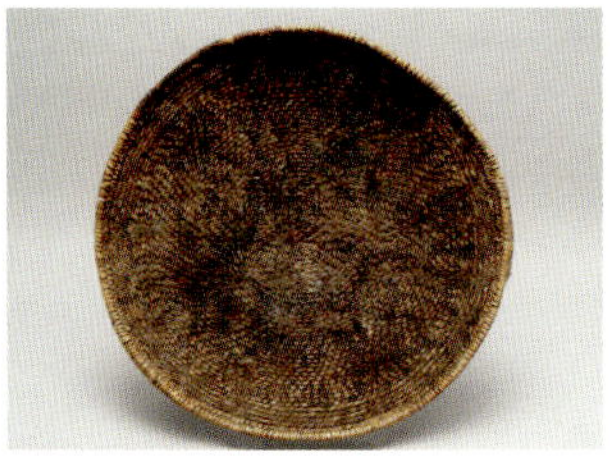

Bowl, c. 1925
Hualapai
Artist unknown
9.1 x 21.1 x 17.1 cm.
Collected by Dr. Alfred L. Kroeber, 10965

CONSTRUCTION: coiling

FOUNDATION: three sumac rods

SEWING ELEMENT: sumac shoots; with dye

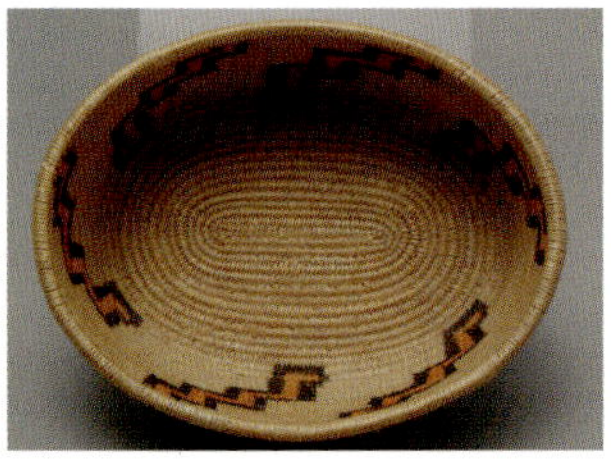

Bowl, c. 1930
Hualapai
Artist unknown
17.7 x 29.5 cm.
Collected by Dr. Alfred L. Kroeber, 10969

CONSTRUCTION: diagonal twining

FOUNDATION: sumac rods

WEAVING ELEMENT: sumac shoots; with dye

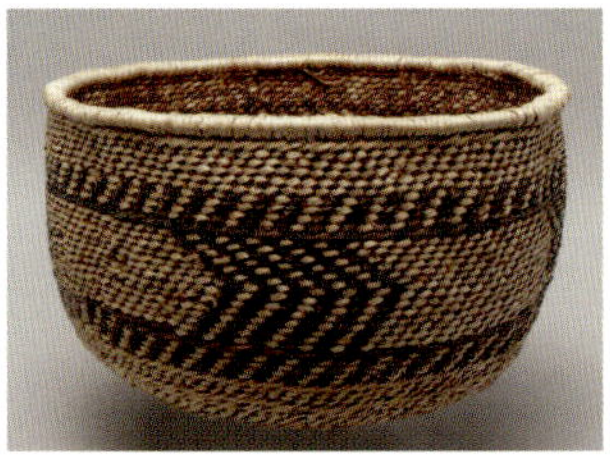

Carrying Basket, c. 1900
Hualapai
Artist unknown
42.9 x 48.0 cm.
Collected by Dr. Alfred L. Kroeber, 10977

CONSTRUCTION: diagonal twining

FOUNDATION: sumac rods

WEAVING ELEMENTS: sumac shoots, devil's claw seedpod; with peach pulp, cloth, buckskin

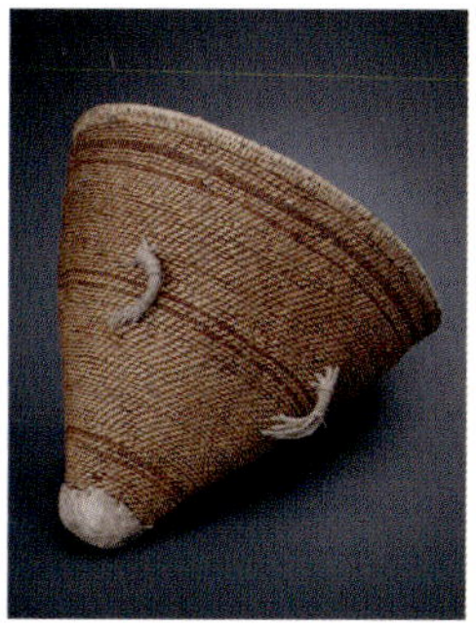

Woman's Cap, 1930
Hualapai
Artist unknown
10.0 x 20.5 cm.
Collected by Dr. Alfred L. Kroeber, 10979

CONSTRUCTION: diagonal twining

FOUNDATION: sumac rods

WEAVING ELEMENTS: sumac shoots

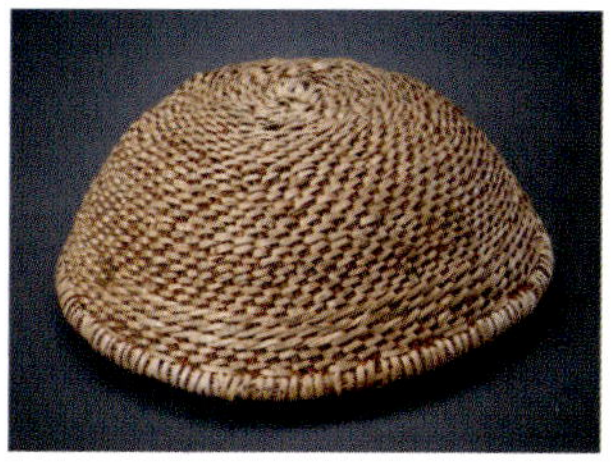

Bowl, c. 1930
Hualapai
Artist unknown
13.3 x 23.6 cm.
Collected by Dr. Edgar L. Hewett, 23722

CONSTRUCTION: diagonal twining

FOUNDATION: sumac rods

WEAVING ELEMENT: sumac shoots; with dye

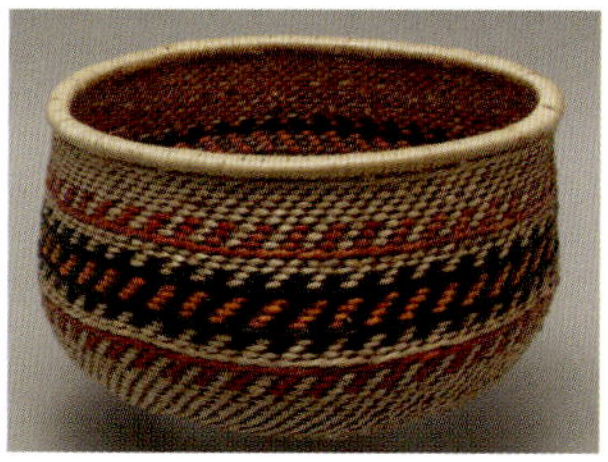

Plaque, 1983
Hualapai
Jenny Imus
0.6 x 18.4 cm.
Museum collection, 50062

CONSTRUCTION: coiling

FOUNDATION: three sumac rods

SEWING ELEMENTS: sumac shoots, devil's claw seedpod

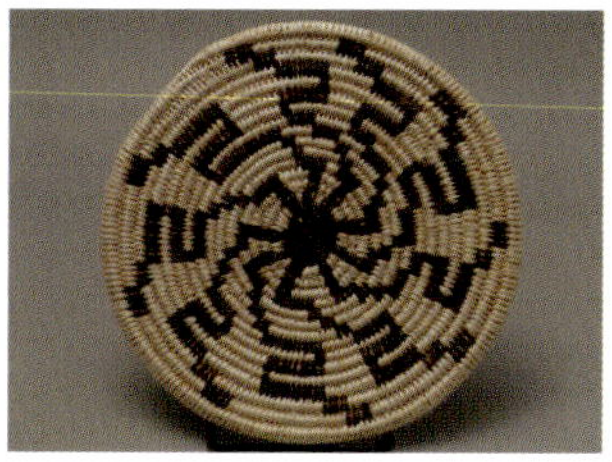

JEMEZ PUEBLO

Sifter Tray, 1961
Jemez Pueblo
Anita Toya
12.0 x 31.5 x 32.0 cm.
Gift of Sally Wagner, 25838

CONSTRUCTION: diagonal plaiting

WEAVING ELEMENT: yucca leaf; with wire

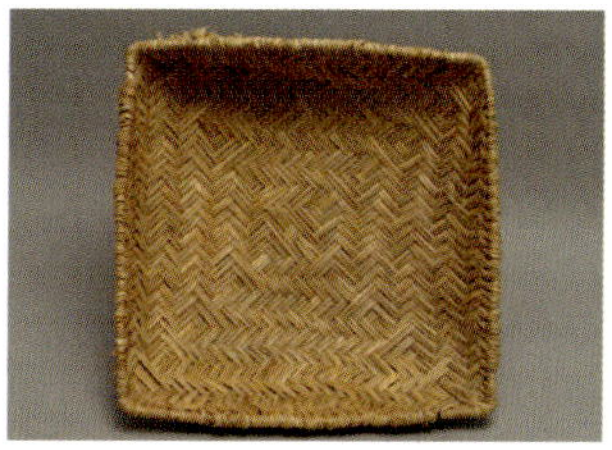

Ring Sifter, 1955
Jemez Pueblo
Artist unknown
16.5 x 50.0 cm.
Museum collection, 37026

CONSTRUCTION: plaiting

WEAVING ELEMENT: yucca leaf; with branch

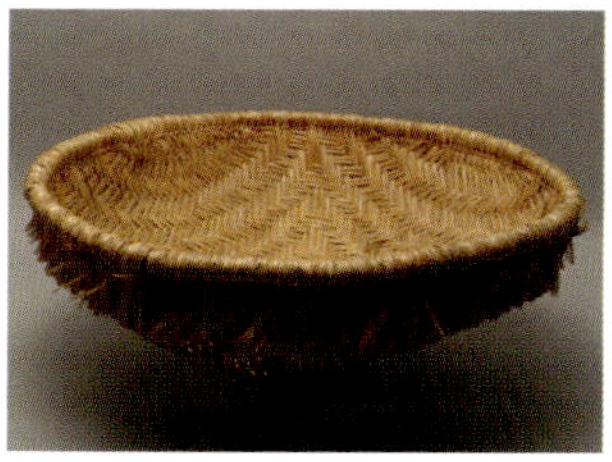

JICARILLA APACHE

Water Jar, c. 1880
Jicarilla Apache
Artist unknown
31.0 x 29.0 cm.
Gift of Bert C. Phillips, 16098

CONSTRUCTION: coiling

FOUNDATION: five willow rods

SEWING ELEMENTS: willow shoots, horsehair; with piñon pitch

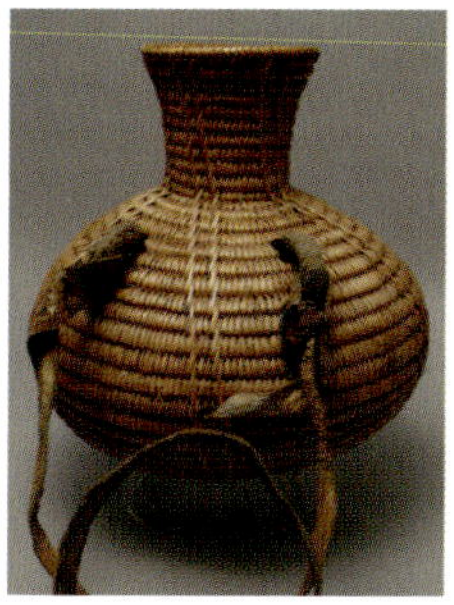

Tray, c. 1920
Jicarilla Apache
Artist unknown
13.0 x 45.0 cm.
Museum collection, 23281

CONSTRUCTION: coiling

FOUNDATION: five willow rods

SEWING ELEMENT: sumac shoots; with dye

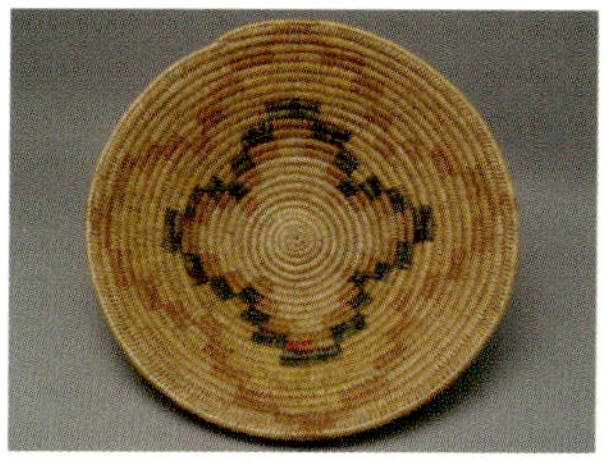

Fruit Bowl, c. 1940
Jicarilla Apache
Artist unknown
9.4 x 33.0 cm.
Gift of Helen Martin, 23476

CONSTRUCTION: coiling

FOUNDATION: three willow rods

SEWING ELEMENT: sumac shoots; with dye

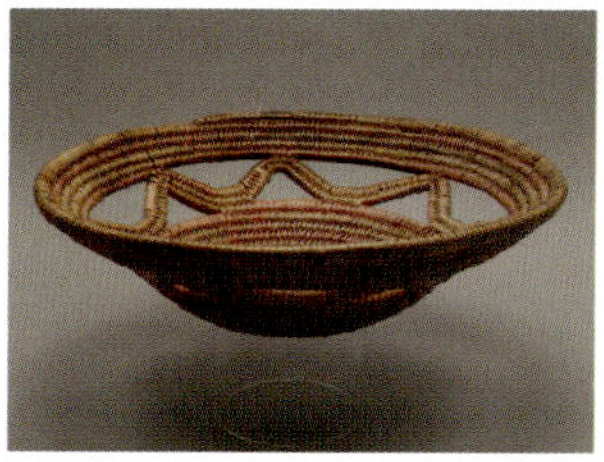

Tray, c. 1925
Jicarilla Apache
Artist unknown
12.5 x 50.5 cm.
Gift of Helen Martin, 23486
CONSTRUCTION: coiling
FOUNDATION: five willow rods
SEWING ELEMENT: sumac shoots; with dye

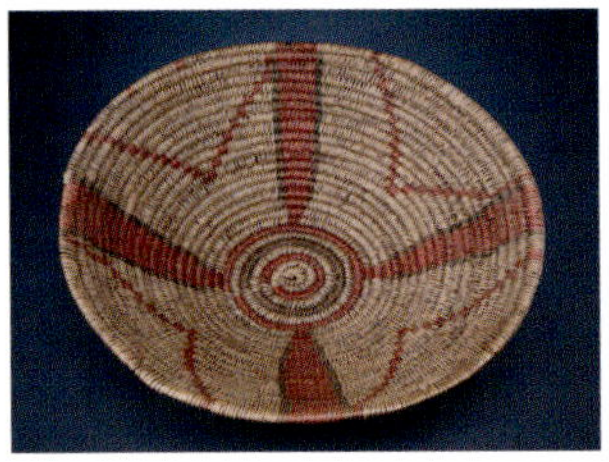

Laundry Basket, c. 1925
Jicarilla Apache
Artist unknown
21.0 x 67.0 cm.
Museum collection, 23488
CONSTRUCTION: coiling
FOUNDATION: five willow rods
SEWING ELEMENT: sumac shoots; with dye

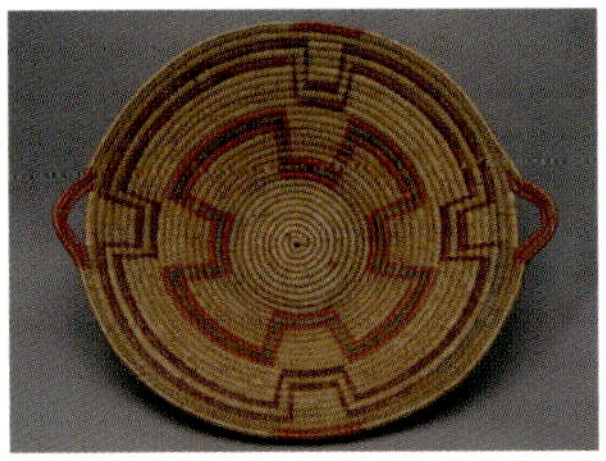

Tray, c. 1930
Jicarilla Apache
Artist unknown
10.5 x 40.5 cm.
Museum collection, 23511
CONSTRUCTION: coiling
FOUNDATION: five willow rods
WEAVING ELEMENT: sumac shoots; with dye

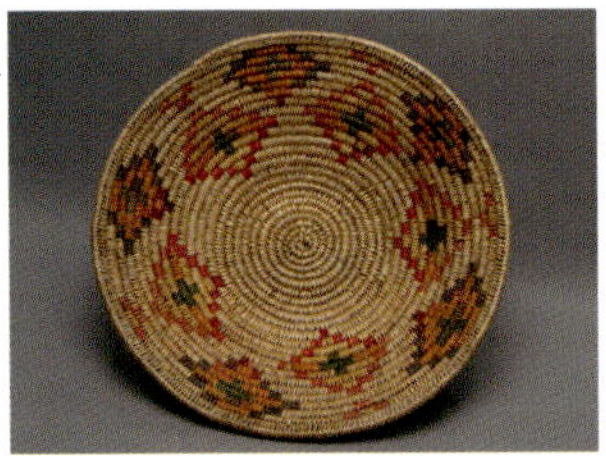

Hat, c. 1930
Jicarilla Apache
Artist unknown
10.5 x 35.0 cm.
Gift of Helen Kelly Kane and Daniel T. Kelly, 23526
CONSTRUCTION: coiling
FOUNDATION: three willow rods
SEWING ELEMENT: sumac shoots; with dye

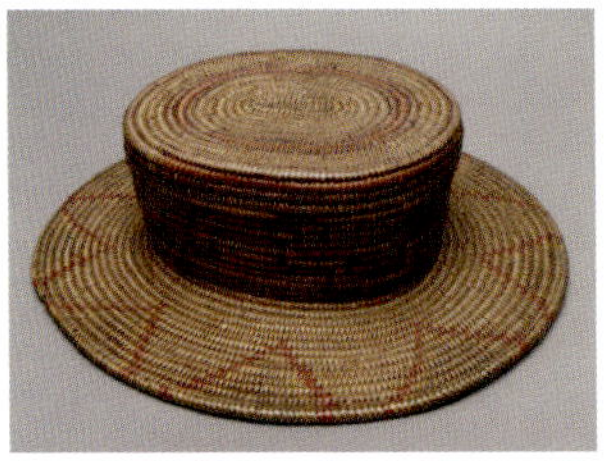

Tray, c. 1930
Jicarilla Apache
Artist unknown
10.0 x 41.0 cm.
Gift of Helen Martin, 23528
CONSTRUCTION: coiling
FOUNDATION: three willow rods
WEAVING ELEMENT: sumac shoots; with dye

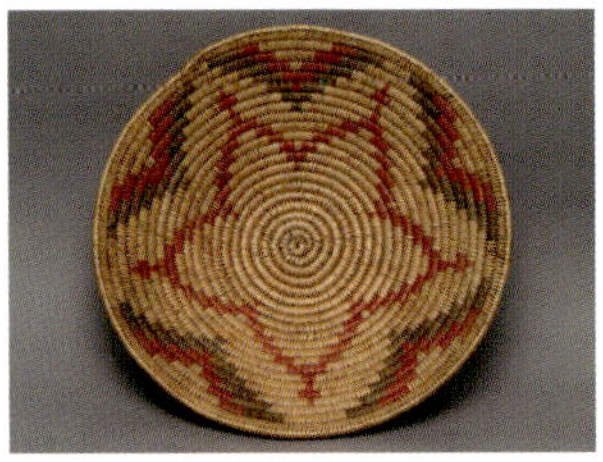

Water Jar, c. 1935
Jicarilla Apache
Artist unknown
28.5 x 25.3 cm.
H. F. Robinson Collection, 23537
CONSTRUCTION: coiling
FOUNDATION: five willow rods
WEAVING ELEMENT: sumac shoots; with dye

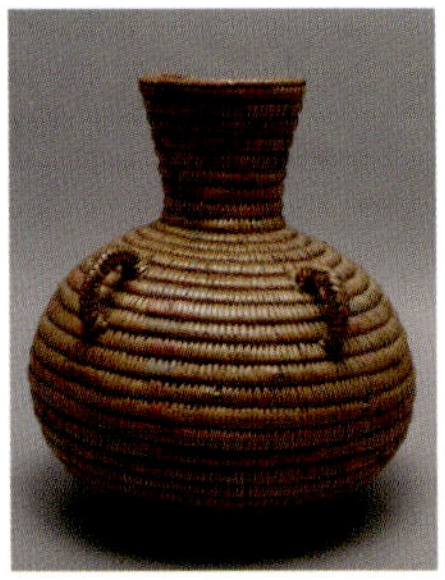

Clothes Hamper, c. 1920
Jicarilla Apache
Artist unknown
48.0 x 32.0 cm.
H. F. Robinson Collection, 23538
CONSTRUCTION: coiling
FOUNDATION: five willow rods
SEWING ELEMENT: sumac shoots; with dye

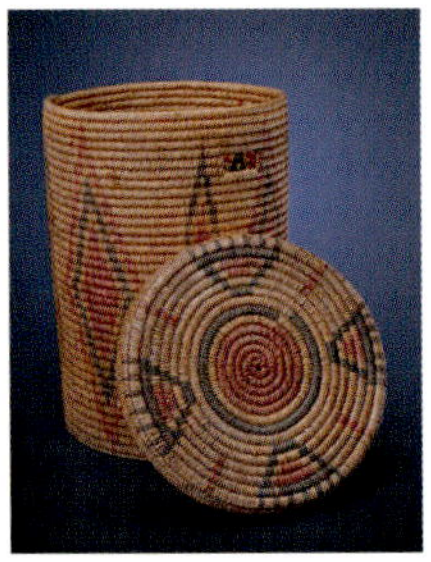

Water Jar, 1920
Jicarilla Apache
Artist unknown
31.0 x 27.0 cm.
Museum collection, 23547
CONSTRUCTION: coiling, vertical overstitching
FOUNDATION: three willow rods
SEWING ELEMENT: sumac shoots; with piñon pitch, buckskin

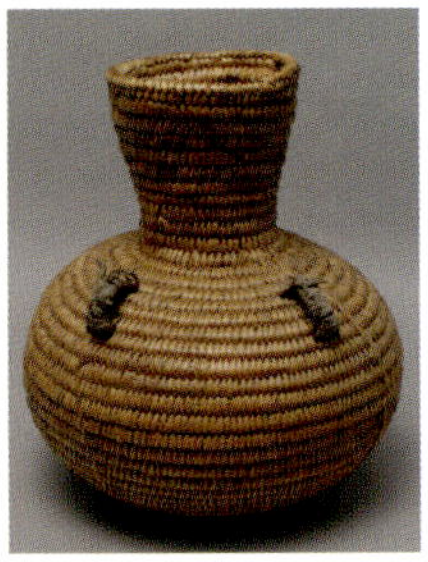

Pitcher, c. 1925
Jicarilla Apache
Artist unknown
30.0 x 28.7 cm.
Gift of Helen Kelly Kane and Daniel T. Kelly, 23555
CONSTRUCTION: coiling
FOUNDATION: five willow rods
SEWING ELEMENT: sumac shoots; with dye

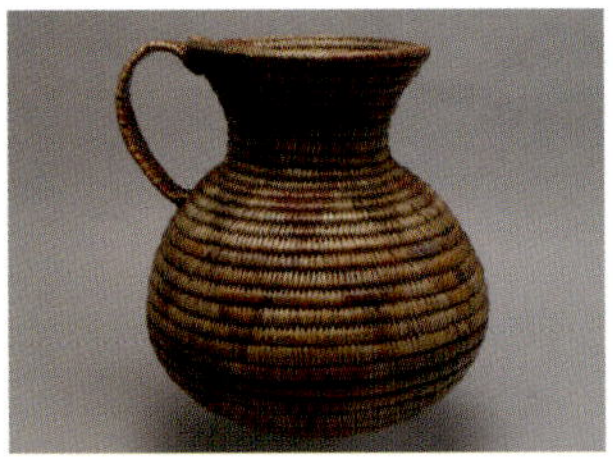

Bowl, 1983
Jicarilla Apache
Lydia Pesata
8.0 x 36.2 cm.
Museum purchase, 50066
CONSTRUCTION: coiling
FOUNDATION: five willow rods
SEWING ELEMENT: sumac shoots; with dye

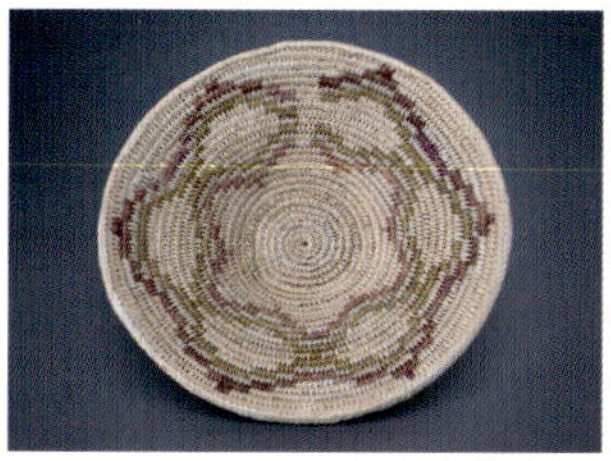

MESCALERO APACHE

Tray, c. 1930
Mescalero Apache
Artist unknown
9.0 x 35.5 cm.
Gift of Herbert Yeo, 11
CONSTRUCTION: coiling
FOUNDATION: two sumac rods, yucca-leaf bundle
WEAVING ELEMENTS: yucca leaf, yucca root

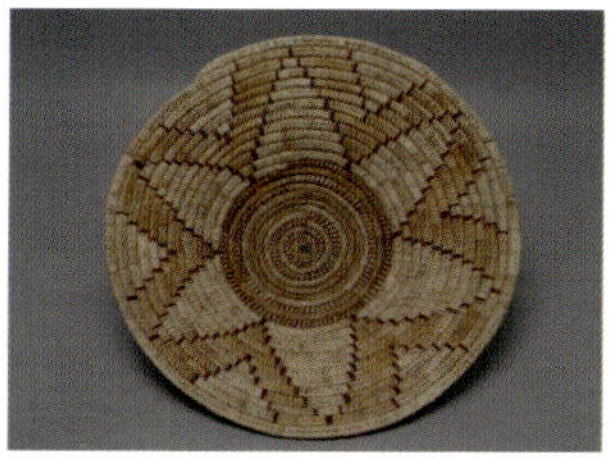

Carrying Basket, c. 1875
Mescalero Apache
Artist unknown
27.0 x 29.0 cm.
Gift of Alden Foss, 25440
CONSTRUCTION: diagonal twining
FOUNDATION: sumac rods
WEAVING ELEMENT: sumac shoots; with dye, buckskin, tin tinklers

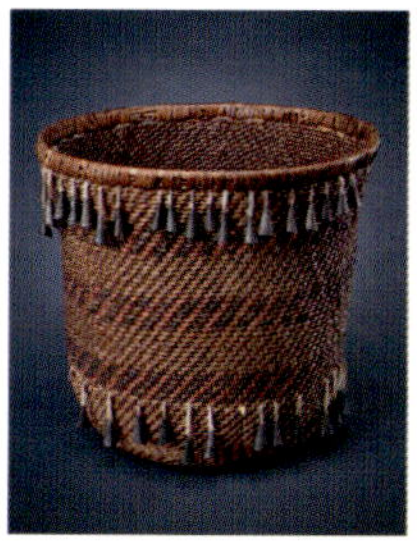

Tray, c. 1905
Mescalero Apache
Artist unknown
9.6 x 52.8 cm.
Herman C. and Bina L. Ilfeld Collection, 48103
CONSTRUCTION: coiling
FOUNDATION: two sumac rods, yucca-leaf bundle
WEAVING ELEMENTS: yucca leaf, yucca root

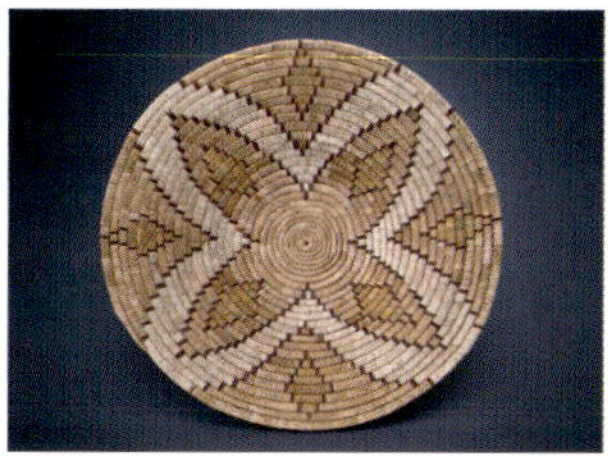

Carrying Basket, c. 1910
Mescalero Apache
Artist unknown
30.5 x 27.9 cm.
Gift of Maurice and Ida May Eby, 56989
CONSTRUCTION: diagonal twining
FOUNDATION: sumac rods
WEAVING ELEMENT: sumac shoots; with dye, buckskin, tin tinklers

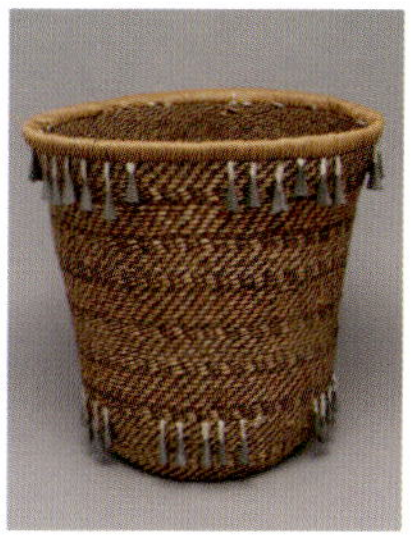

OHKAY OWINGEH PUEBLO

Bowl, 1963
Ohkay Owingeh Pueblo
Stephen Trujillo
13.5 x 36.0 cm.
Museum collection, 22632
CONSTRUCTION: wicker
FOUNDATION: willow rods
WEAVING ELEMENT: willow rods

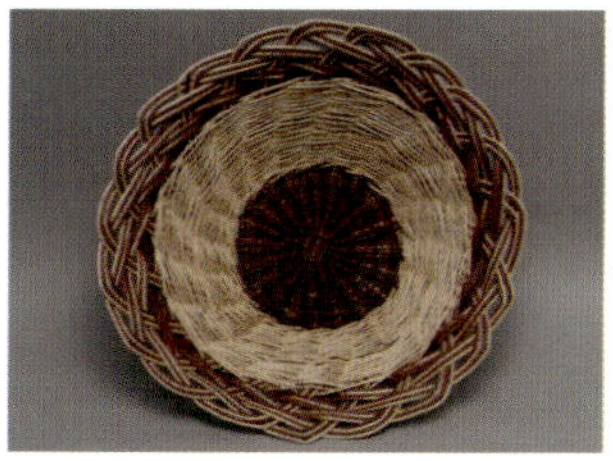

PUEBLO

Bowl, c. 1850
Pueblo
Artist unknown
11.1 x 32.6 cm.
Michael Harrison Collection, 1104
CONSTRUCTION: coiling
FOUNDATION: two sumac rods and sumac bundle
SEWING ELEMENT: sumac shoots; with dye

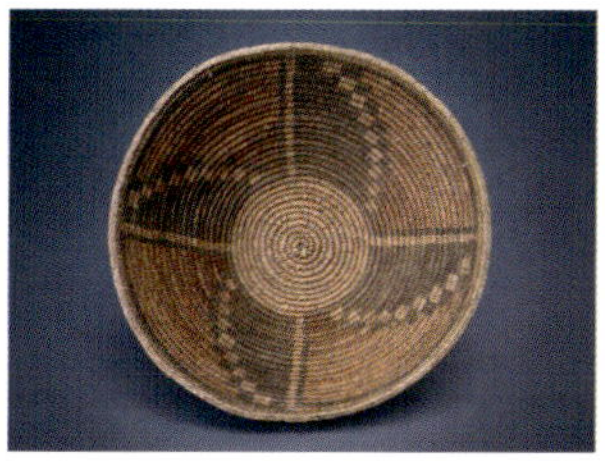

Canteen, c. 1800
Pueblo
Artist unknown
16.5 x 18.0 cm.
Gift of Sam F. Huddleson, 11345
CONSTRUCTION: coiling
FOUNDATION: two rods and sumac bundle
SEWING ELEMENT: sumac shoots; with piñon pitch, wood, buckskin

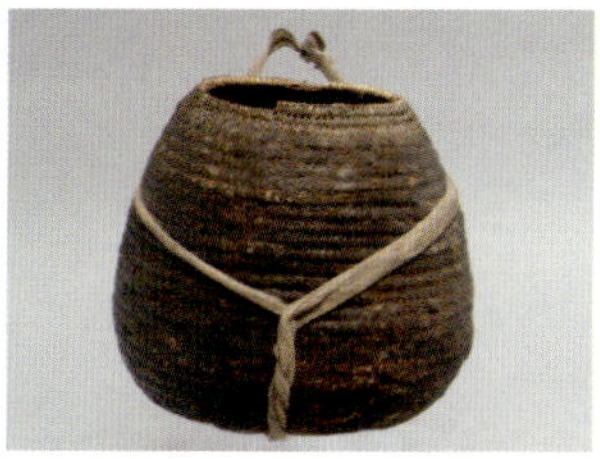

Bowl, c. 1880
Pueblo
Artist unknown
12.5 x 31.5 cm.
Honorable Daniel H. McMillan Collection, 14423
CONSTRUCTION: coiling
FOUNDATION: two sumac rods and sumac bundle
SEWING ELEMENT: sumac shoots; with dye

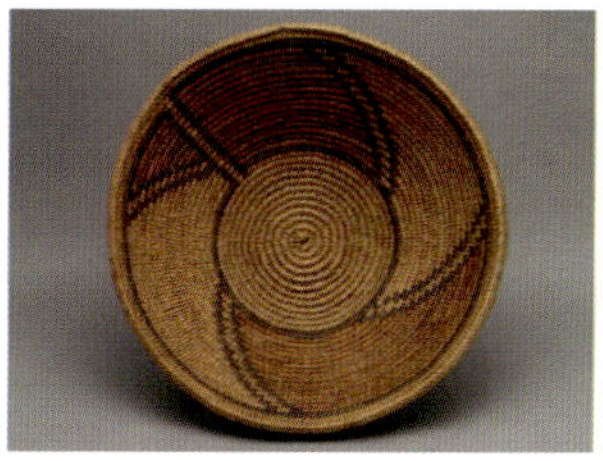

Bowl, c. 1820
Pueblo
Artist unknown
10.8 x 37.4 cm.
Gift of Francis J. McCormack, as a memorial to his late wife, Ada Crawford McCormack, 36689

CONSTRUCTION: coiling

FOUNDATION: two sumac rods and sumac bundle

SEWING ELEMENT: sumac shoots; with dye

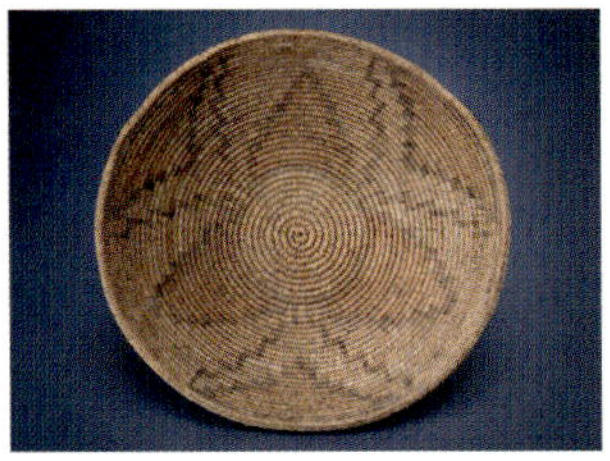

Carrying Basket, c. 1850
Pueblo
Artist unknown
27.0 x 33.0 cm.
Museum collection, 45767

CONSTRUCTION: diagonal and cross-warp twining

FOUNDATION: sumac rods

WEAVING ELEMENT: sumac shoots

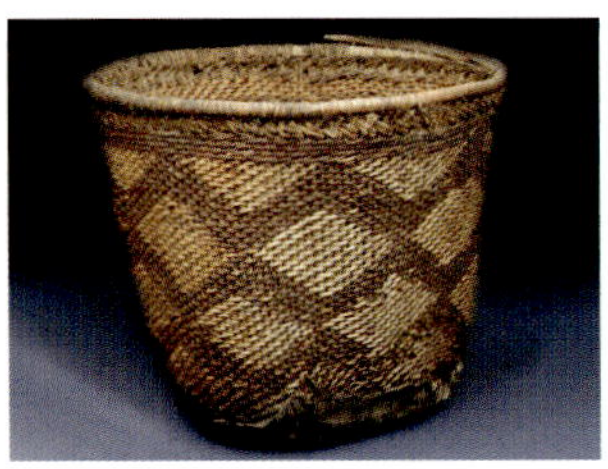

Bowl, c. 1930
Pueblo
Artist unknown
21.0 x 57.0 cm.
Gift of E. Boyd Hall, 47702

CONSTRUCTION: wicker

FOUNDATION: willow rods

WEAVING ELEMENT: willow rods

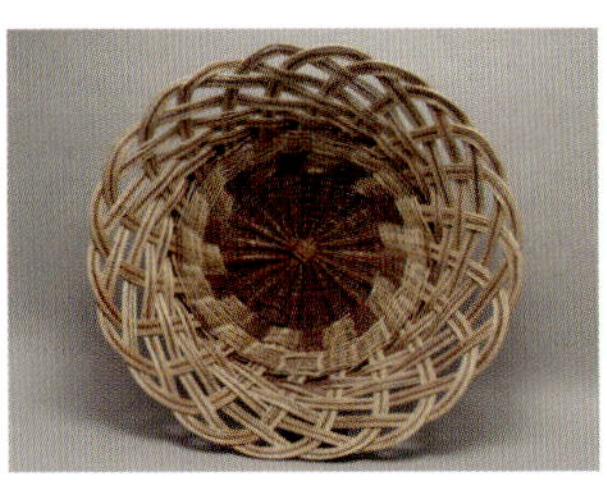

Carrying Basket, c. 1850
Pueblo
Artist unknown
30.0 x 26.0 cm.
Museum collection, 49424

CONSTRUCTION: diagonal and cross-warp twining

FOUNDATION: sumac rods

WEAVING ELEMENT: sumac shoots

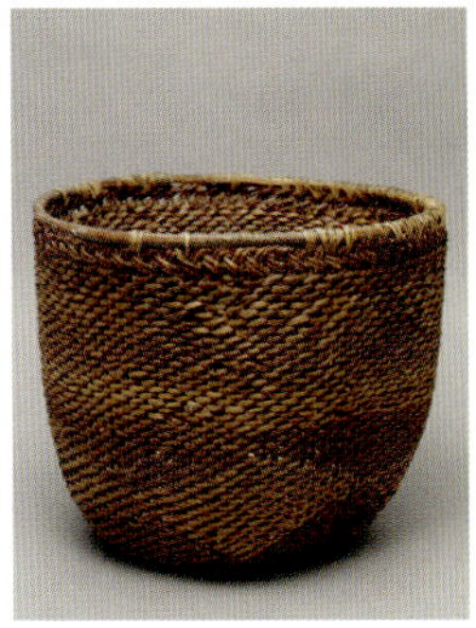

SAN CARLOS APACHE

Carrying Basket, c. 1925
San Carlos Apache
Artist unknown
28.0 x 33.0 cm.
Museum purchase, 1115

CONSTRUCTION: plain, diagonal, and three-strand twining

FOUNDATION: cottonwood rods

WEAVING ELEMENTS: willow shoots, devil's claw seedpod; with red paint, buckskin, wire

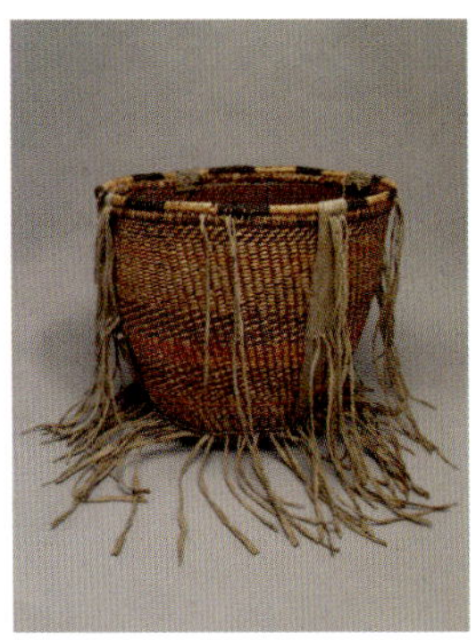

Tray, c. 1910
San Carlos Apache
Artist unknown
9.0 x 39.5 cm.
Gift of Thomas Bahti, 12604

CONSTRUCTION: coiling

FOUNDATION: three willow rods

SEWING ELEMENTS: willow shoots, yucca root, devil's claw seedpod

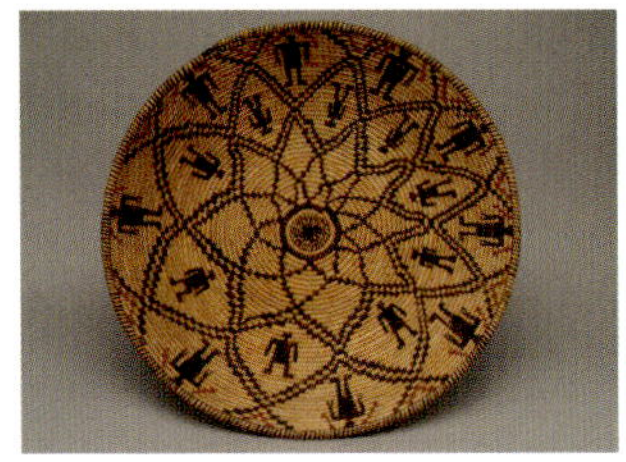

Tray, c. 1900
San Carlos Apache
Artist unknown
7.0 x 51.0 cm.
Ada Crawford McCormack Collection, 23633

CONSTRUCTION: coiling

FOUNDATION: three willow rods

SEWING ELEMENTS: willow shoots, devil's claw seedpod

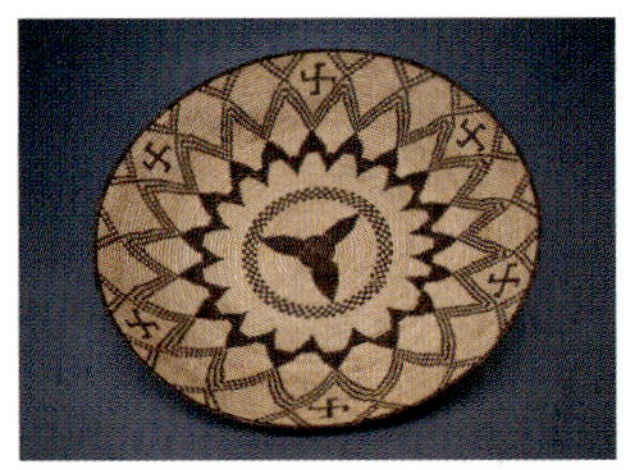

Tray, 1983
San Carlos Apache
Mary Porter
7.62 x 36.2 cm.
Museum purchase, 50065

CONSTRUCTION: coiling

FOUNDATION: three cottonwood rods

SEWING ELEMENTS: cottonwood shoots, devil's claw seedpod

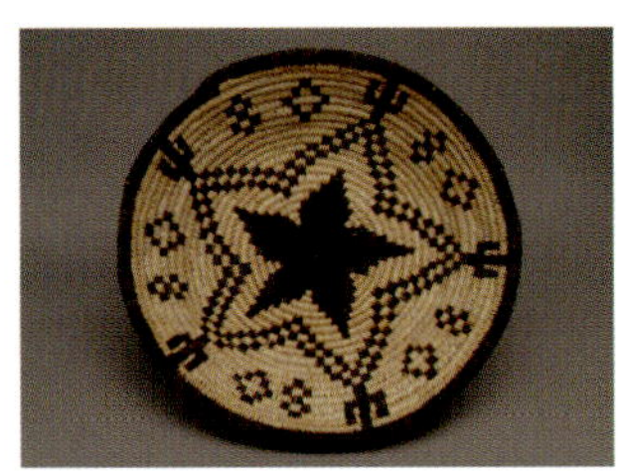

Carrying Basket, 2002
San Carlos Apache
Velveeta Henry
41.7 x 40.0 x 39.5 cm.
Gift of Friends of Indian Art, 56278

CONSTRUCTION: plain twining

FOUNDATION: cottonwood rods

WEAVING ELEMENT: willow shoots; with buckskin, tin tinklers

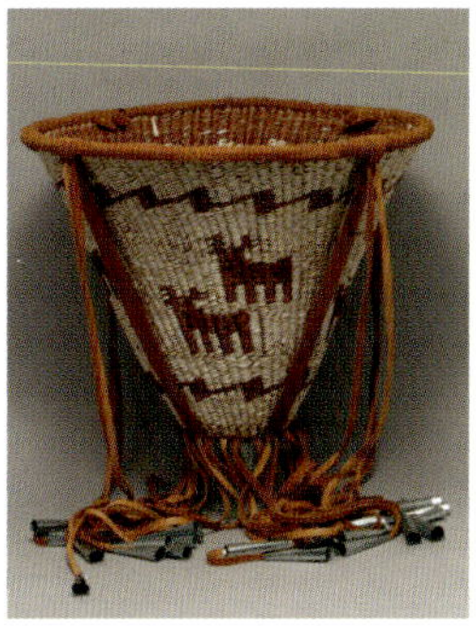

SANTO DOMINGO PUEBLO

Storage Basket, 1949
Santo Domingo Pueblo
Santiago Tenorio
28.0 x 62.0 cm.
Museum collection, 23499

CONSTRUCTION: wicker

FOUNDATION: willow rods

WEAVING ELEMENT: willow rods

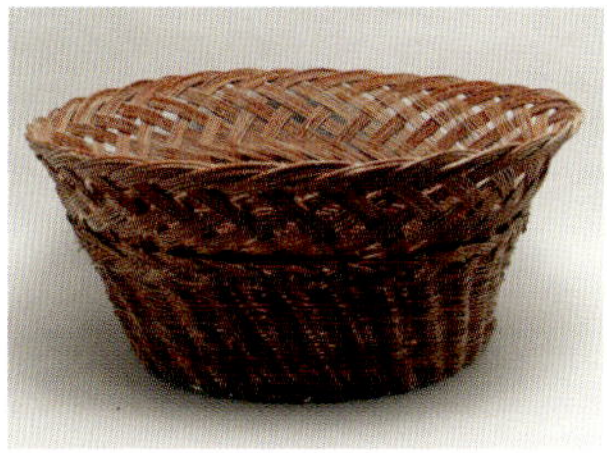

TOHONO O'ODHAM

Unfinished Tray, c. 1930
Tohono O'odham
Artist unknown
3.0 x 37.0 cm.
Ina Sizer Cassidy Collection, 907

CONSTRUCTION: coiling

FOUNDATION: beargrass bundle

SEWING ELEMENTS: yucca leaf, devil's claw seedpod, with dye

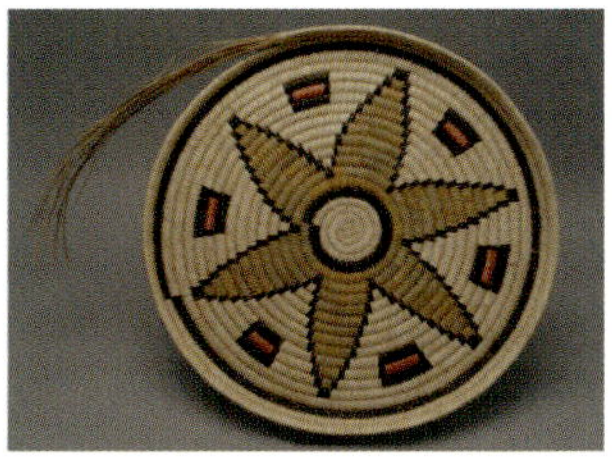

Jar, c. 1915
Tohono O'odham
Artist unknown
24.0 x 26.0 cm.
Gift of Mrs. H. S. Kaune, 1146

CONSTRUCTION: coiling

FOUNDATION: cattail-splint bundle

SEWING ELEMENTS: willow shoots, devil's claw seedpod; with paint

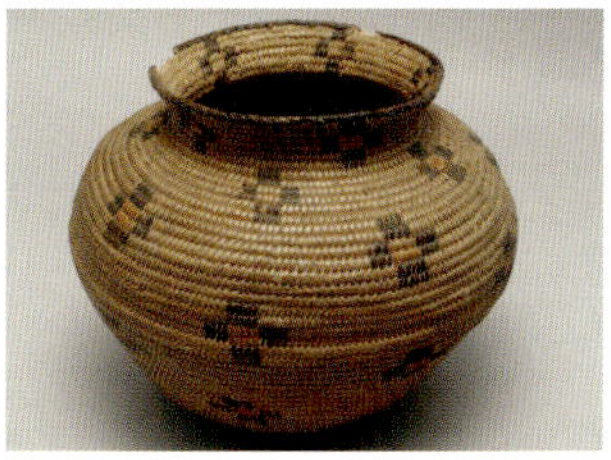

Hat, c. 1920
Tohono O'odham
Artist unknown
8.5 x 25.0 cm.
Gift of Barbara Cotton Seymour, 1730

CONSTRUCTION: coiling

FOUNDATION: beargrass bundle

SEWING ELEMENTS: yucca leaf, devil's claw seedpod

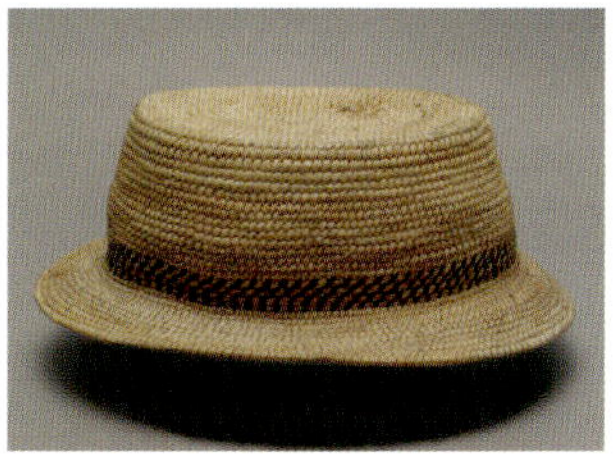

Plaque, c. 1935
Tohono O'odham
Artist unknown
0.5 x 29.2 cm.
Gift of T. B. Williamson, 14249

CONSTRUCTION: coiling

FOUNDATION: beargrass bundle

SEWING ELEMENTS: yucca leaf, devil's claw seedpod

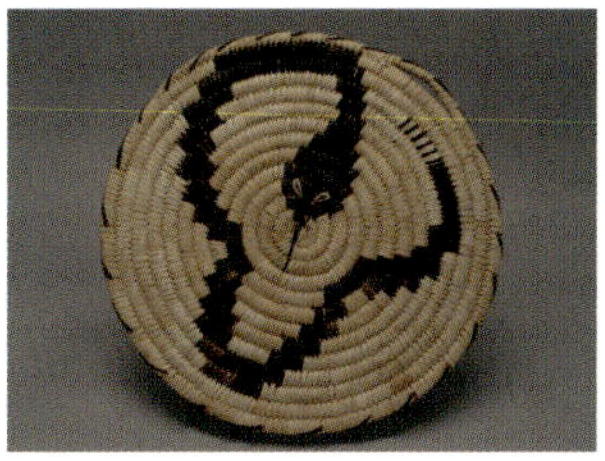

Bowl, c. 1900
Tohono O'odham
Artist unknown
14.0 x 48.0 cm.
Honorable Daniel H. McMillan Collection, 14411

CONSTRUCTION: coiling

FOUNDATION: cattail-splint bundle

SEWING ELEMENTS: willow, devil's claw seedpod

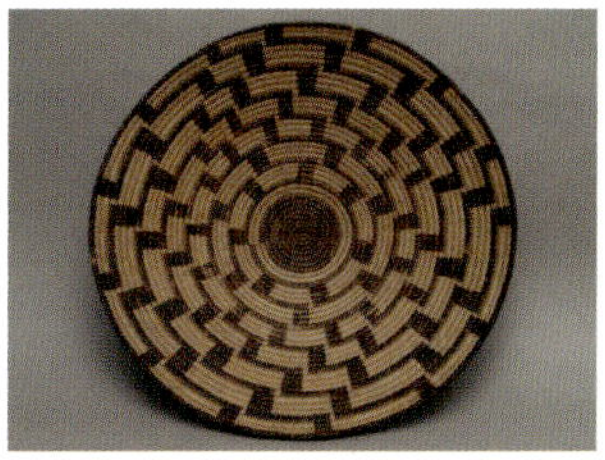

Hat, c. 1960
Tohono O'odham
Artist unknown
6.9 x 28.0 cm.
Gift of Sally Wagner, 25413

CONSTRUCTION: coiling

FOUNDATION: beargrass bundle

SEWING ELEMENTS: yucca leaf, devil's claw seedpod

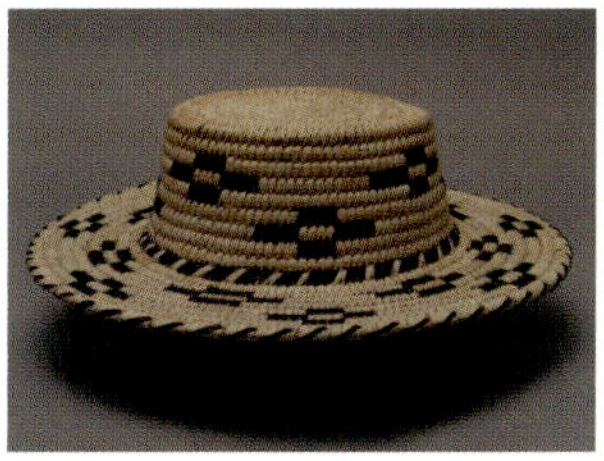

Saguaro-wine Serving Bowl, c. 1885
Tohono O'odham
Artist unknown
21.5 x 48.0 cm.
Gift of Mrs. Julius Gans, 35959
CONSTRUCTION: coiling
FOUNDATION: cattail-splint bundle
SEWING ELEMENTS: willow shoots, devil's claw seedpod

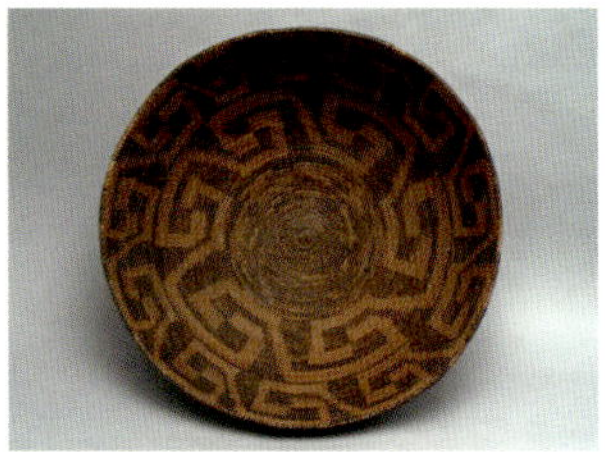

Tray, 1983
Tohono O'odham
Barbara Havier
7.9 x 35.9 cm.
Museum collection, 50014
CONSTRUCTION: coiling, open-and-closed wheat stitch
FOUNDATION: beargrass bundle
SEWING ELEMENT: yucca leaf

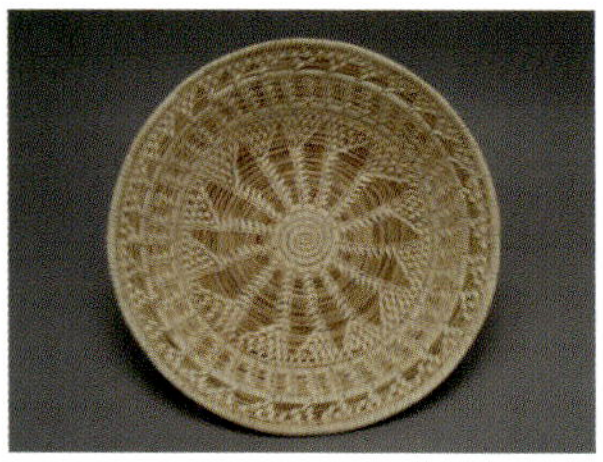

Bowl, c. 1970
Tohono O'odham
Artist unknown
9.6 x 46.0 cm.
Gift of Charmay Allred, 54644
CONSTRUCTION: coiling
FOUNDATION: beargrass bundle
SEWING ELEMENTS: yucca leaf, devil's claw seedpod

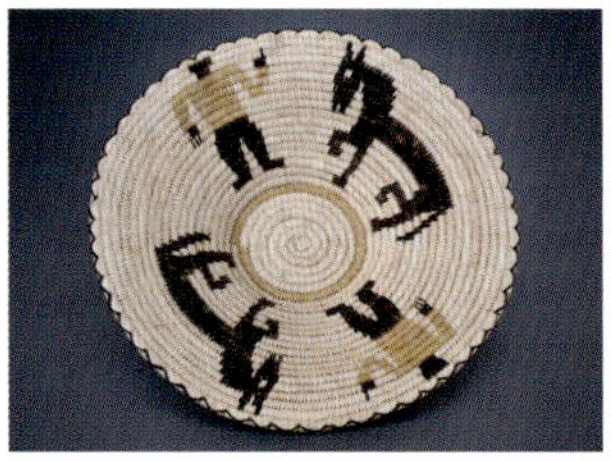

Storage Basket Model, c. 1900
Tohono O'odham
Artist unknown
34.0 x 48.0 cm.
Gift of Rhoda Thomas, 35970
CONSTRUCTION: coiling
FOUNDATION: wheat-straw bundle
SEWING ELEMENT: mesquite root

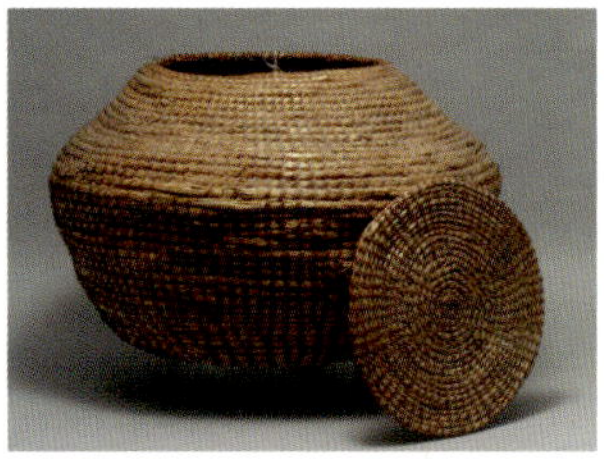

Miniature Basket, 1983
Tohono O'odham
Norma Antone
0.3 x 7.3 cm.
Museum collection, 50125
CONSTRUCTION: coiling
FOUNDATION: horsehair
SEWING ELEMENT: horsehair

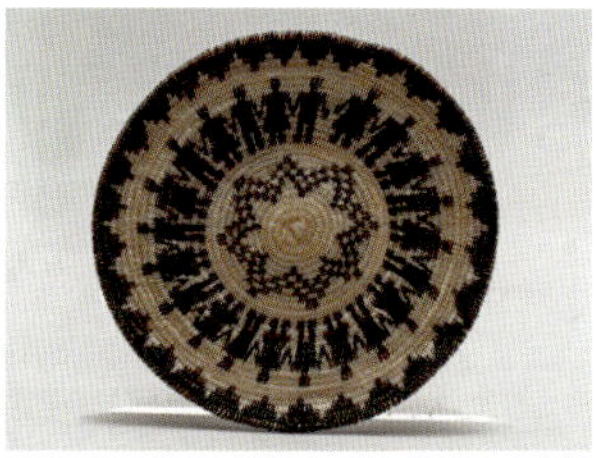

Tray, 1999
Tohono O'odham
Mildred Lewis
7.1 x 32.6 cm.
Museum collection, 55671
CONSTRUCTION: coiling
FOUNDATION: cattail-splint bundle
SEWING ELEMENTS: willow shoots, banana yucca root, devil's claw seedpod

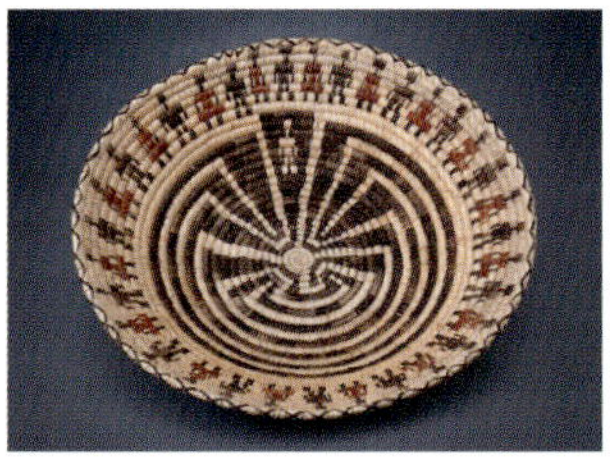

Bowl, 1983
Tohono O'odham
Anita Antone
16.3 x 24.5 cm.
Museum purchase, 50013
CONSTRUCTION: coiling
FOUNDATION: beargrass bundle
SEWING ELEMENTS: yucca leaf, devil's claw seedpod

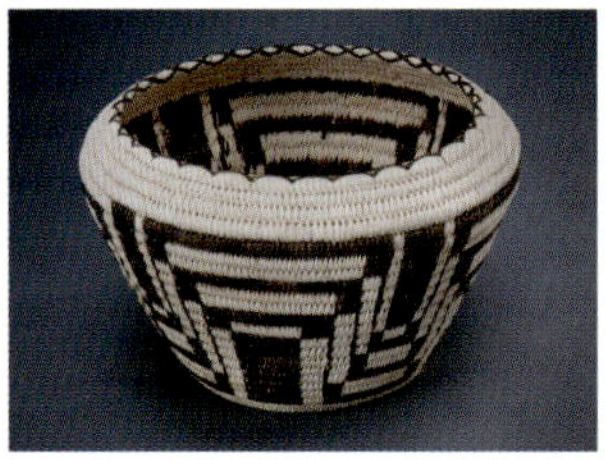

Jar, c. 1900
Tohono O'odham
Artist unknown
34.5 x 29.0 cm.
Gift of Paul and Fredrica Smith, 51196
CONSTRUCTION: coiling
FOUNDATION: cattail-splint bundle
SEWING ELEMENTS: willow, devil's claw seed-pod; with dye

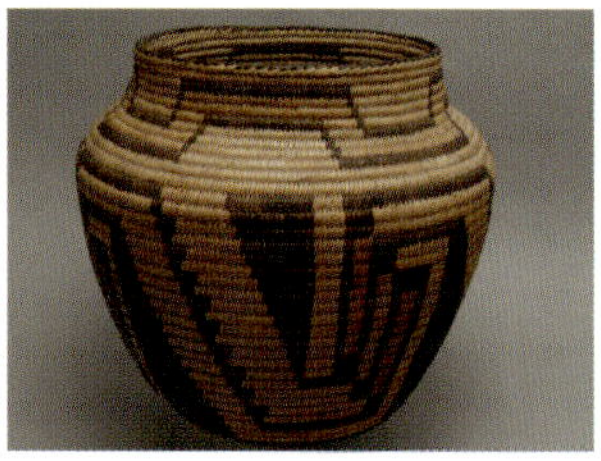

Tray, 2000
Tohono O'odham
Sadie Marks
7.5 x 31.5 cm.
Gift of Friends of Indian Art, 55728
CONSTRUCTION: open-coiling, split stitches, and wheat stitches
FOUNDATION: beargrass bundle
SEWING ELEMENTS: yucca leaf, devil's claw seedpod

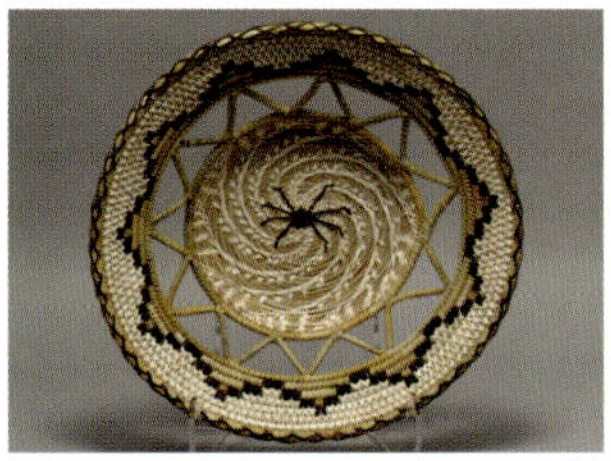

Saguaro-wine Serving Bowl, c. 1910
Tohono O'odham
Mildred Lewis
19.5 x 39.5 cm.
W. S. Stallings Jr. Collection, 57476
CONSTRUCTION: coiling
FOUNDATION: cattail-splint bundle
SEWING ELEMENTS: willow shoots, devil's claw seedpod

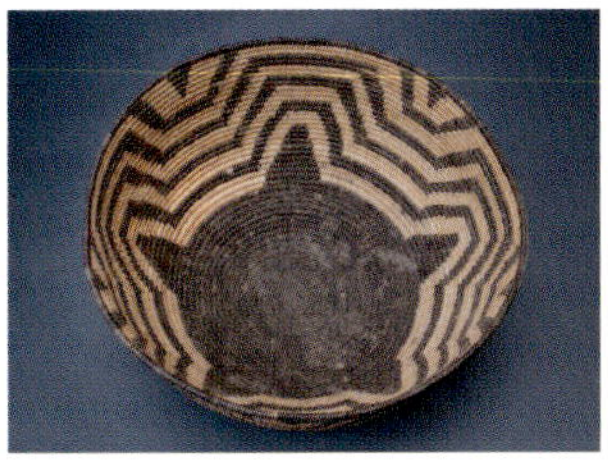

Gourd Basket, 2012
Tohono O'odham
Terrol Dew Johnson
6.8 x 23.1 cm.
Museum purchase, 58315
CONSTRUCTION: carving, sewing
SEWING ELEMENTS: gourd, beargrass

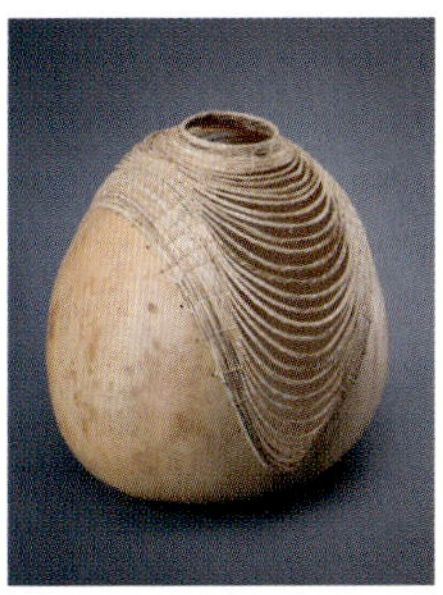

WESTERN APACHE

Jar, c. 1910
Western Apache
Artist unknown
38.0 x 29.5 cm.
Ada Crawford McCormack Collection, 11999
CONSTRUCTION: coiling
FOUNDATION: three willow rods
SEWING ELEMENTS: willow shoots, devil's claw seedpod

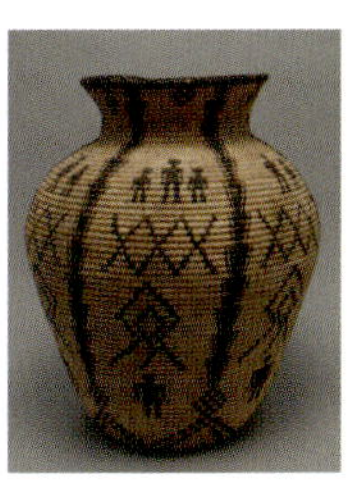

Tray, c. 1900
Western Apache
Artist unknown
10.8 x 78.5 cm.
Museum purchase sponsored by Charmay Allred, 12000
CONSTRUCTION: coiling
FOUNDATION: three willow rods
SEWING ELEMENTS: willow shoots, devil's claw seedpod

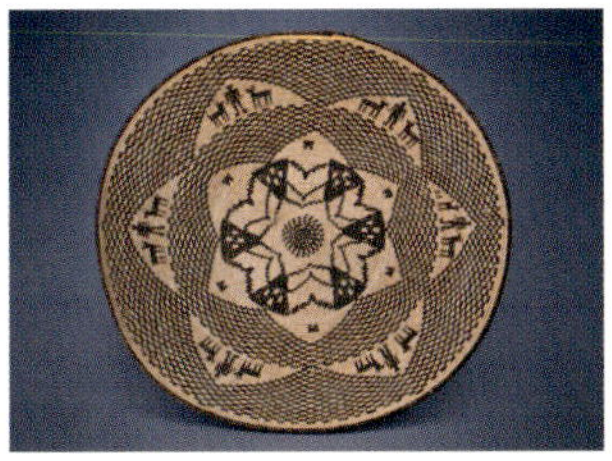

Tray, c. 1890
Western Apache
Artist unknown
12.8 x 49.7 cm.
Gift of Ernest N. Stanton, 14215
CONSTRUCTION: coiling
FOUNDATION: three willow rods
SEWING ELEMENTS: willow shoots, devil's claw seedpod

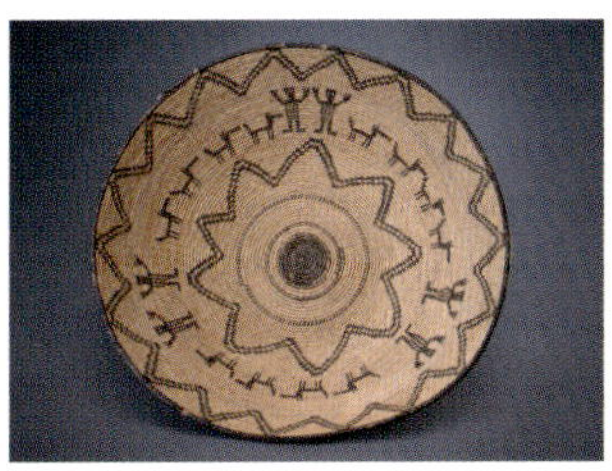

Tray, c. 1895
Western Apache
Artist unknown
13.5 x 46.5 cm.
Honorable Daniel H. McMillan Collection, 14408
CONSTRUCTION: coiling
FOUNDATION: three willow rods
SEWING ELEMENTS: willow shoots, devil's claw seedpod

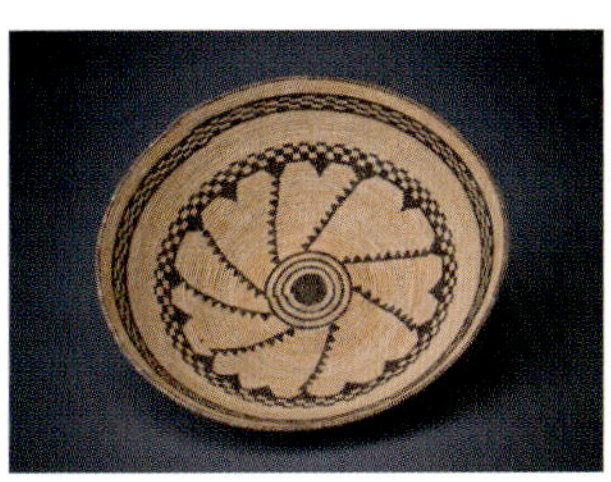

Jar, c. 1930
Western Apache
Artist unknown
36.1 x 28.3 cm.
Ada Crawford McCormack Collection, 23301
CONSTRUCTION: coiling
FOUNDATION: three willow rods
SEWING ELEMENTS: willow shoots, devil's claw seedpod

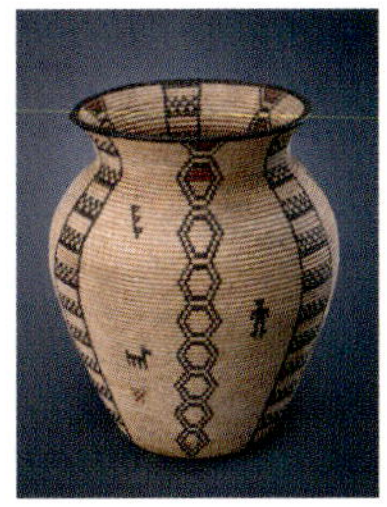

Bowl, c. 1905
Western Apache
Artist unknown
10.0 x 40.5 cm.
Gift of the Historical Society of New Mexico, 23672
CONSTRUCTION: coiling
FOUNDATION: three willow rods
SEWING ELEMENTS: willow shoots, devil's claw seedpod

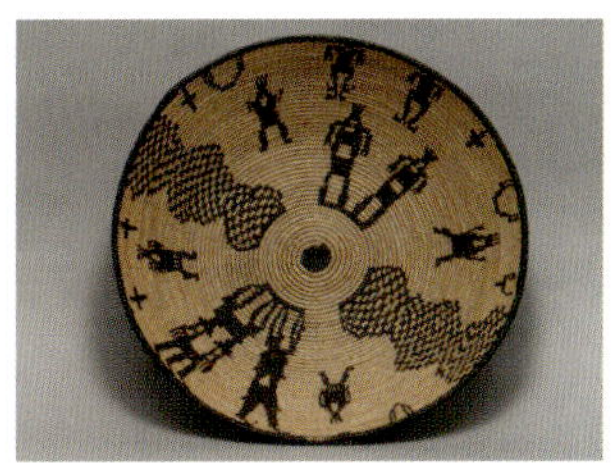

Tray, c. 1900
Western Apache
Artist unknown
6.5 x 30.5 cm.
Gift of Francis J. McCormack, as a memorial to his late wife, Ada Crawford McCormack, 31119
CONSTRUCTION: coiling
FOUNDATION: three willow rods
SEWING ELEMENTS: willow shoots, devil's claw seedpod

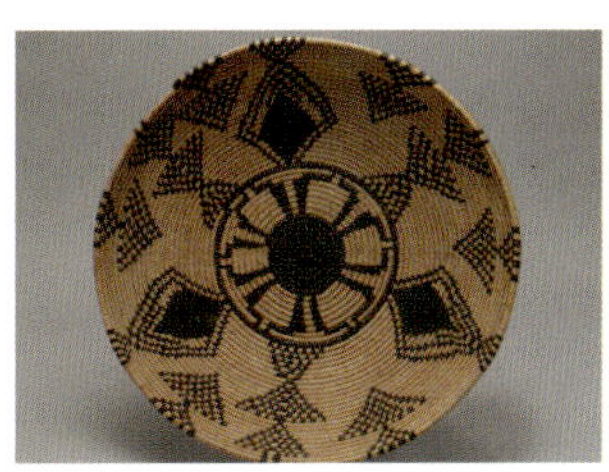

Bowl, c. 1900
Western Apache
Artist unknown
12.5 x 39.5 cm.
Gift of M. T. Faris, 31132
CONSTRUCTION: coiling
FOUNDATION: three willow rods
SEWING ELEMENTS: willow shoots, devil's claw seedpod

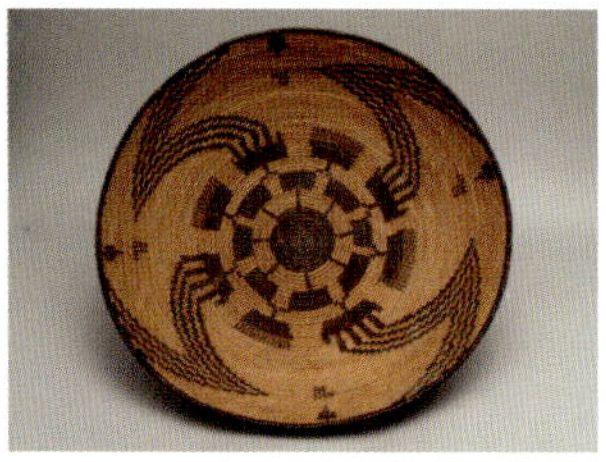

Bowl, c. 1905
Western Apache
Artist unknown
11.0 x 41.0 cm.
Gift of M. T. Faris, 31134
CONSTRUCTION: coiling
FOUNDATION: three willow rods
SEWING ELEMENTS: willow shoots, devil's claw seedpod

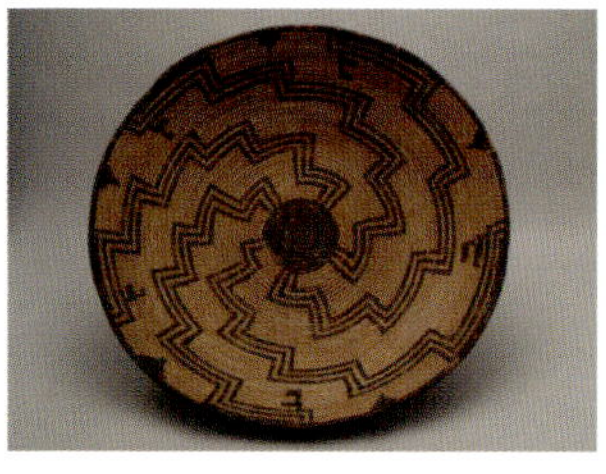

Jar, c. 1900
Western Apache
Artist unknown
53.2 x 46.2 cm.
Museum collection, 35969
CONSTRUCTION: coiling
FOUNDATION: three willow rods
SEWING ELEMENTS: willow shoots, yucca root, devil's claw seedpod

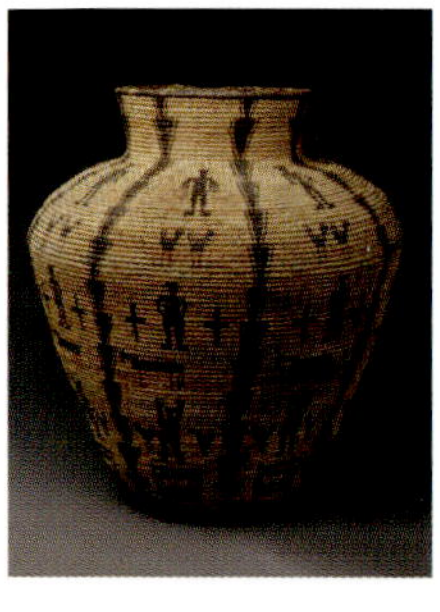

Bowl, c. 1900
Western Apache
Artist unknown
19.0 x 61.5 cm.
Ada Crawford McCormack Collection, 37918
CONSTRUCTION: coiling
FOUNDATION: three willow rods
SEWING ELEMENTS: willow shoots, devil's claw seedpod

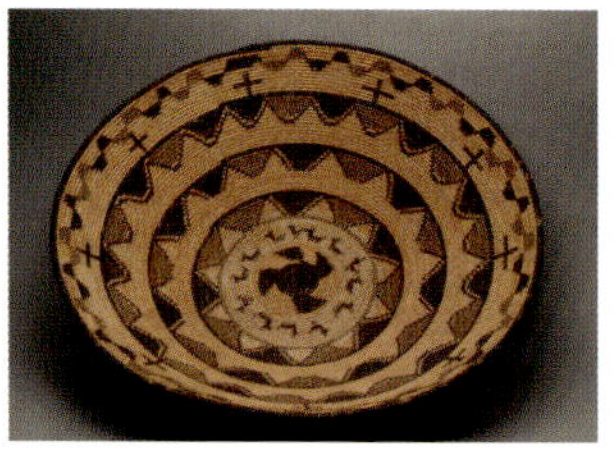

Bowl, c. 1895
Western Apache
Artist unknown
11.5 x 35.0 cm.
Gift of Dr. and Mrs. Russell T. Snip, 45199
CONSTRUCTION: coiling
FOUNDATION: three willow rods
SEWING ELEMENTS: willow shoots, devil's claw seedpod

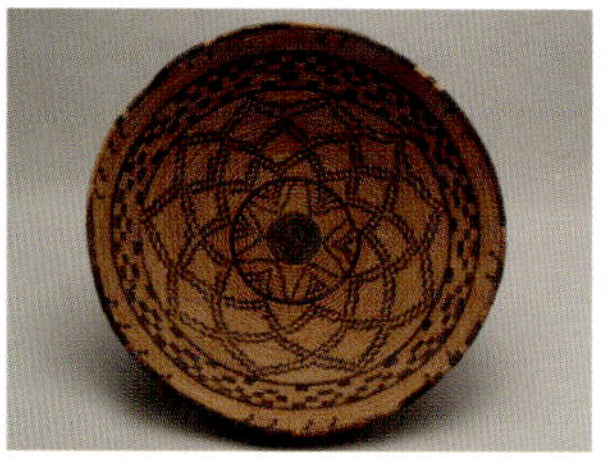

Water Jar, c. 1895
Western Apache
Artist unknown
33.5 x 34.0 cm.
Gift of Joan Higgins Reed, 46562
CONSTRUCTION: diagonal and three-strand twining
FOUNDATION: cottonwood rods
WEAVING ELEMENT: cottonwood shoots; with piñon pitch, mesquite wood

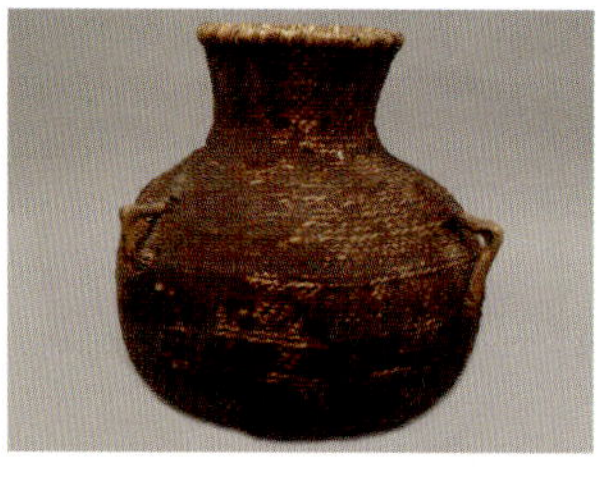

Bowl, c. 1910
Western Apache
Artist unknown
13.5 x 53.5 cm.
Madeleine P. and William C. Ilfeld Collection, 48094
CONSTRUCTION: coiling
FOUNDATION: three willow rods
SEWING ELEMENTS: willow shoots, yucca root, devil's claw seedpod

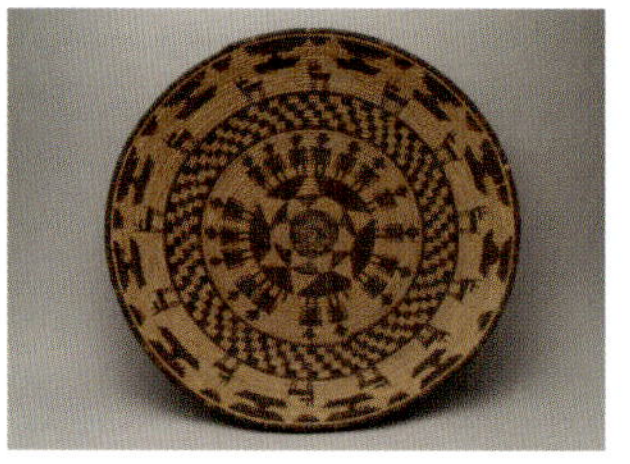

Bowl, c. 1905
Western Apache
Artist unknown
13.5 x 43.5 cm.
Madeleine P. and William C. Ilfeld Collection, 49934
CONSTRUCTION: coiling
FOUNDATION: three willow rods
SEWING ELEMENTS: willow shoots, devil's claw seedpod

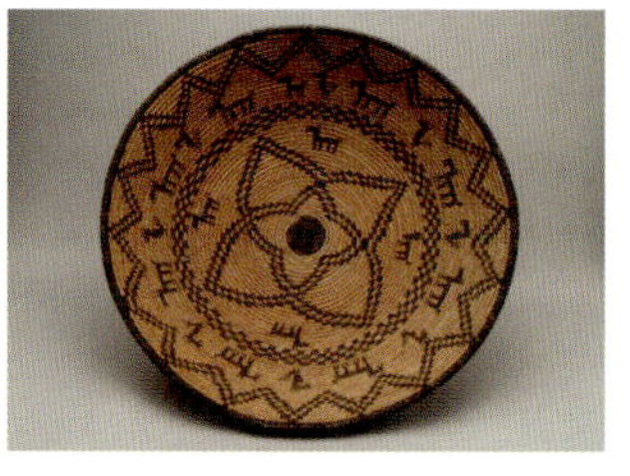

WHITE MOUNTAIN APACHE

Tray, c. 1910
White Mountain Apache
Artist unknown
10.0 x 36.0 cm.
Michael Harrison Collection, 1047

CONSTRUCTION: coiling

FOUNDATION: three cottonwood rods

SEWING ELEMENTS: cottonwood shoots, devil's claw seedpod

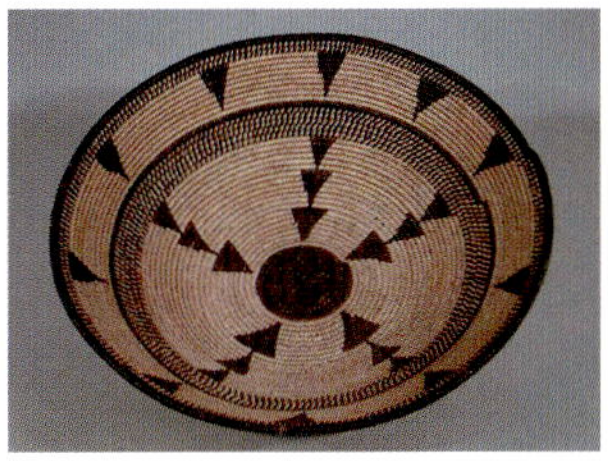

Tray, c. 1915
White Mountain Apache
Artist unknown
8.0 x 42.5 cm.
Michael Harrison Collection, 1050

CONSTRUCTION: coiling

FOUNDATION: three willow rods

SEWING ELEMENTS: willow shoots, devil's claw seedpod

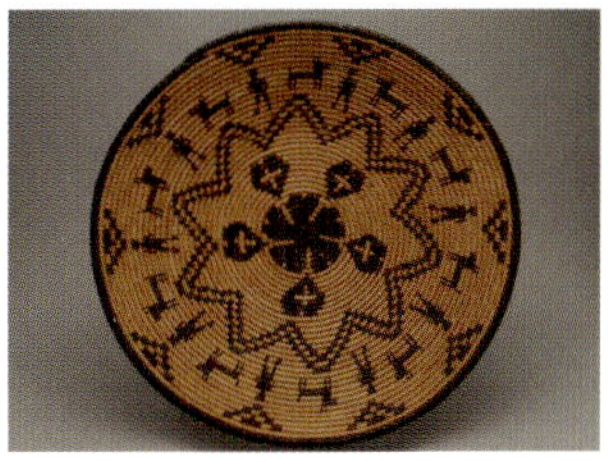

Carrying Basket, c. 1920
White Mountain Apache
Artist unknown
25.0 x 29.0 cm.
Gift of Verda Josey, 12603

CONSTRUCTION: plain and diagonal twining

FOUNDATION: willow rods

WEAVING ELEMENTS: willow shoots, devil's claw seedpod; with dye, cotton, buckskin

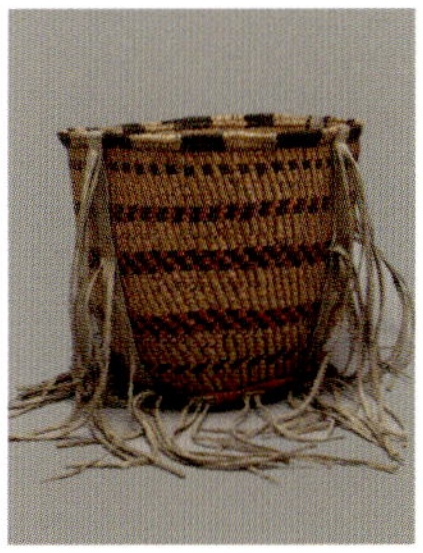

Tray, c. 1890
White Mountain Apache
Artist unknown
5.0 x 32.5 cm.
Gift of Lydia J. Trowbridge, 23277

CONSTRUCTION: coiling

FOUNDATION: three willow rods

SEWING ELEMENTS: willow shoots, devil's claw seedpod

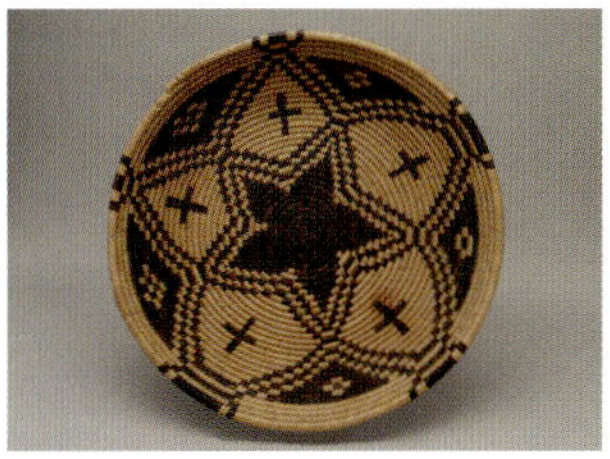

Tray, c. 1900
White Mountain Apache
Artist unknown
10.0 x 39.0 cm.
Ada Crawford McCormack Collection, 31078

CONSTRUCTION: coiling

FOUNDATION: three cottonwood rods

SEWING ELEMENTS: cottonwood shoots, devil's claw seedpod

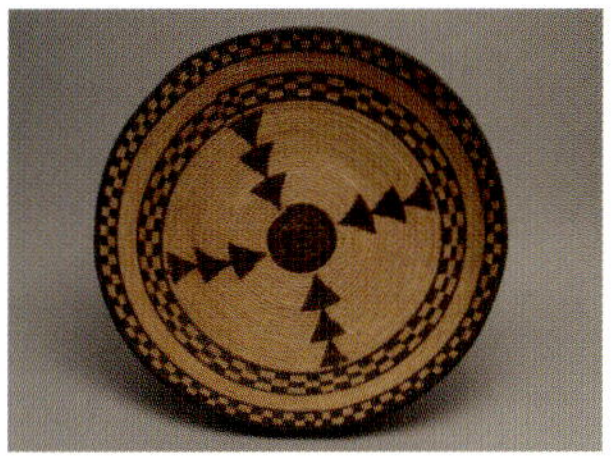

YAVAPAI

Bowl, c. 1895
Yavapai
Artist unknown
10.0 x 41.0 cm.
Museum collection, 23678

CONSTRUCTION: coiling

FOUNDATION: three willow rods

SEWING ELEMENTS: willow shoots, devil's claw seedpod

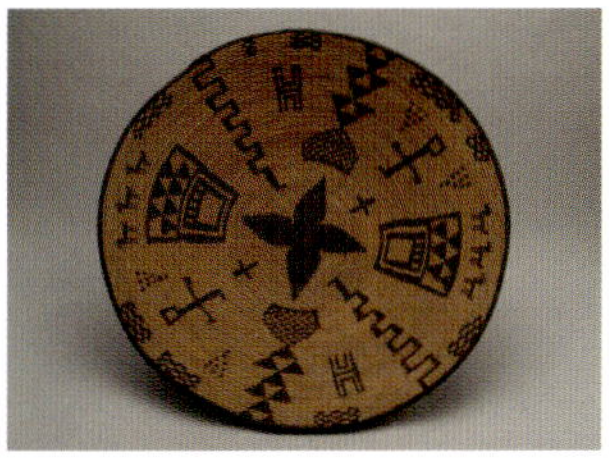

Jar, c. 1935
Yavapai
Artist unknown
42.5 x 36.0 cm.
Gift of Virginia Gladden, 25110

CONSTRUCTION: coiling

FOUNDATION: three willow rods

SEWING ELEMENTS: willow shoots, devil's claw seedpod

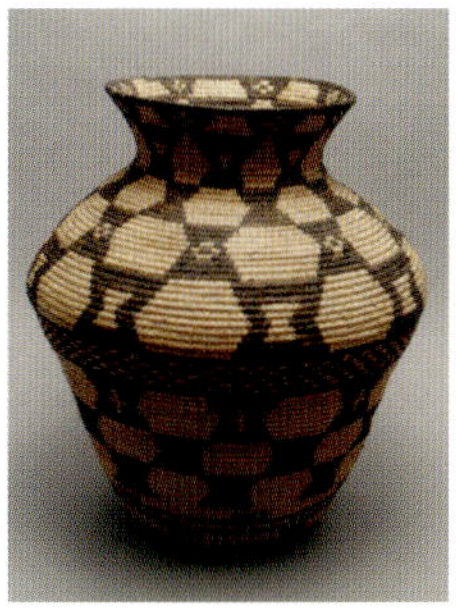

Jar, c. 1890
Yavapai
Artist unknown
36.0 x 36.5 cm.
Gift of Alden Foss, 25424

CONSTRUCTION: coiling

FOUNDATION: three willow rods

SEWING ELEMENTS: willow shoots, devil's claw seedpod

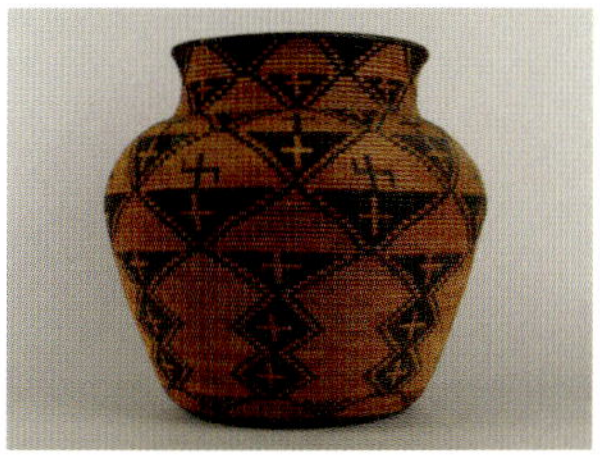

Tray, 1983
Yavapai
Lillian Shenah
5.1 x 26.4 cm.
Museum collection, 50011

CONSTRUCTION: coiling

FOUNDATION: three cottonwood rods

SEWING ELEMENTS: cottonwood shoots, devil's claw seedpod

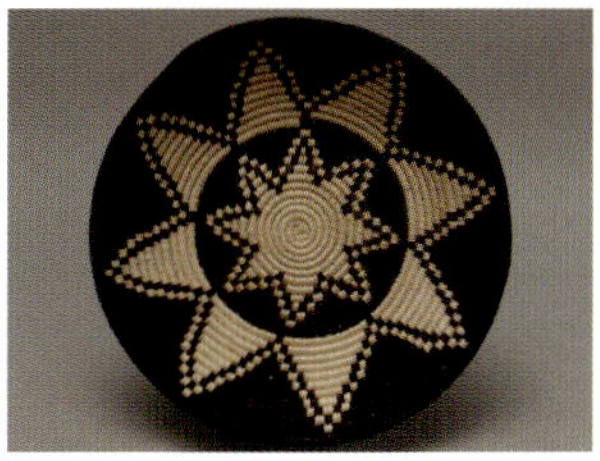

ZUNI

Jar, c. 1800
Zuni
Artist unknown
28.0 x 35.0 cm.
Gift of Dr. Kenneth Chapman, 1118

CONSTRUCTION: coiling

FOUNDATION: two sumac rods and sumac bundle

SEWING ELEMENT: sumac shoots; with dye

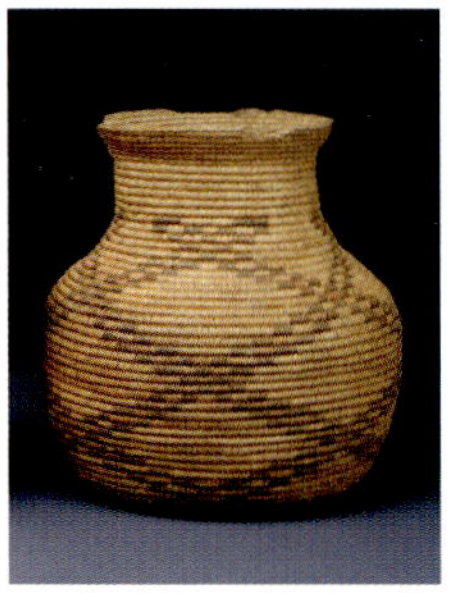

GREAT BASIN

CEDAR PAIUTE

Carrying Basket, 1932
Cedar Paiute
Minnie Tom
62.0 x 52.0 cm.
Collected by Dr. Isabel Kelly, 9971

CONSTRUCTION: diagonal twining

FOUNDATION: willow rods

WEAVING ELEMENT: willow shoots; with buckskin

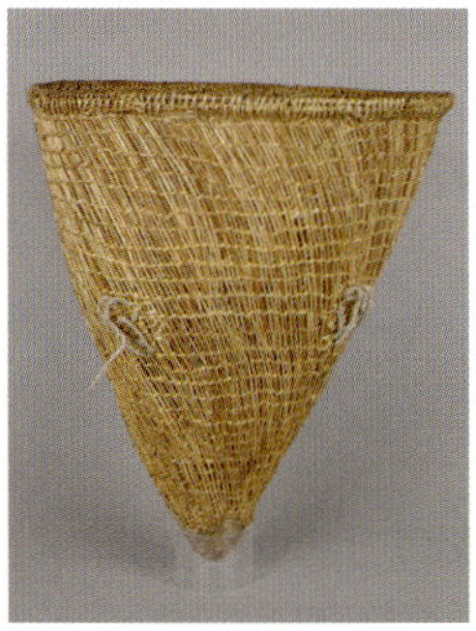

Fancy Basket, 1932
Cedar Paiute
Minnie Tom
5.0 x 23.5 cm.
Collected by Dr. Isabel Kelly, 9978

CONSTRUCTION: coiling

FOUNDATION: three willow rods

SEWING ELEMENTS: willow shoots, devil's claw seedpod

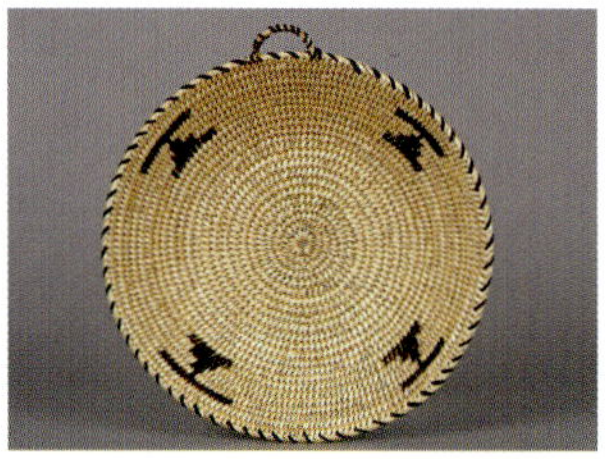

Winnowing Tray, 1932
Cedar Paiute
Minnie Tom
7.0 x 48.0 x 50.0 cm.
Collected by Dr. Isabel Kelly, 9989

CONSTRUCTION: diagonal twining with coiled selvedge

FOUNDATION: willow rods

WEAVING ELEMENT: willow shoots

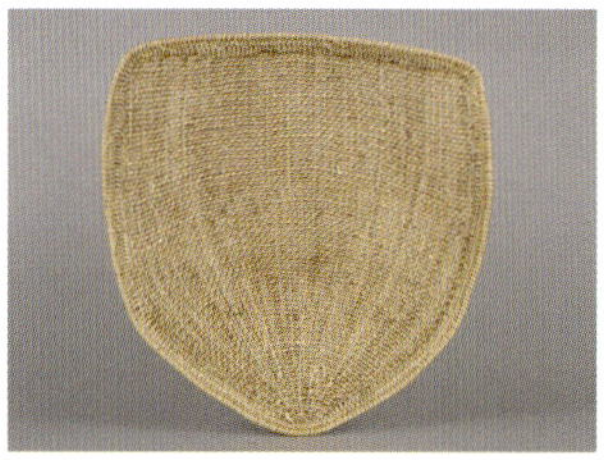

KAIBAB PAIUTE

Seed Beater, 1932
Kaibab Paiute
Sarah Frank
11.0 x 27.5 x 56.5 cm.
Collected by Dr. Isabel Kelly, 900

CONSTRUCTION: diagonal twining

FOUNDATION: sumac rods

WEAVING ELEMENT: sumac shoots; with tin, cotton

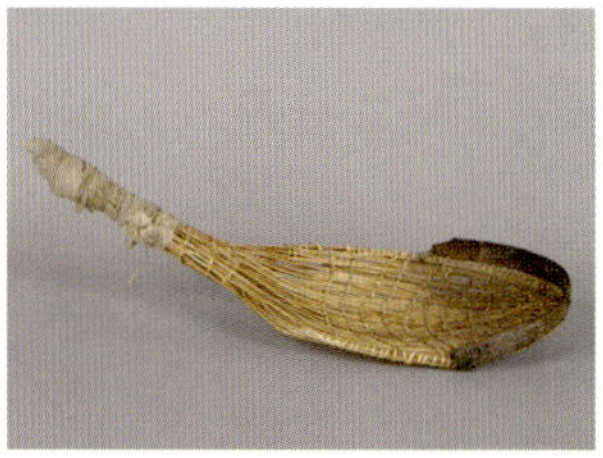

Winnowing Tray, 1932
Kaibab Paiute
Sarah Frank
11.0 x 55.0 x 57.0 cm.
Collected by Dr. Isabel Kelly, 9959

CONSTRUCTION: diagonal twining

FOUNDATION: sumac rods

WEAVING ELEMENT: sumac shoots

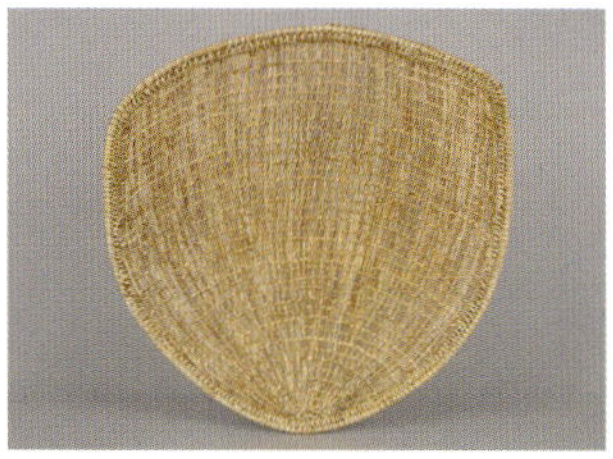

MOAPA PAIUTE

Bag, 1932
Moapa Paiute
Annie Bolin
17.5 x 15.0 x 32.0 cm.
Collected by Dr. Isabel Kelly, 9979

CONSTRUCTION: coiling

FOUNDATION: three willow rods

SEWING ELEMENTS: willow shoots, devil's claw seedpod

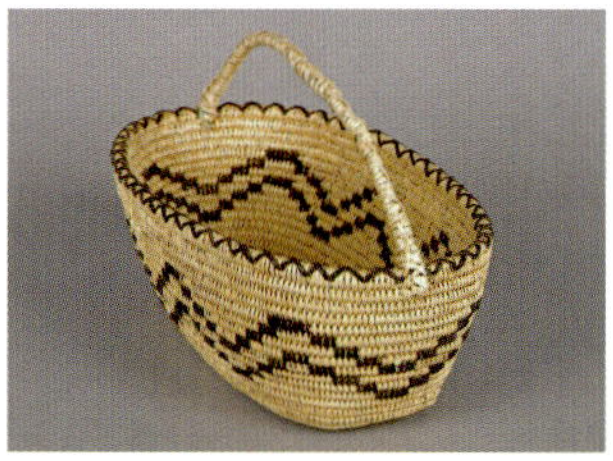

Jar, 1932
Moapa Paiute
Mary Ann Pepo
17.0 x 18.0 cm.
Collected by Dr. Isabel Kelly, 9982

CONSTRUCTION: diagonal twining

FOUNDATION: willow rods

WEAVING ELEMENTS: peeled and unpeeled willow shoots; with buckskin

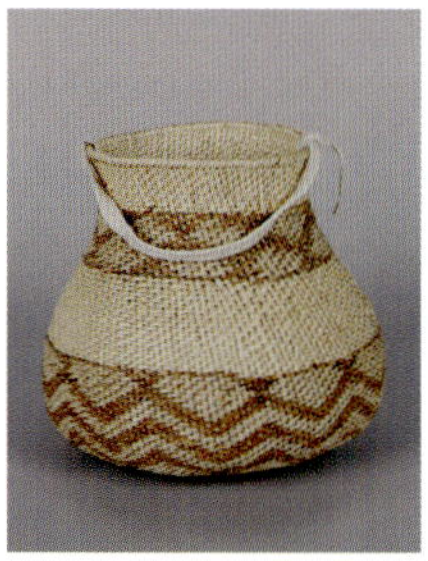

Woman's Cap, 1932
Moapa Paiute
Artist known as "Tangre"
14.5 x 22.0 cm.
Collected by Dr. Isabel Kelly, 9988
CONSTRUCTION: diagonal twining
FOUNDATION: willow rods
WEAVING ELEMENT: willow shoots

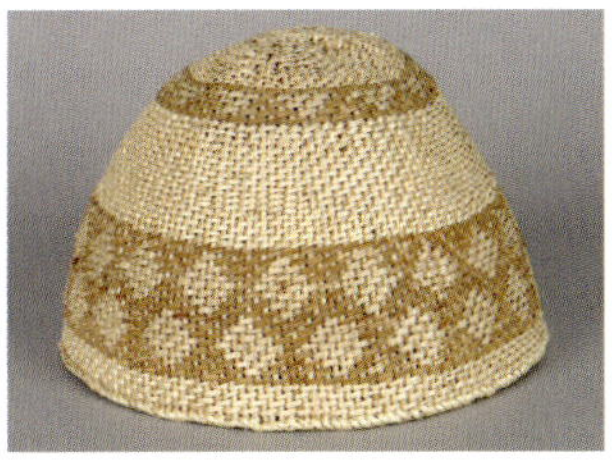

Woman's Cap, 2002
Moapa Paiute
Everett Pikyavit
13.8 x 19.4 cm.
Museum purchase, 56289
CONSTRUCTION: coiling
FOUNDATION: three willow rods
SEWING ELEMENTS: sumac shoots, yucca root, yucca leaf

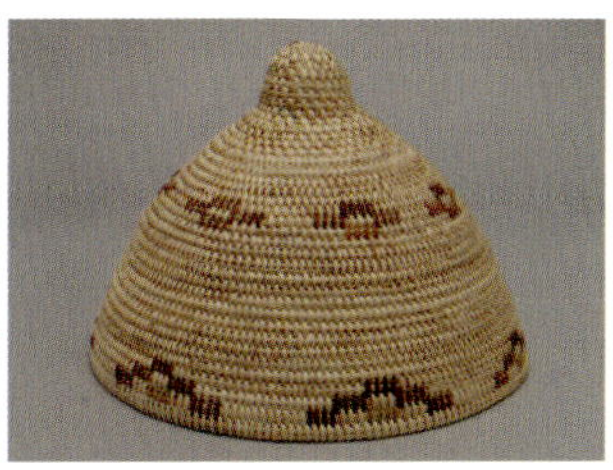

Water Jar, 2012
Moapa Paiute
Everett Pikyavit
21.4 x 13.2 cm.
Gift of Native Treasures, 58188
CONSTRUCTION: diagonal twining
FOUNDATION: willow rods
WEAVING ELEMENTS: willow shoots, cliffrose

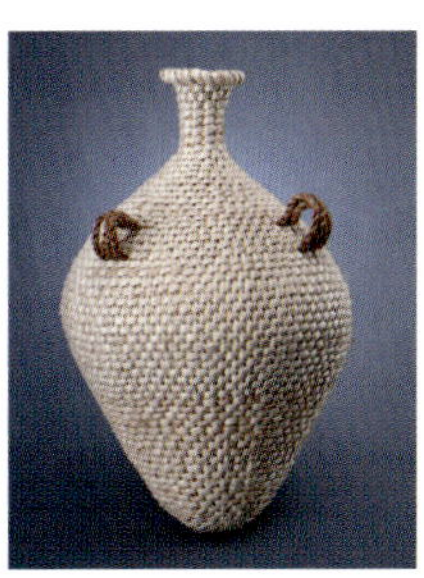

MONO LAKE PAIUTE

Bowl, 1912
Mono Lake Paiute/Miwok
Lucy Parker Telles
17.0 x 21.0 cm.
Homer E. Sargent Collection, 14308
CONSTRUCTION: coiling
FOUNDATION: three willow rods
SEWING ELEMENTS: sedge rhizome, redbud shoots, bracken fern rhizome; with dye

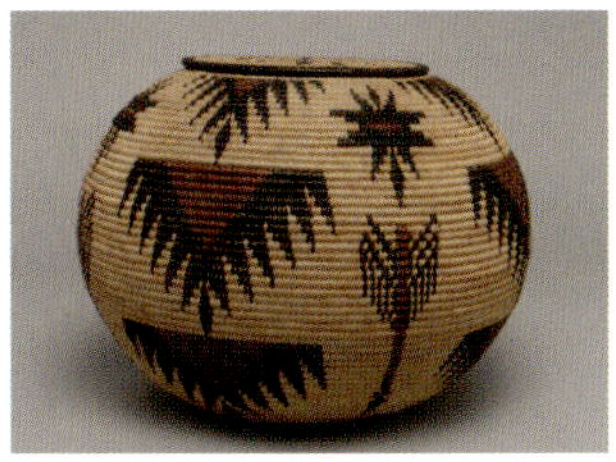

Bowl, c. 1905
Mono Lake Paiute
Artist unknown
11.0 x 26.5 cm.
Honorable Daniel H. McMillan Collection, 14407
CONSTRUCTION: coiling
FOUNDATION: three willow rods
SEWING ELEMENTS: willow shoots, bracken fern rhizome; with dye

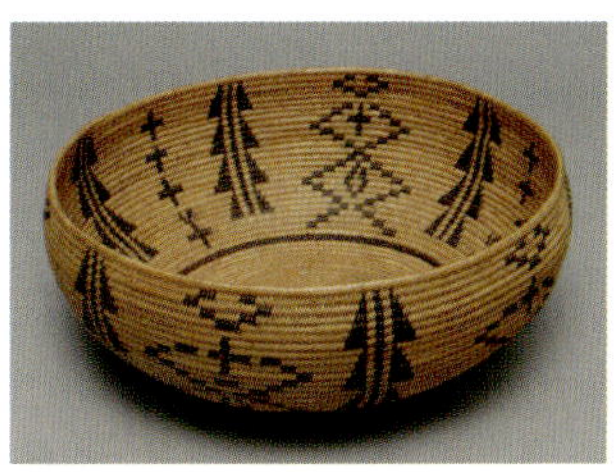

PAIUTE

Seed Bottle, c. 1990
Paiute
Artist unknown
26.0 x 18.0 cm.
Gift of S. J. Hess, 23383
CONSTRUCTION: diagonal and plain twining
FOUNDATION: willow rods
WEAVING ELEMENTS: willow shoots, Indian hemp fiber

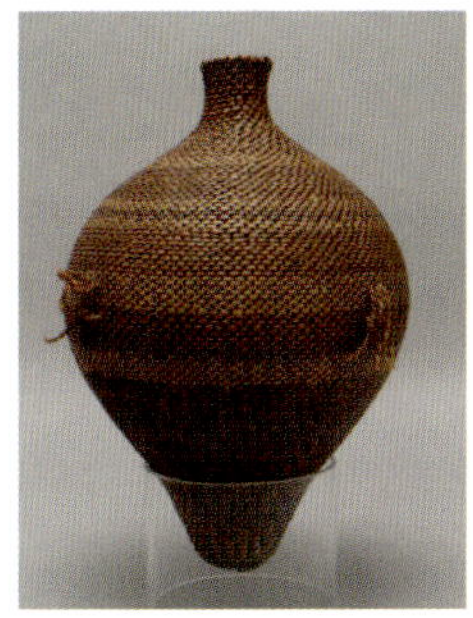

PANAMINT SHOSHONE

Gift Basket, c. 1900
Panamint Shoshone
Artist unknown
12.0 x 17.0 cm.
Gift of Chris and Bob Stengle, 56963
CONSTRUCTION: coiling
FOUNDATION: three willow rods
SEWING ELEMENTS: willow shoots, Joshua tree root, devil's claw seedpod

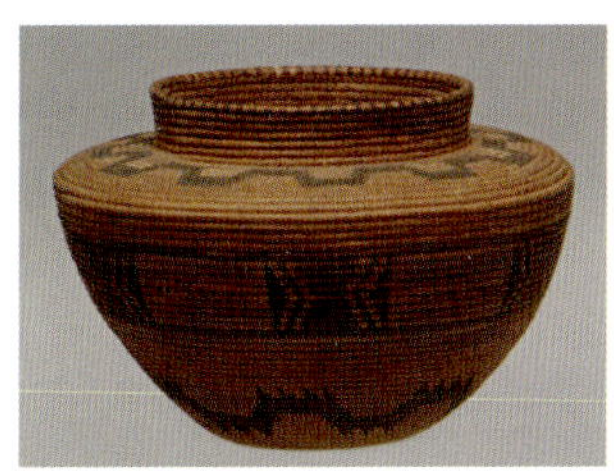

SAN JUAN PAIUTE

Tray, c. 1925
San Juan Paiute
Artist unknown
5.0 x 34.5 cm.
Michael Harrison Collection, 1076

CONSTRUCTION: coiling

FOUNDATION: three sumac rods

SEWING ELEMENT: sumac shoots; with dye

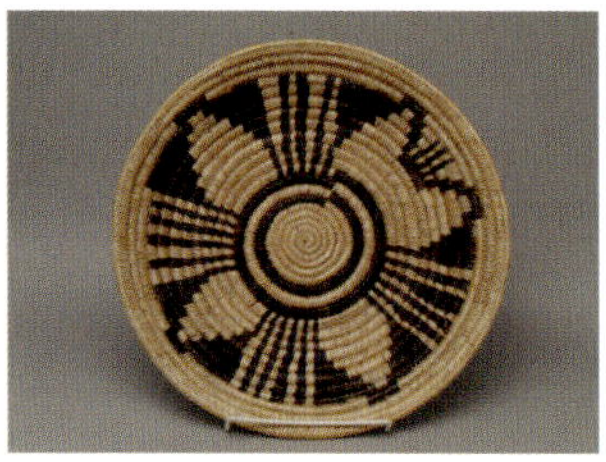

Plaque, c. 1985
San Juan Paiute
Attributed to Lorraine King
4.0 x 28.0 cm.
Gift of Mark and Martha Alexander, 55919

CONSTRUCTION: coiling

FOUNDATION: three sumac rods

SEWING ELEMENT: sumac shoots; with dye

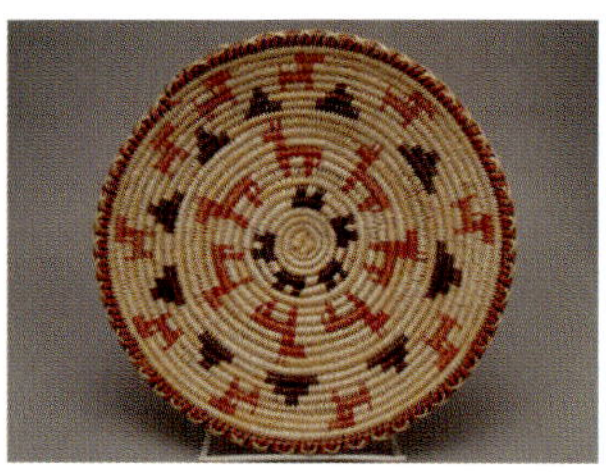

Tray, c. 1985
San Juan Paiute
Lorraine King
5.5 x 38.5 cm.
Gift of Mark and Martha Alexander, 55920

CONSTRUCTION: coiling

FOUNDATION: three sumac rods

SEWING ELEMENT: sumac shoots; with dye

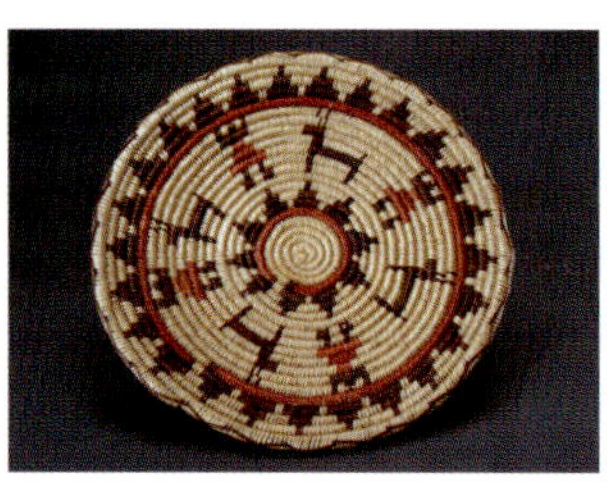

Wedding Tray, c. 1930
San Juan Paiute
Artist unknown
5 x 30.5 cm.
Gift of Zorro Bradley, 57534

CONSTRUCTION: coiling

FOUNDATION: three sumac rods

WEAVING ELEMENT: sumac shoots; with dye, cotton

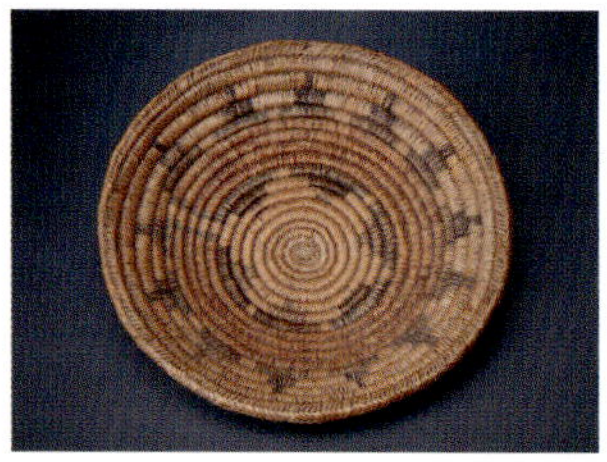

Tray, c. 2005
San Juan Paiute
Louise Owl Tallman
2.9 x 26 cm.
Gift of Blue Rain Gallery, 58025

CONSTRUCTION: coiling

FOUNDATION: two sumac rods and sumac bundle

SEWING ELEMENT: sumac shoots; with dye

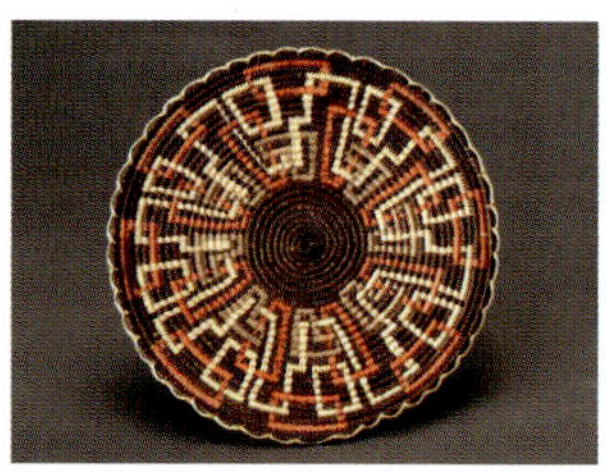

Tray, c. 2005
San Juan Paiute
Louise Owl Tallman
2.0 x 26 cm.
Gift of Elizabeth Baldwin, 58044

CONSTRUCTION: coiling

FOUNDATION: two sumac rods and sumac bundle

SEWING ELEMENT: sumac shoots; with dye

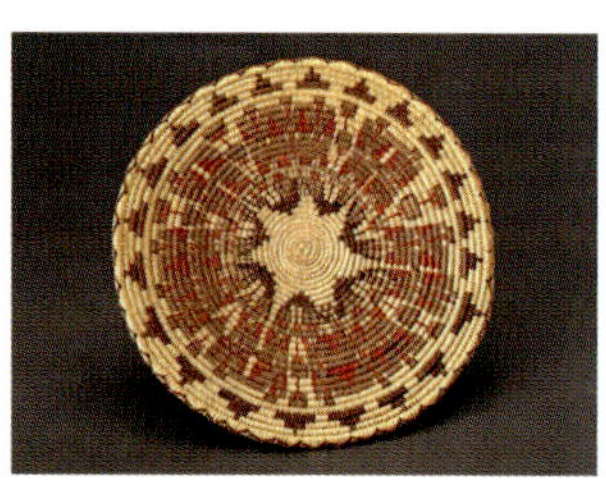

SHIVWITS PAIUTE

Parching Tray, 1932
Shivwits Paiute
Artist known as "Ida"
6.0 x 35.5 cm.
Collected by Dr. Isabel Kelly, 9956

CONSTRUCTION: coiling

FOUNDATION: three sumac rods

SEWING ELEMENT: sumac shoots

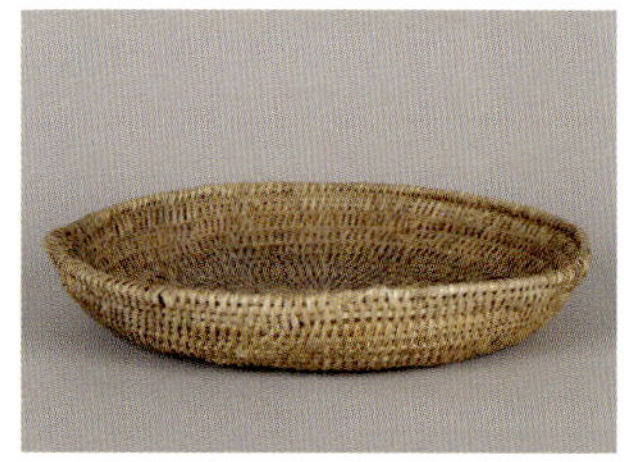

Seed Beater, 1932
Shivwits Paiute
Sarah or Sally Kaputs
8.0 x 29.0 x 47.0 cm.
Collected by Dr. Isabel Kelly, 9992

CONSTRUCTION: diagonal twining

FOUNDATION: sumac rods

WEAVING ELEMENT: sumac shoots

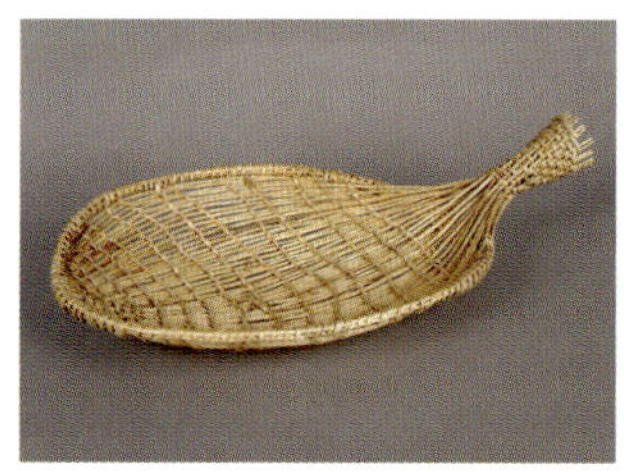

SOUTHERN PAIUTE

Water Jar, c. 1930
Southern Paiute
Artist unknown
25 x 16.5 cm.
Ada Crawford McCormack Collection, 23467

CONSTRUCTION: diagonal twining

FOUNDATION: willow rods

WEAVING ELEMENTS: willow shoots, cliffrose

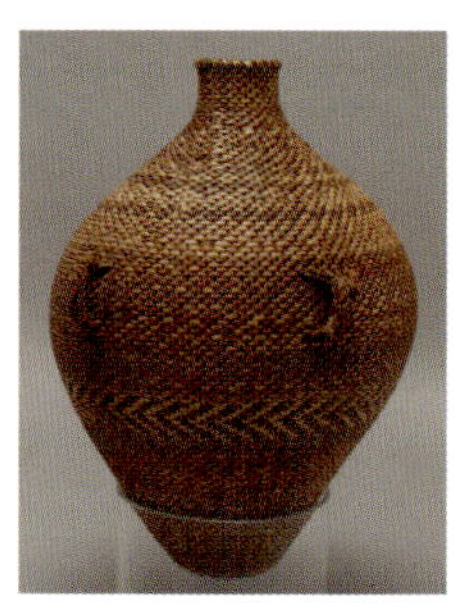

UTE

Water Jar, 1935
Ute
Artist unknown
32.0 x 25.0 cm.
Collected by Dr. Anne M. Cooke, 7498

CONSTRUCTION: coiling, vertical overstitching

FOUNDATION: three-stacked willow rods

SEWING ELEMENTS: willow shoots, horsehair; with buckskin

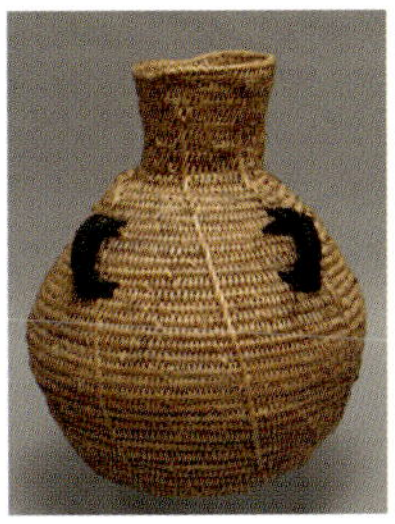

Food Bowl, 1932
Southern Paiute or Ute
Sally Ann
7.0 x 22.0 cm.
Collected by Dr. Isabel Kelly, 9915

CONSTRUCTION: coiling

FOUNDATION: three sumac rods

SEWING ELEMENTS: sumac shoots, devil's claw seedpod

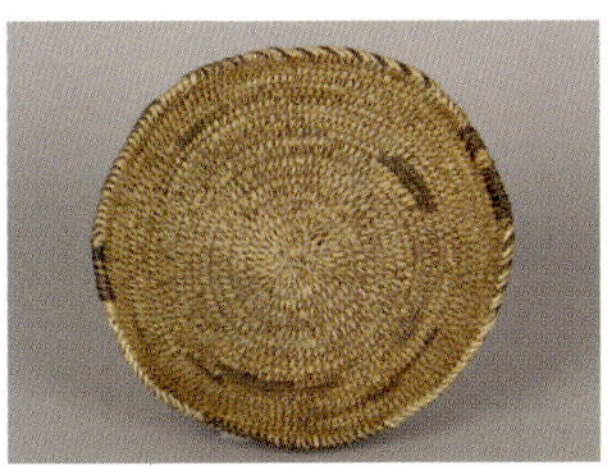

WASHOE

Cooking/Serving Bowl, c. 1920
Washoe
Artist unknown
25.5 x 46.0 cm.
Museum collection, 23772

CONSTRUCTION: coiling

FOUNDATION: single willow rod

SEWING ELEMENTS: willow shoots, redbud shoots, bracken fern rhizome; with dye

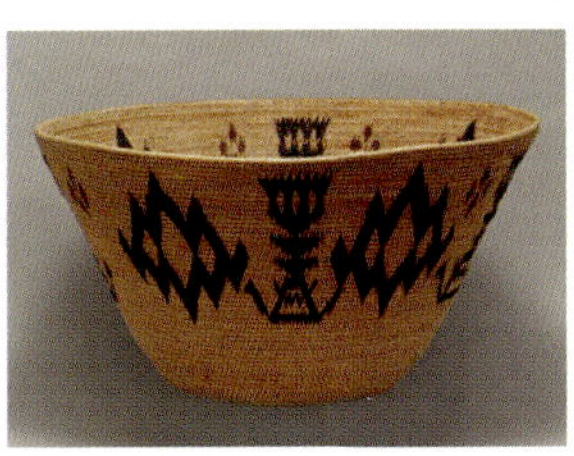

PLATEAU

MODOC

Woman's Hat, c. 1900
Modoc
Artist unknown
10.0 x 20.0 cm.
Gift of Marion Bond, 14260

CONSTRUCTION: plain and wrapped twining

FOUNDATION: twisted tule stem cordage

WEAVING ELEMENTS: tule stem, beargrass, porcupine quill; with dye

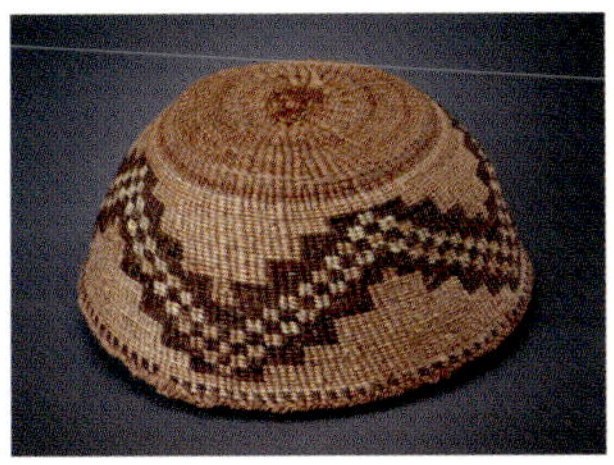

Bowl, c. 1920
Modoc
Artist unknown
10.0 x 18.0 cm.
Wyland Collection, 35703

CONSTRUCTION: plain and wrapped twining

FOUNDATION: twisted tule stem cordage

WEAVING ELEMENTS: bulrush root, cattail fiber; with dye

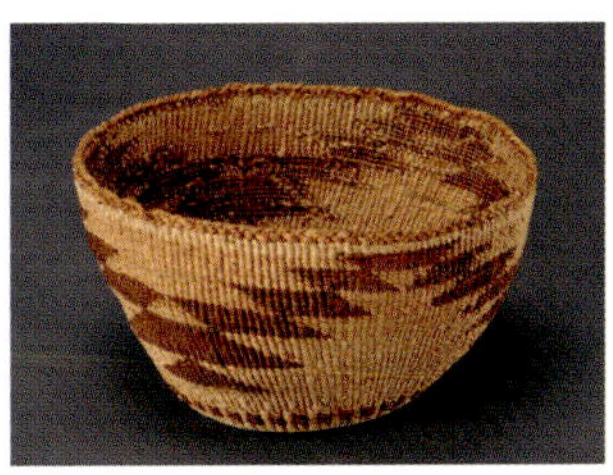

KLAMATH

Bowl, c. 1920
Klamath or Modoc
Artist unknown
10.2 x 15.5 cm.
Gift of Louis C. Mueller, 1786

CONSTRUCTION: plain and wrapped twining

FOUNDATION: twisted tule stem cordage

WEAVING ELEMENT: cattail fiber; with dye

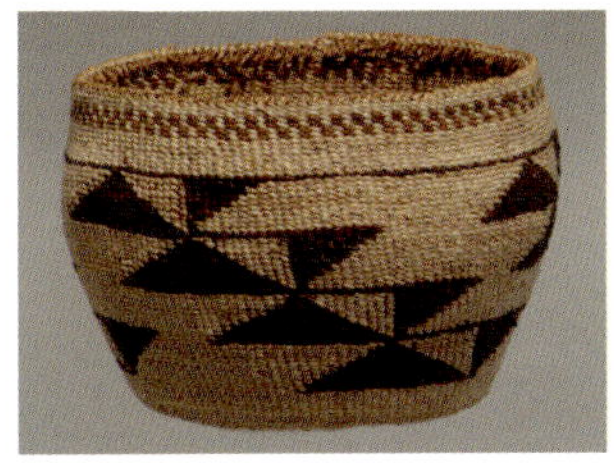

NTLAKAPAMUK

Bowl, c. 1890
Ntlakapamuk
Artist unknown
11.0 x 19.5 cm.
Honorable Daniel H. McMillan Collection, 14401

CONSTRUCTION: coiling, imbrication, slat bottom

FOUNDATION: cedar-root bundle

SEWING ELEMENTS: split cedar-root strand, bitter cherry bark, phragmites

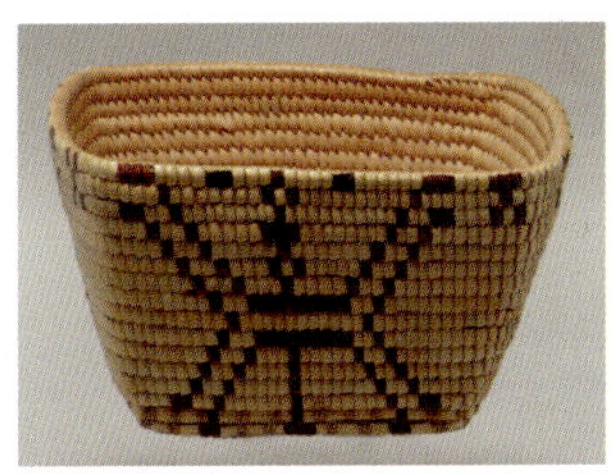

Storage Basket Model, c. 1890
Ntlakapamuk
Artist unknown
23.0 x 42.0 x 33.5 cm.
Gift of Alden Foss, 25438

CONSTRUCTION: coiling, imbrication, beading

FOUNDATION: cedar-root bundle

SEWING ELEMENTS: split cedar-root strand, bitter cherry bark, phragmites; with dye

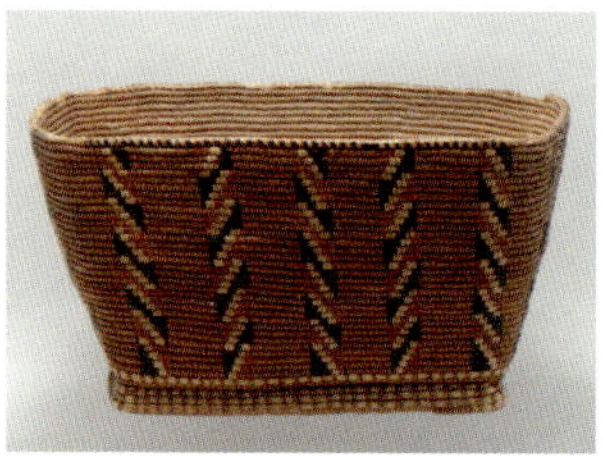

PLATEAU

Carrying Bag, c. 1900
Plateau
Artist unknown
63.0 x 47.5 cm.
Gift of Rosemary Ames, 25030

CONSTRUCTION: plain twining, false embroidery

FOUNDATION: Indian hemp cordage

WEAVING ELEMENTS: Indian hemp fiber, cornhusk fiber, wool; with dye, buckskin

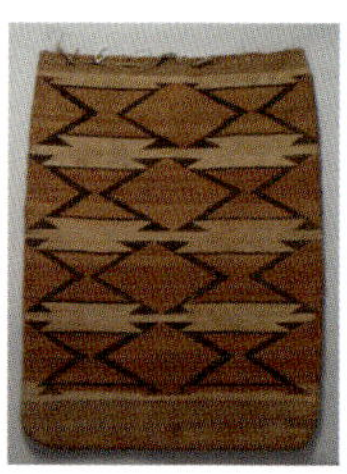

Bag, c. 1885
Plateau
Artist unknown
39.7 x 59.2 cm.
Gift of Thomas B. Catron III, 53234

CONSTRUCTION: twining, false embroidery

FOUNDATION: Indian hemp cordage

WEAVING ELEMENTS: Indian hemp fiber, cornhusk fiber, iris fiber, wool

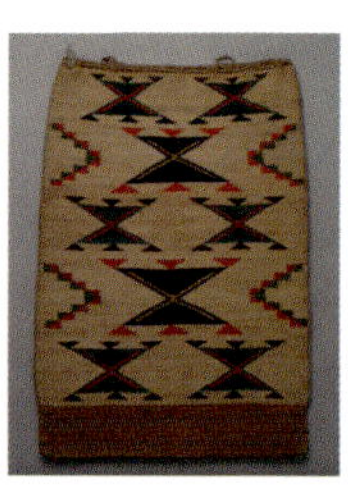

UMATILLA

Bag, c. 1910
Umatilla
Artist unknown
14.0 x 11.0 cm.
Museum collection, 23697

CONSTRUCTION: wrapped and plain twining

FOUNDATION: Indian hemp fiber cordage

WEAVING ELEMENTS: cornhusk fiber, iris fiber; with dye, cloth, beads

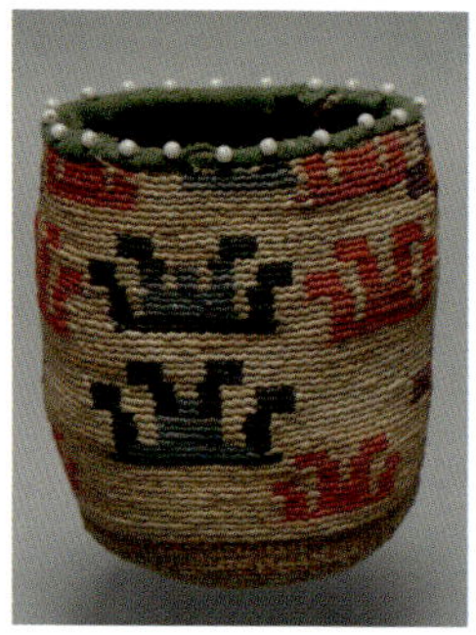

WASCO-WISHRAM

Miniature Gathering Basket, c. 1880
Wasco-Wishram
Artist unknown
10.0 x 13.5 cm.
Ina Sizer Cassidy Collection, 911

CONSTRUCTION: plain twining

FOUNDATION: tule cordage

WEAVING ELEMENTS: tule, Indian hemp fiber; with dye, hide

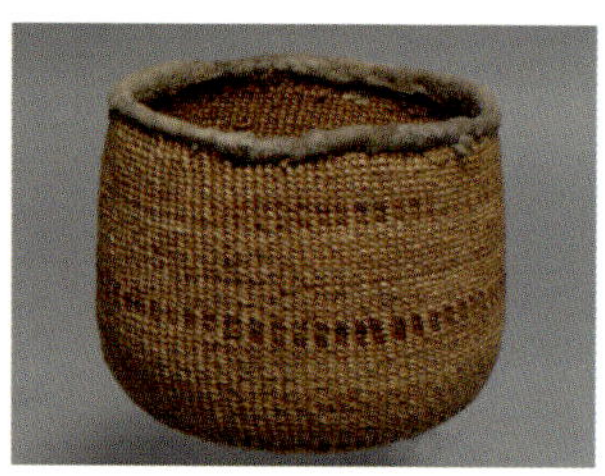

Gathering Basket, c. 1880
Wasco-Wishram
Artist unknown
25.5 x 19.0 cm.
Gift of Agnes E. Hawkins, 14376

CONSTRUCTION: plain twining

FOUNDATION: tule cordage

WEAVING ELEMENTS: tule, Indian hemp fiber; with dye, hide

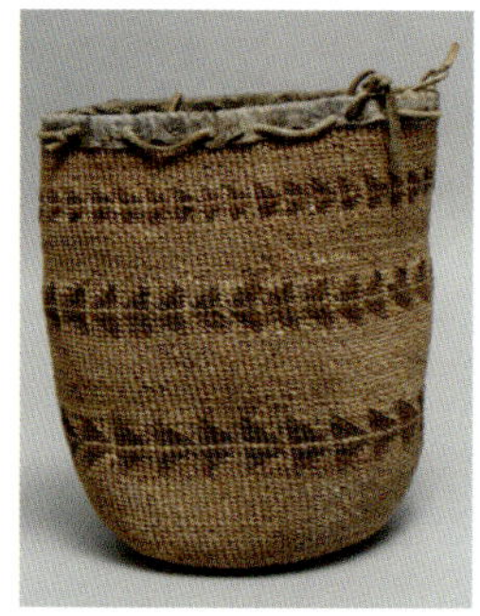

CALIFORNIA

ACHUMAWI

Carrying Basket, c. 1905
Achumawi
Artist unknown
48.5 x 53.0 cm.
Gift of Mary Cabot Wheelwright, 1852

CONSTRUCTION: plain and three-strand twining, overlay

FOUNDATION: conifer-root cordage

WEAVING ELEMENTS: conifer root, redbud shoots, beargrass, maidenhair fern stem

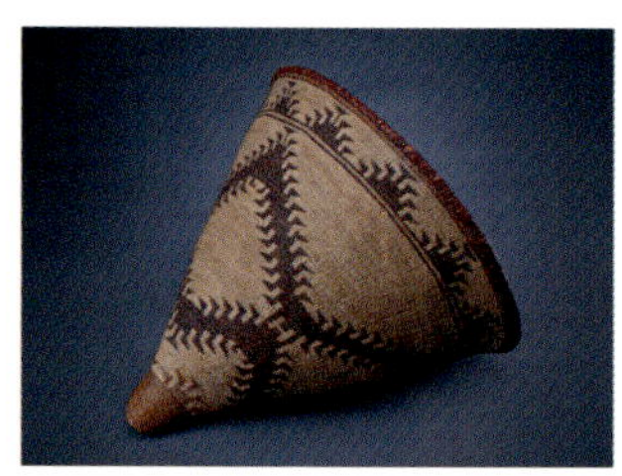

CAHUILLA

Winnowing Tray, c. 1920
Cahuilla
Artist unknown
4.5 x 43.0 cm.
Twitchell Estate, 23236

CONSTRUCTION: coiling

FOUNDATION: deergrass bundle

SEWING ELEMENTS: sumac shoots, juncus stalk; with dye

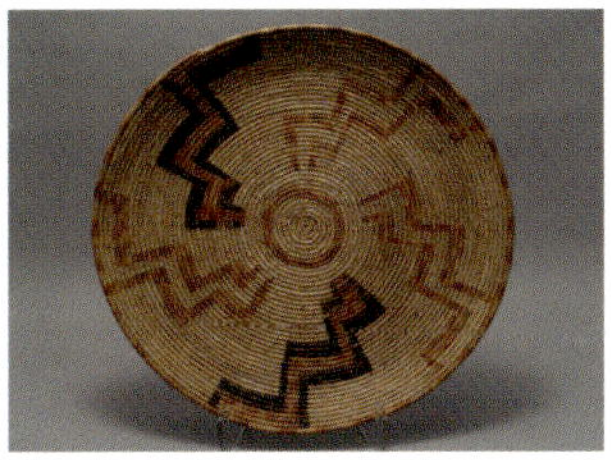

Bowl, c. 1895
Cahuilla
Artist unknown
16.0 x 27.0 cm.
Ada Crawford McCormack Collection, 23468

CONSTRUCTION: coiling

FOUNDATION: deergrass bundle

SEWING ELEMENTS: sumac shoots, juncus stalk

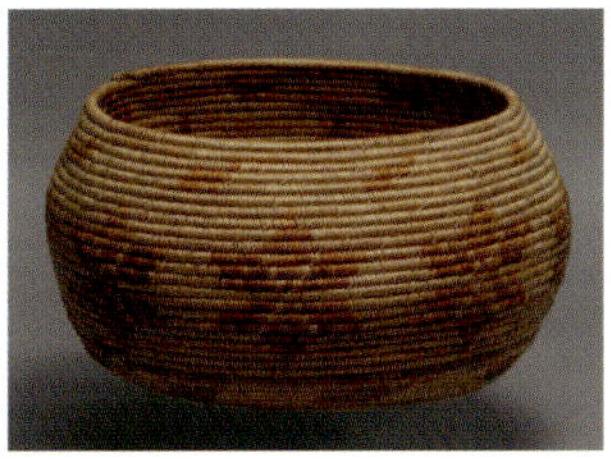

Tray, c. 1920
Cahuilla
Artist unknown
7.0 x 36.0 cm.
Gift of Rose Dugan, 23774

CONSTRUCTION: coiling

FOUNDATION: deergrass bundle

SEWING ELEMENTS: sumac shoots, juncus stalk; with dye

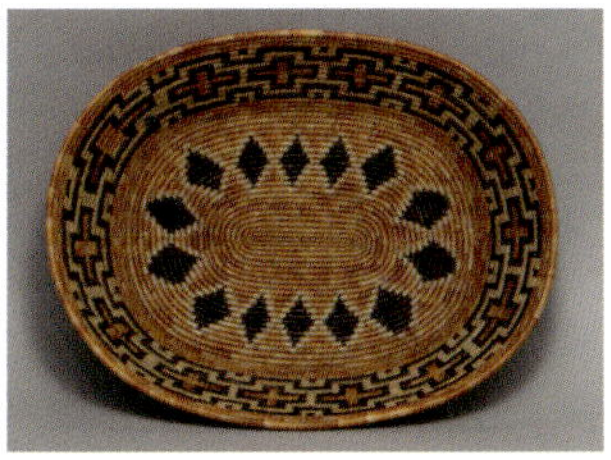

Tray, 1910
Cahuilla
Artist unknown
7.0 x 29.5 cm.
Gift of Rosemary Ames, 25025

CONSTRUCTION: coiling

FOUNDATION: deergrass bundle

SEWING ELEMENTS: sumac shoots, juncus stalk; with dye

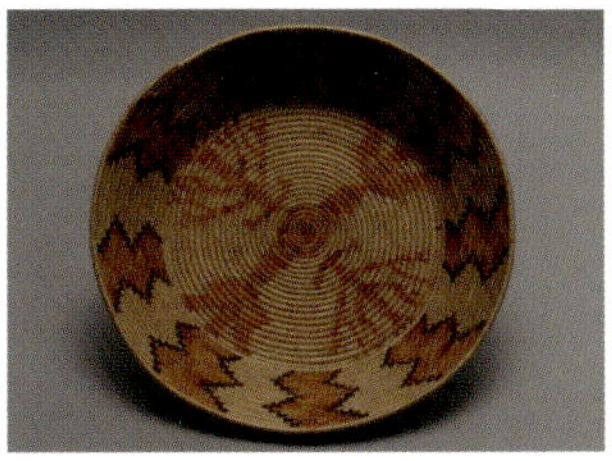

Tray, c. 1890
Cahuilla
Artist unknown
8.0 x 33.5 cm.
Gift of Rosemary Ames, 25026

CONSTRUCTION: coiling

FOUNDATION: deergrass bundle

SEWING ELEMENTS: sumac shoots, juncus stalk

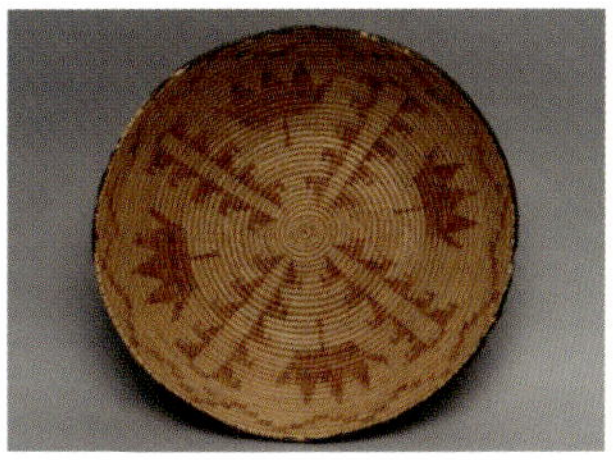

HUPA

Cooking Basket, c. 1900
Hupa
Artist unknown
18.0 x 26.0 cm.
Ada Crawford McCormack Collection, 23495

CONSTRUCTION: plain and wrapped twining, overlay

FOUNDATION: hazelnut rods

WEAVING ELEMENTS: conifer root, beargrass

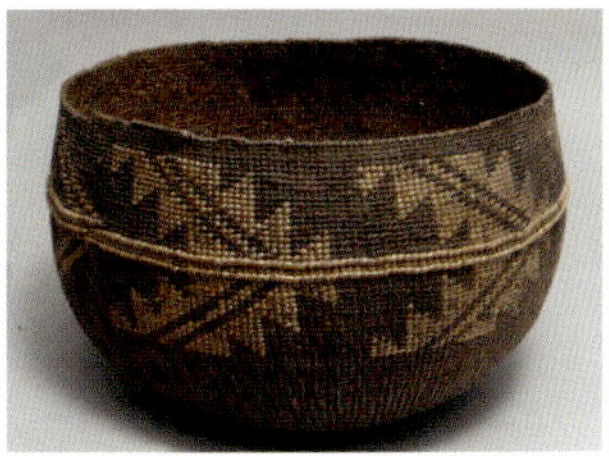

Carrying Basket, c. 1900
Hupa
Artist unknown
38.0 x 44.0 cm.
Gift of Mrs. A. W. Rogers, 23782

CONSTRUCTION: plain, diagonal, and three-strand twining, overlay

FOUNDATION: hazelnut rods

WEAVING ELEMENTS: conifer root, beargrass, maidenhair fern stem

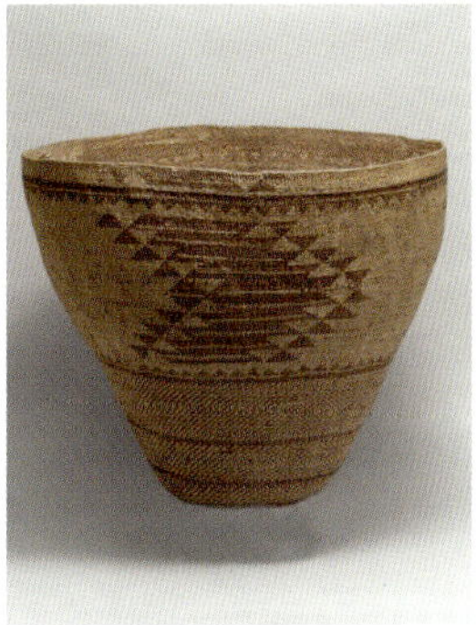

KARUK

Woman's Cap, c. 1920
Karuk
Artist unknown
7.5 x 17.5 cm.
Gift of Esther Cummings, 19

CONSTRUCTION: plain twining, overlay

FOUNDATION: hazelnut rods

WEAVING ELEMENTS: spruce root, beargrass, alder-dyed woodwardia fern stem, maidenhair fern stem

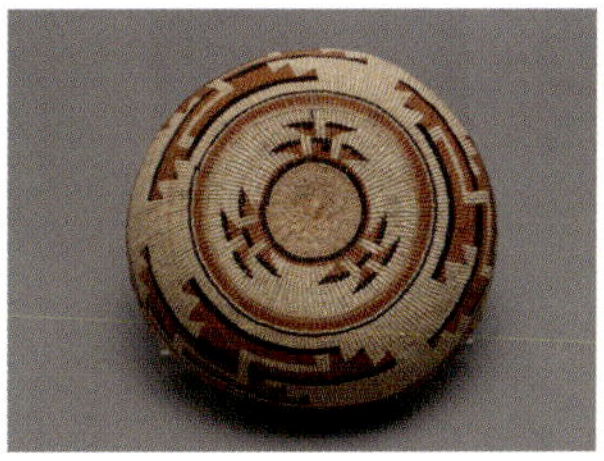

Unfinished Bowl, 1913
Karuk
Artist unknown
32.0 x 7.0 cm.
Gift of Homer E. Sargent, 14294

CONSTRUCTION: plain twining, overlay

FOUNDATION: hazelnut rods

WEAVING ELEMENTS: spruce root, beargrass, alder-dyed woodwardia fern stem, maidenhair fern stem

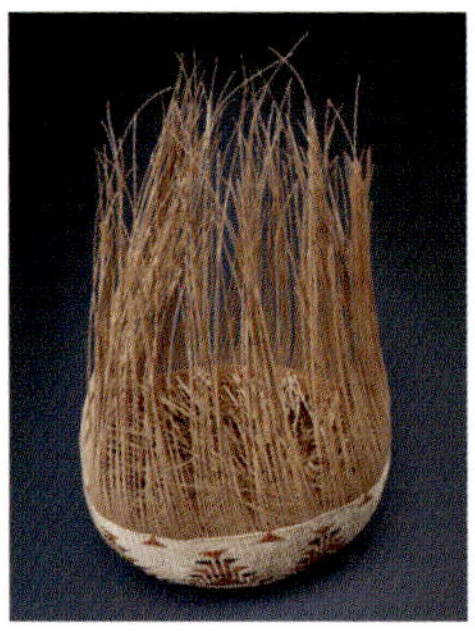

KUMEYAAY

Tray, c. 1910
Kumeyaay
Artist unknown
10.1 x 36.2 cm.
C. T. Cotton Collection, 1742

CONSTRUCTION: coiling

FOUNDATION: deergrass bundle

SEWING ELEMENTS: sumac shoots, juncus stalk; with dye

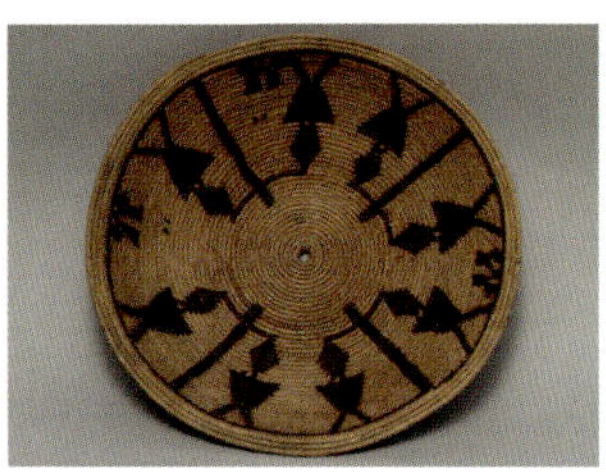

Bowl, 1893
Kumeyaay
Ramona Balenzuela
11.0 x 17.5 cm.
Homer E. Sargent Collection, 14305

CONSTRUCTION: coiling

FOUNDATION: deergrass bundle

SEWING ELEMENTS: sumac shoots, juncus stalk; with dye

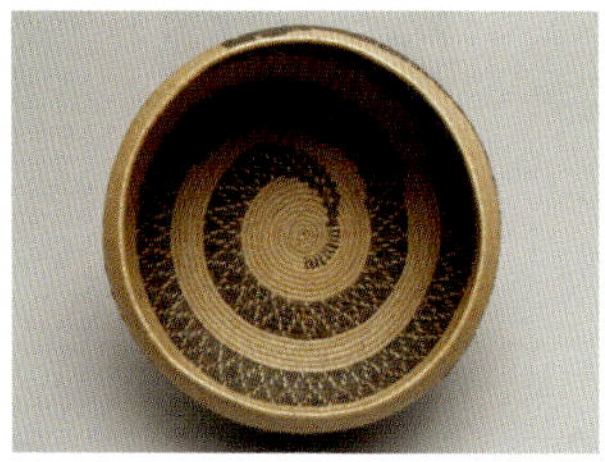

Bowl, c. 1900
Kumeyaay
Artist unknown
13.0 x 39.0 cm.
Gift of Agnes E. Hawkins, 14378

CONSTRUCTION: coiling

FOUNDATION: deergrass bundle

SEWING ELEMENTS: sumac shoots, juncus stalk; with dye

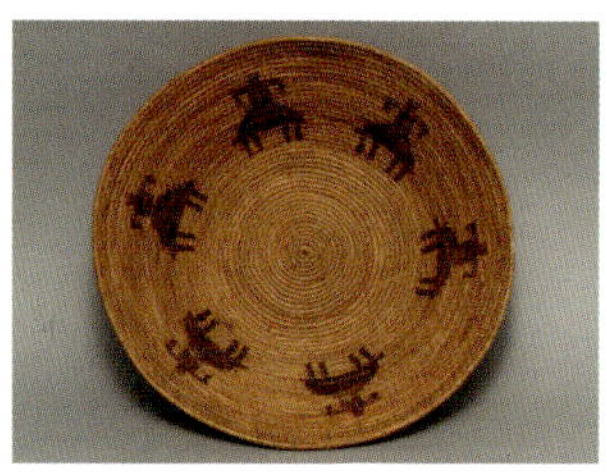

Tray, c. 1910
Kumeyaay
Gregoria Pia
5.5 x 36.5 cm.
Gift of Byron Harvey III, 23235

CONSTRUCTION: coiling

FOUNDATION: juncus-stalk bundle

SEWING ELEMENTS: sumac shoots, juncus stalk; with dye

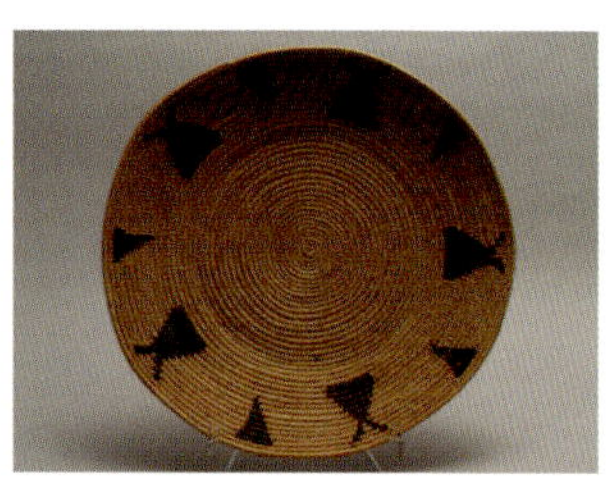

Bowl, c. 1900
Kumeyaay
Artist unknown
11.5 x 25.5 cm.
Gift of Lydia Trowbridge, 23778

CONSTRUCTION: coiling

FOUNDATION: deergrass bundle

SEWING ELEMENTS: sumac shoots, juncus stalk

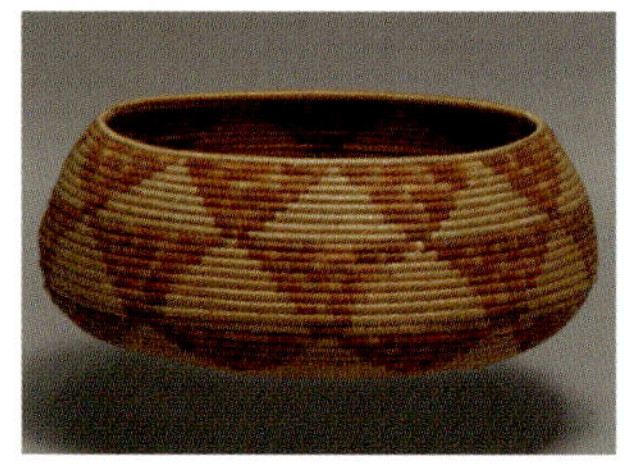

Tray, c. 1900
Kumeyaay
Artist unknown
6.0 x 26.0 cm.
Gift of Rosemary Ames, 25024

CONSTRUCTION: coiling

FOUNDATION: deergrass bundle

SEWING ELEMENTS: sumac shoots, juncus stalk

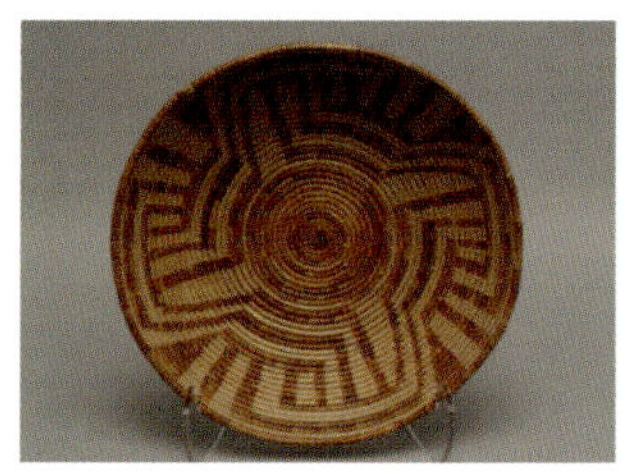

LOWER KLAMATH RIVER

Food Bowl, c. 1910
Lower Klamath River
Artist unknown
9.0 x 16.5 cm.
Gift of Mrs. A. W. Rogers, 23688

CONSTRUCTION: plain, three-strand, and wrapped twining, overlay

FOUNDATION: hazelnut rods

WEAVING ELEMENTS: spruce root, beargrass

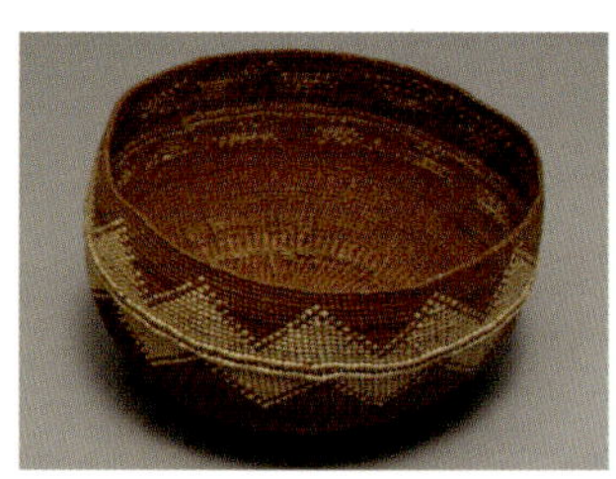

Woman's Cap, c. 1930
Lower Klamath River
Artist unknown
9.0 x 17.0 cm.
Gift of Henry Dendahl, 23715

CONSTRUCTION: plain twining, overlay

FOUNDATION: hazelnut rods

WEAVING ELEMENTS: spruce root, beargrass, maidenhair fern stem

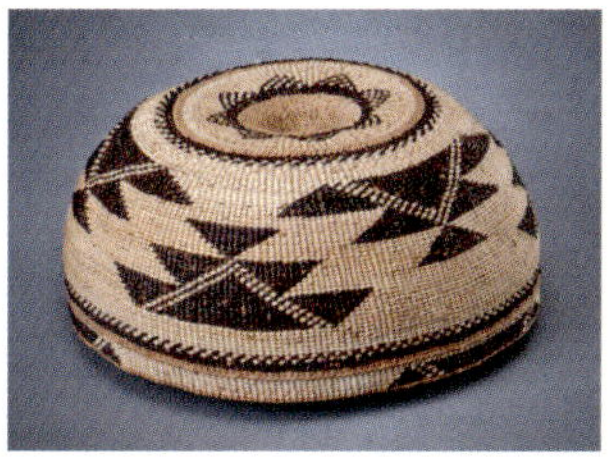

Woman's Cap, c. 1930
Lower Klamath River
Artist unknown
9.0 x 19.0 cm.
Gift of Henry Dendahl, 23716

CONSTRUCTION: plain twining, overlay

FOUNDATION: hazelnut rods

WEAVING ELEMENTS: spruce root, beargrass, maidenhair fern stem

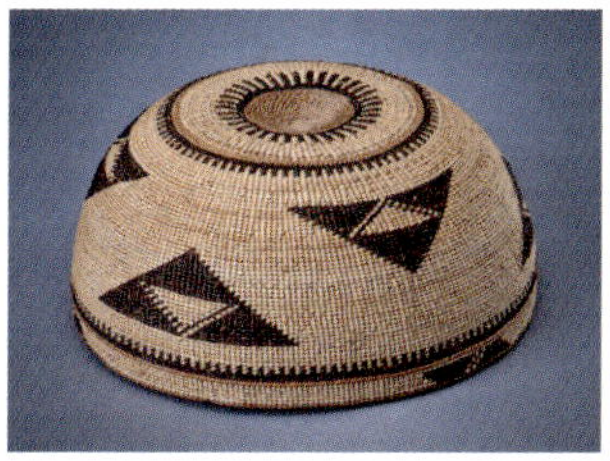

MONACHE

Cooking Basket, c. 1885
Monache
15.4 x 20.8 cm.
Artist unknown
Gift of Alden Foss, 25445

CONSTRUCTION: coiling

FOUNDATION: deergrass bundle

SEWING ELEMENTS: sedge rhizome, bracken fern rhizome; with dye

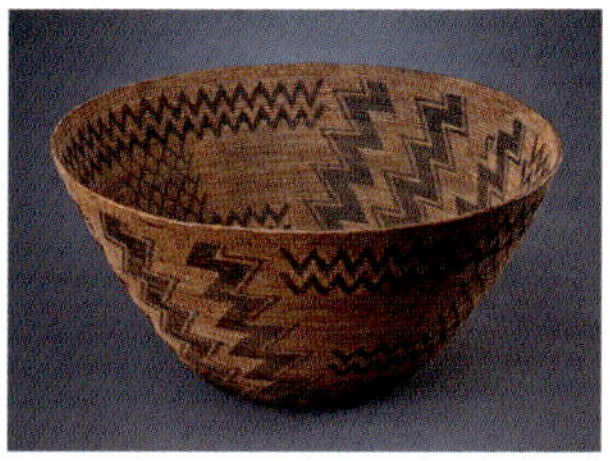

Gift Basket, c. 1950
Monache
Artist unknown
9.0 x 18.0 cm.
Gift of Mrs. Crawford R. Buell, 47664

CONSTRUCTION: coiling

FOUNDATION: deergrass bundle

SEWING ELEMENTS: sedge rhizome, bracken fern rhizome; with dye

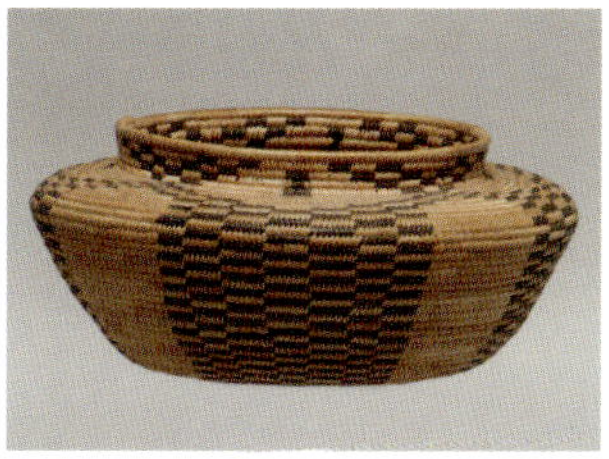

MOUNTAIN MAIDU

Bowl, c. 1907
Mountain Maidu
Artist known as "Young Bob's Woman"
9.0 x 13.0 cm.
Homer E. Sargent Collection, 14306

CONSTRUCTION: coiling

FOUNDATION: three willow rods

SEWING ELEMENTS: maple shoots, bracken fern rhizome; with dye

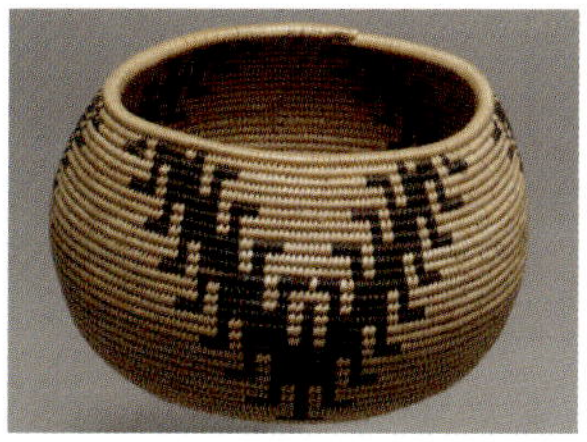

Tray, c. 1905
Mountain Maidu
Artist known as "Big Meadows Susan"
4.0 x 43.5 cm.
Homer E. Sargent Collection, 14312

CONSTRUCTION: coiling

FOUNDATION: three willow rods

SEWING ELEMENTS: peeled and unpeeled redbud shoots

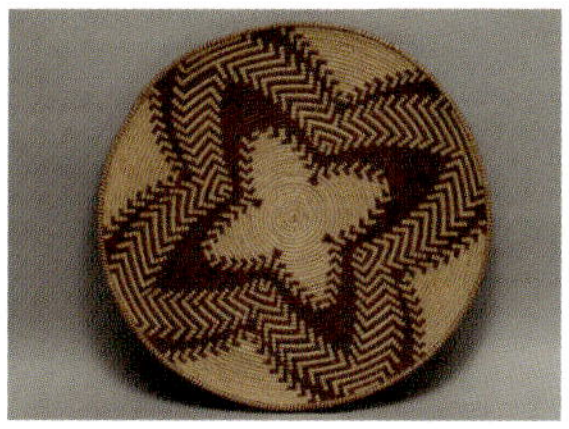

POMO

Storage Bowl, c. 1906
Pomo
Artist known as "Captain Jack's Wife"
20.0 x 31.0 cm.
Gift of E. Boyd Hall, 28

CONSTRUCTION: diagonal, plain, three-strand, and wrapped twining

FOUNDATION: hazelnut rods

WEAVING ELEMENTS: sedge rhizome, redbud shoots

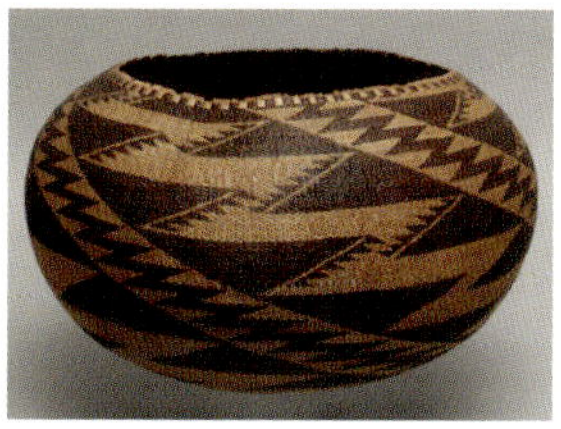

Doctor's Basket, c. 1910
Pomo
Artist unknown
13 x 22 x 30 cm.
Ina Sizer Cassidy Collection, 917

CONSTRUCTION: coiling

FOUNDATION: three willow rods

SEWING ELEMENTS: sedge rhizome, bulrush root; with dye, woodpecker scalp feathers, quail topknots, clamshell disk beads, abalone pendants

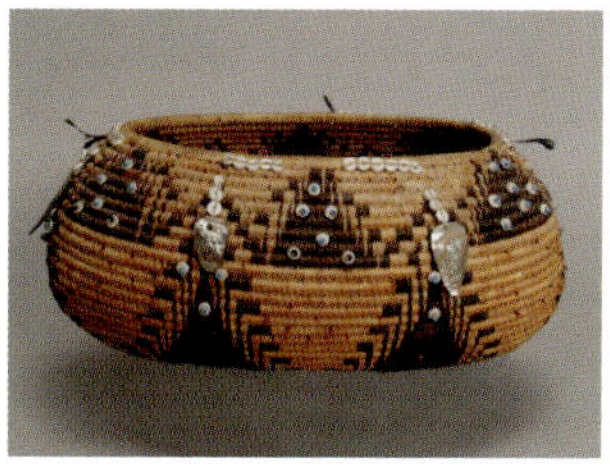

Gift Basket, c. 1920
Pomo
Artist unknown
4.2 x 8.50 cm.
Ina Sizer Cassidy Collection, 924

CONSTRUCTION: coiling

FOUNDATION: single willow rod

SEWING ELEMENTS: sedge rhizome, redbud shoots

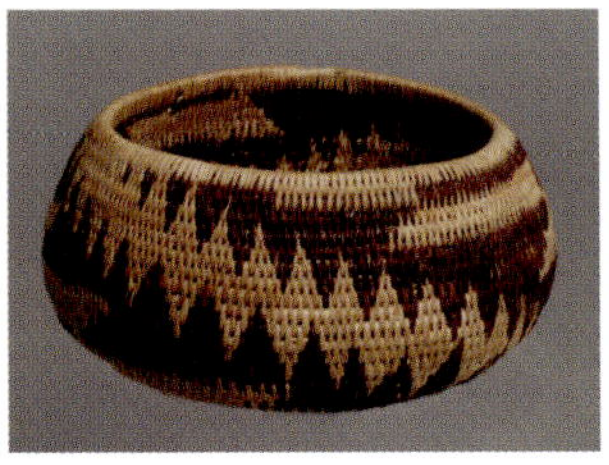

Bowl, c. 1895
Pomo
Artist unknown
9.0 x 16.5 cm.
Homer E. Sargent Collection, 14309

CONSTRUCTION: coiling

FOUNDATION: three willow rods

SEWING ELEMENTS: willow shoots, bulrush root; with dye

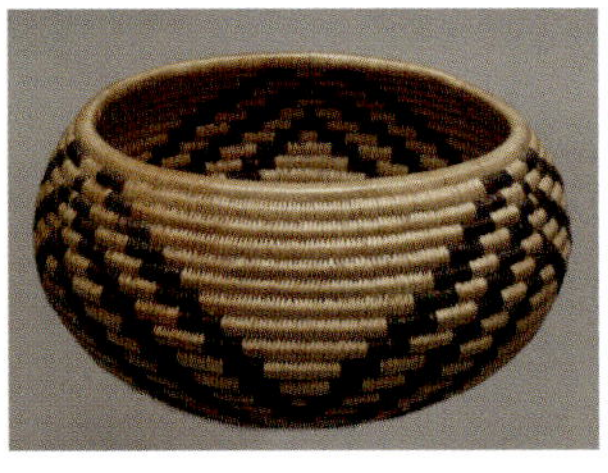

Miniature Carrying Basket, c. 1901
Pomo
Attributed to Mary Knight Benson
9.2 x 9.7 cm.
Homer E. Sargent Collection, 14324

CONSTRUCTION: diagonal and wrapped twining

FOUNDATION: hazelnut rods

WEAVING ELEMENTS: sedge rhizome, redbud shoots

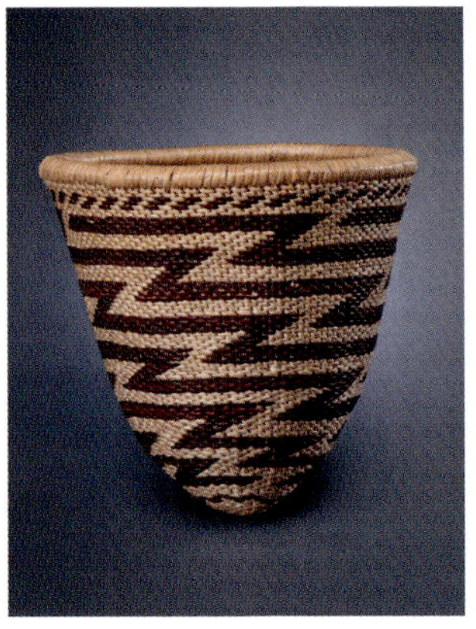

Trinket Basket, 1906
Pomo
Emily Graves
6.7 x 10.5 cm.
Homer E. Sargent Collection, 14325

CONSTRUCTION: three-strand twining

FOUNDATION: hazelnut rods

WEAVING ELEMENTS: sedge rhizome, redbud shoots

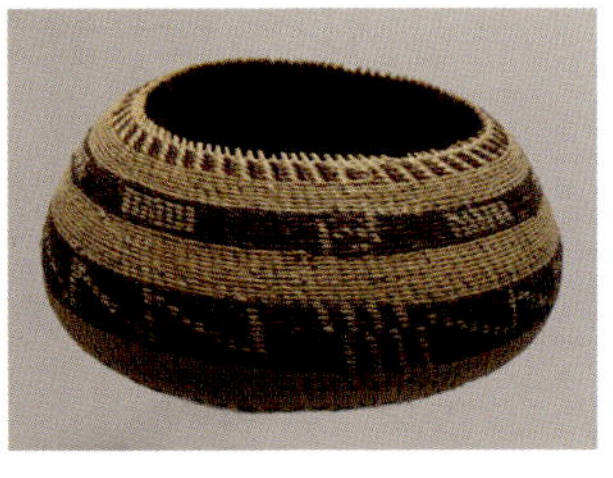

Cooking Bowl, c. 1900
Pomo
Mary Posche
15.5 x 20.5 cm.
Homer E. Sargent Collection, 14327

CONSTRUCTION: plain twining

FOUNDATION: willow rods

WEAVING ELEMENTS: sedge rhizome, redbud shoots

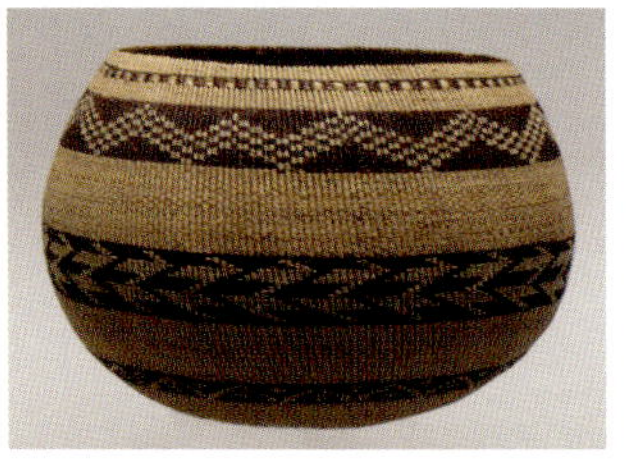

Cooking Bowl Model, 1912
Pomo
Emma Lily
18.5 x 26.5 cm.
Homer E. Sargent Collection, 14328

CONSTRUCTION: plain and three-strand twining

FOUNDATION: hazelnut rods

WEAVING ELEMENTS: sedge rhizome, redbud shoots

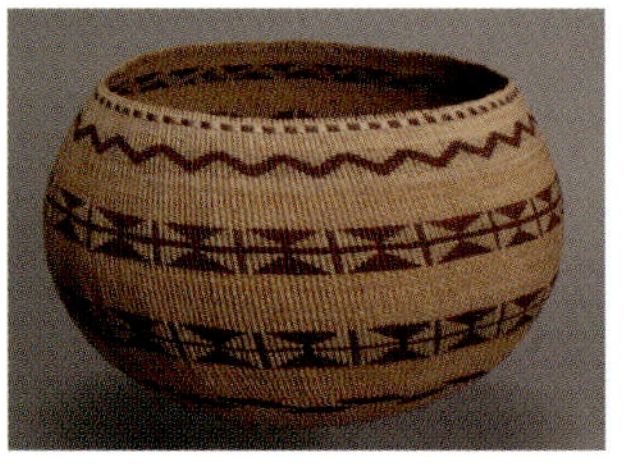

Treasure or Gift Basket, c. 1900
Pomo
Attributed to Laura White Wilbell
10.0 x 26.0 cm.
Homer E. Sargent Collection, 14331

CONSTRUCTION: coiling

FOUNDATION: three willow rods

SEWING ELEMENTS: sedge rhizome, bulrush root; with dye, woodpecker-scalp feathers, oriole feathers, quail topknots, clamshell disk beads, glass seed beads

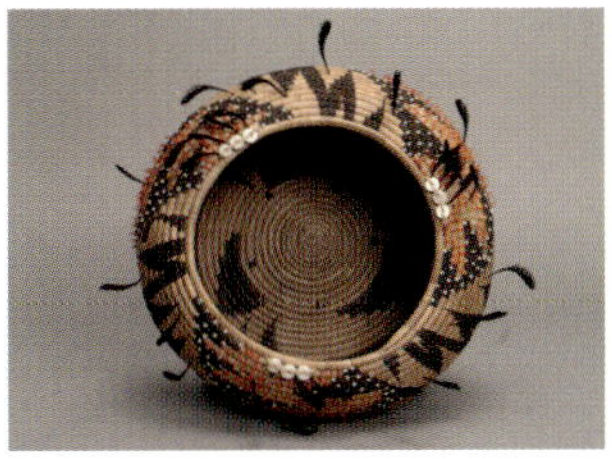

Treasure or Gift Basket, c. 1900
Pomo
Artist unknown
9.5 x 21 x 25 cm.
Homer E. Sargent Collection, 14332

CONSTRUCTION: coiling

FOUNDATION: three willow rods

SEWING ELEMENTS: sedge rhizome, bulrush root; with dye, quail topknots, glass seed beads

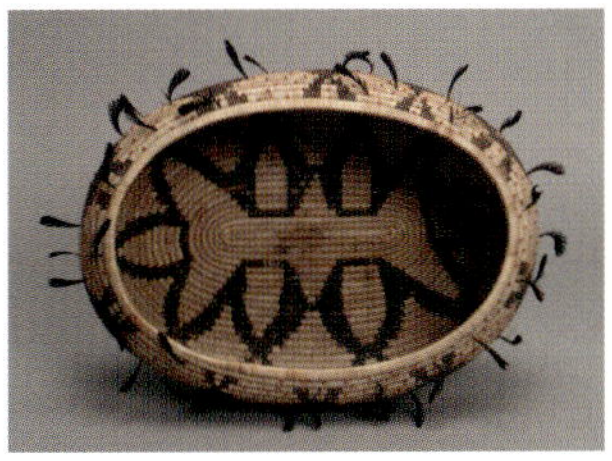

Gift Basket, c. 1906
Pomo
Artist unknown
6.3 x 10.7 cm.
Homer E. Sargent Collection, 14334

CONSTRUCTION: coiling

FOUNDATION: single willow rod

SEWING ELEMENTS: sedge rhizome, bulrush root; with dye

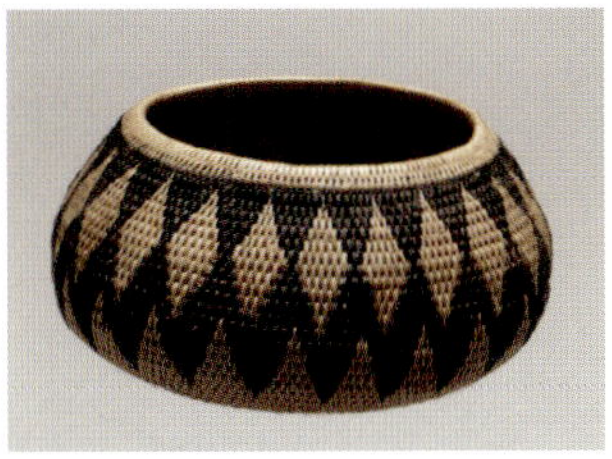

Treasure or Gift Basket, c. 1910
Pomo
Artist unknown
6.0 x 14.1 cm.
Homer E. Sargent Collection, 14335

CONSTRUCTION: coiling

FOUNDATION: three willow rods

SEWING ELEMENTS: sedge rhizome, bulrush root; with dye, woodpecker-scalp feathers, quail topknots

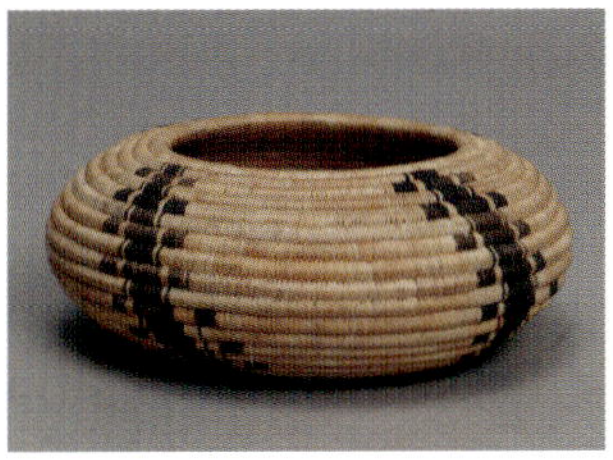

Treasure or Gift Basket, c. 1900
Pomo
Artist unknown
2.5 x 11.6 cm.
Homer E. Sargent Collection, 14351

CONSTRUCTION: coiling

FOUNDATION: three willow rods

SEWING ELEMENT: sedge rhizome; with meadowlark feathers, mallard feathers, quail topknots, clamshell disk beads, abalone pendants

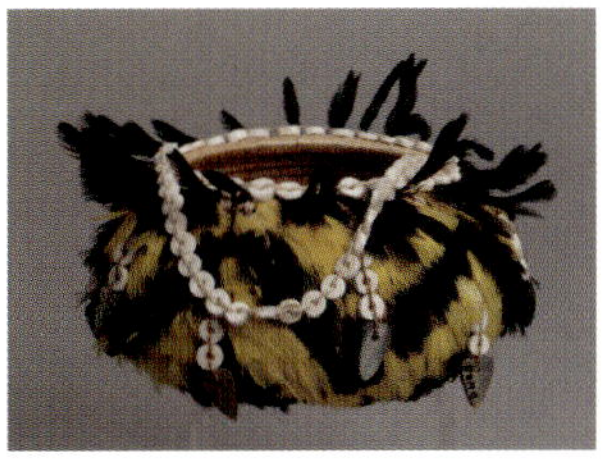

Carrying Basket, c. 1895
Pomo
Artist unknown
48.0 x 58.5 cm.
Ada Crawford McCormack Collection, 23265

CONSTRUCTION: plain and diagonal twining

FOUNDATION: willow rods

WEAVING ELEMENTS: sedge rhizome, redbud shoots

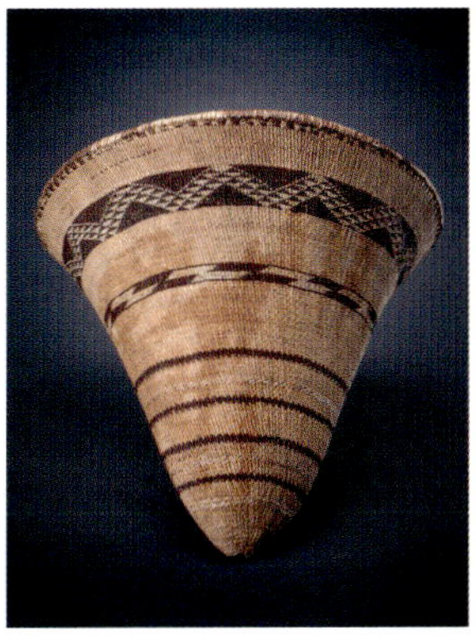

Mortar Hopper, c. 1920
Pomo
Artist unknown
16.0 x 48.5 cm.
Ada Crawford McCormack Collection, 23500

CONSTRUCTION: plain, diagonal, and lattice twining

FOUNDATION: willow rods

WEAVING ELEMENTS: sedge rhizome, redbud shoots; with cotton

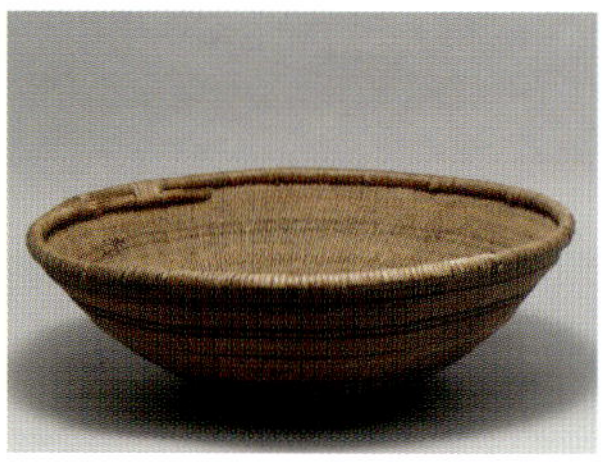

Work Basket, c. 1902
Pomo
Artist unknown
17.0 x 46.0 cm.
Ada Crawford McCormack Collection, 31081

CONSTRUCTION: plain twining

FOUNDATION: hazelnut rods

WEAVING ELEMENT: hazelnut shoots; with cotton

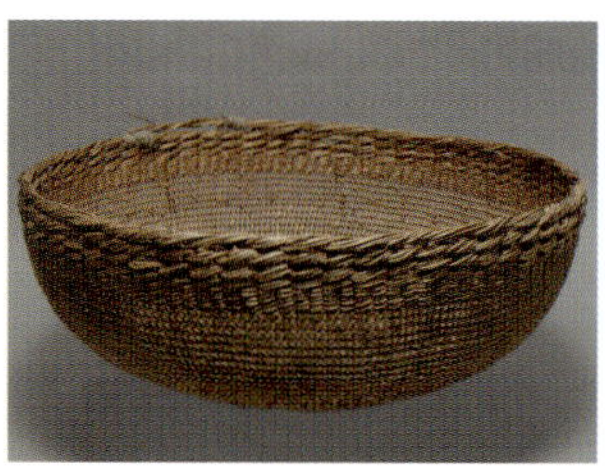

TUBATULABAL

Jar, 1905
Tubatulabal
Artist known as "Lucy"
16.0 x 25.0 cm.
Homer E. Sargent Collection, 14315

CONSTRUCTION: coiling

FOUNDATION: deergrass bundle

SEWING ELEMENTS: sumac shoots, devil's claw seedpod; with quail topknots

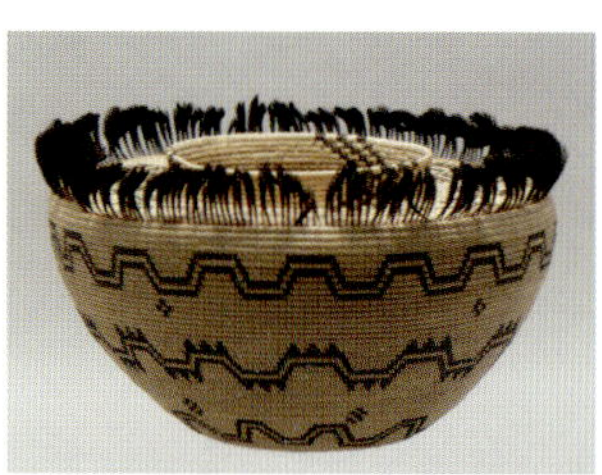

Cooking Bowl, c. 1890
Tubatulabal
Artist unknown
18.5 x 40.0 cm.
Gift of Henry Dendahl, 23682

CONSTRUCTION: coiling

FOUNDATION: deergrass bundle

SEWING ELEMENTS: sumac shoots, Joshua tree root

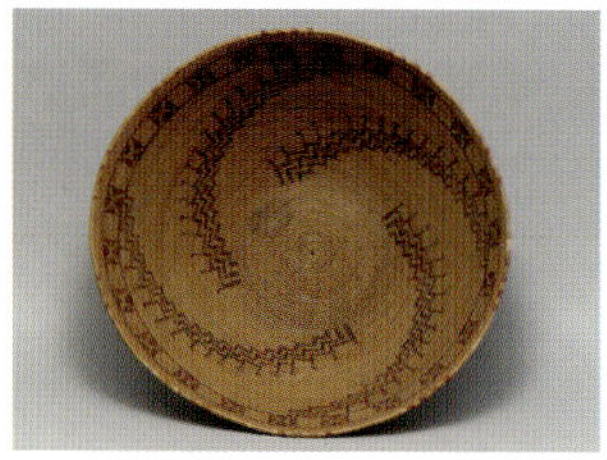

WAPPO

Gift Basket, c. 1910
Wappo
Artist unknown
2.4 x 4.6 x 7.0 cm.
Homer E. Sargent Collection, 14321

CONSTRUCTION: coiling

FOUNDATION: single willow rod

SEWING ELEMENT: sedge rhizome; with glass beads

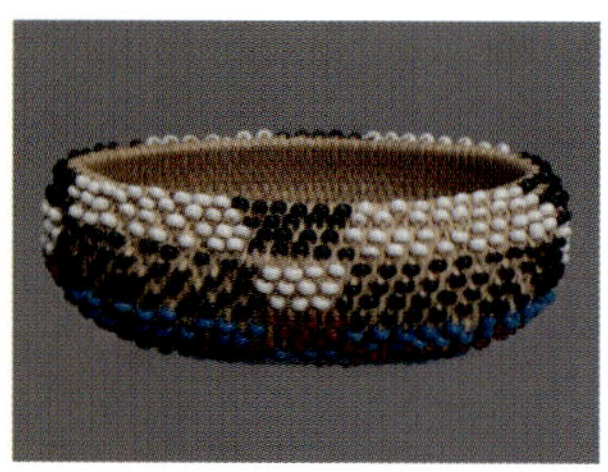

WINTU

Cooking Bowl, c. 1910
Wintu
Artist unknown
19.5 x 24.0 cm.
Ada Crawford McCormack Collection, 23448

CONSTRUCTION: plain twining, overlay

FOUNDATION: hazelnut rods

WEAVING ELEMENTS: spruce root, beargrass, alder-dyed woodwardia fern stem, maiden-hair fern stem

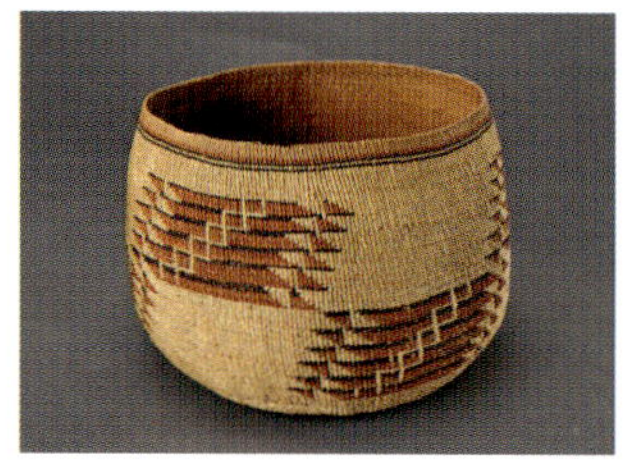

YOKUTS

Jar, c. 1910
Yokuts
Artist known as "Wife of Joe Joloa"
17.5 x 31.0 cm.
Homer E. Sargent Collection, 14300

CONSTRUCTION: coiling

FOUNDATION: deergrass bundle

SEWING ELEMENTS: sedge rhizome, bracken fern rhizome, redbud shoots; with dye

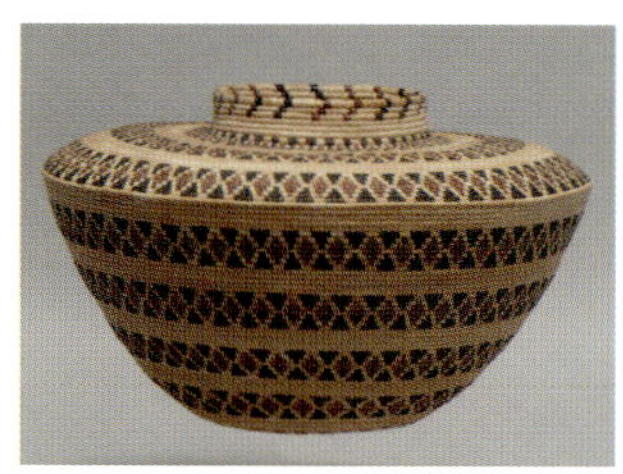

Gift Basket, c. 1910
Yokuts
Artist known as "Old Charley's Wife"
16.5 x 28.0 cm.
Homer E. Sargent Collection, 14304

CONSTRUCTION: coiling

FOUNDATION: deergrass bundle

WEAVING ELEMENTS: sedge rhizome, redbud shoots, bracken fern rhizome; with dye, acorn woodpecker-scalp feathers, quail topknots

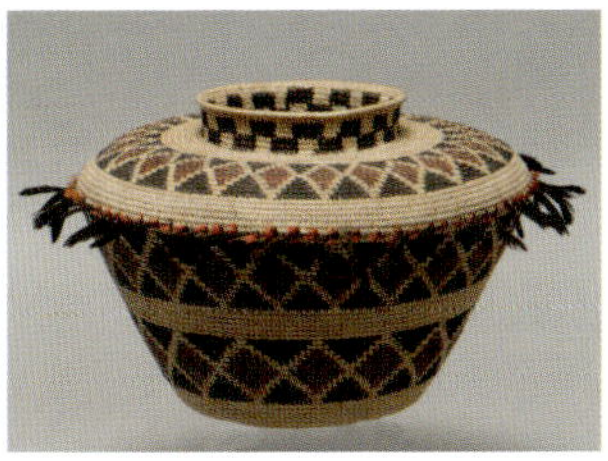

Bowl, c. 1910
Yokuts
Artist unknown
17.0 x 38.0 cm.
Gift of Agnes E. Hawkins, 14386

CONSTRUCTION: coiling

FOUNDATION: deergrass bundle

WEAVING ELEMENTS: sedge rhizome, bracken fern rhizome, redbud shoots; with dye

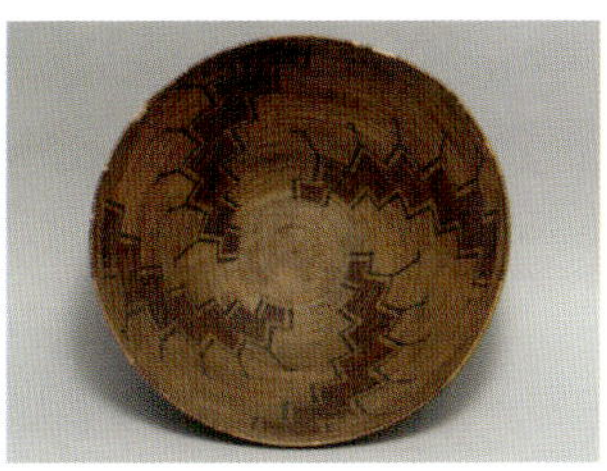

YUROK

Storage Basket Model, c. 1904
Yurok
Mrs. Johnny Jack
38.0 x 32.0 cm.
Gift of A. F. Hartman, 14296

CONSTRUCTION: plain twining, overlay

FOUNDATION: hazelnut rods

WEAVING ELEMENTS: spruce root, beargrass, maidenhair fern stem

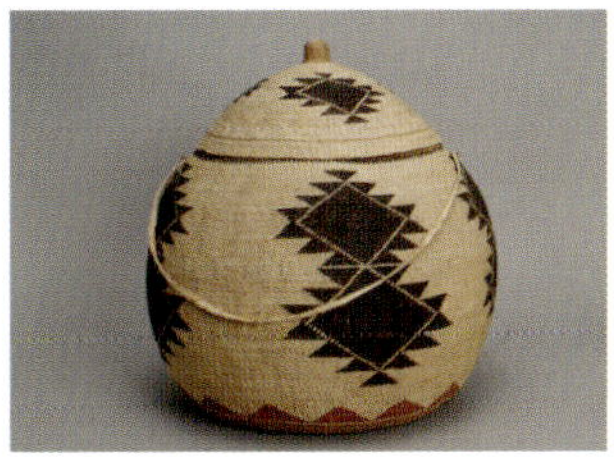

Jump Dance Basket, c. 1900
Yurok
Artist unknown
15.0 x 52.0 cm.
Homer E. Sargent Collection, 14311

CONSTRUCTION: twining, overlay

FOUNDATION: hazelnut rods

WEAVING ELEMENTS: conifer root, beargrass, maidenhair fern stems; with feathers, buckskin

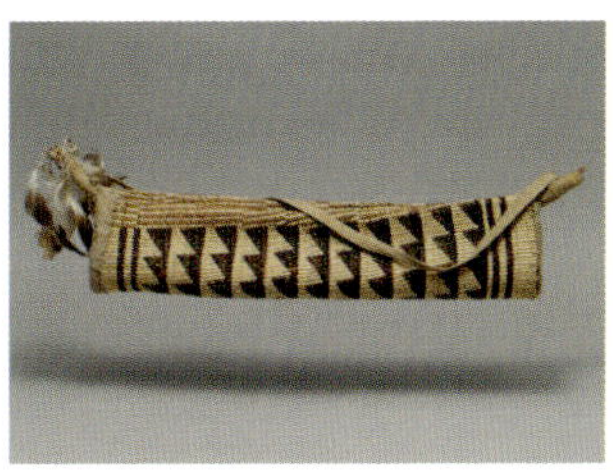

Woman's Cap, c. 1930
Yurok
Artist unknown
9.0 x 18.0 cm.
Feist Collection, 23267

CONSTRUCTION: plain twining, overlay

FOUNDATION: hazelnut rods

WEAVING ELEMENTS: spruce root, beargrass, maidenhair fern stem

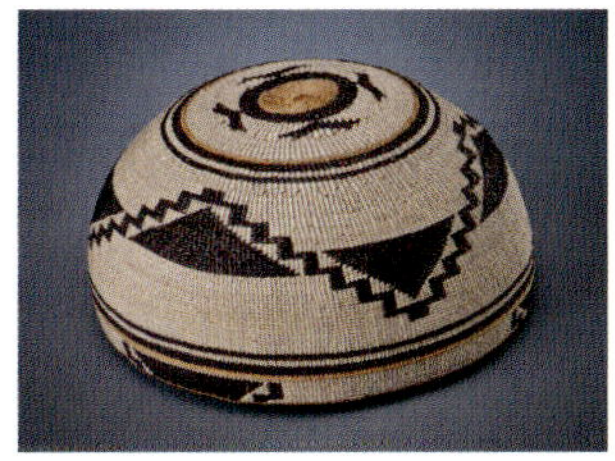

Food Bowl, c. 1920
Yurok
Artist unknown
9.0 x 16.0 cm.
Gift of Mrs. R. Crawford Buell, 47663

CONSTRUCTION: plain twining, overlay

FOUNDATION: hazelnut rods

WEAVING ELEMENTS: spruce root, beargrass

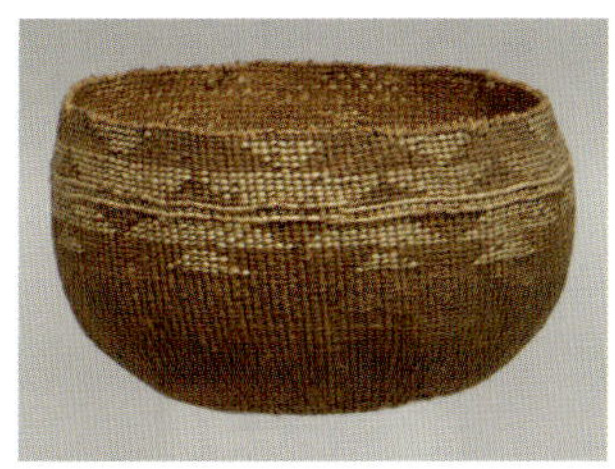

Woman's Cap, c. 1945
Yurok
Artist unknown
8.0 x 17.1 cm.
Gift of Sally Wagner, 54586

CONSTRUCTION: plain twining, overlay

FOUNDATION: hazelnut rods

WEAVING ELEMENTS: spruce root, beargrass, alder-dyed woodwardia fern stem, maidenhair fern stem

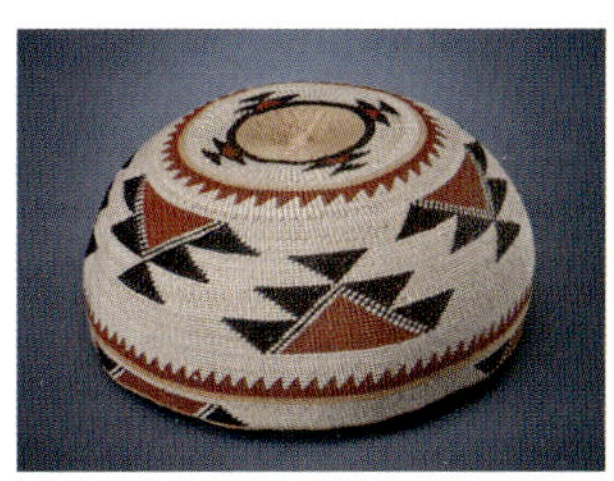

Cradle and Sunshade, c. 1920
Yurok
Artist unknown
63.8 x 29.5 x 19.2 cm.
Gift of Frank H. and Patricia N. Harlow, 57152
CONSTRUCTION: parallel and cross-warp twining
FOUNDATION: hazelnut rods
WEAVING ELEMENTS: hazelnut shoots, conifer root, alder-dyed woodwardia fern; with dentalia, shells, glass beads, cotton string

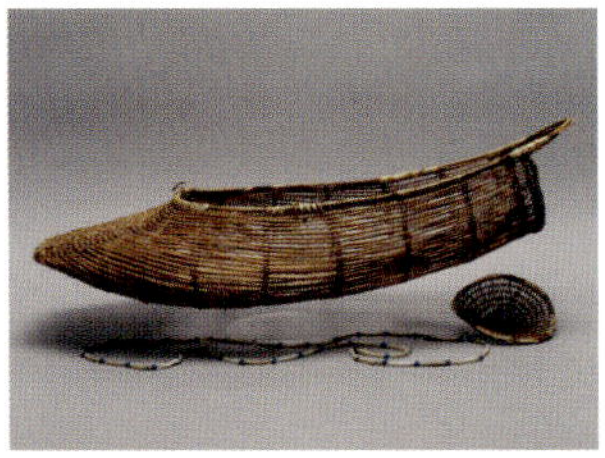

NORTHWEST COAST

CLATSOP

Fancy Gathering Basket, c. 1840
Clatsop
Artist unknown
15.0 x 20.0 cm.
Gift of Mr. and Mrs. A. A. Mosher, 45106
CONSTRUCTION: plain and wrapped twining
FOUNDATION: shredded "cedar bark" bundle
WEAVING ELEMENTS: beargrass, iris fiber, indigo- and cochineal-dyed wool

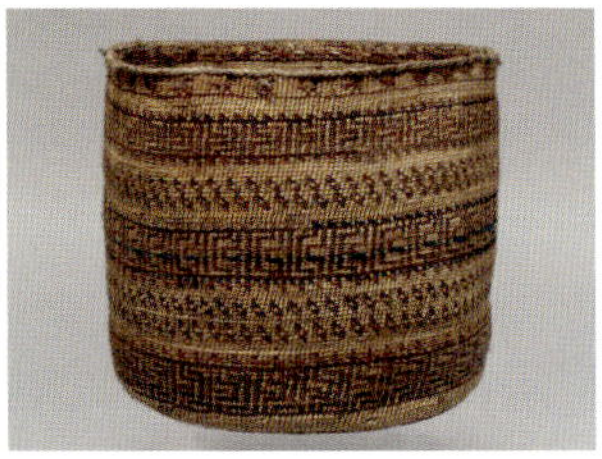

COWLITZ

Bowl, c. 1900
Cowlitz
Artist unknown
8.5 x 18.5 cm.
Ada Crawford McCormack Collection, 31111
CONSTRUCTION: coiling, imbrication, beading
FOUNDATION: cedar-root bundle
SEWING ELEMENTS: cedar root (inner bark), beargrass, horsetail root; with dye

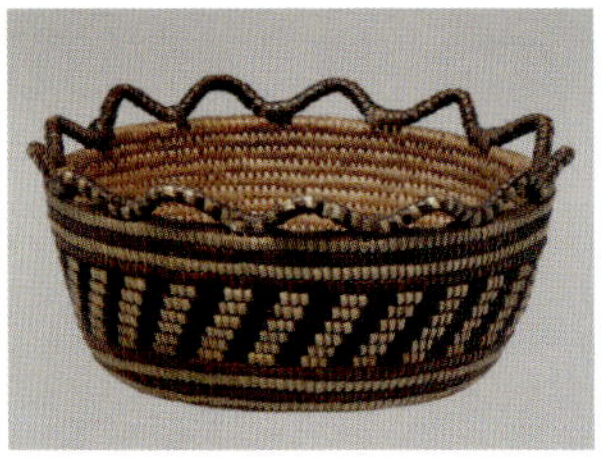

HAIDA

Cylinder, c. 1890
Haida
Artist unknown
18.0 x 20.0 cm.
Gift of Pansy Stockton, 46245
CONSTRUCTION: plain and diagonal twining, false embroidery
FOUNDATION: spruce-root fiber
WEAVING ELEMENTS: spruce root, beargrass; with dye

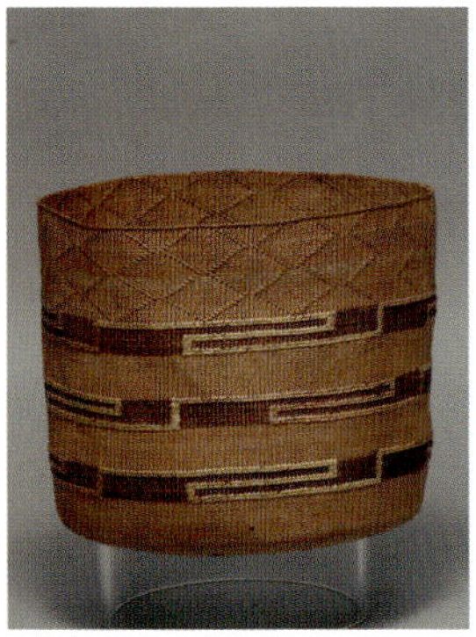

MAKAH

Bottle, c. 1920
Makah
Artist unknown
18.5 x 8.8 cm.
Gift of James G. McNary and Family, 23244
CONSTRUCTION: wrapped twining, plaiting
FOUNDATION: shredded cedar-bark bundle
WEAVING ELEMENT: beargrass; with dye

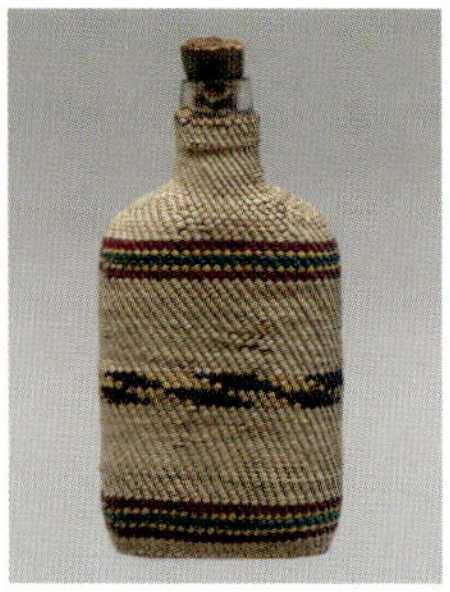

Bag, c. 1915
Makah
Artist unknown
23.0 x 27.0 x 9.5 cm.
Feist Collection, 23342
CONSTRUCTION: wrapped twining
FOUNDATION: shredded cedar-bark bundle
WEAVING ELEMENTS: beargrass, yellow cedar-bark strip; with dye

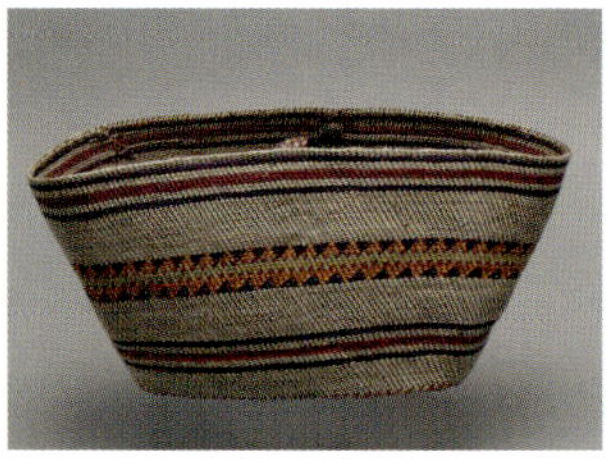

Mat, c. 1910
Makah
Artist unknown
0.1 x 17.4 x 21.7 cm.
Gift of James G. McNary and Family, 23344
CONSTRUCTION: wrapped twining, plaiting
FOUNDATION: shredded cedar-bark bundle
WEAVING ELEMENT: beargrass; with dye

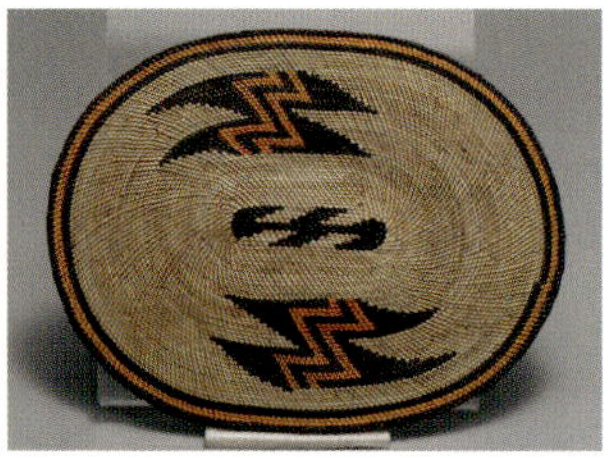

Lidded Bowl, c. 1970
Makah
Artist unknown
6.0 x 8.6 cm.
Feist Collection, 23696

CONSTRUCTION: wrapped twining

FOUNDATION: shredded cedar-bark bundle

WEAVING ELEMENT: beargrass; with dye

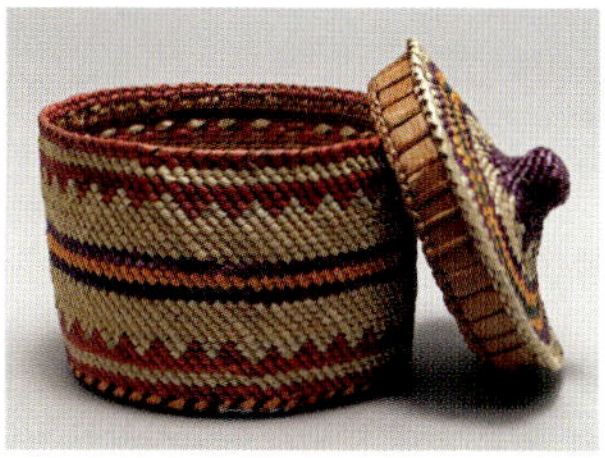

Lidded Bowl, c. 1900
Makah
Artist unknown
8.2 x 12.5 cm.
Gift of Alden Foss, 25427

CONSTRUCTION: plain and wrapped twining, plaiting

FOUNDATION: shredded cedar-bark bundle

WEAVING ELEMENTS: beargrass, sedge rhizome; with dye

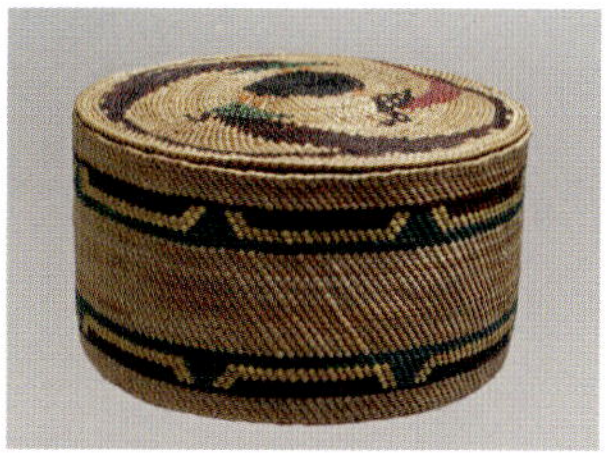

Rectangular Basket, c. 1910
Makah
Artist unknown
16.0 x 29.5 x 22.0 cm.
Ada Crawford McCormack Collection, 31110

CONSTRUCTION: wrapped twining, plaiting

FOUNDATION: shredded cedar bark bundle

WEAVING ELEMENTS: cattail fiber, beargrass; with dye

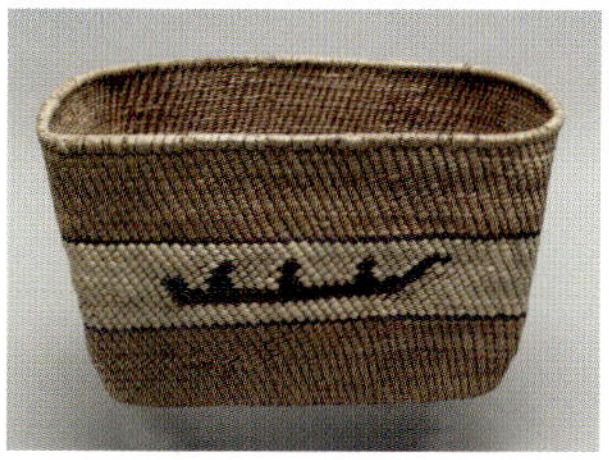

NUU-CHAH-NULTH

Bowl, c. 1920
Nuu-chah-nulth
Artist unknown
5.5 x 11.1 cm.
Feist Collection, 23689

CONSTRUCTION: plain twining, plaiting

FOUNDATION: cedar bark

WEAVING ELEMENT: swamp grass; with dye

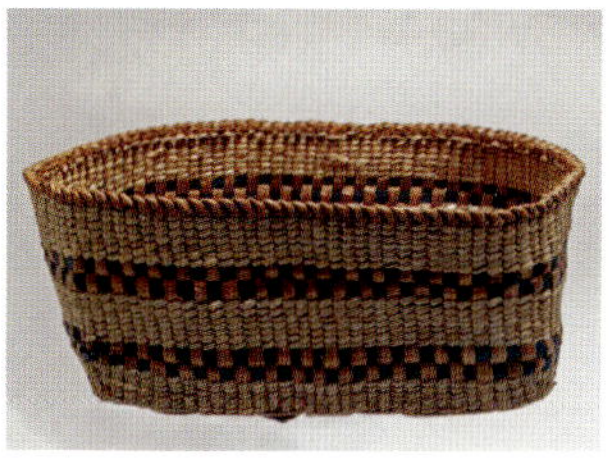

Hat, c. 1900
Nuu-chah-nulth
Artist unknown
17.0 x 35.0 cm.
Gift of Francis J. McCormack, as a memorial to his late wife, Ada Crawford McCormack, 31092

CONSTRUCTION: plain, three-strand, and double twining

FOUNDATION: cedar bark (inner)

WEAVING ELEMENT: cedar bark; with paint

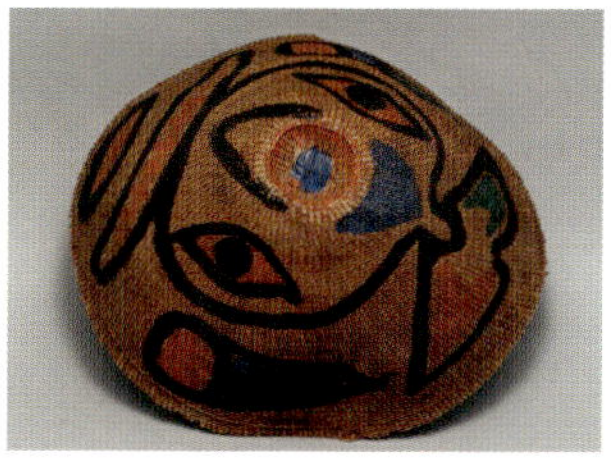

Whaler's Hat, c. 1900
Nuu-chah-nulth
Artist unknown
27.0 x 26.5 cm.
Gift of Mrs. Bryan Forsyth, 48236

CONSTRUCTION: wrapped twining

FOUNDATION: cedar bark (inner)

WEAVING ELEMENTS: cedar bark, wild rye beach grass; with dye

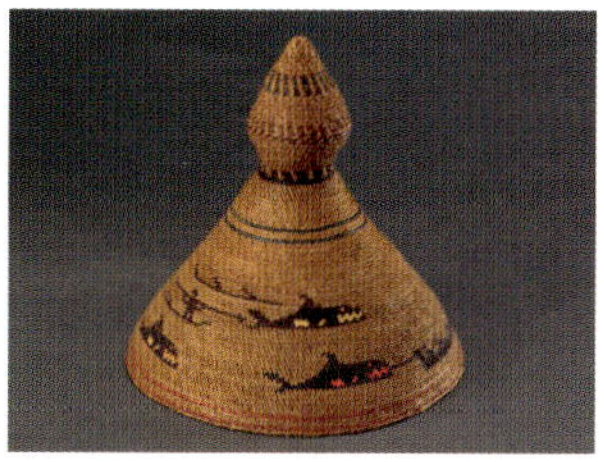

Hat, 1890
Nuu-chah-nulth
Artist unknown
15.6 x 31.4 cm.
Gift of Charmay Allred, 57848

CONSTRUCTION: plain, three-strand, and double twining

FOUNDATION: cedar bark (inner)

WEAVING ELEMENT: cedar bark; with paint

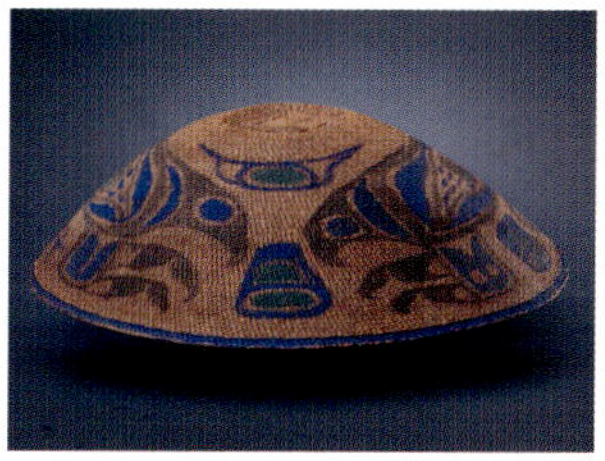

Whaler's Hat, c. 1900
Nuu-chah-nulth
Artist unknown
20.0 x 27.8 cm.
Gift of Charmay Allred, 57849

CONSTRUCTION: wrapped twining

FOUNDATION: cedar bark (inner)

WEAVING ELEMENTS: cedar bark, wild rye beach grass; with dye

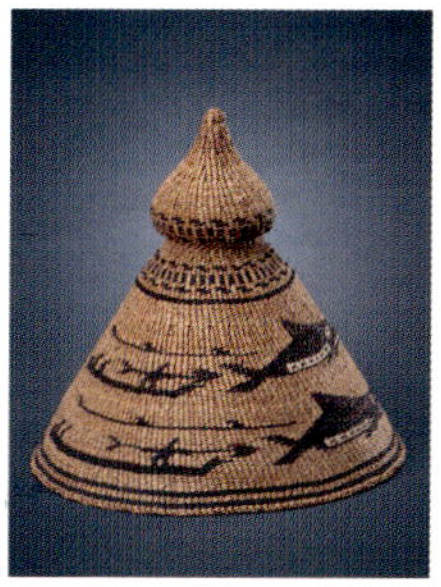

QUINAULT

Gathering Basket, c. 1940
Quinault
Artist unknown
19.0 x 25.5 cm.
Gift of Francis Elmore, 23258
CONSTRUCTION: plain twining, overlay
FOUNDATION: spruce root
WEAVING ELEMENTS: spruce root, beargrass

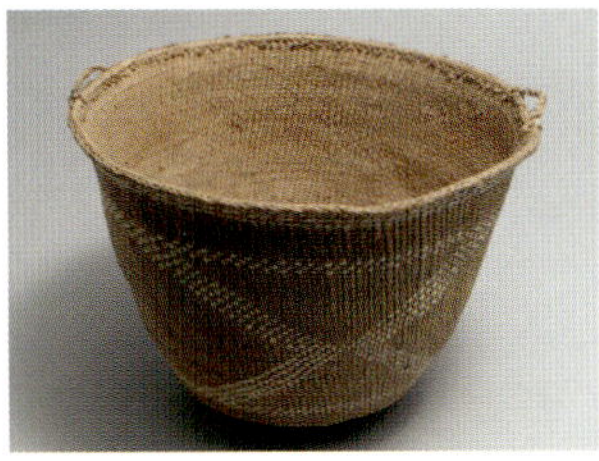

Gift Basket, c. 1870
Quinault
Artist unknown
17.0 x 28.0 x 14.5 cm.
Gift of Lydia J. Trowbridge, 23348
CONSTRUCTION: plain and wrapped twining, plaiting, beading
FOUNDATION: shredded cedar-bark bundle
WEAVING ELEMENTS: tule, beargrass; with dye

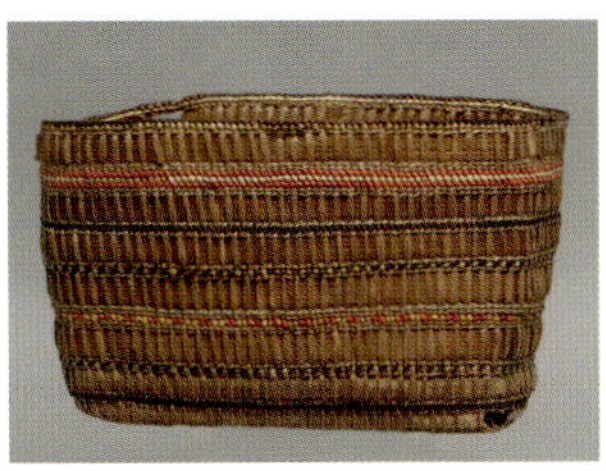

Gift Basket, c. 1870
Quinault
Artist unknown
12.0 x 24.0 x 8.0 cm.
Gift of Lydia J. Trowbridge, 23701
CONSTRUCTION: plain and wrapped twining, plaiting
FOUNDATION: shredded cedar-bark bundle
WEAVING ELEMENTS: tule, beargrass; with dye

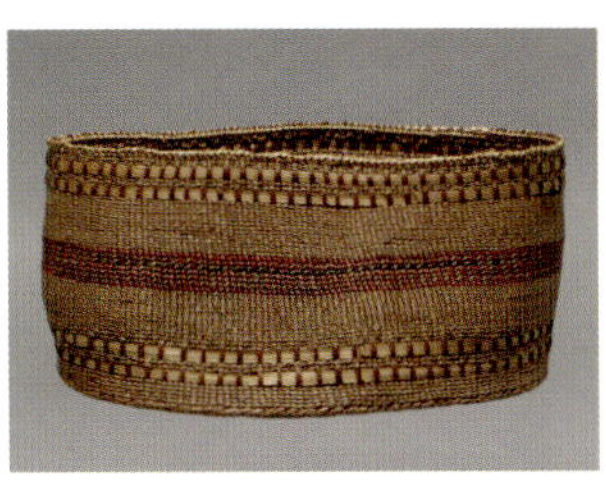

TLINGIT

Fancy Carrying Basket, c. 1900
Tlingit
Artist known as "Mary"
26.2 x 31.0 cm.
Gift of Alice G. Brock, 1901
CONSTRUCTION: plain and three-strand twining, false embroidery
FOUNDATION: spruce root
WEAVING ELEMENTS: spruce root, phragmites; with dye

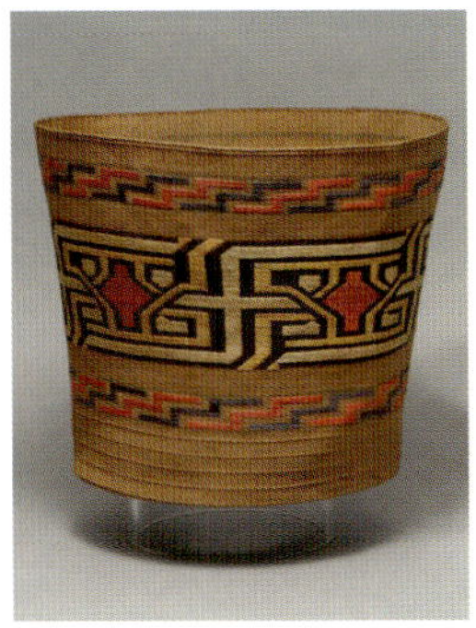

Gift Basket, c. 1900
Tlingit
Artist unknown
8.0 x 14.6 cm.
Homer E. Sargent Collection, 14317
CONSTRUCTION: plain and open cross-warp twining, false embroidery
FOUNDATION: spruce root
WEAVING ELEMENTS: spruce root, phragmites; with dye

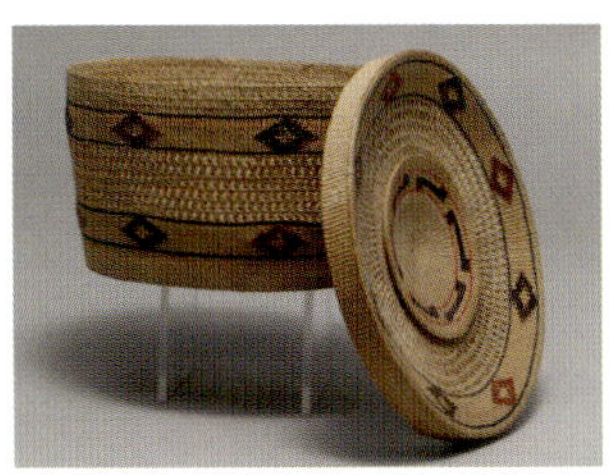

Fancy Gathering Basket, c. 1930
Tlingit
Artist unknown
20.3 x 24.5 cm.
Homer E. Sargent Collection, 14318
CONSTRUCTION: plain twining, false embroidery
FOUNDATION: spruce root
WEAVING ELEMENTS: spruce root, phragmites; with dye

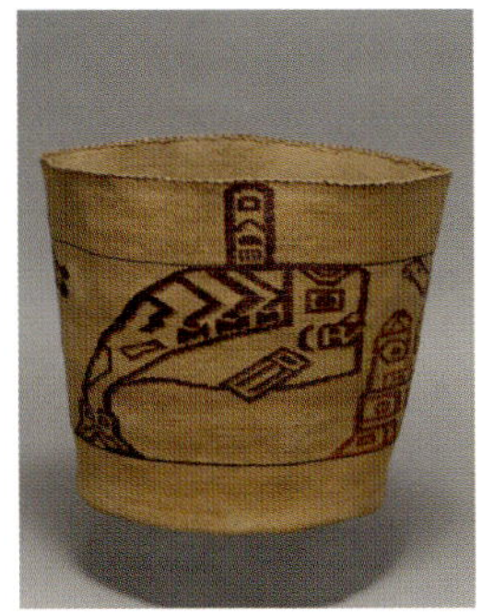

Fancy Gathering Basket, c. 1920
Tlingit
Artist unknown
19.8 x 14.9 cm.
Museum collection, 23445
CONSTRUCTION: plain twining, false embroidery
FOUNDATION: spruce root
WEAVING ELEMENTS: spruce root, wild rye beach grass; with dye

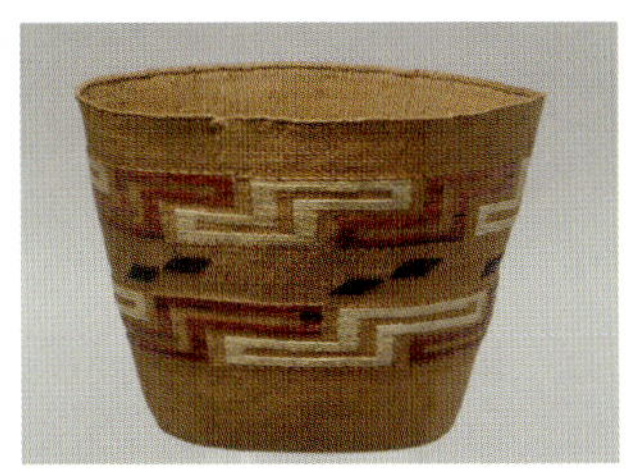

Cylinder, c. 1900
Tlingit
Artist unknown
11.5 x 11.0 cm.
Feist Collection, 23629

CONSTRUCTION: plain and cross-warp twining, false embroidery

FOUNDATION: spruce root

WEAVING ELEMENTS: spruce root, phragmites; with dye

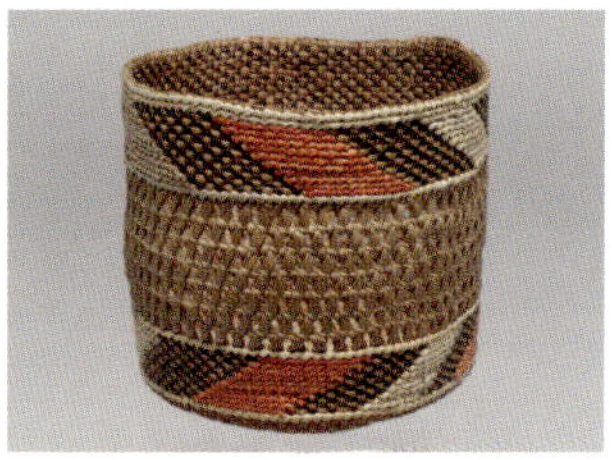

Fancy Gathering Basket, c. 1885
Tlingit
Artist unknown
16.0 x 20.4 cm.
Gift of Alden Foss, 25435

CONSTRUCTION: plain twining, false embroidery

FOUNDATION: spruce root

WEAVING ELEMENTS: spruce root, phragmites; with dye

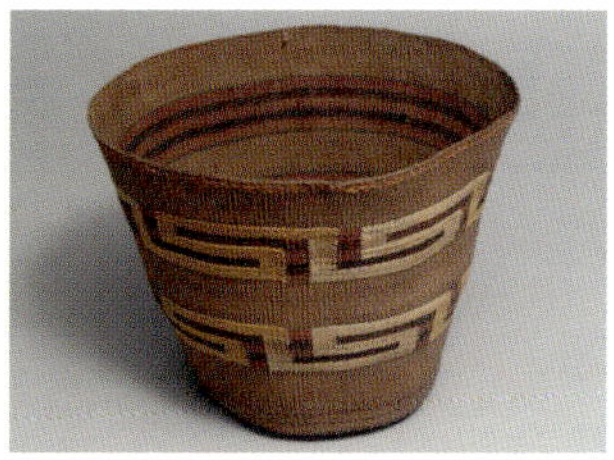

Cylinder, c. 1950
Tlingit
Artist unknown
Museum collection, 48638
15.3 x 18.0 cm.

CONSTRUCTION: plain twining, plaiting, false embroidery

FOUNDATION: spruce root

WEAVING ELEMENTS: spruce root, phragmites; with dye

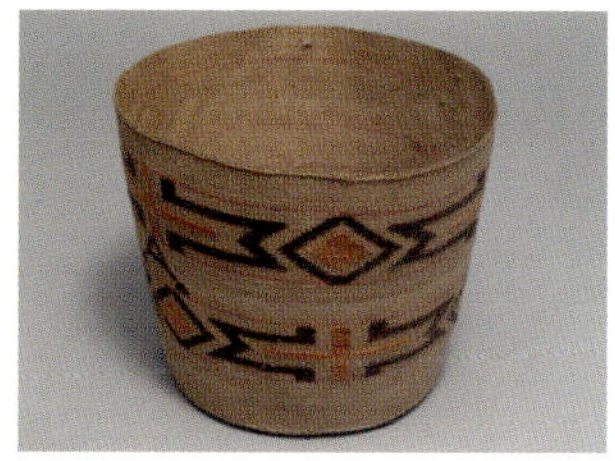

Jar with Rattle Lid, c. 1909
Tlingit
Artist unknown
10.4 x 12.7 cm.
Gift of Alden Foss, 25431

CONSTRUCTION: plain twining, false embroidery

FOUNDATION: spruce root

WEAVING ELEMENTS: spruce root, wild rye beach grass; with dye

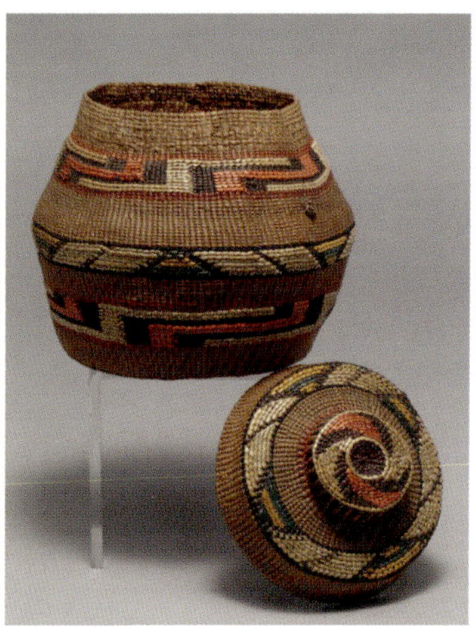

Cylinder, c. 1950
Tlingit
Artist unknown
19.0 x 17.5 cm.
Museum collection, 48637

CONSTRUCTION: plain twining, false embroidery

FOUNDATION: spruce root

WEAVING ELEMENTS: spruce root, beargrass; with dye

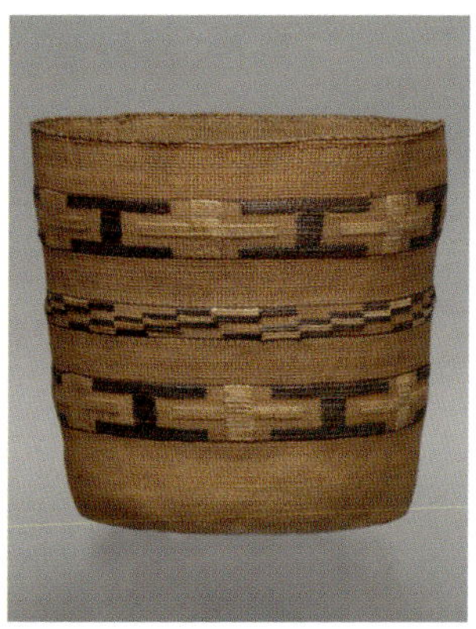

TSIMSHIAN

Carrying/Storage Bag, c. 1900
Tsimshian
Artist unknown
33.0 x 43.0 cm.
Homer E. Sargent Collection, 14293

CONSTRUCTION: checker plaiting

WEAVING ELEMENT: cedar bark; with dye

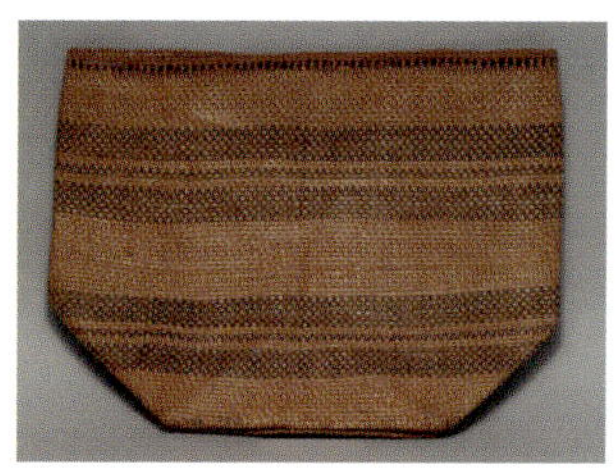

Hat, 2012
Loa Balumnaech Ryan
Tsimshian/Gitlan
16.4 x 30.1 cm.
Museum purchase, 58314

CONSTRUCTION: plain twining, checker plaiting

FOUNDATION: cedar bark

WEAVING ELEMENT: cedar bark

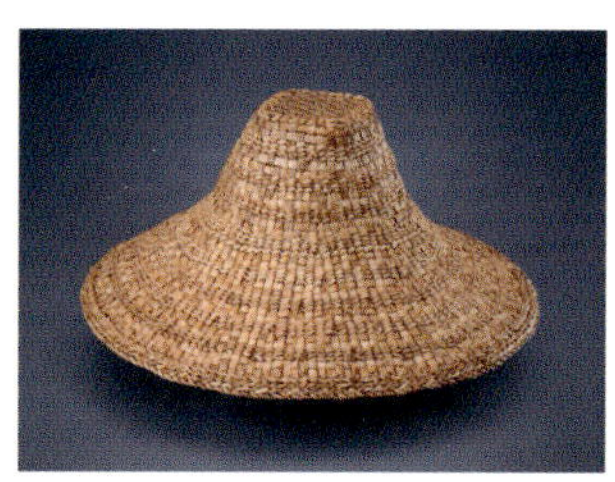

ARCTIC

INUPIAT

Box, 1949
Inupiat
George Omnik
10.0 x 8.0 x 17.5 cm.
Gift of Lily E. Hagerman, 50006
CONSTRUCTION: coiling
FOUNDATION: baleen
SEWING ELEMENT: baleen; with carved ivory

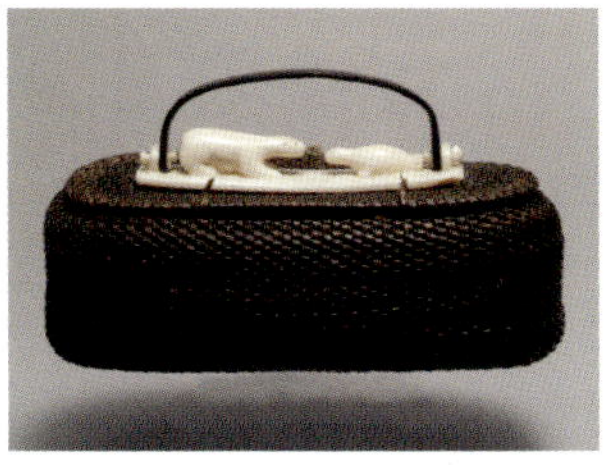

UNANGAN

Cigarette Case, c. 1915
Unangan
Artist unknown
5.0 x 6.2 x 8.8 cm.
Homer E. Sargent Collection, 14299
CONSTRUCTION: plaiting
WEAVING ELEMENT: baleen

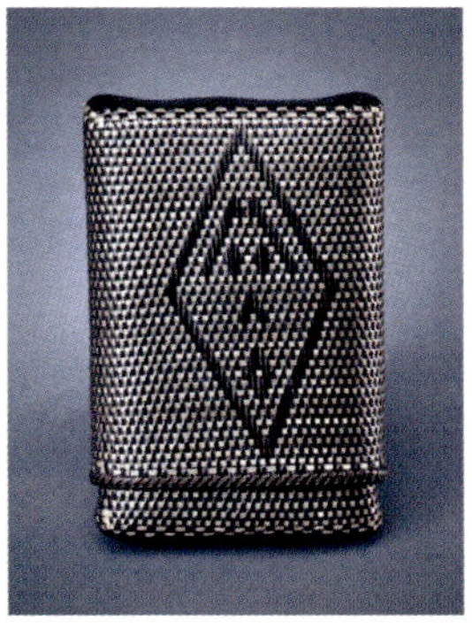

Fancy Carrying Bag, c. 1905
Unangan
Artist unknown
19.5 x 29.0 cm.
Homer E. Sargent Collection, 14319
CONSTRUCTION: plain twining, false embroidery
FOUNDATION: wild rye beach grass bundle
WEAVING ELEMENTS: wild rye beach grass, wool

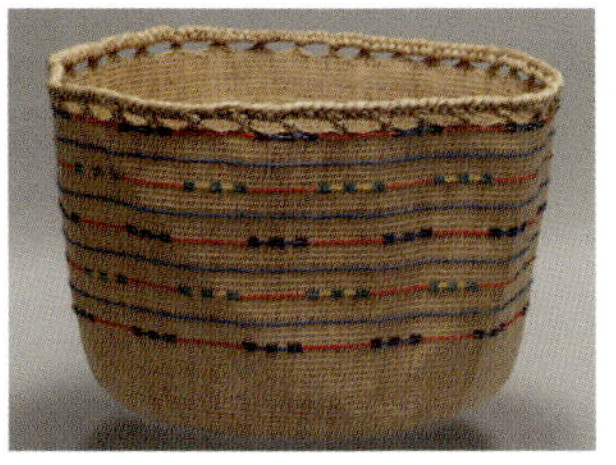

Carrying Bag, c. 1900
Unangan
Artist unknown
20.5 x 31.5 cm.
Homer E. Sargent Collection, 14320
CONSTRUCTION: plain twining
FOUNDATION: wild rye beach grass bundle
WEAVING ELEMENTS: wild rye beach grass, wool

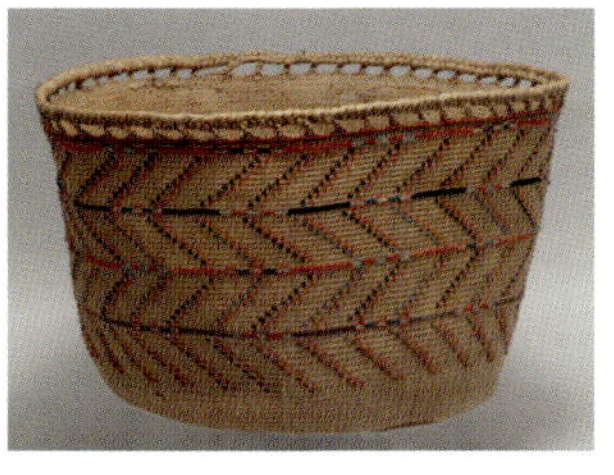

Carrying Bag, c. 1920
Unangan
Artist unknown
22.0 x 17.0 cm.
Gift of Rhoda Thomas, 36008
CONSTRUCTION: plain twining
FOUNDATION: wild rye beach grass bundle
WEAVING ELEMENT: wild rye beach grass; with silk thread

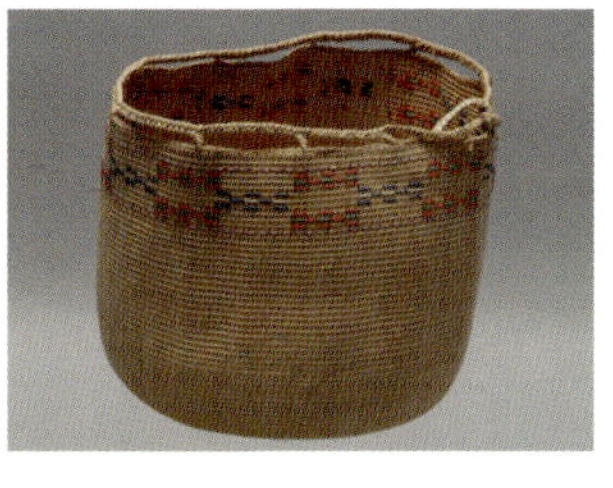

Trinket Basket, c. 1920
Unangan
Artist unknown
8.0 x 8.0 cm.
Gift of Rhoda Thomas, 36010
CONSTRUCTION: plain twining
FOUNDATION: wild rye beach grass bundle
WEAVING ELEMENT: wild rye beach grass; with silk thread

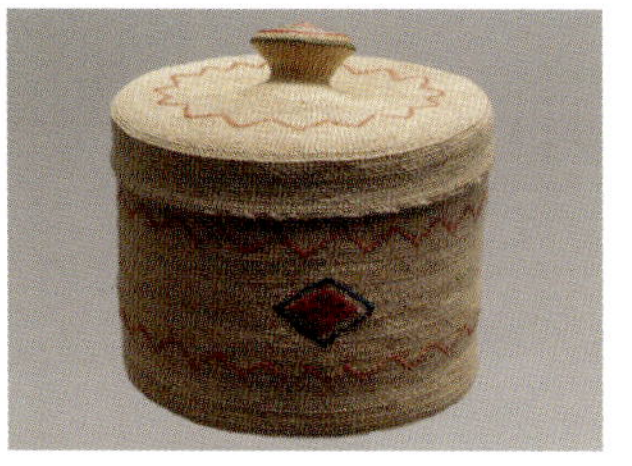

Bottle, c. 1920
Unangan
Artist unknown
7.0 x 3.5 cm.
Gift of Rhoda Thomas, 36011
CONSTRUCTION: plain twining
FOUNDATION: wild rye beach grass bundle
WEAVING ELEMENT: wild rye beach grass; with silk thread

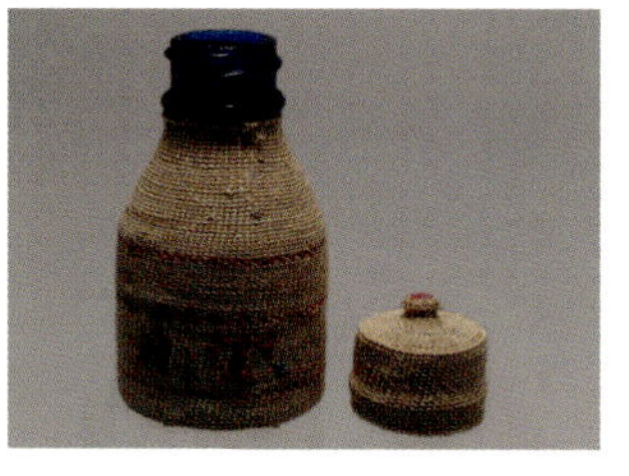

Trinket Basket, c. 1900
Unangan
Artist unknown
8.0 x 9.5 cm.
Gift of Rhoda Thomas, 36013
CONSTRUCTION: plain twining
FOUNDATION: wild rye beach grass bundle
WEAVING ELEMENT: wild rye beach grass; with silk thread

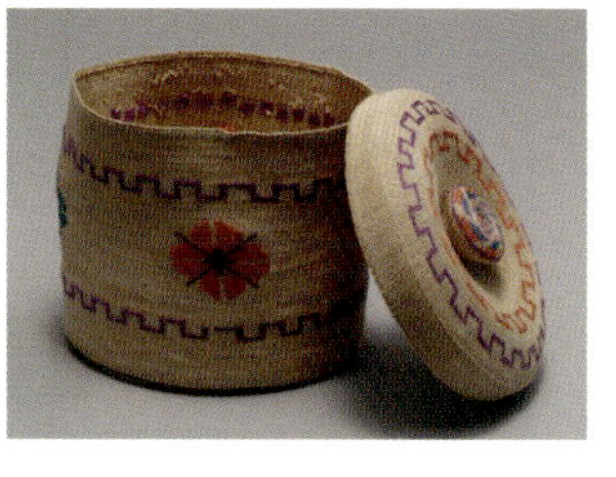

Trinket Basket, c. 1920
Unangan
Artist unknown
4.3 x 5.7 cm.
Gift of Rhoda Thomas, 36014

CONSTRUCTION: plain twining

FOUNDATION: wild rye beach grass bundle

WEAVING ELEMENT: wild rye beach grass; with silk thread

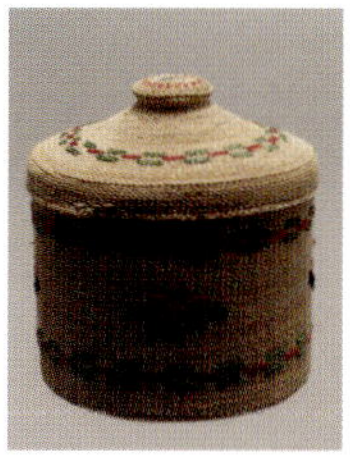

Bowl, c. 1945
Yupik
Artist unknown
25.5 x 32.0 cm.
Gift of Lily E. Hageman, 50005

CONSTRUCTION: coiling

FOUNDATION: wild rye beach grass bundle

SEWING ELEMENT: wild rye beach grass; with dye

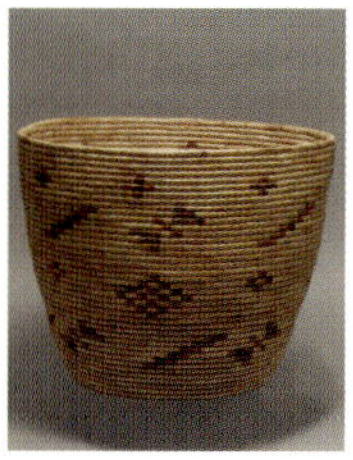

YUPIK

Cup and Saucer, c. 1930
Yupik
Artist unknown
5.5 x 8.5 cm.
Gift of William O. Sweet, 48195

CONSTRUCTION: coiling

FOUNDATION: wild rye beach grass bundle

WEAVING ELEMENT: wild rye beach grass; with dye

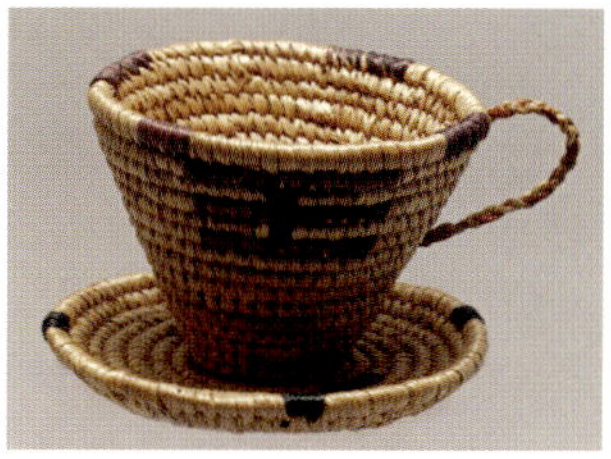

Lidded Jar, c. 1970
Yupik
Artist unknown
19.0 x 15.4 cm.
Gift of Charmay Allred, 54648

CONSTRUCTION: coiling

FOUNDATION: wild rye beach grass bundle

WEAVING ELEMENT: wild rye beach grass; with dye

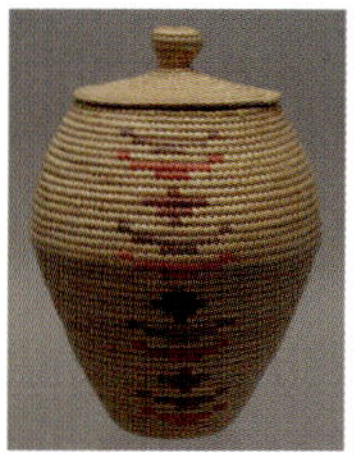

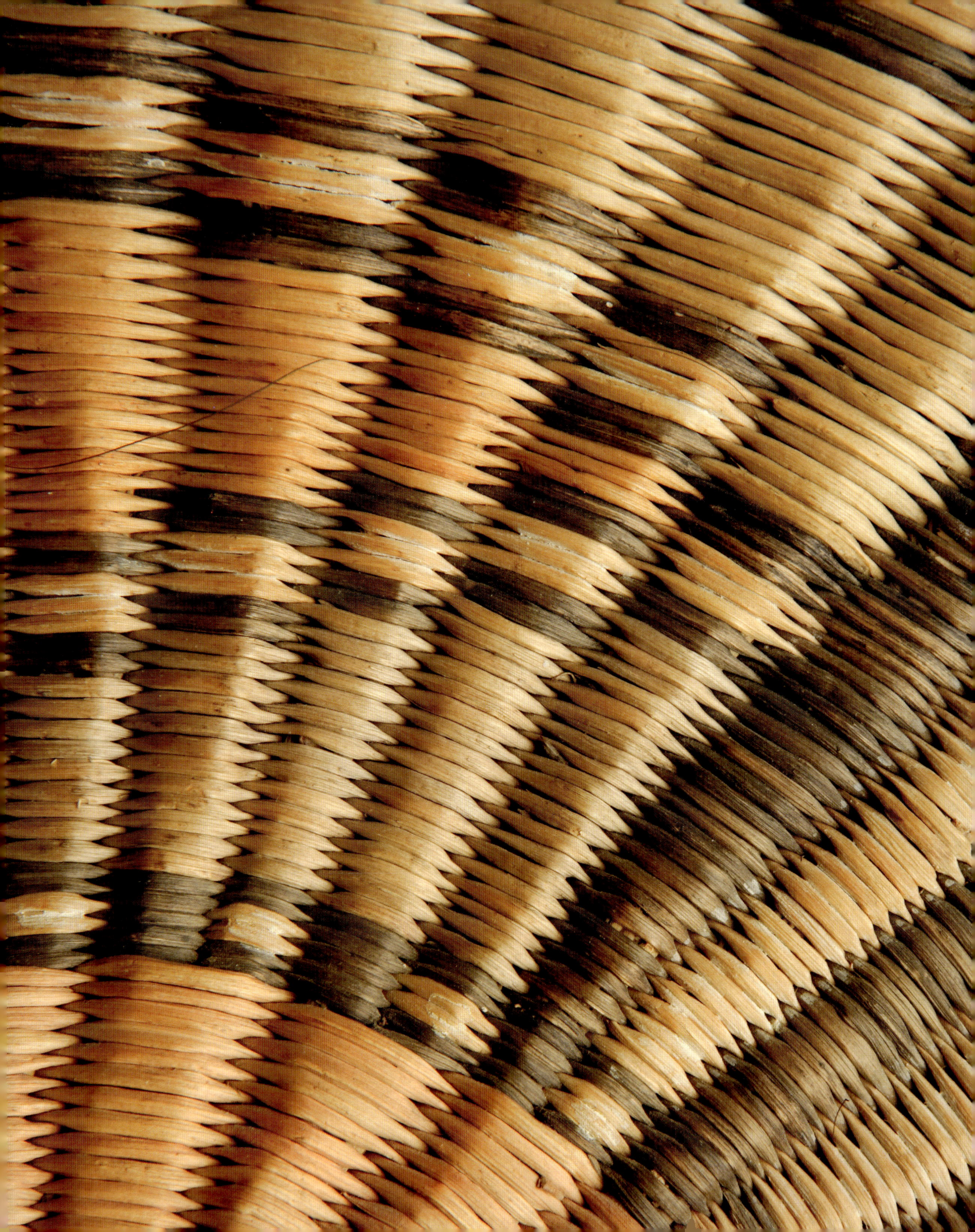

Bibliography

Adovasio, J. M., and R. L. Andrews

1977 Basketry Technology: A Guide to Identification and Analysis. Chicago: Aldine Publishing Company.

Ahtone, Heather

2009 Designed to Last: Striving toward an Indigenous American Aesthetic. *The International Journal of the Arts in Society* 4(2):373–386.

Allan, Derek

2009 Art and the Human Adventure: André Malraux's Theory of Art. Amsterdam: Rodopi.

Allen, Elsie

1972 Tomo Basketmaking: A Supreme Art for the Weaver. Happy Camp, CA: Naturegraphs Publishers.

Anderson, George B.

1907 History of New Mexico: Its Resources and People. Los Angeles: Pacific States Publishing Co.

Anderson, M. Kat

1991 California Indian Horticulture: Management and Use of Redbud by the Southern Sierra Miwok. *Journal of Ethnobiology* 11(1):145–157.

2005 Tending the Wild: Native American Knowledge and the Management of California's Natural Resources. Berkeley: University of California Press.

Aronilth, Wilson

1985 Unpublished manuscript. Quoted in *Molded in the Image of Changing Woman: Navajo Views on the Human Body and Personhood*, by Maureen Trudelle Schwarz, 38–39. Tucson: University of Arizona Press.

Barrett, S. A., and E. W. Gifford

1933 Miwok Material Culture: Indian Life of the Yosemite Region. Yosemite National Park, CA: The Yosemite Association.

Bates, Craig D., and Martha J. Lee

1990 Tradition and Innovation: A Basket History of the Indians of the Yosemite-Mono Lake Area. Yosemite National Park, CA: Yosemite Association.

Baumhoff, Martin A.

1978 Environmental Background. In *Handbook of North American Indians. Vol. 8: California*, edited by William C. Sturtevant, 16–36. Washington, DC: Smithsonian Institution.

Berger, John

1972 Ways of Seeing. London: British Corporation and Penguin Books.

Berger, P. L., and T. Luckmann

1966 The Social Construction of Reality: A Treatise in Sociology of Knowledge. Garden City, NY: Anchor Books.

Berlo, Janet Catherine

1992 The Early Years of Native American Art History. Seattle: University of Washington Press.

Bernstein, Bruce

1979 Panamint Shoshone Coiled Basketry: A Definition of Style. *American Indian Art* 4(4):68–74.

1985 Panamint-Shoshone Basketry 1890–1960. *American Indian Basketry and Other Native Arts* 5(3):4–11, 29.

1990 Weaver's Talk, the Language of Baskets and the Meaning of Aesthetic Judgments: The Patwin of Central California. In *The Art of Native American Basketry: A Living Legacy*, edited by Frank W. Porter III, 213–226. New York: Greenwood Press.

2003 The Language of Native American Baskets: From the Weavers' View. Washington, DC: National Museum of the American Indian, Smithsonian Institution.

Bernstein, Bruce, and Gerald McMaster, eds.

2004 First American Art: The Charles and Valerie Diker Collection of American Indian Art. Washington, DC: National Museum of the American Indian, Smithsonian Institution.

Bibby, Brian

1996 The Fine Art of California Indian Basketry. Sacramento, CA: Crocker Art Museum.

Cohodas, Marvin

1990 Washoe Basketweaving: A Historical Outline. In *The Art of Native American Basketry: A Living Legacy*, edited by Frank W. Porter III, 153–186. New York: Greenwood Press.

1997 Basket Weavers for the California Curio Trade: Elizabeth and Louise Hickox. Tucson: University of Arizona Press and The Southwest Museum.

Croes, Dale R.

1977 Basketry from the Ozette Village Archaeological Site: A Technical, Functional, and Comparative Study. Pullman: Washington State University Press.

Crane, Diana
2000 Fashion and Its Social Agendas: Class, Gender, and Identity in Clothing. Chicago: University of Chicago Press.

Dalrymple, Larry
2000 Indian Basketmakers of California and the Great Basin. Santa Fe: Museum of New Mexico Press.

2000 Indian Basketmakers of the Southwest. Santa Fe: Museum of New Mexico Press.

2008 Southern Paiute Baskets Collected by Isabel T. Kelly. *American Indian Art Magazine* 33(4): 46–55.

Devine, Sue
1980 Nootka Basketry Hats: Two Special Types. Theme issue, "The Twined Basketry of Western Washington and Vancouver Island (Part I)." *American Indian Basketry* 1(3):5.

Dewhurst, C. Kurt, Marsha MacDowell, and Marjorie Hunt
2007 http://www.greatlakesfolkfest.net/glff2007/programs&activities (accessed March 21, 2013.)

Dittemore, Diane, and Cathy Notarnicola
1999 Anonymous Was a Weaver: In Search of Turn-of-the-Century Western Apache/Yavapai Basketry Artists. *American Indian Art Magazine* 24(3):55–65.

Edison, Carol
2006 Contemporary Navajo Baskets on the Utah Reservation. *Utah Historical Quarterly* 74(3):241–258.

Eisenhart, Linda L.
1990 Hupa, Karok, and Yurok Basketry. In *The Art of Native American Basketry: A Living Legacy*, edited by Frank W. Porter III, 241–266. New York: Greenwood Press.

Ferg, Alan, ed.
1987 Western Apache Material Culture: The Goodwin and Guenther Collections. Tucson: University of Arizona Press.

Folwell, Jody, Terrol Dew Johnson, Ann E. Marshall, Diana F. Pardue, Tristan Reader, and Diza Sauers
2001 Hold Everything!: Masterworks of the Basketry and Pottery from the Heard Museum. Phoenix: The Heard Museum.

Fowler, Catherine S.
1986 Subsistence. In *Handbook of North American Indians. Vol. 11: Great Basin*, edited by Warren L. D'Azevedo, 64–97. Washington, DC: Smithsonian Institution.

Fowler, Catherine S., and Judith W. Finger
2011 Southern Paiute Fine Coiled Baskets of Southern Nevada: History & Style. *American Indian Art* 37(1):44–53.

Frigout, Arlette

1979 Hopi Ceremonial Organization. In *Handbook of North American Indians, Vol. 9: Southwest*, edited by William C. Sturtevant, 564–580. Washington, DC: Smithsonian Institution.

Gifford, Edward W.

1932 The Southeastern Yavapai. *University of California Publications in American Archaeology and Ethnology* 29(3).

Gill, Sam D., and Irene F. Sullivan

1994 Dictionary of Native American Mythology. Oxford University Press.

Glassie, Henry

1993 Turkish Traditional Art Today (Indiana University Turkish Studies). Bloomington: Indiana University Press.

Gogol, John M.

1980–81 Nootka/Makah Twined Fancy Baskets. Theme issue, "The Twined Basketry of Western Washington and Vancouver Island (Pt. 2)." *American Indian Basketry* 1(3–4): 4–11.

1982 Indian, Eskimo, and Aleut Basketry of Alaska. Theme issue, "Indian Eskimo, and Aleut Basketry of Alaska." *American Indian Basketry* 2(2):4–10.

1983 Klamath, Modoc, and Shasta Basketry. Theme issue, "Klamath, Modoc and Shasta Basketry." *American Indian Basketry* 3(2):3–18.

Haeberland, H. K., James A. Teit, and Helen H. Roberts

1928 Coiled Basketry in British Columbia and Surrounding Region. In *Forty-first Annual Report of the Bureau of American Ethnology, 1919–1924*, edited by J. Walter Fewkes, 119–484. Washington, DC: Government Printing Office.

Hedges, Ken

1997 Fibers & Forms: Native American Basketry of the West. San Diego: San Diego Museum of Man.

Herold, Joyce

1979 Havasupai Basketry: Theme and Variation. *American Indian Art* 4(4):42–53.

1999 Showing the Sun: Mythological-Ceremonial Foundations of Jicarilla Apache Basketry. *American Indian Art Magazine* 24(3):66–79.

Hudson, Raymond L.

1990 The Influence of Attu Weavers on Aleut Basketry. In *The Art of Native American Basketry: A Living Legacy*, edited by Frank W. Porter III, pp. 335–344. New York: Greenwood Press.

Jonaitis, Aldona.

2006 Art of the Northwest Coast. Seattle: University of Washington Press.

Khera, Sigrid, and P.S. Mariella

1983 The Yavapai. In *Handbook of North American Indians, Vol. 10: Southwest*, edited by Alfonso Ortiz, 38–54. Washington, DC: Smithsonian Institution.

Kirk, Ruth

1986 Tradition & Change on the Northwest Coast: The Makah, Nuu-chah-nulth, Southern Kwakiutl and Nuxalk. Seattle: University of Washington Press.

Kissell, Mary Lois

1916 Basketry of the Papago and Pima. *Anthropological Papers of the American Museum of Natural History* 17(4):150–254.

Kroeber, A. L., and E. W. Gifford

1949 World Renewal: A Cult System of Native Northwest California. Berkeley: University of California Press.

Kroeber, A. L., and S. A. Barrett

1960 Fishing Among the Indians of Northwestern California. In *Anthropological Records, Vol. 21*. Berkeley: University of California.

Kroes, Peter, and Anthonie Mejiers

2002 Dual Nature of Technical Artifacts. *Techné* 6(2):110–116.

Laforet, Andrea

1990 Regional and Personal Style in Northwest Coast Basketry. In *The Art of Native American Basketry: A Living Legacy*, edited by Frank W. Porter III, 281–298. New York: Greenwood Press.

Lamphere, Louise

1983 Southwestern Ceremonialism. In *Handbook of North American Indians, Vol. 10: Southwest*, edited by Alfonso Ortiz, pp. 743–763. Washington, DC: Smithsonian Institution.

Langer, Susanne K.

1966 The Cultural Importance of the Arts. In *Journal of Aesthetic Education, 1(1):5–12.*

Latta, F. F.

1949 Handbook of Yokuts Indians. Oildale, CA: Bear State Books.

Lee, Molly

1983 Baleen Basketry of the North Alaskan Eskimo. Barrow, AK: North Slope Borough Planning Department.

1990 Objects of Knowledge: The Communicative Aspect of Baleen Baskets. In *The Art of Native American Basketry: A Living Legacy*, edited by Frank W. Porter III, 319–334. New York: Greenwood Press.

Lévi-Strauss, Claude

1966 The Savage Mind. Chicago: The University of Chicago Press.

Lobb, Allan

1978 Indian Baskets of the Northwest Coast. Portland, OR: Charles H. Belding.

Malin, Edward, and Norman Feder

1962 Indian Art of the Northwest Coast: The Cultural Background of the Art. Denver: Denver Art Museum.

Malloy, Mary

2000 Souvenirs of the Fur Trade: Northwest Coast Indian Art and Artifacts Collected by American Mariners. Cambridge: Peabody Museum, Harvard University.

Manuel, Frances, and Deborah Neff

2001 Desert Indian Woman: Stories and Dreams. Tucson: University of Arizona Press.

Marr, Carolyn J.

1990 Continuity and Change in the Basketry of Western Washington. In *The Art of Native American Basketry: A Living Legacy*, edited by Frank W. Porter III, 267–280. New York: Greenwood Press.

1991 Basketry Regions of Washington State. *American Indian Art* 16(2):40–49.

Marshall, Ann

2000 Rain: Native Expressions from the American Southwest. Phoenix: Heard Museum.

Mauldin, Barbara

1984 Traditions in Transition: Contemporary Basket Weaving of the Southwestern Indians. Santa Fe: Museum of New Mexico Press.

McGreevy, Susan Brown

1985 Translating Tradition: Basketry Arts of the San Juan Paiute. Santa Fe: Wheelwright Museum of the American Indian.

1999 Embellishing the Spiral: Design Development in Navajo Baskets. *American Indian Art Magazine* 24(3):44–53.

2001 Indian Basketry Artists of the Southwest: Deep Roots, New Growth. Santa Fe: School of American Research Press.

McKee, Barbara, Edwin McKee, and Joyce Herold

1975 Havasupai Baskets and Their Makers: 1930–1940. Flagstaff, AZ: Northland Press.

Miller, G. Lynette

1990 Basketry of the Northwestern Plateaus. In *The Art of Native American Basketry: A Living Legacy*, edited by Frank W. Porter III, 135–152. New York: Greenwood Press.

Miller, Sheryl F.

1999 Katsina Designs on Hopi Baskets. *American Indian Art* 25(1):56–65.

Myers, John, and Robert Gryder

1988 The Salt River Pima-Maricopa Indians. Phoenix: Heritage Publishers.

Newman, Sandra Corrie

1974 Indian Basket Weaving: How to Weave Pomo, Yurok, Pima, and Navajo Baskets. Flagstaff, AZ: Northland Press.

Niethammer, Carolyn

1977 Daughters of the Earth: The Lives and Legends of American Indian Women. New York: Collier MacMillan Publishing.

O'Neale, Lila M.

1932 Yurok-Karok Basket Weavers. Berkeley: Phoebe Hearst Museum of Anthropology, University of California, Berkeley.

Opler, Morris E.

1941 An Apache Life-Way. Chicago: University of Chicago Press.

1983 The Apachean Culture Pattern and Its Origins. In *Handbook of North American Indians, Vol. 10: Southwest*, edited by Alfonso Ortiz, 368–392. Washington, DC: Smithsonian Institution.

Parry, Alison Ruth

1997 "Their Works Do Follow Them": Tlingit Women and Presbyterian Missions. Master's thesis, University of British Columbia.

Paul, Frances

1981 [1944] Spruce Root Basketry of the Alaska Tlingit. Sitka, AK: The Arrowhead Press.

Pearlstone, Zena

2001 Katsina: Commodified and Appropriated Images of Hopi Supernaturals. Los Angeles: UCLA Fowler Museum of Cultural History.

Pye, David

1969 The Nature of Design. New York: Reinhold Books Corporation.

Rhodes, Robert W.

2007 Hopi: Wicker Plaques and Baskets. Atglen, PA: Schiffer Publishing.

Roberts, Helen H.

1972 Basketry of the San Carlos Apache Indians. Glorieta, NM: The Rio Grande Press.

Robinson, Bert

1954 The Basketweavers of Arizona. Albuquerque: University of New Mexico Press.

Rofkar, Teri

2008 Teri Rofkar, Tlingit basket weaver, tours Penn Museum's American Collection Storage. http://www.youtube.com/watch?v=rn9f_zzesy4 (accessed Sept 11, 2012).

2009 NEA Heritage Fellowships. www.nea.gov/honors/heritage/fellows/fellow.php?id=2009_09&type=int (accessed November 11, 2012).

Saxton, Dean, and Lucille Saxton

1973 Legends and Lore of the Papago and Pima Indians. Tucson: University of Arizona Press.

Schlick, Mary Dodds

1994 Columbia River Basketry: Gift of the Ancestors, Gift of the Earth. Seattle: University of Washington Press.

Schwarz, Maureen Trudelle

1997 Molded in the Image of Changing Woman: Navajo Views on the Human Body and Personhood. Tucson: University of Arizona Press.

Shreve, Margaret

1943 Modern Papago Basketry. *The Kiva* 8(2):10–16.

Simpson, Georgiana Kennedy

2003 Navajo Ceremonial Baskets: Sacred Symbols, Sacred Space. Summertown, TN: Native Voices.

Smithsonian Institution

n.d. Alaska Native Collections: Sharing Knowledge. http://alaska.si.edu/record.asp?id=362 (accessed Sept. 11, 2012).

Tanner, Clara Lee

1982 Apache Indian Baskets. Tucson: University of Arizona Press.

1983 Indian Baskets of the Southwest. Tucson: University of Arizona Press.

Teit, James A.

1930 The Salish Tribes of the Western Plateaus. In *Forty-Fifth Annual Report of the Bureau of American Ethnology to the Secretary of the Smithsonian Institution, 1927–1928*, edited by Franz Boas, 45. Washington, DC: Government Printing Office.

Teiwes, Helga

1996 Hopi Basket Weaving: Artistry in Natural Fibers. Tucson: University of Arizona Press.

Turnbaugh, Sarah Peabody, and William A. Turnbaugh

1986 Indian Baskets. West Chester, PA: Schiffer Publishing.

Weber, Ronald L.

1990 Tlingit Basketry, 1750–1950. In *The Art of Native American Basketry: A Living Legacy*, edited by Frank W. Porter III, 299–318. New York: Greenwood Press.

Whiteford, Andrew Hunter

1988 Southwestern Indian Baskets: Their History and Their Makers. Santa Fe: School of American Research.

Whiteford, Andrew Hunter, and Susan Brown McGreevy, eds.

1985 Translating Tradition: Basketry Arts of the San Juan Paiutes. Santa Fe: Wheelwright Museum of the American Indian.

Winther, Barbara

1985 Pomo Banded Baskets and Their Dau Marks. *American Indian Art* 10(4):50–57.

1996 More about Dau Marks: Visiting Four Pomo Basket Makers. *American Indian Art* 21(4):44–51.

2011 Pacific Northwest Onion-Domed Whalers' Hats. *American Indian Art* 36(3):46–53.

Woodbury, Richard B.

1979 Prehistory: Introduction. In *Handbook of North American Indians, Vol. 9: Southwest,* edited by Alfonso Ortiz, 22–30. Washington, DC: Smithsonian Institution.

Wyckoff, Lydia L., ed.

2001 Woven Worlds: Basketry from the Clark Field Collection at the Philbrook Museum of Art. Tulsa, OK: The Philbrook Museum of Art.

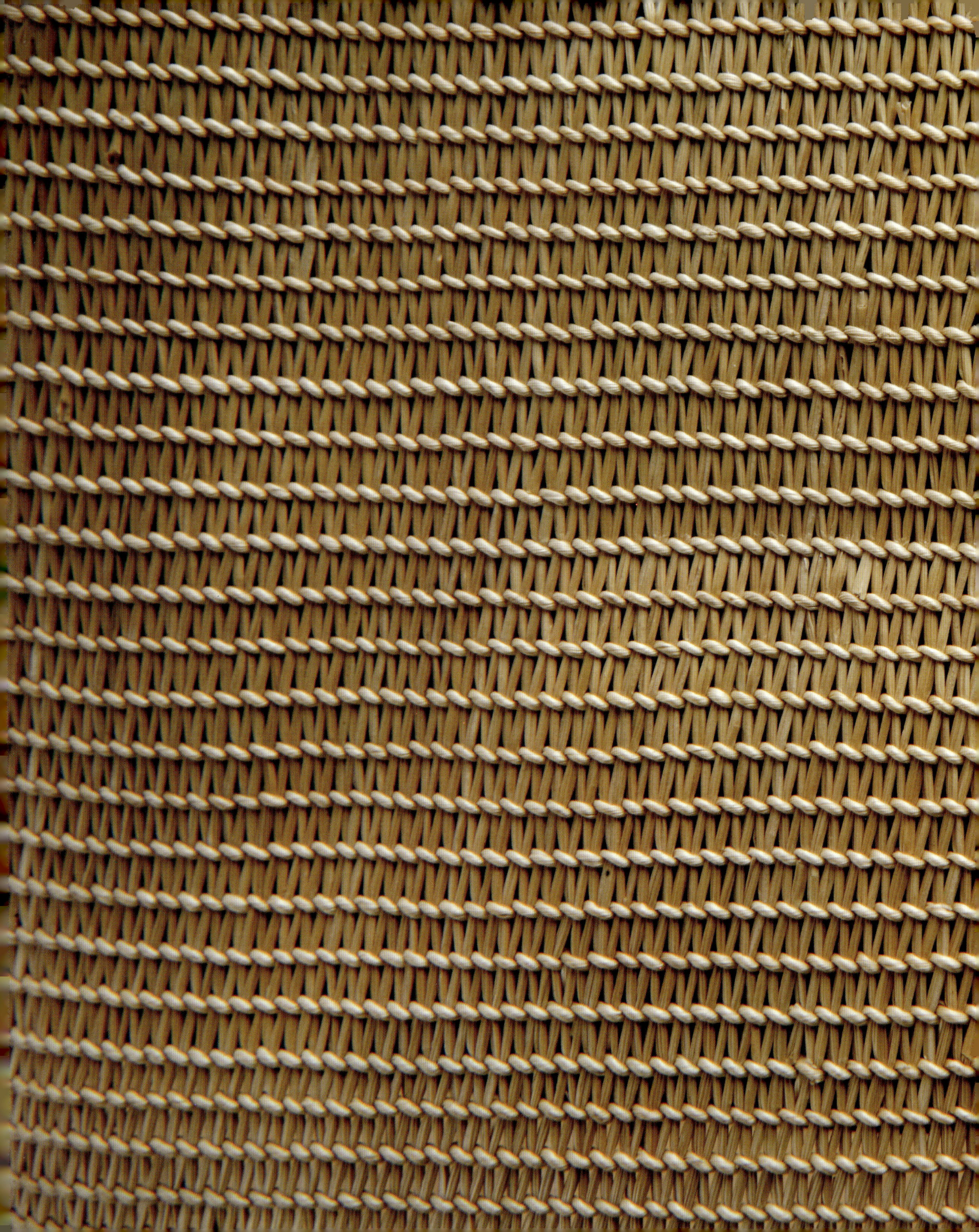

Index

Italicized page numbers refer to illustrations.

Funding for aspects of this project was provided by grants from the National Endowment for the Arts and the Institute for Museum and Library Services.

Project editor: Mary Wachs
Design and production: David Skolkin
Composition: Set in Scala and Scala Sans
Map by Candy Carlson Design
Manufactured in China
10 9 8 7 6 5 4 3 2 1

Library of Congress Cataloging-in-Publication Data

Verzuh, Valerie K.
Woven identities : basketry art of western North America : featuring the collection of the Museum of Indian Arts & Culture / by Valerie K. Verzuh.
pages cm
Includes bibliographical references and index.
ISBN 978-0-89013-584-6 (clothbound : alk. paper)
1. Indian baskets—West (U.S.)—Themes, motives. 2. Basket making--West (U.S.)—History. 3. Museum of Indian Arts and Culture/Laboratory of Anthropology (Museum of New Mexico)—Ethnological collections. I. Title.
E78.W5V47 2013
746.41'08997079--dc23
2013017102

Museum of New Mexico Press
PO Box 2087
Santa Fe, New Mexico 87505
www.mnmpress.org

Photo page 2: Bowl, c. 1900, Akimel O'odham.